1984 AND 1980 PRESIDENTIAL ELECTION RESULTS, POPULAR AND ELECTORAL VOTES

1984
(Unofficial Returns, 11/9/84)

		Popular Vote	Electoral Vote
	Ronald Reagan (R)	53,428,357 (59%)	525
	Walter Mondale (D)	36,930,923 (41%)	13

1980

		Popular Vote	Electoral Vote
	Ronald Reagan (R)	43,899,248 (51%)	489
	Jimmy Carter (D)	35,481,435 (41%)	49
	John Anderson (I)	5,719,437 (7%)	—

AMERICAN GOVERNMENT

Policy and Politics

AMERICAN GOVERNMENT
Policy and Politics

Neal Tannahill
Houston Community College

Wendell M. Bedichek

Scott, Foresman and Company   Glenview, Illinois   London, England

NON NISI PARENDO VINCITUR

LIBRARY OF CONGRESS CATALOGING IN PUBLICATION DATA
Tannahill, Neal R., 1949-
   American government.

   Includes bibliographies and index.
   1. United States-government and politics. 2. Policymaking process.
I. Bedichek, Wendell M.,   II. title
JK274.T36   1985   320.973   84-2031

ISBN 0-673-15838-1

Copyright © 1985
Scott, Foresman and Company
All Rights Reserved
Printed in the United States of America

  2 3 4 5 6 - MPC - 89 88 87 86 85

Preface

When Wendell Bedichek and I first began work on *American Government: Policy and Politics*, we had several goals in mind. First, we wanted a text that would cover thoroughly the basics of American government. Our long experience teaching introductory courses in American government has taught us that many students, even very bright students, lack a knowledge and understanding of many basic concepts. We are no longer surprised when we discover that many of our students cannot explain what a primary election is, do not understand the notion of separation of powers, and haven't heard of NATO. Experience has shown that it is best to assume no prior knowledge and begin by thoroughly explaining the basics.

Second, we wanted to go beyond basic concepts to an analysis of more sophisticated ideas and processes. The public-policy process in America is complex and dynamic, but it is also interesting. We have learned that students are eager to study the policy process in all its glory once they have mastered the basic concepts. Consequently, each section of the book discusses the politics and the dynamics of policymaking.

Third, we wanted to produce a text that would be up-to-date and practical, relevant to our students' experiences. We have found that students become interested in learning about American government when they discover that it is meaningful to their lives. Our classroom experience has taught us that motivation is the beginning of learning. So throughout the text we emphasize the ways policymaking in America affects Americans on a daily basis. A discussion of the United States Constitution, for example, must certainly include consideration of historical, legal, and political points, but we will also include an examination of the impact of the document on the individual in the 1980s.

Fourth, we wanted to include a number of special features that would not only enhance the book's readability but also improve its scholarship. We have scattered short essays called **Perspectives** throughout the text, and we have included short interviews with political scientists on topics of special interest, called **Conversations with Scholars**. These allow the student to benefit from the thinking of a number of the discipline's leading scholars in a form that is less formal and, we think, more interesting than the typical academic essay. Also enhancing the text are an **Appendix**, dealing with the 1984 elections, and an alphabetized **Glossary**, reinforcing the **key terms** that are set off at the end of chapters.

Fifth, we set out to present the text in a readable and attractive fashion. Good scholarship and good writing are not incompatible. This generation of students is the generation of portable television sets, stereo headphones, and cinematic extravaganzas. Never has the written word faced such stiff competition for attention. If scholarly writing is to be read by anyone other than diehard academics, it must be sharp and crisp. Bland, colorless language dulls student interest, undermining motivation for learning. If students are to learn from a text, they must be motivated to read it with their full attention and interest. Therefore, we have tried to write with grace and wit.

Finally, we wanted to produce a text structured around the public-policy approach. We have found the approach to be a useful means of organizing course materials. It is simple enough to be explained to a college sophomore, but sophisticated enough to offer insight into complex political processes. In particular, we have found the public-policy approach to be more interesting to students than more traditional approaches.

Many persons contributed greatly to the writing and production of this book. We were fortunate in having Greg Odjakjian, Bruce Borland, Christine Silvestri, and Trig Thoreson, of Scott, Foresman and Company to give us sympathetic and highly professional help from the project's inception to completion. Ellen Pettengell and Cathy Wacaser provided outstanding efforts in design and editorial liaison to production. We are also grateful to the scholars who reviewed the manuscript: Professors Sharon Z. Alter, William Rainey Harper College; Trudy H. Bers, Oakton Community College; Charles F. Cnudde, University of Texas at Austin; Edward C. Dreyer, University of Tulsa; Kenneth D. Kennedy, College of San Mateo; Burdett Loomis, University of Kansas; and Steven Miller, UCLA. Their comments proved invaluable in preparing the final manuscript.

We wish to thank several individuals for their advice and kind assistance in gathering information. These included Joseph Cooper, Robert Stein, Harold Hyman, Chandler Davidson, and Ferne Hyman of Rice University; Franklin Jones, Glenn Nichols, and Cary Wintz of Texas Southern University; Irving O. Dawson and Thomas Prehoditch of the University of Texas at Arlington; William F. West of Texas A&M University; and Joseph Stewart of Tulane University. Douglas Vecchio and Jeffrey Sterman helped by gathering data for our research.

I am particularly grateful to my mother, Mrs. Roy A. (Ruby) Tannahill who diligently clipped information out of the newspaper. Her efforts proved indispensable to the book's timely completion.

A number of people at Houston Community College gave us encouragement and assistance. These included Randolph G. Wagner, Carol Brown, Raymond Lew, Linda B. Kirkendall, Roderick A. Stamey, Jr., Brenda F. Jones, James L. Steele, Marcella G. Washington, Stephen W. Coates, Donald L. Smith, Manuel O. Reyes, Philip B. Crow, James Smith, Mary Davis, and, above all, Sue A. Cox, our friend and dean.

Many others contributed more than they will ever know to this work's completion: Bruce Felgar, Richard Holt, Don Lapin, David Brown, Steve Darby, Morgan Slusher, Thomas Warshauer, Jon Hanson, Larry Fabiny, George Greanias, John Pizzitola, Marian McWhorter, Warren Holleman, and Wendell Johnson.

Finally, this book is dedicated to the memory of Wendell M. Bedichek, who died suddenly and unexpectedly in May 1982. He was a colleague, a partner, and a friend. Although I completed much of the work on the book after Wendell's death, it is still "our" book. His influence is on every page.

Neal Tannahill

Table of Contents

Perspectives

Conversations

AMERICAN GOVERNMENT

Policy and Politics

Introduction:

STUDYING AMERICAN GOVERNMENT

THE PUBLIC-POLICY APPROACH

THE REALITIES OF POLICYMAKING

OUTLINE OF THE BOOK AND MAJOR THEMES

In April 1983, a presidential commission on excellence in education issued a report that shook the nation. The report was titled "A Nation at Risk" and its conclusions were sobering.

> *The educational foundations of our society are presently being eroded by a rising tide of mediocrity that threatens our very future as a nation and as a people. If an unfriendly foreign power had attempted to impose on America the mediocre educational performance that exists today, we might have viewed it as an act of war.*[1]

The commission found that educational standards in America were sharply in decline. "For the first time in the history of our country," said the report, "the educational skills of one generation will not surpass, will not equal, will not even approach, those of their parents."[2] This means that a whole generation of Americans may be ill-equipped to deal with the new technologies of the late twentieth century. The United States may be unprepared to compete in a global economy. Even the quality of America's democracy may be threatened. "A high level of shared education is essential to a free, democratic society and to the fostering of a common culture, especially in a country that prides itself on pluralism and industrial freedom."[3]

All of this is quite disturbing, especially to those of us who are part of America's educational system. In particular, we are concerned with the political implications of the report. Democracy depends on the informed participation of the citizenry. If Americans participate on the basis of ignorance or prejudice, the quality of life in the nation will likely decline. Democracy may fail.

Our goal in this book is to help you become an informed participant in America's democracy. We believe that your study of how government works is important to the nation, but it will also be beneficial to you personally. All of us need to learn about government because it affects us in our daily lives.

First, all of us enjoy the benefits of government services. We are born in hospitals that probably receive government assistance, either directly or indirectly. We attend public grade schools and high schools and then enroll in public community colleges or state universities. Even if we attend parochial or private schools, we may receive government assistance in the form of transportation, textbooks, or school lunches. We may obtain student loans for college. Eventually, some of us will get jobs working for the government while others will sign on with private companies doing contract work for government agencies or departments. All the while, we drive on government-built streets and highways and ride on publicly subsidized mass transit. We are protected by local police and fire departments and rely on the national government to guard our nation's security. The government gathers our garbage, delivers our mail, vaccinates our children, and insures our bank deposits against loss or theft. If we fall on hard times, government can help with unemployment compensation, food stamps, and Medicaid. When we retire, we collect Social Security and receive Medicare benefits.

Second, many aspects of our lives are regulated directly or indirectly by the government. We are governed by the criminal law, of course, but government also regulates the rates of interest banks and savings-and-loan associations pay us on our savings, the educational and technical requirements individuals must meet in order to engage in many occupations and professions, and the proportion of "meat byproducts" that can be included in a frankfurter. Government regulation affects the quality of our air and water, the mileage performance of our automobiles, and the working conditions in our factories. Regulation attempts to protect us from unsafe products, deceptive advertising, and discrimination based on race, color, sex, religion, national origin, or age.

Finally, all of us pay a sizable share of our income in taxes to the various units of government. Income and Social Security taxes are withheld from our paychecks. We pay sales taxes on many retail purchases and excise taxes on a variety of products, including tobacco, alcohol, tires, and gasoline. We pay property taxes directly on our homes and businesses or indirectly through our rent.

Thus, because we are all touched both directly and indirectly by the hand of government in our homes, on our jobs, and in our personal affairs, we need to know about government. If we understand the workings of government, we will be able to take advantage of the benefits and services government provides and to prepare ourselves to live effectively under government regulation and taxation. We will also have a clearer idea of how we can affect government through our votes, our participation in political organizations, and our personal communications with policymakers. We *can* have an influence on government policy—probably more influence than most of us would ever imagine.

THE PUBLIC-POLICY APPROACH

There are many ways to go about studying government, but we believe that the **public-policy** approach is particularly helpful. Let's begin by defining a few terms. **Public** means governmental, as opposed to **private** businesses, homes, or finances. Policy involves the response, or lack of response, of decisionmakers to an issue. So when we study public policy, we are studying the ways in which governmental decisionmakers respond or do not respond to an issue. In particular, we are interested in the **public-policy process,** that is, the process by which public policy is made.[4]

There are five stages in the policy process: agenda building, policy formulation, policy adoption, policy implementation, and policy evaluation. **Agenda building** is the process through which issues become matters of public concern and governmental action. Sometimes political leaders bring issues to the public's attention. President Carter, for example, helped to raise the energy crisis to the public agenda by calling it "the moral equivalent of war." At other times, events arouse concern about an issue. When the Soviet Union launched its Sputnik satellite in 1957, many Americans decided it was time to enter the space race. Interest groups can also raise issues, such as abortion, nuclear energy, or unemployment. Political parties can publicize problems in their platforms. Some groups can call public attention to problems through protest activity, as did the civil-rights and antiwar protesters of the 1960s. Other issues can be raised to public concern through the news media. In the early 1980s, news reports helped make AIDS (Acquired Immune Deficiency Syndrome) the nation's most talked-about health problem.

The problems that are raised to public concern are known as the **public agenda.** The set of problems that government actually chooses to try to remedy are called the **official agenda.** As students of the public-policy process, we want to know who raises issues in American politics and how those issues are placed on the official agenda. We are also interested in which problems are *not* raised to public attention and debate.

Policy formulation involves the development of courses of action for dealing with the problems of the official agenda. Policy formulation is frequently the work of government officials. A congressional subcommittee, for example, can draft legislation strengthening the powers of the Internal Revenue Service to crack down on tax evasion, or the president can prepare a new approach to arms control. Justices on the Supreme Court can draft an opinion on capital punishment, or the Federal Aviation Administration can develop new standards for airline safety. On many occasions, however, policies are formulated by nongovernmental actors, such as interest groups, private individuals, and the mass media. A labor union, for example, might propose higher tariffs on imported goods in hopes of protecting American manufacturers, or a newspaper columnist might argue in favor of changing a president's term of office.

After issues are raised and policies are formulated, they have to be officially adopted. **Policy adoption** refers to the official decision of a governmental body (for example, the Congress or the Supreme Court) to adopt a public policy. We will examine the legislative process in Congress, the executive role of the president, decisionmaking in the courts, and rulemaking in the bureaucracy.

Policy implementation is the stage of the policy process in which the policies are carried out. We cannot assume that just because a policy has been formulated and adopted, the issue is settled. A policy in operation may evolve far differently from what its architects intended or expected. Sometimes this occurs because the nature of the problem is different from what was expected or because the resources devoted to the policy turn out to be insufficient. Sometimes it happens because of bureaucratic inefficiencies. At other times it results from the resistance of entrenched groups, other branches of government, or other levels of government. It sometimes occurs because bureaucrats have their own interests that may affect policy implementation.[5]

Policy evaluation is concerned with the assessment and appraisal of policy. It involves questions of cost, efficiency, honesty, and effectiveness.

What groups and individuals are benefiting from the policy? Who is being hurt by it? To what degree?

In policy evaluation it is important to make a distinction between **policy outputs** and **outcomes.** Policy out*puts* are what government does; policy out*comes* involve the impact of the policy in operation.[6] Not all outcomes are anticipated, or welcomed. Beginning in 1975, for example, Congress voted to tie Social Security benefits to the rate of inflation. The idea was to shelter the elderly from inflation, but Congress had not anticipated the inflation rates of the late 1970s. Consequently, benefits rose faster than tax receipts and the Social Security trust fund neared bankruptcy.

Evaluation has both objective and subjective aspects to it. Technical, quantitative evaluations of policy can be prepared in order to measure a policy's impact. We can count how many dollars a new tax raises for the government or how many jobs a federal employment program produces. This can be useful in determining whether a policy is fulfilling its stated goals. Many questions, however, are much more subjective. Is the goal a worthy one? Is the program worth its cost? Can the scarce resources of government be put to better use? All of these are judgment calls.[7]

Policy evaluation can be made by many parties. Frequently, evaluation takes place within the government itself. We began this introduction by quoting from a report by a presidential commission that was charged with evaluating education in America. Congress oversees the operation of federal programs through the committee and subcommittee system; the General Accounting Office (G.A.O.) acts as a watchdog agency, preparing reports for the Congress on the general efficiency of government programs and agencies. Within the executive branch, program evaluation is one of the functions of the Office of Management and Budget (O.M.B.).

Evaluation also comes from outside government. Interest groups frequently voice their views about public policy. Oil companies, for example, argue that government regulation has made America excessively dependent on foreign sources of oil. Other evaluations come from the mass media, such as newspaper editorials or special reports on network television. There are even private organizations whose primary function is the evaluation of public policy, including the Brookings Institution and the American Enterprise Institute. Evaluations can also be made by private individuals, including political-science instructors and students.

THE REALITIES OF POLICYMAKING

The picture we have sketched of the policymaking process is quite neatly drawn and compartmentalized. We have presented it that way in order to make it readily understandable. In reality, though, the process is far more complex. First, keep in mind that the public-policy process is not another way of describing "how a bill becomes a law." When Congress passes a bill, it is adopting a policy, but not all policies are drafted into formal legislation.

Judicial decisions are also policy; so are the executive orders of the president. Many policies are made by members of the bureaucracy.

Second, it is not possible to match up each stage of the policy process on a one-to-one basis with a different governmental institution or political actor. Issues may be raised by interest groups or big-city mayors or the president. Policies may be formulated by the president or Congress or federal judges. They may be implemented by the civilian bureaucracy, the military, or state and local governments. Evaluations come from many parties.

Third, there are no clear lines of demarcation among the five steps of the policy process. Agenda setting and policy formulation sometimes overlap. For example, when President Carter emphasized the severity of the energy crisis, he was also lobbying for his own policy proposals. Policy implementation often has an aspect of policy adoption to it as agencies fill in the details of legislation left vague by Congress. Also, policy evaluations are made throughout the policy process, not just at its end. Policy evaluations may lead to demands for more government action and the process begins again.

Finally, it is wrong to assume that the public-policy approach is a completely rational path leading inexorably toward the Ideal Public Policy. Real life does not work that way. After all, public policy is made by humans operating within complicated political structures. In an ideal process, policymakers would act to identify policy issues before the issues reached the crisis stage. There would be great emphasis on problem prevention, not just problem solution. In reality, however, problems are not tackled until they are clearly identified as problems and placed on the public agenda. Little energy is directed toward problem prevention. In an ideal process, policymakers would examine all possible policy options to determine the best possible solution. In reality, though, policymakers tend to settle upon the first policy that appears workable. In an ideal process, one adopts the best possible policy without regard for past practices and procedures. In reality, however, policymakers first consider modifications of current programs and policies instead of looking to dramatic new approaches. There is a tendency to retain practices that once proved successful even if the nature of the problem has changed. Consequently, public policy usually changes incrementally—slowly, by bits and pieces—rather than dramatically.

OUTLINE OF THE BOOK AND MAJOR THEMES

We begin our study of government and policymaking in America in Part One by exploring the historical, socioeconomic, and legal/constitutional backgrounds of policymaking. How has America's past shaped contemporary politics? How does the nation's socioeconomic background influence policymaking? Chapter 1 focuses on America's past and present, with an examination of the nation's political heritage and its contemporary socioeconomic structure. The American Constitution is the subject of chapter 2. We sketch the historical and philosophical backgrounds of the document, profile its main features, and explore its impact on public policy today. Chapter 3 examines federalism and intergovernmental relations. It begins by discussing federalism from the standpoint of the Constitution and constitutional law. Then, it considers the historical development of America's intergovernmental system. The chapter concludes with an essay on the politics of the federal system in the intergovernmental context.

Participation is the subject of Part Two: who participates, in what ways, and with what effect? Chapter 4 discusses public opinion. It studies how public opinion is measured; it examines how political attitudes and beliefs are acquired; it analyzes the content of public opinion; and it discusses the relationship between public opinion and public policy. In chapter 5, the focus is on participation and the electoral process. It considers the ways individuals participate in the policymaking process and discusses the effect of individual participation on the policy process. The latter portions of chapter 5 deal with elections, particularly presidential elections. Chapter 6 examines the role interest groups and political parties play in the policy process.

Part Three profiles the policymaking structures of American government. The United States Congress is the topic of chapter 7, and chapter 8 examines the office of the presidency. Chapter 9 looks at the role of the bureaucracy. Chapter 10 considers the place of the courts in the policymaking process.

Part Four deals with the nature of policymaking and policy in five substantive areas, with specific consideration of these questions: What is public policy in each of these areas? How is it made? What effect does it have on America and Americans? Chapter 11 examines public economics; that is, the role government plays in promoting economic growth, controlling inflation, and reducing unemployment. Chapter 12 looks at the regulatory policies of government in America. In chapter 13 the focus is on civil liberties. Minorities and women are the subjects of chapter 14. Finally, chapter 15 examines foreign and defense policy.

A number of important themes occur and reoccur throughout this book. We will summarize them briefly. First, the policymaking process in America involves a multitude of groups and interests. As we will see in chapter 1, the United States is an extraordinarily diverse nation whose people represent a wide array of backgrounds and perspectives. Consequently, a remarkable variety of groups makes demands on government in America.

Second, the policymaking process involves conflict and controversy. The diverse groups participating in America's policy process have interests that are sometimes opposed to one another. Frequently, the differences involve money: Who will benefit from a given policy? Who will pay the bills? At other times, the conflicts involve gut-wrenching emotional issues, such as abortion, busing, capital punishment, and nuclear weapons.

Third, the structures through which policy is made in America are fragmented. At the national level, three separate branches of government share power: the executive, legislative, and judicial. Political power is further divided among the various levels of government within the federal system—that is, federal, state, and local governments.

Political fragmentation has both positive and negative aspects. On the one hand, it provides a large number of forums in which the diverse interests of American society can be heard. Consequently, nearly every group or interest on the political scene can find an arena where it can air its views. Very few interests are completely shut out of the policy process.

On the other hand, political fragmentation makes policy change more difficult. Fragmentation allows for the development of numerous power centers, each of which must be appeased before new policies can be adopted. Policymaking becomes a slow, laborious process and the end product a hodgepodge of compromises. Consequently, American public policy often has difficulty responding to the rapidly changing conditions of the 1980s.

Finally, policymaking involves **politics.** We can define politics as the authoritative allocation of values for society as a whole[8] or, in simpler terms, as the process that determines who gets what, when, and how.[9] Politics involves competition, bargaining, negotiation, and compromise. In some quarters, politics has gotten a bad name. We sometimes write off policy failures by saying "that's politics." Or government officials promise to reform some area of policymaking by saying they will take it "out of politics." In fact, however, politics is an inevitable, essential element of the policymaking process. In today's diverse society, a multitude of contending groups and interests hold different views about public policy. Politics is the process that determines whose views will prevail and what policies will be enacted. To be sure, politics has its rough edges. There are winners and losers. However, making policy decisions through the political process is far preferable to the alternative: having decisions made by an elite and handed down to the rest of us.

Our central *purpose* in this text, then, is to present the student with a solid, basic grounding in the essentials of American government. Our guiding *focus* is on policy and politics—how they interact, how they conflict and come together, how they ultimately influence and often direct the course of American life. If we can grasp these aspects of our political system, we will have gone a long way toward understanding the essence of current American government.

KEY TERMS

AGENDA BUILDING (3)   *POLICY EVALUATION (4)*

OFFICIAL AGENDA (4)   *POLICY FORMULATION (4)*

POLICY ADOPTION (4)   *POLICY IMPLEMENTATION (4)*

***POLICY OUTCOMES** (5)*   ***PUBLIC** (3)*

***POLICY OUTPUTS** (5)*   ***PUBLIC AGENDA** (4)*

***POLITICS** (8)*   ***PUBLIC POLICY** (3)*

***PRIVATE** (3)*   ***PUBLIC-POLICY PROCESS** (3)*

NOTES

1. National Commission on Excellence in Education, *A Nation at Risk* (Washington: U.S. Government Printing Office, 1983), quoted in *New York Times,* 27 April 1983, Section II, p. 6.
2. Ibid.
3. Ibid.
4. James E. Anderson, *Public Policy-Making* (New York: Praeger, 1975).
5. Robert T. Nakamura and Frank Smallwood, *The Politics of Policy Implementation* (New York: St. Martins, 1980), and John Brigham and Don W. Brown, eds., *Policy Implementation* (Beverly Hills: Sage, 1980).
6. Anderson, p. 134.
7. Stuart S. Nagel, *Policy Evaluation* (New York: Praeger, 1982).
8. David Easton, *The Political System* (New York: Knopf, 1953), ch. 5.
9. Harold D. Lasswell, *Politics: Who Gets What, When & How* (New York: McGraw-Hill, 1936).

SUGGESTED READINGS

ANDERSON, JAMES E. *Public Policy-Making.* New York: Praeger, 1975.

CHELF, CARL P. *Public Policymaking in America: Difficult Choices, Limited Solutions.* Glenview, Il.: Scott, Foresman and Company,1981.

DYE, THOMAS. *Policy Analysis: What Governments Do, Why They Do It and What Difference It Makes.* University, Alabama: University of Alabama Press, 1976.

————. *Understanding Public Policy,* 3rd ed. Englewood Cliffs, N.J.: Prentice-Hall, 1968.

EDWARDS, GEORGE C., AND SHARKANSKY, IRA. *The Policy Predicament: Making and Implementing Public Policy.* San Francisco: Freeman, 1978.

JONES, CHARLES O. *An Introduction to the Study of Public Policy.* North Scituate, Mass.: Duxbury Press, 1977.

LINDBLOM, CHARLES E. *The Policy-Making Process,* 2nd ed. Englewood Cliffs, N.J.: Prentice-Hall, 1980.

LINEBERRY, ROBERT. *American Public Policy: What Government Does and What Difference It Makes.* New York: Harper and Row, 1977.

MAY, JUDITH, AND WILDAVSKY, AARON, EDS. *The Policy Cycle.* Beverly Hills: Sage, 1978.

RAE, DOUGLAS, AND EISMER, THEODORE. *Public Policy and Public Choice.* Beverly Hills: Sage, 1979.

Part One

THE POLICYMAKING SETTING

1 AMERICA PAST AND PRESENT

2 THE AMERICAN CONSTITUTION

3 FEDERALISM

To understand the policymaking process in America we must first understand America. Agenda building, policy formulation, policy adoption, and the like take place within the context of American life. In chapter 1 we begin our study by exploring the philosophical and socioeconomic settings that affect policymaking. Since the contemporary policy process is a product of all that has come before, we start with an essay on the great themes of American history. Next we show how these themes have helped shape the principal policy debates of our own day.

In the latter portions of chapter 1 we turn our attention to contemporary America. First, we attempt to place the United States in the context of its international environment by focusing on the role America plays in the world community and on how that role has changed since World War II. Next, we examine the current socioeconomic context of policymaking in America. The chapter concludes by discussing how the nation's socioeconomic structures affect the policy process.

In chapter 2, we turn our attention to the constitutional context of American policymaking. Although the United States Constitution is now two hundred years old, it is still very relevant to the policy process. We consider the purposes for a written document, and then we study the historical and

philosophical background of America's Constitution. We profile some of the most significant features of the Constitution, including the separation-of-powers and checks-and-balances system, federalism, bicameralism, the Bill of Rights, and the methods of amendment. Next we examine the Constitution as a living, political document that has been able to adapt to changing times. Chapter 2 concludes with a critical analysis of the ways in which the Constitution affects the policy process today.

Chapter 3 ends our discussion of the backgounds of policymaking in America by examining America's federal system. This is one of the more complex features of Ameri-

can government and one of the most important. Virtually every aspect of domestic policy and politics is affected by the federal system and intergovernmental relations. We begin with federalism as it is outlined in the Constitution. We then present a history of intergovernmental relations in America and describe many of the more important features of today's intergovernmental system. The next part of the chapter discusses the politics of the federal system in terms of the public-policy process. We conclude the first section of our book (and chapter 3 as well) with a brief analysis of how background factors affect policymaking.

Chapter One

AMERICA PAST AND PRESENT

America is a land of diversity and contrast. Its people have roots in nearly every continent, representing a kaleidoscopic range of cultures and traditions. Its political structures are based on a unique mix of Western European political ideas and North American political experiences. Its history is a mixture, too, producing a heritage of contrasting elements: democracy and inequality, prosperity and poverty, consensus and conflict. In short, America is a political alloy, a mixed system, and the only constant in the American experience has been change.

To understand the public-policy process in America, we must first understand the land, its people, and their heritage. That's a tall order, of course, too big for one chapter or even one book. Consequently, we will limit ourselves to a discussion of a few of the more prominent elements that form the background of policymaking in America.

In the first portion of this chapter, we will consider a number of political ideas and values that have been important in the nation's political development: equality, democracy, freedom, reform, liberalism and conservatism. These aren't the only ideas that could be discussed, but they are some of the most important historically. Also, they are particularly relevant to contemporary debates about public policy. In the second part of the chapter, we will turn our attention to the socioeconomic background of policymaking in America. Part of our effort will be directed toward placing the United States in a world context. We will compare America with other nations in terms of social and economic development and military strength. Also, we will attempt to place America in the context of her recent past by considering how life in the United States has changed in the years since World War II. In the last section of this chapter, we will discuss how the policy process of the 1980s is affected by the socioeconomic changes that have been taking place in the nation.

AMERICA'S POLITICAL INHERITANCE

Every student knows that history is the study of people, places, and things of an earlier day and age, but history is also about certain intangibles—ideas, ideals, aspirations, and beliefs. Although the tangible aspects of the past may fade in our memories, the intangibles endure, shaping our lives today. Let us begin our study of policymaking in America by examining some of the intangible political ideas and ideals. They are a product of America's political past, but they help shape the present.

EQUALITY

"We hold these truths to be self-evident, that all men are created equal . . . ." When Thomas Jefferson wrote these familiar words in the Declaration of Independence, he was making a bold assertion for the world of the late eighteenth century. Europe was very class-conscious. People certainly weren't born equal there, nor were they likely to achieve equality. Certain definite social distinctions between the aristocracy and the working class were carefully maintained. The children of English common folk were taught this prayer:

God bless the squire and his relations
And keep us in our proper stations.[1]

In America, however, the idea of equality has been at the heart of political rhetoric for more than two hundred years. It is part of the credo of the nation, a symbol of the American dream. Alexis de Tocqueville, a Frenchman who was an astute observer of the American scene, said this about equality in American political life.

Liberty is not the chief object of their [the Americans'] desire; equality is their idol. They make sudden and rapid efforts to obtain liberty, and if they miss their aims resign themselves to their disappointment; but nothing can satisfy them without equality, and they would rather perish than lose it.[2]

Why has equality been so important to Americans? Political scientist Louis Hartz points out that America was a new land settled by people fleeing the oppressions of the old world. The heritage of feudalism that was largely responsible for European class distinctions simply did not exist in America. In fact, the nation was founded in reaction to that tradition.[3]

Historian Frederick Jackson Turner argues that the American environment, especially the frontier, was important in shaping the American ideal of equality. The frontier was a harsh place where class status counted for little in the face of drought, disease, flood, Indian attack, and other hardships. Also, the frontier offered opportunity. Land was cheap on the frontier and that gave the poor the chance to move up in life—with hard work, of course, and a little luck.[4]

Finally, John Locke, a seventeenth-century English political philosopher, provided a theory to support the American doctrine of equality. In his *Second Treatise on Government* (1689), Locke postulated that in a natural state all men are born free and equal and that they possess certain rights. These "natural rights," wrote Locke, were life, liberty, and property. Unfortunately, the good life of the state of nature is marred by evildoers who conspire to deprive others of their life, liberty, or property. It is for this reason, Locke said, that men join together to form governments. The power of government, then, stems from the consent of the governed, who endow the government with responsibility for protecting their lives, liberty, and possessions. When the government fails in this task, Locke continued, it is the right of the people to revolt and institute a new government.[5]

As you can imagine, Locke's ideas were quite attractive to eighteenth-century Americans. The wild continent they inhabited certainly resembled a state of nature, and Locke's description of natural man as free and equal conformed to their conception of the American experience. Also, we should add that Locke's ideas offered the perfect theoretical rationale for the American Revolution. Read the Declaration of Independence reprinted in the Appendix of this text to see how closely the founders of our country followed Locke's theory.[6]

It is important to understand what Americans have meant by equality. It isn't a mathematical equality in which everyone enjoys the same status, nor is it an equality of results in which all receive the same rewards for their labors. Instead, it is *equality of opportunity*. In America, the idea of equality has included a recognition of differences among people in ability and achievement.

Let's consider three aspects of equality in America. First, there is equality before the law. This is the belief that all persons should be treated alike in their dealings with the government. Justice is to be evenhanded. The government is to be fair. Second, Americans believe in political equality. Everyone should have the same say in selecting public officials. Finally, there is economic equality. This is the idea that all Americans should have an equal opportunity to get ahead. Like Horatio Alger, a poor person can become wealthy. Like Abraham Lincoln, a person born in humble circumstances can become president.[7]

The ideal of equality in America hasn't always been achieved in practice. Women, blacks, Hispanics, and other racial and cultural minorities have had less than equal opportunities. Through the years, the nation has gradually recognized these inequalities and sought to remedy them, but barriers to equality still remain. In fact, some observers contend that inequality is still a basic characteristic of American life.[8] The ideal of equality and how to achieve it remains a lively topic of policy debate.

DEMOCRACY

Democracy derives from the belief that men and women can rule themselves; it is, as Lincoln put it, government of the people, by the people, and for the people. In practice, democracy can take several forms. A *pure democracy* is a system in which citizens vote directly on matters of public concern. Except in some localities where town meetings are held, we do not have a pure democracy in America. Instead, we have a *representative democracy*. Citizens elect representatives who then make public-policy decisions on behalf of the citizens they represent.

The founders of our nation believed in democracy, but not in *too much* democracy. They deeply distrusted the judgment of the common people or "the mob," as the founders sometimes referred to the general populace. Consequently, they acted to limit democratic participation. Whole groups of people—women, slaves, nonlandowners—were denied the right to vote. Those who could vote were kept from direct participation in the decision-

John Locke (1632–1704), the British philosopher and author of Two Treatises on Government, *whose writings strongly influenced both the Declaration of Independence and the United States Constitution.*

making process by means of representative democracy. The Constitution's authors believed that members of a House of Representatives elected by the people would be wiser and more deliberate than the people themselves in mass assembly. The founders were even more cautious in the selection of United States senators and the president. They provided that senators be chosen by the state legislatures while the president was to be selected by electors who would first be chosen by the general electorate.[9]

Through the years, many Americans have worked to lessen the disparity between the cherished ideal and the actual practice of democracy in America. The nation has experienced what might be called a great **democratization** as the public-policy process has been opened to meaningful participation by a broad spectrum of Americans, including the propertyless, blacks, and women. In the 1980s, the struggle for greater opportunities for political participation has been joined by new faces and voices: Hispanics, American Indians, gay people, the elderly, and the disabled.

Democracy in the America of the 1980s is far more broadly based than it was in the 1780s, but there are troubling imperfections. The doors to participation in the public-policy process are now open to most Americans, but many choose not to enter. In the 1980 presidential election fewer than 55 percent of us bothered even to vote. We also know that Americans are not really equal participants in the democratic process. Those with money and status are, as political novelist George Orwell might put it, more equal than others.

The nature of democracy in America today is also the object of debate. Some argue that the disparities of political influence in America are so great as to compromise seriously the quality of American democracy. One critic, a proponent of the **elite theory** of American government, charges that the nation is ruled by several groups of powerful corporate and governmental elites. "Democracy for the few," he calls it.[10] Others agree that there are powerful elites, but there are many of them and they compete with one another. The role of the electorate, then, is to choose among these elites. In America's **pluralist democracy,** as these observers call it, public policy results from competition and compromise among different groups of elites.[11]

FREEDOM

Freedom is another important value in America's political tradition. Throughout the nation's history, freedom has been a central theme of political discourse and patriotic rhetoric. It's a concept that is endorsed by virtually all Americans.

Freedom has been important to Americans for several reasons. First, the search for freedom motivated the settlement of the land and the founding of the nation. Many of the immigrants who settled North America were seeking freedom from economic, religious, or political oppression. Also, the Revolution was fought to gain freedom from British authority. "Give me liberty or give me death," said Patrick Henry.

Second, the diversity and size of America nurtured the growth of freedom. In colonial times, the central government in London was simply too far away to monitor and control the lives of Americans. Individuals could escape oppressive local authorities simply by moving to a new colony. Rhode Island in particular became a haven for religious and political dissidents. If all else failed, people could seek their freedom on the frontier, away from the reach of all political authorities.

Finally, John Locke's political philosophy supported the American ideal of freedom. In Locke's state of nature, you recall, humans were not just equal; they were also free. What's more, they were endowed by their Creator with the inalienable rights of life, *liberty,* and property. Thomas Jefferson liked Locke's phrasing so much that he used it in the Declaration of Independence almost verbatim. His one alteration, of course, was to substitute the phrase *pursuit of happiness* for the term *property.*

Despite America's affinity for the ideal of freedom, the nation's history is marked by controversy and tension over the practice of freedom. There are certainly flaws on the record—slavery, for example, and the second-class status that, through the years, has been accorded to black Americans and other racial and cultural minorities. We could also mention the internment of American citizens of Japanese descent during World War II, or the paranoid excesses of the McCarthy period in the early 1950s, when much of the nation went on an anticommunist witch hunt.

If freedom is so basic to America's political tradition, how do we account for the blemishes? Studies show that Americans express near-unanimous support for the ideals of individual liberty when those ideals are stated in relatively abstract terms such as "freedom of speech" and "freedom of religion." When the issue is brought closer to home, however, there is often less support. For example, many Americans who endorse free speech would oppose allowing Nazis, communists, or Ku Klux Klan leaders to speak in their own town. Freedom of religion may be the American way, but to many the Moonies or the Children of God are another question.[12]

Perhaps the most important reason for the shortcomings in the practice of freedom in America is that a tension exists between the ideal of democracy and the ideal of freedom. The basic idea of democracy is that of **majority rule.** Meanwhile, at the heart of the ideal of freedom is the concept of **minority rights,** the idea that freedom of religion, freedom of expression, and other individual rights should be protected and should not be dependent on majority agreement. Majority rule and minority rights are key components of America's political tradition, but there is an inherent conflict between the two.

Consider the case of *The Progressive* magazine and the H-bomb. In 1979, *The Progressive,* a magazine published in Wisconsin, decided to print an article detailing how a hydrogen bomb is made. The government sought to prevent the article's publication, saying it was a threat to the national interest. Eventually, a federal court ruled that the magazine could publish the article. The case illustrates well the kinds of conflicts that arise between the interests of the majority (in this instance the perceived national interest) and individual freedom (the right of the editors to publish the article).[13] We will discuss these questions in greater detail in chapter 13 when we examine civil liberties.

REFORM

America has always had its reformers. They are men and women, usually a small minority of the population, who believe they recognize a disparity between the ideals of equality, freedom, and democracy in America and its practical reality. They want to change America for the better, at least as they understand it. Reformers may be persistent, noisy, disruptive, somewhat self-righteous, and sometimes wrongheaded, but they are the vanguard for some of the noblest ideals of America. They push and they tug at the fabric of society until the nation stirs itself to change, to reform.

America has seen many great reform movements. The abolition movement aimed to end slavery. The Populists strove to improve the lot of the common person, particularly small farmers. The Progressives' reform goals were also directed toward the common folk, but progressivism had an essentially urban focus. The New Deal of Franklin Roosevelt embraced a series of reforms aimed at helping organized labor, farmers, the poor, and the elderly. The 1960s saw great advances in the areas of civil rights for blacks and greater civil-liberties protections for a wide range of minorities, including Jehovah's Witnesses, atheists, students, political protesters, and those accused of crimes. In the 1980s, the causes of reformers are many and varied: women's rights, consumerism, environmentalism, civil rights, the nuclear-freeze movement, and more.

Reform has been a blessing for America, but it has been a mixed blessing. Thanks to the work of reformers, American society today is freer, more democratic, healthier, and more just than it otherwise would have been. Nevertheless, not all reforms have been successes, at least not unqualified successes. Prohibition, after all, was a reform. Many of the reforms of the Progressive Era were designed to make local and state governments more responsive to average citizens, but in practice wound up strengthening the hand of special-interest groups. The New Deal was a great reform movement in its day, but it has become the target of conservative reformers in this day. In the 1960s America's political parties, especially the Democrats, adopted reforms aimed at reducing the role party bosses play in selecting presidential candidates and at increasing the importance of average voters. By the 1980s, however, many party leaders began to believe that the earlier reforms only served to increase the importance of money, interest groups, and television. It became a case of the reforms needing reforming. We shall explore the reasons for this in detail in chapters 5 and 6.

In the 1980s, the impulse of the reformer still lives, but there is increasing disagreement about what the content and nature of reform should be. Some believe the types of reforms begun in the New Deal and extended in the 1960s need to be fine-tuned and carried still further. Others, though, see those reforms as a major cause of today's problems. They believe that America needs to embark on a path of reduced government involvement. The opposing philosophies in this debate are known as **liberalism** and **conservatism.**

LIBERALISM AND CONSERVATISM

Political thought in America is characterized by consensus on the goals of politics but conflict over the means to those goals. Americans have almost universally believed in the ideals of equality, democracy, and freedom. The aim of politics has been the maximization of those ideals. Americans have disagreed, however, on the *means* to be used, and the disagreement has centered on the role of government. One group believes that government action can be an instrument for expanding equality, democracy, and freedom. A second group believes the actions of government only succeed in undermining those goals.

A key focus for reformers in the 1980s: the issue of arms control and nuclear freeze.

The terms *liberal* and *conservative* are often used with imprecision and are shrouded in emotion, but they represent real differences concerning the content of public policy. In the eighteenth and nineteenth centuries, Americans saw government as the greatest threat to liberty. The Revolution was fought to gain freedom from oppressive British rule. The Constitution was written and a Bill of Rights added to establish democracy and protect individual liberty. Toward the end of the nineteenth century, in the midst of the industrial revolution and urbanization, many liberals began to recognize other threats to individual liberty: poverty, illiteracy, disease, discrimination, and business monopolies. They decided that government could be used as a weapon against these evils. For liberals, then, government action, particularly by the national government, came to be seen as an instrument for achieving personal freedom. From then on, the gospel of liberal reform focused on government action designed to improve the lot of the worker, the consumer, the poor, the elderly, the ill, and those suffering from discrimination.

From the days of the New Deal until 1980, liberals succeeded in setting the agenda for policymaking in America. After Franklin Roosevelt was elected in 1932, he proposed (and Congress enacted) a series of programs requiring government action to combat the Great Depression and to help the disadvantaged. Similar liberal programs were at the heart of Harry Truman's Fair Deal, Kennedy's New Frontier, and Lyndon Johnson's

Great Society. Each was a legislative program calling for government action; each was motivated by a desire to maximize human freedom.[14]

After the New Deal, conservatives were left to defend the liberal thought of the nineteenth century, that is, the belief that government action threatens individual freedom. They were reduced to naysaying and pointing out examples of idealistic liberal naïveté. They would echo the tone of that crotchety social critic, H. L. Mencken, who said, "An idealist is someone who, upon observing that a rose smells better than a cabbage, also assumes that it makes better soup." Unfortunately for modern-day conservatives, they never really had a reform program of their own. Neither did they succeed in electing one of their own to the presidency. Conservatives preferred Robert Taft and Barry Goldwater, but they got the more moderate Dwight Eisenhower and Richard Nixon. Instead of repealing the New Deal, Eisenhower consolidated it. Nixon, who resigned in disgrace following the Watergate scandal, succeeded in giving conservatism a bad name. For decades, then, liberals were in the driver's seat. For the most part, they set the policy agenda while the conservatives reacted. Then came 1980.[15]

By the end of the 1970s, New Deal liberalism had run out of steam. Memories of the Great Depression had faded, and a new generation of voters had grown up knowing Franklin Roosevelt only as an historical figure. Vietnam and assorted scandals had sapped liberalism of much of its moral authority. Liberalism was also hurt by its own success. Many of the groups that had been among the disadvantaged of the 1930s—organized labor and farmers in particular—were no longer disadvantaged and frequently no longer liberal. Perhaps most importantly, though, liberals were running out of ideas. Many of the great liberal programs of the 1930s and 1960s were showing signs of wear and tear by the '70s. Their cost was skyrocketing, and their effectiveness was in grave doubt. Indeed, for many, the liberal programs appeared to be a major cause of America's problems. But the liberals had no new ideas and no brave new leaders. The 1930s produced a Franklin Roosevelt, the 1970s a Jimmy Carter.

Meanwhile, the conservatives had been preparing a program of their own. They had always been critical of liberal programs, but now their criticism was finding greater acceptance. Most importantly, they were offering an alternative: a significant reduction of the role of government, particularly the national government, in American society. The election of Ronald Reagan, the first truly conservative president since before the New Deal, offered conservatives an opportunity to put their reforms into effect.

But Reagan's election in 1980 was not the ultimate victory for conservatives. Many voted not for Reagan, but against Jimmy Carter. The poor economy and the hostage situation in Iran may have had more to do with Reagan's victory than political philosophy. Many voters were attracted by Reagan's personal qualities, not by his philosophy.

Also, it's too early to say that liberalism is on the wane. By 1982 liberals had regrouped and had begun vigorously to challenge the conservatives' views. Consequently, the 1980s promise to be years of fundamental debate in America about the future of the nation's politics, a debate of a kind not heard since the 1930s. Let us examine some of the specific issues that are likely to dominate that debate.

Social-welfare policies.   Liberals advocate government action to benefit disadvantaged groups in society, such as the poor, the elderly, and minorities. They want to fine-tune and perfect the social-welfare programs of the New Deal and the 1960s. Conservatives argue that many social-welfare programs are beset by waste, inefficiency, and corruption. Enormous amounts of money are being spent, but little help is going to the truly needy. The conservatives favor paring back federal activity in this area. Instead, they want to rely more on the efforts of state and local government and private charity.

Regulation of business.   Liberals believe in the use of government action to regulate business in the "public interest"—as they define that term, of course. Consequently, liberals support the idea of environmental-protection laws to safeguard air and water quality, consumer-protection laws to protect the buying public, occupational-safety and health standards to insure good working conditions, and careful regulation of utilities to guarantee efficiency. In contrast, conservatives are disturbed about what they see as government interference. They point out the cost, red tape, and inefficiency of bureaucratic regulation. They believe in the motto, "The government that governs least, governs best."

Social policy.   Some of the most controversial issues in American politics today are social issues, such as pornography, abortion, gay rights, school prayer, and women's rights. Liberals see these issues in terms of individual rights, while conservatives see them as matters of traditional morality and family values. Liberals argue that adults should be allowed to decide for themselves what books to read or what films to see. Women should be free to pursue whatever career goals they choose and should be treated equally with men under the law. Women should not be forced to bear unwanted

Drawing by Mort Gerberg; © 1980 The New Yorker Magazine, Inc.

children; gay people should not suffer discrimination; and the government should not prescribe prayers to be recited in public schoolrooms.

In contrast, conservatives regard these issues in terms of traditional values. They see pornography, homosexual liberation, abortion, some aspects of the feminist movement, and the Supreme Court's refusal to allow government-mandated prayer in schools as direct assaults on God, family, and country. Consequently, conservatives tend to support the rigorous enforcement of pornography laws and the passage of a constitutional amendment against abortion and another amendment in favor of school prayer. At the same time, conservatives mount the barricades against the advocates of women's liberation and equal rights for gay people.

If, as Emerson said, "consistency is the hobgoblin of little minds," then neither liberals nor conservatives can be accused of small-mindedness. On the issues of social-welfare policy and government regulation, the liberals support an active role for government while the conservatives oppose it. On social issues, however, the two sides flip-flop. Liberals call for less government involvement; the conservatives call for more.

We should also emphasize that our discussion of American political issues in terms of liberalism and conservatism is an oversimplification.[16] For the sake of illustration, we have painted our picture with bold strokes, but the differences between liberalism and conservatism are often subtle ones of degree and emphasis. Some issues, such as the need for a strong national defense, certain foreign-policy matters, and the importance of honesty in government, cannot really be defined in liberal/conservative terms. Also, few people are down-the-line conservative or liberal on all issues. Most of us are liberal on some matters, conservative on others.

Nevertheless, the terms help define the contours of the public-policy debate of the 1980s. The election of 1980 gave conservatives the opportunity to define the public-policy agenda for the first time in nearly fifty years. They have not wasted the opportunity. President Reagan proposed major changes in American public policy, including substantial funding reductions in a wide range of social-welfare programs, a big increase in defense spending, massive tax cuts, and a major reduction in federal regulatory activity. All of this reflects Reagan's conservative belief that the national government's most "legitimate functions" are national defense and internal security. In Reagan's view, without the heavy hand of government individuals function better—through initiative, hard work, and competition. Reagan has also taken the lead in calling for a constitutional amendment against abortion and for an amendment to allow oral prayer in the classroom.

Naturally, liberals have been highly critical of Reagan's program. They have argued that the tax cuts are unfair and the spending decisions a misplacement of priorities. The tax cuts have given too much back to the rich, they say, and the spending reductions have taken too much away from the poor. They have charged that the Reagan policies have rolled back the clock on federal protection for the environment, workers, consumers, and civil rights for minorities. In addition, they have opposed Reagan's initiatives on abortion and school prayer.

And so the stage is set for an intense and emotional debate on public policy in the 1980s. Americans always argue about contemporary issues, of course, but now the debate is more fundamental. The great themes of American political history—equality, democracy, freedom, and reform— are much nearer the surface and at times are in dispute themselves. It's an exciting time to study public policymaking in America.

A Changing America in a Changing World

America and the world have changed a great deal in the last forty years. The United States emerged from World War II as the foremost economic and military power on earth and the undisputed leader of the Western alliance. Germany and Japan were in ruins, and America was the one major power whose industrial plant had not been severely damaged by the war. Militarily, the United States was the only nation that possessed nuclear weapons.

Here at home images of American life in the postwar years often resembled the Norman Rockwell paintings that adorned the covers of the old *Saturday Evening Post:* images of small-town life and of loving families observing the traditional values. But the postwar years had a darker side, too. There was poverty, illiteracy, and ill-health. Blacks and other nonwhites were segregated from the white population. Women were given unequal pay for equal work. Still, for many Americans—middle-class whites, at least—those were the "good old days." In this section, we will examine the changes that have taken place in America since the postwar years and look at how they have affected the public-policy process.

AMERICA AND THE WORLD

By almost any measure, the United States is a principal actor on the world's stage. The 1980 census revealed that there are now more than 220 million of us, giving the United States the world's fourth largest population after mainland China, India, and the Soviet Union. The nation's land area is 3,628,150 square miles, larger than all other nations but the Soviet Union, Canada, and China.

The United States also has the world's largest economy by far. America's **gross national product (GNP)**—which is the sum total of the goods and services produced by the economy in a year (and a standard measure of an economy's size)—reached $3 trillion in early 1982. That is more than the combined outputs of Japan, West Germany, France, and Great Britain.

Nevertheless, in certain areas the United States' economy has been slipping. America once had the highest standard of living in the world measured in terms of national income per person, but that is no longer true. By 1980, the U.S. had fallen to eleventh place among the world's nations with a per capita GNP of $11,360. Two small oil-producing Arab states, the United Arab Emirates ($26,850) and Kuwait ($19,830) headed the list. Then came Switzerland ($16,440), West Germany ($13,590), Sweden ($13,520), Denmark ($12,950), Norway ($12,650), Belgium ($12,180), France ($11,730), the Netherlands ($11,470), and the United States.[17]

Years of chronic inflation and periodic recession have sapped America's economy. **Inflation** refers to a decline in the purchasing power of a nation's currency. In the early 1970s, the annual inflation rate in America was around 5 percent, but by the end of the decade inflation soared to more than 13 percent a year. Inflation cooled in the early 1980s, only to be replaced by a severe economic downturn—a **recession**—and an unemployment rate of more than 10 percent. The economy recovered in 1983 and early 1984, but many economists were predicting more problems in the near future.

The nation's economy has its short-term ups and downs, but it suffers from a number of deep-seated problems that cast a shadow over its long-term development. First, the energy crisis is still with us. The United States may be the world's leading energy producer and energy consumer, but it has also become one of the world's leading importers of petroleum. More than 40 percent of America's oil comes from foreign sources whose reliability as providers of reasonably priced fuel has sometimes proved suspect. Second, **labor productivity** has been on the decline in America for years. Labor productivity refers to the amount of output generated per worker. Its decline means that the nation's workers are producing less. A major reason for this is that America's industrial base needs to be modernized with new machinery and procedures. This costs money, of course, but the rate of investment in American industry has lagged. Third, American industry often competes poorly with its European and Japanese counterparts. This has been particularly true for the so-called "smokestack industries," such as steel and automobile manufacturing. Now, in the middle 1980s, there is talk of an economic revival in America based on new high-technology industries and increased investment and productivity for older industries. Whether that will materialize or not remains to be seen.

Forty years ago, no nation in the world could boast better educational opportunities and better health care for its citizens than the United States, but today that claim could be challenged. In the 1983 report "A Nation at Risk," the National Commission on Excellence in Education found that American students performed poorly in comparison with students from other industrialized countries. On nineteen academic tests, American students were never first and they were last seven times.[18] As for health care, America clearly has some of the finest medical facilities in the world, but

Sign of the times: Japanese cars on a Newark, New Jersey, loading dock await shipment to U.S. car dealers. Controlling the flow of foreign imports into the United States remains a serious problem for American industry.

there are problems. Physicians tend to concentrate in the middle class suburbs of cities, leaving inner-city neighborhoods and many rural areas with a doctor shortage. Also, the high cost of medical care limits access to medical assistance, especially for the working poor who earn too much money to qualify for government aid.

Finally, America is no longer the world's preeminent military power. Today, the Soviet Union and the United States stand at a position of rough parity, each possessing terrible weapons capable of devastating each other and much of the rest of the world as well. The United States has also learned that the possession of great military might does not guarantee immunity from challenges by lesser powers, nor does it bring with it unquestioned leadership of the Western world. Western Europe and Japan are often unwilling to follow America's lead, looking instead to their own particular interests. Meanwhile, the United Nations is dominated by developing nations who frequently regard America with disdain or contempt.

Policymaking in the America of the 1980s takes place in a world far different from the world of the 1940s. America's place has changed. No longer is it number one according to almost every measure of wealth and power. No longer is it unchallenged economically, militarily, and diplomatically. This should not be viewed as a precipitous decline, however. Change was inevitable. America's position after 1945 was in large part a consequence of the successful war effort and the nation's good fortune not to be on the front lines of the fighting.

Today, America is no longer first among the unequal nations of the world, but it is at or near the top in most categories of socioeconomic strength and development. Japan is an economic titan, but spends very little on defense, relying instead on American protection. The Soviet Union is a military behemoth, but its economy is a shambles. The United States is like the decathlon athlete: perhaps not the best on every measure of achievement, but superior all-around. No other nation can claim that distinction.

It is unclear, however, whether the United States can maintain its position. Since the early 1970s, America has been in a troubling slump that raises questions about the future. Is the country merely pausing to catch its second wind or, like an over-the-hill athlete, has it begun a long-term decline?

AMERICA AT HOME

America and Americans have changed dramatically in the last forty years. There is good news: more people are enrolled in college now than ever before, and the death rate is down. But there is also bad news: both the crime rate and the divorce rate are up sharply.[19] Let's look in detail at the changing face of American society.

The economy.   The purpose of an economic system is to allocate scarce resources among competing ends. It must determine *what* goods are to be produced, *how* they are to be produced, and *for whom* they are to be produced.[20]

There are two major alternative economic models, the **centrally directed economy** and the **market economy.** In a centrally directed economy, decisions on what to produce, how to produce, and for whom to produce are made by the government. Natural resources and industrial plants are government-owned, and most workers are employed by the government. There is a central planning commission that draws up an economic master plan, and the plan is then implemented by regional and local government agencies.

In a market economy, economic decisions aren't made by the government; they are made by the marketplace in which buyers and sellers freely exchange goods and services. Natural resources and industrial plants are owned by private businesspeople or groups of private investors. Most workers are employed by private enterprise. These enterprises compete to provide goods to the consumer at prices the consumer is willing to pay.

In the real world, no economy conforms exactly to either of the two basic economic models. Each nation has a **mixed economy**, combining aspects of a centrally directed economy with those of a market economy. The nature of that mix, however, varies from country to country.

The Soviet Union and other self-proclaimed **communist** countries conform fairly closely to the centrally directed model. Most businesses and industries there are owned by the government, though there are some minor exceptions. The U.S.S.R., for example, permits the private ownership of personal property and some agricultural plots. Economic allocation and pricing decisions are made by central planning in communist countries, although, once again, there are exceptions. The Soviets allow the private sale of farm products raised on private land, and some Eastern European countries, notably Hungary, permit free-market competition in several segments of their otherwise centrally directed economies. Finally, each communist country is governed by an authoritarian regime controlled by the communist party.

The economic mixture in **social democratic countries,** such as Sweden, France, and Great Britain, combines extensive government ownership of industry with democratically elected governments. In social democracies, the government owns basic industries, ususally including transportation, communications, energy, and finance. Other industries and most smaller businesses, however, are privately owned. Also, most production and pricing decisions are determined by market forces.

The United States is the world's leading example of a free-enterprise **capitalist** economy. In America, most of the means of production—farms, factories, stores, and the like—are privately owned and economic decisions are made in the marketplace.[21]

The American economy, however, diverges from the classic free-market model in certain important respects. Some industries are publicly owned. The Tennessee Valley Authority (TVA) is owned by the federal government, for example, and many transportation and electric companies as well as water utilities are operated by state and local governments. Many businesses and industries in America are closely regulated, and government at all levels spends billions of dollars on defense, health, education, welfare, and a host of other services. What's more, government's role in America's mixed economy has grown extensively over the past four decades. Since 1941, total government spending in America has increased from $29 billion to more than $1 trillion. Taxes and total government disbursements currently make up about one third of the national output.

Nevertheless, Americans have more money and more buying power now than they did four decades ago. The average American earned $8872 after taxes in 1981, more than twice the $4073 (in 1981 dollars) he or she made in 1941. Family incomes have risen more sharply, in part because the number of working women has increased. In 1941, only 28.5 percent of women were in the work force. By 1981 that percentage had increased to 52.3 percent.

American spending patterns have also changed. In 1941 Americans spent 23.7 percent of their incomes on food and beverages, 13 percent on clothing. Now these items take relatively less of the consumer's budget: 18.1 percent and 7.4 percent, respectively. Other items, however, cost relatively more, particularly housing (up from 12.9 percent to 16.3 percent), medical care (from 4.1 percent to 9.9 percent), and transportation (from 10.6 percent to 14.5 percent).[22]

There is also poverty in America. The government measures poverty on the basis of subsistence, that is, the amount of money an individual or family needs to purchase basic necessities such as food, clothing, shelter, health care, and transportation for one year. The amount varies with family size, of course, and from year to year because of inflation, but in 1982 the **poverty line,** as it is called, was $9862 a year for a nonfarm family of four. That means that families of four making less than $9862 a year were officially poverty families. By this standard, there were 34.4 million poor people in America in 1982, about 15 percent of the population. (The problems of defining poverty are discussed in the **PERSPECTIVE** on this page.)

Most observers believe that poverty is not as extensive in America today as it was in the 1940s or even the 1960s, but it is nonetheless a serious social problem, particularly for certain groups.[23] Table 1.1 shows that poverty tends to be concentrated among racial minorities, the elderly, and families headed by women when there is no adult male in the household. Moreover, the number of poor people in America has been on the rise since the late

Perspective
DEFINING POVERTY

How do you define poverty? One approach is to define it in terms of *relative deprivation*. Economist John Kenneth Galbraith says that "people are poverty-striken when their income, even if adequate for survival, falls markedly below that of the community." Another approach is the *subsistence approach*. It defines poverty as the lack of sufficient income to purchase the necessities of life.

Each of these approaches presents the political scientist with certain technical difficulties. If we use relative deprivation as our standard of measurement, that will mean computing a different poverty standard for every city and region in the country. Someone who is relatively poor in Hollywood,

California, might be considered relatively wealthy if he or she were living in the Mississippi delta country. The subsistence approach also presents problems of measurement. Just what, for example, is to be included under the heading, "the basic necessities of life"? And even if we agree on what these necessities are, the cost of these things (food, clothing, shelter, energy) will vary considerably from place to place.

Deciding on a definition for poverty also has political ramifications. There's a politics of science just as there is a science of politics. If poverty is defined in terms of relative deprivation, then this suggests that poverty can be ended only by a major redistribution of wealth in Amer-

ica. Government statistics show that in 1981 the poorest one fifth of Americans received only about 5 percent of the nation's total annual income. Meanwhile, the wealthiest fifth earned more than 40 percent. Defining poverty in terms of subsistence points to a set of policy alternatives that are politically less difficult to accomplish. If being poor simply means not having enough money to live on, then poverty can be reduced by increasing the buying power of the poor through guaranteed employment, cash transfers, the provision of necessities such as food and health care, or some combination of these approaches.

Group	Percentage Poor
Whites	12.0%
Blacks	35.6
Hispanics	29.9
Elderly	14.6
Families headed by a woman with no male adult present	40.6

TABLE 1.1
Poverty in America, 1982

SOURCE: U.S. Census Bureau data, quoted in "Poverty Grips More Americans," *Houston Post*, 24 February 1984, p. 11A.

1970s. In 1979, there were 26 million Americans living below the poverty level, more than 8 million fewer than in 1982.

The people. There are more Americans now than in the 1940s, of course—229.8 million in 1981 to 133.4 million in 1941—but the pattern of growth is fascinating. During the war years many Americans put off having families. Then, in the late 1940s and 1950s, they made up for lost time and the birth rate soared. This "baby-boom generation," as it is called, is now in its teens, twenties, and thirties and, as Figure 1.1 shows, it creates quite a bulge in the demographic chart. After the 1950s, the birth rate in America declined until the mid-1970s, when the baby-boom generation began having children of its own—an echo effect from the original boom. Still, the overall growth rate for the nation has been declining, from 18.6 percent in the 1950s, to 12.5 percent in the 1960s, to 11.4 percent in the 1970s. Experts predict further declines into the 1980s and 1990s. If it weren't for Americans living longer and for a sizable immigration flow (more than 1.5 million legal and illegal immigrants a year), the growth rate would be even lower.

Blacks, Hispanics, American Indians, and Asian Americans are far more visible in the America of the 1980s than they were in the America of the 1940s. For one thing, there are more of them. The birth rate for nonwhites in America is greater than for whites, and the last decade has seen a significant influx of immigrants from Mexico, the Caribbean, and Southeast Asia. These newcomers are particularly evident in the Southwest, along the Gulf Coast, and in the nation's big cities. Table 1.2 shows that the percentage of black Americans is greatest in the South and the Northeast. Meanwhile, Hispanics are concentrated in the West. Another reason for the increased visibility of racial minorities has been the changes in laws, judicial rulings, and attitudes that have opened schools, the work places, and the mass media to greater participation by minorities.

Americans have also moved around a great deal in the last forty years. The 1940 census found a majority of Americans living in the Northeast and Midwest, and a sizable proportion of Americans living on the farm (22.6 percent). The 1980 census painted a quite different picture. First, the

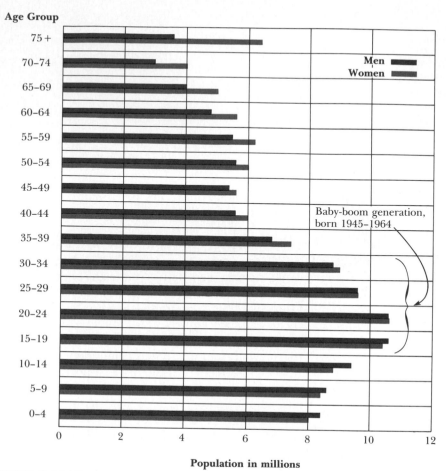

FIGURE 1.1

Distribution of Americans by Age Group, 1980

Age Group

Men
Women

Baby-boom generation, born 1945–1964

Population in millions

SOURCE: *Statistical Abstract of the United States, 1982–83,* p. 27.

South and West, the regions of the country known as the **sunbelt,** are growing much faster than the Northeast and Midwest, the **frostbelt.** The census found that 33.3 percent of Americans now live in the South while 19.1 percent live in the West. The growth of the nation's cities dramatically illustrates the population shift. Table 1.3 shows that nearly all major frostbelt cities lost population in the 1970s while almost every sunbelt city gained population. Second, the 1980 census revealed some interesting facts about where people live. Since the 1940s the United States has become quite urbanized, with 73.7 percent of the population now living in urban areas. Only 2.7 percent of us live on farms. During the 1970s, however, the areas of greatest growth were not the cities (which grew by only 6.7 percent); they were the suburbs (up 17.4 percent) and the nonmetropolitan areas (up 16 percent). Suburban growth is not new, but the significant

Region	Blacks	Pct.	Hispanics	Pct.
Northeast	6,351,036	11.6	2,696,324	4.9
Midwest	5,336,542	9.1	1,276,405	2.2
South	12,539,124	17.9	4,381,109	6.3
West	2,261,516	5.2	6,252,045	14.5
Total	26,488,218	11.7	14,605,883	6.4

TABLE 1.2
Black and Hispanic Population, 1980

SOURCE: *Statistical Abstract of the United States, 1982–83*, p. 32.

population increases in nonmetropolitan areas may signal a new trend in American growth patterns. Some suggest that what is happening is a revitalization of small-town America.[24]

And so the changes go on. America and Americans are different in the 1980s from what they were in the 1940s. But what does all of this mean for the public-policy process?

CONCLUSION: PUBLIC POLICY AND A CHANGING AMERICA

Public policymaking takes place within the socioeconomic context of American society. Politics, economics, and demography are closely entwined, so much so that one cannot be truly understood apart from the others. Several points deserve special notice.

The first is the relationship between political and economic power. Karl Marx, the founder of the communist philosophy, argued that capitalism is the exploitation of man by man. In theory, communism ends the exploitation. In practice, of course, the current Soviet system is highly exploitative. There is a joke told in the Soviet Union that under capitalism man exploits man, but under communism it is just the opposite. The truth is that under communism *political* power leads to *economic* power; under capitalism, *economic* power leads to *political* power. Neither fulfills the ideal of democracy and freedom. The Soviet system has produced a relatively efficient police state but a relatively *in*efficient economy. The American system has produced a relatively efficient economy but a relatively inefficient government.

In America the close relationship between economic and political power means that those most in need of governmental assistance are the least able to bargain for it and vice versa. In general, those with wealth and status are active, influential participants in the policy process, while the poor and disadvantaged remain on the sidelines. That does not mean that the disadvantaged are ignored. Most advantaged Americans, liberals and conservatives alike, share a sincere concern for the well-being of the poor and debate how best to help, whether through government programs or through private initiative. The irony is that those who are most directly affected by the debate, the disadvantaged themselves, are frequently non-participants in it.

A second point concerns the relationship between prosperity and policymaking. The United States has been blessed with an abundance of natural and human resources. Because of our nation's wealth, public-policy decisions in America have been sometimes less agonizing than in poorer nations. The workplace could be opened to greater participation by racial minorities and women because the economy was expanding; more jobs were being created. New workers could be added without taking jobs from old workers. Because of economic growth, there was money for federal social-welfare programs. The nation's economic surplus could be used to

TABLE 1.3

Growth of American Cities

City	1970 population	1970 rank	1980 population	1980 rank	Pct. change
New York	7,895,563	1	7,071,030	1	− 10.4%
Chicago	3,369,357	2	3,005,072	2	− 10.8
Los Angeles	2,811,801	3	2,966,763	3	+ 5.5
Philadelphia	1,949,996	4	1,688,210	4	− 13.4
Houston	1,233,535	6	1,594,068	5	+29.2
Detroit	1,514,063	5	1,203,339	6	− 20.5
Dallas	844,401	8	904,078	7	+ 7.1
San Diego	697,471	14	875,504	8	+25.5
Phoenix	584,303	20	789,704	9	+35.2
Baltimore	905,787	7	786,775	10	− 13.1
San Antonio	654,153	15	785,410	11	+20.1
Indianapolis	736,856	11	700,807	12	− 4.9
San Francisco	715,674	13	678,974	13	− 5.1
Memphis	623,988	17	646,356	14	+ 3.6
Washington	756,668	9	637,651	15	− 15.7
San Jose	459,913	29	636,550	16	+38.4
Milwaukee	717,372	12	636,212	17	− 11.3
Cleveland	750,879	10	573,822	18	− 23.6
Columbus	540,025	21	564,871	19	+ 4.6
Boston	641,071	16	562,994	20	− 12.2

SOURCE: *Statistical Abstract of the United States, 1982–83,* pp. 17–19, 21–24.

In 1970, 7 of the nation's 10 most populous cities were in the frostbelt. As of the 1980 census, there were only 5, and now that's down to 4. Since the 1980 census count, two sunbelt cities have moved up a notch. Houston has overtaken Philadelphia for 4th place, and San Antonio has edged out Baltimore for 10th. Another rapid climber is San Jose, Calif., which leaped from 29th place in 1970 to 16th in 1980. Of 11 northern and midwestern cities that remain in the 1980 top 20 list, all but Columbus, Ohio, lost population.

help the poor. Charity comes easier to a wealthy people whose income is growing than to a poor people whose income is shrinking. Part of the explanation for the current decline of liberalism in America may be that the rate of increase in American abundance has slowed. There is less surplus to spread around and fewer jobs to be filled. Consequently, middle-class Americans may be feeling a bit less charitable.

Finally, demographic and economic change affects policymaking. For example, population shifts are causing growing pains for the sunbelt and contraction pains in the frostbelt. Water has always been a precious commodity in the West and Southwest, but rapid growth is pushing the issue to the top of the political agenda. The 1980s will see increased political disputes over limited water resources among states, among regions, and between the farmers and the rapidly growing urban areas. Rapid growth will also mean increased demands for basic city services for the sunbelt cities. Meanwhile, the depopulation of many northeastern cities has not lessened the demand for services as much as it has reduced the tax base. So, representatives of both the sunbelt and frostbelt will be turning to Washington for assistance.[25]

A second illustration of the effects of socioeconomic changes on the policy process might be called the politics of aging. There are now 25.5 million Americans age 65 and over, representing 11.3 percent of the population. In the future the number and percentage will increase, especially when the baby-boom generation reaches old age after the year 2000. Consequently, the policy agenda will increasingly reflect the interests and demands of the elderly. Health care and retirement income security, for example, will be placed higher on the agenda. Also, we can expect to see an increase in the size and influence of interest groups organized by and for older Americans.

There are many other examples of the ways socioeconomic factors affect the policy process, but the point has been made. The public-policy process takes place within the broad context of American life. To understand the policy process, one must also understand America and its people.

KEY TERMS

CAPITALISM (27)

CENTRALLY DIRECTED ECONOMY (26)

COMMUNISM (26)

CONSERVATISM (19)

DEMOCRACY (15)

DEMOCRATIZATION (16)

ELITE THEORY (16)

FROSTBELT (30)

GROSS NATIONAL PRODUCT (GNP) (23)

INFLATION (24)

LABOR PRODUCTIVITY (24)

LIBERALISM (19)

MAJORITY RULE (17)   *POVERTY LINE (28)*

MARKET ECONOMY (26)   *RECESSION (24)*

MINORITY RIGHTS (17)   *SOCIAL DEMOCRATIC COUNTRIES (27)*

MIXED ECONOMY (26)   *SUNBELT (30)*

PLURALIST DEMOCRACY (16)

NOTES

1. David M. Potter, *People of Plenty* (Chicago: University of Chicago Press, 1954), p. 104.
2. Alexis de Tocqueville, *Democracy in America,* ed. Phillips Bradley, vol. 1 (New York: Vintage Books, 1954), pp. 53–54.
3. Louis Hartz, *The Liberal Tradition in America* (New York: Harcourt, Brace & World, 1955).
4. Frederick Jackson Turner, *The Frontier in American History* (New York: Henry Holt & Co., 1920).
5. John Locke, *Two Treatises on Government,* ed. Peter Leslett (New York: Cambridge University Press, 1965).
6. Donald J. Devine, *The Political Culture of the United States* (Boston: Little, Brown and Company, 1972).
7. Robert Salisbury, *Governing America* (New York: Appleton-Century-Crofts, 1973), ch. 2.
8. Harrell R. Rodgers, Jr. and Michael Harrington, *Unfinished Democracy: The American Political System* (Glenview, Il.: Scott, Foresman and Company, 1981).
9. Richard Hofstadter, *The American Political Tradition* (New York: Alfred A. Knopf, 1964), ch. 1.
10. Michael Parenti, *Democracy for the Few,* 3rd ed. (New York: St. Martin's Press, 1980).
11. Robert Dahl, *Who Governs?* (New Haven: Yale University Press, 1961), and Nelson Polsby, *Community Power and Political Theory* (New Haven: Yale University Press, 1963).
12. James W. Prothro and C. W. Grigg, "Fundamental Principles of Democracy: Basis of Agreement and Disagreement," *Journal of Politics* 22 (Spring 1960): 276–94.
13. *New York Times,* 10 March 1980, p. 1.
14. Eric F. Goldman, *Rendezvous with Destiny* (New York: Vintage Books, 1956).
15. Clinton Rossiter, *Conservatism in America* (New York: Vintage Books, 1962).
16. Pamela Johnson Conover and Stanley Feldman, "The Origins and Meaning of Liberal/Conservative Self-Identification," *American Journal of Political Science* 25 (November 1981): 617–45.

17. Associated Press, "U.S. Now 9th in Per Capita GNP Ranking," *Houston Post,* 16 August 1982, p. 2A.
18. *U.S. News & World Report* (9 May 1983) p. 150.
19. "How the U.S. Has Changed in Four Decades," *U.S. News & World Report* (7 December 1981), pp. 52–53.
20. Roy J. Ruffin and Paul R. Gregory, *Principles of Economics* (Glenview: Scott, Foresman and Company, 1983), ch. 2.
21. Turley Mings, *The Study of Economics* (Guilford: Dushkin Publishing, 1983), ch. 17.
22. "How U.S. Has Changed in Four Decades," pp. 52–53.
23. Michael Harrington, *The Other America* (New York: Macmillan, 1962).
24. Dirk Kirschter, "America on the Move," *National Journal* (14 November 1981), pp. 2016–24.
25. Rochelle L. Stanfield, "Task for Policy Makers: Keeping Up with Change," *National Journal* (14 November 1981), pp. 2025–31.

SUGGESTED READINGS

BEITZINGER, A. J. *A History of American Political Thought.* New York: Dodd, Mead and Co., 1972.

GOLDMAN, ERIC F. *Rendezvous with Destiny.* New York: Vintage Books, 1956.

HARTZ, LOUIS. *The Liberal Tradition in America.* New York: Harcourt, Brace, & World, 1955.

HOFSTADTER, RICHARD. *The American Political Tradition.* New York: Alfred A. Knopf, 1964.

POTTER, DAVID M. *People of Plenty.* Chicago: University of Chicago Press, 1954.

PRATT, HENRY J. *The Gray Lobby.* Chicago: University of Chicago Press, 1976.

RIFLIN, JEREMY, AND BARBER, RANDY. *The North Will Rise Again.* Boston: Beacon Press, 1978.

ROSENBAUM, WALTER A. *Political Culture.* New York: Praeger, 1975.

ROSSITER, CLINTON. *Conservatism in America.* New York: Vintage Books, 1962.

Chapter Two

THE AMERICAN CONSTITUTION

Do you remember studying the theory of evolution in your high-school biology class? Evolution holds that the various types of plants and animals, including man, have evolved over a very long period of time from earlier forms of life through a process of natural selection. Did your teacher also discuss the biblical doctrine of creation, that is, the belief that "in the beginning God created the heavens and the earth"?

The question of whether man is a risen ape or a fallen angel is a longstanding public-policy controversy in America. In 1925, the state of Tennessee made it illegal for any public-school teacher "to teach any theory that denies the story of the divine creation of man as taught in the Bible, and to teach instead that man has descended from a lower order of animals." Shortly after the law's passage, John T. Scopes, a twenty-four-year-old biology teacher, was arrested for teaching evolution.

The Scopes trial was a great sensation, pitting William Jennings Bryan, the great orator and former candidate for president, as the attorney for the state of Tennessee, against Clarence Darrow, the famous trial lawyer who represented Scopes. The jury found Scopes guilty, but the real victory belonged to Darrow, who succeeded in holding Bryan and the law up to public ridicule. Later, the verdict was reversed by a higher court on the basis of a technicality.[1]

After the Scopes trial, the debate over the teaching of evolution died down but did not die out. In the 1970s, groups of fundamentalist Christians once again raised the issue to the policy agenda. For them, the Adam-and-Eve story was literally true and the theory of evolution a challenge to their faith. The fundamentalists were opposed by many educators, the scientific community, and a number of religious leaders who did not believe in a literal interpretation of the Bible's creation story. In 1981, the fundamentalists scored a major victory. The Arkansas legislature passed a law requiring that if public schools teach the theories of "evolution science," they must also teach "creation science."

The fundamentalists' victory was short-lived, however. Opponents of the law filed suit in federal court, charging that the statute violated the First Amendment to the United States Constitution, which reads, in part, "Congress shall make no law respecting an establishment of religion. . . ." In January 1982 federal judge William Overton agreed with the law's opponents. He ruled that teaching creation science is nothing more than teaching religion. Therefore, the law was unconstitutional.[2]

The creation-versus-evolution controversy illustrates well the elements of the policy process. Fundamentalist Christian groups raised the issue to the policy agenda. The Arkansas legislature formulated and adopted a policy for implementation by that state's public schools. Other groups then carried the issue to another forum, a federal district court, where *another* policy was formulated and adopted.

Our story also illustrates the importance of the United States Constitution in the policy process. Throughout the controversy, the Constitution stood in the background. Constitutional questions were raised repeatedly during the debate over the issue and the final policy decision was made on constitutional grounds. Let's begin our study of the Constitution's role in the policy process by examining the background of its writing.

THE BACKGROUND OF THE CONSTITUTION

The United States Constitution is the fundamental law of the land by which the nation is organized and governed. The Congress, the president, the bureaucracy, the courts, the states, and the local governments are all subordinate to it and must conform to its principles. So, if the Arkansas legislature, for example, enacts legislation that is adjudged to be contrary to the provisions of the Constitution, it is struck down as unconstitutional.

Not all constitutions are written (Britain's is not) and not all are obeyed (the Soviet constitution, for example, guarantees religious freedom), but the American document is both. It dates back to 1787, making it the oldest national constitution still in effect in the world. Despite its age, the American Constitution still plays a major role in the political process of today. It deserves our study.

THE HISTORICAL BACKGROUND OF THE CONSTITUTION

To understand America's Constitution one must understand the circumstances that surrounded its composition. The Constitution was written in 1787 by men who had lived through two rather difficult periods: the late colonial period and the period under the government created by the Articles of Confederation. The Constitution is their reaction to these two experiences.

The relationship between Great Britain and her North American colonies was initially quite satisfactory for the Americans. London was very far away, and the Americans were generally allowed to govern themselves. Each colony had its own structures of government, its own laws, and its own locally chosen officeholders. King George's officials were seldom seen. The Americans were generally content with the arrangement.

In 1763, however, British authorities chose to reorganize their colonial system. The French and Indian War left London with a sizable financial burden, and the British looked to America for help. After all, the war had been fought to protect the Americans and the American colonies had contributed little money to the war effort. The primary contributions of the colonists had been manpower and material. Also, the British had other problems to deal with in North America: governing Canada, pacifying the

Indians (which meant limiting westward expansion by the colonies), and controlling smuggling.

Consequently, London decided to play a more direct role in governing her colonies in the New World. This meant more soldiers, more courts, more officials, more regulations, and more taxes. The British motive was to provide better governance in the colonies, but London misunderstood political realities in America and miscalculated the Americans' reaction, which was one of outrage. The colonists had been long used to a large measure of self-government, and they were unwilling to surrender that privilege. They saw the new policies as a violation of local traditions and an abridgement of their rights as British subjects. The dispute worsened, eventually leading to revolution and American independence.[3]

After the Revolutionary War, the United States was governed under the Articles of Confederation. The government created by the Articles had its strengths, more than is usually recognized, but it also had serious faults. The key problem was that the national government was simply too weak. The Articles had been written by men who had just gone through a period of governance by a central government they considered too strong—the British government. In reaction, they created a weak national government for the United States.

Experience proved, however, that the colonists had gone too far. The government under the Articles lacked the power to tax and the power to regulate commerce. It had to rely upon the states for revenue and for the implementation of national policies, but the states frequently failed to cooperate. To make matters worse, when the states did fail to cooperate, the national government had no other choice but to resort to the use of force—not a very satisfactory policy. To complicate matters further, changing the Articles to correct the problems required unanimous approval of the thirteen states and, thanks to stubborn Rhode Island, that could never be achieved. Before long, the United States treasury was empty, the economy was in chaos, and most Americans considered the new national experiment a failure.

This was the setting for the Constitutional Convention of 1787. The men who gathered that year in Philadelphia had lived under one central government they considered too strong (the British after 1763) and another they considered too weak (the government of the Articles). Now, they set about to create a government that would be neither, something more along the lines of their experience under British colonial rule before 1763. This they achieved by setting up a federal system of government (described on page 44).

THE PHILOSOPHICAL BACKGROUND OF THE CONSTITUTION

The men who drafted the United States Constitution were also influenced by the political ideas of their day. America was far distant from Europe

A political procession marks the adoption of the Constitution to replace the old Articles of Confederation. President Washington and members of Congress are shown atop the fort at left. The name of Hamilton at the base of the wagon attests to Alexander Hamilton's importance in bringing about the ratification of the Constitution.

geographically, but not intellectually. As a whole, Americans were a literate people, and the men who wrote the Constitution were among the most learned, well-read people in the world. It should come as no surprise that they were acquainted with and influenced by the great political ideas of their day.

The epoch in which the founders lived is known to historians as the **Enlightenment.** It was the Age of Reason, a time of abiding faith in the capacity of people to solve their problems in a rational manner. The very idea of a written constitution was grounded in the Enlightenment's belief that people were capable of governing themselves.

The Enlightenment was a time of belief in the doctrine of **natural rights.** This was the notion, argued by such thinkers as England's John Locke and France's Jean Jacques Rousseau, that people, in a state of nature, possessed certain rights. These rights existed regardless of any man-made laws, were enjoyed by all, and could not be taken away. This is what Locke meant when he spoke of the "inalienable rights of life, liberty, and property." The framers of America's Constitution put the doctrine of natural rights into practice by including a number of provisions limiting the power of government. Several of these were included in the original document; others were added in the Bill of Rights.[4]

The important constitutional principles of **separation of powers** and **checks and balances** were popular eighteenth-century political ideas as well. The Baron de Montesquieu, a French political philosopher, argued that there are three kinds of political power: the power to make laws **(legislative),** the power to enforce laws **(executive)**, and the power to interpret laws **(judicial).** If liberty is to be preserved, he said, these three powers should not all be held by the same person or the same group of people. There must be a separation of powers, dividing power among three officials or groups of officials. Also, to keep any one of these groups from becoming too strong, there must be a built-in system of checks and balances. The framers of America's Constitution adopted Montesquieu's ideas completely.

PURPOSES OF THE CONSTITUTION

The American Constitution was written to accomplish several purposes. First, it presents a framework for government. Examine Articles I, II, and III of the Constitution reprinted at the back of this book. Those articles prescribe the structures of American government; name the major government officials; and define their roles, powers, and responsibilities. As you can see, the Constitution creates a government of three branches: a legislative branch called the Congress, an executive branch headed by a president, and a judicial branch headed by the Supreme Court. The government established by the Constitution is also a **federal** system, dividing power between a national government (with authority over the whole nation) and a series of state governments.

A second purpose of the Constitution is to define the powers of government. The Preamble of the Constitution identifies the general goals of government: establish justice, ensure domestic tranquility, provide for the common defense, promote the general welfare, and secure the blessings of liberty. Articles I, II, and III enumerate the powers of government with greater specificity. In Article I, Congress is granted a number of powers, including the power to tax, to regulate commerce, to declare war, and to raise and support armed forces. Article II lists the powers of the president, including the power to act as commander in chief of the armed forces, the power to negotiate treaties, and the power to make appointments. Meanwhile, Article III declares that the judicial power of the United States is to be vested in the Supreme Court, and it lists the types of cases the Court may hear.

A third purpose of the Constitution is to limit the power of government. The very idea of writing down the powers of government implies that government is limited, that there are things government cannot do.[5] Yet the Constitution also spells out several important restrictions on governmental power. In Article I, Section 9, the Constitution guarantees the privilege of the **writ of habeas corpus** except in time of war or civil war. A writ of habeas corpus is a court order requiring government authorities either to release a person held in custody or to demonstrate that the person is being held in accordance with the law. Habeas corpus, then, insures that the police or the military may not simply arrest individuals and hold them without filing charges against them or trying them before a court of law. As you know, arrests of this kind occur today in many countries around the world.

Article I, Section 9 also prohibits the passage of **bills of attainder** and **ex post facto** laws. A bill of attainder is a law declaring a person or group of persons guilty of a crime and provides for punishment without benefit of indictment or trial. Meanwhile, an ex post facto law is a retroactive law. It makes a crime out of actions committed before the passage of the law. In other words, under an ex post facto law, someone could be punished for doing something which was not illegal when it was done.

Many other important limitations on the power of government are found in the amendments to the Constitution. The first ten amendments are known as the **Bill of Rights.** Among other things, they guarantee individual freedom of speech, freedom of religion, freedom of assembly, and freedom of the press. They protect against unreasonable searches and seizures, cruel and unusual punishments, and excessive fines. Persons accused of crimes are also guaranteed the right to confront witnesses who are testifying against them, to obtain counsel for their defense, and to be tried by a jury of their peers.

A number of other amendments also include protections of individual liberty. The Thirteenth Amendment prohibits slavery, while the Fourteenth Amendment guarantees all persons equal protection under state laws and forbids the states from taking life, liberty, or property without due process of law. The Fifteenth Amendment gives blacks the right to vote. Women's suffrage is granted in the Nineteenth Amendment. Finally, the Twenty-Fourth Amendment outlaws the poll tax, that is, a tax that must be paid before one is allowed to vote.

PROFILE OF THE CONSTITUTION

The United States Constitution represents a marriage of eighteenth-century political ideas and the practical political experiences of its authors. The marriage has had its rocky moments, during the Civil-War era in particular, but overall it has been a happy one. The document has endured for two centuries. Let us look in detail at some of its key aspects.

SEPARATION OF POWERS AND CHECKS AND BALANCES

Montesquieu's theories had been well accepted in America and most of the thirteen states' constitutions had provided for a balance and separation of powers. It wasn't surprising, then, that the Convention of 1787 divided power among legislative, executive, and judicial branches. The founders also incorporated a number of checks and balances into the system. For example, Supreme Court justices are appointed by the president, but their

THE RESULT OF THE FIFTEENTH AMENDMENT,
And the Rise and Progress of the African Race in America and its final Accomplishment, and Celebration on May 19ᵗʰ A.D 1870.

The adoption of the Fifteenth Amendment in 1870 was interpreted by many as a final step along the road to black participation in the political process. It would, however, be many years before the provisions of the amendment would be implemented with anything resembling full commitment on the part of the government.

appointments must be confirmed by the Senate. The Congress passes bills, but the president has the power to veto them. The Congress in turn can then override the veto with a two-thirds vote. Only the Congress can declare war, but the commander in chief of the armed forces is the president.

This elaborate system of check and countercheck was designed to ensure against any one official or small group of officials becoming too powerful, but in practice it has also guaranteed a certain amount of tension in the political system. The lines of demarcation among the powers of the three branches of government are not clearly drawn. In fact, the phrase *separation of powers* is somewhat misleading. What we really have is a system in which separate institutions *share* powers. Consequently, friction is inevitable.

American history abounds with examples of spokespersons for the president, the Congress, or the courts complaining that another branch is overreaching, usurping powers not rightfully its own. During the late 1950s and 1960s, for example, opponents in Congress and in the states attacked the Supreme Court for going too far in the areas of civil rights and the rights of the criminally accused. Also, in the 1960s and 1970s, congressional critics spoke ominously of an "imperial presidency," charging the president with overstepping his powers in the conduct of the war in

Southeast Asia. Later, Presidents Ford and Carter complained that Congress had placed too many restrictions on the president's power to manage foreign policy and on his power as commander in chief.

FEDERALISM

The Constitution of 1787 created a federal system, dividing political power between the federal government and the state governments. In theory, this was quite a bold step—the "political scientists" of the time held that **federalism** was an unworkable political form. In practice, though, the Americans were merely returning to a practice that had worked happily for them in the past. The pre-1763 British colonial rule in North America functioned much like a federal system. The local, colonial governments were fairly autonomous, operating as states do in a federal system. For the Americans, at least, the system worked well. It offered the opportunity for local control and local response to local problems. In a land far larger and more diverse than Great Britain, this was not only a virtue but a necessity.

In the Articles of Confederation, however, the Americans had gone too far. They created a **confederation,** a league of nearly independent states similar, in form, to the United Nations of the twentieth century. The federal system established in 1787 was designed to meet the need for a reasonably strong national government while maintaining the importance of the states. We will study the effects of federalism on policymaking in America in more detail in chapter 3.

BICAMERALISM

The Constitution created a **bicameral** legislature; that is, a Congress with two chambers, the Senate and the House of Representatives. The Constitution's authors debated long before finally reaching a compromise on how to determine representation for the two houses and how to choose the members of each. Representation in the House was to be based on population, the larger states getting more representatives than the smaller states. Meanwhile, the states would receive equal representation in the Senate, two senators from each. In the House, members would be selected by direct popular election, while members of the Senate would be chosen by the state legislatures. In 1913, however, the Seventeenth Amendment—providing for the direct popular election of senators—was ratified.

BILL OF RIGHTS

Individual rights was an important concept for the framers of the Constitution, but they included no bill of rights in the original document. The national government would not be powerful enough to threaten individual rights, they argued; therefore, no bill of rights was necessary. This became a major issue during the ratification debate, however, and eventually the Constitution's supporters agreed to support the addition of a series of amendments to serve as a bill of rights once the new Constitution took effect. This they did and by December 15, 1791, ten amendments had been adopted by Congress and ratified by a sufficient number of states. These came to be known as the Bill of Rights.[6]

Originally, the Bill of Rights was intended to apply only to the federal government. As the First Amendment states, "Congress shall make no law. . . ." There is no mention of state action. Then, at the close of the Civil War, Congress proposed the Fourteenth Amendment in order to place the civil rights of blacks on a firm footing. The states were forbidden to take life, liberty, or property without "due process of law," or to deny anyone "equal protection of the laws." States were also prohibited from making laws abridging the "privileges or immunities" of their citizens.

The exact intent of this phrasing is unclear, and it may not have been clear even to its authors. Some believed it included protection for basic rights in general; others thought it included all or some of the rights guaranteed in the Bill of Rights. Interpretation has fallen on the shoulders of the Supreme Court. In the twentieth century, the Court has ruled that the "due-process clause" of the Fourteenth Amendment binds the states to honor selective provisions of the Bill of Rights. This is known as the **selective incorporation of the Bill of Rights.** The Supreme Court has never ruled that the Bill of Rights as a whole binds the states, but it has selectively, one at a time, held that virtually all its key provisions affect the states through the due-process clause of the Fourteenth Amendment.[7] Consequently, Judge Overton held the Arkansas creation-science statute unconstitutional on the basis of the First *and* Fourteenth Amendments.

METHODS OF AMENDMENT

A major flaw in the Articles of Confederation was that they could be amended or changed only by unanimous vote. Consequently, correcting faults in them proved impossible because of the obstinacy of one or only a few states. In 1787, then, the Constitution's framers were careful to include a reasonable method of amendment—difficult enough to preclude hasty, ill-conceived changes, yet not impossible.

They provided two methods for proposing constitutional amendments and two methods for their ratification (see Figure 2.1). An amendment can be proposed by either a two-thirds vote of each house of Congress or by a constitutional convention called by Congress upon the application of two thirds of the states. The former method of proposal has been used many times; all twenty-six amendments that have been added to the Constitution were proposed by Congress.

In contrast, the convention procedure has never been used, but it may be soon. By the early 1980s, nearly three fourths of the state legislatures had

FIGURE 2.1

Amending the Constitution

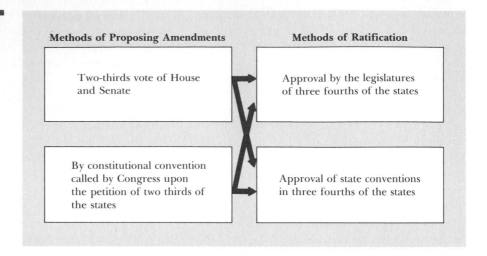

Methods of Proposing Amendments · Methods of Ratification

Two-thirds vote of House and Senate

By constitutional convention called by Congress upon the petition of two thirds of the states

Approval by the legislatures of three fourths of the states

Approval of state conventions in three fourths of the states

submitted petitions to Congress calling for a convention to consider an amendment requiring a balanced federal budget. Since the procedure has never been used, however, no one knows for sure just how the convention process would operate. The Constitution isn't specific. Would Congress *have* to call a convention if the required number of states submitted petitions? How would the convention delegates be chosen? Would the convention be limited to drafting an amendment to balance the budget or could it set about to rewrite the entire document? These are questions that cannot now be answered, but we may soon have the opportunity to find out.

After an amendment is proposed, either by Congress or by a convention, it must be ratified. This can be done either by vote of the legislatures of three fourths of the states or by approval of conventions in three fourths of the states. The former method has been used successfully twenty-five times, the latter only once (to ratify the Twenty-First Amendment repealing Prohibition).

Constitutional amendments have been the vehicles for a number of major policy changes in America. The first ten amendments constitute the Bill of Rights, of course. They and the Fourteenth Amendment have been significant agents of democratization. The same can be said for the Thirteenth Amendment that abolished slavery, the Fifteenth Amendment that gave blacks the right to vote, the Nineteenth that gave women the right to vote, the Twenty-Fourth that outlawed the poll tax, and the Twenty-Sixth that gave eighteen-year-olds the right to vote. Other amendments represent the culmination of major public-policy struggles. The Sixteenth Amendment legalized the income tax. The Eighteenth Amendment began Prohibition and the Twenty-First ended it.

For groups striving to shape the course of public policy, a constitutional amendment offers the closest thing to ultimate victory the American system affords. The United States Constitution is the supreme law of the land;

it is fundamental. All state laws, all acts of Congress, and all actions of executives, courts, and legislatures at all levels of government are subordinate to the Constitution. Amending the Constitution is extraordinarily difficult when controversial issues are involved, but once an amendment is ratified it is just as difficult to repeal (although that can be done as in the case of Prohibition).

The road to a constitutional amendment may be hard, but a number of groups believe their cause is worth the effort. In the 1970s and early 1980s, the Equal Rights Amendment (ERA), guaranteeing equality before the law regardless of sex, passed Congress and came within three states of ratification. Congress set, then extended, a time limit for ratification. That time limit finally expired in 1982, but women's-rights groups have vowed to continue the struggle, starting the process over again in the Congress. In the early 1980s, Congress also passed an amendment to grant the District of Columbia voting representation in the House and Senate. However, that proposal has made little headway toward ratification by the states.

A number of other proposed amendments are now under consideration by Congress. Abortion opponents want an amendment to outlaw abortion. Others are pushing for an amendment to permit oral prayers in public schools. Still others want an amendment requiring a balanced federal budget. Finally, there is sentiment to reform the electoral-college system by means of amendment. None of these seem likely to emerge from Congress in the near future, with the possible exception of the balanced-budget amendment.

Advocates of ratification and extension of the Equal Rights Amendment made a concerted effort in the early '80s, but failed to win congressional approval for their cause. If they are to hope to succeed in adding the ERA to the Constitution, they must begin the difficult and lengthy amendment process all over again.

THE CONSTITUTION TODAY: A LIVING DOCUMENT

The remarkable fact about the American Constitution is not just that it has survived for two hundred years, but that it has grown and matured with the nation, serving still as the fundamental framework for policymaking in America. When the original document was penned in 1787, the nation was rural and agrarian. There were only some four million inhabitants, and many of these were denied full rights of participation in the policymaking process—slaves, women, nonlandowners. Today, the country is dramatically changed, but the Constitution, with only twenty-six formal amendments, endures as the centerpiece of policymaking in America.

THE "MAJESTIC VAGUENESS" OF THE CONSTITUTION

The genius of America's Constitution lies in a quality that is sometimes labeled **"majestic vagueness."** At first, this seems to be a contradiction in terms. "Majestic" is a lofty adjective, but we seldom consider vagueness a virtue. What is the explanation?

The Constitution is a very brief, general document; it is frequently nonspecific. For example, the Eighth Amendment prohibits "cruel and unusual punishments." Just what does that mean? Presumably it forbids Chinese water torture or tying a criminal to an ant hill, but does it outlaw public floggings and placing criminals in the stocks? The latter punishments were used in colonial times. How about the death penalty? It is certainly cruel and fairly unusual in the United States of the 1980s.

Judge Overton found Arkansas' creation-science law unconstitutional because the First Amendment prohibits an "establishment of religion." But, what does "establishment of religion" mean precisely? Does it mean government may not give tax monies to religious organizations? Does it mean government may not grant tax exemptions to them? Does it mean government may not place "In God We Trust" on coins? The term "establishment of religion" is vague and requires interpretation.[8]

There are many other examples of vague terms and phrases in the document. Article I, Section 8 gives the Congress the power to "regulate commerce." What is commerce? Article II, Section 4 says the president may be impeached and removed from office for "treason, bribery, or other high crimes and misdemeanors." How are these defined? The Fourth Amendment prohibits "unreasonable searches and seizures," but what are they?

The Constitution is often vague, but the founders intended it to be so. They set down certain basic, fundamental principles, but they left out the details in order to allow succeeding generations to supply the specifics in light of their own experience. For example, the basic idea behind "cruel and unusual punishments" is that government is not to go too far in punishing criminals. What "too far" is depends on the times. Punishments acceptable in the 1790s might not be acceptable in the America of the 1980s. The prohibition against "unreasonable searches and seizures" means that there are limits on the police. Their exact nature depends on the standards of the day. Had the Constitution's framers decided to spell out everything in detail, they would have produced a document much longer and much less satisfactory than the one we have. Eventually, the nation would have outgrown it and either cast it aside or been forced to amend it repeatedly. Because the Constitution is vague, majestically vague, it has grown and matured with the country. Consequently, the Constitution has been able to change through informal processes, not just through the addition of numbered amendments.

JUDICIAL REVIEW AND THE PROCESS OF CONSTITUTIONAL CHANGE

The Constitution has changed by several means. Frequently, constitutional adaptation has occurred by accident or, at least, been unplanned. Consider the development of the political-party system, the committee structure in Congress, the cabinet, and the use of executive agreements by the president in lieu of formal treaties. There's not a word about any of these in the original Constitution, nor have they been prescribed by amendment. Nonetheless, they are an essential part of America's basic framework of government.[9]

The Constitution has also grown through the workings of the policy process. The role of the presidency today is far broader than it was in George Washington's time, but not because of formal amendment. For the most part, the powers of the presidency have grown through the experience of incumbent presidents, especially during wartime. The role of the bureaucracy in writing specific details of laws has developed because of the general authorization of that power by Congress. Consequently, many regulatory agencies now exercise all three of the basic powers of government: legislative, executive, and judicial.

The most important avenue for constitutional change, however, has been judicial interpretation. In fact, it is no exaggeration to say that what counts most in constitutional law is what the Supreme Court says. The Constitution itself is merely secondary. Many phrases important to constitutional law aren't even in the Constitution, including "war power," "clear and present danger," "interstate commerce," "separation of church and state," and "police power." As constitutional historian Leonard Levy puts it, these phrases are "judicial glosses."[10] Also, as we have seen, many of the phrases in the Constitution are purposefully ambiguous. They call out for continuous reinterpretation and adaptation. In large measure, Levy says, we have an unwritten Constitution whose history is the history of judicial interpretation.[11]

The process by which the courts interpret the Constitution is known as

judicial review. Since the case of *Marbury* v. *Madison* (1803) (see **PERSPEC-TIVE** on this page), it has been accepted practice for the courts, ultimately the Supreme Court, to hold the actions of the states and the branches of the national government up to scrutiny in light of the letter and spirit of the Constitution.[12] If the court finds the actions violate the Constitution, it declares them unconstitutional and hence null and void. This is what Judge Overton did with the Arkansas creation-science statute.

Judicial review requires the courts to interpret the Constitution in light of current circumstances and current judicial thinking. For example, the Sixth Amendment says that a person accused of a crime is entitled to "assistance of Counsel for his defense." Clearly, this means that accused persons have the right to hire an attorney, but what if a defendant cannot afford one? Must he or she go defenseless or is the government to provide a lawyer at public expense? In 1942 in the case of *Betts* v. *Brady*, the

Perspective

MARBURY V. *MADISON*

Today, *Marbury* v. *Madison* is recognized as the first case in which the Supreme Court exercised its power of judicial review by ruling an act of Congress unconstitutional. In its own day, however, the case was more significant for its political overtones.

The controversy had its roots in the election of 1800, when President John Adams was defeated for reelection and his party, the Federalists, lost their majority in Congress. In the time between the election and the inauguration of the new president, Thomas Jefferson, Adams proceeded to nominate, and the Senate to confirm, the appointments of a number of loyal Federalists to the federal courts.

One of these judicial appointments went to William Marbury, who was named a justice of the peace for the District of Columbia. President Adams signed and

sealed Marbury's official commission on the day before he was to leave office. Unfortunately for Marbury, however, the secretary of state failed to deliver the commission. Then, when President Jefferson took office, he ordered his new secretary of state, James Madison, not to deliver the commission. Marbury subsequently sued, asking the Supreme Court to issue a **writ of mandamus** against Madison, that is, a court order directing him to deliver the commission.

The case presented the Court with a difficult dilemma. Chief Justice Marshall and his fellow Federalist judges would have liked nothing better than to blast the Jefferson Administration and order Madison to deliver the commission. Had the Court done so, however, it was quite clear that Jefferson would simply defy the Court. Marshall knew that would destroy the Court's pres-

tige, but he also wanted to avoid ruling for the administration.

Judicial review provided Marshall and the Court with a way out of their dilemma. Marshall used the Court's opinion to scold Jefferson and Madison for refusing to deliver the commission. Marbury was entitled to his commission, said Marshall, and a writ of mandamus was in order, but the Court did not have the power to issue the writ. Marshall ruled that the section of the Judiciary Act that gave the Court the power to issue writs of mandamus was *unconstitutional*. By this means, Marshall was able to deliver a political attack against Jefferson and still avoid risking Jefferson's defiance of the Court's power. At the same time, Marshall established the historic precedent for the Supreme Court's ability to declare certain laws unconstitutional.

NAME_____   NUMBER_____

In The Supreme Court of The United States
        Washington D.C.
Clarence Earl Gideon
        Petitioner—   Petition for a writ
    vs.   of Certiorari Directed
H. G. Cochran, Jr, as   to The Supreme Court
Director, Divisions   State of Florida.
of corrections state   No. 890 Misc.
of Florida.   OCT. TERM 1961
                             U. S. Supreme Court
To The Honorable Earl Warren, Chief
    Justice of the United States
        Comes now The petitioner, Clarence
Earl Gideon, a citizen of The United States
of America, in proper person, and appearing

Clarence Earl Gideon's handwritten petition to the Supreme Court to hear his case involving the right of indigent defendants to legal representation. The result of this petition was Gideon v. Wainwright, *a landmark Supreme Court decision.*

Supreme Court held that indigent defendants need be provided counsel only in special circumstances: when the death penalty is involved or when the accused is illiterate, feebleminded, or underage.[13] Otherwise, indigent defendants must defend themselves. In 1963, however, in the case of *Gideon* v. *Wainwright,* the Supreme Court ruled that the Sixth Amendment (through the Fourteenth Amendment) requires states to provide lawyers for all defendants who cannot afford one.[14] *Betts* v. *Brady* was overturned. No constitutional amendment had been enacted, but the Constitution was changed just as surely as if one had.

CONCLUSION: THE CONSTITUTION AND PUBLIC POLICY

Because of its adaptability, the American Constitution is still a very relevant part of the public-policy process of the 1980s. In one way or another, nearly every important policy issue is affected by the Constitution. It animates policy debates and sets the ground rules for their resolution.

CONSTITUTIONAL ISSUES IN POLICYMAKING

Constitutional questions are frequently raised in policy debates, injecting historical issues into current policy deliberations. The Watergate impeachment proceedings involving President Richard Nixon illustrate this point. The White House, Congress, the press, academicians, and the Supreme

Changing the Constitution
A CONVERSATION WITH PAUL L. MURPHY, UNIVERSITY OF MINNESOTA

Q. One of the most important constitutional developments of our day is the drive to convene a new constitutional convention. Nearly two thirds of the state legislatures have sent petitions to Congress asking it to call a convention to consider constitutional amendments. What is the basis for this?

A. Article V of the United States Constitution provides for two ways of amending that document. Congress by a vote of two thirds of both houses can propose particular amendments. Or a constitutional convention for the purpose of proposing amendments can be convened by Congress if two thirds of the state legislatures ask Congress to do so. In either case, any amendments proposed become part of the Constitution if ratified by three fourths of the states.

Q. Has the convention method ever been used?

Paul L. Murphy teaches in the Department of History and the Program of American Studies at the University of Minnesota. He has written and lectured extensively on American constitutional and legal history, and on the history of civil liberties and civil rights in the United States.

A. No. We have had only one constitutional convention in American history at the national level, the one called in 1787 to amend the Articles of Confederation. Since that time there have been over three hundred applications for conventions from the states, but none has ever been called. In some instances, where such petitions have seemed to have widespread support, Congress has passed the proposed amendments and sent them to the states for ratification rather than risk a convention. The most recent example was in 1913, when the Seventeenth Amendment, providing for direct election of U.S. senators by the people, was adopted. The first such example was in 1789, a move which resulted in the adoption of the Bill of Rights.

Q. So why is a convention being pushed at this time, and by whom?

A. Those currently calling for a convention are seeking a con-

Court all were caught up in ascertaining the precise meaning of such phrases as "high crimes and misdemeanors" and "faithfully execute the office of President of the United States." What Nixon had or had not done was important, but when the impeachment business got serious, the motives of the founders and the constitutional precedents in the late eighteenth and early nineteenth centuries surged to the forefront of the debates and legal briefs.

The virtue of this emphasis on constitutionalism is that it provides an avenue for the resolution of controversies without violence. Americans view the Constitution with great deference. Once the constitutional issue is settled, that ends the controversy for many—at least in the short run. The

stitutional amendment requiring the federal government to have a balanced budget. The support comes principally from conservative groups, especially the National Taxpayers Union, whose aim is to reduce federal-government spending and taxation and cut down sharply on the size and authority of the federal government.

Q. What are the arguments of the opponents of the convention idea?

A. As to the specific amendment, many experts argue that economic policy does not belong in the Constitution, and such an amendment would cripple the government's authority to deal with fluctuations in the economy, especially depressions and recessions. They also worry about potential compliance problems, and how such an amendment could be enforced. But, more generally, critics fear a "runaway convention" which might move quickly to a whole range of amendments, from antiabortion, to antibusing, to school prayer. Some even fear that in the hands of a militantly conservative leadership, such a convention might repeal much of the Bill of Rights, and thus significantly alter American government.

Q. Are these fears in any way justified? Aren't there safeguards in the Constitution that would prevent them?

A. Authorities differ sharply. Regrettably, Article V is quite vague. It does not make clear the procedure to start, stop, pause, or populate such a convention. The precedent of the first constitutional convention is itself disturbing. There the delegates broke every legal restraint designed to limit their power and agenda. They violated specific instructions from Congress to confine themselves to amend-ing the Articles of Confederation and instead discarded the Articles altogether and wrote our present Constitution. This could happen again, and there is no certainty that our nation would survive a modern convention with its basic structures intact and its citizens' basic rights retained. Therefore some fear a new constitutional convention could be dangerous and reckless.

Q. But hasn't the American Bar Association argued that Congress could responsibly structure such a convention?

A. Yes. Some authorities do feel Congress could contain such a movement. Congress can decide whether state applications amount to a legitimate call for a convention for proposing amendments. Congress would also seem to have power to limit the scope of such a gathering. In fact, the Senate in 1971 passed a Constitutional Procedure Act,

(to next page)

losers must turn their attention to amending the Constitution, but that's a long, laborious struggle that usually serves only to dissipate their energies. In the process, passions cool and compromises can be reached.

On the other hand, the raising of constitutional issues has a way of sidetracking the policy process. The Constitution possesses great symbolic force in American politics. To argue a course of action on its merits is one way to conduct a policy debate, but describing that policy as constitutional or unconstitutional packs a more potent political punch. It is perfectly legitimate to invoke the Constitution in policy debates, of course, but the problem comes when constitutional issues obscure practical factors. In the evolution-versus-creation controversy, for example, the debate over the

setting up procedures for limiting the powers of a constitutional convention. But the House rejected the measure, arguing forcefully that neither Congress nor the courts can limit a convention once it begins. Further, many members of Congress are not keen about setting the rules, because such a convention would in effect usurp some of Congress's authority. In fact, some constitutional experts feel that a convention would be *above* the three branches of the government and could thereby disregard Congress' guidelines because it would be above the law. Even if Congress did limit the topics to be considered, the convention would not necessarily feel bound by such limitations.

Q. But isn't it democratic to allow the people to change the Constitution?

A. No, it isn't democratic as long as the rules governing such conventions are so unclear. As it is currently, many of the thirty-plus state legislatures that support the current call for a convention did so with hardly any debate or study at all. In sixteen, there were no full committee hearings and public witnesses were not allowed to testify. In fifteen, there were no committee reports. And in six states there were no recorded votes. In fact, in Colorado, a house committee approved its state petition after discussing it for less than six minutes. This hardly suggests popular participation in the process. Also, the nature of the later steps in the process is unclear. Who would serve as delegates to such a convention and how would they be elected? Could Congress appoint its own members as delegates? Would the states be equally represented as they were in the original constitutional convention in 1787 or would the one person, one vote rule apply as it now does in the elections for all legislative bodies other than the U.S. Senate? Could Congress prescribe rules for the convention, or limit its amending power? How would such a convention be funded? Could Congress withhold appropriations? How long could the convention remain in session? Would its sessions be held in secret as in 1787, or would media coverage be demanded and obtained? Could Congress refuse to submit to the states for ratification any amendment proposed by the convention? Could Congress set a short time limit for ratification? Who would decide such disputes between Congress and the convention?

First Amendment overshadowed what many would call a more pertinent debate over government policy and science education, involving questions over who should determine curricula and on what grounds.

The most important way in which the Constitution affects policymaking today is that it fragments political power. The separation-of-powers provisions divide power at the national level among legislative, judicial, and executive branches. Bicameralism, in turn, splits the legislative branch in two, dividing power between a House and a Senate. The development of the committee system in Congress and the executive bureaucracy have fragmented power even more. Meanwhile, federalism divides power still further among the levels of government—national, state, and local.

Consider the contrast in policymaking between Great Britain and the United States. In Britain, political power is concentrated in the hands of

Constitutional scholars disagree. And no one knows if even the United States Supreme Court would have authority to resolve such disputes. Thus it is unclear how the people could successfully participate in the process.

Q. But couldn't these questions be resolved in advance?

A. Congress could attempt to answer these questions through enacting an enabling statute clarifying all such matters. The question that still nags is whether a constitutional convention would feel bound by such action. The best solution might well be for rules governing such constitutional conventions to be established by a constitutional amendment, thereby assuring that no convention could put itself above the "Supreme Law of the Land."

Q. So you are saying that the convention method of amending the Constitution couldn't work and shouldn't be tried?

A. Certainly at the moment the mechanisms necessary to make it work are not in place. However, it is difficult to argue that it should not be considered. The current single-issue movement for a balanced-budget amendment through the convention process may well be primarily a political maneuver. Its advocates may be using the convention idea as a diversionary attempt to pressure Congress into using the traditional amendment process. Thus the threat of using a highly undefined constitutional technique may be enough to activate the use of procedures that have proved to be workable and accepted. It might be well to leave this provision unimplemented and yet always have it available as a means by which citizens can press legislative bodies to act on issues they might not wish to come to terms with. In this way, the ends sought might be attained through means people are comfortable with and whose limitations are well understood. After all, constitutional history is the story of pragmatic adaptation of the Constitution to democratic problem-solving. This is surely a principal reason why we keep an eighteenth-century Constitution and why we respect it.

Parliament. The prime minister is chosen by the Parliament, and the courts lack the power of judicial review. Consequently, the election of a new parliamentary majority can make for a dramatic change in the direction of public policy in Britain; policy can change rather quickly.

In contrast, the fragmentation of political power in America makes for slow, incremental change. A president needs the cooperation of Congress to have his programs enacted. For its part, Congress has difficulty acting without presidential initiative or at least acquiescence. Both president and Congress need the support of the bureaucracy if their policies are to be faithfully implemented, and frequently they need the cooperation of state and local officials as well. Meanwhile, the courts can reverse or delay policies adopted at other levels or by other branches of government. With so many steps and so many power centers involved in the policy process in

America, change is usually quite slow acoming if it comes at all. What changes do occur are generally incremental, gradual changes, reflecting compromise among the various power centers involved in the process.

Jeff MacNelly. Tribune Media Service, Inc. Reprinted by permission.

America's constitutional system is biased in favor of the status quo, but that's because the founders preferred a system that would ensure deliberation and delay rather than precipitous action. They were cautious people, wary of rapid change and none too confident about the judgment of popular majorities. Consequently, they deliberately created a constitutional apparatus that would work slowly and that would be unlikely to produce dramatic upheavals in public policy. The founders feared that too often rapid, major change would produce more harm than good. With the system they established, they ensured that nothing bad would happen quickly; with luck, it might not happen at all. Cooler heads would have time to prevail.

The framers also wanted to ensure that the diversity of political interests in American society would be represented in the policy process. During the debates at the convention of 1787, one of the major issues concerned how best to protect the small states from large-state domination. Consequently, the authors of America's Constitution created a system that would provide opportunity for the many groups and interests of American society to have a say in policymaking. In the 1980s, many Americans still see this as a virtue.

PROBLEMS IN CONSTITUTIONAL POLICYMAKING

America's constitutional arrangements are not without their critics, however. Some say that the fragmentation of power in America's political structures encourages buck-passing. The president, members of Congress, and state officials can always blame some other branch or some other official for policy failures. According to the critics, the Constitution divides responsibility in so many ways that no one is responsible. The public ends up having to blame everyone or no one.

Another criticism is that America's constitutional arrangements abet the power of interest groups. The constitutional fragmentation of power that presents a range of forums in which different groups can be heard also provides a series of power centers that interest groups can dominate. Because of the complexity of the constitutional process, entrenched groups can frequently muster the influence to halt policy changes they consider unfavorable, even though the changes may be supported by a sizable majority in Congress and a majority in the nation. One critic describes the situation this way: "When we demand a system of fair, general sacrifice, our constitutional machine seems programmed to produce only general selfishness."[15]

The most basic criticism of the Constitution, though, is that it is a blueprint for political deadlock among the branches and units of government. By dividing government against itself, the founders ensured that all proposals for policy change must pass through a labyrinth of power centers. The complexity of the arrangement not only slows the policymaking process, it also gives most of the trump cards to the forces opposing whatever policy proposal is under consideration. It's easier to defeat policy proposals than to pass them.

In today's political world, say the critics, the outcome of the policymaking process is, all too frequently, stalemate. Presidential proposals are thwarted by Congress while congressional initiatives are vetoed by the president. The result is that the elected branches of government are unable or unwilling to govern. Major policy problems remain unresolved or are left to the bureaucracy and the courts to handle.[16]

So who's right—the Constitution's defenders or its critics? That's a question that you will have to answer for yourself. By the end of this book we believe you will be better prepared to make a judgment. After all, the study of public policymaking in America invariably involves the Constitution, either directly or indirectly.

Do you recall the illustration with which we began this chapter? The Arkansas evolution controversy encapsulates the role of the Constitution in today's public-policy process. In the forefront were interest groups, legislators, and educators all debating the merits of a particular policy. In the background, however, stood the Constitution, whose literal language and historic intent were debated by both sides. The Constitution set the ground rules for debate, and it was on constitutional grounds that a federal judge determined the outcome. The evolution-creation debate will not likely end with the Arkansas ruling, of course. There may be appeals or the enactment of similar laws in other states. One thing is certain, though: the debate will be shaped by constitutional questions. Such is the importance of the Constitution for policymaking in today's America.

KEY TERMS

BICAMERAL *(44)*

BILL OF RIGHTS *(42)*

BILLS OF ATTAINDER *(42)*

CHECKS AND BALANCES *(40)*

CONFEDERATION *(44)*

ENLIGHTENMENT *(40)*

EXECUTIVE *(40)*

EX POST FACTO *(42)*

FEDERAL *(41)*

FEDERALISM *(44)*

JUDICIAL *(40)*

JUDICIAL REVIEW *(50)*

LEGISLATIVE *(40)*

"MAJESTIC VAGUENESS" *(48)*

NATURAL RIGHTS *(40)*

SELECTIVE INCORPORATION OF THE BILL OF RIGHTS *(45)*

SEPARATION OF POWERS *(40)*

WRIT OF HABEAS CORPUS *(41)*

WRIT OF MANDAMUS *(50)*

NOTES

1. Lawrence W. Levine, *Defender of the Faith* (London: Oxford University Press, 1965).
2. Max Woodfin, "Adam and Eve Expelled," *Texas Observer,* 29 January 1982, pp. 1, 4–6.
3. Alfred H. Kelly and Winfred A. Harbison, *The American Constitution,* 4th ed. (New York: W. W. Norton, 1970); and Jack P. Greene, *The Reinterpretation of the American Revolution* (New York: Harper and Row, 1968).
4. Jethro K. Lieberman, *Understanding Our Constitution* (New York: Walker and Co., 1967).
5. C. Herman Pritchett, *The American Constitutional System,* 3rd ed. (New York: McGraw-Hill, 1971).
6. Robert Rutland, *The Birth of the Bill of Rights, 1776–1791* (Chapel Hill: University of North Carolina Press, 1955).
7. Henry J. Abraham, *Freedom and the Court,* 4th ed. (New York: Oxford University Press, 1982), ch. 3.
8. How has the Supreme Court answered these questions? In order: yes, no, and no.
9. Pritchett, ch. 1.
10. Leonard Levy, *Judgments: Essays on American Constitutional History* (Chicago: Quadrangle Books, 1972), p. 17.
11. Ibid., ch. 2.
12. *Marbury* v. *Madison,* 1 Cranch 137 (1803).
13. *Betts* v. *Brady,* 316 U.S. 455 (1942).
14. *Gideon* v. *Wainwright,* 372 U.S. 335 (1963).
15. Robert M. Kaus, "Power to the People: Making the Constitution Work Again," *Washington Monthly* 11 (October 1979): 51.
16. Ibid.

SUGGESTED READINGS

ABRAHAM, HENRY, J. *Freedom and the Court.* 4th ed. New York: Oxford University Press, 1982.

BEARD, CHARLES A. *An Economic Interpretation of the Constitution.* New York: Macmillan, 1913.

CORWIN, EDWARD S., AND PELTASON, JACK W. *Understanding the Constitution.* Rev. ed. New York: Dryden Press, 1958.

FERRAND, MAX. *The Framing of the Constitution of the United States.* New Haven: Yale University Press, 1913.

GARVEY, GERALD. *Constitutional Bricolage.* Princeton, N. J.: Princeton University Press, 1971.

GOLDWIN, ROBERT A., AND SCHAMBRA, WILLIAM A., eds. *How Democratic is the Constitution?* Washington, D.C.: American Enterprise Institute, 1980.

KELLEY, ALFRED H., AND HARBISON, WINFRED A. *The American Constitution: Its Origins and Development,* 5th ed. New York: Norton, 1976.

LEVY, LEONARD. *Judgments: Essays on American Constitutional History.* Chicago: Quadrangle Books, 1972.

ROSSITER, CLINTON. *1787: The Grand Convention.* New York: Macmillan, 1966.

SMITH, PAGE. *The Constitution: A Documentary and Narrative History.* New York: Morrow, 1978.

WOOD, GORDON S. *The Creation of the American Republic,* 1776–1787. Chapel Hill, N.C.: University of North Carolina Press, 1969.

Chapter Three

FEDERALISM

FEDERALISM AND THE CONSTITUTION

The Powers of State and Nation
The limits of power / National powers / Guarantees to the states

Judicial Interpretations and *McCulloch* v. *Maryland*

THE DEVELOPMENT OF THE FEDERAL SYSTEM

1789–1913: The System Established

1913–1950: Cooperative Federalism

The 1950s: Federalism in Transition

The 1960s: Federalism in Turmoil

The 1970s and 1980s: Federalism in Crisis

INTERGOVERNMENTAL PROGRAMS: POLICY AND POLITICS

Setting the Agenda

Formulating Policy

Adopting Policy

Implementing the Programs

Evaluating the System

Reforming the System

CONCLUSION: THE BACKGROUND OF POLICYMAKING

On January 26, 1982, President Ronald Reagan used the first State of the Union address of his presidency to propose significant changes in America's federal system, which, he said, had become unresponsive to the people.

> *Our citizens feel they have lost control of even the most basic decisions about the essential services of government, such as schools, welfare, roads, and even garbage collection. They are right. A maze of interlocking jurisdictions and levels of government confronts average citizens in trying to solve even the simplest problems. They do not know where to turn for answers, who to hold accountable, who to praise, who to blame, who to vote for or against.[1]*

The president called for taking certain powers and responsibilities away from the national government and distributing them among state and local authorities. "Let us solve this problem with a single bold stroke," he said, "the return of some $47 billion in federal programs to state and local government, together with the means to finance them."[2]

The details of Reagan's "New Federalism," as it was soon labeled, involved a swap of intergovernmental responsibilities. He proposed that the national government take over total control and financing of the Medicaid program of health care for the poor while states would assume responsibility for two other welfare programs: Food Stamps and Aid to Families with Dependent Children (AFDC). A host of other programs operated by the federal government would be turned over to state and local governments as well, including most federal highway and bridge projects, aid to mass transit and airports, sewerage treatment programs, rural water and sewer projects, vocational rehabilitation programs, child nutrition aid, low-income energy aid, various health and social-service programs, and virtually all education programs. To help the states finance these programs, Reagan called for the creation of a "federal trust fund." The fund would be phased out after eight years, however.

President Reagan's "New Federalism" can be seen as part of his administration's emphasis on reducing federal government involvement in the everyday lives of citizens. One way of reducing this involvement, in Reagan's view, is by giving states and localities greater responsibility and authority over local projects; another is by encouraging private business and individuals to rehabilitate their own communities, such as this devastated section of the South Bronx.

61

Disputes over federalism are nothing new in American politics. The nature of the federal system was a topic of hot debate at the Constitutional Convention of 1787, and the issue has arisen again and again throughout American history. As long ago as 1822, President James Monroe vetoed federal money for tollgates on the Cumberland Road, saying they threatened the integrity of the federal system. In modern times, calls for reforming the system have been frequent. Lyndon Johnson offered what he called "Creative Federalism" and Richard Nixon proposed a "New Federalism" program of his own.

President Reagan's New Federalism proposals have revived a perennial debate about federalism in America that is as complicated as it is longstanding, involving philosophical, practical, and political questions. In this chapter, we will attempt to explain this most complex feature of American government. Certainly it is an important topic to understand. We can think of few aspects of policymaking in America that are not profoundly affected by the federal system. In the pages ahead, we will examine the constitutional background of federalism, its historical development, and the politics of intergovernmental relations today.

Before we begin, however, it might be helpful to define both federalism and **intergovernmental relations.** As we noted in chapter 2, federalism refers to a system of government in which power is shared between a national government and a series of state or regional governments. Intergovernmental relations refers to the interactions among the various units of government in America—the nation, the states, cities, counties, townships, school districts, and other units of local government. Federalism and intergovernmental relations are not synonymous, but they are closely related. For our purposes, we will use the two terms roughly interchangeably as we discuss the distribution of political power among the various units of government in America.

FEDERALISM AND THE CONSTITUTION

As you recall from our discussion in chapter 2, the men who gathered in Philadelphia in 1787 to write a constitution had lived under several different constitutional arrangements. In the beginning, the British North American colonies were part of a **unitary system** in which ultimate political power was concentrated in the hands of a single government in London. The colonial governments had been created by Parliament and were allowed to exercise only the powers specifically granted to them. In practice, before 1763 London had permitted the colonists a great deal of freedom in managing their local affairs, and the Americans had been satisfied with the arrangement. After 1763, however, the British authorities decided to exert more direct control over their North American possessions. The Americans' deep displeasure with this new arrangement eventually led to revolution and American independence.

The United States' first national constitution, the Articles of Confederation, established a *confederal* form of government, a **confederation.** It was a league of nearly independent states, somewhat like the United Nations of today. Individual Americans were citizens of their respective states; there was no such thing as national citizenship. The national government had no power for dealing directly with individuals, only with the governments of the thirteen states.

The government under the Articles proved a failure, however, and in 1787 the states sent delegates to Philadelphia to remedy the situation. Their goal was to create a governmental system that would be capable of effective government but that would not be a threat to liberty. They created the federal system.

On the one hand, federalism provided a means of political representation that could accommodate the diversity of American society.[3] Individual Americans would be citizens of both their states and the nation and would participate in the selection of representatives to both governments. The constituents of the government under the Articles were the thirteen states, but under the new federal system the national government would be able to deal directly with individuals. No longer would disputes over tax collection and the enforcement of national laws inevitably develop into conflicts between nation and state. Now, they could be settled on an individual basis; a national judiciary was established to facilitate that process.

On the other hand, federalism was also a mechanism for protecting individual freedom from governmental interference. Bicameralism and

According to this 1788 cartoon, once the states of Virginia and New York ratified the Constitution, the federal system would be solidly in place and a new golden age could begin, even if Rhode Island and North Carolina failed to ratify.

the separation of powers were created to insure against the concentration of power within the national government. Federalism was designed to provide a check and balance on the power of both state and nation.[4]

THE POWERS OF STATE AND NATION

The founders created a federal system in which the national and state governments share power, but they did not totally separate the powers of each level. Let's consider what the Constitution has to say about the powers of government.

The limits of power.   The first and perhaps most important point is that the Constitution restricts the powers of government. Indeed, the very idea of a written constitution implies that the powers of government are limited. Turn to the Appendix in the back of this book and read Article I, Sections 9 and 10 of the United States Constitution. Both the national and state governments are prohibited from enacting ex post facto laws and bills of attainder, from taxing interstate commerce, and from granting titles of nobility. Other limitations on the power of the national government include the provision that money cannot be withdrawn from the treasury unless it is duly appropriated. Also, Congress may not grant preferential treatment to any state nor suspend the writ of habeas corpus except in dire circumstances. States are prohibited from making treaties or alliances and from entering into confederacies. They may not coin money, nor may they impair the obligation of contracts.

Other important restrictions on the powers of government are found in the amendments to the Constitution. The Bill of Rights, for example, limits the powers of the national government by guaranteeing certain individual rights and liberties. In the twentieth century, the Supreme Court has interpreted the Fourteenth Amendment so as to apply most of the provisions of the Bill of Rights to the states as well. Other amendments also impose restrictions on governmental power in America. The Fifteenth and Nineteenth, for example, give blacks and women the right to vote in elections for offices at all levels of government. The Twenty-fourth Amendment prohibits the poll tax in national elections.

National powers.   The Constitution discusses the powers of the national government in Articles I, II, III, and VI. Articles I and VI, in particular, deserve our scrutiny. Article I, Section 8 lists what are known as the **delegated powers.** "The Congress shall have Power," it says, "to lay and collect Taxes, Duties, Imposts and Excises, to pay the Debts and provide for the common Defense and general Welfare. . . ." Among other powers, Congress is granted the authority to borrow money, regulate commerce, coin money, declare war, create courts, raise and support armies and navies, govern the District of Columbia, and establish post offices.

The last of the delegated powers is more general than the others. It is known as the **necessary and proper clause:** "To make all Laws which shall

t and South.
most serious
pression. In
tates passed
or example,
Baltimore
business in
re wanted.
and Mary-
se: Does a
Does the

by Chief
aryland's
power to
n out of
tax an
national
ture of
refore,

bank
at the
rticle
rrow
ked
Th
s

g into Execution the foregoing Powers,
Constitution in the Government of the
nt or Officer thereof."

the issue of the powers of the national

of the United States which shall be made in
aties made, or which shall be made, under the
shall be the supreme Law of the Land; and the
bound thereby; any Thing in the Constitution or
rary notwithstanding.

al supremacy clause.

The founders also included a number of guar-
icle IV, the Constitution declares that states may
lated without their permission. They are guaran-
of government, protection against invasion, and
estic violence when requested. Article V pledges
eprived of equal representation in the Senate. The
promises that the federal courts will not hear law-
a state by individual citizens. Finally, there is the
which we quote in full: "The powers not delegated to
by the Constitution, nor prohibited it by the States, are
tates respectively, or to the people."

INTERPRETATIONS AND
CH v. MARYLAND

n see, the Constitution draws few clearcut lines of demarcation
the powers of the national government and those of the state
ments. Constitutional guidelines in this area are fairly general and
vague. Consequently, as controversies have arisen, the United States
Supreme Court has played the role of umpire.

The Court's most important precedent in the area of nation-state relationships and the powers of government came in the famous case of
McCulloch v. *Maryland*, decided in 1819.[5] The background of the case dates
to 1791, when Congress chartered a national bank, the First Bank of the
United States, amid great controversy. Thomas Jefferson and others argued that the national government should adhere strictly to the letter of
the delegated powers of the Constitution. Since the power to charter banks
is not expressly granted, they contended, Congress' action was unconstitutional. On the other hand, Alexander Hamilton argued that Congress'
action was justified as an exercise of authority reasonably *implied* by the
delegated powers. Despite the debate, there was never a legal challenge.
The bank operated until its charter expired in 1811.

In 1816, Congress chartered the Second Bank of the United States and it

too became the subject of controversy, especially in the Wes
Accusations of corruption and inefficiency arose, but the
charge was that the bank was responsible for an economic de
response to the public outcry against the bank, a number of s
restrictions on it or imposed heavy taxes against it. Maryland, f
required payment of an annual tax of $15,000 on the bank'
branch, which was a sum large enough to drive the bank out of
the state. This, of course, was just what the Maryland legislatu
McCulloch, the bank's cashier, refused to comply with the law,
land sued. Two basic constitutional issues were raised by the ca
state have the power to tax an arm of the federal government?
national government have the authority to charter a bank?[6]

The unanimous opinion of the Supreme Court was written
Justice John Marshall. On the one hand, the Court ruled that M
tax was unconstitutional. The power to tax, said Marshall, is the
destroy, since a very high tax can drive the object of the taxatio
existence. Consequently, if Maryland or any state has the power to
arm of the national government, it could effectively shut down the
government. That, concluded Marshall, would be contrary to the na
the federal union as stated in the national supremacy clause. The
Maryland's tax was unconstitutional.

On the other hand, the Court upheld Congress' power to charter
on the basis of the doctrine of **implied powers.** Marshall admitted th
power to incorporate a bank is not among the delegated powers, but A
I, Section 8 does include the powers to lay and collect taxes, to bo
money, and to raise and support armies and navies. What if, he a
money raised in the North is needed in the South to support the army?
creation of a national bank to transport that money would be a "neces
and proper" step to execute the delegated power and would therefor
constitutional. The power to charter the bank, Marshall held, was *implied*
the necessary and proper clause. Then, in one of the most famous passa
in constitutional law, Marshall broadly defined the extent of impli
powers:

> Let the end be legitimate, let it be within the scope of the Constitution, and all
> means which are appropriate, which are plainly adapted to that end, which are not
> prohibited, but consistent with the letter and spirit of the Constitution, are constitu-
> tional.[7]

In sum, the Marshall Court found few constitutional limitations on the
powers of the national government. It stressed national supremacy and the
doctrine of implied powers while totally ignoring the Tenth Amendment as
an independent curb on the powers of the national government. Essentially, the Court of Marshall's day interpreted the Tenth Amendment as
little more than the truism that states have all the powers not denied them
by the Constitution.[8]

Between the 1870s and the 1930s, however, the *McCulloch* precedent

*John Marshall, chief
justice of the United
States, 1801–1835.*

gathered dust as successive generations of Supreme Court justices developed a different vision of the federal system that one scholar has labeled **dual federalism**.[9] According to this doctrine, the states are equal partners with the national government in the federal system; each level of government has its own set of powers, which are fixed and immutable. During this period, especially in the early 1930s, the Court used dual federalism as justification for striking down both national and state laws as unconstitutional invasions of the prerogatives of the other level of government.

In 1937, however, the Supreme Court changed its course and returned to the Marshallian view of the federal system. *McCulloch* v. *Maryland* was back in vogue. Once again, the Court discounted the Tenth Amendment's provision of powers reserved to the states as a barrier to the expansion of federal power. In fact, since 1937, the Court has ruled only once that an act of Congress was an unconstitutional encroachment on state powers, and that ruling was probably an aberration.[10] Today, the Court has generally left the development of the federal system in the hands of the other branches of government to be resolved through the political process. And the federal system *has* grown, as the **PERSPECTIVE** on page 68 clearly shows. Let's turn our attention to the course of that development.

THE DEVELOPMENT OF THE FEDERAL SYSTEM

One of the most important points to understand about America's federal system is that it is changing. The intergovernmental system of today is far different from the arrangement of one hundred years ago or even of twenty years ago. And, if Mr. Reagan has his way, the federal system of tomorrow will be considerably different from that of today. Let's examine the evolution of America's federal system.

1789–1913: THE SYSTEM ESTABLISHED

In the early years of the nation, the division of responsibilities in the federal system was relatively clearcut. The national government defended the borders, delivered the mail, and promoted westward expansion. Meanwhile, most domestic public services were provided by state and local governments.

By the end of the nineteenth century, the role of government in American society was growing. The societal changes brought about by industrialization and urbanization created problems that Americans asked government to solve. Most of the growth of government came at the state and local level, but there was an increase in the functions of the national government as well. In 1887, for example, Congress created the Interstate Commerce Commission in response to public demands to regulate the railroads. Then, in 1890 and 1914, it passed first the Sherman and then the Clayton Antitrust Acts in an effort to control monopolies.[11]

PLENTY OF RICH
GOVERNMENT LANDS
FOR HOMESTEADS
STOCK-RAISING.

In the nineteenth century, the government promoted westward expansion by opening up lands to homesteaders and by offering substantial amounts of public land to the railroads.

1913–1950: COOPERATIVE FEDERALISM

Perhaps the most important event in the development of the modern federal system was the ratification of the Sixteenth Amendment, the "income-tax amendment," in 1913. This provided Washington with a substantial source of revenue that could be used to finance federal programs. Beginning in 1916 with the enactment of the Federal Highway Act, Congress created a series of programs providing federal money to states and, occasionally, local governments. Over the next several decades, Congress created programs in the fields of vocational education, aid for disabled veterans, agriculture, old-age assistance, education, housing, and aid to the blind, among others. The most rapid expansion of federal programs came during the 1930s as the national government moved to help states and localities recover from the Great Depression.

The best way to describe the intergovernmental system during this period was **cooperative federalism.** An effective partnership developed between Washington and state and local governments. States and localities asked Uncle Sam for assistance in accomplishing their goals. The national government responded.[12]

THE 1950s: FEDERALISM IN TRANSITION

The 1950s were a time of transition for the federal system. First, the role of the national government expanded so rapidly as to make state action clearly secondary. By the end of the decade, there were some eighty federal

Perspective
THE GROWTH OF GOVERNMENT

One of the most important developments in the federal system has been the growth of government at all levels. Since 1789, the size and scope of the federal government have grown in ways probably inconceivable to the founders. When George Washington was elected president, there were fewer than four million Americans in the entire country. Today, if we include the two million people on active duty in the armed forces, nearly five million Americans *work* for the federal government. In

Andrew Jackson's time, the executive branch operated out of four buildings. Today, there are 470,400 federal buildings scattered over the United States and the world. The average federal budget in Washington's day was a mere $1.4 million. Today, the budget is well over $900 billion. The Code of Federal Regulations is now more than 85,000 pages long.

State and local governments have grown as well. They now employ more than eleven million workers; their total budgets ex-

ceed $450 billion. In the words of one observer, states are like "miniature Washingtons" in that many are heavily involved in social-welfare and regulatory activities. All but eighteen states have environmental protection agencies, and thirty-five have transportation agencies. Also, like the federal government, states tend to spend money faster than they can raise it. In 1980, the total debt hit $119 billion.[1]

[1]Gregg Easterbrook, "50 Miniature Washingtons," *Washington Monthly* (January 1982), pp. 11–21.

grants-in-aid programs in operation, and state and local governments were growing more and more dependent on federal aid.

Second, many of the programs enacted during the 1950s were the result of pressure from relatively narrowly based interest groups. The older federal programs, such as the Highway Act, had been enacted in response to broad public pressure and demands from state authorities. In the 1950s, however, interest groups learned that they frequently could have more success lobbying the U.S. Congress than lobbying their state legislatures or city councils. Consequently, Congress enacted federal programs that were frequently greeted with indifference and sometimes even hostility by state and local officials.[13]

THE 1960s: FEDERALISM IN TURMOIL

The 1960s saw a dramatic change in both the quantity and quality of federal programs. During the decade, especially during the heyday of Lyndon Johnson's Great Society (1964–66), Congress enacted scores of new grants-in-aid programs dealing with education, employment, health care, the environment, urban development, poverty relief, and other matters. In the process, many policy areas that had once been the exclusive responsibility of state and local governments became "intergovernmentalized," including rural fire protection, libraries, jellyfish control, police pensions, local law enforcement, historical preservation, urban gardening, training for use of the metric system, urban rat control, junkyard control, arson, home insulation, snow removal, development of bikeways, pothole repair, fire-ant control, school security, and art education.[14] Many of these new programs dealt directly with cities and other local governments, bypassing state governments in the process.

There was also an important change in the way federal programs were initiated. Initiatives for federal programs now came from *within* the federal bureaucracy. Federal bureaucrats with scientific or professional expertise identified what they saw as problems and proposed federal programs for their solution. Frequently, the bureaucrats (in alliance with interest groups) had the political power to win congressional approval for their programs, despite the opposition of state and local officials. Consequently, the old pattern of the national government assisting state and local authorities to attain state and local objectives was stood on its head. Now, federal programs represented an effort by Washington to impose national goals on states and localities.[15]

Another important development affecting the federal system during the 1960s was the civil-rights movement. In order to protect citizens against discrimination, Washington took an active hand in voter registration, public education, access to housing, employment opportunities, public accommodations, and other matters that traditionally had been the sole responsibility of state and local government.

This expansion of the federal role in the 1960s proved quite controversial. On the one hand, officials in the Johnson Administration and their supporters spoke in favor of setting national goals in such policy areas as health care, education, welfare, housing, police protection, conservation, and civil rights. To achieve these goals would require a massive federal effort, they argued. Only Washington, they said, could supply the large amounts of money needed to do the job. Also, national power was needed to stamp out discrimination and insure the equitable treatment of all Americans.

On the other hand, there was a backlash from state and local governments. The cooperative federalism of an earlier era now gave way to conflict. State and local officials welcomed federal money, of course, but they resented the red tape and federally imposed conditions that came with it. They complained about confusion, duplication, overlap, and a breakdown of intergovernmental communication and coordination.[16]

THE 1970s AND 1980s: FEDERALISM IN CRISIS

During the 1970s, there was a great deal of talk about strengthening the role of state and local governments in the federal system, but there was more talk than action. Presidents Nixon, Ford, and Carter all proposed reforms in the federal system, but by the end of the decade state and local dependency on federal money was greater than ever before. There were more than five hundred federal grants-in-aid programs, totaling in excess of $90 billion. More than one fourth of the total budgets of state and local governments in America now came from Washington.[17] Many large northern cities had become virtual wards of the national government.

In 1981 Ronald Reagan came to the White House promising a revolution in the federal system to return power to state and local authorities. He proposed a realignment of nation-state responsibilities with the elimination of some federal programs and the consolidation of many others. To top it all off, the president proposed a sharp reduction in federal money for grants-in-aid programs to states and localities.[18]

The reaction to Reagan's New Federalism program was mixed. Conservatives hailed Reagan's ideas as a long overdue shift of governmental responsibilities to state and local governments, which, they argued, are closer to the people. Liberal critics of the Reagan proposals saw in them a Trojan horse. Reagan's New Federalism, they charged, was merely a strategy to eliminate social programs. The net result would be fewer services for the needy.[19]

Reagan was unable to deliver on his entire New Federalism package— revolutions don't come easily in Washington politics. His proposal for shifting welfare programs between the state and federal governments never got off the ground, but Congress did agree to the consolidation of a number of programs. Reagan's greatest success, however, came on his budget-cut proposals. In 1981 and 1982, Congress agreed to slash $19.2 billion from the budget for federal aid to states and localities. By the end of

1983, the federal contribution to state and local budgets had been reduced from a high of 26 percent in 1978 to 20 percent.[20]

The budget cuts came at the worst of all possible times for state and local governments. On the one hand, the nation was in the midst of a deep recession that shrank state and local tax revenues while increasing the demand for public services. On the other hand, since the late 1970s, public opinion had grown quite hostile to tax increases, as evidenced by the passage of California's tax-cutting Proposition 13 in 1978. Consequently, the twin blows of recession and federal-aid reductions left many states and localities caught in a dilemma between two politically unpopular alternatives: raising taxes or cutting public services. In the eyes of many, the federal system was in crisis.[21]

By late 1983, things began to look up a bit for state and local governments. The economy began to improve, and that helped their financial picture. Also, the tax increases and spending decreases enacted by states and localities during 1980 and 1981 began to pay off. A number of states even reported budget surpluses. Nevertheless, state and local officials were wary of the possibility of more federal-fund reductions or another economic downturn.[22]

INTERGOVERNMENTAL PROGRAMS: POLICY AND POLITICS

The intergovernmental system today is a complex maze, involving interest groups, state and local officials, members of Congress and their staffs, federal bureaucrats, and scores of complicated and sometimes contradictory federal regulations. It is a confusing system that one expert has likened to an oozing, slithering, squishing mass.[23] Nevertheless, it is important because virtually all aspects of domestic public policy are affected by intergovernmental programs. If we are to understand public policy in America, we need to understand the policies and politics of the intergovernmental system.

SETTING THE AGENDA

Intergovernmental programs are the concern of interest groups, state and local officials, and federal bureaucrats. Some of the older federal programs, such as the highway program, have survived and flourished because of the effective lobbying support of a coalition of groups that stand to benefit from highway construction. These include highway contractors, cement and asphalt dealers, trucking interests, and elected officials from states with a great amount of highway mileage. Many of the newer programs were created at the behest of interest groups. For instance, the National Education Association (NEA), a teachers' lobby group, has been a major supporter of federal aid to education. Also, many of the strings attached to federal programs are the result of interest-group pressure. Minority-rights groups support nondiscrimination requirements, for example, while environmentalists demand that federal construction contracts include environmental-impact statements. Labor unions and manufacturers join forces to push for "Buy American" requirements on aid programs involving major purchases of equipment.

Some of the most active and effective lobbying in the intergovernmental process comes from within government itself. At the national level, bureaucrats have interests and perspectives of their own. In fact, the initiative for many of the federal programs enacted in the last twenty-five years has come not from the states nor from private interest groups, but from within the federal bureaucracy itself. Once the program is enacted, a coalition of interest groups that benefit from it then develops to support its continuance.

Other lobbying efforts come from state and local governments. Thirty states and one hundred cities are now represented by professional lobbyists in Washington.[24] New York City, for example, has seven people in its Washington lobbying office plus separate consultants for employment and taxation. The New York City Board of Education has three people in Washington. What's more, the New York Municipal Labor Union, the New York-New Jersey Port Authority, and the New York Transit Authority all contribute to the area's lobbying efforts—which nets about $2 billion a year in federal funds.[25] State and local governments also lobby through national associations. The most important of these are the National League of Cities, the U.S. Congress of Mayors, the National Governors Conference, the National Association of County Officials, and the International City Management Association.

FORMULATING POLICY

The formulation and adoption of intergovernmental programs in Congress is a highly political process. Frequently, interest groups, officials of a government agency, and key members of Congress form three-sided alliances in support of particular federal programs. These **policy triangles** or "iron triangles," as they are sometimes called, are mutually beneficial to the parties involved. The interest groups benefit from the program. Highway contractors win contracts to construct highways, for example, or medical researchers gain more money to do their work. Bureaucrats in the executive branch favor the program because it increases their responsibility and authority. The increase in federal aid to education eventually led to the establishment of the Department of Education, for instance. Finally, members of Congress benefit since the interest groups will contribute to their reelection campaigns and the bureaucracy will see to it that the home district gets special treatment, with the representative getting the credit. The NEA works for Senator X's reelection, for example, or the Highway Department makes the completion of the interstate in Representative Y's district a top priority. Over time, policy triangles can become so well entrenched that the federal programs they support become almost immune to dissolution or serious reduction.[26]

Then there's the politics of computer printouts. Some of the hottest battles in Congress are fought over whose districts will benefit the most from a particular federal-grant program. Consequently, as the elements of the progam are debated, members send their staffers scurrying to fetch computer printouts showing how their particular district will fare as the program's details are changed.

Many of these printout battles are fought between the frostbelt and the sunbelt. In the early 1970s, members of Congress from the Northeast and Midwest produced statistics showing that frostbelt states generally paid more money in federal taxes than they received in federal aid, but for the sunbelt it was just the opposite. Using these statistics as a rallying point, in 1976 frostbelt representatives organized the Northeast-Midwest Congressional Coalition to counter what they saw as an unfair distribution of federal programs, jobs, and contracts.[27]

The frostbelt coalition succeeded in revising some federal programs to benefit their region. One example was the Community Development Program. When Congress enacted the program in 1974 to help cities revitalize blighted neighborhoods, funding was based on a formula that included population, poverty, and overcrowded housing. This formula tended to favor sunbelt cities because of their rapid growth and housing shortages. In 1977, however, the frostbelt coalition won a battle when Congress revised the formula to emphasize the percentage of a city's housing built before 1940. Naturally, this shifted funding away from the young cities of the sunbelt to the older cities of the Northeast and Midwest.[28] Another example of a victory by the frostbelt came in 1979 when Congress enacted a program to assist poor families in paying their home heating bills.

Before long, however, representatives from the sunbelt were organized and fighting back. Their computers produced statistics showing that the sunbelt wasn't really getting more than its fair share of the federal largesse. As a region, they pointed out, the sunbelt is still poorer than the frostbelt, despite recent economic trends and migration patterns.[29] The sunbelt may pay less in taxes and receive more aid, they said, but that's because the region is poorer and the need is greater. What's more, rapid population growth can produce problems nearly as severe as population decline.

By the early 1980s, the sunbelt forces had won a few victories. They had succeeded, for example, in getting the energy-assistance program expanded to include aid to low-income people in paying home-cooling as well as home-heating bills.[30]

The political future looks bright for the sunbelt. The 1980 census figures translated into a shift of some seventeen seats in the U.S. House of Representatives from frostbelt to sunbelt states. As you can see in Figure 3.1, the South and West now have a majority in the House. They can use this in the future to direct the spending of federal dollars.

ADOPTING POLICY

Federal programs come in a variety of forms. Table 3.1 will help you sort them out. **Category grants** are federal grants-in-aid programs that provide federal funds to state and local governments for fairly narrow, specific purposes. Little discretion is left to state and local officials in deciding how the money is to be spent.

There are two types of category grants that differ in the criteria by which funding is awarded. For **project grants,** state and local governments are required to present detailed grant applications to federal agencies; the agencies then evaluate them and make funding decisions on a competitive basis. In contrast, **formula grants** provide federal funds to state and local governments based on a formula established by Congress. The Federal Highway Act of 1916, for example, provided money to states based on a formula that included a state's size, population, and rural-mail-route mileage.

In contrast to category grants, **block grants** provide funding for pro-

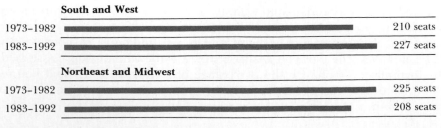

FIGURE 3.1
The Power Shift in the House, 1973–1992 (Projected)

South and West

| 1973–1982 | | 210 seats |
| 1983–1992 | | 227 seats |

Northeast and Midwest

| 1973–1982 | | 225 seats |
| 1983–1992 | | 208 seats |

SOURCE: U.S. Census Bureau.

Type of Grant	Recipient Discretion	Program Scope	Funding Criteria	
Category				**TABLE** 3.1
a. Project	low	narrow	administrative review	*Federal Grant Programs*
b. Formula	low	narrow	legislative formula	
Block	medium	functional area	legislative formula	
General Revenue Sharing	high	broad	legislative formula	

SOURCE: Adapted from George E. Hale and Marian Lief Palley, *The Politics of Federal Grants* (Washington, D.C.: Congressional Quarterly Press, 1981), p. 12.

grams in a broad, general policy area. In recent years, this approach has been proposed as a means of giving state and local officials more discretion to use federal money in accordance with local needs. In 1981, for example, Congress agreed with President Reagan's request and folded some fifty-seven category grants into block grants based on formulas set by Congress.

Both category and block grants come with plenty of strings attached. First, there are usually matching-fund requirements. Uncle Sam picks up only part of the tab. Although some federal programs are totally financed by the national government (Food Stamps, for example), most require matching funds. Sometimes the match from state and local funds may be as low as 10 or 20 percent, but other times Congress has required a 50-percent match. Second, federal money for category and block grants comes with numerous across-the-board requirements for virtually all federal programs, including provisions in the areas of equal rights, equal access for the disabled, environmental protection, historic preservation, and wage rates for contractors' personnel.[31]

In 1972 Congress created **general revenue sharing,** a program designed to provide federal financial aid to states and localities with only a few strings attached. The money could not be spent in a discriminatory fashion, for example, but otherwise state and local officials could use the money as they saw fit. Funds were awarded on the basis of a legislative formula and checks were sent to all the states and every general-purpose local government in America. In 1980, however, the program was changed to exclude states.

IMPLEMENTING THE PROGRAMS

After intergovernmental policies have been formulated and adopted, they must be implemented. Sometimes Congress creates a new bureaucracy at the same time that it creates a new program. In the early 1970s, for

example, when Congress decided to establish a program to provide federal money for mass transportation, it set up a new agency to administer the program, the Urban Mass Transit Administration (UMTA). At other times, Congress uses an existing bureaucracy to implement new programs.

Much of the actual work of implementing federal programs, however, falls on the shoulders of state and local governments. Bureaucrats in Washington may write program guidelines, approve grant applications, and review reports, but state and local officials actually operate the programs. The Food Stamp program, for example, is paid for entirely by federal funds, but the task of administration (and its cost) is borne by state governments.

Congress prefers this approach to the administration of federal programs, but state and local officials generally resent it. Members of Congress like it because it allows them to accomplish their objectives without having to vote to hire more federal employees, a politically unpopular move. In contrast, state officials complain about the costs and headaches of administering complex federal programs. One state official phrases it this way: "Now, four out of ten state and local employees are actually federal employees in disguise, marching like a secret army to the guidelines and regulations of Washington."[32]

Congress often leaves the details of program implementation to the judgment of bureaucrats in the executive branch or in state and local governments. Consider Congress' mandate for providing access to the disabled. In the 1973 Rehabilitation Act, Congress legislated that "no otherwise qualified individual . . . shall . . . be excluded from participation in . . . any program or activity receiving federal financial assistance." On the basis of this rather broad language, the federal Department of Transportation wrote detailed regulations for transit systems receiving federal funds, stipulating the need to provide elaborate systems of elevators and escalators and transbuses for the disabled.[33]

The language of grant programs is often vague because it reflects political compromise. Federal programs are inevitably the consequence of disparate coalitions in which policymakers cannot agree on just what they want to achieve, what can be accomplished by government action, or how to go about it. Congress can agree on the principle of equal access for the disabled, for example, but not on how that goal can be defined or achieved in practice. Consequently, it is easier politically for Congress to adopt general policy and leave the messy details to the bureaucracy. The members of Congress can claim credit for supporting the ideal, but when problems of implementation crop up they can blame the bureaucracy. The bureaucrats "fade the heat" for Congress. They are in Washington, they're hard to pin down, and they don't have to run for reelection. Nevertheless, the bureaucracy likes the system the way it is because it enhances their power over policy. State and local officials generally prefer it too, because it gives them more leeway than they would otherwise enjoy.[34]

The awarding of federal grants is a highly political process as well. As we have seen, the bureaucracy likes to keep congressional allies happy and that often means steering grant money to the states or districts of friendly legislators. Election-year politics can also affect the awarding of federal grants. Presidents running for reelection love to announce the award of a federal grant to the city or state in which they are making a campaign appearance. The withholding of grants can even be used to punish political opponents. In 1979 Chicago's Democratic Mayor Jane Byrne announced her endorsement of Senator Edward Kennedy against President Jimmy Carter. Thereafter, Neil Goldschmidt, Carter's secretary of transportation, announced he had "lost confidence" in Mayor Byrne and would not look favorably on Chicago's applications for federal funds.[35]

Politics is also involved at the receiving end of the federal pipeline. The proliferation of federal grants has seen the emergence of a new type of employee at the state and local levels of government—the federal grants specialist. These individuals often work full-time identifying the grants for which their state or locality is eligible, applying for the grants, and following up on the application.

EVALUATING THE SYSTEM

In general, the motivations behind federal programs are worthy, and some noteworthy achievements have been recorded. First, federal programs have helped state and local governments provide more services for their citizens than they otherwise could. Federal money is behind most public-housing developments, many sewerage-treatment plants, and some parks. Meanwhile, federal programs such as the School Lunch Program, Food Stamps, Medicaid, Aid to Families with Dependent Children, and the Energy Assistance Program have provided much-needed aid to millions of poor Americans.

Second, intergovernmental programs have allowed the national government to provide technical assistance to states and localities. Thanks to federal programs, many states and localities have been able to obtain national assistance for dealing with such troubling societal problems as drug abuse, alcoholism, family violence, and the spread of communicable disease.

Finally, federal programs have been an instrument for injecting a public-interest perspective into state/local operations. The federal guidelines that accompany federal programs can require state and local governments to practice nondiscrimination, to provide access to public facilities for the disabled, to show a concern for the environment, and to pursue other socially desirable goals. The threat of a cutoff of funds can be a powerful weapon for achieving compliance. In the late 1960s and throughout the 1970s, for example, many school districts proceeded with desegregation only because of the danger of losing federal money if they did not.[36]

Despite these achievements, most observers are in agreement that the intergovernmental system today is in crisis. Liberals argue that the role of the national government in the federal system should be one of setting national standards and then furnishing the resources to see that those standards are met nationwide. Two observers describe this conception of the system in these words:

> If we decide as a nation that we want a certain level of education, or welfare, or health care for all persons as U.S. citizens, then only the application of the Robin Hood principle through the national government can achieve this goal.[37]

According to the liberals, the problem with the contemporary federal system is that the growth of federal programs and federal aid has not been matched by a concomitant increase in federal personnel. The system is plagued by problems of implementation since the national government must rely on state and local officials whom it can neither hire nor fire to promote its policies. Consequently, the liberals argue, the system is uneven and inefficient. Many inequities remain and the system's goals have not been achieved.[38]

In contrast, conservatives see the problem with federalism today as too much rather than too little national control. The federal government, they argue, is overloaded by being involved in all policy matters, including many that should be strictly local in jurisdiction. The result is an increase in the costs of bureaucratic overhead, a loss of program flexibility, a decline of governmental responsiveness, and a sacrifice of public accountability.[39]

There are other criticisms of the federal system that cannot easily be labeled either conservative or liberal. One standard criticism is that the intergovernmental system simply isn't neat. The structure of authority isn't a pyramid; it's a matrix and a badly coordinated one at that.[40] There is waste, red tape, project delays, and duplication. For example, in 1978 there were seventy-eight categorical grants for health alone, seventy for education.[41] Lines of authority become hopelessly tangled as agencies apply for and receive multiple grants from several different agencies.

Another important criticism holds that it is simply bad policy for money to be raised at one level of government and spent at another. In the federal system today, most of the money is raised by the national government, but the folks who spend it are at the state and local levels. Consequently, there's a tendency to think of federal money as "free money." The local or state official might be inclined to say, "So what if some is wasted, it's only federal money." The truth, of course, is that all money is tax money. There will be more accountability, the argument goes, if the officials who spend the money are the ones who raised it in the first place.

Finally, many criticisms of the federal system aren't so much philosophical as they are political. State officials complain because they feel that they are bypassed by direct federal aid to cities. Members of Congress criticize block grants and revenue sharing because those approaches reduce their control over programs. Liberals attack programs that don't happen to benefit the groups about which they are most concerned. Meanwhile, conservative business types oppose federal aid in general but welcome federally funded projects that improve property values, such as freeway construction. Perhaps a "federal handout" is something somebody else gets.

REFORMING THE SYSTEM

There is no shortage of ideas for reforming the federal system. Liberals are distressed by the recent reductions in federal grants-in-aid money and the trend toward greater autonomy for state and local governments in the federal-grants process. There are major societal problems in the areas of health, welfare, and education that are unmet, they say. What's more, the problems are too great for most state and local governments, especially considering that some of the areas with the greatest needs are the least able to meet them because of low tax bases.[42] Liberals also fear that the poor and minorities will be left out of social programs if federal guidelines are relaxed. Consequently, liberals would like to see more money for federal grants for social programs and close federal supervision of program implementation.

In contrast, conservatives see the slowdown in intergovernmental programs as a development long overdue. They have long complained about the waste and inefficiency that they see as endemic to the system. Conservatives believe that less money from Washington coupled with the effects of the recent taxpayers' revolt against high taxes will force state and local governments to be more efficient, innovative, and accountable. Conservatives also favor the trend toward decentralization in the federal system. They argue that state and local officials are best able to know what their areas' needs are, not Washington bureaucrats. Consequently, conservatives generally favor the basic thrust of Reagan's New Federalism while liberals oppose it.[43]

Officials and citizens alike couch proposals for intergovernmental reform in high-flown moral and legal terminology, but the most important element in the intergovernmental policy process is politics. Federal programs invariably result from political conflicts among highly organized groups. And the conflicts usually take the form of arguments over who gets the money and who controls fund allocations. For example, federal grants to cities grew rapidly during the Great Society years, with northeastern and midwestern cities benefiting the most. This reflected President Johnson's political concerns and the impact of large Democratic majorities in Congress. Then, as President Nixon sought to consolidate his votes in 1968 with those of Governor George Wallace in a new political alliance (sometimes called Nixon's "southern strategy"), federal outlays between 1972 and 1975 aided southern and western cities more than those in other areas. After the Watergate scandal and the recession of the mid-1970s, President Jimmy Carter and a large Democratic majority in Congress effected a slight shift back toward the urban areas of the frostbelt.[44] The Reagan proposals reflected a tilt back toward the sunbelt and Reagan's political allies.

In the years ahead, it's certain that the federal system will continue to be the object of great debate in American politics. The policy stakes are too high for it to be otherwise. There will be changes, of course—the intergovernmental system is quite dynamic—but it is unlikely that there will be upheaval. Each element in the current intergovernmental system is supported by powerful, well-entrenched forces. As the political winds change, various types of programs, policies, or political interests will fall in or out of favor. There will be evolution in the federal system, but probably no revolution.

CONCLUSION: THE BACKGROUND OF POLICYMAKING

We began the first part of this book with the assertion that one cannot understand the policymaking process in America unless that process is placed in the context of American life. In chapter 1 we explored the philosophical and socioeconomic backgrounds of policymaking. In Chapter 2 we looked at the importance of the Constitution. Finally, in this chapter we examined the federal system. What have we learned from this study of public policy in America?

First, more public policy is being made now than ever before. Since the 1930s, government involvement in the areas of social welfare, regulation, and economic management has grown remarkably. Consequently, the range of subjects considered appropriate for inclusion on the public-policy agenda is far broader in the 1980s than it was in the 1920s.

Second, most public policies have a federal component. The liberal reforms of the New Deal and beyond invariably involved federal action; so much so that now most areas of public policy in America cannot be understood without considering the role of the national government. National politics affects local politics and vice versa.

Whether this is good or bad depends upon your point of view. Government has grown; federal involvement has increased. Liberals see these developments as necessary to improving the quality of life for all Americans. Conservatives warn against the danger of government stifling initiative and restricting individual freedom.

The debate is generally placed in a constitutional framework, but the issues are decided through the political process. Increased federal activity after 1932 was a response to public demands for government action. The Constitution and the federal system neither prevented nor mandated the federal response, but they did serve to define its contours.

In the 1980s the question of the power and size of the federal government is again at the top of the policy agenda. The issue will be decided through the democratic political process, but, as always, the areas of debate will be defined by the Constitution and limited by the structure of the federal system. Such is the nature of America's political process.

KEY TERMS

BLOCK GRANTS (74)

CATEGORY GRANTS (74)

CONFEDERATION (63)

COOPERATIVE FEDERALISM (68)

DELEGATED POWERS (64)

DUAL FEDERALISM (67)

FORMULA GRANTS (74)

GENERAL REVENUE SHARING (75)

GRANTS-IN-AID (69)

IMPLIED POWERS (66)

INTERGOVERNMENTAL RELATIONS (62)

NATIONAL SUPREMACY CLAUSE (65)

NECESSARY AND PROPER CLAUSE (64)

POLICY TRIANGLES (73)

PROJECT GRANTS (74)

UNITARY SYSTEM (62)

NOTES

1. *New York Times,* 27 January 1982, p. A1b.
2. Ibid.
3. Samuel H. Beer, "Federalism, Nationalism, and Democracy in America," *American Political Science Review* 72 (March 1978): 9–21.

4. Gottfried Dietze,*The Federalist* (Baltimore: Johns Hopkins, 1960); and Beer.

5. *McCulloch* v. *Maryland*, 4 Wheaton 316 (1819).

6. Robert E. Cushman and Robert F. Cushman, *Cases in Constitutional Law*, 3rd ed. (New York: Appleton-Century-Crofts, 1968).

7. *McCulloch* v. *Maryland*, 4 Wheaton 316 (1819).

8. Michael D. Reagan and John G. Sanzone, *The New Federalism* (New York: Oxford University Press, 1981), ch. 1.

9. Edwin S. Corwin, *The Twilight of the Supreme Court* (New Haven: Yale University Press, 1934), ch. 1.

10. *National League of Cities* v. *Usery*, 426 U.S. 833 (1976).

11. George E. Hale and Marian Lief Palley, *The Politics of Federal Grants* (Washington, D.C.: Congressional Quarterly Press, 1981), ch. 1.

12. Daniel J. Elazar, "The Evolving Federal System," *Proceedings of the Academy of Political Science* 34 (1981): 5–19.

13. Donald H. Haider, "The Intergovernmental System," *Proceedings of the Academy of Political Science* 34 (1981): 20–30.

14. David B. Walker, "Dysfunctional Federalism—The Congress and Intergovernmental Relations," *State Government* 54 (1981): 53–57.

15. James L. Sundquist, *Making Federalism Work* (Washington, D.C.: Brookings Institution, 1969).

16. Haider.

17. Joseph A. Pechman, ed. *Setting National Priorities: The 1983 Budget* (Washington, D.C.: Brookings Institution, 1982), p. 156.

18. Albert J. Davis and S. Kenneth Howard, "Perspectives on a 'New Day' for Federalism," *Intergovernmental Perspective* 7 (Spring 1982): 9–21.

19. Rochelle L. Stanfield, "Governors, Mayors Turn from Seeking More Power to Fending Off Aid Cuts," *National Journal* (2 January 1983), pp. 356–62.

20. David S. Broder, "Reagan's Feat on Federalism," *Washington Post*, National Weekly Edition, 12 December 1983, p. 4.

21. Stanfield.

22. Neal R. Peirce, "State Deficits Becoming Surpluses," *Houston Chronicle*, 25 November 1983, Sec. 2, p. 10.

23. Charles V. Hamilton, *American Government* (Glenview: Scott, Foresman and Company, 1982), ch. 3.

24. Hale and Palley, p. 57.

25. Kathy Lewis, "Washington Connection," *Houston Post*, 14 February 1982, p. 1A.

26. Harold Seidman, *Politics, Position, and Power*, 3rd ed. (New York: Oxford University Press, 1980).

27. "The New 'Civil War' for Federal Dollars," *U.S. News & World Report* (19 April 1982), pp. 81–84.

28. Hale and Palley, p. 62.

29. Bernard L. Weinstein and John Rees, "Sunbelt/Frostbelt Confrontation?" *Society* 17 (May/June 1980): 17–21.

30. "The New 'Civil War'."
31. Neal Peirce and Jay Hamilton, "Flypaper Federalism," *National Journal* (12 September 1981), pp. 1636–39.
32. Richard A. Snelling, "American Federalism in the Eighties," *State Government* 53 (Autumn 1980): 168.
33. Hale and Palley, p. 72.
34. Carl E. Van Horn, *Policy Implementation in the Federal System* (Lexington: Lexington Books, 1979).
35. *New York Times,* 30 December 1979, p. 4E.
36. Reagan and Sanzone, pp. 60–75.
37. Ibid., p. 43.
38. Ibid.
39. David B. Walker, *Toward a Functioning Federalism* (Boston: Little, Brown, 1981).
40. Elazar, p. 17.
41. Hale and Palley, p. 83.
42. Robert B. Lucke, "Rich States—Poor States: Inequalities in Our Federal System," *Intergovernmental Perspective* 8 (Spring 1982): 22–28.
43. Susannah Calkins and John Shannon, "The New Formula for Fiscal Federalism: Austerity Equals Decentralization," *Intergovernmental Perspective* 8 (Winter 1982): 23–29.
44. Ann Markusen, Annalee Saxenian, and Marc Weiss, "Who Benefits from Intergovernmental Transfers?" *Publius* 11 (Winter 1981): 5–35.

SUGGESTED READINGS

ADRIAN, CHARLES R., AND PRESS, CHARLES. *Governing Urban America.* 4th ed. New York: McGraw-Hill, 1972.

DERTHICK, MARTHA. *The Influence of Federal Grants.* Cambridge: Harvard University Press, 1970.

ELAZAR, DANIEL J. *American Federalism: A View from the States.* 2nd ed. New York: Thomas Y. Crowell, 1972.

GRODZINS, MORTON. *The Federal System.* Englewood Cliffs, N.J.: Prentice-Hall, 1960.

HAIDER, DONALD H. *When Governments Come to Washington.* New York: Free Press, 1974.

HALE, GEORGE E., AND PALLEY, MARIAN LIEF. *The Politics of Federal Grants.* Washington, D.C.: Congressional Quarterly Press, 1981.

REAGAN, MICHAEL D., AND SANZONE, JOHN G. *The New Federalism.* New York: Oxford University Press, 1981.

RIKER, WILLIAM. *Federalism: Origin, Operation, Significance.* Boston: Little, Brown, 1964.

SUNDQUIST, JAMES L. *Making Federalism Work.* Washington, D.C.: Brookings Institution, 1969.

WALKER, DAVID B. *Toward a Functioning Federalism.* Boston: Little, Brown, 1981.

Part Two

PARTICIPATION

Public policy is made by people, participating individually or collectively. Issues become part of the public agenda when large numbers of ordinary people or smaller numbers of influential people begin to perceive those issues as problems for government to address. Individually, we influence policymaking through our votes and our voices. Collectively, we work through interest groups and political parties. Participation, then, is the foundation of policymaking. What issues appear on the official agenda, what policies are proposed to deal with those issues, which policies officeholders decide to adopt, how policies are put into practice, and, finally, how we evaluate the end results all depend upon who participates and how.

Chapter 4 examines what Americans know and believe about policies—public opinion. It begins by studying the methods used to measure public opinion. Then it discusses political socialization, the process whereby individuals acquire knowledge, attitudes, and beliefs about politics. The next portion of the chapter deals with the content of public opinion. It considers political knowledge, support for democracy, political trust, political efficacy,

and political ideology. The chapter concludes with a discussion of the effect of public opinion on public policy.

Chapter 5 examines the ways Americans participate in politics. It discusses who participates, how they participate, and the effects of participation on public policy and vice versa. The latter portion of the chapter focuses on elections as a part of the public-policy process. It details the elections process for president and for Congress, studying the factors involved and their ultimate impact on public policy.

In the last chapter of this section, chapter 6, we turn our attention to group participation. First, we look at interest groups. What kinds of interest groups are there in America and what are their goals? What effect does group politics have on the policy process? The second part of chapter 6 deals with political parties. We will examine the history, organization, and composition of political parties in America. Finally, the chapter and the section conclude with a short analytical essay on participation and public policy.

Chapter Four

PUBLIC OPINION

MEASURING PUBLIC OPINION

Sampling

Question Wording and Timing

POLITICAL SOCIALIZATION

The Process of Socialization

The Agents of Socialization
Family / School / Peer groups / Media / Events

The Politics of Socialization

THE CONTENT OF PUBLIC OPINION

Political Knowledge

Support for Democracy

Political Trust

Political Efficacy

Political Ideology
Social class / Race / Religion / Region / Gender

CONCLUSION: PUBLIC OPINION AND PUBLIC POLICY

By fall of 1979, President Jimmy Carter was in deep political trouble. Public-opinion polls showed that barely a third of the electorate approved of Carter's performance. Carter faced a serious potential challenge for the Democratic presidential nomination: a poll taken in October showed that Senator Edward Kennedy was the favorite of 60 percent of Democrats while only 30 percent supported Carter. The rest were undecided.[1] Consequently, when Kennedy declared his candidacy in early November, many observers believed that the president was in for a tough fight just to win his party's nomination.

Shortly after Kennedy's announcement, however, an event occurred that dramatically changed the course of American politics. In Tehran, Iran, an angry mob of radical students stormed the American embassy and took some fifty Americans hostage. The American public rallied around the president. Carter's approval rating in the Gallup Poll soared to 61 percent. In December 1979, a poll revealed that Carter led Kennedy by 46 to 42 percent, with 12 percent undecided.[2]

Subsequently, Carter defeated Kennedy in the early presidential primaries and held on to win the Democratic nomination. As the hostage crisis wore on, however, Carter's popularity waned, eventually sinking below the low point it had reached before the seizure of the hostages. Finally, in November 1980 Carter was soundly defeated for reelection by Republican Ronald Reagan.

The Iranian hostage crisis at first caused a surge in popularity for President Carter. As the months dragged by, however, with no satisfactory resolution, the president's popularity steadily waned.

This story illustrates several important points about public opinion in America. First, public opinion is dynamic. In a matter of days, President Carter's popularity rose nearly 30 percentage points. Then, over the course of the next year it fell back again. Second, public opinion *responds* to events, the event in this case being the hostage crisis. Third, public opinion has a clear impact on politics. To some degree at least, the events in Iran helped Carter defeat Kennedy for the Democratic nomination and later aided Reagan against Carter in November. Finally, our example illustrates the complexity of public opinion. The immediate public response to the hostage seizure was one of support for the president, but the reaction didn't so much reflect approval of Carter's policies as it did a patriotic showing of national unity against a foreign adversary. After the immediate crisis passed, the president's popularity in the polls fell as the public again began to evaluate his performance, including his handling of the crisis.

Public opinion is a slippery subject, but it is important to our understanding of political participation and policymaking. Whether one participates or not in the policy process will depend on what one thinks of politics. The way one chooses to participate will depend in large part on one's knowledge of the policy process. And the focus and intent of participation will be shaped by one's opinions on the political issues of the day.

So we begin our study of political participation in America by exploring public opinion. First, we will discuss the technical science of opinion measurement. What are the strengths and weaknesses of modern survey-research methods? Second, we will focus on the process by which individuals acquire their political knowledge, attitudes, and beliefs—**political socialization.** How do Americans learn about politics? What factors shape their attitudes and opinions? Third, we will study the content of public opinion. What do Americans know about government? How do they feel about the political system? What are their opinions on political issues? Finally, we will explore the relationship between public opinion and public policy.

MEASURING PUBLIC OPINION

Survey research, or public-opinion polling, is now a familiar part of the American scene. Businesses use market surveys to assess public tastes for their products and services. Political campaigns employ polls to plan campaign strategy. The media use polls to gauge public reaction to political events and to predict election results. Scholars rely on survey reseach as a tool for studying political knowledge, attitudes, and beliefs. Consequently, measuring public opinion is big business, and the major national pollsters employed by political and commercial clients are household words to many Americans—Gallup, Harris, Roper, Yankelovitch. The Center for Political Studies (CPS), formerly the Survey Research Center (SRC), at the University of Michigan is the most prominent center for academic survey research.

SAMPLING

The theory behind survey research is that one can accurately measure the opinions of a large population or **universe**—such as all Americans, all Californians, or all Catholics—based on interviews with a relatively small **sample.** Probability theory tells us that a sample of only a thousand persons will produce results that are accurate within three percentage points (plus or minus) 95 percent of the time. This means that if our survey shows that 60 percent of this particular sample of Americans favor gun control, then the odds are ninety-five in one hundred that the true value for the universe of all Americans is within 3 percent of this result.

The key is for our sample to be representative of our universe. If we are interested in the views of all Americans, a sample of one thousand people from Pittsburgh, one thousand women, or one thousand callers to a radio talk program would hardly be representative. In fact, one of the most famous polling errors in history was caused by an unrepresentative sample. During the 1920s and '30s, a highly publicized presidential poll was conducted by a magazine called the *Literary Digest.* In 1936, the *Digest* mailed some ten million "ballots" to individuals whose names and addresses were drawn from telephone directories and from automobile registration lists across the country. More than two million responded. On this basis the *Digest* predicted that Alf Landon, the Republican challenger, would defeat

Democratic President Franklin Roosevelt by a resounding 57 to 43 percent. Instead, Roosevelt was reelected by the biggest landslide in American history.

What went wrong? The *Digest*'s sample was drawn exclusively from people who owned telephones and automobiles. In the midst of the Great Depression, these were mostly middle- and upper-income folks who tended to vote Republican. In contrast, the many poor and working-class people who could not afford cars and telephones weren't sampled by the poll. On election day, they voted for Roosevelt.

There is no foolproof way to guarantee a representative sample 100 percent of the time, but the ideal approach is a **random sample,** in which each member of the universe has an equal chance of being included. If our universe were students at a college, we could draw a random sample by picking every fifth or tenth student from a master list. Taking a true random sample of all Americans or all Californians, however, is virtually impossible since no master list is available to researchers. At any rate, a completely random sample of one thousand Americans would likely be so scattered about the country that it would be prohibitively expensive for interviewers to meet with each one. Respondents could be telephoned, of course, but that would omit those who didn't have phones. A mail survey is an even less desirable alternative since many people would likely not reply and since we would have no way of knowing whether those who did respond were similar in important respects to those who did not. This was another fault of the *Literary Digest* poll.

Today, almost all reputable survey research uses a technique known as **cluster sampling.** This involves taking a sample by stages. For a national sample, the country would first be divided into geographic regions. Within each region, several counties would be selected at random. Then, within each county, a number of census tracks (fairly small areas for which census data are available) would be chosen randomly. Next, several city blocks would be selected from each track. In each block, certain households would be chosen based on an established rule—the second house from the northeast corner, for example. Finally, one person of voting age would be interviewed. Technically, cluster sampling is random in that every individual has an equal chance of being interviewed, but for statistical reasons it is not as efficient as a simple random sample. In general, though, a national cluster sample of some 1500 persons is as accurate as a simple random sample of 1000.[3]

QUESTION WORDING AND TIMING

The best of samples is worthless if the survey questions are invalid. If the researcher wants to ask the members of the sample if they prefer Ronald Reagan or Walter Mondale for president, that is straightforward, and the results will be clear. Asking questions about issues, however, is much more complex. Changes in the wording of questions, for instance, can produce rather dramatic variations in response. For example, in 1980 the *New York Times* commissioned a poll in which individuals were asked if there should be a constitutional amendment prohibiting abortion. Some 29 percent favored the amendment, 62 percent were opposed, and 9 percent had no opinion. Then, later in the same poll, respondents were asked if there should be a constitutional amendment protecting the life of an unborn child. This time, 50 percent said yes, 39 percent no, and 11 percent had no opinion.[4] Did either question accurately measure public opinion on the issue? No one can say for sure. This also illustrates the potential for mischief from those who would like to manufacture survey data to support their own point of view. Jerry Falwell, the head of the Moral Majority, surveyed his supporters using this question: "Do you approve of the present laws legalizing abortion on demand that result in the murder of 1.5 million unborn babies every year?" It's easy to see which side he's on, and it's easy to imagine the kind of responses he received.

Many people may not have an opinion on an issue but will nevertheless give an answer to the interviewer in order not to appear uninformed. Survey researchers call these "doorstep" opinions because that's where they originate. Professional pollsters generally try to reduce these by offering respondents a relatively painless opportunity to confess they haven't heard of an issue or don't have an opinion. Still, doorstep opinions are a potentially serious problem for any survey.

Researchers also know that even the characteristics of an interviewer can affect poll results. In a poll conducted several years ago on racial issues, responses varied depending on the race of the interviewer. When the interviewers were white, for example, 35 percent of the black people surveyed agreed that whites could be trusted. When the interviewers were fellow blacks, however, agreement fell to only 7 percent. Similarly, 56 percent of the whites surveyed said that students of both races should attend the same schools when questioned by white interviewers. But when the interviewers were black, 91 percent of the whites supported school integration.[5]

Finally, it's important to keep in mind that even the most professionally conducted survey is only a snapshot of public opinion taken on the day of the poll. Polls don't make good crystal balls because of the variability of public opinion. In 1980, for example, the final Gallup and Harris surveys taken the week before the presidential election showed the race too close to call, yet on election day Reagan won by a substantial margin. Were the polls wrong? No, but they turned out to be poor prognosticators. Polls conducted for the candidates also showed an extremely close race right up to the weekend before election day. At that point, both the Carter and Reagan camps' polls indicated that the undecided vote had turned dramatically against President Carter. The Gallup and Harris Polls had apparently been correct when they were taken; by election day, the climate of opinion had changed.

Polls have become an integral part of the political process. As we shall see in chapter 5, surveys are frequently used to direct election campaigns. They are a major part of the news media's coverage of election campaigns; in fact, controversies have arisen over journalists using election-day polls to call election winners even before the polls close (see **PERSPECTIVE** on page 92). Polls can also have an effect on public policy. On the one hand, it can be argued that polls help officeholders better fulfill their role as representatives. How better to determine what the folks back home think than to read the results of a scientifically conducted poll? On the other hand, does government-by-opinion-poll necessarily produce good policy? What a majority of Americans want today may not be what they will want tomorrow and may not be in their long-term best interests. There is something to be said for political leaders who lead rather than wait to see where the crowd is going and then rush to get in front. After President Reagan ordered the marines to invade the Caribbean island of Grenada in 1983, for example, most of the leading candidates for the Democratic presidential nomination withheld judgment on the invasion for several days or longer. Perhaps they were waiting for all the facts to be known; cynics would suggest that they were waiting to read the opinion polls.

POLITICAL SOCIALIZATION

Political socialization is the process whereby individuals acquire political knowledge, attitudes, and beliefs. It is a learning process, but most of what we learn about politics isn't the result of formal teaching. To be sure, some of our knowledge about government was taught us in the classroom or explained to us by our parents when we were youngsters. Much of what we know and believe about politics, however, we learn informally throughout our entire lives. We are socialized politically when we see our parents go to vote, or hear our schoolmates discuss the use of illegal drugs, or listen to a newscast, or serve on a jury, or pay property taxes, or wait for the police to come after we discover that our home has been burglarized. Let's examine what political scientists have learned about the process of political socialization and then discuss some of the agents that help bring about socialization.

THE PROCESS OF SOCIALIZATION

Studies have found that very young children tend to personalize and idealize the political system. By the age of five or six, most children are able to identify police officers and the president with the government. Also, children's attitudes toward these figures are quite positive. They see police officers as friends and helpers and say that the president is someone who is "smarter" and "more honest" than most people. Apparently, patriotism develops early. Most children are able to distinguish the American flag

Perspective

THE POLITICS OF EXIT POLLS, OR, CALLING THE RACE BEFORE IT'S OVER

On election night 1980, the NBC television network projected Ronald Reagan as the winner of the presidential election at 8:15 P.M. Eastern Standard Time. For hours already, all three television networks and other news organizations had been strongly hinting that Reagan was on his way to victory. In many areas, however, especially on the West Coast, the polls were still open. Would these early projections discourage potential voters from going to the polls? Could this in turn affect the outcome of some state and local races?

The major television networks and other news organizations are able to project election winners early through means of election-day exit polls. The pollsters select a sample of precincts from around the nation. NBC used four hundred in 1980. Interviewers are stationed at the selected precincts and told to confront each *k*th voter leaving the polls, perhaps every tenth or fifteenth. The voters are given a "secret" ballot on which they mark the names of the candidates for whom they voted. They are also asked their views on various issues and asked to supply some background information on themselves, such as race, age, and income level. The inter-

WITH ONE PER CENT OF THE VOTE IN, OUR COMPUTER AT ELECTION CENTRAL PREDICTS WILBUR FUNT WILL WIN THE U.S. SENATE SEAT IN OHIO... IN 1985 HE WILL MARRY HIS DEVOTED SECRETARY... THEY WILL HAVE TWO CHILDREN... IN 1989 HE WILL BECOME SERIOUSLY ILL AND...

By Peters for The Dayton Daily News

[1]John E. Jackson, "Election Night Reporting and Voter Turnout," *American Journal of Political Science* 27 (November 1983): 615–35; Mark R. Levy, "The

from others and say that it is their favorite.[6] Perhaps this helps explain the intense public reponse to the hostage seizure in Iran. As children we learn to love our country and to identify the person of the president with it. Consequently, our gut reaction to foreign crisis is one of outrage and support for the president.

As children grow older, their knowledge increases but still they recognize people and symbols more readily than they understand procedures and processes. Grade-school youngsters are able to identify such terms as *Congress, political parties, voting,* and *democracy*. Their understanding, though, is still rudimentary. Most children see the Congress as a group of men and women who help the president. Many are able to name the political party their family supports, but they are unable to note differences between the

viewers periodically phone in totals to the polls' managers throughout election day.

News organizations have used exit-poll data both to analyze voting patterns and to project election outcomes. During the 1984 Democratic primary season, for example, exit-poll data were used to analyze the nature of Walter Mondale and Gary Hart's popular support. The most controversial use of exit polls is to project election results, sometimes even before the polls close. In March 1984, NBC "called" the Alabama primary an hour and a half before the polls closed there. NBC then proceded to interview candidate John Glenn, asking him what he would do now that he had lost in Alabama. Glenn chided the network for its haste and urged Alabamans to go vote. As it turned out, NBC was right. Glenn lost in Alabama.

In fact, the track record of exit polls has been quite good.

But do they keep people from voting? There is not a great deal of research on this subject, but a recent study reports that potential voters who learned of early projections in 1980 were less likely to vote than those who had not gotten the word. Also, some evidence in the study showed that Reagan supporters were more likely to be affected than Carter backers. Although many observers have expressed the fear that early projections may become self-fulfilling prophecies, these data suggest that projected winners may be hurt more than losers.

Finally, we must ask what, if anything, should be done about exit polling and early projections. In 1984, one newspaper columnist encouraged voters to lie to the interviewers to sabo-

tage the projections. That may be one way to put the suspense back into election night, but if large numbers of people were to take that advice, it would destroy a valuable means of gathering data for post-election analysis. Another approach is for Congress to legislate an end to early projections. That, however, probably falls afoul of the Constitution's First Amendment guarantee of a free press. Perhaps the best solution to the problem of early projections is for the news media to use restraint and not call elections while the voting continues. Public pressure is growing for the media to do just that, but news organizations are also under great competitive pressures to be first with the news. So far, the latter pressures have been the stronger.[1]

Methodology and Performance of Election Day Polls," *Public Opinion Quarterly* 47 (Spring 1983): 54–67.

parties. Although most young children declare democracy to be the best form of government, few have much understanding of the term's meaning.

In adolescence, young people begin to resemble adults politically. They are now able to separate individual from institutional roles. They recognize that it is possible to criticize the president, for example, while still supporting the presidency. Procedures and processes such as voting and lawmaking are more visible and important to adolescents, and their general knowledge of the political process is more sophisticated. Also, in adolescence the attitudes of different groups toward the political system begin to diverge. Studies have found that the socialization experiences of young children are quite similar.[7] In adolescence, though, minority children grow less trustful of authority figures, especially police officers.[8] In contrast, young people from middle-class white families remain supportive of the system.

Political socialization continues throughout one's life, of course, but few systematic studies have been done of the process beyond adolescence. In part, this is because adults are much more difficult to pin down than school-age children. Also, there are so many factors, past and present, that can influence the political knowledge, attitudes, and beliefs of adults that it is quite difficult to separate them out for individual study.

THE AGENTS OF SOCIALIZATION

The family, school, peer groups, the media, and dramatic events are all **agents of socialization.** They shape the level, intensity, and direction of our thoughts and actions about government. Let's consider the effects of each of these factors on our political development.

Family. The family's influence on socialization is important, but it is difficult to assess precisely. The family's power is private, subtle, and ongoing. We know, however, that families filter information about politics for children and transmit signals about political events. In particular, researchers have found that the family is a key factor in the development of political-party loyalties. One researcher found that 60 percent of the fourth-graders he interviewed identified with a political party. The children had virtually no knowledge of party history, issues, or candidates. Instead, they merely adopted the party of their parents in much the same way that they accepted their parents' religious preference. For children, proclaiming "We're Democrats" is as natural as saying "We're Baptists."[9]

At the same time, other research has found that the correlation between the attitudes of high-school students and their parents on several political *issues* is not particularly strong, although young people still usually share their parents' party identification.[10] Thus, children may inherit a political-party identification from their parents, but a complete set of political ideas and values is not part of the legacy.

Family background also affects interest and involvement in politics. Children whose parents are politically active are more likely to grow up to be politically active adults than are children from families with little political involvement.[11]

Finally, the influence of the family can strengthen or weaken the impact of other socializing forces, such as the school or peer groups. For example, one study has found that children from lower-class and middle-class families experience different patterns of political socialization.[12] This may help explain differences in political attitudes among adults.

School. The school is another important agent of political socialization, but generally not because of civics education. Children learn some of the basic mechanics of government in elementary school, but high-school civics classes add very little to their knowledge and understanding. Research has found that civics courses have almost no effect on students' knowledge, participatory skills, political tolerance, or support for democracy.[13] Perhaps this is simply an indicator of the general weakness of American education. Some studies do show that high-school civics teachers often know little about the subject they teach.[14]

On the other hand, schools *are* effective at teaching patriotism, at molding children into little Americans. In the classroom, students pledge allegiance to the flag, sing patriotic songs, learn about national holidays, and study the lives of great American heroes and heroines. Schools also give young people first-hand experience in working within a power structure. A school is a self-contained political system, with peers, authorities, rules, rewards, and punishments. The young person inevitably develops attitudes about rules and authority and about his or her expected role as a participant in the system. Schools aren't democracies, of course; principals and teachers are often more interested in discipline than in participation. Some scholars suggest that the school's primary focus on compliance hinders the development of political participation skills.[15] Research has found that this is particularly true of schools in working-class areas.[16]

The effects of college on political socialization are difficult to measure. Students who attend college differ politically from their peers who do not, but college-bound young people tend to be different from their peers even before they go to college. Studies have found that high-school graduates who go on to college are more knowledgeable and interested in politics and feel more capable of influencing the policy process than the noncollege-bound.[17]

However, the college experience does seem to loosen family ties as far as political attitudes are concerned. College is often a broadening experience in which students are exposed to a greater variety of ideas and people than they were in high school. Consequently, collegians are less likely to share their family's political views than those people who do not attend college. We should add, though, that the political impact of college depends on the type of institution students attend, their major field of study, and whether or not they work their way through college.

Peer groups.   Our peers are the people with whom we associate socially and professionally throughout our lives. Peer-group influence on political socialization is found in many places: back-fence conversations between neighbors; beauty and barber-shop visits; and at union meetings and in boardrooms. Studies have found that peers are more important in shaping young peoples' issue positions than parents[18] and that when adults change peer groups because of a new job or a move to a different city, their political views are likely to change as well.[19] Still, this is another area in which more research is needed.

A major problem for scholars is that the agents of political socialization are often quite closely interrelated. Family background often determines choice of school, and schools affect peer groups. Both of these influence the types of careers individuals pursue. With so much overlap, it is difficult for social scientists to separate out individual influences.

Media.   Most scholars believe that the mass media are important agents of political socialization. After all, Americans spend a great deal of time watching television, listening to radio, and reading newspapers and magazines. Unfortunately, little definitive research has been done on the political effects of the media. Polls show that most Americans get most of their news from TV, yet only about 20 percent of the public regularly watches news programs.[20] Also, research shows that newspapers are generally a better source of information than TV.[21] We know that this is the age of television campaigning, but one study suggests that TV may actually diminish political participation because it adds to a climate of cynicism about politics and because it encourages a degree of passivity on the part of viewers.[22]

The political role of the media is quite controversial. In the late 1960s, the Nixon Administration, spearheaded by Vice-President Spiro Agnew, attacked the news media for an alleged liberal bias. "Nattering nabobs of negativism," Agnew called the press. In contrast, others suggest that the media act to reinforce society's dominant values. One critic argues that the media try not to offend anyone for economic reasons. Consequently, radical ideas generally don't receive a hearing.[23]

Scholarly research on the subject has provided no clear answers on the

The media are ever-present at political events. They transmit, edit, interpret, and summarize what occurs. In so doing, they serve as important agents of political socialization.

issue of political bias in the press. On the one hand, studies have found that newspapers editorially endorse Republican presidential candidates over Democrats by a three-to-one margin and that these editorial views sometimes spill over into the news.[24] On the other hand, research has found that most national news journalists hold liberal views.[25] Still other studies have found no appreciable bias in the television network news.[26]

Many observers do agree, however, that the media are often able to *set the agenda* for public debate. Studies have found that the public considers headline and lead news stories to be more significant than stories that receive less attention. Consequently, the credibility of a cause, issue, or candidate often depends on media coverage.[27]

Thoughtful Americans have long recognized the importance of an active, free press in a democratic society. Thomas Jefferson phrased it this way: "Were it left to me to decide whether we should have a government without newspapers, or newspapers without government, I should not hesitate a moment to prefer the latter." In recent years, the media have played an important role in uncovering the Watergate scandal and in educating the public about the war in Vietnam.

Perhaps the most important point to remember about the mass media in general is that they are private businesses seeking profit. For television stations, the primary goal is good ratings. The higher the ratings, the more the station can charge for advertising. Similarly, the rates newspapers charge advertisers depend on circulation. Consequently, the media are faced with a multitude of temptations to shade or simply hype the news. And, many succumb to temptation, at least a bit. Lively stories that increase ratings or newspaper circulation increase advertising revenue. The great majority of media owners are honorable people who take the news seriously, but their game is a savagely competitive one. America has some of the world's best newspapers, but it also has supermarket tabloids, and the tabloids sell better. Meanwhile, television can be credited with producing some first-rate documentaries. Unfortunately, they invariably wind up at the bottom of the ratings chart. So it's not surprising that commercial stations push entertainment at the expense of information and analysis. "The A-Team" outsells "Meet the Press."

Since most of us get the bulk of our political news through the television tube, several points should be kept in mind about that medium. First, television news is condensed. On the network news programs, major stories must be covered in a few minutes, the entire day's news in less than half an hour. Local news shows are usually even shorter. Consequently, television news tends to be superficial, akin to reading the headlines and maybe the first paragraph of a few major stories in the newspaper. There's nothing wrong with reading headlines, of course, but television viewers who want detailed information must turn to other sources.

Second, television does a poor job of explaining political issues. Instead of exploring the substance of complex issues, television is preoccupied with easily grasped confrontations. Too often the nightly news pits extreme views against each other while ignoring sensible viewpoints in the middle ground. Many such television events can only be called mutual exchanges of ignorance. The time limitations of television are also a factor. One early-morning program offers a forum for debate that restricts the actual exchange of views to about three minutes of air time. The result: the participants (often articulate and well-informed individuals with much of value to say) can only bark at one another for a few minutes before being cut off in mid-sentence by the moderator. Even a respected show such as "Sixty Minutes" sometimes uses the "ambush" style of journalism, featuring short, dramatic jousts between star journalists and those being questioned.

Local news programs tend to be the worst offenders. Reporters are trained in communications and journalism, not political science, economics, law, business, or foreign affairs. They must learn the substance of public affairs on the job, but rapid turnover in local television makes that difficult. As soon as reporters begin to get a feel for city-hall politics, they move on to a new job in a different town and must begin again. Consequently, local stations often present "happy talk" news shows, playing up the silly, but seldom the significant, aspects of the local news. They do stories on spectacular wrecks and bizarre killings. They laugh a lot on camera, but detailed examinations of local issues are rare.

Finally, television news stories are generally constructed around considerations of drama, visual imagery, and action. In 1963, the executive producer of the NBC Evening News wrote this memo to his staff:

Every news story should, without any sacrifice of probity or responsibility, display the attributes of fiction, of drama. It should have structure and conflict, problem and denouement, rising action and falling action, a beginning, a middle and an end. These are not only the essentials of drama; they are the essentials of narrative.[28]

In the eyes of news producers, the best stories are those with dramatic action shots, such as political demonstrations or natural disasters. Hurricanes aren't covered at the weather bureau, but on the beach with palm trees swaying and waves crashing. Even a "nonvisual" story, such as a report on the latest inflation statistics, is illustrated with shots of supermarket shoppers. Television covers election campaigns much as it follows a baseball pennant race. Instead of the candidates' issue positions, viewers are treated to "horserace and hoopla."[29] Television focuses on who's ahead, who's behind, who's catching up, and who's slipping. In all of this, there is a tendency to exaggerate. The good is made to seem better than it really is; the bad, worse. It's "gee-whiz show biz," showing us what happened, but seldom telling us why.

Events.   Events are not as tangible as parents, schools, and peers, but they too are important agents of political socialization. Elections, for example, provide children and adolescents with much information about the political process and institutions.[30] During an election campaign, young people become more aware of political authority.[31] Moreover, a parent's electoral choice in a presidential contest probably cues the young child's adoption of a political party.[32]

Adults are also socialized by political events. Dramatic episodes of action and intrigue attract a glut of media attention and interpretation. The more famous and controversial an event becomes, the more discussion it prompts among citizens. Chances increase that peoples' normal understanding of the political world will be challenged and perhaps even altered. Clearly change occurred in Americans' attitudes during the 1960s. That decade of political violence and failures, including assassinations, civil disobedience, and the Vietnam war, prompted disillusionment with the two major political parties and with government leaders in general.[33]

THE POLITICS OF SOCIALIZATION

As we have seen, much of our political socialization is the result of incidental experiences. As children, we overhear our parents discussing politics, or a police officer helps us when we become lost. As adults, we watch a television movie about nuclear war, or we lose a job during an economic downturn. Although we "learn" things about politics and government from each of these experiences, our learning isn't the result of conscious teaching.

At other times, however, socialization is the result of conscious efforts by political authorities and others to shape our attitudes and beliefs. In the late nineteenth and early twentieth centuries in particular, the public schools worked diligently to teach "Americanism" to the children of a nation of immigrants. Today, political leaders manipulate symbols and images in hopes of influencing public opinion. After the invasion of Grenada, for example, President Reagan criticized reporters who insisted on calling the marine landing an "invasion." It was a "rescue mission" for the American medical students there, he said. Reagan also insisted on referring to the MX missile as the "Peacekeeper Missile." Moreover, political leaders use events to influence public attitudes as well. Trips abroad during an election year, for example, give the incumbent president the opportunity to look presidential.

Around the world, public attitudes and opinions are the concern of political leaders. In authoritarian regimes, such as the Soviet Union, the government devotes enormous resources to controlling what citizens hear and are taught about government in the schools and in the media. Dissent is sharply limited and the press is controlled. In the United States and other democratic political systems, a free press and the democratic process provide a check on government's efforts to shape public attitudes. In the pages ahead, we will be discussing the ways in which public opinion can affect policymaking, but it is important to recognize that policymakers can also affect public opinion.

THE CONTENT OF PUBLIC OPINION

Public opinion consists of the combined personal opinions of adults toward issues of relevance to government.[34] Discussing public opinion is difficult, however, because there is no single opinion that is held by everyone, few people hold opinions on every issue, and people hold views with varying degrees of intensity.

First, on any particular issue, part of the public will have an opinion and part will not. The bulk of the citizenry on an issue are part of the **mass public**—they are uninformed and uninterested in the issue. In contrast, the **attentive public** are those people who have an active and continuing interest in the subject. Finally, **opinion leaders** are people who lead opinion, make decisions, and muster support for policies among the other two publics.

The relative size of these three groups varies from issue to issue. During the 1960s, most Americans belonged to the attentive public on the issues of the war in Vietnam and the civil-rights movement. In contrast, few of us today are particularly interested or attentive to the machinations of the International Monetary Fund. Opinion leaders, however, are almost always a relatively small group. They are political activists who are also in positions of influence. Depending on the issue, they may be newspaper editors, television journalists, elected officials, church leaders, community figures, business people, or famous personalities.

Second, views are held with varying degrees of intensity. You may feel quite strongly about abortion or nuclear energy, or you may not feel much one way or the other. Few Americans were neutral about Watergate. On the other hand, the 55-mph speed limit has not provoked many protest demonstrations.

Finally, public opinion waxes and wanes as issues grow in importance or recede from view. In 1977 and 1978, many Americans were fired up over the Panama Canal Treaty that returned sovereignty over the Canal Zone to Panama. After the Senate ratified the treaty, however, passions cooled and the issue faded. In the 1980s, nuclear-arms control may be the issue "whose time has come."

With these considerations in mind, we will do our best to discuss what Americans know, believe, and think about politics. We will examine the public's knowledge of government, support for democratic principles, political trust and efficacy, and political ideology. These aren't just topics for the academically curious; they are also important to those concerned about the quality of democracy in America. Do Americans have the knowledge to participate intelligently in the policy process? Do they support the democratic process? Are they satisfied with our present form of government? Do they believe their participation can affect the policy process? Are Americans liberal or conservative?

POLITICAL KNOWLEDGE

Americans in general are not very well-informed about politics. Recent surveys have found that only some 80 percent of us can name the vice-president of the United States, only half knows which party has a majority in each house of Congress, and less than a third of us knows that the term of a member of the House is two years. More Americans know their astrological sign than can name their representative in Congress.[35] To be sure, a minority of Americans is quite knowledgeable about public policy, and most Americans are probably informed on at least a few matters of concern to them. It is difficult to imagine, however, that the majority of adult Americans understands enough about public affairs to participate intelligently in the public-policy process. As one group of scholars puts it, it appears the American public includes a "hard core of chronic know nothings."[36]

Who's to blame? One prominent political scientist, the late V. O. Key, Jr., points the finger at the political system itself. Candidates and officeholders often do a poor job of explaining issues to the voters.[37] We might also suggest that the media do a poor job of educating the public about politics as well. An additional explanation is that most people are more interested in matters other than politics. Some of us may be political junkies, but most Americans would rather devote their time and energy to earning a living, raising a family, and enjoying life than to learning about politics.

SUPPORT FOR DEMOCRACY

Do Americans support the democratic principles of majority rule and minority rights? In 1960, two political scientists, James W. Prothro and

"Put me down for 'no comment' on that one . . . I really haven't read enough polls on the subject to form an opinion!"

C. W. Grigg, published a classic study on the issue. Their sample of Americans overwhelmingly endorsed the statements that democracy is the best form of government, that public officials should be chosen by majority vote, and that the minority should have the right to convince others of their views. When Prothro and Grigg asked about specific, concrete situations, however, they found dramatically less support for the practice of majority rule and minority rights. Many respondents in their survey agreed that a communist should not be allowed to take office even if legally elected. Many also agreed that atheists should not be allowed to speak publicly against religion.[38] In the years since the Prothro and Grigg study was first published, other research has confirmed that Americans are more likely to support democratic principles in the abstract than in specific application. One famous study found a majority of Americans opposed to many of the specific provisions of the Bill of Rights.[39]

This disturbs some observers. Political theorists often argue that maintenance of a free and democratic society requires a high degree of popular support for democratic principles. How, then, can one explain the stability of democracy in America in the face of research that has often found a lack of support for the fundamental principles of democracy?

The answer most frequently given by political scientists involves something we might call **"democratic elitism."**[40] Studies have found that practical support for democratic principles is not evenly distributed across the population. It seems that the people who are most active politically are more supportive of democratic values than the people who are politically uninvolved. Consequently, the saving grace for America's democracy is that those who are most directly involved in policymaking—the political "elites"—are the most supportive of the principles of majority rule and minority rights.[41]

In addition, survey research has shown that Americans in general have grown considerably more tolerant of diversity over the last twenty years. In the mid-1950s, less than 40 percent of Americans polled agreed that a speech against religion should be permitted or that anti-religious books should be allowed in the library. In the 1970s, however, about 60 percent of those surveyed agreed to both of those propositions.[42] Perhaps this is the result of a younger, more urbanized, better-educated population.

This sort of basic change in people's values can have an important influence on public policy. Students of history will recall that the 1950s was the decade of "McCarthyism," a frenzied search for communists and communist sympathizers led by Senator Joseph McCarthy. Many innocent persons were falsely accused and their careers ruined. Although we cannot say for sure, we suspect that today a Senator McCarthy would be unable to generate the fear and hysteria that characterized the 1950s. At least it would be easier for responsible political leaders to oppose McCarthy in the 1980s than it was in the 1950s.

POLITICAL TRUST

Many scholars argue that political trust is essential to the preservation of a healthy democracy. For the most part, democracy depends on the voluntary cooperation of its citizens rather than on their coercion. People pay taxes and obey the law essentially because they believe it is the proper thing to do. They work to redress grievances through the political system, and they peacefully accept the outcome of the election process.

If a significant proportion of the population ceases to trust the political system, however, the quality of democracy begins to decline. Tax evasion and disregard for the rule of law increase. The potential for a revolutionary change in the political order may develop. Political battles may be fought not with ballots but bullets.[43]

Political scientists have tried to study political trust in America by means of a series of questions regularly asked of national samples of Americans by the Center for Political Studies (CPS) at the University of Michigan. The questions probe the degree to which citizens think government leaders in Washington are honest (or crooked) and competent (or incompetent). When the CPS first began asking these questions in 1958, only a minority of the respondents chose distrustful responses. That remained true until the middle 1960s. Thereafter, the proportion giving the most distrustful answers rose steadily and sharply. By 1976, more than 40 percent of the sample chose the most mistrustful response for each of the questions.[44]

These data aren't good news, but they do not necessarily signal the demise of democracy in America. Dislike of public officials, disapproval of public policies, and unhappiness with the consequences of those policies do not necessarily add up to a rejection of the political system. Some scholars argue that the CPS questions measure degrees of support for public officials and their policies rather than a general level of trust in the political system. What with Vietnam, Watergate, inflation, recession, and the turmoil of the 1960s, it is easy to understand how many Americans could lose confidence in political leaders and their policies. But does this lost confidence in institutions extend to the political system as a whole? Perhaps not, for other CPS surveys have found that more than 85 percent of those sampled still agree that they were "proud of many things about our form of government."[45]

"If you were to cast your ballot today, who would you consider to be the lesser-of-two-evils?"

POLITICAL EFFICACY

Political efficacy refers to the extent individuals believe they can have an effect on the public policymaking process. In theory, efficacy should be closely related to political participation. After all, if citizens feel they can

TABLE 4.1

Americans' Political Philosophy, Self-Identification

Time of Poll	Liberal	Moderate	Conservative	Don't Know
March 1981	17%	46%	30%	7%
August 1978	22	37	30	11
September 1976	20	38	26	16

SOURCE: *The Gallup Report* (April 1981).

have little influence on the policy process, why bother voting or working on a campaign?

The Center for Political Studies has attempted to measure political efficacy by means of the following questions (respondents were asked if they agreed or disagreed with each of these):

1. I don't think public officials care much what people like me think.
2. People like me don't have any say about what the government does.
3. Sometimes politics and government are so complicated that a person like me can't really understand what's going on.

The survey results suggest that Americans have grown considerably less confident in their ability to affect government decisions. In 1960, CPS data showed that while more than 50 percent of the sample said that government is too complicated to understand, less than 30 percent agreed to the other two statements. By 1976, however, more than 40 percent of those questioned believed they had no say in government, more than 50 percent said officials don't care what they think, and more than 70 percent said that government is too complicated.[46] It is interesting that this apparent decline in the public's belief in political efficacy was accompanied by a decline in voter turnout.

POLITICAL IDEOLOGY

Are Americans liberal or conservative? By their own admission, they lean toward the conservative side and are more conservative now than in the mid-1970s (see Table 4.1). However, one must be careful not to put too much credence in self-appraisals of political ideology. Studies have found that many Americans cannot accurately define liberalism and conservatism. It is not unusual for many individuals to call themselves conservatives and then express liberal views on particular issues. Also, many Americans hold liberal views on some issues, conservative opinions on others.[47]

It is sometimes useful to see how Americans in general feel about certain issues, regardless of political affiliation or ideology (see the **PERSPECTIVE** on page 105). It can also be instructive to look at how public opinion varies among different subgroups of the population. In fact, membership in a subgroup may, in many cases, be a more significant political identifier than the self-assigned label of liberal or conservative. Let's look briefly at the political viewpoints associated with a few important subgroups.

Social class. Studies have found a number of interesting differences of opinion between working-class and middle-class Americans.[48] On the one hand, working-class people tend to be more liberal on social-welfare issues than middle-class individuals. Low-income groups see themselves as beneficiaries of these programs, while middle-income people think in terms of paying the bills. On the other hand, working-class individuals are often more conservative than other Americans on noneconomic issues. They are less supportive of women's rights and the rights of the criminally accused. Working-class whites are less supportive of civil rights for blacks.[49] In foreign-policy matters, working-class individuals are more isolationist than middle-income people but also more supportive of the use of force in

Perspective
AMERICANS ON THE ISSUES

How do Americans feel about the basic policy issues of the day? The following poll results are taken from recent national surveys conducted by the Gallup Poll. In your evaluation of this data, consider question wording. Also, remember that the survey results reflect opinion on the date the survey was taken.

Would you favor or oppose an agreement between the United States and the Soviet Union for an immediate, verifiable freeze on the testing, production, and deployment of nuclear weapons?

Favor	70%
Oppose	21
No opinion	9

March 11–14, 1983

There is much discussion as to the amount of money the government in Washington should spend for national defense and military purposes. How do you feel about this? Do you think we are spending too little, too much, or about the right amount?

Too little	16%
Too much	41
About right	31
No opinion	12

November 5–8, 1982

Some people say the U.S. should give military assistance to governments in Central America that are friendly to us. Others say we should not get involved in the internal affairs of these nations. Which point of view comes closer to the way you feel—that we should give military assistance to these nations or that we should not get involved?

Give military assistance	35%
Don't get involved	55
No opinion	10

July 26–August 1, 1983

In general, do you feel that the laws governing the sale of handguns should be made more strict, less strict, or kept as they are now?

More strict	59%
Less strict	4
Kept as now	31
No opinion	6

May 13–16, 1983

The U.S. Supreme Court has ruled that a woman may go to a doctor to end pregnancy at any time during the first three months of pregnancy. Do you favor or oppose this ruling?

Favor	50%
Oppose	43
No opinion	7

June 24–27, 1983

SOURCE: *The Gallup Report* (January, May, August, and September 1983).

dealing with other nations. In contrast, middle- and upper-income people have a more internationalist perspective; they tend to favor free trade, foreign aid, and negotiated settlements of disputes.[50] Some scholars suggest that the key variable accounting for differences between working-class and middle-income individuals is education.[51]

Race.   Studies have found that the political attitudes of blacks differ notably from those of white Americans. One would expect blacks to be more liberal than whites on civil-rights issues, of course, but black liberalism extends to economic issues as well. What's more, middle-income blacks are just as liberal on economic issues as low-income blacks.[52] Perhaps the best explanation for black liberalism is that blacks as a group frequently have benefited from the use of federal power.

Religion.   There are also differences in public opinion based on religion. On economic issues, for example, Catholics have tended to be more liberal than Protestants, though this may be class-related (historically, Catholics have held a disproportionately large number of low-income jobs). Jews have tended to be liberal on issues across the spectrum, though this may be a consequence of education (as a group, Jews have tended to be better educated than Americans in general). In some cases, political differences among religious groups can be explained on the basis of theology. Catholics, for example, tend to be more conservative on the issues of abortion and divorce than other religious groups. Jews tend to be very supportive of U.S. aid for Israel. Fundamentalist Protestants, such as Southern Baptists, are more inclined to favor the teaching of creationism in the public schools and more likely to oppose legalized gambling and drinking.[53]

Region.   Differences among people from different geographical regions are fewer now than they once were, but differences do still exist. In general, people from the East or the West Coasts are more liberal than those from the South, Midwest, or Rocky Mountain areas. On civil rights in particular, the South is more conservative than other areas. Most of these regional differences can be explained by other factors, however—class, race, education, religion. Nevertheless, some bona fide regional variations, based on unique historical and cultural factors, may play a role in the political fabric of the nation. The South's lingering identification with the old Confederacy is perhaps the most notable example of how history can shape the political thinking of a region.[54]

Gender.   Through the 1970s, scholars found few differences between the attitudes of men and those of women. Even on so-called women's issues, such as abortion or the Equal Rights Amendment, the views of men and women were quite similar.[55] Recently, however, the phrase **"gender gap"** has become a prominent part of the political vocabulary. Surveys have found major differences between women and men on a number of issues, particularly those concerning war and peace. Men are more prone to favor the use of military force in the conduct of foreign affairs while women are more concerned about the danger of war. In October 1983, a poll commissioned by the *Washington Post* and ABC News found that 73 percent of the men surveyed agreed with President Reagan's decision to invade the Caribbean island of Grenada compared to only 45 percent of the women.[56] Surveys have also found women to be more liberal than men on some social issues. Women, for example, are more often opposed to the death penalty than men and more frequently oppose the relaxation of environmental standards.[57]

Conclusion: Public Opinion and Public Policy

To what extent does public opinion affect public policy? In high-school civics class, we may have gotten the impression that public opinion translates directly and immediately into policy. Now we know that view is naive. In contrast, some critics of American government say there is *no* relationship between public attitudes and policy. But that view is too cynical. The truth lies somewhere in between.

Several studies have found a relationship between public opinion and policy at least some of the time. One researcher argued that national policy corresponds to public attitudes about two thirds of the time,[58] and his research has been supported by another study of state policies and public opinion within states.[59] Other research has indicated that a politically active community can affect policy at the local level.[60]

Whether or not public opinion affects policy depends on the issue. When the attentive public is fairly sizable and feelings are intense, public opinion may become important. Issues such as abortion, environmental protection, civil rights, and American support for Israel attract large and often influential attentive publics. Policymakers have to take public opinion into account on these issues.[61] There is not a perfect matchup, however, and, for years on end, opinion and policy may differ. Frequently, this is because of the power of entrenched groups. Polls show, for example, that a majority of Americans favor tighter federal controls on the availability of hand guns. Nevertheless, the National Rifle Association has been able to use its considerable influence to defeat all recent efforts at gun control.

Even on issues on which there is a sizable attentive public, political decisionmakers, especially the president, are often able to swing majority support behind the policies they wish to pursue. This is particularly true in foreign affairs. In the late 1960s, for example, opinion surveys consistently showed that a large majority of Americans opposed American recognition of mainland China. Then President Nixon traveled to Peking and American opinion turned around overnight, especially among Republicans who, as a group, had once been the ones most adamantly opposed to direct dealings with the Chinese communists. In the early 1980s, polls showed that few Americans endorsed the idea of American military intervention in Central America. Yet in 1983 President Reagan ordered the invasion of Grenada and won broad public support for that action.

On many issues, the attentive public may be small and/or relatively uninfluential. When this is true, it stands to reason that public opinion may be an unimportant part of the policy process. We suspect, for example, that public opinion plays little role in shaping American government policy on the status of Tibet and the Dalai Lama. The Tibetan community in America is quite small and most Americans probably think of the Dalai Lama as either a painter or a Peruvian beast of burden. Consequently, there is little public opinion on this matter, leaving American foreign policymakers free to set policy on other grounds.

Considering the American public's general ignorance of public affairs, policymakers enjoy considerable leeway in many, perhaps most, policy areas. This does not mean, however, that policymakers can disregard the public. Studies show that many voters hold public officials accountable for perceived policy outcomes.[62] For officeholders, reelection depends on policies that the public considers successful. Public opinion may offer little specific guidance to policymakers on how to conduct economic policy, for instance, but voters do know the difference between a healthy economy and a weak one and will vote to reward or punish officeholders accordingly.

In sum, in most cases public opinion acts as an after-the-fact, *retrospective* check on public policy. The public tells leaders how they've done in the past, not necessarily what to do in the future. To be sure, on some issues there is an important attentive public with fairly clear policy demands— abortion, the rights of women, and civil rights, for example. On a number of policy issues, however, public opinion simply hasn't crystallized. Consequently, public officials generally enjoy a great deal of policymaking freedom. The public cannot be ignored, however, since voters do react to policy outcomes.

Let's return to our illustration of the Iranian hostage seizure. As the hostage crisis wore on, the American public had no strongly held, clearcut view of the best course to follow in resolving the situation. At least as far as public opinion was concerned, the Carter Administration enjoyed considerable leeway in devising a policy to free the hostages. In fact, considering the dynamics of public reaction to international crises, Carter could probably have expected public support for whatever course he took. Nevertheless, public opinion was very strong and very clear about one point: the American people wanted the crisis ended and the hostages freed. Public opinion may have been vague about the means to end the crisis, but it was quite exacting about the goal it wanted achieved. The public's demands weighed heavily on the president. Carter failed to win an early release of the hostages. He lost the election.

Key Terms

AGENTS OF SOCIALIZATION *(94)*

ATTENTIVE PUBLIC *(100)*

CLUSTER SAMPLING *(89)*

DEMOCRATIC ELITISM *(102)*

GENDER GAP *(106)*

MASS PUBLIC *(100)*

OPINION LEADERS *(100)*

POLITICAL EFFICACY *(103)*

POLITICAL SOCIALIZATION *(88)*

RANDOM SAMPLE *(89)*

SAMPLE *(88)*

SURVEY RESEARCH *(88)*

UNIVERSE *(88)*

NOTES

1. *The Gallup Report* (December 1979), pp. 3–5.
2. Ibid.
3. Alan D. Monroe, *Public Opinion in America* (New York: Dodd, Mead, 1975), ch. 2; and Frederick F. Stephen and Philip J. McCarthy, *Sampling Opinions: An Analysis of Survey Procedures* (New York: Wiley, 1958).
4. *New York Times,* 18 August 1980, p. A15.
5. Howard Schuman and Jean Converse, "The Effects of Black and White Interviewers on Black Response in 1968," *Public Opinion Quarterly* 35 (Spring 1971): 44–68; and Shirley Hatchett and Howard Schuman, "White Respondents and Race of Interviewer Effects," *Public Opinion Quarterly* 39 (Winter 1975): 523–28.
6. Fred I. Greenstein, *Children and Politics* (New Haven: Yale University Press, 1956); Robert D. Hess and Judith V. Torney, *The Development of Political Attitudes in Children* (Chicago: Aldine, 1967); and David Easton and Jack Dennis, *Children in the Political System: Origins of Political Legitimacy* (New York: McGraw Hill, 1969).
7. Edward Greenberg, "Orientations of Black and White Children to Political Activity," *Social Science Quarterly* 5 (December 1970): 561–71; and Chris F. Garcia, *Political Socialization of Chicano Children* (New York: Praeger, 1973).
8. Harrell Rodgers, "Toward Explanation of the Political Efficacy and Political Cynicism of Black Adolescents: An Exploratory Study," *American Journal of Poltitical Science* 18 (May 1974): 257–82.
9. Greenstein, pp. 71–75.
10. M. Kent Jennings and Richard G. Niemi, "The Transmission of Political Values from Parent to Child," *American Political Science Review* 62 (March 1968): 169–84.
11. Paul Allen Beck and M. Kent Jennings, "Pathways to Participation," *American Political Science Review* 76 (March 1982): 94–108.
12. Robert E. Lane, "Fathers and Sons: Foundations of Political Beliefs," *American Sociological Review* 24 (August 1959): 502–11.

13. Kenneth P. Langton, *Political Socialization* (New York: Oxford University Press, 1969), pp. 84–119.
14. Byron Massialas, *Education and the Political System* (Reading: Addison-Wesley, 1969), p. 172.
15. Robert Cleary, *Political Education in the American Democracy* (Scranton: Intext, 1971).
16. Edgar Litt, "Civic Education, Community Norms, and Political Indoctrination," *American Sociological Review* 28 (February 1963): 69–75.
17. Langton, p. 116.
18. Jennings and Niemi.
19. Herbert P. Hyman, *Political Socialization* (Glencoe: Free Press, 1959), pp. 109–15.
20. John P. Robinson, "The Audience for National TV News Programs," *Public Opinion Quarterly* 35 (Fall 1971): 403–5.
21. Thomas E. Patterson and Robert D. McClure, *The Unseeing Eye* (New York: G. P. Putnam's Sons, 1976).
22. Joseph Wagner, "Media Do Make a Difference: The Differential Impact of Mass Media in the 1976 Presidential Race," *American Journal of Political Science* 27 (August 1983): 407–30.
23. W. Lance Bennet, *Public Opinion in American Politics* (New York: Harcourt Brace Jovanovich, 1980), ch. 11; Eric Barnow, *The Sponsors: Notes on a Modern Potentate* (New York: Oxford University Press, 1978).
24. John P. Robinson, "The Press as Kingmaker: What Surveys Show from the Last Five Campaigns," *Journalism Quarterly* 49 (Summer 1972): 239–55; and Ben H. Bagdikian, "The Politics of American Newspapers," *Columbia Journalism Review* 10 (March/April 1972): 30–42.
25. S. Robert Lichter and Stanley Rothman, "What You Always Wanted to Know About the Media Elite," *Houston Chronicle*, 28 January 1982, Sec. 2, p. 11.
26. C. Robert Hofstetter, *Bias in the News* (Columbus: Ohio State University Press, 1976).
27. Shanto Iyengar, Mark D. Peters, and Donald R. Kinder, "Experimental Demonstrations of the 'Not-So-Minimal' Consequences of Television News Programs," *American Political Science Review* 76 (December 1982): 848–58.
28. Reuven Frank, quoted in Edward Jay Epstein, *News From Nowhere* (New York: Vintage Books, 1973), pp. 4–5.
29. Patterson and McClure.
30. R. W. Connell, *The Child's Construction of Politics* (Carlton, Victoria: Melbourne University Press, 1971).
31. Hess and Torney.
32. Philip E. Converse, "Public Opinion and Voting Behavior," in Fred I. Greenstein and Nelson W. Polsby, eds., *Handbook of Political Science*, vol. 2 (Reading: Addison-Wesley, 1975).
33. Gerald Pomper, *Voter's Choice: Varieties of American Electoral Behavior* (New York: Dodd, Mead, 1975).

34. Robert S. Erikson, Norman L. Luttbeg, and Kent L. Tedin, *American Public Opinion*, 2nd ed. (New York: Wiley, 1980).

35. The data are from surveys conducted in the 1970s by Gallup, Harris, and the Center for Political Studies quoted in Erikson, et al., p. 19; and Bennet, ch. 2.

36. Angus Campbell, Philip E. Converse, Warren E. Miller, and Donald Stokes, *The American Voter* (New York: Wiley, 1960), p. 186.

37. V. O. Key, Jr., *The Responsible Electorate* (Cambridge: Harvard University Press, 1966).

38. James W. Prothro and C. W. Grigg, "Fundamental Principles of Democracy: Bases of Agreement and Disagreement," *Journal of Politics* 22 (Spring 1960): 276–94.

39. Robert Chandler, *Public Opinion: Changing Attitudes on Contemporary Political and Social Issues*, A CBS News Reference Book (New York: R. R. Bowker Co., 1972), pp. 6–13.

40. V. O. Key, Jr., *Public Opinion and American Democracy* (New York: Alfred A. Knopf, 1961).

41. Herbert McClosky, "Consensus and Ideology in American Politics," *American Political Science Review* 58 (June 1964): 361–82.

42. Samuel A. Stouffer, *Communism, Conformity, and Civil Liberties* (Garden City: Doubleday, 1955); and National Opinion Research Center, 1977.

43. Arthur H. Miller, "Political Issues and Trust in Government: 1964–1970," *American Political Science Review* 68 (September 1974): 951–72; and William A. Gamson, *Power and Discontent* (Homewood: Dorsey Press, 1968), ch. 9.

44. Data from the Survey Research Center, University of Michigan, quoted in Miller, p. 953.

45. Jack Citrin, "Comment: The Political Relevance of Trust in Government," *American Political Science Review* 68 (September 1974): 973–88; and James S. House and William M. Mason, "Political Alienation in America, 1958–1968," *American Sociological Review* 40 (April 1975): 123–47.

46. Norman H. Nie, Sidney Verba, and John R. Petrocik, *The Changing American Voter* (Cambridge: Harvard University Press, 1976), pp. 125–28.

47. Philip E. Converse, "The Nature of Belief Systems in Mass Publics," in David Apter, ed., *Ideology and Discontent* (New York: The Free Press, 1964), pp. 206–61.

48. Erikson, et al.

49. Seymour Martin Lipset and Earl Rabb, *The Politics of Unreason* (New York: Harper and Row, 1970).

50. Eugene R. Wittkopf and Michael A. Maggiotto, "Elites and Masses: A Comparative Analysis of Attitudes Toward America's World Role," *Journal of Politics* 45 (May 1983): 303–34.

51. Lewis Lipsitz, "Working Class Authoritarianism: A Re-Evaluation," *American Sociological Review* 30 (1965): 103–9.

52. Lloyd A. Free and Hadley Cantril, *The Political Beliefs of Americans: A Study of Public Opinion* (New York: Simon and Schuster, 1968), p. 217.
53. Gerhard Lenski, *The Religious Factor: A Sociological Study of Religion's Impact on Politics, Economics, and Family Life,* rev. ed. (Garden City: Doubleday, 1963).
54. Erikson, et al., p. 175.
55. Monroe, ch. 5.
56. *Washington Post,* Weekly Edition, 14 November 1983, p. 43.
57. Gallup Poll, reported in *Houston Post,* 15 August 1983.
58. Alan D. Monroe, "Consistency Between Public Preferences and National Policy Decisions," *American Politics Quarterly* 7 (January 1979): 3–19.
59. Robert S. Erikson, "The Relationship Between Public Opinion and State Policy: A New Look at Some Forgotten Data," *American Journal of Political Science* 20 (February 1976): 25–36.
60. Sidney Verba and Norman H. Nie, *Participation in America* (New York: Harper and Row, 1972), Part III.
61. Warren E. Miller and Donald E. Stokes, "Constituency Influence in Congress," *American Political Science Review* 57 (March 1963): 45–56.
62. Morris P. Fiorina, *Retrospective Voting in American National Elections* (New Haven: Yale University Press, 1981).

SUGGESTED READINGS

EASTON, DAVID, AND DENNIS, JACK. *Children in the Political System: Origins of Political Legitimacy.* New York: McGraw-Hill, 1969.

ERIKSON, ROBERT S., LUTTBEG, NORMAN G., AND TEDIN, KENT L. *American Public Opinion: Its Origins, Content, and Impact,* 2nd ed. New York: Wiley, 1980.

GEORGE, JOHN. *Public Opinion: Coalitions, Elites, and Masses.* New York: St. Martins, 1979.

GRABER, DORIS A. *Mass Media and American Politics.* Washington, D.C.: Congressional Quarterly Press, 1980.

GREENSTEIN, FRED I. *Children and Politics.* New Haven: Yale University Press, 1956.

HALBERSTAM, DAVID. *The Powers That Be.* New York: Knopf, 1979.

HESS, ROBERT D., AND TORNEY, JUDITH V. *The Development of Political Attitudes in Children.* Chicago: Aldine, 1967.

KEY, JR., V. O. *Public Opinion and American Democracy.* New York: Knopf, 1961.

MEADOW, ROBERT G. *Politics as Communication.* Norwood, N. J.: Ablex, 1980.

MONROE, ALAN D. *Public Opinion in America.* New York: Dodd, Mead, 1975.

Chapter Five

POLITICAL PARTICIPATION AND ELECTIONS

On February 28, 1984, the voters of New Hampshire trudged through a heavy snowstorm to vote in the nation's earliest presidential primary election. In so doing, each voter was both performing an act of individual participation in the policy process and taking part in the larger drama of presidential selection. President Reagan had no serious opposition for the Republican nomination so this year most of the attention was focused on the Democratic challengers. Walter Mondale, Gary Hart, Jesse Jackson, John Glenn, and the other contenders had been campaigning in the state for months. All of these men knew the stakes were high. Since New Hampshire's primary is the first, it receives an extraordinary amount of media attention, and its winner gets a big boost toward the nomination.

This year the smart money was betting on former Vice-President Mondale. He had more money, more endorsements, a better organization, and better name recognition than his opponents. What's more, only a week earlier Mondale had won a resounding victory in the Iowa caucuses, easily outdistancing the second place finisher, Senator Hart.

The big news on election night, however, was that Gary Hart had pulled a major political upset, winning 37 percent of the vote to Mondale's 28 percent. Exit polls showed that many voters were concerned that Mondale had made too many promises and was too beholden to "special interests." Meanwhile, Hart's second-place finish in Iowa had projected him as an alternative to Mondale. Also, his campaign of "new ideas" caught on with many voters. Once again, the voters of New Hampshire had confounded the experts. Thanks to them, the struggle for the 1984 Democratic presidential nomination wasn't over; it was just beginning.[1]

The 1984 New Hampshire primary vaulted Gary Hart (left) into the political limelight for the first time in his presidential campaign. From that point on, Democratic frontrunner Walter Mondale (right) had to give serious attention to Hart's bid for the nomination.

The story of the New Hampshire primary introduces the two major themes of this chapter—individual political participation and elections. In the first section of this chapter, we will examine the ways individuals take part in the policy process, the extent of participation in America, and the effect of participation on policy. The second section of the chapter will deal with elections. We will consider presidential and congressional elections, examine the operation of the electoral process, and evaluate the impact of elections on public policy.

POLITICAL PARTICIPATION

Individuals try to influence the policy process through various forms of political participation, but the most common political act is voting. Americans have the opportunity to vote for president every four years. Every two years all the members of the House of Representatives and one third of the Senate membership must stand for election as well. Meanwhile, voters are periodically asked to elect a host of state and local officials. At times, they must also vote to approve state constitutional amendments and city-charter changes, and to vote in bond elections and in state or local referenda elections.

Voting is not the only way people can participate in politics, of course. Some of us decide we want to do more for our candidate or political party than just vote so we get involved in election campaigns. We contribute money, stuff envelopes with campaign literature, phone potential voters, put up yard signs, and work at the polls on election day.

Another way to participate in politics is through groups. One person working alone or casting a single ballot is not as effective as a group of people working together. Consequently, many Americans try to have their voices heard by participating in such political organizations as the League of Women Voters, the Sierra Club, Common Cause, or the National Rifle Association.

We can also participate in politics by contacting government officials. We may write our senator about the nuclear-arms race. We may send a mailgram to our state legislator asking for tougher laws against drunk driving. We may telephone our city-council representative to ask about getting a pothole fixed in our neighborhood. (The PERSPECTIVE on page 116 illustrates the best way to compose a letter to your legislator.)

Finally, some Americans participate through dramatic acts such as protest demonstrations, sit-ins, or even riots. During the 1960s, thousands of Americans took to the streets on behalf of the civil-rights movement or in opposition to the Vietnam war. In recent years, the United States has witnessed demonstrations for and against abortion, women's rights, draft registration, nuclear weapons, and American policy in Central America and the Middle East.

THE LEVEL OF PARTICIPATION

The level of political participation in America is relatively low and, at least until very recently, it has been declining. No political event in America is the object of more media ballyhoo than a presidential election, yet only a few more than half the eligible voters bother to vote—in 1980, the figure was only 53.9 percent. Compared to other western democracies, that figure is low.[2] The French presidential election of 1981, for example, attracted 81 percent of the French electorate. In Italy, voter turnout hit 90 percent in the general election of 1979. Turnout in other types of elections in America is usually even lower than in presidential contests. In 1982, for example, only 42 percent of eligible voters took part in the midterm congressional elections.[3] Local-election turnout is frequently lower than that. What's more, voter turnout in America fell steadily in every national election between 1960 and 1980.[4] Table 5.1 shows this recent decline. Participation in congressional elections declined as well, falling from 48 percent in 1962 to a low of 38 percent in 1978.

Perspective

HOW TO WRITE YOUR REPRESENTATIVE

Writing a letter to a United States representative or senator is one of the more effective means individuals have of influencing the policy process on issues that concern them. Yet it is surprising how few people ever do this. Many people believe that their representatives in Washington haven't the time or inclination to read their mail and that one letter won't make a difference anyway. Public officials are busy, of course, but their *job* is to represent constituents' views. What's more, in many cases, thoughtful, factually based presentations of ideas can either change officials' views or at least cause them to rethink their judgments.

Letters should be addressed as follows:

The Honorable___(full name)___
United States Senate
Washington, D.C. 20510 (Dear Senator _____)

The Honorable___(full name)___
House of Representatives
Washington, D.C. 20515 (Dear Mr./Mrs./Ms./Miss ____)

To communicate effectively with your elected representatives, it is important to remember a number of *do*'s and *don'ts*. Be factual and to-the-point in presenting your point of view. Emotional appeals or argumentative presentations are seldom effective. Make sure your information is correct, and be sure you understand how the policy process works. In other words, know your political science. Also, be original. Communicate in your own words, not someone else's.

It's important to use courtesy in dealing with public officials as well. Show them that you recognize their problems and are willing to consider their point of view. Don't use threats or make the issue a personal confrontation. Even if public officials don't do what you want this time, it's important to keep the lines of communication open for next time. Finally, take the time to say "thank you" when a public official does something you like.[1]

---

[1]Adapted from "Communicating with Your Legislators," *Texas Town & City* (January 1983).

Year	Turnout
1960	64.5%
1964	62.0
1968	61.0
1972	55.5
1976	54.4
1980	53.9

TABLE 5.1
American Presidential Election Turnout, 1960–80

SOURCE: U.S. Bureau of the Census, *Statistical Abstract of the United States*; Federal Election Commission, reported in *Houston Post*, 2 November 1981.

Studies show that fewer Americans participate by campaigning, working in groups, contacting officials, and marching in the streets than by voting. In a survey-research study conducted by political scientists Sidney Verba and Norman H. Nie, 72 percent of those sampled claimed they voted regularly in presidential elections and 47 percent said they participated in local elections. In contrast, only 30 percent claimed to be involved in an organization and only 25 percent said they had ever taken part in a campaign. About 20 percent reported that they had ever contacted a government official about a problem. Moreover, these figures are probably a bit on the high side since some people may be reluctant to admit how little they actually participate politically.[5]

Now, in the mid-1980s, however, there is evidence that political participaton may be on the upswing. Turnout in the 1982 congressional election rose by two percentage points over 1978, the first increase in turnout in a national election in twenty years. Participation in a number of local elections in 1983 was up as well.

Much of this increase results from heightened political activism on the part of women and blacks. One effect of the defeat of the Equal Rights Amendment (ERA) was to galvanize women to greater political involvement. At one time, women voted in smaller percentages than men. That is no longer the case. What's more, the recent emergence of the gender gap shows that women are developing a political consciousness of their own. Similarly, the election of Harold Washington as the first black mayor of Chicago in 1983 stimulated a dramatic nationwide increase in black voter registration and electoral turnout. In 1984, the candidacy of Jesse Jackson for the Democratic presidential nomination spurred black participation still further.

WHY SOME PARTICIPATE AND SOME DO NOT

Why is it that some of us take part in politics and some of us do not? Part of the answer involves time and convenience. Most American elections take place on Tuesdays, not the most convenient day of the week. Europeans hold elections on weekends or declare election day a holiday so people can vote more easily. Registration is another inconvenience. Before people can vote they must register, and when they move they must update their registration. One study estimates that registration procedures may keep 6 to 10 percent of the potential electorate away from the polls.[6] Registration and voting take some time and effort, and other types of participation can be even more time-consuming. Many Americans are simply too busy earning a living and raising a family to become political activists. Meanwhile, advanced age and ill-health prevent others from taking a very active role in the policy process.

Sometimes, there are coincidental factors that affect our participation. We may not go to the polls because we have to work late or we have car trouble or the weather is bad. On the other hand, we may decide to take part in an election campaign because a friend or relative is involved or because we can get extra credit in a political-science course we are taking. We may decide to phone our city-council member in hopes of untangling a problem with our property-tax assessment.

The most important factors affecting participation, however, are psychological. Many Americans find time to be involved politically because they think politics is interesting. Some people enjoy collecting stamps, some like to watch major-league baseball, and some like politics. Many of us enjoy reading about government and following the course of an election campaign or the struggle to get a bill through Congress. We may be fascinated by the personalities of political leaders and enjoy the camaraderie of a campaign headquarters or a political organization. Writing our senator or visiting our city-council representative may give us a feeling of influence and importance.

Some of us are active politically because we know that government is important and believe that it is our civic duty to participate. When we were children, we listened to our parents discuss public affairs and observed them going to the polls on election day. We learned, we were *socialized*, to believe that political activity was something adults ought to do. Today, we would feel guilty if we did not vote. We always try to read the newspaper and watch the news on television and, when we can, we get involved in the affairs of our community. Some others may feel no such obligation. They can take politics or leave it, but they don't feel guilty either way. They were socialized differently.

Political efficacy and political trust also influence participation. People who have confidence in their ability to affect the policy process are more likely to participate than those who reason that their votes won't count or their voices won't be heard. Similarly, cynics who believe that all politicians are crooks are less likely to participate than those who think that government is working to create a better world for all of us.

In recent decades, Vietnam, Watergate, the growth of government, and other factors have reduced political efficacy and trust in America and, consequently, have lowered political participation rates as well.[7] As we saw in chapter 4, recent surveys have shown a decline in the number of Americans expressing trust in public officials. For example, a 1983 study found that less than 15 percent of a national sample said they had "a great deal of confidence" in the leaders of Congress and the executive branch.[8]

WHO PARTICIPATES?

Who participates in American politics? People who are interested, people who are informed, people who have the time, people who believe they can affect the policy process, and people who believe that participation is their civic duty. These people are found among all groups of Americans, but some people are more likely to participate than others.

First, participation is related to age. Studies show that young people are less likely to take part in politics than their elders. In fact, one important reason for the recent decline in voter turnout was the ratification of the Twenty-sixth Amendment in 1971, which lowered the voting age from twenty-one to eighteen. This act substantially increased the pool of eligible voters, but it did so with young people who were less likely to participate than their elders. As you saw in Table 5.1, electoral turnout in 1972 fell more than five percentage points below turnout in 1968 (when the eighteen-year-old vote was not in effect). Many young adults are political no-shows because they frequently have matters on their minds other than politics—finishing school, starting a career, beginning a family, buying a home. They are relatively inexperienced politically and probably less informed about public affairs than their parents. Also, since young people tend to move more frequently than older people, they are less likely to keep their voter registration current.

Studies show that participation increases steadily with age until advanced age and ill-health force the elderly to slow down. As people approach middle age, they settle down and establish roots in their community. Naturally, they are more concerned about taxes, schools, public services, and regulations than eighteen-year-olds. What's more, they have more experience participating and, probably, more time for political activism than younger people.

Second, political participation is related to socioeconomic status, that is, educational, income, and occupational status. Middle-class people are more active politically than low-income individuals; the college-educated participate more than those with high-school educations; professionals and business people are more likely to take part than clerical workers or laborers. The most important factor in this relationship is education. Better-educated people are exposed to more information about politics, they better understand how government works, and they feel more confident in their own ability to affect the policy process. We should add, however, that middle- and upper-income people probably have more time and certainly have more money to devote to politics than others.

A final factor affecting participation is what we might call "group iden-

A volunteer organizer in East Los Angeles explains the registration process to prospective Hispanic voters. In recent years, minority groups have become increasingly conscious of the power they can wield once they become a political force at the ballot box.

tity." All of us belong to groups in the sense that we are all black or white or Asian or female or under thirty or Presbyterian. Group identity becomes important politically when group members begin to develop a group consciousness and to perceive that certain desired goals can be achieved through collective political action. Because of socioeconomic status, for example, black participation tends to be lower than that of whites; yet because of group identity blacks participate more than other groups with similar socioeconomic profiles. Political participation by Jewish Americans is enhanced by feelings of group identity as well. Also, in recent years, women, Hispanics, and gays have become more active politically because of increased group identity.[9]

THE EFFECT OF INDIVIDUAL PARTICIPATION

How much influence can the average individual have on the policy process in America? The answer depends on the level of government and the issues involved. We think voting is important, but we would be naive to suggest that one person's vote will change the outcome of very many elections. There have been occasions, of course, when an election contest has been decided by one vote or just a few votes, but that is quite rare.

To have much effect on elections, individuals need to work actively in campaigns. A good campaign volunteer can be worth dozens, maybe even hundreds, of votes. Although that isn't enough to swing many national or statewide elections, it can have a real impact at the local level.

An individual's influence on issues is limited as well. On major, national political issues, the average individual is simply outgunned. No individual's arguments, no matter how persuasive, are going to outweigh those of powerful interest groups. Consequently, the effectiveness of individual contacts is generally limited to issues that don't concern the heavyweights of American politics. And for the most part, these are local issues, narrow in scope.

In sum, the political effectiveness of the average individual acting alone is usually limited to local-election contests and local issues of narrow scope. Does this mean, then, that political participation for the average American is a sham at worst and a waste of time at best? We don't think so. The truth is that our lives are probably more directly affected by city government, counties, and other units of local government than by events that take place in Washington, D.C., or in state capitals. Also, "narrow" issues, such as the location of a police substation or the expansion of vocational-education programs at the local community college, are often very important to us. Just because the impact of individual participation is limited doesn't mean it isn't important. What's more, individuals can increase the impact of their participation significantly through group participation. That, however, is the subject of chapter 6.

ELECTIONS

A presidential election is the greatest political show on earth. It's a combination of democracy and show business, and it features some of the best and some of the worst aspects of American politics. On the one hand, presidential elections are the showcase of American democracy, in which millions of citizens debate the course of public policy and participate in selecting the nation's leaders. One observer says this about presidential elections: "I sit here . . . and hear the Soviet Union's [leaders] . . . tell the Soviet people what to think, while in the U.S. everybody and his dog is down in the public arena kicking each other around. It is wonderful. It is the melody of democracy."[10] On the other hand, presidential elections are long, expensive, banal, garish, and shallow. They are media events in which image is often more important than character and in which style outweighs substance. Some observers suggest that those most capable of leadership cannot be elected, while those who can be elected are often least capable of leadership.[11]

QUALIFICATIONS

The Constitution requires the president to be at least thirty-five years old, a natural-born American citizen, and to have lived in the United States at least fourteen years. In practical terms, a presidential candidate must have other qualities to be successful. Among these are desire and stamina. Running for president is a complex, often demeaning endurance test. One has to want to be president badly to stay with it, and many qualified people either do not try or drop out early. Presidential candidates must also have access to gigantic sums of money; it helps to be independently wealthy. Another quality is image potential. Candidates should be smooth but not too smooth; "down-home" and "just plain folks" but not hicks. They must be sincere but not maudlin; experienced but not an "old face." One suspects that the gawky Abraham Lincoln would have difficulty looking presidential enough for today's standard.

ORGANIZING THE CAMPAIGN

Serious candidates for the presidency start early, very early. Walter Mondale, Gary Hart, and John Glenn, for example, were hot on the campaign trail back in 1982, two years before the 1984 election. Jimmy Carter spent four years running for the White House. Ronald Reagan's quest for the presidency dates back to 1964. Today, prospective candidates are laying the groundwork for 1988 and 1992.

It's important to begin early because there is much to be done. One of the first chores for a serious candidate is to assemble a top-notch campaign team. A modern presidential campaign is no more a one-person operation than a professional football team consists of just the quarterback. Big-time campaign organizations usually include pollsters, fundraisers, media consultants, scheduling coordinators, speech writers, issue consultants, volunteer coordinators, a press secretary, a manager, and perhaps even a joke writer. John Glenn, for example, hired for his campaign team Bob Orben, who used to write jokes for Bob Hope and Jerry Ford. A quality campaign team is indispensable to the serious candidate. A good organization can make a winner out of even a mediocre candidate, and a bad organization would probably doom even the best candidate to defeat.

Once the organizational groundwork is laid, it's time to prepare the candidate for the long haul of the campaign. This often means outfitting the candidate with a new wardrobe, a new hairstyle, and a slimmer waistline. Candidates are coached to smile, to appear presidential, and to give better speeches. They memorize a basic campaign speech and rehearse answers to questions reporters might raise. By the time the serious campaigning begins, the candidates have been carefully trained to stick close to their scripts. Campaign managers know that impromptu remarks can sometimes be embarrassing or even fatal to a campaign. In 1968, for example, George Romney, the frontrunner for the Republican nomination, saw his campaign collapse after he remarked that he had been "brainwashed" about the war in Vietnam. After all, who wants a president who can be brainwashed? In the 1980 campaign, Ronald Reagan made so many ad-lib blunders that his handlers went to extraordinary lengths to limit his opportunities to make spontaneous remarks.

An early start is also important for serious candidates because it gives them time to build nationwide support. By making public appearances they can increase their name recognition among the general public. It helps, of course, to be well-known already, as were astronaut John Glenn, war-hero Dwight Eisenhower, movie-actor Ronald Reagan, or Vice-Presidents Richard Nixon or Walter Mondale. What's more, serious candidates can stockpile IOUs by campaigning for local party officials. During the 1982 congressional elections, for example, Mondale gave 150 speeches in 38 states.[12] Two years later, all that work paid off as Mondale gathered scores of endorsements from Democratic officeholders.

Candidates also start early so that they can begin raising the massive amounts of money needed to run a credible campaign. In 1980, for example, President Carter spent $18.6 million to win his party's nomination; Reagan spent $21.4 million. At one time, candidates could often rely on a few big donors to bankroll their campaigns. In both 1968 and 1972, for instance, W. Clement Stone, a Chicago tycoon, contributed a million dollars to Richard Nixon's presidential campaign. In 1974, however, after the Watergate scandal, Congress passed legislation in order to reduce the opportunities for financial misconduct in presidential elections and created the Federal Election Commission (FEC) to enforce the new regulations. The new rules limited the amount of money an individual or **political action committee (PAC)** could give to a candidate or a party and provided for public disclosure of contributors giving $100 or more. Now, candidates can't rely on a few sugar daddies, but must work harder to get many small contributions.[13] The new regulations are summarized in the **PERSPECTIVE** on page 124.

The new legislation also provided for partial federal funding of presidential campaigns to be financed from an annual one-dollar checkoff on federal income-tax returns. Candidates can qualify for federal money by raising $5000 in each of twenty states in contributions of $250 or less. Thereafter, Uncle Sam provides dollar-for-dollar matching funds for contributions of $250 or less up to $8 million. If candidates accept the federal money, they must agree to a $24-million total-spending limit in the preconvention period and a series of limits on spending in each state. Candidates who reject the federal dollars can raise and spend as much as they are able, although they must still abide by contribution limits and disclosure rules.

In practice, nearly all candidates who can qualify accept the federal funds. In 1980, for example, Carter received $5.1 million in federal funds while Reagan collected $7.3 million from the government.[14]

Finally, candidates must seek interest-group endorsements. Interest groups can provide money, organization, and, in some cases, a bloc of votes. In 1980, Reagan won the Republican nomination with the help of conservative groups. For the 1984 race, Mondale cornered endorsements from organized labor, teachers' groups, the National Organization for Women (NOW), and several black groups.

This is known as "brokerage politics." Candidate A runs for office, and

During the Watergate investigation, the nation was shocked by allegations suggesting that political contributions to the 1972 Nixon reelection campaign had sometimes arrived in suitcases stuffed with hundred-dollar bills and that potential contributors had allegedly been warned to come up with the cash or face a possible Internal Revenue Service audit. Those days are now gone, thanks in part to a series of new laws regulating campaign financing and providing for partial federal funding of presidential elections. The following is a summary of some of the more important regulations.

Individual Contribution Limits

*An individual can give no more than
- $1000 to any candidate running for Congress or the presidency per primary, runoff, or election;
- $5000 a year to any one political action committee (PAC);
- $25,000 a year in total contributions to candidates for federal office, PACs, and party committees.

*However,
- individual candidates can give as much as they like to their own campaigns;
- there are no federal restrictions on contributions to candidates for state and local office, although states and localities may enact their own limitations.

Limits on Political Action Committees

*PACs can give
- no more than $5000 to any candidate running for Congress or the presidency per election;
- no more than $15,000 a year to a party committee.

*However,
- there are no limits on overall PAC contributions;
- there are no federal restrictions on PAC contributions to state and local candidates although states and localities may enact their own limitations.

Disclosure Requirements

*Candidates for federal office are required to keep careful records of campaign contributions and contributors and to report the names of those who give $250 or more to the Federal Election Commission.

Government Financing

*Presidential candidates can qualify for government financing by raising $5000 in each of twenty states in individual contributions of $250 or less.

*For candidates who qualify, the government will match dollar-for-dollar all contributions of $250 or less.

*After the major-party nominees are chosen, they are eligible for about $40 million in federal money for the November election.

*Candidates who accept the $40 million may neither raise nor spend additional funds.

*Third-party and independent candidates can be eligible for federal funds *if* they win 5 percent of the vote in November, but they must wait until after the election to collect.

*All of the monetary figures presented here are regularly adjusted for inflation.

*There are now no provisions for the federal financing of any elections other than presidential elections.

*There is a major loophole in the law in that there are no restrictions on individuals or PACs "independently" raising and spending money to elect or defeat a candidate as long as they do not coordinate their efforts with the candidate's campaign.

Interest Group J makes demands. Candidate A promises to fulfill those demands if elected. Group J then works to elect A. Brokerage politics is as old as democracy, but it has its pitfalls. Candidates who go through the campaign promising something for everyone leave themselves little room to maneuver once they have gained the White House. They must either break their promises or try to deliver on the promises at the risk of sacrificing more general goals. Either way can be a prescription for a failed presidency. Also, interest-group endorsements can sometimes be used against a candidate during the campaign. In the 1984 Democratic nomination race, for example, Gary Hart scored points by branding Walter Mondale as the candidate of the big labor-union bosses.

THE DELEGATE-SELECTION PROCESS

The first stage of the presidential-election process involves candidates competing for their political party's nomination. In the summer of an election year, the two major parties hold conventions to which the local party organizations in every state, the District of Columbia, and the various territories send delegates. The convention's primary task is to select presidential and vice-presidential nominees to be the party's ticket for the general election in November. This is done by majority vote of the delegates at the convention. Until the conventions have done their work, the real contest is not between Democrats and Republicans, but among Democrats for the Democratic presidential nomination and among Republicans for the Republican nomination. Since the convention delegates make the actual selection, the presidential candidates must focus on the delegate-selection process in each state, hoping to get their supporters selected as delegates to the national convention.

The process of selecting delegates to the party conventions varies in a crazy-quilt pattern from state to state and even from party to party within the same state. Today, about half the states (twenty-six in 1984) employ some method of **primary election.** In these elections party voters have the opportunity to cast their ballots for the presidential candidate they prefer or for delegates pledged to support a particular candidate at the convention. In most of the states using the primary-election method of selecting convention delegates, candidates win delegate support in rough proportion to their popular-vote totals.

Other states choose national-convention delegates by the **caucus** method. This process begins with party members going to local meetings, or *caucuses.* There they elect delegates to district meetings. At the district meeting delegates are selected to go to the state party convention. Finally, the state convention chooses delegates to attend the national convention. Caucuses are not as well-publicized or well-attended as primary elections;

"How binding are campaign promises made only in primaries?"

the key to success for a presidential candidate is to cultivate supporters who will be committed enough to take the time to attend the caucus meetings. In caucus states, it's more important to have a few strong supporters who will attend the caucuses than many lukewarm supporters who will stay home.

The delegate-selection process has changed a great deal in recent years. For more than a century, the major parties' candidates were nominated by conventions dominated by elected officials and state and local party leaders. This began to change in the 1950s and '60s as primaries and television became more important to the process. These changes were accelerated after 1968 by the efforts of a group of reformers within the Democratic party. The reformers criticized a system that allowed Hubert Humphrey to win the 1968 Democratic presidential nomination without even entering a primary. They charged that too much power remained in the hands of party bosses such as Mayor Richard Daley of Chicago. Consequently, in the 1970s the Democratic party adopted a number of reforms in the delegate-selection process to open the process to more participation by "grassroots Democrats" and to increase the number of women, minority, and youth delegates.

By the end of the decade, many Democrats thought that the reforms had gone too far. The attempt to reduce the power of party bosses had worked so well that many Democratic members of Congress and many Democratic governors even ceased attending conventions after 1968. Their power over delegates had been largely lost to candidates and interest-group representatives. After the 1980 election, the Democratic party leaders counterattacked. A new plan was adopted for the 1984 convention that set aside 561 of the 3931 delegate seats for party officials and elected officeholders.

While the Democrats have struggled over reforming delegate-selection procedures, the Republican party has been content to leave most delegate-selection decisions in the hands of the state parties. The Republicans have taken some steps, however, to insure more participation by underrepresented groups, especially women.[15]

THE LONG ROAD TO THE NOMINATION

The road to the nomination is long and grueling. Back in the 1960s, candidates could focus on primary elections in fewer than a dozen states. By 1980, however, candidates faced a back-breaking schedule of primaries and caucuses, including a record-setting thirty-seven primary elections. In 1984, the number of primaries was reduced, but candidates were tested by a "front-loaded" system of twenty-five primaries and caucuses by March 20, including six primaries and four caucuses on "Super Tuesday," March 13. The large number of caucuses and primaries places a premium on organization, name recognition, and media techniques. It also forces candidates to make strategic decisions on how to allocate resources among caucuses and primaries.

Some primaries and caucuses mean more than others. The big states are important, of course, because many convention delegates are at stake. Others are important because of timing. Traditionally, the Iowa caucus and the New Hampshire primary are key because they are first. Success there means momentum, or the "Big Mo," as George Bush called it.

You either have momentum or you don't, and campaign contributions and voter support respond quickly to media portrayals of how the campaign is going. In early 1976, for example, Jimmy Carter was a little-known former governor from Georgia who had once appeared on "What's My Line" and stumped the panel. He was running for president, but the Gallup Poll pegged his support at only 4 percent. Then Carter finished first in the Iowa caucus. *Time* and *Newsweek* wrote 726 lines about him to only 30 for all the other candidates combined. Next, Carter finished first in the New Hampshire primary, even though he gathered only 28 percent of the vote. For this, he made the cover of *Time* and *Newsweek* and received 2630 lines of coverage. Morris Udall, the second-place finisher, got a paltry 96 lines. All of Carter's opponents combined were given 300 lines. When the smoke cleared and the ink dried, Carter's standing in the Gallup Poll shot up to 26 percent—not a bad increase in two months' time.[16] In 1984, Gary Hart's second-place finish in Iowa provided him the media attention he needed to win in New Hampshire.

Media momentum makes some campaigns, but it breaks others. In 1972, Edmund Muskie won the New Hampshire primary, but the media decided his margin wasn't big enough so he lost ground to George McGovern. Candidates are aware of all of this, of course, and not above trying to manufacture a little momentum on their own. Imagine, for example, that a candidate anticipates receiving 31 percent of a state's primary vote. He tells the media he expects about 24 percent. Then he gets 27 percent and zips into the next primary with this self-created "momentum," even when he did slightly worse than he expected. Welcome to the bizarre world of presidential politics.

As the primary season progresses, candidates begin to drop out. The relentless polls contribute to this weeding-out process, building up some individuals and tearing down others. The media buzzards begin to circle over the faltering candidates and, by Memorial Day, the race has usually come down to a handful, perhaps only two or three. By midsummer, when convention time rolls around, one candidate may well have the nomination sewed up.

THE PARTY CONVENTIONS

The national conventions of the Republican and Democratic parties are grand shows, resembling a cross between a three-ring circus and an old-

The Presidential Candidate Selection Process

A CONVERSATION WITH PROFESSOR WILLIAM CROTTY, NORTHWESTERN UNIVERSITY

Q. Now that the 1984 presidential election is history, there is a great deal of discussion about the election process, especially the nominating process through which the major parties select their candidates for president and vice-president. Just what do we expect from our presidential nominating system?

A. A little bit of everything. Politicians want somebody who will win the presidential election while unifying their political party and in the best way possible meeting the commitments the party makes to the electorate. Political scientists and other academicians want a presidential nominating system that provides the very best man or woman the nation has to offer: one equal to the task of leading a nation and a world community in transition; one who has the political ability and personal skills required to conduct the business of government; and one who can identify and then work to achieve the goals that best advance the nation's interests and best repre-

William Crotty, Professor of Political Science at Northwestern University, has written numerous books and articles on political parties, party reform, the presidential nominating system, and comparative election procedures. Professor Crotty has served on a variety of commissions studying election procedures in Central and South America, and was recently a guest scholar at the Brookings Institution.

sent its people. It seems all of us want the presidential nominating system to turn up a candidate

who is accessible, who can deal with a variety of competing individual and group demands, who is fair and open and accessible in manner, who is able to communicate with friend and foe alike, who is committed to the democratic ideals and democratic processes, and who can give meaning to the term "national purpose" and direction to the nation's people. In short, we want a new Lincoln or Franklin Roosevelt or at least someone who comes close to satisfying the demands of the nation for courageous, popular, and successful leadership. Needless to say, the presidential nominating system does not always turn out candidates of this caliber. As a consequence, it is often a subject of controversy and criticism. This has been particularly true over the last two decades.

Q. Hasn't the nominating system been changed a great deal in recent decades?

A. It has and it hasn't. The rudiments of the nominating system

fashioned revival meeting. Everything—the convention's location, the order of speakers, the demonstrations—is geared toward prime-time media coverage. The convention is a giant, week-long pep rally for the party faithful aimed at convincing the voters watching on TV at home that the party deserves their support.

In addition to all the hoopla and media hype, the conventions have some serious business to transact. One of the first orders of business is to seat the various state delegations. The size of each state's delegation is based on a formula that includes both the state's population and the success of party candidates in the state. Normally, the seating of a delegation is a mere

and its basic forms go back to the beginning of the Republic. The basic structure of the national convention system is little changed since its inception in the years 1831–32. There have been numerous changes, however, in the delegate-selection process.

Q. Would you discuss those changes?

A. Yes. Up until the 1960s, the delegate-selection process for both parties was relatively loose and unstructured. The state parties were permitted to adopt whatever rules they chose, and the result was that presidential delegate selection operated in a relatively closed manner that gave disproportionate power to established party leaders and interest-group representatives. The weaknesses in the system were exposed by the events surrounding the Democratic convention of 1968. The violence in the streets and in the convention hall that characterized the 1968 Chicago convention led to a commitment on the part of the Democratic party to formalize the presidential delegate-selection structures, open its procedures, and make them more democratic. The end result has been, in effect, a virtually new nominating structure within the Democratic party. This new nominating structure has been characterized by

• a centralization of power over delegate-selection procedures in the national party (these had formally been a prerogative of the state parties);

• the relocation of the decisive power over presidential nominations in the party's rank and file, as represented by those who participate in the local party's caucuses and state-level primaries; and

• an effort to provide wider participation in party decision-making more generally and a greater representativeness and coherence to the party's policy formulations through the inclusion of more grassroots members, minorities, and other previously underrepresented groups (women, youth, nonparty professionals).

Q. These changes haven't come easily have they?

A. No, they have been resisted, often intensely, by party regulars up until this day. After each election there has been a new party reform commission established to review the nominating rules and to recommend changes for the next presidential selection cycle. By the 1980s, these party committees came to reflect primarily the interests of the potential presidential contenders and the major interest groups within the party. The result has been an extraordinarily complex set of rules and procedures which are modified for each new presidential election year.

Q. Have the changes introduced by the post-1968 reforms resulted in any positive consequences?

A. Yes. The old nominating system had gotten to the point that

(to next page)

formality, but occasionally a delegation's credentials will be challenged by a group, charging that its selection violates party rules. Sometimes these challenges can be politically significant. In 1953, for example, a delegate-certification dispute at the Republican convention turned into a showdown between the forces supporting Robert Taft for the nomination and those backing General Eisenhower. In the 1950s and '60s, the Democrats fought a number of bitter disputes over the seating of southern delegations that excluded blacks.

Another task for the convention is to adopt a **platform.** A platform is a statement of party principles and issue positions. The conventional wisdom

it was divorced from the party base and was not representative, or at least many people believed it not to be representative, of the policy concerns and changes taking place in the electorate. For example, when Eugene McCarthy announced as a candidate against incumbent President Lyndon Johnson in November 1967, a year prior to the actual election, two thirds to three fourths of the delegates to the national party convention in 1968 had already been selected. Under such a system, change and a response to the immediate concerns of the electorate, no matter how severe these may be, is made difficult. This is basically what happened in 1968. The new system instituted during the 1970s allows for greater participation and greater representation of a variety of group interests. Participation in Democratic caucuses and primaries at the state level increased from 8.4 million in 1968 to 18.1 million in 1980. The changes instituted by the Democratic party have of necessity affected the Republican party as well. Overall, the level of participation in both parties' nominating processes increased from roughly 13 million to 32 million in the period 1968 to 1980. At the same time, the proportion of blacks participating in Democratic conventions has about doubled, and the proportion of women, the biggest gainers in the reform era, has increased from roughly 13 to 50 percent in Democratic conventions. According to present rules, one half of the delegates to the Democratic convention have to be women.

Q. Have there been any losers in the process?

A. Of course. The biggest decrease in participation in Democratic conventions can be seen among national party representatives. Under the old system, about 75 percent of Democratic U.S. senators attended the convention. In 1980, however, that percentage was only 14 percent. After the 1980 convention the rules were changed again to set aside a percentage of the delegate seats, between 400 and 500 in 1984, for Democratic-party elected and organizational offcials. Nonetheless, under the new system the basic decision as to who will be the party nominee is made at the state level by the grass-roots party electorate in the caucuses and the primaries. This is a major change from the old party system.

Q. Can the nominating process be improved?

A. Of course, anything can be improved. The real queston is what do you want? Whom do you want represented in the process? What type of conditions do you want weighted most heavily in the decisionmaking? What

is that party platforms are both bland and meaningless, forgotten by Labor Day, but that's overstating the case. At times platforms do include rather general language, but that's because they usually represent compromises among different factions within the party. Nonetheless, there are often clear differences between the Democratic and Republican platforms, as you can see from Table 5.2. Republican platforms generally emphasize defense and government-management issues such as a balanced budget while Democratic platforms stress labor and welfare issues. Also, there is evidence that platform promises aren't so meaningless after all. One study finds that three fourths of platform promises are kept.[17] At any rate, the convention delegates don't consider platforms irrelevant. In 1948, for example, a Democratic platform fight over civil rights led to a southern

values do you want to see maximized? The problem is there is serious disagreement on each of these. That has not stopped people from coming forward with a number of proposals. For instance, there have been proposals

- to restrict the delegates' selection to a three- or four-month period during the election year, which the Democrats already do;
- to funnel all funds for candidate organization from the Federal Election Commission through the national parties, thus giving the national parties more direct control over individual candidacies;
- to create a national commission to simplify the state nomination rules and require them to coordinate these so that they would be relatively the same in each of the states.

These are some of the more modest suggestions. There are others. Among the more radical departures from present processes is the call for a national primary to select all national-convention delegates through a direct vote by all party members in one election. Another proposal is for a series of regional primaries, that is, primaries or caucuses held on the same day in each of the regions, with the country divided into North, South, Midwest, Far West, and so on.

Q. Do you think change is needed?

A. Before we decide on some drastic change in present procedures, I think two points are worth noting: first, the system works relatively well now. A simple, clear, and fair system of delegate selection open to party members, in my opinion, should be the goal. In many respects we are beginning to approach that at present. Second, the country and its people get about the type of nominating system they want. The present system appears to serve the national needs relatively well. Therefore, some discretion in advancing any type of significant changes might well be in order. And, finally, the burdens placed on the presidential nomination system are enormous. So much is expected from it in terms of righting the ills of a society in change that it can never reasonably achieve all of its goals. If we realize that the presidential nominating system is simply one aspect, although certainly a critical one, in the entire process of governance, perhaps less attention could be paid to changes in the nominating process and more to changes in other areas of the government that might improve representation.

walkout and the formation of the splinter "Dixiecrat" party. Then, in 1972 the Democrats had another particularly bloody fight over the Vietnam war and social and economic policy.

The most important business of most conventions is to select a presidential nominee. Traditionally, this takes place during prime time on the third evening of the convention. The festivities begin as speakers place the names of prospective nominees before the convention and their supporters respond with exuberant (and planned) demonstrations of support. Eventually, the time comes to call the roll of the states and the delegates vote. Nominees are chosen by majority vote and at every convention for the last thirty years a winner has been selected on the first ballot. At most conventions there hasn't even been suspense as the eventual winner has come to

TABLE 5.2 *Democratic and Republican Party Platform Positions in 1984, Selected Issues*

Issue	Democratic Platform Planks	Republican Platform Planks
Tax Policy	Supports the graduated, progressive income tax. Endorses 15 percent minimum corporate tax. Favors rescinding some of the Reagan tax cuts for those making more than $60,000 a year.	Supports consideration of modified flat-rate tax. Strongly opposes tax increases. Calls for repeal of windfall profits tax on oil. Proposes doubling the $1000 personal income tax exemption and reducing tax rates on interest income.
Deficit Reduction	Proposes to "reassess" defense spending, create an "adequate and fair" tax system, control health costs, and "eliminate other unnecessary expenditures." Opposes a constitutional amendment to balance the budget.	Proposes to work toward a balanced budget by promoting economic growth and by cutting spending (but mentions no specific cuts). Favors an amendment to balance the budget.
Defense	Favors slowing the rate of increase in defense spending. Opposes production of the MX missile and the deployment of a space weapons system.	Favors increasing defense spending. Endorses both the MX missile and a space weapons system.
Nuclear Freeze	Seeks a comprehensive, mutual, and verifiable nuclear weapons freeze.	Opposes any nuclear freeze but calls for mutual reductions in nuclear weapons.
Central America	Opposes Reagan policies in Central America. Calls for international cooperation to solve region's problems and opposes aid to guerrillas in Nicaragua.	Supports Reagan initiatives in Central America. Favors continued military aid to the government of El Salvador and to the guerrillas in Nicaragua.
Middle East	Affirms support for Israel and moderate Arab states.	Affirms support for Israel and moderate Arab states.
Women's Rights	Endorses the ERA and supports the concept of equal pay for work of comparable value.	Supports equal rights for women but ignores the ERA. Opposes concept of equal pay for work of comparable worth.
Civil Rights	Supports affirmative action to end discrimination.	Deplores racism, bigotry, and anti-Semitism. Opposes quotas.
Homosexual Rights	Supports legislation to prohibit job discrimination based on sexual orientation.	Does not mention homosexual rights.
Abortion	Affirms reproductive freedom as a fundamental human right and opposes an amendment to outlaw abortion.	Affirms the unborn child's fundamental right to life and calls for an amendment to outlaw abortion.
School Prayer	Endorses the separation of church and state but does not mention school prayer.	Advocates voluntary school prayer.
Gun Control	Supports strong restraints on the availability of handguns.	Opposes gun control.

SOURCES: *Houston Post,* 18 July, 1984, p. 14B, and 18 August 1984, p. 3A; *Houston Chronicle,* 22 August 1984, Sec. 1, p. 16.

town with a majority of delegates already in tow. If no candidate should receive a majority on the first ballot, however, another vote will be taken and then another until a nominee is chosen. When this happens, it is an occasion for high political drama as old candidates drop out, new ones enter the field, and party leaders wheel and deal behind the scenes. Unfortunately for those who like high political drama, however, today's delegate-selection process makes multiple ballots unlikely.

The final business of the convention is to choose a vice-presidential nominee. The selection process is formally identical to the method for choosing a presidential nominee, but, in practice, the presidential nominee makes the choice and the convention ratifies it. Presidential nominees look for running mates who will help them win in November. Frequently, this means trying to "balance the ticket" by selecting a vice-presidential candidate from a different region, a different political background, or perhaps, a different wing of the party than the presidential candidate. Vice-presidential selections can sometimes be used to help unify a divided party. Also, it's helpful if the vice-presidential candidate comes from a large state. By these criteria, George Bush made an excellent running mate for Ronald Reagan. Reagan was a westerner, Bush a southwesterner with East Coast ties. Reagan was regarded as a conservative, Bush a moderate. Reagan was an outsider to Washington, Bush an insider. What's more, Bush's selection helped unite the party since he was Reagan's major opponent for the nomination and Bush came from a big state—Texas.

EVALUATION OF THE NOMINATING PROCESS

Is this system a desirable way to select presidential nominees? In 1980 over thirty million voters participated in primary elections in more than three dozen states. The primaries are open to large numbers of candidates and a relative unknown, such as Jimmy Carter in 1976, or Gary Hart in 1980, can suddenly catch on. Supporters of the system say that, while it is not perfect, still it is a reasonably open, representative way to do the job.

Critics disagree. How good is the system, they ask, if it produces the likes of Richard Nixon, George McGovern, Gerald Ford, Jimmy Carter, Walter Mondale, and Ronald Reagan? Are these the best leaders America has to offer? Critics see a process that places more emphasis on the ability to raise money and manipulate the media than on the ability of a candidate to govern.

Some critics of the present system want a one-day national party primary arrangement. However, that would probably just aggravate the money problem and emphasize television even more. Others want a series of regional primaries scattered across the country every few weeks in the spring. That would reduce confusion but might not substantially affect the present characteristics of the primary process. At any rate, it seems certain that America's system for selecting presidential nominees will be the target of reformers in the years ahead.

THE ELECTORAL COLLEGE

As the candidates prepare for the general election in November, many of their strategic calculations must be based on the workings of the **electoral college.** As with most other aspects of politics in America, the electoral process takes place within the context of the Constitution. For presidential elections, that means the electoral college. The authors of America's Constitution were not unqualified believers in democracy. They did not trust in the collective wisdom of the common people to select the right person for president. Consequently, they devised a system for choosing the president *indirectly*: the electoral college. Instead of voters picking a president and vice-president themselves, they select electors who do it for them. The intent of the founders was that these electors be community leaders, people of stature who could be trusted to act prudently.

The number of electors each state is entitled to select is based on the sum of its representation in the U.S. Senate and House. Since every state has two senators and at least one representative, every state has at least three electoral votes. Texas, for example, with its twenty-seven representatives and two senators is able to choose twenty-nine presidential electors; California with forty-five representatives and two senators picks forty-seven. Altogether, there are 538 electors, based on 435 members of the House, 100 senators, and three electors for the District of Columbia. It takes a majority (270 electors) to be elected president.

In practice, the electoral college does not operate quite the way the Constitution's authors planned. Political parties have emerged to put forward slates of electors pledged to cast their electoral ballots for their party's presidential and vice-presidential candidates. So, when you vote for president in November, you are actually voting for a slate of electors pledged to support the candidate for whom you are voting. The slate of electors supporting the candidate winning the most popular votes in a state wins the right to cast that state's electoral votes. Come December, the electors gather in the state capital to mark officially their ballots for president and vice-president. Theoretically, they can vote for whomever they like, but in practice almost all will honor their promise and vote for their party's candidates. In January, the Congress convenes, opens the ballots, and formally confirms that the individual we all thought was elected president in November has indeed been constitutionally named president.

What happens if no one receives a majority of the electoral votes? Then Congress picks the president and vice-president. The Constitution says that the House must choose the president from among the three candidates with the most electoral votes. Each state delegation gets one vote, and a majority is needed for election. Meanwhile, the Senate names the vice-president from the top two candidates. Each senator has one vote, and a majority is required for election.

Few aspects of America's political system are more frequently criticized than the electoral college. In the eyes of many, it is a constitutional crisis waiting to happen—something we had better fix before disaster strikes. First, there is the problem of the "faithless elector." Since electors can legally vote for whomever they choose, some electors may break their pledges and vote contrary to the popular vote in their state. This has happened on occasion. In 1976, for example, two electors pledged to Gerald Ford cast their electoral votes for Ronald Reagan. It's highly unlikely, though, that enough electors would be so perfidious as to change the outcome of any but the very closest of elections.

Second, if more than two strong candidates are in the race, it is possible for no one to get a majority; in such a case, the election would have to be decided by Congress. This would be in accord with the Constitution, of course, but we suspect many Americans would be uncomfortable with the idea that a president could be chosen through behind-the-scenes maneuvering. In 1824, the last time Congress picked the president, the selection of John Quincy Adams over Andrew Jackson was marred by dark rumors of backroom deals. In recent years, the closest we have come to seeing the election go to Congress was in 1968, when independent candidate George Wallace gathered forty-six electoral votes. In 1980, the candidacy of John Anderson presented a similar possibility.

Finally, the candidate with the most popular votes could actually fail to win the most electoral votes and thus not be elected president. The electoral-college system awards a candidate all of a state's electoral votes whether he or she has a victory margin of one vote or one million votes. So, if Candidate A wins several states by large margins while Candidate B wins other states by small margins, Candidate A could very well garner *more* popular votes than Candidate B but *fewer* electoral votes. It happened to Samuel Tilden in 1876, when he lost to Rutherford B. Hayes despite getting a larger popular vote. In 1888 it happened again: Grover Cleveland won a majority of the popular vote, but lost the electoral college—and the presidency—to Benjamin Harrison. It almost happened again in 1976. Gerald Ford would have returned to the White House if only some 9245 voters in Ohio and Hawaii had voted for him instead of Jimmy Carter, even though Carter would still have enjoyed a 1.7 million-vote lead nationwide.

What can be done about the electoral college to head off these potential crises? There are nearly as many reform proposals as there are critics, but the simplest and probably most popular idea would be to abolish the electoral college altogether and choose the president by direct popular vote. Proponents say that direct popular election of the president would be more democratic—the most popular candidate nationwide would be assured of winning.

Nonetheless, direct popular election has its critics. Some opponents worry that campaigners would make fewer public appearances than they do now and that television would be even more important. Others are concerned that parties would be weakened further by a proliferation of independent and minor-party candidates. Spokespersons from small states argue that their regions would be totally ignored if direct popular elections were adopted.

Then there are those who fear a loss of political influence if the electoral college were eliminated. The present system forces candidates to concentrate on the largest states with the most electoral votes: in particular, California, New York, Texas, Illinois, Ohio, Pennsylvania, Michigan, Florida, and New Jersey. Presidential races in these states tend to be close; groups that are powerful in each of these states thus have their influence magnified. For example, 14 percent of the population of New York is Jewish. To win New York's thirty-six electoral votes a candidate needs to appeal to Jewish voters. Does it surprise you that both major-party candidates go out of their way to emphasize their unswerving commitment to American support for Israel? And, of course, it's not just Jewish groups that benefit directly from the workings of the electoral-college system. Large states also tend to be areas where organized labor is strong and where racial and ethnic minority groups are relatively well-organized. Thus, these groups have a political stake in the preservation of the electoral college as well.

Perhaps the greatest barrier to reforming the electoral college is public apathy. Americans don't believe in fixing something if it's not broken, and they aren't convinced the electoral college is broken and probably won't be until it presents us with a constitutional crisis. In the middle 1970s a constitutional amendment providing for the elimination of the electoral college and its replacement by direct popular election came to a vote on the floor of the Senate. It received fifty votes, far short of the required two thirds. Notably, there was no outcry, one way or the other. The electoral college may be a constitutional albatross, but it's a familiar one we will have to live with for some time.

THIRD PARTIES AND INDEPENDENTS

Independent candidate John Anderson of Illinois made a serious bid for the presidency in 1980 and captured 7 percent of the vote.

The general-election campaign is primarily a showdown between the Democratic and Republican party tickets, but others may be involved as well. In recent elections, the ballot has included candidates for a number of small parties, such as the Libertarians and Socialist Workers, as well as several independent candidates, including George Wallace, Eugene McCarthy, and John Anderson. The most successful of these were Wallace, who won 13.5 percent of the vote and forty-six electoral votes in 1968, and Anderson, who polled 7 percent of the vote in 1980 although he won no electoral votes.

In general, minor-party and independent candidates face an uphill fight. First, they have a problem just getting on the ballot. Getting a place on the ballot is automatic for the Democrats and Republicans, but many states make it exceedingly difficult for others to get their names before the voters. In 1980, John Anderson did make the ballot in every state but only after expending a great deal of time, energy, and money on the effort.

Second, America's winner-take-all election system works against third-party and independent candidates. Candidates get nothing for finishing second or a strong third in a state. Consequently, Anderson had no electoral votes to show for his 5.5 million popular votes since he failed to carry any states.

Third, candidates other than Democrats and Republicans have difficulty being taken seriously by the media and the voters. For one thing, they don't get nearly the amount of free publicity the major-party candidates receive. In addition, many of their potential supporters wind up voting Democratic or Republican rather than "throwing away" their votes on someone who stands little realistic chance of capturing the White House.

Money is also a serious problem for minor-party candidates and independents. Federal money is available to the major-party candidates shortly after the conventions. In 1984, the Republican and Democratic party tickets each received about $40 million. By accepting that amount, however, they agreed not to raise or spend additional funds. The law provides money for other candidates, too, but only if they receive at least 5 percent of the vote. They receive funds in proportion to their vote total but must wait until November to collect. In the meantime, they must raise money from private contributors or borrow in hopes of reaching the magical 5-percent mark on election day. In 1980, Anderson's 7 percent of the vote was good for $4.2 million in federal funds.

FROM CONVENTION TO ELECTION

More than any other election, the race to November is a media contest directed by skilled media consultants and professional pollsters.[18] Campaign managers have polls taken throughout the race to chart the course of voter attitudes about the candidates and the issues. Media consultants then use this information to prepare campaign advertising and plan strategy. What if your polls show that your candidate is perceived as too old by some voters? Run television spots showing him chopping wood or riding a horse. Do the polls show that some voters are apprehensive that your opponent's policies may lead to higher taxes? Then run advertising that hammers away on the spend-and-spend, tax-and-tax theme.

The strategy for the presidential contest is similar to that employed by football teams in the Super Bowl. You seldom see teams in that contest playing wide-open, risky football. Similarly, presidential candidates often focus on trying not to lose the election rather than on trying to win it. If you are ahead or even, stick to the familiar, safe, general themes of getting America moving again or reelecting a winning combination. Wait for mistakes by the other side and then pounce with all your media guns blazing. Only if you are behind should you dare gamble.

If the president is running for reelection, that greatly affects the direction and tempo of campaign strategy. Incumbents frequently like to use a "rose-garden strategy"; that is, they campaign for reelection from the White House, trying to appear "presidential" rather than political. In this, presidents enjoy certain advantages. Challengers can only talk, but the president can act—by holding press conferences, meeting foreign heads of state, making "nonpolitical" trips to dedicate public-works projects, controlling the release of news favorable and unfavorable to the administration, and, especially, controlling the timely announcements of federal grants and projects in closely fought states and cities. This approach worked well for Lyndon Johnson in 1964 and for Richard Nixon in 1972. On the other hand, presidents work from the disadvantage of having to defend their records. Challengers are much freer to criticize and offer alternatives. Also, at times presidents can become the captives of events beyond their control, as, for example, with Jimmy Carter and the hostage situation in Iran.

The campaign begins after Labor Day, but doesn't really heat up until October. The candidates spend a great deal of time in airplanes crisscrossing the country in their attempts to shore up a weakness here or make a breakthrough there. Because of the electoral college, the campaign focuses on the most populous states, particularly on those in which the election is perceived to be most closely fought. Candidates give "the speech," a term used by journalists to describe the basic issues statement the candidate has been peddling for years (tailored, of course, to the particular audience being addressed). Late in the campaign, tempers begin to fray, exhaustion approaches, and mistakes are made. Presidential debates, such as the one between Carter and Reagan in 1980, presumably contribute to the public's knowledge of the issues and its sense of the candidates' abilities to govern. One observer, however, calls them uninteresting, uninformative, and unedifying.[19]

THE VOTERS DECIDE

Finally, election day arrives and the voters make their decision. Barring a glitch caused by the electoral college, a president is chosen. But why did the voters act as they did? That question has long been the subject of scholarly debate.

Studies based on survey data from the 1950s painted a picture of the American voter that was fairly unbecoming. This research found little evidence of issue-voting. It found that most citizens were unable to consider political life in broad abstract terms and did not hold consistent views across a range of issues. What's more, the studies discovered that many voters simply adopted the issue positions of their favorite candidate while others misperceived their candidate's views to make them coincide with their own.

These studies concluded that the major determinant of the voters' choice was party identification. The best informed, most politically active citizens had fairly strong, long-term commitments to a political party, and in any one election the large majority of these (usually more than 70 percent) supported their party's presidential candidate. In a low-interest election, these people comprised most of the electorate, and the outcome would be a **normal vote** reflecting the underlying party balance in the electorate. In this the Democrats held the edge by a 54-to-46 margin. Most presidential elections, however, are high-interest contests, attracting many marginal voters who might otherwise stay home. The studies found that these people tended to be independents or ticket-splitters who were often poorly in-formed about politics. They would make their voting decision based on the short-term factors that had attracted them to the polls in the first place—a particularly attractive candidate or a "hot" issue. When most of these marginal voters were drawn in the same direction, they could swing the outcome of an election well away from what the result would otherwise have been. Ironically, then, the best campaign strategy was thought to be one aimed at the least interested and least informed among us.

This approach was used to create an interesting classification scheme. An election in which the normal voting patterns prevail and the party balance remains unchanged was called a **maintaining election.** An example of this was Harry Truman's victory in 1948. In contrast, a **deviating election** was one in which short-term forces upset the normal balance, giving one party an exceptionally large margin or the other party an upset victory. The election of the popular Dwight Eisenhower in 1952 and 1956 were exam-ples of deviating elections. A **reinstating election** was one that restored "normal" voting habits after a brief deviation. John Kennedy's 1960 victory was called a reinstating election. The most important type of election, however, was a **realigning election.** Here, voters change basic party loy-alties and trigger a long-range change in the balance of party strength. This occurred last in 1932 with the election of Franklin Roosevelt.[20]

In recent years, political scientists have substantially revised the earlier studies' conclusions about the behavior of American voters. Some of the revisions are the consequence of different research approaches and analy-tic techniques. More importantly, however, it seems that the voters them-selves have changed. For one thing, political-party identification now has less effect on voting. Survey data show that the percentage of Americans identifying with a political party fell from 75 percent in 1964 to 63 percent in 1976.[21] What's more, party identifiers today are more willing to defect to the other party's candidate than they were in the 1950s, and ticket-splitting has become the norm. All of this makes it more difficult to predict election results and helps explain the dramatic swings in voter sentiment from one election to the next.

Studies have also found that issues have become significantly more important in the voting decision. More voters now have issue positions, and many of the new independents are quite well-informed about politics.[22] The 1960s and '70s saw a significant rise in issue-voting as issues such as civil rights and Vietnam became important in the minds of many Ameri-cans.[23] Part of the explanation for this may be that voters are becoming more astute, but the most important reason seems to be that the candidates

Voting today is often done by machine, on which the voter is asked to punch out tabs on a ballot card. The ballot itself can be several pages long.

have been presenting clearer choices. One can't expect much issue-voting when the candidates don't articulate policy differences. Today, the major political parties are more *polarized* than they were in the 1950s. The Democrats are more liberal than before; the Republicans more conservative. Consequently, the two parties are more likely to nominate candidates with rather clear policy differences. Given a choice, most voters are able to recognize that the candidates have different positions on issues, and many voters are apparently making their decisions based on that choice.[24]

OTHER ELECTIONS

Elections are big business in America, and nothing quite matches the extravagance of presidential races. But many local contests in fact are rather modest affairs. The candidates, their families, and a few friends shake some hands, knock on a few doors, put up some signs, and, perhaps, raise enough money to buy a small ad in the local newspaper. The contest may be hard-fought, but the stakes aren't usually high enough to support a major-league campaign effort. Not so, however, with statewide races for governor or senator, local elections in big cities, and many elections for Congress and state legislatures. These contests feature big-time campaign techniques.

Above all else, that means they are expensive. In 1983, for example, Edwin Edwards spent about $13 million on his successful race for governor of Louisiana.[25] The year before, Bill Clements spent almost that much in his unsuccessful effort to be reelected governor of Texas, and in the same year Mark Dayton shelled out $7 million in a losing race for the U.S. Senate from Minnesota.[26] One expert estimates that total campaign spending in 1980 reached a record $1.2 billion.[27] Most observers say that serious candidates for the U.S. House need to spend at least $250,000 on their race, while Senate campaigns run upwards of $1.5 million. A well-financed campaign, of course, doesn't guarantee success, but money is almost a political necessity for serious candidates, especially for challengers who lack name recognition.[28] In 1980, for example, the thirty-two candidates for the House who defeated incumbents were all well-financed, spending an average of $350,000 apiece for their campaigns.[29]

Where does all the money go? The biggest single item in the big-time campaign budget is media, especially television. Modern campaigns use the media to increase candidates' name recognition and to create favorable images for them. Many campaigns also invest money in media specialists and in polling firms who employ the same types of techniques used in presidential campaigns. Other money goes for campaign literature, office space, postage, telephones, and salaries for a professional campaign staff.

Where does the money come from? Candidates who are well-to-do can bankroll their own campaigns or at least "loan" themselves money in hopes of paying themselves back when contributions come rolling in. Governor

Jay Rockefeller of West Virginia, for example, is a multi-millionaire who hasn't been afraid to spend his own money to get elected. Most campaign money, however, comes from contributions by individuals and groups. A surprisingly large amount of money is raised by mail in the form of thousands of contributions of $50 or less,[30] though major campaigns must usually rely on big contributions (see **PERSPECTIVE** on this page). In 1982, for example, Clements raised $3.5 million at a Texas-size fundraiser in Houston.[31] A great deal of the big money comes from interest groups, who contribute through their political action committees. In 1982, for example, PACs gave a cool $87 million to candidates for the U.S. House and Senate.[32] We will talk more about PACs in chapter 6.

Perspective
P.S.: SEND MONEY

One of the newest and most effective methods for raising political money is direct mail. The basic technique is quite simple. An interest group, a candidate, or a political party mails out letters asking for contributions. In the hands of experts such as Richard A. Viguerie, however, direct mail has become both a science and big business.

Certainly, it is big business. Viguerie, who usually works for conservative causes and candidates, heads a conglomerate that employs more than three hundred people. In 1982 alone, Viguerie's group mailed 80 million letters. Roger Craver is Viguerie's less well-known liberal counterpart, heading a firm with some 105 employees. All told, Viguerie, Craver, and other direct-mail operations sent out more than a half billion pieces of mail soliciting money in 1982; some 5.5 million people responded. The National Conservative Political Action Committee (NCPAC), for example, raised almost all its $10-million war chest by direct mail. Meanwhile, the Republican party raised about $30 million by mail.

Direct mail begins with a mailing list. Lists can be compiled from earlier campaigns, but they can also be bought and sold. In fact, list compiling is a business in itself. Anyone who has ever given money to a cause or candidate knows how easily it is to get onto mailing lists. Generally, groups purchase lists of people they think likely to contribute to their cause. NCPAC, for example, might buy the National Rifle Association's mailing list. There's usually a little guesswork involved in mailing lists, though. In 1972, for example, the McGovern campaign bought a list of Volvo owners on the hunch they would be independently wealthy and liberal.

The next step is to write a fundraising appeal. Experience has shown that the most effective letter is long and emotional. There's always some impending calamity that can only be prevented by your writing a twenty-five-dollar check and returning it in the enclosed, stamped envelope. President Reagan, for example, began a fundraising letter this way: "We are in the midst of the biggest political battle waged in our country in the last forty years. . . ." Thanks to computer technology, each letter can be personally addressed and the recipient mentioned by name within the text.

All that's left, then, is to wait for the money to arrive in the mail. Most purchased lists will produce a response rate of 5 percent or less, but lists of past contributors will generally respond at an 8-to 15-percent rate. The averge contribution is about twenty-five dollars. The names of those who responded to the mailing can be fed into the computer to be asked for money again, in about six weeks.[1]

[1]Dom Bonafede, "Part Science, Part Art, Part Hokum, Direct Mail Now a Key Campaign Tool," *National Journal* (31 July 1982), pp. 1332–36.

Many of the factors that influence the outcome of presidential races affect other elections as well. Political-party affiliation is still important. Many congressional districts, for example, are long-standing strongholds for one party or the other. Issues make a difference as well. One study found a high degree of policy-oriented voting in the 1980 congressional elections.[33] Also incumbents usually enjoy a big advantage, especially in races for the U.S. House.

At times, national factors can influence state and local election contests. In presidential-election years, a strong presidential candidate can often provide a boost to candidates of the same party in other races. This is known as a **coattail effect.** In 1980, for example, the Reagan sweep apparently helped Republicans win a number of close Senate races. In contrast, sagging presidential popularity can work against fellow party members. The national recession and the uncertainty over Reagan's economic policies may have helped do in a number of Republican candidates in 1982. Nevertheless, we suspect that local factors, such as candidate image, campaign organization, and local issues, are more important to the outcome of most local contests than national influences.

CONCLUSION: ELECTIONS AND PUBLIC POLICY

What part do elections play in the public-policy process? That's an important question, but one that is difficult to answer. Critics of American elections label them as fetishes, frauds, irrational responses, and public pacifiers. R. W. Apple, Jr., for example, characterizes our elections as "exhausting, fragmented, irrational, superficial, and ridiculously expensive."[34] Michael Parenti argues that they are essentially rich people's games: they might be a symbol of democratic government, but they do not guarantee it.[35] Others tell us that elections don't matter because appointed bureaucrats, judges, and special-interest groups govern us, not elected officials. Elections, in this view, are mere illusions of policy determination and, anyway, our electoral process discourages qualified people from running for office.

To be sure, American elections frequently fall short of the democratic ideal presented in many civics texts. Election campaigns are often long, expensive, televised extravaganzas that concentrate on image rather than on substance. The winning candidates are expert fundraisers and are expert at the use of media, but are frequently inexpert at economics, foreign policy, defense issues, energy, or other substantive concerns. As social critic H. L. Mencken once put it, sometimes it seems that the electoral odds are with individuals who have aroused the least suspicion among the voters by having not discussed issues.[36]

American elections do, however, often serve as mandates for government to enact certain policies. Several states and many localities provide for processes called **initiative** and **referendum,** whereby citizens gather signatures in order to place a proposal on the ballot, where it can be voted into law by the electorate. Sometimes this procedure has been used to enact major policy changes. In 1978, for example, California voters passed "Proposition 13," a significant tax limitation/tax rollback measure. Subsequently, similar measures were adopted by many states and localities across the nation.

Elections for office, however, seldom indicate voter preferences on policy matters, at least not very clearly. For that to be the case, issues would have to play a prominent role in election campaigns; candidates would have to articulate clear and differing positions on those issues; the electorate would have to be aware of those differences; and the voters would cast their ballots accordingly. If all of this were true, then we could say that elections provide clear policy guidelines for public officals. Some issues are important to some voters in some elections, of course, but we know that this sort of policy voting is not the general case in American politics. Also, when it does occur, it is aimed more at general policy goals than the details of policy. In sum, the evidence is that election results seldom represent **prospective voting** in the sense that voters choose Candidate A on the prospect of seeing the adoption of Policies X, Y, and Z.

That does not mean, however, that most election results are unrelated to policy. There is evidence that election decisions are frequently **retrospective;** that is, the voters decide on the basis of their perceptions of how things have been. Instead of voting for promises (prospective voting), they vote for performance (retrospective voting).[37] Members of Congress are judged on their overall effectiveness, on their service to constituents, on their ability to win policy concessions for their district or states, and on their success as advocates for the special interests that best represent the needs of their constituents. Presidents are evaluated on the perceived quality of their leadership and the success or failure of their policies.[38]

For an example of retrospective voting, consider the 1968 New Hampshire primary election between President Lyndon Johnson and anti-Vietnam-war candidate Eugene McCarthy. McCarthy did surprisingly well in the race, but not entirely because of his opposition to the war. One study found that many of those who voted for McCarthy weren't antiwar doves but hawks who wanted the U.S. to go all out to win the war. They weren't voting *for* McCarthy, in support of his antiwar position; they were voting *against* the limited-war policies of Johnson.[39]

The 1980 election provides another example. Studies of that race show that Reagan did not win because of his positions on the issues or his conservative ideology. In fact, many of those who voted for Reagan opposed him on those points. Instead, it appears that Carter *lost* because of widespread dissatisfaction with his first-term performance and uncertainty over his competence as a political leader.[40]

What, finally, can we say about the relationship between elections and public policy? Elections determine the selection of government personnel and sometimes affect the general direction of policy. In general, however, citizens care more for practical results than policy approaches. This means that politicians are free to choose the details of policy, but may have to pay the price at the ballot box if the voters judge those policies to be a failure.

KEY TERMS

CAUCUS (125)

COATTAIL EFFECT (142)

DEVIATING ELECTION (139)

ELECTORAL COLLEGE (133)

INITIATIVE (143)

MAINTAINING ELECTION (139)

NORMAL VOTE (139)

PLATFORM (129)

POLITICAL ACTION COMMITTEE (PAC) (123)

PRIMARY ELECTION (125)

PROSPECTIVE VOTING (143)

REALIGNING ELECTION (139)

REFERENDUM (143)

REINSTATING ELECTION (139)

RETROSPECTIVE VOTING (143)

NOTES

1. *Time* (12 March 1984), pp. 16–27.
2. Jeff Fishel, ed. *Parties and Elections in an Anti-Party Age* (Bloomington: Indiana University Press, 1978).
3. *National Journal* (27 November 1982), p. 2038.
4. Arthur T. Hadley, *The Empty Polling Booth* (Englewood Cliffs: Prentice-Hall, 1980).
5. Sidney Verba and Norman H. Nie, *Participation in America* (New York: Harper and Row, 1972).
6. Steven J. Rosenstone and Raymond E. Wolfinger, "The Effects of Registration Laws on Voter Turnout," *American Political Science Review* 72 (March 1978): 22–45.
7. Paul R. Abramson and John H. Aldrich, "The Decline of Electoral Participation in America," *American Political Science Review* 76 (September 1982): 502–21.
8. National Opinion Research Center, reported in *Time* (12 December 1983), p. 79.
9. Verba and Nie; Richard D. Shingles, "Black Consciousness and Political Participation: The Missing Link," *American Political Science Review* 75 (March 1981): 76–91.
10. Political analyst Richard Scammon, quoted in *Time* (3 January 1983), p. 44.
11. David Halberstam, "How Television Failed the American Voter," *Parade* (11 January 1981), pp. 4–8.
12. *Time* (3 January 1983), p. 14.

13. Paul Taylor, "Fishing for Money During 'The Year Before'," *Houston Chronicle,* 15 May 1983, Sec. 1, p. 16.

14. Thomas B. Edsell, "The Ins and Outs of the American Political Money Machine," *Washington Post,* Weekly Edition, 12 December 1983, pp. 6–7.

15. Michael J. Malbin, "Democratic Rule Makers Want to Bring Party Leaders Back to the Conventions," *National Journal* (2 January 1982), pp. 24–28.

16. Thomas E. Patterson, "Press Coverage and Candidate Success in Presidential Primaries: The 1976 Democratic Race," (Paper delivered at the annual meeting of the American Political Science Association, Washington, D.C., September 1–4, 1977), p. 6. Quoted in Stephen J. Wayne, *The Road to the White House* (New York: St. Martins, 1980).

17. Gerald M. Pomper, *Elections in America: Control and Influence in Democratic Politics* (New York: Dodd, Mead, 1968), chs. 7 & 8.

18. Larry J. Sabato, *The Rise of Political Consultants* (New York: Basic Books, 1981).

19. Austin Ranney, ed. *The Past and Future of Presidential Debates* (Washington: American Enterprise Institute, 1979), p. 186.

20. Angus Campbell, Philip E. Converse, Warren E. Miller, and Donald Stokes, *The American Voter* (New York: Wiley, 1960); Campbell et al., *Elections and the Political Order* (New York: Wiley, 1967).

21. Helmuth Norpoth and Gerald G. Rusk, "Partisan Dealignment in the American Electorate: Itemizing the Deductions Since 1964," *American Political Science Review* 76 (September 1982): 522–37.

22. Walter Dean Burnham, *Critical Elections and the Mainsprings of American Politics* (New York: Norton, 1970).

23. David E. Repass, "Issue Salience and Party Choice," *American Political Science Review* 65 (June 1971): 389–400.

24. Norman H. Nie, Sidney Verba, and John R. Petrocik, *The Changing American Voter,* enlarged edition (Cambridge: Harvard University Press, 1979).

25. *Houston Post,* 23 October 1983, p. 6A.

26. *Houston Chronicle,* 7 January 1983, Sec. 1, p. 4.

27. Herbert Alexander, quoted in *Houston Chronicle,* 8 May 1983, Sec. 1, p. 33.

28. Gary C. Jacobson, "The Effects of Campaign Spending in Congressional Elections," *American Political Science Review* 72 (June 1978): 469–91.

29. Richard E. Cohen, "Giving Till It Hurts: 1982 Campaign Prompts New Look at Financing Races," *National Journal* (18 December 1982), 2144–53.

30. Dom Bonafede, "Part Science, Part Art, Part Hokum, Direct Mail Now a Key Campaign Tool," *National Journal* (31 July 1982), pp. 1332–36.

31. *Houston Chronicle,* 12 December 1982, Sec. 1, p. 16.

32. *Houston Chronicle,* 1 May 1983, Sec. 1, p. 25.

33. John C. McAdams and John R. Johannes, "The 1980 House Elections: Re-Examining Some Theories in a Republican Year," *Journal of Politics* 45 (February 1983): 143–62.

34. R. W. Apple, Jr., "There Must Be a Better Way," *New York Times*, 28 March 1976, Sec. 4, p. 4.

35. Michael Parenti, *Democracy for the Few*, 3rd ed. (New York: St. Martins, 1980), p. 204.

36. H. L. Mencken, *On Politics: A Carnival of Buncombe*, ed. Malcolm Moos (New York: Vintage Books, 1960), pp. 19–21.

37. V. O. Key, Jr., *The Responsible Electorate* (Cambridge: Harvard University Press, 1966).

38. Morris P. Fiorina, *Retrospective Voting in American National Elections* (New Haven: Yale University Press, 1981).

39. Philip E. Converse, "Continuity and Change in American Politics: Parties and Issues in the 1968 Election," *American Political Science Review* 63 (December 1969): 1083–105.

40. Gregory B. Markus, "Political Attitudes During an Election Year: A Report on the 1980 NES Panel Study," *American Political Science Review* 76 (September 1982): 538–60.

SUGGESTED READINGS

ALEXANDER, HERBERT. *Financing Politics: Money, Elections, and Political Reform*. Washington, D.C.: Congressional Quarterly, 1976.

BURNHAM, WALTER DEAN. *Critical Elections and the Mainsprings of American Politics*. New York: Norton, 1960.

CAMPBELL, ANGUS, CONVERSE, PHILIP E., MILLER, WARREN E., AND STOKES, DONALD. *The American Voter*. New York: Wiley, 1960.

FIORINA, MORRIS P. *Retrospective Voting in American National Elections*. New Haven: Yale University Press, 1981.

HADLEY, ARTHUR T. *The Empty Polling Booth*. Englewood Cliffs, N.J.: Prentice-Hall, 1980.

KEY, V. O., JR. *The Responsible Electorate*. Cambridge: Harvard University Press, 1979.

NIE, NORMAN H., VERBA, SIDNEY, AND PETROCIK, JOHN R. *The Changing American Voter*. Enlarged ed. Cambridge: Harvard University Press, 1979.

PAGE, BENJAMIN I. *Choices and Echoes in Presidential Elections*. Chicago: University of Chicago Press, 1978.

POLSBY, NELSON W., AND WILDAVSKY, AARON B. *Presidential Elections*. 5th ed. New York: Scribner's, 1980.

VERBA, SIDNEY, AND NIE, NORMAN. *Participation in America*. New York: Harper and Row, 1972.

Chapter Six

INTEREST GROUPS AND POLITICAL PARTIES

In 1983, the United States government purchased $2.5 billion worth of dry milk, butter, and cheese. Some of it was used in the school-lunch program; some was given as foreign aid; but most went into storage. There, to this day, some 1.3 million tons of unwanted dairy products bought by the government simply sit and spoil.

This is known as the *Milk Fund.* A government agency called the Commodity Credit Corporation is required by law to buy surpluses of milk and milk products in unlimited quantities. The corporation buys at prices designed to maintain the income of dairy farmers at between 75 and 90 percent of **parity** (a price determined by farm wages, the price of tractors, the price of fertilizer, and many other factors). The concept of parity is based on the idea that farmers' purchasing power should not be allowed to slip below a certain predetermined level. So, when farm prices fall, government steps in to prop them up. In the case of dairy products, government guarantees that farmers will receive a base price for their product. In 1981, the government paid $1.50 a pound for butter and 95¢ a pound for dry milk, even though the world-market price was only $1 and 25¢ a pound, respectively.

What does this mean for farmers? It means guaranteed prices, irrespective of the law of supply and demand. Think of it this way. Imagine that you are a shoemaker. If there were a "Shoe Fund" comparable to the Milk Fund, the government would promise to buy all the shoes you made at a price designed to maintain your standard of living. What if you worked very hard and made twice as many shoes this year as last? The government would buy the extra pairs. Also, if the cost of leather, tools, electricity, and other expenses went up, the government would increase the amount it gave you.

In addition, Congress has recently "reformed" the Milk Fund to make it an even better deal for the dairy industry. In 1983, Congress passed and President Reagan signed a bill to pay farmers not to produce milk. Now, in addition to purchasing excess milk, the government has agreed to pay farmers nearly 80 percent of the full price for milk they don't produce, up to 30 percent of their average annual output. Not a bad deal if you can get it.

What does the Milk Fund mean for consumers? Higher prices and higher taxes. Since government guarantees farmers a minimum price, consumers end up paying artificially high prices. No farmer is going to sell his product to a retailer at less than what government pays. Also, as the parity price rises, so do prices at the supermarket. Consumers end up paying twice, of course, since the $2.5-billion fund is tax money.

In this day of budget-cutting and $100-billion budget deficits, how has the Milk Fund survived and prospered? Plain and simple, it is a monument to **interest-group** influence. The program dates back to 1949, when it was established to compensate for a basic fact of nature—cows give more milk in the spring than they do in the winter. In the winter there was a shortage of milk and high prices; in the spring there was a surplus and low prices. In order to smooth out the market fluctuations, Congress created the milk program with the idea of purchasing milk products in the spring, storing them, and then selling them to consumers during the winter months. Theoretically, this was designed to stabilize both prices and supply, making life easier both for farmers and consumers.

Although free-enterprise advocates would argue that government should have kept out of the dairy market, one can see at least some justification behind the creation of the milk-price support system. Thanks to the political power of the dairy lobby, however, the parity price has risen faster than supply and demand would have dictated. Consequently, farmers have overproduced and the government has had to purchase the surplus.[1]

INTEREST GROUPS

Congress and the president are responsible for the Milk Fund, of course, but much of the credit must be laid at the feet of the National Milk Producers Federation. It is an interest group and an effective one. Interest groups are composed of people who join together voluntarily on the basis of a shared interest. Perhaps they are all dairy farmers, or they work in the same industry, or they are women's-rights advocates. They come together to try to influence public policy to their advantage. They may seek a change in public policy to benefit their cause, or they may simply want to preserve the status quo. Interest groups are an ubiquitous part of the policy process, and their role must be understood if we are to comprehend the dynamics of policymaking in America.

A farmer today must be politically and economically astute in order to compete effectively in world markets. The existence of the Milk Fund is a tribute to the effectiveness of the dairy industry's influence on the policymaking process.

TYPES OF INTEREST GROUPS

In America, interest groups represent every cause imaginable, from the Chamber of Commerce to the United Farm Workers, from the Conservative Caucus to the National Gay Task Force, from the American Medical Association to the Hawaiian Golfers for Good Government. Interest groups can be found at work on every level of the American political system and at every stage of the policy process.

However, interest groups are not created equal. Some operate nationwide; others are effective only at the state or local level. Some groups exert a powerful influence on the policy process; others are fairly ineffective. In general, an interest group's political power depends on the size of its membership, the characteristics of its membership, and its access to resources. First, all other things being equal, larger groups are more influential than smaller groups. They make up a bigger voting bloc and offer a larger worker pool for group activities. Second, groups of wealthier, better-educated individuals such as doctors and lawyers, are generally more powerful than groups of poorer, less-educated people. Higher-status individuals are more likely to participate in politics, and they are likely to possess greater financial resources and personal skills than persons from lower-status groups. Finally, groups that are able to raise large sums of money or muster an army of volunteers are more effective than those that cannot. As California politician Jesse Unruh once said, "money is the mother's milk of politics." Also, volunteer workers are an invaluable asset. Let's examine some of the influential groups in America's policy process, discussing what they want from government and how successful they have been in obtaining it.

Business and trade groups.   Business and trade groups are the most potent of America's interest groups. Other groups may be influential at particular levels and at certain points in the policy process, but business groups are powerful everywhere, from the White House to the courthouse, from Congress to state legislatures. Their voices are heard on virtually every major policy issue.

Business and industry embrace many diverse interests, and their concerns reflect that diversity. The oil and gas industries, for example, are concerned about government regulation and the "windfall-profits" tax. Auto manufacturers are interested in laws and regulations affecting pollution controls, exhaust emissions, safety, and the threat of import competition from Japan. Chrysler, the automaker that found itself on the verge of bankruptcy in the late 1970s, had a special interest in federally guaranteed loans. The coal industry is concerned about mine-safety regulations and pollution-control laws affecting coal-burning power plants. In general, business and trade groups worry about tax laws, interest rates, environmental regulations, labor laws, and similar matters.

Business groups are effective because they are organized, well-financed, and skilled in advocating their positions. Firms in the same general field form associations to present a unified political front. The American Petroleum Institute, for example, speaks for the interests of the oil and gas industries; the National Association of Manufacturers represents larger manufacturing concerns; and the Chamber of Commerce is an articulate advocate for smaller business concerns.

Business groups are powerful, but it's important to remember that business and industry are not monolithic. The images they project of themselves and outside appraisals of their interests and concerns frequently gloss over internal fault lines. Big business and small business have different perspectives. Corporate decisionmakers think about long-term and broadscale trends, while small businesses must focus on the immediate neighborhood and the attitudes of retail customers. "Economies of scale" (the greater efficiencies that result from doing business on a large scale) not only make for big corporate profits but also produce chain operations that hurt the family grocery store, restaurant, dry cleaners, auto-parts store, and five-and-dime. Cyclical changes in the economy often mean that big business gets bigger and small businesses face trouble and/or mergers with larger firms.

Consequently, big business and small business often fight over policy issues. Big oil companies and independent operators often view government regulation, or deregulation, differently. City-planning decisions that promote the growth of large shopping malls may hurt family-owned businesses. The big bank holding companies may welcome the deregulation of the financial industry while small, country banks may bitterly oppose it.

Business and professional groups in different fields sometimes clash as well. Railroads and utilities squabble over coal slurry pipeline authorization (which would allow coal companies to pump ground coal mixed with water to utility-company purchasers rather than shipping it by rail). Banks and savings-and-loans feud over banking regulations. Meanwhile, fishing interests on the east and west coasts don't see eye-to-eye on international fishing agreements.

Labor. Organized labor is a powerful political force in America, but, unlike business groups, labor's influence is not important at all levels across the land. Moreover, labor's strength is perhaps on the decline, its membership decreasing. The largest union federation in the nation is the American Federation of Labor-Congress of Industrial Organizations (AFL-CIO). It is composed of some 110 separate unions with 14 million members. The United Mine Workers and the Teamsters are the largest unions not affiliated with the AFL-CIO.

Organized labor is strongest in the large, industrialized states of the Northeast and Midwest. In Michigan, for example, there is no more potent political force than the United Auto Workers. In these regions, the labor force is well-organized and skilled at flexing its political muscles at city hall, the state capital, and the nation's capital as well.

In contrast, labor is not nearly so well-organized nor so politically influential in the sunbelt. There, labor is hamstrung by antilabor laws and a diverse and divided work force, many of whose members are antiunion. So far, unionization in the South and Southwest has come only in a few areas. Consequently, labor's power in most of the sunbelt is confined to certain local areas. In fact, the general political climate is often so antiunion that labor support for a candidate or a cause can be counterproductive.

Not only have the leaders of organized labor failed significantly to expand union power into the sunbelt, they are increasingly hard-pressed to maintain a united political front in their strongholds. In 1980, for example, the leaders of the AFL-CIO and most other unions endorsed the reelection of Jimmy Carter. Nevertheless, a *New York Times* election-day poll found that Carter outpolled Reagan among members of labor-union families by a mere 47 to 44 percent.[2]

What does organized labor want politically? Conventional wisdom holds that organized labor and big business counterbalance each other, invariably taking opposing views on public-policy issues. At times, that's the case. Management and labor generally disagree on labor-relations laws, occupational-safety and health regulations, and minimum-wage laws. At other times, though—more often than most people imagine—big business and big labor find themselves on the same side in public-policy disputes. For example, the United Auto Workers and the auto manufacturers both like the idea of restricting Japanese import competition. Both labor and business leaders argue in favor of higher defense spending because it means more defense contracts and more jobs. Both frequently oppose environmental regulations that might threaten the closing of offending plants and the loss of jobs.

Public-employee groups. Public-employee groups are a part of organized labor, but we are considering them separately because of their unique position. Public-employee groups are among the fastest-growing labor organizations in the nation. In the last several decades, they have become powerful influences on governments at all levels.

What do public employees want? As with other workers, public employees want higher wages, better benefits, and improved working conditions. But, unlike other workers, the demands of public employees *visibly* affect the public-policy process. Money for public employees' wages and salaries comes from tax revenues, of course. The demands of public employees may also directly affect the everyday workings of government, as when teachers go on strike and effectively shut down entire school systems.

Public-employee groups are strongest in those parts of the country where organized labor as a whole is strongest, particularly in the Northeast and Midwest. In Detroit, for example, city typists, janitors, park workers, stenographers, and refuse collectors all earn around $10 an hour. Firefighters there make more than $13 an hour and police officers more than $15. In 1983, the average Detroit city employee made nearly $18,000 a year. In New York City, garbage personnel earn more than $12.50 an hour, and police officers in San Francisco make more than $17 an hour.

Meanwhile, back in Washington, federal workers have been quite successful in winning wage and benefit gains. A University of Pennsylvania study found that in 1981 the average postal employee earned $23,300 a year, including fringe benefits. That's $6591 more per year than comparable private-sector employees, $5238 more than local-government workers, and $1514 more than public-utility workers. Only mining-industry workers and, you guessed it, other federal employees earned more per year. What's more, postal workers negotiated a new contract in 1981 granting them a $2100 raise spread over three years.[3]

There is a cloud to public employees' silver lining, however. Federal budget cuts and the erosion of local tax bases have made it more difficult for big cities in America to make ends meet, particularly in the frostbelt. Consequently, in recent years public workers there have frequently faced the danger of layoffs and salary freezes. Also, public sentiment in general is mixed at best about public-employee groups. Great resistance to public-

The president is the focal point for a seemingly limitless number of contending interest groups. Somehow he must strive to please a number of different groups while still adhering to the general outlines of his administration's policy goals.

employee unionization exists in sunbelt states, and President Reagan's dismissal of the striking air traffic controllers in 1981 found wide public support.

Professional associations.   Auto workers, postal clerks, and truck drivers aren't the only American workers who are organized; so are doctors, lawyers, realtors, and other professionals. Their numbers are not as great as those of blue-collar workers, of course, but professional associations are nonetheless influential because of the relatively high socioeconomic status of their membership. They have the resources to make their voices heard, and they enjoy an added advantage in that many elected officials come from the ranks of professionals, especially lawyers. As one wag put it, we haven't a government of laws; we have a government of lawyers.

Professional associations are concerned with public policies that affect their members. The American Medical Association (AMA), for example, worries about the possibility of Congress' passing some form of national health insurance. The lawyers' association, the American Bar Association (ABA), is interested in no-fault auto insurance, the selection of judges, and legal/constitutional questions in general. Realtors are active in state and local government on issues of development and land-use regulation. Professional associations in general are concerned with professional licensing and regulation. Also, it is not unusual for professional associations to take stands on public-policy issues outside the immediate concerns of their membership, such as tax cuts, budget deficits, defense spending, and women's rights. On these matters, most professional groups are conservative.

Farm groups.   The dairy producers aren't the only farmers who are organized politically. So are the wheat, rice, sugar, peanut, and tobacco farmers, and they are some of America's most successful interest groups. Farmers' groups are often politically astute, well-organized, and know how to exert influence where they are strongest: in the state legislatures in farming regions and in Washington. Their success can be measured in dollars and cents. In 1983, the federal government spent $18.8 billion in farm subsidies for peanuts, sugar, tobacco, wheat, and, of course, dairy products. The debate about farm subsidies is intensifying, however, so farm lobbyists may not be as successful in the future as they have been in the past.

Racial/ethnic groups.   There are innumerable racial and ethnic minority groups in America: blacks, Hispanics, American Indians, Southeast-Asians, and Japanese-Americans, to name some of the larger groups. Blacks, Hispanics, and American Indians have been the more active politically, organizing a variety of groups to promote their political goals, including the National Association for the Advancement of Colored People (NAACP), the Congress of Racial Equality (CORE), the Urban League, the League of United Latin American Citizens (LULAC), and the American Indian Movement (AIM).

In general, racial and ethnic minority groups in America share certain goals: equality before the law, representaton in elective and appointive office, freedom from discrimination, and economic equality. Specifically, minorities are interested in the enforcement of the federal Voting Rights Act, the appointment and election of minorities to federal, state, and local offices; and the extension of government programs geared to fighting poverty.

The 1960s were the salad days of the civil-rights movement in America. The nation's conscience was stirred, and the worst aspects of discrimination were eliminated by the courts and Congress. Lyndon Johnson and the Congress launched a war on poverty. The nation soon learned, however, that it couldn't fight poverty and the war in Vietnam at the same time. Both wars were lost.

The 1970s were years of lost momentum. The most blatant aspects of discrimination were in disrepute, but more subtle forms persisted. Also, for many minority Americans poverty remained a way of life.

In the 1980s, racial and ethnic minority groups are a force to be reckoned with in most big cities and in the South and Southwest, where their numbers translate into political power. In addition, minorities—particularly blacks and, to a lesser degree, Hispanics—remain important in national politics. Unfortunately, the problems facing minorities in America today are particularly obstinate—subtle discrimination, inadequate housing, disease, malnutrition, and illiteracy. These groups hope that the recent increases in minority participation in politics will lead to the adoption of public policies beneficial to minority interests. In an age of huge federal deficits and budget cuts, however, minority groups may find themselves hard pressed merely to hold the gains they have already won.

Religious groups.   Some of the most politically active groups in America are religious groups. Religion and politics are both firmly implanted in American culture; it is not surprising the two sometimes intermix. The abolition movement and Prohibition had strong religious overtones. The same was true of the civil-rights movement of the 1960s. In 1928 and 1960, respectively, powerful feelings were stirred up over the candidacies of Roman Catholics Al Smith and John Kennedy. State aid for parochial schools has long been a cause dear to members of the Catholic Church, and in recent years Catholics have led the fight against legalized abortion. Meanwhile, Jewish groups have kept a close watch over American policy toward Israel.

The political influence of conservative, fundamentalist Christians has become increasingly visible as groups such as the self-proclaimed Moral Majority have gained skills in the use of slick media presentation. The gap separating church and state has narrowed as television preachers such as Jerry Falwell and James Robison have mounted the pulpit of the electronic church to call for a Christian crusade against the "evils" of abortion, pornography, sex and violence on television, homosexuality, sex education, the Equal Rights Amendment, budget deficits, welfare chiselers, federally funded day-care centers, the Panama Canal Treaty, the Department of Education, and communism. They have likewise spoken out in favor of teenage chastity, prayer in schools, and increased defense spending. As Professor William Martin puts it, for some the Spirit of the Lord has descended in the form of a hawk.[4]

The ability of traditional, mainline Protestant, Catholic, and Jewish groups in America to exert a moral influence on issues such as civil rights, the threat of nuclear war, and poverty is longstanding and ongoing, but there is considerable debate about the actual influence of the television preachers. In 1980, the Moral Majority and other conservative Christian groups actively worked for the election of Ronald Reagan and the defeat of a number of liberal Democratic senators. Reagan won and most of the Democratic senators lost, so the religious conservatives claimed credit. Many observers, though, have questioned their impact on the election. Professor Martin points out that the typical congregant of the television church is a working-class, poorly educated, white woman past middle age and living in the rural South, and that the size of the viewing audience is much smaller than the preachers claim.[5]

Perhaps the best explanation for the rise of groups like the Moral Majority is that they represent a reaction on the part of some people to rapid social change. In quickly changing times, people have a tendency to turn toward religion because of its stabilizing influence. In America and around the world, times of rapid change are frequently accompanied by religious revival. It's a phenomenon, however, that's generally short-lived.

Today, groups such as the Moral Majority function partly as a refuge for people uncomfortable with the notion of women out of the kitchen, blacks out of the cotton patch, and gay people out of the closet. If history is any guide, though, such groups are a passing phenomenon.[6]

Public-interest groups.   Some interest groups claim not to be "special" interest groups but advocates of the "public" interest. They see themselves as spokespersons for the general good, at least as they define it. Common Cause, for example, calls itself "the citizens' lobby." It has worked for, among other things, the reform of campaign financing laws. In particular, it wants to see the power of PACs reduced.

Probably the best known spokesperson for public-interest groups is Ralph Nader. He has organized a number of public-interest groups, including Public Citizen, Congress Watch, the Tax Reform Research Group, and Public Interest Research Groups (PIRGs) which operate on the campuses of many colleges and universities. Nader and his groups have been involved with such issues as auto safety, consumer rights, and environmental protection.[7]

Public-interest groups are not, perhaps, among the super heavyweights of American politics, but they have frequently been effective in selling their points of view to the general public, and they have won their share of battles in Congress. What's more, when the Carter Administration took office, many of the leaders of these groups were appointed to posts in the bureaucracy from which they could administer the reforms they had lobbied through Congress. During the Reagan Administration, however, that practice was not continued. Instead, most of the so-called public-interest advocates were replaced by individuals from the business interests that the public-interest groups had long opposed.

MADD (Mothers Against Drunk Driving) is a single-issue group that has had some success in pushing for tougher drunk-driving laws.

Single-issue groups.   American politics is enlivened by the presence of a variety of **single-issue groups.** These groups focus their efforts on a single issue or a group of related issues. For Right to Life, the cause is opposition to abortion; for the National Organization for Women (NOW), it's women's rights; for the Sierra Club, it's the environment; for the American Civil Liberties Union (ACLU), it's the zealous protection of the rights of the individual as outlined in the Bill of Rights.

The influence of single-issue groups is generally limited to their pet causes; and in these areas they have achieved some notable successes. Mothers Against Drunk Driving (MADD), for example, has succeeded in generating a great deal of public support for tougher driving-while-intoxicated (DWI) laws. In many states and localities, tax-protest groups have forced tax rollbacks or limitations, such as California's Proposition 13. The National Rifle Association (NRA) has been able to prevent the adoption by Congress and most state legislatures of all but the mildest gun-control laws.

Ideological groups.   Recent years have seen the emergence of a number of groups organized to promote either the conservative or the liberal cause. The Americans for Democratic Action (ADA), a liberal group, has been around for decades, and various conservative groups have gained prominence lately. These latter include the National Conservative Political Action Committee (NCPAC), Young Americans for Freedom (YAF), and the Congressional Club. Along with other conservative goals, these groups have pushed for constitutional amendments to outlaw abortion, permit school prayer, and require a balanced budget (see the **PERSPECTIVE** on this page). A high point of the conservatives' influence came in 1980. The conservative groups claimed credit for electing their favorite, Ronald Reagan, to the White House and turning out a half-dozen liberal senators they had targeted for defeat. Reagan in turn named some of the conservative activists to posts in his administration.

Since 1980, however, the conservatives' fortunes have waned somewhat. Congress failed to enact many of the conservatives' key programs: proposals on abortion, school prayer, and a balanced budget all failed. Some of the conservatives blamed Reagan, but others pointed the finger at the actions of pragmatic White House aides such as James Baker. "Let Reagan be Reagan," they exclaimed. Then, 1982 turned out to be a bad year for the conservative groups. NCPAC, for example, targeted some twenty-four senators and representatives for defeat, but only one lost.[8] Meanwhile, liberals counterattacked, organizing groups such as the Progressive Political Action Committee (PROPAC) and the National Committee for an Effective Congress.

Neighborhood groups.   Finally, a large number of neighborhood and community groups across the nation involve themselves in the policy

Perspective
THE "ATTACK" PAC

Politics can be rough business, of course, but NCPAC, the National Conservative Political Action Committee, has developed quite a reputation for playing hardball. Its enemies would say it plays dirty ball. NCPAC targets liberal officeholders it considers vulnerable and then spends millions of dollars to mount hard-hitting advertising campaigns against them. In 1980, NCPAC took credit for ousting a number of liberal Democrats from the Senate, including George McGovern, Frank Church, and Birch Bayh.

In 1982, however, many felt NCPAC's tactics backfired. Officeholders under NCPAC attack went on the offensive, making the organization's negative tactics a campaign issue. This time nearly all of the incumbents won reelection. Nevertheless, NCPAC continues raising money and planning negative, antiliberal campaigns.[1]

[1]*Time* (25 October 1982), p. 26.

process. Most urban subdivisions have civic clubs or some other sort of neighborhood improvement associations. Many schools have very active Parent Teacher Associations (PTAs).

Neighborhood groups can be important at the local level, but their overall influence on policy is limited. Most of these groups see politics as a secondary activity, and many are not very skilled at it. Also, their concerns are usually focused on highly specific issues of local concern.

STRATEGY AND TACTICS

The tactics of interest groups vary, ranging from electioneering to lobbying to propaganda to protest activity to litigation. Some groups specialize in one particular type of political activity. The ACLU, for example, focuses most of its energy on litigation. The most successful groups in American politics, however, are those that use the entire arsenal of political warfare. Let's consider the various ways interest groups attempt to influence the policy process.

Electioneering.   Interest groups live by the motto, "Elect your friends; defeat your enemies." Groups with large membership and/or influence hope to affect election outcomes by endorsing favored candidates and delivering bloc votes on their candidates' behalf. In 1983, for example, the AFL-CIO, NOW, and the National Education Association (NEA) all endorsed Walter Mondale for the 1984 Democratic presidential nomination. The problem with this strategy is that groups are not always successful in persuading their members to vote for the endorsed candidate.

Perhaps the most effective means interest groups have for influencing elections is by contributing money to election campaigns. In general, it is illegal for corporations and unions to contribute to political candidates directly from corporate or union funds, but it is permissible for corporate executives and union members to give money as private individuals. Consequently, business and labor groups may form political action committees (PACs) to collect money from group members, pool it, and then give it to campaigns under the label of the PAC.

Many PACs have names that clearly connect them with the interest groups they represent. Build-PAC, for example, is organized by the National Association of Home Builders. Some PAC names are even clever, such as SixPAC for beer distributors, or WhataPAC for Whataburger, Inc. In some cases, however, PACs seem to prefer to operate incognito. Not many would guess that the Good Government Fund is tied to Tenneco Oil or that HOUPAC is organized by oilmen from Houston, Texas. Another big-spending PAC, the National PAC, is, despite the seemingly all-embracing name, organized to support Israel.

In the 1981–82 election cycle, some 3371 PACs raised and spent nearly $200 million, $87 million of which was given directly to campaigns. The biggest fundraisers were the conservative ideological groups such as

NCPAC and the Congressional Club each of which raised and spent some $10 million during that period. Other big spenders were the National Association of Realtors ($3 million) and the AMA ($2.4 million). PACs representing the dairy industry gave more than $1.8 million to candidates for Congress. All told, PACs associated with corporations gave $43.2 million to candidates in 1982, trade and health PACs contributed $41.7 million, and labor-union PACs gave $35 million.[9]

Interest groups give money to election campaigns in hopes of making winners out of their friends and friends out of winners. On the one hand, groups give money to whichever candidates are most favorably disposed to their point of view. Corporate and trade PACs lean toward Republicans while union PACs give almost all their contributions to Democrats.[10] On the other hand, interest groups also want to build ties with those who will actually wield power, and that means giving money to likely winners. Consequently, most PAC money goes to incumbents. This tends to help Democrats, who in 1982 received about 54 percent of total PAC contributions.[11] In close races, PACs may even give money to both candidates. That way, no matter who wins the election, the interest group comes out on top.

PACs are among the most controversial features of contemporary American politics. Their defenders argue that they are a means whereby thousands of people can participate in politics through financial contributions. In addition, they say, politicians can't be bought for a mere $5000, the maximum amount a PAC is allowed to give in a campaign to a member of Congress. In contrast, critics contend that PAC money now plays such a big role in political campaigns that it distorts the traditional relationship between elected officials and their constituents. Why should representatives reach out to appeal to a broad base of constituents for support, ask the critics, when they can raise hundreds of thousands of dollars of campaign money from PACs? The result of such a system is that the Republicans tend to become the party of big business rather than small business, while the Democrats will answer to big labor instead of the working people.[12]

Lobbying.   Between election campaigns, interest groups attempt to influence policymaking by lobbying. **Lobbyists** are paid representatives of interest groups whose job is to present their groups' point of view to government decisionmakers. They are at work at every level of American government and at every stage of the policy process.

Professional lobbyists today are skilled technicians, knowledgeable both in how to approach public officials and in the subject matter vital to their group. Occasional scandals demonstrate that lobbyists sometimes use blatantly illegal methods, but such approaches are unusual. The basic stock-in-trade of the skilled lobbyist is information. In fact, lobbyists perform a number of beneficial functions for the political system: they provide input into decisionmaking; they represent a segment of the population and its interests to policymakers; and they provide expertise on complex issues to government officials.

A busy legislator hurries into the House chamber as lobbyists discuss the MX missile with Democrat James R. Jones (center) of Oklahoma. Lobbyists perform valuable services for legislators, who often find themselves in need of the information, expertise, and diverse viewpoints the lobbyists can provide.

Other tactics.   Groups employ other tactics to influence public policy. One technique is propaganda; groups launch public-relations campaigns to convince the general public of the correctness of their views and the righteousness of their cause. In 1983, for example, the banking industry conducted a drive to persuade the public that income-tax withholding on interest and dividend income was a bad idea. Congress passed the requirement in 1982 in an effort to reduce tax evasion, but the banking industry opposed it because of the additional paperwork it would require. The banks managed to convince much of the general public that withholding was a new tax (it wasn't), and members of Congress were flooded with more than 22-million letters in opposition. Eventually, Congress caved in to pressure and repealed withholding.

Groups that cannot afford public-relations experts and expensive advertising costs pursue similar goals by means of protest demonstrations. Civil-rights groups used this technique in the 1960s. Today, it is occasionally employed by a variety of groups pursuing many different goals, ranging from school teachers protesting low pay to Ku Klux Klansmen denouncing Vietnamese immigration. In general, protest demonstrations are a tactic used by groups unable to achieve their goals through other means. Sometimes the protest catches the fancy of the general public, and pressure is brought to bear on behalf of the protesting groups. In most cases, however, protests have only a marginal impact on policy.

Occasionally, frustrated groups go beyond peaceful protest to violent, illegal activities. During the 1960s, some extremist groups opposed to the war in Vietnam took over college administration buildings. The decade of the 1960s was also a time when riots erupted in many inner-city ghettos. Today, international terrorism sometimes spills over into America.

The problem with violence as a political tool, however, is that it invites a violent response from the political authorities. Nevertheless, one can make a case that violence does occasionally succeed in calling the public's attention to an issue that might otherwise be ignored.

Finally, a number of groups have become expert in the use of litigation to achieve their goals. The NAACP, for example, has found in the federal courts a powerful ally in its efforts to achieve equality under the law. Other groups that have been frequent litigants include the Sierra Club, the ACLU, and the Mexican American Legal Defense Fund (MALDEF). Litigation has been an important political tool for interest groups, but it has its limitations. Lawsuits are both time-consuming and expensive. Also, litigation reacts rather than initiates; lawsuits are invariably filed to overturn public policy that is already in place. Although court action sometimes succeeds in overturning policies, the real political power remains in the hands of those who make the policies in the first place.

INTEREST GROUPS AND PUBLIC POLICY

Interest groups are active in every stage of the public-policy process, at every level of government, and in every institutional branch. They propose items for the policy agenda, suggest policies, urge their adoption, monitor their implementation, and evaluate their results. They lobby every public official from the Speaker of the House of Representatives to a county commissioner in rural Oklahoma. They attempt to influence policymaking in the Congress, in the courts, in the bureaucracy, and in the White House. In short, interest groups are everywhere, trying to exert influence over all types of policies, at all levels of government.

Their influence is important, particularly on issues about which the general public is relatively uninformed and unaware, such as the Milk Fund. The attentive public for the issue of farm price supports consists primarily of farmers and the groups representing them. Does it surprise you that Congress responds favorably to a relatively small group that is actively concerned with a particular area of public policy when the general public is apathetic?

Congress (and every other part of government) responds to political pressure and public demands. Interest groups have power because they actively make demands and exert pressure while others do not. An active, informed public along with strong, representative political parties could serve as counterbalances to interest-group power, but neither exists in America today. Election turnout has been at a low point, and parties are weaker than at any time in this century. So interest groups hold sway, and the more money they have the more sway they hold.

There are intense debates in American politics about who runs the country. Some say that power is in the hands of a small, cohesive elite. Others argue that America is pluralist; that is, power is divided among competing groups of elites. Probably the truth lies somewhere between the elitist and the pluralist approaches. Powerholders vary from one issue to another and from one locale to another. In some states, business groups

Interest Groups in American Politics

A CONVERSATION WITH PROFESSOR BURDETT LOOMIS, UNIVERSITY OF KANSAS

Q. Are "special interests" too powerful in America's policymaking process?

A. Yes and no.

Q. That's a typical academic response. Perhaps you'd like to elaborate.

A. There's no denying that interest groups have grown in number and sophistication over the past twenty years. The dairy lobby is only one example of a group that vigorously and successfully pursues its interests. Some folks, such as those associated with Common Cause or with Ralph Nader's groups, would have us see American politics as a kind of "Special Interest State," where powerful interests get their way most of the time.

Q. But you don't see that as cause for alarm?

A. Not necessarily. Interests have always been with us, and the framers created a system that works to reduce the "evils of faction." In many ways, more interests are more ably represented today than ever before in our history. Look, for instance, at the emergence of strong environmental groups, consumer groups, antiabortion groups, and the like. In addition, at the local level many groups have grown up around neighborhood issues, school concerns, zoning, and a host of other topics. A lot of people are directly involved in the political process.

Burdett Loomis, Associate Professor at the University of Kansas, is author of numerous articles on interest groups and congressional politics. His current research deals with contemporary political careers. A Congressional Fellow, he has coauthored an American politics text and edited the collection, Interest Group Politics.

Q. You make interest-group participation sound like the foundation of democracy in America.

A. Group participation is important, but there are also problems. Today, there are so many interests represented in the policy process that the system may well bog down under their weight. Even the government itself has become a major voice for many interests. Take the Department of Education. The National Education Association (NEA) worked diligently on behalf of Jimmy

Carter in the 1976 election. Subsequently, he "delivered" on the NEA's desire for a separate cabinet department of education. Once established, however, the department took on a life of its own. Even in the conservative Reagan Administration, the Department of Education tends to represent its constituents in the education community whose interests are often at odds with mainstream administration policies.

Q. You mean that governmental officials within the national bureaucracy end up acting like lobbyists?

A. Yes. Generals lobby on defense, agriculture officials lobby on farm issues, and transportation bureaucrats lobby on behalf of their own particular transportation interests (highways, mass transit, railways, etc.). Beyond that is the whole world of officials from other levels of government who lobby continually in Washington.

Q. That gets us to lobbying. Do you think we'd be better off without it?

A. Probably not, but let's begin by defining lobbying. Although we may think of lobbying as the buying of favors or as attempts to sway policymakers through "wining and dining" them, lobbying ordinarily consists of interests seeking to provide information to those who make policy. It's mostly communications.

Q. That sounds a bit simplistic, and perhaps naive. Isn't there more?

A. Of course. The process is often complex and difficult to view in its entirety. Communications, nevertheless, remain central, and two particular types of information—technical and political—are especially valuable. Many decisionmakers and most members of Congress are policy amateurs. They continually need data and analyses in order to make reasonably well-informed judgments. Much lobbying consists of attempts to convey useful technical information, on nuclear energy, agriculture, welfare— whatever—to policymakers.

Q. Wouldn't lobbyists just put forward self-serving information that supports their own point of view?

A. To an extent. And politicians expect some bias. At the same time, lobbyists seek to foster long-term relationships with policymakers. Such ties are based on trust, and lobbyists cannot afford to stray far from the truth. Thus, they generally provide information that is technically competent and reasonably neutral.

Q. What about the other type of valued information—the political side of things?

A. Decisionmakers, and especially members of Congress, want to know what their constituents think about policies, both actual and proposed. In this age of speedy and extensive communication, members hear surprisingly little about most policies. Good political information is at a premium. Lobbyists can keep members informed on how a policy is received back home.

Q. Finally, what about political action committees (PACs)? We hear a lot about them, but it's unclear what effects they have on the political system.

A. I'm glad you asked because, in a real sense, this gets us back to the initial question of special-interest power in American society. There are two distinct schools of thought here. The first, most vociferously represented by Common Cause, states that larger numbers of PACs, increased campaign costs, and the expanding number and level of PAC contributions combine to produce a Congress that is the "best that money can buy." Some particular examples do seem to support this argument. The used-car dealers, for instance, gave over a million dollars to congressional candidates prior to the 1982 elections, and there does appear to be some fairly strong relationship between donations and congressional voting on the issue of whether to require these dealers to disclose

known defects in the cars they sold. More generally, in the last decade congressional campaigns have become more expensive, the number of PACs has grown tremendously, and PACs have greatly increased their contribution levels, both to incumbents and, more recently, challengers.

On the other hand, the PAC patterns may simply reflect the ways in which money is currently channeled into politics. Running for office has always been fairly costly, and PACs, so the second school of thought argues, are merely conduits for the money that would be spent anyway. Indeed, since PACs can contribute only limited amounts ($5000 per candidate per campaign) and must report the names of both donors and recipients, we may be better off with PACs than with the old system of large, secret contributions.

Q. This is beginning to get complicated.

A. So it is. Let's conclude by taking note of James Madison's observation that faction is sown into the nature of man. And the structure of American politics encourages groups (factions) to attempt to influence policies in many arenas and in many ways. This is both the bane and wonder of our unique system.

dominate; elsewhere they must compete with labor and other groups. Single-issue groups are frequently effective on their particular issues. Ethnic and racial minority groups are powerful in many big cities and may be influential nationwide. Farm groups usually get their point across on issues directly affecting them.

We should keep in mind, however, that not all interests are organized. In late 1983, it was estimated that there were 2.5 million homeless people in America.[13] What interest group speaks for them? For that matter, what group represents the children of the poor? Or persons suffering from mental illness? American politics features group competition, but it's important to remember that groups are not equally influential and that not all Americans are represented by groups.

How are we, finally, to evaluate the role played by interest groups in American politics? The answer depends on one's point of view. When the late Robert Benchley, the American humorist, was a student at Harvard, he was asked to write an essay on the international whaling industry from the viewpoint of Britain, France, or the United States. He wrote that since he was unfamiliar with any of those viewpoints, he preferred to discuss the issue from the viewpoint of the whale.

Similarly, one's evaluation of interest-group politics will depend on one's perspective. If you are a consumer, for example, you may be outraged that billions of taxpayers' dollars are going to farm subsidies. On the other hand, if you're a farmer, you may think farm subsidies are the best thing since air-conditioned tractor cabs. As with the story of Robert Benchley and the whaling industry, it all depends on your point of view.

POLITICAL PARTIES

Political parties are groups of people organized to seek political office in order to make public policy. They may be small or large, well-organized or confused, broadly or narrowly based. American politics has seen parties of all sizes, all varieties of popular appeal, and all organizational formats, but successful parties in America are invariably large, broadly based "umbrella" parties, with decentralized organizations.

THE PARTY SYSTEM

The American party system seems able to accommodate only two major parties at any one time. Since the Civil War, those parties have been the Republicans and the Democrats. To be sure, there have been others—the Progressive, Populist, Libertarian, American Independent, Socialist Workers, and Communist parties—but the system isn't very kind to minor parties. There are no consolation prizes for finishing second or a strong third. The candidate with the most votes wins the office; all others wait until next time. Consequently, voters, political activists, and potential financial backers think twice about signing on with a party whose chances appear slim. Once in a while, a minor party will get over the hump and become a major party. (After all, the Republican and Democratic parties didn't sail over on the Mayflower.) But, minor-party success invariably accompanies the demise of one of the former major parties. In the 1850s and '60s, for example, the Republicans rose to major-party status over the dead body of the Whig party.

Another problem for minor parties is the adaptability of the major parties. Both the Republican and Democratic parties are broadly based, mass parties with a diverse membership holding a variety of viewpoints. Every major economic, racial, ethnic, religious, regional, and ideological group in America can be represented to a greater or lesser degree in one or both of the major parties. Whenever a minor party comes up with an idea that proves popular with the electorate, the major parties are flexible (and opportunistic) enough to adopt it as their own, leaving the minor party without a cause all its own.

PARTY ORGANIZATION

Much of the flexibility of parties in America comes from their extreme decentralization. In a sense, there are fifty-one Republican and fifty-one Democratic parties: the national parties and the party organizations in each state. Every four years the national parties assemble in convention to adopt a platform and nominate candidates for president and vice-president. At other times, the national parties exist as names, offices, and committees, with most of the day-to-day party affairs being conducted by state and local organizations that are largely independent of national control. The state parties choose their own candidates, conduct their own campaigns, and raise most of their own money.

Significant differences exist within each party from one region to another, say, for example, between Republicans in New York and Texas or between Democrats in Illinois and Florida. Because of the decentralized nature of America's party system, political parties in each state tend to reflect the political contours of the state. Organized labor, for instance, is a major component of Democratic parties in the industrial Midwest and Northeast, but is relatively unimportant in the Democratic parties of the South and Southwest where the labor movement is weak. Similarly, Hispanics are an important part of the Democratic coalition in Texas and other states in the Southwest, but not in the Midwest. The most important regional variation in the party system is in the South. To understand the southern difference, we must turn our attention to the history of America's party system.

HISTORY OF THE PARTY SYSTEM

The two most important events affecting America's party system were the Civil War and the Great Depression. The Republican party emerged from the Civil War as the nation's dominant party. After all, the "Grand Old Party" (GOP), as it is called, was the party of Lincoln, the party of the Emancipation Proclamation, and the party of Reconstruction. For decades, the Republicans controlled Congress and the White House while waving the flag of Civil War victory and nominating ex-Union generals to the presidency.

All of this played very well in Peoria, but not at all in Birmingham or the rest of the South. For those whose eyes grew moist at the first strains of "Dixie," Republican was a dirty word. The Republican party was a symbol of patriotism and triumph in the North, but in the South it symbolized defeat and oppression. Among southerners, the GOP could count on the loyalty only of blacks, immigrants from the North, and a few white southerners who had long supported the Union. The South became the "Solid South," solidly *Democratic,* and remained so for nearly a hundred years as families passed along memories, loyalties, and allegiances from generation to generation. Old times there were not forgotten.

To be sure, Republican dominance after the Civil War was by no means absolute. The GOP was strongest in the Midwest; the Democrats controlled the South. And at times the Democratic party was able to challenge the Republicans successfully nationwide. Toward the end of the nineteenth century, for example, the two major parties competed on fairly even terms, and Democrat Grover Cleveland captured the presidency twice. In 1912, Democrat Woodrow Wilson won the White House, primarily because the GOP was divided; in 1916 he was reelected. Nevertheless, the Republicans resumed their political dominance in the 1920s.

Then came the Great Depression. The economy collapsed, and many voters blamed President Hoover and the Republican party. They elected Franklin Roosevelt to the presidency; the shape of America's party system was changed forever.

The coalition of voters who elected FDR was broad and diverse and, for many years, constituted a clear majority of the electorate. It included organized labor; blue-collar voters; the poor; the unemployed; Jews; Catholics; Hispanics; Irish-, Italian-, and Polish-Americans; white southerners; and blacks, who switched from their traditional Republican loyalties. It was quite a varied group, this Democratic coalition, but it was united by support for Franklin Roosevelt the man and for the liberal programs of the New Deal. Who did that leave in the camp of the GOP? Primarily middle- and upper-class white, Anglo-Saxon Protestants (WASPs) living outside the South.

DEMOCRATS AND REPUBLICANS TODAY

The portrait of party alignment drawn in the 1930s is basically the same today, only the lines are not so clear, the colors not so sharp. For years, the

Democratic coalition was a great juggernaut, crushing most Republican candidacies in its path. It swept Democratic presidential candidates to victory in 1932, 1936, 1940, 1944, and 1948 and kept the party in control of the U.S. Congress for most of the period from 1930 to 1980. Since the 1940s, however, Democratic momentum has slowed. Republicans won the White House in 1952, 1956, 1968, 1972, and 1980. Also, in 1980, the election of Ronald Reagan was accompanied by the return of a Republican majority in the Senate.

Today, the Roosevelt coalition may no longer represent an electoral majority, at least certainly not an overwhelming majority. Yet it does still influence electoral politics. The 1976 Jimmy Carter-Gerald Ford presidential contest, for instance, produced a classic Democratic-Republican voter division. As Table 6.1 shows, Carter did well among traditionally Democratic groups—southerners, blacks, Hispanics, Jews, Catholics, lower-income persons, blue-collar workers, less-educated individuals, the unemployed, and labor-union families. Ford did best among groups that are normally Republican—white, Anglo-Saxon Protestants, midwesterners, middle- and upper-income voters, college graduates, professionals, and white-collar workers. Yet Carter barely won, receiving 51 percent of the popular vote compared to Ford's 48 percent.

What has happened to the once mighty coalition of Franklin Roosevelt? First, short-term factors have had their effects. In the 1930s and 1940s the Democrats were aided immeasurably by the personal charisma of FDR. In the 1970s and 1980, however, they were hindered by the blandness of a George McGovern or a Jimmy Carter. Meanwhile, General Eisenhower's personal appeal gave the GOP a big boost in the 1950s. The short-term

FDR's Democratic coalition embraced a wide variety of people, including workers, intellectuals, ethnic minorities, liberals, and the poor. The coalition lasted until well past Roosevelt's death, and still provides the general population base that Democratic candidates try to reach.

TABLE 6.1

Two-Party Presidential Election Voting by Groups, 1976 and 1980

Group	1976 Carter	1976 Ford	1980 Carter	1980 Reagan
Democrats	77%	22%	66%	26%
Independents	43	54	30	54
Republicans	9	90	11	84
East	51	47	43	47
South	54	45	44	51
Midwest	48	50	41	51
West	46	51	35	52
Blacks	82	16	82	14
Hispanics	75	24	54	36
Whites	47	52	36	55
Catholics	54	44	40	51
Jews	64	34	45	39
Protestants	44	55	37	56
Income:				
less than $10,000	58	40	50	41
$10–14,999	55	43	47	42
$15–24,999	48	50	38	53
$25–50,000	36	62	32	58
Over $50,000	–	–	25	65
Professional or manager	41	57	33	56
Clerical, sales, or other white collar	46	53	42	48
Blue-collar worker	57	41	46	47
Looking for work	65	34	55	35
Agricultural	–	–	29	66
High-school education	57	43	46	48
Some college	51	49	35	55
College education	45	23	35	51
Labor-union household	59	39	47	44

SOURCE: *New York Times*, 9 Nov. 1980. Based on interviews conducted with more than 10,000 voters leaving the polls on election day, 1976 and 1980.

influence of various issues has also influenced election outcomes. The Republicans were helped in the 1950s by voter unhappiness with Democratic handling of three big issues: communism, corruption, and Korea. In the 1968 election, the issues of Vietnam and domestic unrest helped defeat Democrat Hubert Humphrey. Economic and foreign-policy issues played a role in Carter's defeat in 1980.

Second, in recent years the glue holding the Democratic coalition together has been coming unstuck, at least around the edges. For many younger voters, Franklin Roosevelt is now an old newsreel figure. The liberal reforms of the New Deal and of subsequent Democratic administrations are themselves under attack and serve as targets of reformers.

Most importantly, though, many of the working-class groups who, in the 1930s, cast their lot with FDR and the New Deal for economic reasons are no longer working-class in the 1980s. Auto assembly-line workers earning eighteen dollars an hour own campers, pay mortgages, and send their kids to college. They may have working-class jobs, but their income is middle-class and so, frequently, are their political concerns: taxes, inflation, crime.

In 1980, the Republican strategy was to appeal to certain segments of traditional Democratic voters, and it worked. The Democratic coalition has always had its internal divisions, including as it does such diverse and divergent groups as conservatives and liberals; northerners and southerners; southern whites and blacks; Catholics, Jews, and southern white Protestants; academics and labor-union bosses. Politics may make strange bedfellows, at times, but political marriages are not forever. Reagan appealed to Catholics on the issue of abortion. To attract working-class voters he attacked Carter's record on the economy. He wooed white southerners by taking a hard line on national defense and by opposing school busing for purposes of racial integration. As Table 6.1 shows, Reagan did much better among these groups of voters than Republicans usually do.

Finally, party affiliation in general has become less important to the electorate. For decades, the Gallup Poll has been asking voters, "In politics today, do you consider yourself a Republican, Democrat, or an independent." Table 6.2 shows that since the 1930s more people have called themselves Democrats than Republicans. In recent years, though, the major development has been an increase in the number of people who call themselves independent, that is, people who do not feel personal ties or allegiance to either major party.

There are a number of reasons for the decline in party identification. The Vietnam war, Watergate and other scandals, high taxes, and inflation have turned many voters off to politics and political parties. Reforms enacted to make the presidential-nomination process more democratic have weakened parties as well. Also, professional political-campaign media specialists have made party organization less significant as candidates appeal directly to the voters through the television tube instead of through a party organization.

With lessened party identification, turnout is lower, the electorate more volatile, and ticket-splitting more common. (**Ticket-splitting** occurs when a voter chooses one party's candidate for president or senator, and then votes the other party for the lower offices.) Short-term factors such as issues and personalities become more important. As a result, we have a smaller and smaller electorate producing larger and larger voting swings.

The 1980 election clearly demonstrated the power of the independent

TABLE 6.2
*Party Affiliation
1937–1983*

Year	Republican	Democrat	Independent
1983	25%	45%	30%
1976	23	48	29
1960	30	47	23
1949	32	48	20
1937	34	50	16

SOURCES: *The Gallup Report*, April 1981; *Houston Post*, 22 September 1983, p. 3B.

voter. Reagan won largely because he ran well among independents and enticed some traditional Democrats to cross over and vote for him.

Publication deadlines make it impossible for us to discuss the 1984 election in this chapter, but it is covered in an appendix at the end of this book. Read that now before continuing with the chapter.

POLITICAL PARTIES AND PUBLIC POLICY

Political parties are an important part of the policymaking process in a democracy. They are a mechanism through which individuals and groups can make claims on government on a broad range of issues. Parties raise issues to the public agenda, propose policies, push for their adoption and implementation, and then evaluate the consequences.

Strong parties make for strong democracy. After all, the idea of representative democracy is that elected officials represent their constituents. Parties are instruments for recruiting qualified men and women to run for office and for conveying, through the candidates, the views and interests of party participants. Also, strong parties are able to enforce discipline on the party's elected officials, making them more responsive to their constituents. That's the notion of **responsible parties,** that is, parties that clearly spell out issue positions in their platforms and, when in office, faithfully carry them out.

In the best of times, however, American parties are neither particularly strong nor responsible. They are extremely decentralized with structures paralleling the federal system and the separation-of-powers system. Each state's party organization is independent of national direction. In addition, no formal connection or method of control unites a president and members of his party in Congress. Consequently, American parties are not particularly effective instruments for formulating, adopting, and implementing public policy. The party in Congress or the party that controls the White House may or may not live up to the promises in its platform. Even if it tries, the separation-of-powers and checks-and-balances system may make the platform well nigh impossible to carry through.

What does this mean for policymaking in America? Less participation, stronger interest groups, and a greater role for television. First, parties are an important tool for involving people in the political process. They organize campaigns, educate voters on the issues, and work to get out the vote. It is no coincidence that the decline of parties in America has been accompanied by a decline in participation.

Second, strong parties act as an important counterbalance to interest groups. In general, parties represent a broader segment of the society than interest groups. Consequently, party issue positions reflect more general concerns than the narrow perspectives of a special-interest group. Also, since parties can generally command greater political resources than most interest groups, party-backed public officials are better able to resist interest-group pressures. With the decline of parties, however, public officials are likely to find themselves tempted to cave in to interest-group demands in order to protect their political hides.

Finally, strong party organization is an effective campaign force. It can raise money for campaign expenses and rally the faithful to work in the campaign. By acting as a key element in campaigns, strong parties can be a mechanism through which citizens make claims on public officials, thus influencing policy. When officials are able to win office without the aid of party organization, this tie is weakened. With parties weakened, candidates will turn to Madison Avenue for slick television advertising.

What does the future hold for the American party system? In the last few years, the Democratic and Republican parties have been trying to reassert themselves politically. As we saw in the last chapter, the Democrats have reformed their procedures for picking a presidential candidate in an effort to give party leaders more influence. Both parties have tried to regain a more prominent role in political campaigns by developing their fundraising abilities and their capacity to provide technical assistance to candidates. In this, the GOP has a head start on the Democrats. For the 1982 election, for example, the Republican National Committee raised $168.8 million compared to the Democrats' $23.7 million. The Republicans also do a better job of recruiting and training candidates than the Democrats.[14] Nevertheless, whether all of this will be enough to turn the tide and instill greater party discipline and party loyalty among officeholders remains to be seen.

Conclusion: Participation and Public Policy

Political participation is at the heart of democratic theory. The ideal of representative democracy is that of an informed, interested citizenry conscientiously choosing public officials to represent their interests in the policymaking process. This assumes, first, that the citizenry is knowledgeable about public-policy issues and has certain preferences about the future course of public policy. A second assumption is that the public will carefully select officials whom they believe will effectively represent their interests.

Finally, the theory assumes that citizens will evaluate public officials on their record, either rewarding them with reelection or punishing them with defeat.

In reality, however, we have learned that participation in America falls well short of the ideal. First, many Americans are simply uninformed about their government and about the public-policy process. Second, we also know that many Americans don't bother to participate, not even taking the time to cast their ballot for president once every four years. Finally, we know that money and media play a major role in the process.

We know as well that those who are most skilled at organization and best able to marshal financial resources are also best equipped to shape the policy process. Socioeconomic status often carries with it political influence. The poor, the uneducated, the very old, and the very young tend to get left by the wayside. They aren't ignored by government; public policy touches their lives directly and profoundly. But, they *are* frequently unheard.

Perhaps we expect too much from ourselves. After a hard day's work, the average person just wants to relax with family and friends and watch a little television. Keeping a close eye on political events or becoming a political activist just aren't high on most people's list of things they want to do. In its ideal form, representative democracy demands more time, energy, and commitment than most of us are willing and able to supply on a regular basis. We are willing to pay attention to politics in a general sort of way, but we stir ourselves to become actively involved only when there's a crisis we see affecting our daily lives. Otherwise, we live our lives, skim the newspapers, and vote—occasionally.

KEY TERMS

INTEREST GROUP (148)   *RESPONSIBLE PARTIES (170)*

LOBBYIST (159)   *SINGLE-ISSUE GROUP (156)*

PARITY (148)   *TICKET-SPLITTING (169)*

POLITICAL PARTY (164)

NOTES

1. *National Journal* (26 September 1981), p. 1737; *Time* (21 November 1983), p. 23.
2. *New York Times,* 9 November 1980, p. 28.
3. *Houston Post,* 25 July 1981, p. A14.
4. William Martin, "Onward Christian Voters," *Texas Monthly* (June 1980), p. 93.
5. *Houston Post,* 10 April 1982, p. 10A.

6. Anson Shupe and William A. Stacey, *Born Again Politics and the Moral Majority* (New York: Edwin Mellen Press, 1982).
7. Jeffrey M. Berry, *Lobbying for the People: The Political Behavior of Public Interest Groups* (Princeton: Princeton University Press, 1977).
8. David S. Broder, "Conservative Group Spent Much, Achieved Little," *Houston Chronicle*, 10 November 1982, Sec. 1, p. 26.
9. *Time* (25 October 1982); *Houston Chronicle*, 1 May 1983, Sec. 1, p. 25; and Richard E. Cohen, "Business, Conservative PACs—Bigger Yet, But Their Influence May be Waning," *National Journal* (7 August 1982); pp. 1368–73.
10. "How PACs Are Spending Their Money," *National Journal* (9 October 1982), p. 1730.
11. *Houston Chronicle*, 1 May 1983, Sec. 1, p. 25.
12. Jack W. Germond and Jules Witcover, "PACs Coming Between Officials and People Who Elected Them," *Houston Post*, 26 January 1983, p. B3; Richard E. Cohen, "Giving Till It Hurts: 1982 Campaign Prompts New Look at Financing Races," *National Journal* (18 December 1982); pp. 2144–53.
13. *Houston Post*, 28 December 1983, p. 12A.
14. Richard E. Cohen, "You Say You Want to Run for Congress? Step Right Up, 1982 May Be Your Year," *National Journal* (3 October, 1981); Cohen, "Giving Till It Hurts," pp. 1752–56.

SUGGESTED READINGS

BERRY, JEFFREY M. *Lobbying for the People.* Princeton: Princeton University Press, 1977.

CHAMBERS, WILLIAM, AND BURNHAM, WALTER DEAN. *The American Party System.* 2nd ed. New York: Oxford University Press, 1975.

CROTTY, WILLIAM J. *Political Reform and the American Experiment.* New York: Crowell, 1977.

GELB, JOYCE, AND PALLEY, MARIAN LIEF. *Tradition and Change in American Party Politics.* New York: Thomas Y. Crowell Co., 1975.

GREENSTEIN, FRED I. *The American Party System and the American People.* 2nd ed. Englewood Cliffs, N. J.: Prentice-Hall, 1970.

GREENWALD, CAROL S. *Group Power: Lobbying and Public Policy.* New York: Praeger, 1977.

KEEFE, WILLIAM J. *Parties, Politics, and Public Policy in America.* 3rd ed. New York: Holt, Rinehart & Winston, 1980.

LOWI, THEODORE J. *The End of Liberalism.* New York: W. W. Norton, 1969.

ORNSTEIN, NORMAN J., AND ELDER, SHIRLEY. *Interest Groups, Lobbying and Policymaking.* Washington, D.C.: Congressional Quarterly Press, 1978.

SUNDQUIST, JAMES L. *Dynamics of the Party System.* Washington, D.C.: Brookings Institution, 1973.

Part Three

THE POLICYMAKING STRUCTURES

In the next four chapters we will carefully describe the structures of government in America: the Congress in chapter 7, the presidency in chapter 8, the federal bureaucracy in chapter 9, and the judiciary in chapter 10. We will outline the constitutional structures of each branch of government, identify key decisionmakers, and discuss their qualifications, backgrounds, powers, duties, responsibilities, and limitations. All of this will be done, however, against a backdrop of policymaking and politics.

Do you remember the five stages of the policymaking process: agenda building, policy formulation, policy adoption, policy implementation, and policy evaluation? In this section of the book we will examine how these stages are incorporated in the institutions of American government and how each institution plays its part in the overall policy process. What role do the structures of government play in agenda building? How are policies formulated? How are policies formally adopted by Congress, by the courts,

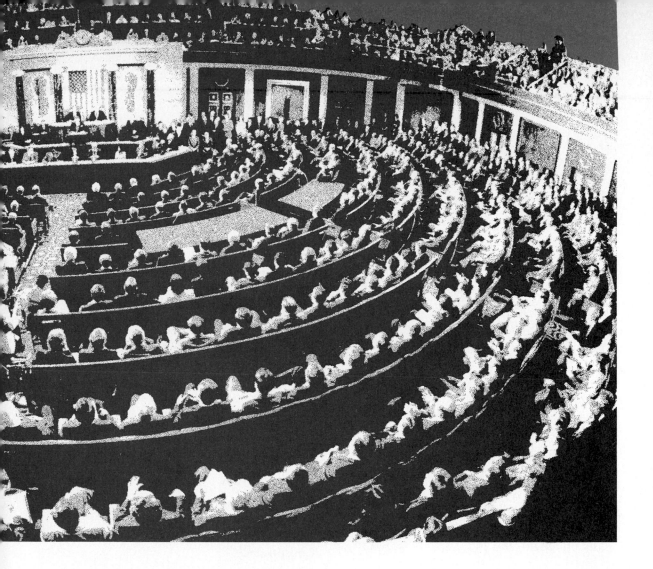

and by the executive branch? What governmental agencies implement which policies? How does that implementation affect the nature of the policies themselves? What role do the structures of government play in the evaluation of public policy?

We are also concerned with politics: who gets what, when, and how. Who benefits from policymaking in America and who pays the bill? Who has influence and who has none? Why are some policies adopted while others are not?

The theme of this section, therefore, is the theme of the book—policymaking and politics. Each chapter looks at a segment of the institutional structure of American government, asks how the structures are involved in policymaking, and looks at the factors involved in the governmental process. Focusing on politics and policymaking is more than simply describing the formal powers of the president or reciting "how a bill becomes a law," but such a focus is probably more revealing and important.

Chapter Seven

THE CONGRESS

PROFILE OF CONGRESS AND ITS MEMBERS

The Congress Today

Formal and Informal Qualifications

The Quality of the Job

THE ROLE OF CONGRESS

THE LEGISLATIVE PROCESS

Origin and Introduction

Committee Action

Floor Action

Conference Committee Action

Presidential Action

ANALYZING THE LEGISLATIVE PROCESS

Political Parties

Committees and Subcommittees

Interest Groups

Constituency

Ideology

Congressional Norms

Personalities

The White House

CONCLUSION: **CONGRESS AND PUBLIC POLICY**

The A-10 Thunderbolt II aircraft is not the most sophisticated weapon in America's defense arsenal. It is designed to provide close combat support for ground troops, though pilots sometimes joke that it's so slow it loses races to birds. Critics point out that it is also more expensive than its more sophisticated rival, the F-16 Fighting Falcon. Even top Pentagon officials agree, saying they need no more A-10s and want F-16s instead. Nonetheless, Congress included hundreds of millions of dollars in the 1982 federal budget for the purchase of *both* planes. The story behind this particular piece of public policy illustrates the dynamics of the policy process in Congress.

The key figure in the House of Representatives was Joseph Addabbo, a Democrat from Queens, New York, who chairs the Defense Subcommittee of the House Appropriations Committee. Like most representatives from New York, Addabbo is a strong supporter of the A-10, which is manufactured by Fairchild Republic Company at a plant on Long Island, New York. The plane had another powerful friend in the person of Speaker of the House Thomas P. "Tip" O'Neill; it seems the plane's engine is built in O'Neill's home state of Massachusetts. So when the appropriations bill passed the House, it included funding for the A-10.

The Senate treatment of the bill was a different story. The chairman of the Senate Armed Services Committee was John Tower, a Republican from Texas. The F-16 is made by General Dynamics Corporation in Fort Worth, Texas. When the appropriations bill cleared the Senate, it contained funding for the F-16 but no money for the A-10.

How was the impasse resolved? The House and Senate eventually reached a compromise acceptable to both sides: money was included for the purchase of some of both planes, the A-10 and the F-16.[1] Thus, in a time of soaring budget deficits and anxious concern about America's defense preparedness, the Congress appropriated millions of dollars for a plane the Pentagon didn't want.

Who's to blame for this example of public policymaking gone awry? The individual members of Congress involved, the Congress as a whole, or the congressional policymaking process itself? To understand how and why Congress works as it does, we need to begin with a brief profile of Congress and its members.

PROFILE OF CONGRESS AND ITS MEMBERS

Congress today is a product of both its constitutional/historical legacy and its immersion in the realities of contemporary politics. At the Constitutional Convention of 1787, a great debate took place over the organization of the legislative branch. One side wanted representatives to be chosen by popular vote with states represented on the basis of population. Delegates

The F-16.

from small states, however, worried that under such a plan the government would be dominated by large states. They preferred a system in which states would have equal representation, with the state legislatures selecting the representatives.

Eventually a compromise was reached, creating a bicameral Congress composed of a Senate and a House of Representatives. Each state would be represented by two senators chosen by its state legislature. Meanwhile, members of the House would be elected by direct popular vote, with the size of a state's delegation dependent on the state's population.

THE CONGRESS TODAY

Through the years, the formula has remained the same, except that senators are now selected by popular vote, thanks to the ratification of the Seventeenth Amendment in 1913. Today, fifty states mean one hundred senators, running at large to serve six-year staggered terms. One third must stand for reelection every two years.

By law, the size of the House is fixed at 435 members plus delegates from the District of Columbia, American Samoa, the Virgin Islands, and a resident commissioner from Puerto Rico. These "extra" members may not vote on the floor of the House, but they are allowed to join in debate. They also serve on committees where they may vote.

The House's 435 seats are apportioned among the states on the basis of population, with every state having at least one representative. Every ten years, after the census is taken, the House **reapportions** its seats to reflect population shifts. Rapidly growing states gain representation; more slowly growing states lose it. Members of the House run from single-member

The A-10.

districts for two-year terms, so the entire House is up for reelection every two years.

The actual task of drawing House district lines falls to the state legislatures, but they must work under certain restrictions. First, the United States Supreme Court has held in its famous "one person, one vote" rulings that the equal protection clause of the Fourteenth Amendment requires legislative districts to be nearly equal in population. For years, many state legislatures had neglected to **redistrict,** ignoring the dramatic population shifts that had occurred because of urbanization. As a result, congressional districts in urban areas were often far more heavily populated than rural districts. In Illinois, for example, one congressional district in Chicago had a population of 914,053 while another in rural southern Illinois had only 112,116 people.[2] Since the cases of *Baker* v. *Carr* (1962)[3] and *Wesberry* v. *Sanders* (1964),[4] this sort of population disparity is no longer constitutionally permissible. Consequently, after each census, state legislatures must redraw congressional district boundaries both to accommodate a gain or loss in representation and to account for population movement within the state.

The Court's reapportionment rulings, as they were called, have had some important effects on congressional representation and policy. In the late 1960s, when the rulings were first implemented, rural areas lost representation while the nation's big cities gained seats. Urban problems, such as housing, education, employment, transportation, and the like took center stage on the congressional agenda. The overall initial impact of reapportionment was to make Congress more liberal. The 1980 census showed, however, that during the 1970s America's population shifted away from the generally liberal inner cities to the more conservative suburbs and surrounding metropolitan areas. This time reapportionment meant fewer representatives from constituencies who demand big government and more from constituents who are wary of it. In the 1980s, therefore, Congress will likely have a more conservative focus.[5] (See the PERSPECTIVE on page 181.)

Second, state legislatures in areas with histories of voter discrimination, particularly in the South and Southwest, are required by the federal Voting Rights Act to safeguard the voting rights of blacks and non-English-speaking minorities, such as Hispanics. On the one hand, state legislatures must be careful not to dilute minority voting strength by spreading minority voters among several white-dominated districts. On the other hand, state legislatures cannot go so far as to pack minorities into a single district in order to reduce their influence in other districts.

FORMAL AND INFORMAL QUALIFICATIONS

The United States Constitution requires that members of the House be at least twenty-five years old, American citizens for at least seven years, and residents of the state in which their district is located. Senators must be thirty, citizens for nine years, and residents of the state they represent. Informally, however, the voters tend to elect people to Congress who are white, middle-class, small-town in origin, middle-age, and male. Most come from a legal or business background.

Because of the reapportionment ruling, the Voting Rights Act, and changing social mores, the "good old boy" network has been breaking down a bit in recent years. In 1983, Congress included more blacks, Hispanics, and women than ever before. The Black Congressional Caucus in the House numbered twenty-one members, including the nonvoting delegate from the District of Columbia. There were also twenty-one women and eleven Hispanics in the House. Although no blacks or Hispanics served in the Senate in 1983, there were two women senators, Nancy Landon Kassebaum from Kansas and Paula Hawkins from Florida, both Republicans. What's more, the body as a whole included more Catholics (142) than at any time in its history. Nevertheless, women, blacks, Hispanics, and other minority groups remained underrepresented in Congress.

THE QUALITY OF THE JOB

How good a job is it being a member of Congress? In 1984, each member of the House and Senate earned $72,200 in salary. House members were allowed to supplement their salaries up to 30 percent from other earned income and from honoraria received for speeches and appearances. Senators, meanwhile, were limited to a 30-percent cap on honoraria only. In addition to their earnings, members of Congress enjoy quite a few "perks" that go with the office, including enough expense money to take at least

Republican Senator Nancy Landon Kassebaum of Kansas. Senator Kassebaum is one of two women senators to serve in the 1984 Congress. The other is Senator Paula Hawkins of Florida, also a Republican.

Perspective
POLITICS AND THE 1980 CENSUS

For some, the census may be nothing more meaningful than a nosy intrusion into one's private affairs, but to political leaders it's nothing less than the raw material of political power. The 1980 census revealed a dramatic shift in America's population from the big cities of the Northeast and Midwest to the suburbs of the South and West. In political terms, this translated into a net shift of sixteen House seats from the frostbelt to the sunbelt. As Figure 7.1 shows, the big losers were the states of New York (−5), Pennsylvania (−2), Ohio (−2), and Illinois (−2). Florida (+4), Texas (+3), and Califor-

nia (+2) were the big winners.

It also looked like a bonanza for the Republican party, at least at first. Most of the areas losing population were Democratic strongholds, and many of the rapidly growing districts were areas of Republican strength. But a funny thing happened on the way to the ballot box. Thanks to a little creative map drawing by Democratically controlled legislatures, the Republican gains from reapportionment failed to materialize. Cartography can have its political side—there's even a word for it: **gerrymandering.** When the smoke cleared from the 1982

elections, the effect of reapportionment on the party balance in Congress was slight and, if anything, probably benefitted the Democrats.[1]

Although the shift of sixteen seats from the frostbelt to the sunbelt may have had little effect on the party balance in Congress, one cannot dismiss its importance for policy. Subtract sixteen seats from one region and add them to the other and that's a net swing of thirty-two votes. On policy issues involving regional differences, such as energy, that could have a major impact.

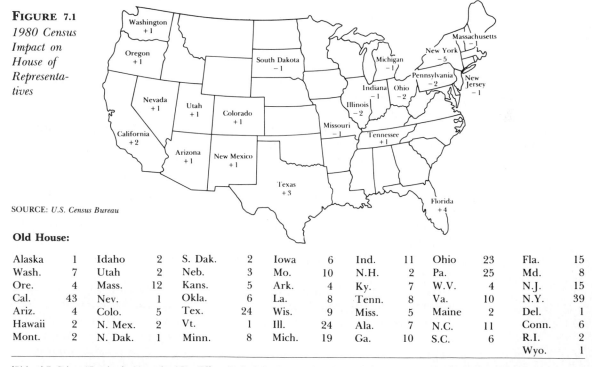

FIGURE 7.1
1980 Census Impact on House of Representatives

SOURCE: *U.S. Census Bureau*

Old House:

Alaska	1	Idaho	2	S. Dak.	2	Iowa	6	Ind.	11	Ohio	23	Fla.	15
Wash.	7	Utah	2	Neb.	3	Mo.	10	N.H.	2	Pa.	25	Md.	8
Ore.	4	Mass.	12	Kans.	5	Ark.	4	Ky.	7	W.V.	4	N.J.	15
Cal.	43	Nev.	1	Okla.	6	La.	8	Tenn.	8	Va.	10	N.Y.	39
Ariz.	4	Colo.	5	Tex.	24	Wis.	9	Miss.	5	Maine	2	Del.	1
Hawaii	2	N. Mex.	2	Vt.	1	Ill.	24	Ala.	7	N.C.	11	Conn.	6
Mont.	2	N. Dak.	1	Minn.	8	Mich.	19	Ga.	10	S.C.	6	R.I.	2
												Wyo.	1

[1]Richard E. Cohen, "Despite the Mapmakers' Best Efforts, Redistricting Won't Help Either Party," *National Journal* (1 May 1982), pp. 752–56.

thirty-two trips home every year; money to hire a personal staff (about $270,000); free postage for official business (franking privileges); free furniture, pictures, and potted plants for the office; access to cut-rate barber shops, beauty salons, and restaurants; the use of a gymnasium and a health clinic; and a comfortable pension.[6]

Congressional salaries, while more than adequate by most standards, are less than those of upper-level corporate executives and probably less than most senators and representatives could make in private business or in their legal practices. Also, Washington is an expensive town, and most members of Congress must maintain two residences—one back home and one in Washington.

As for status and prestige, it's certainly an ego-builder to be addressed as *senator* or *representative,* but the job has its down side as well. Being a politician isn't all that reputable in many people's eyes. One recent poll found that no more than 13 percent of those surveyed have "a great deal of confidence" in those running Congress.[7] Another poll discovered that in terms of "honesty and ethical standards," Americans rank politicians last among the members of twenty-four occupations, lower than realtors, used-car salespeople, and insurance agents.[8]

There are also enormous pressures that come with the office, many of which involve the nearly constant need to campaign for reelection. Incumbents have an advantage, of course, but probably not as much as they once did. For most of the 1970s, about 90 percent of House members and three fourths of Senate incumbents seeking reelection were successful. In 1980, however, these proportions declined to 79 percent and 55 percent. That's not too bad a batting average, of course, but there are fewer "safe seats" these days, seats that incumbents can count on winning in walkaway elections. As Professor Thomas Mann points out, most members of Congress no longer *feel* safe, especially from the challenge of a well-financed opponent. Almost everyone is running scared; consequently, members devote more time and energy to campaign fundraising and weekend trips back home to get in a little politicking.[9]

Other pressures come from the job, from constituents, from the media, and from interest groups. More subcommittees exist now than fifteen years ago, and that means more meetings. Also, individual constituents more frequently ask their representatives for assistance in dealing with the federal bureaucracy. This takes members' time as well. One recent study revealed that the average member of Congress works more than eleven hours a day.[10]

All of this has led to a high turnover in the membership of Congress. It was once said of members of Congress that few died and none retired. Now that's no longer true. Some have been defeated for reelection, but many others—burned out, broke, or frustrated—have simply chosen not to run again.[11] In 1984, for example, three of Congress' most able men chose retirement over another reelection bid—Senate Majority Leader Howard Baker, Senate Armed Services Committee Chairman John Tower, and Congressman Barber Conable, the senior Republican on the House Ways and Means Committee. All three were relatively young and in apparent good health. Turnover has opened the door for younger members to assume a greater role in the legislative process. A price has been paid, however, in the loss of talent and experience.

THE ROLE OF CONGRESS

The Constitution outlines the formal duties of Congress: to declare war, to propose constitutional amendments, to impeach and remove the president. The Senate, by two-thirds vote, is empowered to ratify treaties and, by majority vote, to confirm or reject certain presidential appointments. But by far the most prominent policymaking activity of Congress is *legislating*.

When the founders organized America's government, they expected Congress to be the dominant branch. In the nineteenth and early twentieth centuries, they were right; Congress was active, assertive, innovative. Writing in the 1880s, Woodrow Wilson, a political-science graduate student who later made good, argued in his doctoral thesis that Congress was the dominant branch of government.[12]

Since 1932, however, innovative policy programs have generally come from the White House rather than from Capitol Hill. First we had the New Deal of Franklin Roosevelt, then Truman's Fair Deal. Kennedy proposed the New Frontier, Lyndon Johnson the Great Society. In the 1980s we have "Reaganomics." Presidents have proposed; the Congress disposed. The only major exception to the pattern came in the 1950s when President Eisenhower was content to allow Congress to assume the policymaking lead and Congress, under the leadership of Speaker of the House Sam Rayburn and Senate Majority Leader Lyndon Johnson, was willing to take it. At other times, however, Congress has acted only after being presented with policy proposals by the president and then nudged along. Sometimes the Congress was recalcitrant, rejecting or delaying the president's program, but seldom was it innovative, proposing programs of its own.

In the late 1960s and early '70s, Congress hit bottom; its constitutional role in the policy process had seemingly been taken over by the White House. For all practical purposes, it had lost the power to declare war or control the budget process. The Korean war and then the Vietnam war were fought without congressional declarations of war: they were waged instead by the president, using his authority as commander in chief. What's more, much of the Vietnam war was conducted in secret, from the people and from Congress. Congress felt deceived, left out, powerless. Similarly, in the early 1970s, President Nixon, claiming extraordinary executive powers, began "impounding" funds; that is, refusing to spend money duly appropriated by Congress. He even went so far as to use impoundment to eliminate programs he opposed.

The Vietnam war was lost, Nixon met his Watergate, and Congress rebounded. The latter part of the 1970s was a season of reform as Congress struggled to reestablish itself as an equal branch of government. First, Congress passed legislation to reassert itself in relation to the president. In 1973, it passed the War Powers Act (over Richard Nixon's veto) restricting the president's power to wage an undeclared war without Congress' authorization. In 1974 and 1976, it amended the Foreign Military Sales Act to give Congress the power to veto arms sales abroad. Both of these measures included provisions known as the **legislative veto,** the idea that Congress, or one house of Congress, or even a committee could vote to reject or veto a program or an action by the executive branch. The Foreign Military Sales Act, for example, allowed Congress to void arms sales if both houses so voted. In 1983, however, in the case of *Immigration and Naturalization Service* v. *Chadha,* the United States Supreme Court ruled that legislative-veto provisions such as those found in the War Powers Act (see the PERSPECTIVE on page 185), the Foreign Military Sales Act, and more than one hundred other laws, are unconstitutional.[13]

Congress passed other measures to limit executive authority. The Budget and Impoundment Control Act was enacted in 1974 to control the president's ability to impound appropriated funds and to give Congress more power over the budgetary process. Then, in 1976, Congress passed the National Emergencies Act, limiting the president's power to declare a national emergency and to exercise extraordinary powers.[14]

Congress also moved to improve its own ability to function as an active part of the policymaking process. In 1973, the Office of Technology Assistance was created to provide expertise on policy issues related to science and technology. The House Information Services and the Congressional Research Service were upgraded better to help members with data gathering, research, and computer operations. At the same time, Congress increased the staff size for committees and individual members and provided for permanent staffing for subcommittees. By the early 1980s, Congress' staff had grown to some 30,000 people compared to 7000 in 1960. Congress also expanded the functions of the General Accounting Office (GAO) beyond its traditional accounting role to include the review and evaluation of executive branch programs already in operation.

Finally, Congress reformed itself to make its own procedures more open and democratic. In the middle 1970s, standing committee and subcommittee proceedings were made fully open, and voting procedures were changed to ensure more roll-call votes. In 1975, the Democratic party decided to elect committee chairmen and appropriations-subcommittee chairmen by a secret ballot vote of all party members. The Republicans decided to choose committee chairs by a vote of committee members. Also, in a series of moves sometimes called the "subcommittee bill of rights," Congress moved in the '70s to give subcommittees more authority over legislation and more independence from control by the committee chairmen.[15]

The result of all this reform has been a more assertive Congress. As Richard Nixon, Gerald Ford, and Jimmy Carter learned, Congress is less willing to be led, more willing to defeat presidential initiatives, and, occasionally, more willing to override presidential vetoes. For the most part, however, the reassertion of Congress has been reactive. Congress has been feeling its oats, all right, but primarily to thwart presidential initiatives, not to offer policy proposals of its own. Congress has become a better check and balance, but it still has not assumed the role of policy initiator.

In fact, Congress' effectiveness as a policymaking institution is under

Perspective
THE WAR POWERS ACT

Congress passed the War Powers Act in 1973 in direct response to what it saw as presidential infringement on its constitutional powers to declare war. First, the act required the president to consult with Congress "in every possible instance" before introducing American forces into situations where hostilities would be likely. Second, the president was also required to make detailed, periodic reports on the necessity and scope of the operation. Third, the act declared that American forces must be withdrawn after sixty days of the first reports of fighting (with a thirty-day grace period to ensure safe withdrawal), unless Congress declares war or specifically authorizes their presence. Finally, the War Powers Act gave Congress the power to order the withdrawal of American forces by majority vote of both parties at any time, even before the sixty-day period had expired.

From the beginning, the War Powers Act was controversial. President Nixon called it an unconstitutional challenge to his powers as commander in chief of the armed forces and vetoed it. Congress promptly overrode the veto. Although questions about the act's constitutionality have continued, no direct challenge has yet reached the Supreme Court for a ruling. In the *Chadha* case in 1983, however, the Court invalidated legislative-veto provisions such as the one giving Congress authority to order the withdrawal of forces short of the sixty-day limit. However, the ruling apparently left the rest of the War Powers Act untouched.

In general, presidents have chafed under the restrictions imposed by the War Powers Act and have sought ways to circumvent them. Jimmy Carter, for example, chose not to consult congressional leaders before ordering the ill-fated hostage-

rescue mission in Iran. Rescue missions aren't combat situations, he said. President Reagan argued that the presence of American troops in Lebanon wasn't affected by the War Powers Act since they weren't in combat. After casualties were taken in Lebanon, however, Reagan was forced to compromise. The War Powers Act was invoked in the fall of 1983, and Congress voted to allow the marines to stay up to eighteen months.

The War Powers Act raises some important policy questions. What roles should Congress and the president play in making American policy? Is Congress capable of playing a constructive role in military policy abroad or is its best role that of a check and balance on presidential action? If Congress is to be a check on the president, is the War Powers Act an effective instrument for that purpose?

fire. In the eyes of many critics and much of the general public, Congress is an archaic institution. It is slow, cumbersome, and outdated. To be sure, the framers of the Constitution never intended the wheels of Congress to grind quickly. Separation of powers, bicameralism, and the system of checks and balances were designed to ensure a slow, deliberate legislative process.

Today, however, many critics contend that Congress' wheels are not only slow, but their product is coarse. There was a time when Congress finished its work by June or earlier. Now Congress frequently remains in session through November or early December. By June, it may not yet have voted on any major legislation. Major pieces of legislation are often delayed or postponed indefinitely. The budget is almost never approved in time for the start of a new fiscal year. When Congress eventually does act, its product reflects the desires of an ever growing array of special-interest groups rather than the public interest. Bills that finally pass, such as the 1977 energy bill or the 1981 tax-cut bill, are not just compromises, they are often "Christmas tree" bills, jerryrigged to offer a plum to every interest group in sight. Witness the story of the A-10 Thunderbolt II.

THE LEGISLATIVE PROCESS

The legislative process is shaped by the Constitution and molded and refined by practice and politics. It's slow, cautious, laborious, and byzantine, reflecting some of the best aspects of American politics, but also some of the worst. The process begins when a bill is introduced, and proceeds as shown in Figure 7.2.

ORIGIN AND INTRODUCTION

Only members of Congress may actually introduce a bill, but the origins of the policy proposals contained in the measure may be many and varied. Many bills are introduced at the urging of constituents to resolve personal problems with the government, such as immigration status. Interest-group representatives initiate many legislative proposals. Frequently, officials from state and local government or from federal agencies request members of Congress to propose legislation as well. And, of course, senators and representatives generally put their own stamp on the legislation they introduce. In modern times, however, the most significant source of major legislation has been the president. In this case, members of the White House staff or executive-department officials draft a bill embodying the president's program. The president then invites sympathetic members of Congress to introduce the measure.

With one exception, bills can be introduced first in either the House or the Senate or in both chambers simultaneously. That exception involves tax bills, which the Constitution says must originate in the House. By custom, appropriations bills usually begin in the House as well. All bills, however, must pass both chambers in order to pass Congress.

COMMITTEE ACTION

Committees are an important part of the legislative process. First, they allow the members to split up the work. In each session, some 20,000 bills are introduced. It would be impossible for each member even to read that many; so Congress is divided into committees. As you can see from Table 7.1, there are twenty-two **standing committees** in the House and sixteen in the Senate. These are permanent committees, but there are also **special** or **select committees** that are established for a limited period only. There are three of these in the Senate and four in the House. Congress also has four **joint committees** that include members from both houses. Committees are organized on the basis of substantive area—for example, foreign relations, agriculture, judiciary, or veterans' affairs. Consequently, members have the opportunity and are expected to specialize in one or two policy areas.

House	Senate
Agriculture	Agriculture, Nutrition, and Forestry
Appropriations	Appropriations
Armed Services	Armed Services
Banking, Finance, and Urban Affairs	Banking, Housing, and Urban Affairs
Budget	Budget
District of Columbia	Commerce, Science, and Transportation
Education and Labor	Energy and Natural Resources
Energy and Commerce	Environment and Public Works
Foreign Affairs	Finance
Government Operations	Foreign Relations
House Administration	Government Affairs
Interior and Insular Affairs	Judiciary
Judiciary	Labor and Human Resources
Merchant Marine and Fisheries	Rules and Administration
Post Office and Civil Service	Small Business
Public Works	Veterans' Affairs
Rules	
Science and Technology	
Small Business	
Standards of Official Conduct	
Veterans' Affairs	
Ways and Means	

TABLE 7.1
Standing Committees in the House and Senate, 1983

SOURCE: *Congressional Directory* 1983–84 (Washington, D.C.: U.S. Government Printing Office, 1983).

FIGURE 7.2 *How a Bill Becomes Law*

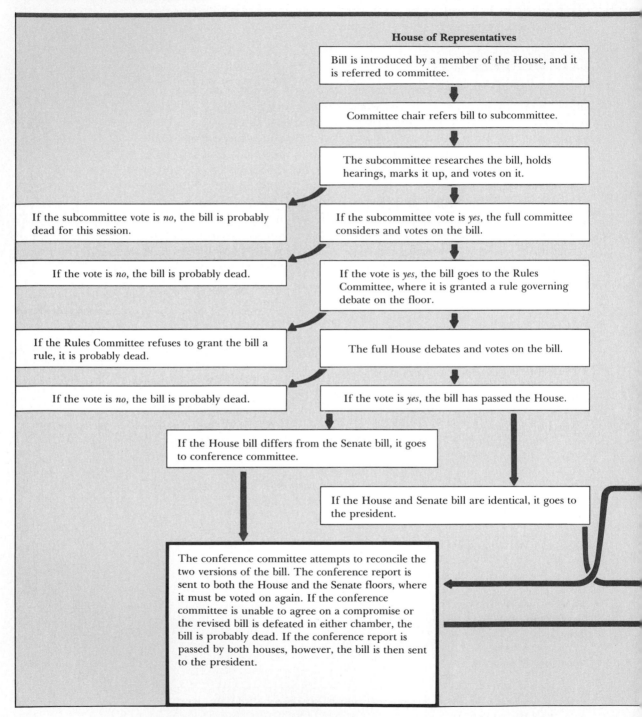

188

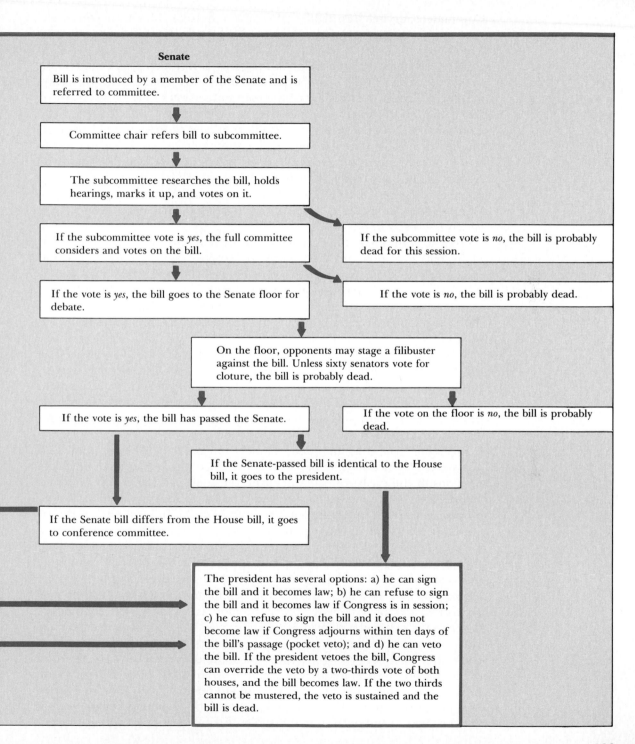

Senate

Bill is introduced by a member of the Senate and is referred to committee.

Committee chair refers bill to subcommittee.

The subcommittee researches the bill, holds hearings, marks it up, and votes on it.

If the subcommittee vote is *yes*, the full committee considers and votes on the bill.

If the subcommittee vote is *no*, the bill is probably dead for this session.

If the vote is *yes*, the bill goes to the Senate floor for debate.

If the vote is *no*, the bill is probably dead.

On the floor, opponents may stage a filibuster against the bill. Unless sixty senators vote for cloture, the bill is probably dead.

If the vote is *yes*, the bill has passed the Senate.

If the vote on the floor is *no*, the bill is probably dead.

If the Senate-passed bill is identical to the House bill, it goes to the president.

If the Senate bill differs from the House bill, it goes to conference committee.

The president has several options: a) he can sign the bill and it becomes law; b) he can refuse to sign the bill and it becomes law if Congress is in session; c) he can refuse to sign the bill and it does not become law if Congress adjourns within ten days of the bill's passage (pocket veto); and d) he can veto the bill. If the president vetoes the bill, Congress can override the veto by a two-thirds vote of both houses, and the bill becomes law. If the two thirds cannot be mustered, the veto is sustained and the bill is dead.

Committees, in turn, are divided into subcommittees. The A-10, you recall, was considered by the Defense Subcommittee of the House Appropriations Committee.

Once a bill is introduced, it is assigned a number and sent by the presiding officer of the chamber to a committee or committees for examination. No major reshuffling of the committee system has occurred since 1946, and jurisdictions sometimes overlap. New issues such as energy, the environment, and consumer protection don't easily fit in the old pattern, though this problem may be solved by sending bills to two or more committees.[16] That makes the process repetitive, complicated, and wasteful of resources; still, it's easier than refereeing a jurisdictional dispute among members of Congress jealous to preserve their entrenched powers. Reforming the system of committee jurisdictions is an idea whose time has not yet come to Congress.

Once in committee, the chairman refers the bill to a subcommittee. Too many bills are introduced for each to receive close scrutiny, hence the subcommittee chair may exercise some discretion. In practice, subcommittee chairmen give most attention to bills they favor personally, bills that enjoy broad support in the Congress as a whole, and measures pushed by the White House. Bills without much support or that are opposed by the subcommittee chair usually lose out.

Subcommittees and committees do the detailed work of Congress. The subcommittee chairman will ask the subcommittee's professional staff to prepare a report on the bill's merits. Perhaps a hearing will be scheduled, particularly if it's a major piece of legislation. The purpose of the hearing is to allow the measure's supporters and opponents the opportunity to present their cases.

Eventually, the subcommittee will meet to "mark up" the bill; that is, to go over it line by line. The members may revise, rewrite, amend, or delete portions of the measure. In most cases, the final product will represent a compromise. Once the bill has been marked up, the subcommittee will vote on whether or not to recommend its passage to the full committee. Defeat at this point usually means the bill is dead.

If the bill clears the subcommittee, it is sent to the full committee. When the subcommittee is fairly united in support of a bill, the full committee may vote with little debate. If the measure is controversial, however, the arguments may spill over into the full committee. New amendments may be added; old provisions dropped. In most cases, however, committees defer to the judgment of their subcommittees. For one thing, the political balance on subcommittees often mirrors that of the full committee. Also, committee members recognize that subcommittee members have acted on the basis of more complete information than they have before them. Committee members want to respect the judgment of subcommittee members just as they hope their own judgment will be respected when the roles are reversed. If the full committee tables the bill (that is, postpones consideration to some later date) or votes the measure down, the bill is probably dead, at least for this session. If the bill is passed, however, it is sent to the floor for consideration by the entire House or Senate.

FLOOR ACTION

Unless a bill is quite noncontroversial, it will be debated on the floor of the House and Senate before a vote is taken. In the Senate, scheduling is the responsibility of the head of the majority political party in the chamber, the **majority leader.** Scheduling can be a matter of time and convenience, but it can have its political side as well. Sometimes delay is a wise course, if, for example, some of the legislators you were counting on are out of town or wavering. On the other hand, if you're confident your side can win now, you may wish to rush to a vote before anything happens to upset the balance.

The scheduling of a bill in the Senate is done by the majority leader. In 1984, the responsibility fell on the shoulders of Republican Senator Howard Baker of Tennessee.

Once a bill passes committee in the House, it is sent to the Rules Committee, which must "grant a rule" for the bill before it can go to the floor. This means the committee sets a time limit on debate and specifies whether or not amendments will be considered and if so, which amendments. For example, the Rules Committee might grant a rule limiting debate to twenty hours: ten for proponents, ten for opponents, and two hours on each amendment. Amendments would be limited to the three specific amendments first proposed in the original committee. After a bill has been granted a rule, the Speaker of the House and the House majority leader will consult on scheduling a time for floor debate.

On the surface, the Rules Committee fulfills the functions of a doorkeeper, but in practice it uses its power to accomplish subtle and not-so-subtle political goals. Back in the 1950s, the committee was controlled by a conservative coalition of Republicans and southern Democrats who used the committee to kill liberal legislation they opposed; they simply refused to grant rules to liberal bills. Then, in 1961, President John Kennedy succeeded in getting the committee membership enlarged so that the party leadership could appoint additional Democrats who would be loyal to the president's program. Since then, the majority-party leadership has been careful to maintain a loyalist majority on the committee.

Now it is the majority-party leadership that can use the Rules Committee to its own advantage. In 1977, President Carter proposed legislation to deal with the energy crisis. In the House, the energy bill was sent to the Ways and Means Committee chaired by Al Ullman, an Oregon Democrat generally sympathetic to the bill. When the bill passed committee it was fairly near the president's original proposal. The Rules Committee then granted a rule allowing no amendments; House members could either take it or leave it, and they took it. Otherwise, the House would almost certainly have changed the bill dramatically.

Congress has a reputation as one of the great debating bodies of the world, but it's unusual for debates to sway many votes. Tourists are often shocked at how poorly attended floor debates sometimes are and at how many of the members present may not be paying much attention. The real work of Congress, however, doesn't take place on the floor, but in committee and subcommittee, in congressional offices, in the cloakroom, and elsewhere around the capitol. Debates allow members to read into the record the case for and against a bill and to justify their own position to their constituents. They are done more to inform the world outside the halls of Congress than to sway opinion within.

In the Senate, though, debate can become a weapon for defeating legislation. Unlike the House, there is no set limit on the amount of time a senator or the Senate as a whole can spend discussing a bill. Consequently, a bill's opponents may attempt to defeat a measure by talking it to death, a **filibuster.** No vote can be taken until the debate is over; the idea is to prolong debate until the bill's supporters give up. There is a procedure for shutting off debate and ending the filibuster; it's called **cloture,** but it takes sixty votes to put into effect.

The filibuster is a powerful weapon. With it, a minority of senators can almost surely delay a bill, possibly defeat it, and probably force a compromise with its backers. It is not surprising, then, that the filibuster has more critics than defenders. Yet the same folks aren't always on the same sides on the filibuster issue. During the 1950s and '60s, conservatives sometimes employed the filibuster to defeat civil-rights bills, and liberals deplored the action. In the early 1980s, however, the sides sometimes reversed as liberals occasionally turned to the filibuster against conservative-backed legislation, such as measures designed to halt court-ordered busing for purposes of school desegregation.

CONFERENCE COMMITTEE ACTION

A bill has not passed Congress until it has cleared both houses in identical form. By the time a measure has wound its way through the legislative labyrinth, it has probably changed from the original. It's also likely that the bills finally passed by each house will differ. If the differences are slight, one house or the other may reconcile the differences by voting to accept the other's changes. For major legislation, however, the differences are likely to be more substantial and not so easily resolved. Then, a **conference committee** is formed to negotiate a compromise.

Conference-committee members, or conferees, are appointed by the leadership of each house, and usually include the chairman and senior members of the standing committee that originally considered the bill, along with other interested members. Once a compromise has been agreed upon by a majority of each house's conferees, the revised bill, or the *conference report,* is sent back for more debate. If both houses accept the compromise, the bill has passed the Congress and goes to the president.

PRESIDENTIAL ACTION

The Constitution gives the president several options in dealing with a bill that has passed Congress. He may sign it: the bill becomes law. If he doesn't sign it, it becomes law anyway after ten days elapse, unless Congress is no longer in session. If Congress has adjourned, the bill dies. This is known as the **pocket veto.** In practice, these last two options are seldom used by modern presidents. For one thing, Congress stays in session nearly year-round now, so there are few opportunities for the pocket veto. More importantly, however, image-conscious contemporary presidents seem to believe it appears more decisive either to sign a bill or to veto it outright. When the president vetoes a bill, he returns it to Congress along with his objections. Congress can override the veto by a two-thirds vote of the House and Senate; the bill then becomes a law. If either house falls short of two thirds, however, the president's veto is sustained and the measure has failed.

ANALYZING THE LEGISLATIVE PROCESS

Step by step, that's how "a bill becomes a law," but it is not the whole story of the legislative process or of Congress' role in public policymaking. We aren't yet ready to answer our questions about the A-10 Thunderbolt. We still must analyze several of the factors affecting the process.

POLITICAL PARTIES

Since the 1930s, the Democratic party has controlled Congress most of the time. They have been in the majority; the Republicans in the minority. There have been exceptions, of course. In the 1947–48 and 1953–54 sessions, the GOP enjoyed majorities in both the House and Senate. Also, in 1980, the Republicans won control of the Senate although the Democrats continued to hold a majority in the House. After the 1982 elections, the party balance in the Senate was 54 Republicans to 46 Democrats; in the House it was 269 Democrats to 166 Republicans.

To control the House or the Senate means to control the flow of business on the floor. The Constitution designates the vice-president as the Senate's presiding officer, but in practice his role is not particularly important. He is regarded as an outsider and seldom attends unless it appears his vote may be needed to break a tie. In his absence, the Constitution says the Senate **president pro tempore** presides. He or she is selected by vote of the Senate as a whole, but customarily the post goes to the senator from the majority party with the longest tenure or seniority in the chamber. In practice, the job of president pro tempore is more honorary than substantive; the rather tedious chore of presiding is left to junior members of the majority party.

Real power on the floor of the Senate and the House is in the hands of the political-party organizations. At the beginning of each session, the Republican and Democratic members of each chamber *caucus,* or meet separately, to select leaders. In the Senate, the head of the majority party is called the majority leader. The majority leader's first assistant is called the **majority whip.** Meanwhile, the minority party is led by the **minority leader** and a **minority whip.** Each party will also elect a policy committee to consider party positions on legislation and another committee to appoint party members to standing committees.

The majority leader's power stems from the ability to control scheduling on the floor of the Senate, the power to appoint conference-committee members, and a role as a communications link among party members in the Senate and, if the majority leader's party controls the White House, between the president and the majority party in the Senate. No one else is in a better position to advise the president about his program's prospects in the Senate or to inform fellow senators about the wishes of the chief executive. At times, the majority leader is an adviser to the president on legislative strategy, a spokesperson for the president's program, and a field general supporting the president's position.

The minority leader plays a similar role with one major difference: his party is in the minority. He can serve as a spokesperson for his party in the Senate and, if his party holds the presidency, he can enjoy an important role as a communications liaison and adviser to the White House.

In the House of Representatives, the Speaker is the presiding officer. He is formally elected by the entire membership of the House, but since party members always vote for their party's candidate, the Speaker is invariably the leader of the majority party. As in the Senate, the Democratic and Republican members of the House caucus at the beginning of each session to choose leaders. The majority party selects its leader, who will become the Speaker of the House. In the House, it is the *second*-ranking figure in the majority party who is called the majority leader. There is also a majority whip and assistant whips. Meanwhile, the minority party chooses a minority leader, a minority whip, and assistant whips.

The powers of the House leadership are similar to those of the Senate leadership, except that presiding is more important in the House. The House is larger than the Senate, of course, so it has to have stricter rules of procedure. As the presiding officer, the Speaker can have an impact on policy in the House by making rulings on such matters as whether a motion is in order and on other parliamentary questions.

The people elected to party-leadership posts in the House and Senate are generally moderates who have shown a capacity for getting along with the different segments of the party. Experience is important, but party leaders aren't usually the members with the most seniority. Qualities such as even temperament, knowledge of the rules, ability to compromise, and a reputation for fairness are more important. In the Congress elected in

1980, for example, both the Republican minority leader of the House, Robert Michel of Illinois, and Howard Baker of Tennessee, the majority leader in the Senate, captured their party's leadership posts despite possessing somewhat less conservative outlooks than the majority of their colleagues. Michel won because of his reputation for hard work and his knowledge of the rules. Baker won because of his reputation for fairness and generosity, and his ability as a legislator.

Historically, the congressional party leadership has played a key role in America's public-policy process. Party leaders such as Speaker of the House Sam Rayburn and Senate Majority Leader Lyndon Johnson, for example, were expert at maneuvering important legislation through the legislative maze. Rayburn and Johnson understood the Congress—its rules, procedures, and personalities—and their impact on public policy was considerable.

Today, party leaders in Congress may not measure up to the leadership standard set by Rayburn and Johnson. It would be difficult for them to do so, partly because members of Congress are simply less willing to be led. Of course, there never has been true party discipline in Congress. All Democrats or all Republicans have never consistently voted as a bloc in support of their party's position. Still, calls for party unity and party loyalty once meant much more than they do now.

Political party is now less important for the electorate, less important in campaigns, and, consequently, less important in Congress. As journalist Neil McNeil puts it, the new members of Congress have gotten there pretty much on their own, pushing and arguing their own pet issues, not the party's.

> *They tend to come from outside the political parties, without working their way up through the ranks. They tend to owe nothing to political-party organizations beyond the convenience of a political label necessary for nomination. They certainly have no emotional commitment to a party organization—including the party organization in Congress. This has bred in them an extraordinary political independence that has played havoc in Washington . . . .*[17]

Strong, disciplined political parties can play an important role in the policymaking process. They can join with a president of their own party to formulate policies and see them enacted. They can present alternatives to the policies of a president from the other party. In short, strong, disciplined parties can get things done.

Today, however, the parties in Congress are weaker than at any time in this century. There is little party loyalty, and the party leadership enjoys few tools for disciplining wayward members. So members go their own way, following their own private agenda; the parties offer a weakened counterbalance to interest-group influence. Congress accomplishes less, and more slowly.

At a House subcommittee hearing on aid to El Salvador, a Defense Department official hands a document to a member of the State Department. Sitting between them, an assistant secretary of state provides testimony to interested legislators.

COMMITTEES AND SUBCOMMITTEES

To understand Congress one must understand the committee system, because that's where the real, detailed work of the legislative process takes place. When senators and representatives are first elected to Congress, they will be named to serve on one or more committees by the Republican party's Committee on Committees or the Democrats' Steering Committee, depending on the members' party label. Some assignments are better than others, of course. Committees that deal with taxes and spending have no trouble finding volunteers. These committees are Appropriations, Budget, and Finance in the Senate; Appropriations, Budget, and Ways and Means in the House. Freshman lawmakers probably won't rate such coveted assignments, but other committees can be attractive as well. A representative from farmbelt Iowa, for example, would be more interested in the Agriculture Committee than would a representative from Brooklyn. A senator from Texas might value service on the Energy and Natural Resources Committee more than one from Rhode Island. An important policy consequence of this process is that many committees and subcommittees are composed of members whose constituents are directly affected by the committee's work. Agricultural committees are populated by members from farm areas while representatives from coastal districts flock to the Merchant Marine and Fisheries Committee.

If members of Congress are unhappy with a committee assignment, they may request a transfer when openings occur on other, preferred committees. Switching committees has its drawbacks, however. Influence on a committee is closely related to **seniority** on that committee. If members change committees, they must start over on the seniority ladder of the new committee. This works to prevent very much committee-assignment reshuffling, although it's not unusual for a member to request a transfer to one of the really choice committees.

Power on congressional committees is based on political-party affiliation, seniority, and chairmanship. The party balance on each committee reflects the party balance in the chamber as a whole. If the Democrats have a majority in the House, they will enjoy a majority on every committee and subcommittee, and every committee and subcommittee chairman will be a

Democrat. After the 1980 election, for example, the Democrats controlled the House, the Republicans the Senate. The House Judiciary Committee had twenty-eight members—sixteen Democrats and twelve Republicans. It was chaired by Peter Rodino, a New Jersey Democrat. The Senate Foreign Relations Committee, however, had seventeen members—nine Republicans and eight Democrats, and its chairman was a Republican, Charles Percy from Illinois.

Seniority is another key factor on committees. The longer one's tenure, the greater one's influence. Committee and subcommittee chairmen are no longer selected solely on the basis of their seniority, but seniority remains probably the single most important factor in the selection process. Even the seating arrangement at committee meetings reflects seniority as members are ranked from greatest seniority at the center of the horseshoe-shaped table to least seniority at the end.

The most powerful individuals on a committee are its chairman and the subcommittee chairmen. Before the reforms of the 1970s, committee chairmen had the power to run their committees like personal fiefdoms, and some did just that. They decided which bills would get a hearing, who would testify at the hearing, when it would be held, and whether it would be open to the public. Committee chairmen controlled subcommittees by appointing their chairs and their members and by deciding what bills to refer to them. Consequently, committee chairmen had the power to push along bills they favored while acting as one-person logjams to block bills they opposed.

Then came the reforms of the 1970s. First, the procedures for selecting committee chairmen were changed. Before, the majority-party member with the most seniority was automatically the chair. In the early '70s, however, the Democrats decided to let the whole Democratic caucus select Democratic committee chairmen by secret ballot. The Republicans gave that responsibility to their party members on each committee. Most of the time since then, the member with the most seniority has still won, though in 1975 the Democratic caucus ousted three committee chairmen whose high-handed behavior had offended many of their colleagues.

Second, the number and power of subcommittees was significantly increased. In the House, for example, rules were passed to require every committee with as many as twenty members to have at least four subcommittees, each with a chair, a staff, a budget, and a jurisdiction. Subcommittee chairmen are elected by the majority party members on each committee (except for House Appropriations Subcommittee chairmen, who are elected by the party caucus), and committee members are allowed to volunteer for subcommittee assignments in the order of their seniority. Also, committee chairmen are now required to refer bills to subcommittee within two weeks of receiving them. Consequently, much of the power committee chairmen once had over a bill's fate is now dispersed among the subcommittee chairs.[18]

All of this means that power in Congress is more fragmented than ever. The 1983 Senate had 16 standing committees with 103 subcommittees; in the House the numbers were 22 and 136. Since each committee/subcommittee is part of the policymaking process, working out a legislative compromise is more difficult than ever. With this proliferation of subcommittees, a significant proportion of the members of the House and Senate now chair a committee or subcommittee. With 103 subcommittees in the Senate, every member of the majority party, even freshmen, chairs at least one subcommittee.[19]

What does this mean for the legislative process? The appearance of independent, powerful subcommittees means another step in the legislative process. That makes it slower and adds another point at which legislation can be defeated. Since power is further dispersed, it makes it more difficult to put together a compromise that will be acceptable to all sides. The addition of numerous subcommittees, each needing to justify its existence, means more hearings, more sessions, and a greater workload for the average member of Congress. These days it is not unusual for a senator to have a dozen or more committee assignments.[20] Also, all the new chairs mean the involvement of younger, less experienced members in key roles in the legislative process. Frequently, the end result is legislation that is less well-drafted and a process that works less smoothly.

INTEREST GROUPS

Interest groups have always been a vital part of the legislative process, but now they are more important than ever. Ironically, one of the reforms of the 1970s designed to reduce the influence of special interests has probably had the opposite effect. Before the 1970s, most committee proceedings were held behind closed doors, and many key votes were taken without a roll call. Members would file past a teller and be counted, but no record was kept on who voted which way. During the 1970s, however, reformers succeeded in opening most committee and subcommittee proceedings to the public and placing teller votes on the record. The reformers argued that members would now have to be more responsive to all of their constituents, not just a few powerful interest groups. What the reformers did not foresee, however, was that the new procedures would also make it easier for interest groups to see who's naughty and who's nice.

The woods are full of interest groups determined to defeat senators and representatives who don't vote their way. Single-issue groups, such as Right to Life and the Moral Majority, keep scorecards on members of Congress, targeting for electoral extermination those who dare oppose them. Business and trade groups have become more active in the legislative process as well. Perhaps as many as 15,000 lobbyists are at work in Washington, spending more than $1 billion a year in direct lobbying.[21]

One of the new weapons in the interest-group arsenal is the political action committee (PAC). Through the first four months of 1982, for example, the Savings Association Political Elections Committee gave $37,500 in campaign contributions to ten members of the Senate Finance Committee, which handles legislation dealing with banks and savings and loans. At about the same time, the bankers' PAC contributed $33,500 to nine of the ten. Meanwhile, over in the House, fourteen members of the tax-writing Ways and Means Committee received contributions of $250 each from the Distilled Spirits Council Political Action Committee. It seems the liquor industry was concerned about higher taxes on booze. Also, Las Vegas gambling interests decided to cover their bets by giving $1000 each to sixteen of the committee's members through their Western Enterprise Political Action Committee.[22] In 1983, incumbent members of Congress received more than $20 million in PAC contributions with eleven senators and eleven representatives collecting more than $100,000 each.[23]

Interest groups have become more important because parties have become less. Party labels and party organization don't mean as much in elections now; personal organization, media campaigning, and, of course, money mean much more. Consequently, members of Congress find themselves obliged to become political PAC-men and PAC-women, gobbling up interest-group dollars to finance their reelection campaigns.

CONSTITUENCY

Another factor affecting Congress is **constituency**, that is, the people a member of Congress represents. There are different theories about the

Congress And Industrial Policy
A CONVERSATION WITH MORRIS P. FIORINA, HARVARD UNIVERSITY

Q. Lately we've heard a great deal about a national industrial policy. During the 1984 election campaign, for example, Walter Mondale and other Democrats adopted the idea as an alternative to Reaganomics. Do you think industrial policy is a good idea?

A. First, let's make sure we're talking about the same thing—industrial policy is a term which covers a great deal of ground. I take it to mean a more extensive and deliberately planned government role in the American economy. The goal would be to make U.S. business more competitive in the global economy over the long term. In practice this means that the government would encourage the withdrawal of resources from declining sectors of the economy such as heavy manufacturing and promote the investment of resources in rising sectors such as hi-tech. This would be done by subsidizing research and development in favored areas, by retraining workers, and by otherwise easing the pain of economic change in specific localities. Taxes and sub-

Morris Fiorina, Professor of Government at Harvard University, received his Ph. D. from the University of Rochester and taught for eleven years at the California Institute of Technology. A member of the American Academy of Arts and Sciences, Fiorina has been a Guggenheim Fellow, and a Fellow at the Center for Advanced Study in the Behavioral Sciences at Stanford. His writings revolve around the theme of electoral accountability—its nature, extent, and consequences. He has written three books and numerous articles and is currently at work on a book describing the constituency service practices of American members of Congress and British MPs.

sidies could also be used to encourage patterns of investment consistent with the country's policy.

Is that a good idea? There are a couple of ways to take that question. Assuming that it works as intended, liberals and conservatives would have very different views, with conservatives opposing additional governmental intervention in the economy, and liberals generally favoring a more extensive governmental role. But regardless of ideology, there's also the prior question of whether industrial policy would work as intended.

Q. Are you implying that it would not?

A. I'm not saying that it couldn't, only that I can see some real problems. The Achilles heel of the notion is that it largely ignores how our governmental institutions work, Congress in particular. If you think Congress did a super job dealing with inflation and energy in the late 1970s, you'll love what it would do with industrial policy. If not, you'd better give

way representatives and senators should represent their constituents. One is that they should be **agents** for their constituents. They should do their best to determine what the folks back home think about an issue, and they should vote accordingly. Another approach is for members of Congress to act as **trustees.** This is the idea that representatives should use their own judgment to decide what's in the best interest of their constituents. After all, members of Congress have more information at their disposal than do their constituents.

industrial policy some sober second thoughts.

Q. Please elaborate.

A. Sure. Looking across our history, you'd have to say that for members of Congress jobs and incomes are bread and butter—from one election to another, nothing is of more continuing concern to them than how people *in their districts* are getting along economically. Members of Congress see their job as representing the people in their districts, and equally as important, getting reelected by those people. This simple fact leads them to see all policies through district lenses.

Q. To be sure, there would be disagreement about the precise shape of an industrial policy, but isn't there always disagreement over any significant policy issue?

A. Not just disagreement. In theory, everyone in Congress could agree on what the best *national* policy is, but that doesn't mean they'd support it. Whenever an important local interest is at stake, the typical member of Congress sacrifices the national interest. The story of the A-10 is not just an extreme example; it's all too typical. Most members of Congress will usually ignore the national costs of a program which helps their district, or the national benefits of a program which hurts their district. That's a large part of the reason why Jimmy Carter, a Democrat president with a two-thirds Democratic majority in each House, couldn't make a serious attempt to deal with energy or inflation from 1976 to 1980.

Q. So you're saying that Congress would pervert an industrial policy.

A. Yes, but let me say that I don't mean to imply that members of Congress are evil life forms who would intentionally pervert a policy. The vast majority of them are honorable people doing their jobs as they see them. It's just an unfortunate fact of life that what's best for a majority of geographic districts in the short term (or perhaps just for the organized groups in those districts) is not necessarily best for the nation in the long run.

Q. One of the most prominent advocates of industrial policy, Robert Reich, claims that the U.S. already has an industrial policy—special tax provisions, all kinds of subsidies, Chrysler bailouts. But, it's a policy by default made through numerous uncoordinated political decisions. Could a formal policy be any worse than what we now have?

A. Yes, I think so. Reich has a point in saying that all the little things we do now have some pretty big implications. But notice that when something major is proposed—the Chrysler bailout, for example—it generally leads to a big fight. The media, economists, and other experts all jump in, public-interest groups lobby, and citizens write. Even so, the political pressures are so strong that these things often carry, for better or for worse. Now, imagine if a new administration announced the principle that government intervention was proper and desirable, and that only the details needed to be decided. Members of Congress would trample each other in a rush to

(continued on next page)

In practice, most members of Congress combine the two approaches. On some issues, they behave as agents; on others, as trustees. In large part, it depends on the visibility and intensity of the particular issue combined with the proximity of the next election and the representatives' perceptions of their own electoral vulnerability. If the attentive public among representatives' constituents is fairly large and/or fairly powerful, the representative will be obliged strongly to consider constituents' feelings. Members of Congress from farm states, for example, usually back farm price supports

propose new special-tax provisions, new subsidies, protection, government investments, and so forth. The floodgates would be opened.

Q. You're painting a very unflattering portrait of our representatives. The idealist in me feels uncomfortable.

A. Again, let me emphasize the forces at work. Our repre-

sentatives are not bad people, as I've already said. Any of us would behave the same way in their shoes. Let's say that the nation's industrial policy proposes that we let domestic steel go down the drain. How do you think the representatives from affected areas would react? Do you think they would go home and say, "Not to worry, the jobs we lose will be more than made

up by jobs gained in other areas and by the jobs we'll gain in the future when our policy pays off"? Don't hold your breath. Any member of Congress who says anything like that won't go back to Washington! Even if they say "Never fear, the government will retrain those who lose their jobs and get them new ones," that won't do either. Maybe the affected constituents can't be re-

whether they are Democrats or Republicans, liberals or conservatives. Representatives from oil-producing states such as Texas, Oklahoma, Louisiana, and Alaska generally endorse the oil industry's position on energy matters. And, as we have seen, members from New York support the A-10 Thunderbolt II. On the other hand, representatives from rural states face few constituent pressures on issues like the A-10, while oil-state representatives enjoy leeway on farm bills.

Constituency pressures are an important influence on policymaking in the Congress, but it's often difficult to separate the overlapping effects of party, ideology, and constituency. Take the case of two adjacent congressional districts in Houston, Texas, the Seventh and the Eighteenth. Texas' Seventh Congressional District is carved out of Houston's affluent western suburbs. It's the home of much of the city's prosperous business community, whose major concerns are high taxes, inflation, too much government regulation, and crime. For more than a decade, the district has been represented in Congress by Republican Bill Archer.

In contrast, the neighboring Eighteenth District is one of the poorest in the nation. It is an inner-city district with a substantial percentage of blacks and Mexican Americans. The chief concerns of the Eighteenth District's residents include minority rights, poverty, housing, unemployment, and government assistance for blighted inner-city areas. Since the late 1970s, Mickey Leland, a black Democrat, has represented the district in Washington. He won the seat in 1978 when Democrat Barbara Jordan decided to retire from Congress.

In the halls of Congress, Representatives Archer and Leland are usually on opposite sides. According to the Congressional Quarterly Press, on ten key votes in 1979–1981, the two voted against each other every time.[24] Why

trained in the new skills, or maybe they don't want to move to Houston, a perfectly understandable reaction.

Put more simply, industrial policy is inherently national and long-range in its perspective. Our representative system is inherently local and short-term in its perspective. You can't expect a member of Congress willingly to sacrifice the jobs and incomes of real flesh-and-blood constituents, even temporarily, for the benefit of other people in other places or at other times who are unknown to him or her. Any industrial policy passed by Congress would be conservative in the sense that it would protect the economic status quo. Rather than ease the movement of resources to more productive uses, it would hinder the process.

Q. What you are saying, then, is that government should do nothing because everything is doomed to fail.

A. No, not at all. What I am saying is that proposed policies which ignore or overlook politics are doomed to fail.

---

did this happen? Is it because Leland is a Democrat and Archer a Republican? Is it because Leland is a dyed-in-the-wool liberal and Archer a staunch conservative? Or is it because each man is voting what he perceives to be the dominant wishes/best interests of his constituents? The answer is probably "all of the above." Party, ideology, and constituency overlap. Both Archer and Leland are safely entrenched in their own districts, but neither would stand a chance of being elected in the other's. If the two suddenly switched voting positions, each would surely face a primary challenge from a more conservative or more liberal challenger. And each would almost certainly lose.

Today, many observers believe that constituency has become of increased importance in congressional policymaking. Declining party strength is one reason. Also, members of Congress are spending more time in their districts than ever before. In the old days, most representatives and senators who didn't represent the Middle Atlantic states would travel to Washington in January and might stay for the session's duration. Now, not only do members maintain full-time offices in the district, but air travel has created a large and growing "Tuesday-Thursday Club." These are members who fly home for extended weekends in the district two, three, or four times a month, all of them worried about the next election and concerned not to "lose touch" with the district.[25]

Constituency influence in the congressional process is an important part of the theory of representative democracy. After all, that's what we mean by the term *to represent*. On the other hand, too much constituency influence can have its drawbacks. People tend at times to be selfish and short-sighted; it's human nature. They want programs that benefit themselves and their district, even though, in a broader sense, the programs may not be beneficial for the nation as a whole. Cut the budget, they say, but don't close down the air-force base in our district. Eliminate wasteful spending, but keep the Thunderbolt A-10. A government handout is something someone *else* gets; spending for our district is necessary and justified. The danger of constituency pressure is that it forces members of Congress to focus primarily on the needs of their district rather than on the needs of the nation. If everyone in Congress is looking after the nation's parts, will there be anyone left to look after the whole?

IDEOLOGY

Another factor that has grown in importance in recent years has been the ideology of the legislators, that is, whether they are liberal or conservative. An analysis of Senate and House votes in the early 1980s found that Congress had become more ideological and more conservative than it had been in the recent past, although there were some inconsistencies. Some representatives were down-the-line conservatives on all types of issues; others were consistently liberal. Others were conservative on economic issues but liberal on social issues. Democrats as a group were found to be more liberal/less conservative than Republicans as a group, yet significant exceptions existed within each party. There are liberal Republicans and conservative Democrats.[26]

These ideological divisions have long been a factor in congressional policymaking. Since the late 1930s, a conservative coalition of sorts has existed between Republicans and southern Democrats. As a region, the South has historically been more conservative than the Northeast and Midwest, particularly on social issues. Consequently, its representatives and senators have often teamed up with northern Republicans against northern Democrats. Frequently, these coalitions have constituted legislative majorities.[27] In 1981, for example, conservative southern Democrats joined Republicans in passing President Reagan's tax-cut and spending-cut proposals in the House despite the Democrats' numerical majority.

In the 1980s, however, Congress is ideologically more fragmented than ever. Speaker Tip O'Neill says there are five Democratic parties in the House, ranging from extreme liberal to extreme conservative.[28] The groups are even starting to take on entomological nicknames. The conservative Democrats, mostly from the sunbelt, call themselves the "boll weevils." In 1981 and 1982, they supported Reagan's economic program in the House. Then there were the "gypsy moths." These are the liberal-to-moderate Republicans worried about the effects of the Reagan budget cuts on their constituents. In the early '80s, many of them wound up voting with liberal Democrats against Reagan's proposals.

The effect of all this ideological fragmentation is to make it more difficult for Congress to make policy. It's becoming harder and harder to put

Democrats Thomas ("Tip") O'Neill, Speaker of the House, and House Majority Leader Jim Wright preside over a party that embraces a great diversity of political philosophies and constituency pressures. Party fragmentation has been a difficult problem for party leaders in recent years.

together a majority coalition in support of a measure, and easier and easier to assemble one in opposition. Fragmentation means more power centers to be consulted, more compromises to be made, and, in all probability, less satisfactory public policy.

CONGRESSIONAL NORMS

Congress is an organization where men and women meet and work together on a regular basis. It has formal rules of procedure, of course, but it also has informal rules or *norms*. Norms are unwritten but expected modes of behavior. They exist in any social group—a university sorority, a softball team, or the United States Congress.

One of the norms of Congress is seniority; members with longer tenure enjoy more status. Another is "reciprocity." This is the idea that members will cooperate with each other, exchanging favors. Consider the farm bloc, for example. Dairy-state representatives vote for tobacco subsidies, and members from tobacco-growing states return the favor by voting for the Milk Fund. Wheat-state representatives support sugar subsidies; representatives from sugar states vote for rice supports. It's called you-scratch-my-back-and-I'll-scratch-yours.

"Apprenticeship" is also a norm. Freshmen are expected to be seen and not heard, at least until they have had a chance to learn the ropes. Ideally, new representatives or senators should focus much of their energy on committee work, developing some expertise. This is the norm of "specialization." Learn one thing very well and then speak out on it. That shows you're holding up your share of the load.

A final norm is "institutional loyalty." Members are expected to respect the institution of the Congress. It's understood that a number of senators have an eye on the White House and that many representatives would like to be senators or governors, but the ideal legislator would be the man or woman who sees the House or the Senate as a career.

The House and Senate are different bodies, of course; so the norms in each differ in certain respects. The Senate is smaller. That means it can be more relaxed, freshmen will be able to take on a larger role, and there will be less time for specialization. The House is far larger. Stricter rules will be needed if it is to function well. Consequently, the pressures for specialization will be greater, the opportunities for newer members fewer.

Norms are informal rules; they are enforced informally, by peer disapproval. Members who bend the norms may be told by more experienced members that they need to get their act in order. As Sam Rayburn put it, you get along by going along. If members go too far, flaunting the norms of the body, they may discover that their pet legislation never seems to get anywhere.

In recent years, however, the norms of Congress have begun to erode. The considerable turnover in membership in the 1970s has brought in a crop of younger members, less familiar and less concerned with the traditional norms of the body. The seniority system has been undermined by the reforms of the 1970s, and the increase in subcommittees has forced freshmen and only slightly more experienced members into positions of power quite early in their careers. Freshmen now are not only seen and heard—they sometimes chair subcommittees.

The weakening of the norms of Congress weakens the legislative process. Norms serve a purpose: they order behavior and establish patterns for getting things done. When norms begin breaking down, issues that were once taken for granted must be constantly negotiated and renegotiated. More sources of conflict arise, and there are more opportunities for disagreements. The consequence is more sand in the wheels of Congress.

PERSONALITIES

Another factor affecting the legislative process is personality. Some members of Congress are bright; others slow. Some are capable; others inept. Some are broadminded; others are petty. All of this affects the policymaking process.

Some members of Congress get things done because they master the legislative process with all its subtleties and nuances. Lyndon Johnson, for example, developed a well-deserved reputation as a wheeler-dealer armtwister. He always seemed able to find the votes to pass his legislation.

In contrast, some members of Congress are so disliked or clumsy that their support for a bill is more a hindrance than a help. A few years ago one senator earned the reputation as the "dumbest man in the Senate" after he revealed in a speech that he believed missile silos were used for storing grain. Another senator reportedly asked an aide to get him a pair of rubbers to keep his feet dry during a rainy day on the campaign trail. The aide rushed off to the nearest Thom McAn store and purchased a pair of galoshes. When he returned with the overshoes, the senator asked, "Where did these come from?"

"Thom McAn," replied the aide.

"That's nice," said the senator. "Please thank Tom for me."[29]

THE WHITE HOUSE

In the twentieth century, perhaps the most important factor affecting congressional policymaking has been the White House. The president is involved in every stage of the legislative process. He is a prime source of legislation. He actively lobbies for his legislative program during committee and subcommittee proceedings; his cabinet officers may testify at hearings. He uses his influence to try to round up votes on the floor and, if things aren't going his way, he can threaten to use his veto, thus perhaps forcing a compromise. Indeed, the role of the president in the policymaking process is so important as to deserve an entire chapter's consideration. This it receives in chapter 8.

CONCLUSION: CONGRESS AND PUBLIC POLICY

In the 1980s, the United States Congress is an institution adrift, searching for direction. Public confidence in Congress is at an all-time low, and serious questions have been raised concerning Congress' role in the public-policy process.

America's constitutional arrangements divide power among institutions and officeholders, so there has always been a potential for political stalemate. In today's Congress, however, fragmenting forces are multiplying, unifying forces are in retreat. Interest groups, constituency, and ideology have grown in importance; political party, leadership, and norms have lost importance. Consequently, power is so dispersed that it becomes nearly impossible for the Congress to make rational public policy.

The story of the A-10 Thunderbolt II illustrates the problem. The outcome of this controversy depended not so much on the merits of the A-10, but on the political influence of two powerful lawmakers. Both Addabbo and Tower stood up for the interests of his district, as perhaps they should have, but who spoke for a national, public interest? Furthermore, the final compromise wasn't between local concerns and national concerns, it was between two particular local concerns.

No one in Congress speaks for the nation, and no single individual speaks for the Congress itself. The so-called reassertion of Congress in the 1970s involved Congress' strengthening its will and ability to say *no* to the president. Presidents Nixon, Ford, and Carter learned that firsthand. Of course, Congress may also say *yes* to presidential leadership. In 1981, President Reagan succeeded in getting his tax cut and spending cuts through Congress virtually intact. What Congress hasn't shown, however, is the consistent ability to say "Here is an alternative" or to provide strong leadership on its own. Congress is able to respond more or less effectively to leadership from the White House but doesn't seem capable of providing national leadership on its own.

In part, Congress' troubles are the result of national political trends: the weakness of political parties, the strength of interest groups, the decline in participation. Some of Congress' injuries, however, have resulted from self-inflicted wounds: the unanticipated consequences of the reforms of the '70s. The increase in the number and power of subcommittees, the elimination of unrecorded teller votes, and the opening of committees to public scrutiny were all well-intentioned reforms, but they served further to fragment power in an already fragmented Congress and to slow a process that is already quite deliberate.

The upshot is that Congress, in wanting to make itself responsive to the public interest, has succeeded primarily in making its members more responsive to local, special interests rather than the national interest. Representatives and senators now find themselves devoting more and more time and attention to the narrow interests of their districts or states and less and less notice to a national perspective. Thus in the 1980s, Congress, in representing the nation's parts, often fails to represent the nation as a whole, and we are all the worse for it.

Key Terms

AGENT *(200)*

CLOTURE *(192)*

CONFERENCE COMMITTEES *(192)*

CONSTITUENCY *(199)*

FILIBUSTER *(192)*

GERRYMANDERING *(181)*

JOINT COMMITTEES *(187)*

LEGISLATIVE VETO *(184)*

MAJORITY LEADER *(191)*

MAJORITY WHIP *(194)*

MINORITY LEADER *(194)*

MINORITY WHIP *(194)*

POCKET VETO *(193)*

PRESIDENT PRO TEMPORE *(193)*

REAPPORTION *(178)*

REDISTRICT *(179)*

SELECT OR SPECIAL COMMITTEES *(187)*

SENIORITY *(196)*

STANDING COMMITTEES *(187)*

TRUSTEE *(200)*

NOTES

1. *Time* (24 May 1982), p. 30.
2. Robert E. Cushman and Robert F. Cushman, *Cases in Constitutional Law,* 3rd ed. (New York: Appleton-Century-Crofts, 1968), p. 42.
3. *Baker* v. *Carr,* 369 U.S. 186 (1962).
4. *Wesberry* v. *Sanders,* 376 U.S. 1 (1964).
5. Michael Barone and Grant Ujifusa, *The Almanac of American Politics 1984* (Washington, D.C.: 1983).
6. Jack Craig, "It Pays To Be a Congressman," *Houston Post,* 11 April 1982, pp. 2BB, 24BB.
7. Harris Survey, reported in *Houston Post,* 27 November 1982, p. 3C.
8. *Gallup Report* (July 1983), p. 4.
9. Thomas Mann, *Unsafe at Any Margin* (Washington, D.C.: American Enterprise Institute for Public Policy Research, 1978).
10. House Commission on Administrative Review, *Administrative Reorganization and Legislative Management,* 95th Cong., 1st sess., 1977, H. Doc. 95-232.
11. Joseph Cooper and William F. West, "Voluntary Retirement, Incumbency, and the Modern House," *Political Science Quarterly* 96 (Summer 1981): 279–300.
12. Woodrow Wilson, *Congressional Government* (New York: Meridian Books, 1956).
13. *Immigration and Naturalization Service* v. *Chadha,* 51 U.S.L.W. 4907 (1983).
14. Harvey G. Zeidenstein, "The Reassertion of Congressional Power," *Political Science Quarterly* 93 (Fall 1978): 393–410.
15. Malcolm Shaw, "Congress in the 1970s: A Decade of Reform," *Parliamentary Affairs* 34 (Summer 1981): 272–90; Steven Haeberle, "The Institutionalization of the Subcommittee in the United States House of Representatives," *Journal of Politics* 40 (November 1978): 1054–65.
16. Shaw.
17. Neil McNeil, "The American Congress: Its Troubled Role in the 1980's," *Modern Age* 24 (Fall 1980): 372–73.
18. Shaw, Haeberle.
19. *Congressional Directory 1983–84* (Washington, D.C.: U.S. Government Printing Office, 1983).
20. *Time* (23 January 1978), p. 10.
21. McNeil, pp. 370–78.
22. Timothy O. Clark, "Tax Lobbyists Scrambling in the Dark to Fight Taxes That Hit Their Clients," *National Journal* (22 May 1982), pp. 896–901.
23. Mary Beth Franklin, "Political Action Committees Protect Incumbents, Study Says," *Houston Chronicle,* 14 February 1984, Sec. 1, p. 11.
24. *Politics in America: Members of Congress in Washington and at Home,* ed.

Alan Ehrenhalt (Washington, D.C.: Congressional Quarterly Press, 1981).

25. Richard Fenno, *Home Style: House Members in Their Districts* (Boston: Little, Brown, 1978).
26. Richard E. Cohen, "Rating Congress—A Guide to Separating the Liberals from the Conservatives," *National Journal* (8 May 1982).
27. David W. Brady and Charles S. Bullock III, "Is There a Conservative Coalition in the House?" *Journal of Politics* 42 (May 1980).
28. Richard Cohen, "A Liberal Freshman Perspective," *National Journal* (29 May 1982), pp. 944–48.
29. Eleanor Randolph, "The Best and the Worst of the U.S. Senate," *Washington Monthly* (January 1982), pp. 30–43.

SUGGESTED READINGS

DAVIDSON, ROGER H., AND OLESZEK, WALTER J. *Congress and Its Members.* Washington D.C.: Congressional Quarterly Press, 1981.

DODD, LAWRENCE C., AND OPPENHEIMER, BRUCE I., eds. *Congress Reconsidered.* 2nd ed. Washington, D.C.: Congressional Quarterly Press, 1981.

FENNO, RICHARD. *Home Style: House Members in Their Districts.* Boston: Little, Brown, 1978.

FIORINA, MORRIS P. *Congress—Keystone of the Washington Establishment.* New Haven: Yale University Press, 1977.

_____. *Representatives and their Constituencies.* Lexington, Mass.: Heath, 1974.

JONES, ROCHELLE, AND WALL, PETER. *The Private World of Congress.* New York: Free Press, 1979.

MALBIN, MICHAEL J. *Unelected Representatives: Congressional Staff and the Future of Representative Government.* New York: Basic Books, 1980.

MANN, THOMAS. *Unsafe at Any Margin.* Washington, D.C.: American Enterprise Institute for Policy Research, 1978.

_____, AND ORNSTEIN, NORMAN J., eds. *The New Congress.* Washington, D.C.: American Enterprise Institute, 1981.

RIPLEY, RANDALL, AND FRANKLIN, GRACE. *Congress, the Bureaucracy, and Public Policy.* 2nd ed. Homewood, Il.: Dorsey, 1980.

Chapter Eight

THE PRESIDENCY

THE CONSTITUTIONAL PRESIDENCY

Qualifications and Background

Compensation and Term of Office

Impeachment and Removal

Presidential Succession and Disability

The Vice-Presidency

Constitutional Powers and Duties

THE DEVELOPMENT OF THE MODERN PRESIDENCY

The Modern Presidency and Domestic Policymaking

The Modern Presidency and Foreign Policymaking

The Modern Presidency and the Media

THE ORGANIZATION OF THE MODERN PRESIDENCY

The White House Staff

The Executive Office of the President

The Growing White House Bureaucracy

The Presidential Bureaucracy and Presidential Decisionmaking

Problems of the Presidential Bureaucracy

CONCLUSION: **THE PRESIDENCY AND PUBLIC POLICY**

The Power to Persuade

The Presidential Character

Presidential Popularity

The Presidential Dilemma

This chilling picture is neither of a German concentration camp nor of a military prison for captured Vietnamese soldiers. It is an internment camp in southern California, where American citizens of Japanese descent were detained during the early years of World War II. The creation of these camps by Franklin Roosevelt illustrates the sometimes awesome power possessed, and exercised, by American presidents.

The presidency is an office cloaked in paradox. At times presidents have exercised awesome power. During World War II, for example, President Roosevelt used his emergency powers to order the internment in detention camps of native-born American citizens of Japanese descent. President Truman ordered American armed forces into the Korean conflict without the benefit of a congressional declaration of war. In 1956, President Eisenhower dispatched the national guard to Little Rock, Arkansas, to ensure the peaceful desegregation of Little Rock High School. In the 1960s and '70s, Presidents Johnson and Nixon ordered secret and illegal bombing raids into Laos and Cambodia in Southeast Asia. Finally, if nuclear war ever threatens, we suspect it will be the president alone who will make the final, fateful decision concerning whether to join the conflict.

At other times, however, presidents have displayed pitiful weakness. In 1919 President Wilson was unable to persuade the Senate to ratify the Treaty of Versailles. In 1974, President Nixon was ordered by a unanimous Supreme Court to turn over transcripts of private conversations to a special prosecutor. Then he resigned rather than face certain impeachment by the House of Representatives. In 1977, Bert Lance, the Director of the Office of Management and Budget and a close friend and adviser to President Carter, was investigated by the Senate and forced to resign over charges of wrongdoing. And Carter himself was generally unable to get his programs approved by Congress despite lopsided Democratic majorities in both chambers.

There is a paradox in the way we view the presidency. As Professor Erwin Hargrove puts it, Americans alternately make heroes and villains of their presidents.[1] On the one hand, the president often seems the only figure capable of policy leadership at the national level. There is the image of the **Heroic President.** Like Franklin Roosevelt, such a president offers a bold program to solve our domestic troubles. Like Kennedy, he challenges us to realize our highest ambitions, to reach for the moon. Like Lyndon Johnson, he speaks to the nation's conscience, calling for equal rights for all. In short, the Heroic President articulates the American Dream and leads the nation to a higher road toward peace, prosperity, and justice for all.

On the other hand, we fear that a president will become too powerful, creating what Arthur Schlesinger, Jr., calls the "**Imperial Presidency.**"[2] After Vietnam, after Watergate, we worry about presidential decisions to enter wars in distant lands with secret agreements and secret bombing. We are apprehensive about the misuse of presidential power via illegal break-ins and coverups.

Since the 1930s national policymaking leadership in America has most often centered in the institution of the presidency, but it is an institution that is difficult to study. There are paradoxes, contradictions, and myths. Presidents can be strong (FDR in 1933, Johnson in 1964 and '65, Reagan in 1981) and they can be weak (Truman in 1951–52, Johnson in 1968, Nixon in 1974.) They can be popular (Roosevelt and Eisenhower) or they can be disliked (Truman after Korea, Johnson after Vietnam, Nixon after Watergate). Our job in this chapter is to separate the myth from the reality, to describe and analyze the power and the limitation of the office of the presidency and to explain the president's role in the policymaking process. Let's begin at the beginning by exploring the constitutional/legal background of the office.

THE CONSTITUTIONAL PRESIDENCY

The basic qualifications, powers, and responsibilities of the president are outlined in Article II of the United States Constitution. The passage itself is relatively brief, but it serves as the backdrop for the development of the single most important office in American government.

QUALIFICATIONS AND BACKGROUND

The Constitution says a president must be thirty-five years old, a natural-born American citizen, and a resident of the United States for at least fourteen years. In practice, all of our presidents have been white males of

Western European ancestry. All but one, John Kennedy, have been Protestants. Most have been fairly well-to-do and the majority have been experienced politicians. Ronald Reagan was a professional actor, of course, but he was also a two-term governor of California. Jimmy Carter had been governor of Georgia. Gerald Ford had spent a lifetime in the U.S. House of Representatives, and Richard Nixon had been vice-president, a U.S. senator, and a congressman from California. Both Lyndon Johnson and John Kennedy had been men of the Senate. The only recent president without experience in the rough-and-tumble world of party politics was Dwight Eisenhower, who had been general of the army.

What's the ideal background for a president? There's no magic formula, but the more diverse the background the better. Ronald Reagan came to office with superb skills in communications and more than an adequate supply of political savvy. He was generally unprepared, however, to deal with the substance of public policy, particularly foreign policy. Jimmy Carter had been a nuclear engineer, a peanut farmer, and governor of Georgia, but he was uninformed about policymaking in Washington. During the campaign he bragged about being an outsider and said it was a virtue. It wasn't; he lacked the political knowledge and skills necessary to accomplish his goals.

Today's media-oriented electoral process imposes other qualifications on would-be presidents. One needs the stamina to persevere for years on the campaign trail and the ability to raise millions of dollars in contributions to finance the long march to the presidency. Most importantly, potential presidents need to be able to project a good media image. Journalist David Halberstam says that Ronald Reagan was the "prototype of the modern media candidate. He had access to big money, which is important; he had the looks; above all, he had the confidence of working around the camera."[3] Communications skills are an important asset for a president, but they aren't the only skills a president needs. As Halberstam asks, "Are our politicians as good at the substance of politics as they are its style? Can those who run and win govern? Equally important, can those who govern run and win?"[4]

In 1982 a reporter asked former President Richard Nixon what advice he'd offer Senator Edward Kennedy on getting elected president. Lose twenty pounds, Nixon said, and then get some new ideas for the 1980s. That answer tells a great deal about the state of contemporary American politics. Image comes first, then issues. It's more important to be lean and trim around the waistline than to be up-to-date on the substance of public policy.

COMPENSATION AND TERM OF OFFICE

The president's salary is $200,000 a year plus $50,000 for expenses. He and his family live rent-free at the White House, and an additional $100,000 may be used for official entertainment and travel. He also re-

ceives a $66,000 a year pension for life once he leaves office, plus an allowance for an office staff.

The president's constitutional term of office is four years. In the original Constitution no limit was set on how many terms a president could serve, but George Washington established the custom of serving two terms and then retiring. When Franklin Roosevelt violated that tradition by successfully seeking a third and a fourth term, sentiment arose to limit the president to two terms constitutionally. This was done with the Twenty-second Amendment, ratified in 1951.

Today, some would like to amend the Constitution again to provide for a single six-year presidential term. Its advocates, who include former Presidents Nixon, Ford, and Carter, believe that would relieve the president of the political pressures of running for reelection and allow him to concentrate on shaping sound public policy. On the other hand, critics say that a single six-year term would weaken the president's political bargaining power, making him a "lame duck" from inauguration day. Critics also say that six years is too short a term for a good president, too long for a bad one. At any rate, it seems unlikely this particular reform will be adopted any time soon.

IMPEACHMENT AND REMOVAL

A president can be removed at the ballot box but also by means of **impeachment.** The Constitution says that a president may be impeached for "treason, bribery, or other high crimes and misdemeanors." As we have seen earlier in this book, the Constitution is often vague, and this is an illustration of that quality. Constitutional scholars tell us that the founders foresaw two broad, general grounds on which a president could be impeached and removed from office. First, impeachment could be used against a president who abused his power and thereby threatened to become a tyrant. Second, it could be employed against a president who simply refused to carry out the duties of his office.[5]

The actual process of impeachment and removal from office involves both the House and the Senate. It begins with the House drawing up articles of impeachment. Technically, the word *impeach* means to accuse; so when the House impeaches the president by majority vote, it is simply accusing him of committing offenses that may warrant removal from office. The president is then tried in the Senate, with the chief justice acting as judge and the senators as jury. A two-thirds vote is needed in the Senate to remove the president from office.

The impeachment process has twice been initiated against presidents. In the 1860s Andrew Johnson, Lincoln's successor as president, was impeached by the House, but the Senate fell one vote short of removing him from office.[6] Then, in the 1970s the House began impeachment proceedings against President Richard Nixon. In 1974, however, Nixon resigned in the face of certain impeachment by the House and probable removal by the Senate.

PRESIDENTIAL SUCCESSION AND DISABILITY

If a president is removed from office, resigns, or dies in office, he is succeeded by the vice-president. After the vice-president, the line of succession goes to the Speaker of the House, the president pro tempore of the Senate, the secretary of state, and on through the cabinet. In our history, nine vice-presidents have succeeded to the presidency but no Speakers or Senate presidents and, thanks to the Twenty-fifth Amendment, it's unlikely that the order of succession will need to extend beyond the office of vice-president.

The Twenty-fifth Amendment was ratified in 1967 after the assassination of President Kennedy focused public attention on the problems of presidential succession and disability. Now, if the office of vice-president becomes vacant, the president can appoint a replacement subject to majority confirmation of both the House and the Senate. This was first used in 1973 when Vice-President Spiro Agnew resigned under fire for criminal wrongdoing. President Nixon nominated Gerald Ford to fill the vacancy. In 1974, Nixon resigned, Ford became president, and Ford in turn nominated Nelson Rockefeller to the vice-presidency. Consequently, in 1974 the United States was led by a president and a vice-president both of whom had been appointed rather than elected.

Other provisions of the Twenty-fifth Amendment established procedures for the vice-president to become acting president if the president is disabled and incapable of performing the duties of the office. The president may declare his disability by written notice to the Senate president pro tempore and to the Speaker of the House. The vice-president then becomes acting president until the president declares in writing that he is able to resume his responsibilities. If the president is unable or unwilling to declare his disability, such a declaration can be made by the vice-president along with a majority of the cabinet. Should there ever be disagreement between the vice-president/cabinet and the president, the question of the president's disability will be settled by the Congress. In such a case, the president can be declared disabled only by a two-thirds vote of both houses.

THE VICE-PRESIDENCY

The vice-presidency has always been an office with a great deal of potential, but until recent administrations, the vice-president has usually been the forgotten man of Washington. John Nance Garner, one of FDR's vice-presidents, once told fellow Texan Lyndon Johnson that the job wasn't worth a "bucket of warm spit." Incredibly, Harry Truman was kept so uninformed regarding the nation's war effort that he learned of the existence of the atomic bomb only after becoming president. Vice-presidents Nixon, Johnson, and Humphrey all had little to do except make political speeches, and Nixon's first vice-president, Spiro Agnew, spent most of his time acting as political hatchet-man for the administration. After Agnew resigned, some said Nixon selected Ford to be vice-president because he believed Congress would think twice about voting impeachment if Ford were to be Nixon's successor.[7]

In the last two administrations, however, vice-presidents have actually become involved in policymaking. President Carter used Walter Mondale as an adviser, a troubleshooter, and an emissary to different interest groups and to Congress. No outside observer can know for sure just how important a role any one person plays in an administration, but both Carter and Mondale said the vice-president's responsibilities were significant. Similarly, George Bush has apparently been given a major policy role in the Reagan Administration, especially in the areas of regulatory reform and foreign policy.

CONSTITUTIONAL POWERS AND DUTIES

The Constitution outlines the powers and duties of the president primarily in Article II, Sections 2 and 3. The sections aren't long, but they grant the president important powers in certain key policy areas. First, the Constitution gives the president the tools to be a significant part of the legislative process. From time to time, it says, the president shall "give to the Congress Information of the State of the Union, and recommend to their Considera-

The application of presidential power to foreign policy was demonstrated when Richard Nixon "opened the door" to China. After Nixon, the process of diplomatic recognition and normalized relations was virtually a foregone conclusion.

tion such Measures as he shall judge necessary and expedient." Traditionally, the president gives his State-of-the-Union address in January each year before a joint session of Congress and a national television audience. It is an excellent opportunity for the president to set the policy agenda for the upcoming session of Congress by presenting proposals to solve national problems. The president can influence policy formulation and policy adoption in Congress by use of his constitutional power to veto or by merely *threatening* to veto legislation. Also, the Constitution gives the president the power to call special sessions of Congress. These days, however, that particular power is fairly insignificant since Congress is in session almost year-round anyway.

Second, the Constitution gives the president, as the official head of the government or **head of state,** broad diplomatic powers for conducting foreign relations. He has the power to grant diplomatic recognition to other nations and to receive and appoint ambassadors. President Nixon, for example, began the process of normalizing relations with mainland China, a country the United States had never officially recognized. Under President Carter, the process was completed and ambassadors were exchanged. The only limitation on the president's power of diplomatic recognition is that his ambassadorial appointments must be approved by majority vote of the Senate, and generally they are. The president also has the power to negotiate treaties with other nations subject to a two-thirds vote of ratification by the Senate. Most treaties receive Senate approval, but there have been several celebrated rejections, including the defeat of the Treaty of Versailles negotiated by President Wilson. More recently, the Strategic Arms Limitation Treaty (SALT II), negotiated by President Carter with the Soviet Union, was never brought to a vote in the face of strong opposition, especially after the Soviet invasion of Afghanistan.

Third, the Constitution names the president the commander in chief of the armed forces. This constitutional provision embodies the important concept of **civilian supremacy of the armed forces.** It is based on the idea that war is too important to be left to the military; political considerations frequently outweigh military ones. It also reflects the belief that the preservation of representative democracy depends on keeping the military out of politics. In many nations, political power grows out of the barrels of the guns of the armed forces. Soldiers rule. In the United States, however, the president, a civilian, stands at the head of the armed forces' command structure. He has the power to make final military decisions. For example, as commander in chief, Franklin Roosevelt decided on the time and place of the Normandy invasion in World War II; Harry Truman made the decision to drop the atomic bomb on Japan; Truman also ordered American intervention in Korea and fired General Douglas MacArthur for contesting his war policy; Richard Nixon ordered an invasion of Cambodia; Jimmy Carter dispatched an expedition to attempt to rescue the American hostages held in Iran; and Ronald Reagan ordered the marines to invade the Caribbean island of Grenada.

Fourth, as part of the checks-and-balances system, the president is given a role in judicial policymaking. The president nominates all federal judges pending majority-vote confirmation by the Senate. The Senate usually confirms the president's nominees, but not without careful scrutiny, especially for Supreme Court nominees. Mr. Nixon saw two consecutive Supreme Court appointments rejected before he came up with a candidate the Senate would approve. The Constitution also gives the president the power to grant pardons and reprieves. A pardon frees an accused or convicted person from all penalty for an offense while a reprieve delays punishment. Most presidential pardons and reprieves are noncontroversial, but there are exceptions—President Ford's pardon of former President Nixon, for example.

Finally, the Constitution gives the president substantial powers of administration to effect policy implementation. The president is the chief executive; that is, he heads the executive branch of government and, the Constitution says, he may require written reports from department heads. More broadly, the Constitution enjoins the president to "take Care that Laws be faithfully executed."

THE DEVELOPMENT OF THE MODERN PRESIDENCY

The Constitution gives the president certain important powers with a significant potential for growth, but the framers hardly could have foreseen the development of the modern presidency. They anticipated that Congress would be the dominant branch of national government. Until the 1930s their expectation was, for the most part, fulfilled. It was Congress, for example, that clamored for the War of 1812 and that shoved President McKinley along toward war with Spain in the 1890s. Congress dominated domestic policymaking as well, and scholars and presidents alike testified to the weakness of the presidential office. "The president has not influence enough, and is not independent enough," said John Adams.[8]

There were important exceptions to the pattern of presidential weakness before the 1930s. Thomas Jefferson, Andrew Jackson, Abraham Lincoln, Theodore Roosevelt, and Woodrow Wilson were activist presidents who effectively used the resources of their offices and successfully defined new dimensions of presidential responsibility and power. Nevertheless, these activist presidents were exceptions to the pattern of presidential leadership before the 1930s. After Lincoln's assassination, presidential power went into eclipse with Andrew Johnson's impeachment and U. S. Grant's ineptitude. Theodore Roosevelt was followed by the unassertive William Howard Taft; Wilson was succeeded by the incompetent Warren G. Harding and the sleepy Calvin Coolidge.

Then came the Great Depression, Franklin Roosevelt, the New Deal, and World War II. A new era of presidential leadership began, in which the activist president became the norm. The modern president takes the lead in domestic policymaking, dominates foreign policymaking, and commands center stage in the media. Let's consider each of these aspects of the modern presidency in turn.

Theodore Roosevelt, whose active and aggressive leadership style prefigured the development of the modern presidency.

THE MODERN PRESIDENCY AND DOMESTIC POLICYMAKING

The Depression generated great public pressure for the federal government to act to revive the nation's staggering economy, to help those hardest hit by the collapse, and to regulate business and industry in an effort to prevent the disaster's reoccurrence. The 1932 election was viewed as a sweeping mandate for President Roosevelt to lead, and lead he did. He used his skills as a politician to become a major force in policy formulation and adoption. He used his administrative talents to play a key role in policy implementation. In so doing, Franklin Roosevelt set that pattern for the role of the modern president in domestic policymaking.

The modern president is the principal actor in the national domestic policymaking process. He proposes issues for the policy agenda, offers programs for their resolution, bargains with Congress for their adoption, and oversees their implementation by the bureaucracy. This is not to say, of course, that the president gets his way in domestic policy matters all of the time or even most of the time. While there have been times of great presidential success in domestic policymaking—FDR's first hundred days, Lyndon Johnson in 1965–66, and Ronald Reagan in 1981—most of the time presidents win some, lose some. The distinguishing characteristic of the modern president in domestic affairs is that his role is one of leadership. The modern president enters office planning to lead, the Congress expects it, and, at times, the nation demands it.

Since FDR, presidents have been more or less assertive in domestic policymaking. President Truman proposed the Fair Deal, Kennedy the New Frontier, Johnson the Great Society, and Reagan the New Federalism. Each program was composed of a series of domestic-policy reforms. In contrast, President Eisenhower was fairly reticent about offering major domestic policy proposals.

The president who tried to claim the greatest authority in domestic-policy matters was Richard Nixon. He asserted the power of **impoundment,** that is, the power to refuse to spend money already appropriated by Congress. Altogether, Nixon impounded more than $18 billion in areas of health, manpower, housing, education, and environmental protection. Eventually, however, impoundment was struck down as a policymaking instrument. On one front, federal courts found the practice unconstitutional. Meanwhile, Congress reasserted itself by passing the Congressional Budget and Impoundment Control Act of 1974 to outlaw the practice.

THE MODERN PRESIDENCY AND FOREIGN POLICYMAKING

Since World War II the president has also taken the lead in foreign policymaking. Historically, presidents have typically dominated foreign and defense policy during wartime, and then Congress has asserted itself again after the war. Remember Wilson and the Treaty of Versailles? Such was not the case after World War II, however. Because of the nuclear age, America's emergence as a world power, the Cold War, and the nation's commitment to maintaining peace around the globe, the modern president is the dominant figure in American foreign policymaking.

In fact, some observers go so far as to say that there are **two presidencies,** one for domestic affairs and another, far stronger presidency for foreign policy (stronger because the president is considered to have more policy leverage in foreign affairs than in domestic policymaking).[9] Since World War II several presidents have used their powers as commander in chief to fight undeclared wars in Korea and Southeast Asia. On many occasions, modern presidents have negotiated military and economic understandings with other nations and adopted them in the form of **execu-**

tive agreements that have the force of treaties but don't require Senate ratification (see the PERSPECTIVE on this page).

Developments in the wake of Vietnam, however, have demonstrated that the two-presidencies thesis was a bit exaggerated. Congress moved to restrain the president's foreign policymaking powers by enacting the War Powers Act, the Foreign Military Sales Act, and other measures. Just as

Perspective
EXECUTIVE AGREEMENTS

The framers of America's Constitution intended for the president and Congress to share diplomatic powers. The president was given sole authority to negotiate treaties with other nations, but all treaties had to be ratified by a two-thirds vote of the Senate. Since the days of George Washington, however, "executive agreements" have been a source of conflict and controversy between the executive and legislative branches. Executive agreements are international agreements between the president and foreign nations that do not require Senate ratification. Under international law and in the eyes of the U.S. Supreme Court, executive agreements have the same standing as treaties.[1]

They are also more numerous than treaties. Between 1940 and 1977, presidents negotiated some 420 treaties, but they concluded another 7715 executive agreements.[2] Many of these agreements involved relatively trivial matters, and many were negotiated with congressional authorization. Some executive agreements, however, involved important policy matters and, in some cases, Congress was not even informed that agreements were being made. America's military involvement in South Vietnam stemmed in part from commitments contained in executive agreements. Meanwhile, executive agreements which were kept secret from the Congress led the U.S. to send military advisers to Laos and to conduct secret bombing raids against communist insurgents.

On several occasions, Congress has attempted to assert some control over the president's use of executive agreements. In 1950, Congress legislated to require the secretary of state to publish annually all executive agreements negotiated during the previous year. Many agreements were kept secret, however, as presidents claimed that national-security concerns necessitated secrecy. Congress tried again in 1972 with the Case Act. This act required the secretary of state to submit to Congress the final text of all executive agreements within sixty days of their negotiation. Agreements involving national security could be submitted to the Senate Foreign Relations Committee or to the House Foreign Affairs Committee on a classified basis. In practice, however, the Case Act, too, has been relatively ineffective. It included no provisions for Congress to reject agreements. It also failed to define executive agreements, leaving it to the executive to determine what must be submitted to Congress.

Executive agreements remain a source of conflict between the executive and legislative branches. Presidents point to a need for secrecy in the conduct of foreign affairs and argue for a free hand in foreign negotiations. In response, Congress contends that it has a constitutional right to act as a check on presidential power in foreign affairs. Conflict is an inherent part of America's separation of powers, however, and it's likely this conflict will be with us for some time.

---

[1]*United States* v. *Belmont*, 301 U.S. 324 (1937).

[2]Louis Fisher, *President and Congress* (New York: Macmillan, 1972); and Thomas E. Cronin, *The State of the Presidency*, 2nd ed. (Boston: Little, Brown, 1980).

important, presidents since the Vietnam war have been limited in their ability to commit armed forces overseas since such actions have often brought with them widespread public resistance, especially in cases where the nation's interests were not very clearly at stake.

Nonetheless, the modern president takes the initiative in foreign policymaking and, in general, enjoys more leeway on foreign affairs than in the domestic arena. The president has more constitutional tools at his command for foreign policymaking, and Congress is less able and often less willing to get involved in the details of foreign policy. After all, most members of Congress were elected because of their knowledge about and interest in taxes, soybeans, and natural gas, not the Straits of Hormuz, Nicaragua, or the Law of the Sea Treaty. Also, fewer interest groups pressure Congress on foreign policy than on domestic policy.

Perhaps the most important foundation for presidential dominance of foreign policymaking is the president's ability to muster broad public support in times of international crisis. Domestic crises divide the nation; foreign crises usually unite it. When the nation appears threatened from abroad, the political criticism that generally accompanies presidential actions is frequently muted. Americans support their president, at least in the short run, whether the news is good or bad. President Kennedy's popularity rose dramatically with both the disaster of the Bay of Pigs invasion and the triumph of the Cuban missile crisis. President Johnson's standing in the polls rose both when he ordered the bombing of North Vietnam and then when he ordered the bombing halted.[10] President Carter's popularity increased with the success of the Camp David accord between Israel and Egypt and with the crisis of the Iranian hostage-taking. However, support declines if things work out badly. This happened to Truman with the Korean War, Johnson with Vietnam, and Carter with the hostage crisis in Iran.

THE MODERN PRESIDENCY AND THE MEDIA

In the television age, the modern president has become a media figure. Television is "up close and personal"; it focuses on the national level of government and on the person of the president. Because of television, the president comes to personify government in general and not just the national government. People are more familiar with the president than they are with the member of Congress elected from their district or the city-council member representing their neighborhood. Americans feel a kinship with the president. When John Kennedy was assassinated many Americans grieved deeply, and felt a sense of personal loss.

The media focus makes the modern president the nation's policy leader. The president can use TV to determine the way issues are shaped and to focus national attention on what he wants to accomplish. He can create news for his own political advantage.[11] Former TV producer Fred Friendly says this about the uses of TV for the modern president: "No mighty king, no ambitious emperor, no pope, no prophet ever dreamt of such an awesome pulpit, so potent a magic wand."[12]

But the media can be a two-edged sword. It has helped to weaken political parties, and that has in turn weakened the president's ability to lead. Calls for party loyalty in support of the president no longer mean as much as they once did.

Then there is the danger of overexposure. Television puts the president at the center of the policymaking stage, but it also makes him more familiar to the public, thereby magnifying his faults.[13] Too much attention tends to trivialize the office—causing a focus on Jimmy Carter's peanuts, for example, or Ronald Reagan's jelly beans. Familiarity can breed contempt, even for presidents. When Gerald Ford's name is mentioned, how many of us still think of his banging his head on helicopter doors? There was a time when the press was fairly discreet. Franklin Roosevelt was never pictured in his wheelchair. Stories about John Kennedy's legendary womanizing never made it into the serious press. Today, however, nothing is sacred, not Brother Billy Carter's drinking, and not First Lady Betty Ford's mastectomy.

Televison increases expectations, and it is impatient for their fulfillment. During the campaign, TV broadcasts the promises of a better America. "I will never lie to you," said Jimmy Carter. Ronald Reagan promised a tax cut, an increase in defense spending, and a balanced budget, all at the same time. Once the new president's term begins, the media focuses on the president's policy initiatives. Hopes are high. Within six months, however, television journalists begin recalling campaign promises, all carefully preserved on tape, and begin asking why the president's program isn't working.

Finally, if things start to go sour, the press can make the president the nation's number one scapegoat.[14] Being at the center of the policymaking stage can have its disadvantages. Bad news generally makes for a better story than good news, and in the last few years, since Vietnam and Watergate, the press has become more distrustful of public officials and frequently indulges in moralizing. On the cover of *Newsweek* magazine on April 5, 1982, was a photograph of a poor, tattered little girl with a forlorn expression. The headline read, "Reagan's America . . . And the Poor Get Poorer." Those who live by the media sword die by the media sword.

THE ORGANIZATION OF THE MODERN PRESIDENCY

The development of the modern presidency has been accompanied by a significant growth in both the size and the power of the presidential bureaucracy—that is, the White House staff and the Executive Office of the President. In the days of Franklin Roosevelt only some ten to twelve assistants worked in the White House, and the total White House staff comprised only about fifty employees. During the Eisenhower Administration the number jumped to 320. Today, there are more than 550 White House employees and more than 1000 people working in the Executive Office.[15]

THE WHITE HOUSE STAFF

The White House staff consists of personal aides, assistants, and advisers to the president, including a press secretary, several speech writers, an appointments secretary, a national security adviser, a legislative liaison, a counselor to the president, a host of special assistants to the president, and a chief of staff. Each of these individuals has at least one deputy, secretarial assistance, and a support staff. The White House staff is chosen by the president without need of Senate confirmation. They are his most loyal supporters; the modern president has grown to rely heavily upon them. Jimmy Carter's staff was headed by Hamilton Jordan, Jody Powell, and other young men from Georgia who went from managing Carter's election campaign to managing the White House. They guided the cabinet, screened key appointments, and influenced politics and policies. When Reagan took office, he brought with him his own collection of political associates. In the first two years of the Reagan Administration, a triumvirate of White House aides—James Baker, Michael Deaver, and Edwin Meese—orchestrated the Reagan presidency and sometimes competed with one another for influence with their boss. By 1983, however, Baker had emerged as Reagan's principal adviser, at least on domestic policy.

Political infighting is not unusual in an administration. Some disputes center on policy, but others involve petty rivalries and jealousies. During the Carter Administration, for example, several cabinet members, including Secretary of Health and Human Services Joseph Califano, were asked to resign by President Carter because of "disloyalty." The truth was that they couldn't get along with the White House staff. In the Reagan Admin-

President Reagan and his top White House aides, 1983. From left: James Baker, William Clark, the president, Edwin Meese, and Michael Deaver.

istration, bitter and often rather public disputes arose over who would manage foreign policy—the secretary of state (first Alexander Haig, then George Shultz), the secretary of defense (Caspar Weinberger), the national security adviser (Richard Allen, William Clark, and then Robert McFarlane), the U.N. ambassador (Jeane Kirkpatrick), or members of the White House staff. President Reagan, meanwhile, seemed unwilling or unable to settle the squabbling.[16] The Reagan Administration suffered another bitter internal battle over economic policy. The main combatants in this feud were Secretary of the Treasury Donald Regan and Martin Feldstein, President Reagan's chief economic adviser. Once again, Reagan failed to step in to halt the public discord.

THE EXECUTIVE OFFICE OF THE PRESIDENT

The Executive Office of the President was established after the Committee on Administrative Management, appointed by Franklin Roosevelt in 1936, concluded that the responsibilities of the presidency were too great for any one individual. "The president needs help," the committee said. Congress responded with the Executive Reorganization Act of 1939, authorizing the Executive Office and allowing the president to create and disband components as he saw fit, without congressional approval.[17] Although the act gave either house of Congress the power to reverse the president's action within sixty days, the Supreme Court's recent ruling on the legislative veto apparently invalidates that provision. Now, the major components of the Executive Office are the Office of Management and Budget, the National Security Council, the Council of Economic Advisers, the Council on Environmental Quality, the Office of Science and Technology Policy, the Office of the Special Representative for Trade Negotiations, and the Intelligence Oversight Board. Of these, the first three are probably the most important.

The Office of Management and Budget (OMB) assists the president in drawing up a budget, serves as a clearing-house for bills drawn up by the cabinet departments to see that they don't conflict with the president's budgetary goals, and monitors expenditures by executive-branch departments. The Director of the OMB is nominated by the president and must be confirmed by the Senate. In recent administrations the OMB has become an increasingly important instrument for presidential control of the executive branch. Under Nixon, it was reorganized to focus more directly on evaluating and coordinating programs. President Carter reorganized the OMB again and assigned it the task of drawing up proposals for reorganizing the federal bureaucracy. Under President Reagan, the OMB and its director, David Stockman, were given the task of cutting billions of dollars from the budget and establishing new budgetary priorities.

The National Security Council (NSC) is composed of the president, the vice-president, the secretaries of state and defense, and others the president may choose to include, such as the national security adviser, the head of the Joint Chiefs of Staff, and the director of the CIA. Its job is to advise the president on national security matters. Under Presidents Kennedy and Johnson, the National Security Council played a prominent policymaking role, but during the Nixon and Ford Administrations it was overshadowed by National Security Adviser and later Secretary of State Henry Kissinger. President Carter usually chose to consult individually with its members or with small groups of foreign-policy advisers rather than deal with the NSC as a whole. President Reagan has generally followed a procedure similar to Mr. Carter's.

The Council of Economic Advisers includes three professional economists whose appointments must be confirmed by the Senate. Its job is to inform and advise the president on economic matters and economic policy. As economic policy has become a larger part of the presidential agenda, the council has played an increasingly prominent part in policymaking. It must usually share that role, however, with other presidential aides and advisers. In the Reagan Administration, the president's chief economic advisers were OMB Director David Stockman, Secretary of the Treasury Donald Regan, and the council.

THE GROWING WHITE HOUSE BUREAUCRACY

The size and policymaking importance of the White House staff and the Executive Office of the President have grown for a number of reasons. First, the role of the president in the policymaking process has expanded significantly. The job is literally too big for one person, and today's complex policy problems require expertise most presidents don't have, especially if they must spend four to ten years on the campaign trail.

Second, the presidential bureaucracy has been augmented by the addition of public-relations media experts whose job is to sell and resell the president. It's as if the campaign for reelection begins on inauguration day. In the Carter Administration, for example, the White House staff included an assistant to the president for public liaison, a liaison with the American Jewish community, a liaison for minority affairs, and a media aide. Some of Carter's more irreverent critics referred to the latter as a presidential assistant in charge of symbolism.

Third, growth has a way of feeding on itself. Every new council needs a staff; every new adviser needs a deputy. Also, people hired to deal with a crisis seldom depart once the crisis is passed. Instead, they drum up some new business for themselves and stay on as part of the permanent White House bureaucracy.[18]

Finally, the White House is generally uncomfortable with what is called the "permanent government," the federal bureaucracy. Bureaucracies are slow, often intractable, and that makes activist presidents impatient. Bureaucrats also have interests of their own: they are loyal to their jobs, their departments, and the programs they administer, but not necessarily to the president, especially if the president wants to reorganize the bureaucracy or cut back their programs. This makes reformist presidents distrustful. The department heads (i.e., the cabinet) are appointed by the president, but they are often chosen for political reasons and not specifically for their loyalty to the president and his programs. Also, over time there is a tendency for department heads to adopt the perspectives of the bureaucracies they head—it's a phenomenon Nixon aide John Ehrlichman once referred to as "marrying the natives." Consequently, presidents turn to those whose loyalty is more certain: the White House staff.

THE PRESIDENTIAL BUREAUCRACY AND PRESIDENTIAL DECISIONMAKING

The White House staff and the rest of the presidential bureaucracy are so important to the modern presidency that the success or failure of an administration may depend on the quality of presidential aides and how well the president uses them. Many observers believe that the ideal method of presidential decisionmaking involves the use of aides and advisers in a **multiple advocacy system.**[19] In this system, the president solicits advice from a broad range of perspectives, perhaps even assigning certain aides the task of playing devil's advocate against certain policy suggestions. Ideally, the president doesn't tip his hand about his own leanings until he has heard all the arguments. It's a good idea for the president to at least appear to maintain an open mind because there's a very strong tendency for aides to tell a president what they think he wants to hear. Lyndon Johnson, for example, was too personally insecure to tolerate criticism; few of his advisers dared suggest that his Vietnam war policy was not working. Consequently, it took him three years to learn that he could not win the war.[20]

The modern president whose decisionmaking style came closest to the multiple-advocacy approach was Franklin Roosevelt. FDR was never wedded to any one adviser or small group of counselors. Instead, he looked to a wide variety of sources—aides, cabinet members, diplomats, experts outside government, friends, and family—for information and advice. On major policy questions, Roosevelt called upon different individuals and factions within the executive branch to argue their cases to him, all the while concealing which way he was leaning at the time. Then, he, the president, would make the decision. This system provided for a certain amount of competition, rivalry, and insecurity within the executive branch, but it also insured a steady flow of ideas.[21]

PROBLEMS OF THE PRESIDENTIAL BUREAUCRACY

The presidential bureaucracy is essential to the effective operation of the presidency, but it can also present problems. First, there is the danger that the White House staff may isolate the president. President Nixon, for example, allowed his chief of staff, H. R. Haldeman, to build a "Berlin Wall" around the president. Consequently, Nixon had to depend on a few staff members—and Haldeman in particular—to present him with a variety of views and ideas.

Second, there is the danger that the White House staff may go into business for themselves, becoming in effect "assistant" presidents. In the Ford Administration, it was widely believed that Secretary of State Henry Kissinger was acting president for foreign policy. During the first year of the Reagan presidency, two Libyan aircraft, after firing on American fighter jets, were shot down over the Mediterranean Sea. Word reached Reagan's ranch in California (where he was vacationing) during the middle of the night, but presidential aide Ed Meese decided not to wake the president. Reagan didn't learn of the incident until several hours later.

Was this an example of an aide overstepping his authority? Many thought it was. After all, the White House staff is unelected, their appointments don't have to be confirmed by the Senate, and, thanks to the doctrine of executive privilege, they cannot be required to reveal to Congress what advice they give the president. Professor Hargrove is particularly cynical about the problems of aides exceeding their authority. "Each successive White House," he writes, "no matter who the president is, seems to be populated by arrogant, careerist, and often ignorant men, who do their president more harm than good in their relations with others and their advice to him. But the headiness of power is intoxicating."[22]

Finally, there is the problem that the White House staff and the Executive Office of the President have grown into large bureaucracies themselves. The presidential bureaucracy has grown because of the White House's impatience with the slowness and intractability of the traditional bureaucracy. Now, ironically the White House bureaucracy is suffering from many of the same ills. As Thomas Cronin phrases it: "The presidency has become a large, complex bureaucracy itself, rapidly acquiring the many dubious characteristics of large bureaucracies in the process: layering, overspecialization, communication gaps, interoffice rivalries, inadequate coordination, and an impulse to become consumed with short-term, urgent operational concerns at the expense of thinking systematically about the consequences of varying sets of policies and priorities and about long-range problems."[23]

CONCLUSION: THE PRESIDENCY AND PUBLIC POLICY

Why are some presidents more successful than others? It's not an easy question to answer; it's not even easy to define success. Is a successful president one who gets his program through Congress? If so, then Franklin Roosevelt in 1933, Lyndon Johnson in 1965–66, and Ronald Reagan in 1981 were successful presidents. But how does one evaluate Dwight Eisenhower, who offered no broad congressional program, but was more interested in administration? Or Richard Nixon, who perennially quarreled with Congress, but who achieved several important foreign-policy goals?

In defining presidential success, shouldn't we also include an evaluation of the president's goals? Congress may enact a president's program, but once in place it may not work well. Lyndon Johnson, for example, proved a master at getting Congress to enact his Great Society program, but he was largely indifferent to problems of administration. This, by the way, is not an uncommon political failing. Most presidents, governors, and mayors find it more politically rewarding to propose new programs than to see to it that old ones work well. Policy implementation frequently takes a back seat to agenda building, policy formulation, and policy adoption.

The difficulty with evaluating the substance of a president's work is that it is very subjective—much lies in the eye of the beholder. Some see Franklin Roosevelt as a savior; others see him as a scoundrel. Some think Ronald Reagan has the right idea; others believe he will lead the nation straight to perdition.

Defining presidential success or failure requires the inclusion of both objective and subjective components (for some subjective evaluations, see the PERSPECTIVE on page 231). Objectively, what kind of success did a president have in terms of his stated goals? Did he get his program through Congress? Was he able to reorganize the bureaucracy? Were his foreign-policy goals achieved? On this criterion, the Carter Administration would generally be considered a failed presidency. To be fair, Carter had some successes—Camp David, the Panama Canal Treaty—but he had more failures: the SALT II Treaty, his proposed consumer protection agency, his energy program, the Iranian crisis. Conversely, by this criterion, Ronald Reagan was a success in 1981 and 1982. Congress passed his budget, approved his tax cut, and upheld his decision to sell the AWACS reconnaissance aircraft to Saudi Arabia.

A second objective evaluation involves results. Did Camp David lead to a lasting peace for the Middle East? Did Reagan's economic program usher in a new era of prosperity? Naturally, these questions must be answered after the passage of some time; presidents often look different after a few years have passed. Today, for example, Harry Truman is highly regarded by both scholars and nonscholars. In his own day, however, Truman's standing in the polls reached a record low that was only surpassed by Jimmy Carter more than twenty years later. Who knows? Perhaps twenty years from now Americans will think fondly of Richard Nixon and look back on Jimmy Carter with nostalgia.

Another difficulty in evaluating presidential success involves this question: Do the times make the president or does the president make the times? If Abraham Lincoln had been elected in 1880 instead of 1860, would he still be ranked as a great president? What impact would Franklin Roosevelt have had were it not for the Great Depression and World War II?

On the other hand, if the Civil War had come four years earlier, would President Buchanan's picture be on the five-dollar bill, or would you need a passport to travel from New York to Richmond?

These are questions that can't be answered, at least not for sure. Times of crisis, such as wartime or depression, do call for greatness. They provide the opportunity for bold leadership. In quieter times, it is more difficult for a president to leave his mark. Still, we suspect that Lincoln would have been a good president in any era and that Buchanan would probably have been a bad one.

That brings us to the elusive question of *why*. What qualities make for effective presidential leadership? Let's examine that by exploring the nature of the president's role in the policy process in a bit more depth.

THE POWER TO PERSUADE

Political scientist Richard Neustadt says that the power of the president is the power to persuade others in political life to cooperate voluntarily to

Perspective
RATING THE PRESIDENTS

Who was the best president in American history? That's a subjective question, and different people offer differing responses. In the fall of 1983, the Gallup Poll asked a national sample of Americans which president, living or dead, they would like to see in the White House today. The big winner was John Kennedy, named by 30 percent of the sample. Franklin Roosevelt was mentioned by 10 percent, followed by Harry Truman with 9 percent, Ronald Reagan at 8 percent, Jimmy Carter tied with Abraham Lincoln at 5 percent, Dwight Eisenhower with 4 percent, Richard Nixon with 3 percent, Theodore Roosevelt at 2 percent, and Gerald Ford,

Lyndon Johnson, and George Washington all tied with 1 percent. In the eyes of the general public, then, Kennedy outshines everyone, Reagan outranks Lincoln, and Carter is ahead of Washington. At the risk of sounding elitist, we can't help but think that a great many people must have slept through social-science classes in high school and college.[1]

Scholarly assessments of presidential performance are quite different from that of the general public. In 1982, two historians, Robert K. Murray and Tim H. Blessing, conducted a survey of American historians, asking them to rank each president from Washington to Carter

as either "great," "near great," "above average," "average," "below average," or "failure." In the judgment of the 846 historians who completed the survey, the greatest president was Lincoln, followed by Franklin Roosevelt, Washington, Thomas Jefferson, Theodore Roosevelt, Woodrow Wilson, Andrew Jackson, Harry Truman, John Adams, and Lyndon Johnson. In contrast, the historians judged Warren G. Harding to be America's worst president. He was followed in ascending order by U. S. Grant, Nixon, James Buchanan, Andrew Johnson, Franklin Pierce, Calvin Coolidge, Millard Fillmore, John Tyler, and Benjamin Harrison.[2]

[1]*Newsweek* (28 November 1983), p. 64.
[2]"Ranking of U.S. Presidents by American Historians," *Washington Post*, National Weekly Edition, 6 February 1984, p. 38.

help him reach his goals.[24] He has to resort to persuasion because there are relatively few in the political arena over whom he has the power to command. He can command his staff and the cabinet, and he is commander in chief of the armed forces, but the separation and balance-of-powers system denies him the power to order about the Congress or the federal judiciary. The federal system means he generally cannot command state officials. Finally, federal law and sheer size make it difficult or impossible for the president to command the federal bureaucracy very much or very closely.

Also, we know that the interests of other political actors don't always coincide with those of the president. Members of Congress have to worry about reelection from their own districts or states, and they are jealous to preserve the prerogatives of their branch of government. The reassertion of Congress in the 1970s involved a conflict over institutional powers. State and local officials are primarily concerned with the well-being of their own areas. Farm-belt governors oppose reductions in farm-price supports. Big-city mayors oppose budget cuts in aid for urban areas. Federal judges are the most independent of all.

The president cannot even count on the cooperation of the whole executive branch. The federal bureaucracy is the permanent government. Presidents and presidential programs come and go, but the bureaucracy stays. Except for the White House staff, the Executive Office of the President, and the cabinet, all of whom serve at the pleasure of the president, the loyalty of federal employees lies with their jobs in their own little niches in the bureaucracy and not with the president's program. A president who wants to reorganize the bureaucracy or cut federal programs invariably meets resistance from within the executive branch.

Consequently, the president has to bargain with other political individuals and groups to try to win their cooperation. He is a broker, a consensus builder. In this task, the president has several assets he can work with. There are a number of appointments he can make; he prepares the budget; he can be of assistance in raising funds for a reelection campaign; and he can appeal to others on the basis of the "national interest" or party loyalty.

To use these assets to their fullest, a president needs to understand the dynamics of political power. Lyndon Johnson, for example, learned as majority leader in the Senate how to build a political coalition to get legislation enacted. In the White House, he put those skills to work and won passage for his Great Society program. In contrast, Jimmy Carter never really understood the mechanics of political power. He ran for president as an "outsider," someone who would ride into Washington and clean up the town. Once in office, Carter was standoffish. He had won the Democratic nomination and had been elected president without having to bargain with the so-called "Washington establishment," and he thought he could govern without bargaining. He was wrong. Politics involves negotiation, give-and-take, compromise. Carter never understood that and consequently was frustrated in most of his goals.

Another useful skill for a president is the ability to communicate. Theodore Roosevelt once called the presidency a "bully pulpit." The modern media make it more so. Certainly a portion of Franklin Roosevelt's success must be attributed to his talent as a communicator. In his famous fireside chats, FDR made the radio listener feel the president was talking directly to him, one-on-one. Much of John Kennedy's appeal can be traced to his gifts as a public speaker and the at-ease, often witty style he employed at press conferences. Ronald Reagan's acting background has been the object of some ridicule, but his skill as a communicator, particularly before the camera, has served him well in getting his message across to the American people.

It's also important for a president to understand the significance of images and symbolism. In Franklin Roosevelt's first term it was just as important that the federal government was doing *something* about the Depression as it was that certain programs were enacted. The relative inaction of the Hoover Administration led to despair; the activity of the New Deal bred hope. Images can produce a substantive result. Lyndon Johnson understood the importance of symbols when he threw the prestige of the presidency behind the cause of civil rights for black Americans. He closed an important speech with the words that symbolized the civil-rights movement: "We shall overcome." At his inauguration, Jimmy Carter symbolized his desire to take some of the pomp and circumstance out of the office of the presidency by walking down the parade route rather than riding in a limousine. Finally, Ronald Reagan symbolized a commitment to women's rights by appointing a woman, Sandra Day O'Connor, to the United States Supreme Court.

THE PRESIDENTIAL CHARACTER

The way a president uses his power of persuasion depends heavily on his personality. Political scientist James David Barber says a president's performance in office is strongly affected by personality traits that are shaped primarily in childhood, but also in adolescence and early adulthood.[25] Barber classifies personality along two dimensions. The first involves the amount of energy an individual brings to what he does. Does he throw himself into the job or does he sit back and wait for events to take place? According to Barber, Presidents Franklin Roosevelt, Harry Truman, John Kennedy, Lyndon Johnson, Richard Nixon, Gerald Ford, and Jimmy Carter were *active* presidents; Warren G. Harding, William Howard Taft, Calvin Coolidge, and Dwight Eisenhower were *passive.*

The second dimension to Barber's personality-classification scheme involves the way an individual feels about what he does. Does he enjoy the job? Is he optimistic? Is he *positive*? Or, is he sad, pessimistic, *negative*? Barber points to Roosevelt, Truman, Kennedy, Ford, and Carter as positive personalities. On the other hand, he sees Lyndon Johnson and Richard Nixon as negative.

Barber uses these two dimensions to create four general types of presidential personalities. According to Barber, the best type of personality for a president is *active-positive*. He is self-confident, optimistic, flexible, and enjoys his job. Franklin Roosevelt, for example, was a supremely self-confident man who set out to master his job. He was a flexible, skillful politician who truly enjoyed being president. Barber also classifies Harry Truman, John Kennedy, Gerald Ford, and Jimmy Carter as active-positive presidents.

Barber says that the most dangerous type of president is the *active-negative*. He puts great energy into his work, but derives little pleasure from it. He suffers from low self-esteem and tends to view political disputes in terms of personal success or failure. He tends to be pessimistic and inclined toward rigidity. Richard Nixon is an example of a president Barber classifies as active-negative. He was personally insecure, combative, tough, and vindictive. He was a loner who saw himself as a righteous leader besieged by enemies. Other examples of active-negative presidents include Herbert Hoover and Lyndon Johnson.

Barber lists two other categories of presidential personalities, *passive-positive* and *passive-negative*. There haven't been many recent examples of passive personalities in the White House. Barber lists Eisenhower as an example of a passive-negative president, that is, one who is involved in politics out of a sense of duty. The passive-negative president avoids conflict and uncertainty and just plain dislikes politics. Finally, the passive-positive president (Barber's most recent example is Taft) is indecisive and superficially optimistic. He tends to react rather than to initiate.

There are clearly some problems with Barber's scheme of classifying presidential personalities—Jimmy Carter and Franklin Roosevelt in the same category?!—but the scheme has been useful in the study of the presidency because it points out the importance of character and personality. To understand the way a president uses his powers of office and his tools of persuasion, one must understand his particular personality.

Consider, for example, how certain aspects of Ronald Reagan's personality have affected decisionmaking in the Reagan White House. Reagan came to Washington a firm believer in the correctness of the basic principles and priorities that he has been espousing most of his adult life. In Reagan's eyes, the source of most of our problems here at home is big government. His solution: cut taxes, cut social spending, reduce regulation. In foreign affairs, Reagan sees the Soviet Union as an implacable adversary and his proposed policy approach is a major buildup of America's armed forces. The result has been a rigid decisionmaking style that has forced advisers to perform intellectual somersaults in order to present alternative policy proposals in terms that seem to be consistent with the Reagan philosophy.[26]

PRESIDENTIAL POPULARITY

A final important factor affecting the president's role in the public-policy process is his popularity. The president is a bargainer. To win cooperation from other political actors he offers inducements from the stock of benefits and advantages his office provides. If the president is politically popular, his inducements are far more valuable than if he is unpopular. A popular president seems more likely to be reelected; his campaign help is more valuable; his support for legislative proposals is more effective; and he can claim to speak for the national interest with greater credibility. Consequently, Lyndon Johnson after his landslide victory in 1964 enjoyed considerably more political credibility than did Richard Nixon in the midst of the Watergate scandal of early 1974.

Thanks to Gallup, we know quite a bit about presidential popularity. For nearly forty years now the Gallup Poll has asked a national sample of Americans the same question every few months: "Do you approve of the way _____ is handling the job as president?" Figures 8.1, 8.2, and 8.3 show the course of presidential popularity for Presidents Ford and Carter, and for the first three years of the Reagan presidency.

The data in the figure illustrate a number of points about presidential popularity. First, presidents usually begin their administrations with high approval ratings. Carter, for example, enjoyed a 65-percent popularity rating after his inauguration, even though he was elected only a few months before with only 51 percent of the popular vote. Apparently Americans give a new president the benefit of the doubt. They are optimistic about his chances for success.

Second, the data show that a president's popularity responds to events.[27] The big jump in Carter's approval rating in the third year of his presidency followed the Iranian hostage seizure—Americans were rallying round the

FIGURE 8.1
*Carter Popularity
Chart*

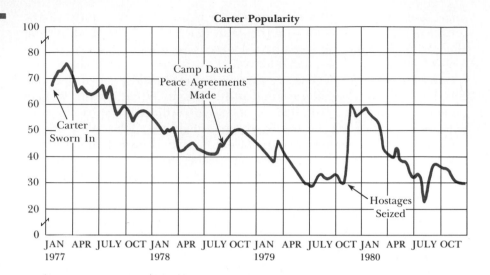

president. Reagan's popularity rose suddenly early in his term after he was wounded in an assassination attempt. It also increased after the invasion of Grenada. In contrast, the big drop in Ford's rating came after he pardoned Richard Nixon.

Finally, a president's popularity tends to decline throughout his term. Every president since Eisenhower has ended his tenure far less popular than when he began. Over time events and conditions erode a president's support. Mounting casualties in Vietnam hurt Johnson; Watergate damaged Nixon; the seemingly endless hostage crisis eventually defeated Carter. Another reason for the decline in presidential popularity is that different groups and factions may jump *off* the bandwagon. In 1976, for example, Jimmy Carter won election with strong labor support. By 1980, however, unhappiness with his economic policies had succeeded in eroding much of that backing. A last explanation is that great expectations foster disappointment. Today's public is cynical. We expect more from the president than he can deliver, sooner than is reasonable, and we are too harsh in our judgments. The irony is that our reduced support for a president is translated through the polls into a reduction in presidential power.

THE PRESIDENTIAL DILEMMA

Such is the dilemma of the modern president in the 1980s. Since the 1930s the role of the federal government has grown dramatically, and the president has become the central figure in the public-policy process. One political scientist has described the role of the modern president by using such extravagant phrases as "leader of the executive branch," "leader of the

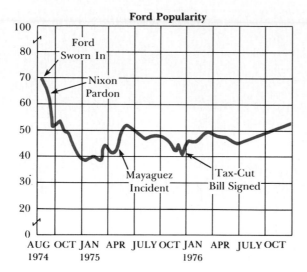

FIGURE 8.2
Ford Popularity Chart

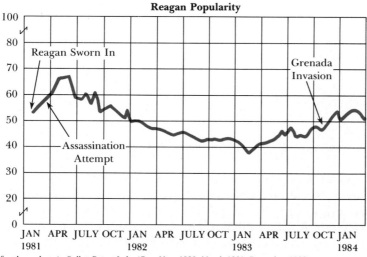

FIGURE 8.3
Reagan Popularity Chart

SOURCES (for three charts): *Gallup Report Index* (Oct.–Nov. 1980, March 1981, December 1983)

forces of peace and war," "leader of Congress," "leader of his party," "leader of public opinion," "leader of the rituals of American democracy," and "leader of the free nations."[28]

Our demands are high and so are our expectations. Madison Avenue campaign techniques succeed in selling presidential candidates, but they also raise expectations. Once a candidate becomes the president-elect and then the president, media hype takes over. The new president's picture is on the cover of *Time* and *Newsweek* and the television news shows are filled with interviews of newly appointed cabinet officers who praise the virtues of the president's new programs. The angry words of the fall campaign are

All presidents must be aware of the symbolic nature of their office, and must strive to present the appropriate public images, from down-home log-splitter (right) to sophisticated head of state (opposite, top).

now forgotten as leaders of both parties speak with optimism about the prospects of cooperation between the Congress and the White House.

But Americans are also impatient. Our favorite television series resolve complicated problems in thirty minutes (and that includes time for three or four deodorant commercials). Is it asking too much for the president to solve our nation's problems in six months or a year? Just as we focus our demands and expectations on the office of the presidency, we focus our impatience there as well. After all, it's easier to blame the president for unemployment, inflation, high interest rates, and the nuclear arms race than it is to unravel the details of policy formulation, policy adoption, and policy implementation.[29]

The challenge for the modern president is enormous—we expect him to turn his simplistic campaign promises into workable solutions to complex problems and to produce discernable results quickly. Does the American electoral system produce individuals capable of meeting this challenge? Professor Cronin doesn't think so: "However much we seek the well-rounded leader for all seasons, we invariably get ambitious, vain, and calculating candidates who rarely know what is to be done (though they are willing to try)."[30] Cronin may be a bit cynical, but it is true that the qualities

needed to *win* the presidency aren't necessarily the qualities required to *be* the president, at least not a good president. Few people would argue that Ronald Reagan, Jimmy Carter, Gerald Ford, and Richard Nixon—whatever their personal strengths and abilities—were the best this nation had to offer during the decades of the '70s and '80s.

Invariably, then, the new president makes mistakes. The pressures for immediate performance are enormous, the problems are exceedingly difficult, and the person in the White House is inexperienced and perhaps unprepared for the job. Eventually, he may get his bearings and grow into the office. Harry Truman had to learn on the job; John Kennedy matured considerably in his three years. Today, however, the president may not get much of a chance to grow. The public and the media are impatient and, since Watergate and Vietnam, are not particularly willing to give a president the benefit of a doubt, at least not for long.

So, when slipups or bad luck come, the president's popularity falls, and we become aware of the decline almost immediately. Just as the Nielsen ratings service tells the network moguls how many people were tuned in to "The A-Team" or "Dallas" last night, the polls tell us how many of us still think the president is doing a good job. If a TV show has bad ratings, it gets cancelled. If a president's popularity falls, he loses political clout. Less political influence means the president will be less successful in getting his programs off the ground, and his popularity will likely fall some more. It becomes a vicious circle; the only thing that can break the pattern is a foreign crisis or an assassination attempt. Even then, the respite may be only temporary, as Carter found out with the Iranian hostage crisis.

One danger presidents must face is the temptation to govern by opinion poll. With poll data coming out every week or so, how much courage does it take for the president to take a stand that he knows will be unpopular, at least in the short run? Can a president afford to ask the nation to sacrifice, to endure temporary hardships in hope of long-term gain? Will today's image-conscious, public relations-oriented White House even consider unpopular positions? What does this mean for public policy?

We seem to have lost sight of the founders' notion of a balance of powers among three separate branches of government. Instead, we focus our attention, our demands, and our expectations on the leader of one of the branches, the president. We demand more from the office than it was intended to provide; we expect more from the president than most mortals can deliver; and we elect people to the office whose temperament is usually far from heroic. Then we rush to judgment—and our judgment is harsh. By the end of the president's term, sometimes well before four years have elapsed, the president's popularity is lost, his political influence is weakened, and he is reduced to being a target for the endless ridicule of stand-up comedians.

Key Terms

CIVILIAN SUPREMACY OF THE ARMED FORCES *(219)*

EXECUTIVE AGREE-MENTS *(221–22)*

HEAD OF STATE *(218)*

HEROIC PRESIDENT *(213)*

IMPEACHMENT *(215)*

IMPERIAL PRESIDENCY *(213)*

IMPOUNDMENT *(221)*

MULTIPLE ADVOCACY SYSTEM *(228)*

"TWO PRESIDENCIES" *(221)*

NOTES

1. Erwin C. Hargrove, *The Power of the Modern Presidency* (Philadelphia: Temple University Press, 1974).
2. Arthur M. Schlesinger, Jr., *The Imperial Presidency* (Boston: Houghton Mifflin, 1973).
3. David Halberstam, "How Television Failed the American Voter," *Parade* (11 January 1981), pp. 4–8.
4. Ibid.

5. Raoul Berger, *Impeachment: The Constitutional Problems* (Cambridge: Harvard University Press, 1973).

6. Michael Les Benedict, *The Impeachment and Trial of Andrew Johnson* (New York: W. W. Norton, 1973).

7. "Walter Mondale: Just Another Veep?" *Economist* (1 September 1979), pp. 26–27.

8. Louis W. Koenig, "Reassessing the 'Imperial Presidency,'" *Proceedings of the Academy of Political Science* 34 (1981): 34.

9. Aaron Wildavsky, "The Two Presidencies," *Trans-Action* 4 (December 1966): 7–14.

10. John E. Mueller, "Presidential Popularity from Truman to Johnson," *American Political Science Review* 64 (March 1970): 18–34; Richard Brody, "International Crises: A Rallying Point for the President?" *Public Opinion* 6 (December/January 1984): 41–43, 60.

11. Richard L. Rubin, "The Presidency in the Age of Television," *Proceedings of the Academy of Political Science* 34 (1981): 138–52.

12. Quoted in Newton Minow, John Bartlow Martin, and Lee W. Mitchell, *Presidential Television* (New York: Basic Books, 1973), p. vii.

13. Don Bonafede, "The Washington Press—It Magnifies the President's Flaws and Blemishes," *National Journal* (1 May 1982), pp. 767–71.

14. Koenig, 31–44.

15. Robert E. DiClerico, *The American President* (Englewood Cliffs: Prentice-Hall, 1979), p. 210.

16. Joseph Kraft, "Our Gangs," *Houston Post,* 16 November 1983, p. 2B; Lou Cannon, "Who's in Charge of Foreign Policy?" *Washington Post,* National Weekly Edition, 5 March 1984, pp. 16–17.

17. Hargrove, p. 81.

18. Thomas E. Cronin, *The State of the Presidency,* 2nd ed. (Boston: Little, Brown, 1980), pp. 229–81.

19. Alexander L. George, "The Case for Multiple Advocacy in Making Foreign Policy," *American Political Science Review* 66 (September 1972): 751–85.

20. Hargrove, pp. 36–40; Eric F. Goldman, *The Tragedy of Lyndon Johnson* (New York: Dell, 1968).

21. Arthur M. Schlesinger, Jr., *The Age of Roosevelt—The Coming of the New Deal,* Vol. II (Boston: Houghton Mifflin, 1958).

22. Hargrove, p. 152.

23. Cronin, p. 244.

24. Richard E. Neustadt, *Presidential Power: The Politics of Leadership* (New York: Wiley, 1960).

25. James David Barber, *The Presidential Character: Predicting Performance in the White House,* 2nd ed. (Englewood Cliffs: Prentice-Hall, 1977).

26. "How Reagan Decides," *Time* (13 December 1982), pp. 12–17; David S. Broder, "Who is Reagan Fooling?" *Washington Post,* National Weekly Edition, 27 February 1984, p. 4; Max Lerner, "Reagan Still Has to Iron

Out his Contradictions," *Houston Chronicle,* 16 December 1983, Sec. 1, p. 30.

27. Samuel Kernell, "Explaining Presidential Popularity," *American Political Science Review* 72 (June 1978): 506–22.

28. Clinton Rossiter, "The Presidency—Focus of Leadership," in Aaron Wildavsky, ed., *The Presidency* (Boston: Little, Brown, 1969), pp. 44–49.

29. Koenig, pp. 31–44.

30. Cronin, p. 33.

SUGGESTED READINGS

BARBER, JAMES D. *The Presidential Character.* 2nd ed. Englewood Cliffs, N.J.: Prentice-Hall, 1977.

CRONIN, THOMAS E. *The State of the Presidency.* 2nd ed. Boston: Little, Brown, 1980.

CUNLIFFE, MARCUS. *American Presidents and the Presidency.* New York: American Heritage Press/McGraw-Hill, 1972.

DiCLERICO, ROBERT E. *The American President.* Englewood Cliffs, N.J.: Prentice-Hall, 1979.

HARGROVE, ERWIN C. *The Power of the Modern President.* Philadelphia: Temple University Press, 1974.

HESS, STEPHEN. *Organizing the Presidency.* Washington, D.C.: Brookings Institution, 1976.

KESSEL, JOHN. *The Domestic Presidency: Decision-Making in the White House.* North Scituate, Mass.: Duxbury, 1975.

KOENIG, LOUIS W. *The Chief Executive.* 3rd ed. New York: Harcourt Brace Jovanovich, 1975.

NEUSTADT, RICHARD. *Presidential Power.* Rev. ed. New York: Wiley, 1976.

PIOUS, RICHARD M. *The American Presidency.* New York: Basic Books, 1979.

POLSBY, NELSON W. *Congress and the Presidency.* 3rd ed. Englewood Cliffs, N.J.: Prentice-Hall, 1976.

ROSSITER, CLINTON. *The American Presidency.* Rev. ed. New York: Harcourt Brace Jovanovich, 1960.

WAYNE, STEPHEN J. *The Legislative Presidency.* New York: Harper and Row, 1978.

Chapter Nine

THE FEDERAL BUREAUCRACY

In early 1981, the Reagan Administration announced a controversial change in government policy: private, nonprofit schools that practice discrimination would once again be eligible for tax-exempt status. Since 1970, the Internal Revenue Service (IRS) had followed the policy of denying tax exemptions to schools that practice discrimination. In 1981, two schools that had been denied exemptions under the ruling—Bob Jones University in Greenville, South Carolina, and the Goldsboro Christian Schools of Goldsboro, North Carolina—had filed suit against the United States Treasury Department, challenging the IRS's policy. In lower federal court, the government, represented by the Justice Department, had won its case, but the decision was appealed to the United States Supreme Court. On Friday, January 8, the administration reversed the long-standing policy. The president ordered the Justice Department to drop the case and asked the Supreme Court to annul the lower-court decision. The reason for the change was political. Conservative Christian groups had pressed the administration for the change and so had several prominent southern Republican congressional leaders.[1]

The announcement of the policy change touched off a firestorm of controversy. Civil-liberties lawyers from the American Civil Liberties Union (ACLU) were appalled by the move and predicted a proliferation of segregationist private schools. Benjamin Hooks of the NAACP took the administration to task for giving official sanction to racial discrimination. In the meantime, Democrats in Congress leaped at the chance to question the Reagan Administration's commitment to racial equality.[2]

In the face of mounting criticism, the president made a strategic retreat. On Tuesday Reagan announced that he was unalterably opposed to racial discrimination and to the schools, colleges, and universities that practice it. Then he called on Congress to pass legislation instructing the IRS to deny tax-exempt status to such schools—exactly what it had been doing for the past eleven years, with the backing of the Justice Department. What is at issue, argued President Reagan, is not whether schools that discriminate can receive favorable tax treatment, but where the policy decision on tax exemptions is made—in the bureaucracy or in Congress.[3]

From there the issue exploded into a many-sided debate. Two Republican senators, embarrassed by their party's association with the controversy, introduced legislation to instruct the IRS, but a pair of crusty southern colleagues hinted they just might block the effort. Meanwhile, Speaker of the House Tip O'Neill, a Reagan nemesis, huffed that legislative instruction already existed in the 1964 Civil Rights Act. One thing was certain: Congress wasn't going to act quickly to resolve the matter.

In the midst of this controversy there emerged another political force determined to have its say—the bureaucrats working within the administration. The Reagan Administration's decision no longer to deny tax-exempt status to schools that discriminate had been made by two top-level Reagan appointees, Attorney General William French Smith and Treasury

Secretary Donald Regan. But many career officials working under these two men disapproved of the change. Long before Smith and Regan had set foot in Washington, IRS officials had been making policy on this issue. For over a decade they had annually turned down tax-exempt petitions from Bob Jones University, Goldsboro Christian Schools, and scores of other private institutions that discriminate racially. When the schools challenged this federal policy in court, lawyers in the Civil Rights Division of the Justice Department had always defended it. And won.

Now many bureaucrats were actively resisting Reagan's policy switch. At first the bureaucratic dissent was expressed only internally. As early as January 8, the day the announcement was made, Theodore B. Olson, head of the Justice Department's Office of Legal Counsel, wrote a memorandum to his boss, Smith, disputing the legal arguments used to justify the policy change.[4] Smith was obviously unconvinced so the bureaucrats raised the ante. More than 100 of the 176 lawyers in the Civil Rights Division signed a letter to the division's head, William Bradford Reynolds, another Reagan appointee, expressing their protest. Then the letter was leaked to the press.[5]

Secretary of the Treasury Donald Regan. Along with Attorney General William French Smith, Regan helped shape the policy of granting tax-exempt status to schools that discriminate. Pressures from within the federal bureaucracy caused the administration later to reverse this policy.

The letter fanned higher the flames of controversy and undermined the administration's position. It was further evidence that the policy was ill-conceived—even officials in the president's own administration disapproved. It was another reason for interest groups to renew their attacks and for members of Congress to resist the president's proposals. It damaged the president's prestige, making him appear a weak leader.

This little episode of Washington policymaking illustrates the role of the federal bureaucracy in the public-policy process. The traditional concept of bureaucracy is that it is composed of competent organizations, responding in a politically neutral manner to the initiatives of Congress and the president. In the real world, however, bureaucracy isn't like that.

Our story tells several things about the realities of the federal bureaucracy. First, bureaucracy is involved in making policy. The original decision to withhold tax exemptions from schools that discriminate, you recall, was made not by Congress or the White House, but by the IRS. It was defended by Justice Department lawyers. Second, bureaucrats have political perspectives of their own. The men and women in the IRS and the Justice Department who had been involved with this particular policy for the last decade believed in it. They thought it was right and they defended it. Finally, bureaucracy has power. By going public with their disagreement, the lawyers in the Justice Department aided the cause of administration critics within Congress and without, and undermined the administration's efforts to settle the matter quietly.

Incidentally, the bureaucrats' position was upheld in the end. The Supreme Court refused to drop the case. Instead, it invited William T. Coleman, Jr., the chair of the NAACP's Legal Defense and Educational Fund, to argue the position that the Reagan Administration had chosen to abandon. Then the Court proceeded to hear the case. In May 1983, the Court announced its decision and it was a stinging rebuke for the White House. By an eight-to-one margin, the Court held that private schools that discriminate are ineligible for tax exemptions. The IRS rules, said the Court, were "wholly consistent with what Congress, the executive, and the courts had repeatedly declared." Moreover, the Court made it clear that "racial discrimination in education violates a most fundamental national policy, as well as rights of individuals."[6]

ORGANIZATION OF THE BUREAUCRACY

The United States Constitution is virtually silent on the organization of the federal bureaucracy. It makes some vague references to executive departments, but it doesn't spell out many details. Instead, the bureaucracy as we know it today, with more than 2.8 million civilian employees working in more than 140 departments, commissions, agencies, and bureaus, has been gradually created by the Congress over a period of about two hundred years. Like a coral reef, the bureaucracy has grown by accretion, its structures more reflective of political compromise and historical accidents than any conscious organizational philosophy or scheme. Consequently, today's federal bureaucracy is so vast and complex that its organization defies simple classification. But we will do our best.

THE EXECUTIVE DEPARTMENTS

A significant share of the activities of the federal government is administered by cabinet-level executive departments. In George Washington's day, there were five departments: State, Treasury, War, Navy, and the Attorney General. Subsequently the War and Navy Departments were merged to form the Defense Department, the Attorney General's Department became the Justice Department, and nine other departments have been added by Congress: Interior, Agriculture, Commerce, Labor, Housing and Urban Development, Transportation, Energy, Health and Human Services, and Education. The two largest of these are Defense and Health and Human Services. The Defense Department has more than a million civilian employees and a budget greater than $200 billion, while Health and Human Services employs some 156,000 workers with a budget of $228 billion.

Each of the departments is divided into many smaller administrative units. The Agriculture Department, for example, includes the Forest Service, the Soil Conservation Service, and the Farmers Home Administration. The Census Bureau, the Small Business Administration, and the National

Oceanic and Atmospheric Administration are all part of the Commerce Department.

All of this division makes for a certain amount of intradepartmental conflict and rivalry. At times, subdepartmental agencies develop political power of their own. When J. Edgar Hoover was alive, nobody messed with the Federal Bureau of Investigation (FBI). For decades, FBI Director Hoover was one of the most powerful and feared men in Washington, even though the FBI was part of the Justice Department and the Attorney General was officially Hoover's boss. Today, no agency below the departmental level has the clout that Hoover's FBI once had, but some have developed power bases of their own. These include the Federal Highway Administration in the Department of Transportation, the Army Corps of Engineers within the Defense Department, the Public Health Service in the Department of Health and Human Resources, and the Forest Service in the Agriculture Department.[7]

Each of the executive departments is headed by a secretary or, in the case of the Justice Department, the attorney general. They are appointed by the president with Senate confirmation to serve "at the president's pleasure"; that is, the president may remove a department head when he wishes. The Senate usually approves the president's cabinet choices although presidential appointeees have been scrutinized more closely in recent years than in the past. This, coupled with tighter conflict-of-interest requirements for cabinet members, the high cost of living in Washington, and comparatively low pay offered cabinet members have made it more difficult for presidents to find qualified men and women willing to accept cabinet posts.[8]

Most presidents come to Washington promising to use their cabinet as a policymaking body, but before very long it's the White House staff and the Executive Office, not the cabinet, that are at the center of presidential decisionmaking. Jimmy Carter began his presidency holding weekly cabinet meetings, but before long the meetings became less frequent as Carter looked inward to his staff for policy advice. In 1980 Ronald Reagan pledged to revitalize cabinet government, but by 1982 that promise was forgotten. "Cabinet government is a myth," said an aide.[9]

Why doesn't cabinet government work? First, the cabinet contains too many people working from too many different perspectives. There are thirteen department heads, and the president usually invites the budget director, the United Nations ambassador, and, perhaps, the national security adviser to sit in as well. That's just too many people for smooth decisionmaking.[10] There are few issues on which everyone in the group has an interest or can contribute. Why include the secretary of labor in a discussion of U.S. policy toward Israel? Is the time of the secretary of defense well spent arguing rice subsidies?

Second, the criteria a president uses in selecting a cabinet don't necessarily guarantee a body that can work together effectively to make policy. The president looks for knowledge, administrative competence, experience, loyalty, and congeniality, but there are other considerations as well. Presidents try to include women and minorities, and they like to have a geographic balance. Some cabinet posts may go to party leaders to reward campaign assistance. Presidents look for secretaries that will fit the style and image of their department. It may also be important that secretaries be acceptable to the interest groups the departments work with most closely. The secretary of the treasury, for example, is always a conservative, sound-money individual who dresses like a banker. The secretary of agriculture is a farmer, usually from the Midwest. Meanwhile, the secretary of interior is a rugged outdoors-type who organizes hikes and goes mountain climbing. Women are most likely to be named secretaries of education or housing and urban development.[11]

Finally, the White House usually grows to distrust the cabinet. Eventually members of the White House staff begin to suspect that department heads are growing too attached to the programs their departments administer and the clientele groups they represent. Remember John Ehrlichman's line about "marrying the natives"? Charles O. Dawes, who was Calvin Coolidge's vice-president, put it like this: "Cabinet members are vice presidents in charge of spending, and as such they are natural enemies of the president."[12]

The traditional image of the cabinet is that its members' primary responsibilities are, first, counseling the president on policy formulation and, second, leading their department in implementing policy. In practice, most cabinet members don't do much of either. For policymaking assistance, the president turns to smaller groups of aides, advisers, and selected cabinet officers, frequently including the secretaries of state, defense, and treasury, and the attorney general. In fact, these four are sometimes referred to as the **inner cabinet.** Full cabinet meetings tend to become forums for presidential pep talks or "show-and-tell" sessions for cabinet members to discuss the latest developments in their departments. As for leading their departments, many secretaries soon learn that their departments are not always willing to be led. Ask Reagan's Attorney General Smith about the lawyers in the Justice Department. Also, most department heads haven't time to concentrate on the details of administration. They are too busy dealing with Congress, doing public-relations work with their department's constituents, selling the president's program, and campaigning for the president's reelection.[13]

INDEPENDENT REGULATORY COMMISSIONS

To the uninitiated, the independent regulatory commissions may seem lost in an alphabet soup of acronyms: ICC, FTC, FCC, FPC, SEC, NLRB, and on and on.[14] In actuality, though, these agencies are quite relevant to the lives of most Americans. Since 1887 when the Interstate Commerce Commission was established to regulate the railroads, Congress has seen fit to create a number of independent commissions with the authority to regulate significant portions of economic life. The Federal Trade Commission, for example, enforces antitrust laws and protects against deceptive advertising. The Federal Communications Commission licenses and regulates radio and television stations. The Securities and Exchange Commission regulates the stock market.

One of Congress' motivations in making these agencies independent has been to remove them from political influence, especially from the White House. The independent regulatory commissions are headed by boards of three to eleven members appointed by the president with Senate approval. Unlike cabinet members, however, the president cannot remove commissioners except for just cause, such as neglect of duty or malfeasance (misconduct) in office. Commissioners serve for fixed, staggered terms ranging from three to fourteen years. Consequently, a new president cannot have much impact on the boards' composition until he has served several years. Congress also generally requires that no more than a bare majority of board members be from the same political party.

A second reason for establishing independent regulatory commissions is to provide closer, more flexible regulation than Congress itself can offer through **statutory laws,** that is, law that emerges from the legislative process. Consequently, Congress has delegated broad, general powers to these agencies to control various business practices in the "public convenience, interest, or necessity."

The stock market is regulated by the Securities and Exchange Commission.

One means of regulation used by the commissions is known as **rulemaking.** Rules, which are sometimes also called regulations or guidelines, are often legally binding in the same sense as statutory law. The process begins when the agency gives advance notice that it is considering issuing a rule in a particular area. The tentative text of the proposed rule is published and interested parties are given the opportunity to comment on the rule. When the commission finally and officially adopts a rule, it is published in the Code of Federal Regulations.

Just how important is rulemaking? The Code of Federal Regulations takes up considerably more library shelf space than the United States Code in which statutory laws are published. More significantly, the independent regulatory commissions make important decisions affecting major segments of society.

These agencies are also the targets of frequent criticism. One line of attack is along theoretical grounds: they violate the doctrine of separation of powers. Not only do the commissions make rules, they also interpret their meaning in concrete applications, and they enforce them. A second criticism is focused on their procedures. The commissioners decide issues on a case-by-case basis, the argument goes, instead of making general policy. Consequently, there is little long-range planning. Finally, a third major criticism is that the commissions have been "captured" by the industries they are supposed to be regulating. It's not the public interest that's served, say the critics, it's the private interest.[15]

In practice, some agencies work better than others. The SEC, for exam-

"We understand you tore the little tag off your mattress."

ple, is generally highly regarded. Since it deals with a single industry, the stock exchange, it has been able to frame consistent policies and stick with them. Also, both the public and the industry understand and accept the need for regulation in this area. In contrast, the FTC is frequently the object of severe criticism from industry and consumer groups. Consumer advocates such as Ralph Nader charge the agency doesn't police advertisers closely enough, while industry spokespersons often question the necessity for government regulation at all.[16]

GOVERNMENT CORPORATIONS

Government corporations are organized much like private corporations, except that they are owned by the government instead of by stockholders. Congress creates them in order to remove a particular activity from direct political influence and to give an agency greater operational flexibility than it otherwise would have. The Postal Service, for example, is headed by an eleven-member board of governors who serve nine-year, overlapping terms. The board names a postmaster general who is in charge of the day-to-day operations of the service.

An important principle behind the Postal Service and other government corporations is that they are self-financing. In the case of the Postal Service, the cost of operation is to be borne by the postal users through service charges rather than through revenues raised by taxes. In addition to the Postal Service, the list of government corporations includes the National Rail Passenger Service Corporation (AMTRAK), the Corporation for Public Broadcasting, the Federal Deposit Insurance Corporation (FDIC), the Federal Savings and Loan Insurance Corporation (FSLIC), the Commodity Credit Corporation, and the Tennessee Valley Authority (TVA).[17]

MISCELLANEOUS AGENCIES

Other government agencies come in a variety of shapes and forms. The Veterans Administration (VA), Central Intelligence Agency (CIA), Environmental Protection Agency (EPA), and the General Services Administration (GSA) are all executive-branch agencies whose heads are named by the president with Senate approval. They report to the president and serve at his pleasure. Other agencies are headed by boards rather than by a single individual—the Federal Election Commission and the National Transportation Safety Board, for example. Still other agencies really can't be classified at all, including the Smithsonian Institution, the Legal Services Corporation, and the National Parks Foundation.

Finally, there are several dozen organizations, including the Rand Corporation, the Institute for Defense Analysis, the Aerospace Corporation, and the Institute for Urban Studies, that exist in a twilight zone between the public and private sector. These organizations technically are not part of the federal bureaucracy. They are private, not-for-profit corporations. In general, however, they have been created at government's initiative. Virtually their entire workload involves providing technical and advisory assistance to such governmental agencies as the Departments of Defense, Energy, Labor, and State, and to the National Aeronautics and Space Administration (NASA) on a contract basis.[18]

THE POLITICS OF ORGANIZATION

Charting the organization of the federal bureaucracy seems a mundane activity, but by doing it we can learn some important lessons about politics and policymaking. As we shall see, organization reflects politics.

Traditional organization theory holds that the ideal bureaucratic model resembles a pyramid. At the bottom are a number of functional units, each responsible for a particular activity. Each of these units is headed by an executive officer who reports to a middle-level executive who in turn is in charge of overseeing the activities of several related functional units. At the top of the pyramid is a chief executive who has final authority over the whole organization.

In contrast to the ideal bureaucratic model, the organization of the federal bureaucracy often seems haphazard or eccentric. Sometimes agencies share responsibilities for a single activity. For example, the Departments of Interior and Agriculture and the U.S. Army Corps of Engineers are all involved in water-resource management. The system developed incrementally and each step was logical in itself. The end result, however, is not. The present system involves an overlapping of responsibilities, duplication of effort, and wasteful competition among the agencies. Yet Congress is unlikely to make any significant changes in the system. Each of the agencies involved is under the jurisdiction of a different set of congressional committees and subcommittees, each of which jealously guards its prerogatives. The creation of a single agency in the bureaucracy to oversee water-resource development and conservation would require a reshuffling of committee and subcommittee jurisdictions in Congress and that would not be achieved without a bloody, bone-shattering fight.[19]

The bureaucracy is disorganized, and Congress, interest groups, and the bureaucrats themselves like it that way. Powerful committee and subcommittee heads stand ready to protect the powers of their own particular policymaking kingdoms. Through the years interest groups have developed understandings with committee and agency staffs, and they don't want to see those arrangements disturbed. Meanwhile, bureaucrats oppose any reorganization that might threaten their positions.

Examples of the politics of organization abound. In 1966, Congress created two separate agencies to administer the highway-safety program and authorized the president to name a single administrator to head both agencies. That way two Senate committees could have a voice in confirming the agency head.[20]

The structure of the independent regulatory commissions reflects politics, too. Most organization theorists argue that administration by a single executive officer is more efficient than by a plural executive. With a plural executive, no one is in charge; it's government by committee. Nevertheless, Congress has prescribed a plural executive for the independent regulatory commissions. Why? Because Congress is concerned that a single executive could be too easily controlled by the president. A plural executive may be less efficient, but, Congress hopes, it will also be independent of the White House and more responsive to the legislative branch.[21] When politics and organization theory clash, politics wins (for an example see the **PERSPECTIVE** on page 253).

Then there's the case of the nonprofit corporations. The argument for the nonprofits is that they can do certain activities faster and better than the government can. But there are political reasons for their existence as well. The bureaucracy is frequently too inflexible to undertake new and complex tasks. Agencies work under personnel ceilings that can't easily be raised. After all, no one in Congress wants to be accused of voting to enlarge the federal bureaucracy. Reorganizing existing agencies can't be accomplished without a political dogfight. Consequently, Congress assigns activities to private nonprofit corporations. It's simply easier for government to spend money than it is to hire more personnel or to reorganize the bureaucracy. The result is a political shell game: the federal government's activities and expenditures expand while its work force remains surprisingly stable.[22]

PERSONNEL

As the size and scope of federal activities have grown, so has the federal bureaucracy. In John Adams' day, only some 3000 individuals worked for the federal government. The number was up to 95,000 in 1881 and 500,000 in 1925. Today, the federal bureaucracy is the largest civilian work force in the noncommunist world with some 2,869,000 employees stationed in every state and city in the country and almost every nation in the world. Since about 1970, however, the number of federal employees has leveled off, thanks to political pressures to limit the "bloated bureaucracy" and to the use of nonprofit corporations to perform some governmental services.

Employment practices in the early days of the republic emphasized character, professional qualifications, and political compatibility with the administration in office. Under President Andrew Jackson, however, political considerations became the primary qualification for federal employment. When a new president took office, he fired all the old government workers and replaced them with his friends and supporters. To the victors belong the spoils, they said, and federal jobs were the spoils.

For years, the **spoils system,** as it was known, was a prime target for reformers. They were unsuccessful, however, until 1881, when President

Perspective
TWO COMMISSIONS ARE BETTER THAN ONE

The Commission on Security and Cooperation in Europe is an obscure government agency whose history illustrates how politics can shape bureaucratic structures. Congress created the commission in 1976 to monitor compliance with international agreements on human rights and other matters. Its membership included six senators, six House members, and three presidential appointees. Democratic Representative Dante Fascell from Florida was named the commission's head while a member of the Senate cochaired the commission.

This arrangement worked smoothly until 1981 when Republican Senator Robert Dole from Kansas was added to the committee and named cochair. Almost immediately, Dole and Fascell were at odds over the commission's operations. The dispute reached a head in 1983 when Dole, who chairs the powerful Senate Finance Committee, won Senate approval of an amendment to a spending-authorization bill that would cut off all money for the commission unless the House agreed to install Dole as chairman, deposing Fascell. This action resulted in a

deadlock in conference committee between House and Senate conferees, a deadlock that was finally resolved by a classic political compromise. A second commission was created to duplicate the work of the original commission and to be headed by Dole. The compromise satisfied everyone except, perhaps, the taxpayers, who will be out $250,000 a year, the budget of the new commission.[1]

[1]Phil Gailey, "Congressional Power Struggle Ends in Duplicate Commissions," *New York Times,* 24 November 1983, p. 12.

Public-Employee Unions

A CONVERSATION WITH PROFESSOR IRVING O. DAWSON, UNIVERSITY OF TEXAS AT ARLINGTON

Q. How extensive is unionism in the public sector?

A. Public-employee unions have existed since the early 1800s, but the big push for unionization came in the 1960s with the advent of collective bargaining. Now, about 60 percent of the federal work force and 50 percent of state and local government employees are represented by unions, compared to only 20 percent of employees in the private sector.

Q. Why do public employees join unions?

A. For the same reasons other workers join: low wages, unhappiness with working hours and conditions, inadequate grievance procedures, a desire to participate in decisionmaking, and political activism. A more favorable legal climate for collective bargaining has aided the cause of unions. Also, the increased numbers of government employees at all levels have made them a target for unionizing efforts.

Q. Will the growth of public employee unions continue?

A. In the last few years union growth among public employees has leveled off and even declined because of the recession.

Irving Dawson, chairman of the Department of Political Science at the University of Texas at Arlington, is a graduate of the University of Texas (Austin) and has worked for the U.S. Civil Service Commission and the U.S. Department of Labor in the field of public-sector labor relations. He teaches this subject and others in public administration, has written several articles on public-sector unions, and is currently at work on a textbook in this area.

When times are hard, employers, both public and private, cut back on hiring. Unions go on the defensive, worrying about the job security of their members as management cuts back on services and personnel and emphasizes worker productivity.

Once the economy improves, however, public-sector unions should prosper again. In particular, keep your eye on the American Federation of State, County, and Municipal Employees (AFSCME). It's an aggressive union with more than a million members, and it is likely to be in the forefront of organizing activities.

Q. You mentioned collective bargaining. Is that part of the labor-management system for public employees?

A. Yes, it is. In 1962, President Kennedy issued Executive Order 10988 which emphasized that collective bargaining for federal employees was in the public interest. Then, in 1978, collective bargaining for federal employees became law. Collective-bargaining policies for government workers below the federal level differ from state to state.

Q. Would you briefly define collective bargaining and explain how it works?

A. Collective bargaining is used by management and labor to channel and resolve conflict. You might say the two sides "exchange promises" about their future relationship. In the first

---

James Garfield's assassination at the hands of a disgruntled officeseeker provided all the impetus the reformers needed. Congress responded in 1883 with the Pendleton Act (the Civil Service Act), creating a Civil Service Commission. The commission was charged with establishing a hiring system based on competitive examinations and with the protection of federal

part of the collective-bargaining process, labor organizes and usually seeks to force management to the bargaining table, where both sides attempt to negotiate a written agreement. This written agreement forms the second part of the process since it serves as a contract in which management manages and the union polices the contract through the grievance procedure. Finally, the collective-bargaining process provides for the resolution of impasses through mediation, fact-finding, and arbitration by third parties.

Q. Is collective bargaining the same in the public sector as in the private?

A. There are important differences because politics and political bargaining are the dominant themes in the public sector. The bargaining is over public money, public policy, and public services. So there is public pressure to reach a settlement. Government officials aren't just employers; they are also politicians. Meanwhile, the bargaining power of the employees is determined by the political clout of their unions, who support their allies and punish their enemies in elections. Ultimately at issue in negotiations is who represents the public interest.

Q. As a matter of public policy, should public employees have the right to unionize and engage in collective bargaining?

A. Yes. We are talking about the constitutional freedom to assemble and associate. For many years, public employees were looked upon as second-class citizens insofar as labor relations were concerned. Government was a sovereign employer. The struggle has been hard and long, but through laws, court decisions, and executive orders at both the national and state levels, public employees have generally won the right to band together as their counterparts in the private sector do. The right of public-employee unions to engage in collective bargaining is still controversial, though, and public policy varies from state to state. Ultimately, Congress and the courts may have to decide on a national policy.

Q. Should public employees have the right to strike?

A. That's a more difficult question. Federal employees are prohibited from striking by law, but that hasn't meant there have been no work stoppages. The postal workers walked out in 1970, and in 1981 the Professional Air Traffic Controllers Organization went on strike. At the state level, only eight states permit strikes under certain conditions. Economic distress in many cities, though, has caused a decrease in strikes. In 1981 there were only 200 work stoppages by public employees compared with 536 in 1980 and 593 in 1979.

I don't expect we'll see most public employees getting the right to strike anytime soon. Old ideas of government as a sovereign still prevail when it comes to strikes and are not likely to change in the near future. And I'm not so sure that that's not good public policy. In the private sector, the strike is the ultimate economic weapon. In the public sector, though, the strike is principally political. Public-employee unions now enjoy the same political weapons as other interest groups. The right to strike would mean a particularly potent addition to their arsenal. If public employees are not granted the right to strike then certainly there must be alternatives when impasses occur, alternatives such as compulsory arbitration.

---

workers from dismissal for political reasons. At first, the civil-service system covered only about 10.5 percent of federal jobs, but Congress expanded coverage through the years to include most career federal workers. In 1939 Congress enacted another reform, the Hatch Act, to restrict the political activities of federal employees to voting and the private expression of views. The rationale behind the law was to protect government workers from being coerced into political activities.

Civil service ended the spoils system, but it also came in for its share of criticism. Many critics charged that the system was too inflexible to reward merit, to punish sloth, or to transfer top civil servants from one agency to another without having to scale a mountain of red tape. It was frequently easier to promote incompetent or recalcitrant employees than to fire them. Other critics attacked the **veterans' preference** system that awarded extra points on civil-service exams to armed-forces veterans. They charged that it violated the principle of merit selection and discriminated against non-veterans, particularly women.[23]

Consequently, in 1978 President Carter proposed a package of civil-service reforms. First, he asked Congress to establish a Senior Executive Service (SES) composed of 8000 or so top civil servants who could be hired, fired, and transferred more easily than ordinary federal workers. They would be eligible for substantial incentive bonuses, but could also be demoted out of the SES. Second, Carter proposed eliminating the Civil Service Commission and replacing it with two new agencies: an Office of Personnel Management to manage the federal work force and to establish hiring criteria and pay scales; and a Merit Systems Protection Board to hear employee grievances. Third, the president asked Congress to legislate protection for "whistle-blowers"—workers who report government wrong-doing or mismanagement. Fourth, Carter proposed that federal workers be granted the legal right to join unions and bargain collectively on matters other than wages. He did *not* ask, however, that federal employees be given the right to strike. President Reagan dramatized this point in 1981 when he fired several thousand air traffic controllers for engaging in an illegal strike. Fifth, Carter suggested that procedures for dismissing incompetent employees be streamlined. Finally, he asked Congress to limit veterans' preference to those who served in Vietnam.

Jimmy Carter has been frequently criticized for dealing ineffectually with Congress, but in the case of civil-service reform he was both skillful and successful. Reforming the bureaucracy is often a thankless political task; it attracts few friends but many enemies. Nonetheless, Carter successfully overcame misgivings on the part of Congress and many federal employees, and the opposition of several interest groups. Congress passed everything Carter wanted except the veterans' preference reform. Chalk one up for the veterans' lobby.[24]

As government has become more complex and its tasks more technically oriented, the people staffing the bureaucracy have assumed more substantive roles in the policy process. Each government job is assigned a Government Service (GS) classification ranging from one to eighteen, with higher classifications requiring more skill and/or experience and receiving more pay. The highest classifications, sixteen through eighteen, are called the **supergrades.** The 11,000 or so men and women holding these positions, or their equivalent, are the executives and the technical managers of government. They have substantive knowledge, technical skill, and an under-standing of the workings of the executive branch.

Government managers and technicians come from a broad range of professional fields—the law, medicine, engineering, and the like—but they tend to concentrate within departments and agencies. Consequently, the character of an agency's activities is often molded by the professional perspectives of its personnel.[25] For example, the Federal Housing Admin-istration (FHA), the agency that insures home mortgages, has long re-flected the professional values and prejudices of the real-estate people and mortgage bankers who staff it. Their primary concern is in insuring safe loans. Consequently, the FHA tends to avoid low-risk clients—the poor, minorities, inner-city residents. This results in a remarkably low default rate on FHA loans, but should that be the sole criterion for judging the effectiveness of the program? Are other public-policy goals being ne-glected?

There are many other examples of professional perspectives affecting agency behavior. The U.S. Army Corps of Engineers is responsible for the construction of dams, levees, harbors, waterways, and the like. It is domi-nated by engineers who decide which projects to undertake primarily on the basis of engineering design. The independent regulatory agencies are the domain of lawyers. They see problems as "cases," and look to precedent and trial-like proceedings to produce solutions.[26]

Finally, consider the case of government policy toward tobacco products. Observers frequently point out the inconsistency of the federal govern-ment's subsidizing tobacco farmers while at the same time warning con-sumers about the health hazards of smoking. There's a logic to the incon-sistency, however—a bureaucratic logic. Tobacco-subsidy programs are formulated by the agricultural committees of the House and Senate and are administered by the Department of Agriculture. All three are populated by individuals with agricultural backgrounds and all are vigorously lobbied by agricultural interests. To them, tobacco is simply another crop whose growers should be supported and whose sales promoted. It's the natural order of things. In contrast, the Public Health Service is the turf of the medical professionals. Naturally enough, their primary concern is health. Consequently, while the Agriculture Department subsidizes tobacco farm-ers, the Surgeon General's office cranks out scientific reports on the health dangers of smoking.

THE POLITICS OF ADMINISTRATION

The federal bureaucracy is very much a part of the policymaking process. It collects and spends hundreds of billions of dollars in revenue. It makes and enforces thousands of regulations. Its activities and operations directly affect the lives of all of us every day. It should come as no surprise, then, that the bureaucracy is often the focus of intense political conflict.

THE PRESIDENTIAL PERSPECTIVE

Presidents have two basic underlying goals: reelection and the achievement of their policy goals. Both these goals are affected by the bureaucracy. Presidents have a personal stake in the faithful and efficient implementation of their own programs, of course, but they also want to place their stamp on the operation of ongoing federal programs. Also, presidents are in a hurry. The bureaucracy is sometimes called the permanent government, but presidents have only four years, eight years at most, in which to make their mark.

Presidents have several tools at their disposal for controlling the bureaucracy. First, there's the power of appointment. The president has the authority to appoint most of the top administrators in the bureaucracy, including cabinet secretaries and undersecretaries, agency heads, and regulatory commissioners, although, as we pointed out earlier in the chapter, this doesn't guarantee presidential control.

A second instrument of control is the White House staff. Staff members are loyal to the president, but they are usually less experienced and less expert than department heads. Also, the bureaucracy is still large and sprawling. One result, though, is guaranteed: tension and conflict among the staff, the department heads, and career bureaucrats. In 1979, for example, Jimmy Carter asked for the resignations of several cabinet members primarily because of conflict between them and the White House staff.

A third presidential tool is the Office of Management and Budget. This office evaluates agency performance and scrutinizes budget requests on behalf of the president, who in turn submits a budget request to Congress. The president's role in the budgetary process provides him with a very attractive carrot and a rather imposing stick for keeping the bureaucracy in line, but it's not without its limitations. Congress has the final say on the budget and, as we shall see, agencies can sometimes make end runs around the White House to protect their particular slice of the budgetary pie. On several occasions in the early 1980s, for example, Congress approved more money for various agencies than the Reagan Administration had requested.

Finally, the president may propose a reorganization of the executive branch. Franklin Roosevelt, for example, would ask Congress to create new agencies when he wanted to overcome the inertia of the old. In general, however, getting Congress to agree to a reorganization is easier said than done. Jimmy Carter came to Washington promising an overhaul of the bureaucracy, but most of his ideas never left the drawing board.

Recent presidents haven't been particularly successful in managing the bureaucracy. It's just too big, and their tools of management are not particularly effective. When the Justice Department lawyers openly opposed the administration's policy on tax-exempt status for private schools that discriminate, President Reagan could invite them all to resign (which he did), but he couldn't fire them, reduce their pay, or have them all transferred to Frostbite Falls, Minnesota.

Also, most presidents aren't particularly skillful at administration. We don't elect presidents for their administrative ability, and it's unusual when we get one who has any. President Nixon, for example, took office determined to have a strong cabinet. Before long, however, he decided he preferred the White House staff for making policy because strong, independent-minded cabinet officers got in the way of his efforts to run the bureaucracy. Consequently, Nixon decided to dump the independent voices in his second term and replace them with relative unknowns who, he hoped, could more easily be controlled by the White House. The scheme failed, however, thanks to the intervention of the Watergate scandal.[27]

THE CONGRESSIONAL PERSPECTIVE

Congress' powers to manage the federal bureaucracy are considerably greater than those of the president. After all, it was Congress that created the bureaucracy, and it is Congress that delegates authority to it. What Congress giveth, Congress can take away. Specifically, Congress can abolish an agency, reorganize its structure, change its jurisdiction, cut its budget, investigate its performance, and overrule its decisions.

There have been occasions when Congress has seen fit to clamp down on particular agencies. In the late 1970s, for example, Congress overrode the Food and Drug Administration's ban on over-the-counter sales of saccharine after laboratory tests discovered a link between it and cancer in white rats. After the 1979 crash of a DC-10 in Chicago that killed 275

After the crash of a DC-10 airliner near Chicago in 1979, officials of the Federal Aviation Agency (FAA) were called before Congress to explain how such a tragedy could have occurred under current agency standards and guidelines.

people, Congress summoned officials of the Federal Aviation Agency (FAA) to explain the agency's procedures for setting and enforcing air-traffic safety requirements.

Then there's the case of the Architectural and Transportation Barriers Compliance Board. This obscure federal agency is authorized by Congress to establish reasonable guidelines for access by disabled individuals to federal facilities. In January 1981, however, the board became much less obscure when it announced guidelines that would require the remodeling of entrances, corridors, elevators, toilets, and meeting rooms in all federal buildings. Access for the disabled is a desirable goal, of course, but many observers thought the board had gone well beyond the "reasonable" in its guidelines. One rule, for example, would have required every federal office with as many as two telephones to purchase an expensive teleprinter for use by the deaf. After the board announced its new guidelines, opposition from other federal agencies began to mount and Congress began to apply pressure against the board. There were some thinly veiled suggestions that the board just might become a casualty of the Reagan budget cuts. Consequently, by December 1981, the board was in full retreat, and the guidelines were scaled back.[28]

Congress has the power to manage the bureaucracy, but it is only interested in doing so on a piecemeal basis (see the **PERSPECTIVE** on page 261). The goals of the members of Congress are reelection and, in some cases, moving up to higher office—the Senate or even the presidency. For the most part, then, their interest in the administration of federal programs is limited to those most directly affecting their districts or their states. Representatives from farm-belt Iowa are concerned about agricultural programs; senators from Nevada worry about federal land management. Consequently, members of Congress volunteer for committees that supervise the programs closest to their hearts, where they can oversee the administration of the programs.

In practice, Congress supervises the *parts* of the bureaucracy, but not the whole. Power in Congress is fragmented and uncoordinated, and that's how Congress oversees the bureaucracy. Each committee and subcommittee is concerned with the agencies within its jurisdiction, but little incentive exists for overall supervision. Ironically, Congress has the power to coordinate control of the bureaucracy, but doesn't have the incentive; the president has the incentive, but doesn't have the power.[29]

THE INTEREST-GROUP PERSPECTIVE

For every agency there's at least one and maybe dozens of interest groups vitally concerned about the programs it administers. For the FAA, it's the airlines; for the Food and Drug Administration (FDA), it's pharmaceutical manufacturers. The Army Corps of Engineers has the Rivers and Harbors Congress while the Soil Conservation Service has the National Association of Soil and Water Conservation Districts. Agricultural interest groups keep a weather eye on the Department of Agriculture, and the Defense Department is the concern of a legion of defense-related industries. Western land interests and environmentalists monitor the activities of the Interior Department while the postal workers' unions worry about the Postal Service. The list goes on and on.

Perspective
THE LEGISLATIVE VETO

During the 1970s and early 1980s, the legislative veto became one of Congress' most important tools for controlling the bureaucracy. As you recall from our discussion in chapter 7, the legislative veto is a device Congress has written into a number of statutes delegating authority to the executive branch. Executive officials or agencies are empowered to make certain decisions or take certain actions subject to the approval or disapproval of Congress—the legislative veto. In many cases, the legislative veto is not subject to presidential veto.[1]

The legislative veto has come in a wide variety of forms. Some veto provisions give Congress the authority to disapprove agency decisions before they go into effect. Others require Congress' advance approval. Still others establish a waiting period in which Congress may act to overturn bureaucratic decisions through the legislative process. The authority to approve or disapprove executive-agency decisions has been vested in either house

of Congress, both houses, a committee or committees from either house, committees from both houses, or some combination of houses and committees.

As Congress has delegated more and more authority to administrative agencies, it has turned more frequently to the legislative veto to maintain control over the bureaucracy. Congress passed legislative veto provisions affecting a broad range of administrative actions, including all rules issued by the FTC, the Department of Education, and the Consumer Product Safety Commission. In recent years, Congress has used the legislative veto to disallow an FTC rule regarding the sale of used cars and to keep former Interior Secretary Watt from opening federal wilderness land to oil drilling.[2]

In 1983, the United States Supreme Court dealt a severe blow to the legislative veto in the *Chadha* case.[3] The Court held one-house legislative-veto provisions unconstitutional as a violation of bicameralism. It also

invalidated veto provisions that allow Congress to disapprove agency actions without presidential involvement as a violation of separation of powers. The Court's decision effectively knocked out most legislative-veto provisions then on the books, although it left intact measures requiring a waiting period before agency rules go into effect and veto provisions that require Congress' explicit approval of agency decisions.

Where does the *Chadha* ruling leave Congress' power to oversee administrative agencies? In the long run, a resourceful and imaginative Congress can probably devise other ways to accomplish the goals it once achieved through the now-defunct legislative-veto provisions. In the short run, however, the Court's ruling not only ensures confusion over the limits of congressional and executive power, it also guarantees a power struggle between the two branches over the control of administrative policymaking.[4]

---

[1]Barbara Craig, *The Legislative Veto: Congressional Control of Regulation* (Boulder, Colorado: Westview Press 1983).
[2]William West and Joseph Cooper, "The Legislative Veto and Administrative Rulemaking," *Political Science Quarterly* 96 (Summer 1983): pp. 285–304.
[3]*Immigration and Naturalization Service* v. *Chadha*, 51 U.S.L.W. 4907 (1983).
[4]Anthony Lewis, "Legislative Veto Decision Ensures Heightened Power Struggle," *New York Times*, 3 July 1983, Sec. 4, p. 5.

What means do interest groups have to influence the bureaucracy? For one thing, groups can lobby the agencies. Department heads devote a significant proportion of their time to dealing with the interest groups of their departments' constituents. For example, the secretary of agriculture meets with farm groups; the secretary of commerce with business groups. We have seen that the relationship can sometimes become so close that the White House will begin to regard cabinet secretaries or agency heads as spokespersons for the interests rather than for the president.

Second, groups can lobby Congress to pressure the bureaucracy or to change the laws under which the agencies work. For years, industry groups have lobbied Congress to lean on the Federal Trade Commission. Business groups have asked Congress to limit the activities of the Occupational Safety and Health Administration (OSHA). The auto industry has lobbied Congress for a relaxation of the auto-exhaust emissions standards enforced by the Environmental Protection Agency (EPA).

Third, when all else fails, groups can file suit to block or reverse an agency's decisions. Environmental groups in the 1980s became frequent litigants in their efforts to stop Interior Secretary James Watt from opening federally owned wilderness land to development. In 1981, when the National Highway Traffic Safety Administration announced it was repealing requirements that new cars have automatically inflated air bags installed as safety devices, State Farm Insurance Company filed suit.

Finally, interest groups have influence in bureaucratic policymaking through an exchange of personnel. It's not unusual for political appointees in the bureaucracy to come from a constituent group their agency serves/regulates and then return to the interest group after their tenure in government. It's a revolving door. Regulatory commissioners, for example, are often recruited from law firms representing the industry regulated by the commission. High officials in the Department of Defense and the military often retire from government to serve on the corporate boards of defense contractors.

THE BUREAUCRATIC PERSPECTIVE

Bureaucrats have goals of their own. As Professor Harold Seidman puts it, "within the professional bureaucracy, primary loyalty is given to the profession, program, bureau, and department, probably in that order."[30] The president's program falls somewhere further down the list. Consequently, lawyers in the Justice Department rally to the defense of a policy they have long defended and oppose the administration's decision to grant tax breaks to schools that discriminate. Bureaucrats in the Department of Health and Human Services close ranks to oppose budget cuts in the programs they administer. Career officials in the Departments of Education and Energy dig in to prevent President Reagan from having their departments eliminated, as he promised in the 1980 election campaign.

Also, bureaucrats have the resources to defend their turf. Sometimes career employees resort to subtle, behind-the-scenes resistance to policy changes they oppose, sort of a bureaucratic guerrilla warfare. In an organization as large as the federal bureaucracy, presidential initiatives can be opposed in a number of quiet ways. Changes can be delayed. Bureaucrats may follow the letter but not the spirit of directives. Officials may "forget" to pass along orders to subordinates. News of mistakes or internal bickering can be leaked to the press.[31]

At other times, however, bureaucrats roll out the heavy artillery to fight their public-policy battles. One weapon is expertise. Today's public-policy problems are so complex that technical expertise and experience are virtually indispensable. Therein lies power. Professor Samuel Beer goes so far as to argue that government specialists with in-depth training and experience have actually taken the policymaking lead in many important policy areas.

> *In the fields of health, housing, urban renewal, transportation, welfare, education, poverty, and energy, it has been, in very great measure, people in government service, or closely associated with it, acting on the basis of their specialized and technical knowledge, who first perceived the problem, conceived the program, initially urged it on the President and Congress, went on to help lobby it through to enactment, and then saw to its administration.*[32]

Bureaucracy also finds power in alliances with important members of Congress and with interest groups. Executive-branch agencies are some of Congress' most vigorous and effective lobbyists. Agencies work to build friendships with key members of Congress by assisting them with problems involving constituent complaints. Also, most agencies enjoy an interest-group constituency that is often willing to use its political resources on behalf of the agency. For the Veterans' Administration it's veterans' groups. Teachers' groups lobby for the Department of Education; defense contractors fight for the defense budget. Medical professionals support the Public Health Service.

CONCLUSION: PUBLIC POLICY AND ADMINISTRATION

Bureaucratic policymaking reflects a complex political process involving government agencies, Congress, the White House, interest groups, and the courts. Each of the participants has its own particular perspective and its own set of political resources for achieving its goals. The process varies from one policy area to another, but there are general patterns that we can discuss.

POLICY TRIANGLES AND CAPTURED AGENCIES

Frequently, federal agencies, interest groups, and congressional committees and subcommittees reach understandings on how their particular part of public policy ought to be managed. These **policy triangles** are cozy relationships in which all three sides benefit. Interest groups and bureaucrats prosper because federal programs near and dear to their hearts are enacted, maintained, and extended. Members of Congress are happy because the interest-group PACs contribute to their reelection campaigns while the bureaucracy sees to it that the folks back home get taken care of and the member of Congress gets the credit.

Take, for example, the highway triangle. On the one side are interest groups that benefit from highway construction: auto manufacturers, autoworkers' unions, tire companies, asphalt and cement dealers, road contractors, and oil companies. Then there's the federal agency, the Federal Highway Administration, which, of course, is interested in the preservation of the programs it administers. On the third side of the triangle are the congressional committees and subcommittees that consider highway-construction bills. In the Senate, it's the Transportation Subcommittee of the Environment and Public Works and Transportation Committee, while in the House it's the Surface Transportation Subcommittee of the Public Works and Transportation Committee. Also involved are senators and representatives from states with extensive interstate highway systems, such as Texas, California, and Oklahoma. Each side of the triangle serves and is served by the other two. The members of Congress involved work to maintain federal support for highway maintenance and construction. This keeps the interest groups and the bureaucrats happy. The interest groups

Reform of the federal bureaucracy is often made complicated and difficult by the existence of "policy triangles" and "captured agencies."

lobby Congress in behalf of highway programs and their PACs contribute campaign money for members of Congress on key committees and sub-committees. Meanwhile, the federal agency makes sure that the districts and states of the legislators involved get more than their share of new highways and bridges. Also, if some town back in the district wants a special favor, town officials call their representative or senator, who passes the request along to the agency. The agency is eager to please and just as eager to give the member of Congress the credit. The people back home are happy, and the representative or senator gets reelected.

A great deal of public policy is made just this way: through cozy, behind-the-scenes understandings among interest groups, key members of Congress, and the federal bureaucracy. What President Eisenhower once re-ferred to as the "military-industrial complex" is a triangle composed of the Department of Defense, defense-related committees and subcommittees in Congress, and an army of interest groups that benefit from defense spend-ing, including defense contractors and their unions.

There are triangles supporting virtually every federal program, and they are powerful. In 1978, President Carter's plan to limit veterans' preference was shot down by the veterans' triangle. The Department of Education, the youngest executive department, was created through the efforts of the education triangle and kept alive despite President Reagan's expressed desire to merge it with Health and Human Services, thus recreating the old Department of Health, Education, and Welfare. The Milk Fund is pro-tected by the dairy triangle.

A similar relationship sometimes exists between regulatory agencies and the industries they are charged with regulating. Critics say these are **cap-tured agencies.** This type of relationship is most common when an agency is created to regulate one industry or a small number of related industries. The Federal Maritime Commission, for example, historically has worked closely with the shipping industry. The old Civil Aeronautics Board (CAB) had close ties to the airline industry. The Federal Power Commission has been accused of working for the electric-utility industry.

Policy triangles are not invincible, however. Captured agencies may not remain captive. During the 1960s and '70s, for example, environmental-protection laws were enacted despite the opposition of numerous business-industrial triangles. Also in the 1970s, the tobacco triangle was beaten when Congress voted to ban cigarette advertising from radio and television. The airline triangle was defeated when Congress voted to deregulate the airline industry and phase out the CAB. In 1981, Ronald Reagan succeeded in persuading Congress to cut funding for a number of programs favored by policy triangles.

POLICY CONFLICT

Many policy areas are not controlled by triangles at all. Policy triangles emerge when interest groups, bureaucrats, and key members of Congress are able to agree on the shape of public policy in a particular policy area. More frequently than not, however, interest groups, bureaucrats, and members of Congress are unable to agree. Instead, policy alternatives are fought over by loose coalitions of interest groups, members of Congress, and federal bureaucrats. The president, the courts, and state and local officials may be involved as well. For example, environmentalists and their friends in the executive and legislative branches compete against prodevelopment forces over federal land-management policy. Consumer interests and industry supporters quarrel over consumer-protection regulations.

A good illustration of how political infighting can surround policy administration involves the Environmental Protection Agency (EPA). The creation of the EPA in 1970 was a victory for environmentalist forces. Congress consolidated some fifteen different programs—managed by five different councils—into a single agency. Although the EPA attracted a professional staff that was, for the most part, sympathetic to the environmentalist cause, William D. Ruckelshaus, the EPA's first director, charted a middle-of-the-road course between the views of industry and environmental groups. This brought the agency criticism from both sides, but many observers gave the early EPA high marks.[33]

During the Carter Administration, however, the EPA moved closer to the side of the environmentalists. Carter was elected with strong environmentalist support and proceeded to appoint environmental activists to manage the agency.[34] The EPA soon found itself more controversial than ever. In 1980, Congress attached legislative-veto provisions to EPA authorizations for rules regarding pesticides and hazardous substances.

In 1981, Ronald Reagan came to the White House determined to overhaul the EPA. For the next two years, the agency was a battleground as interest groups, career officials, appointed administrators, members of Congress, and the White House fought over environmental policy and control of the EPA. Reagan fired the first shot by appointing proindustry advocates to head the agency and by asking Congress to cut significantly the agency's budget and work force. Environmentalist forces fought back in the courts and in Congress. They filed lawsuits in hopes of preventing the agency from relaxing tough environmental standards. Meanwhile, sympathetic members of Congress launched investigations of alleged wrongdoing by the Reagan appointees, evidence of which was conveniently leaked by disgruntled career employees of the EPA. By early 1983, most of Reagan's initial appointees to the EPA had resigned under fire. The president then asked William Ruckelshaus to return to head the agency and try to restore smooth operations. For the time being, at least, open warfare over the agency's policies was at an end. Nevertheless, there remained a deep underlying disagreement among policymakers and interest groups as to the future course of the EPA and the nature of environmental policy.[35]

ADMINISTRATIVE POLICYMAKING IN THE 1980s

It is tempting to try to explain all administrative policymaking on the basis of policy triangles and captured agencies, but that is not the reality.To be sure, policy triangles do exist, and they are powerful. Some regulatory agencies are closely tied to interest groups. But policy triangles frequently compete with one another over scarce governmental resources, and captured agencies are sometimes "liberated" by a determined president and Congress. Also, many policy areas are not controlled by a policy triangle at all; they are the focus of conflict among competing groups. Many agencies are not captured. The EPA illustration is not unique. Other agencies that frequently have been policy battlegrounds include the Federal Trade Commission (FTC), the Consumer Product Safety Commission, the National Highway Traffic Safety Board, and the Occupational Safety and Health Administration (OSHA).

In reality, then, bureaucratic policymaking is probably more frequently characterized by conflict than by cooperation. The White House distrusts the bureaucracy; the bureaucracy distrusts the White House. Career employees have one set of priorities; appointed administrators have another. Competing sets of interest groups frequently fight for control of a single agency. Rival power centers in Congress contend for influence. The courts are often called upon to mediate disputes, and so they become participants in the policy process as well. It is a complex process that cannot be simply explained, but that's the reality of administrative policymaking in the 1980s.

Key Terms

Captured Agencies (265)   *Rulemaking (249)*   *Supergrades (256)*

Inner Cabinet (248)   *Spoils System (253)*   *Veterans' Preference (256)*

Policy Triangles (264)   *Statutory Law (249)*

NOTES

1. *New York Times,* 9 January 1982, p. 1; Jim Mann, "Reagan Administration Misgauged Public, Court on Racial Bias Question," *Houston Chronicle,* 29 May 1982, Sec. 1, p. 22.
2. *New York Times,* 10 January 1982, p. 19.
3. *New York Times,* 13 January 1982, p. 1.
4. *New York Times,* 4 February 1982, Sec. 2, p. 12.
5. *New York Times,* 12 February 1982, p. 20.

6. *New York Times,* 25 May 1983, p. 22; Anthony Lewis, "Bob Jones II: Humiliating Defeat for Reagan," *New York Times,* 26 May 1983, p. 27.

7. Harold Seidman, *Politics, Position, and Power,* 3rd ed. (New York: Oxford University Press, 1980), p. 135.

8. G. Calvin Mackenzie, "The Paradox of Presidential Personnel Management," in Hugh Heclo and Lester M. Salamon, eds., *The Illusion of Presidential Government* (Boulder, Colorado: Westview Press, 1981).

9. "Cabinet Government Fades Away Once More," *U.S. News & World Report* (29 March 1982), p. 28.

10. Thomas E. Cronin, *The State of the Presidency,* 2nd ed. (Boston: Little, Brown, 1980), pp. 263–68.

11. Nelson W. Polsby, "Presidential Cabinet Making: Lessons for the Political System," *Political Science Quarterly* 93 (Spring 1978): 15–25; Seidman, pp. 133–35.

12. Quoted in Kermit Gordon, *Reflections on Spending* (Washington, D.C.: Brookings Institution, 1967), p. 15.

13. Seidman, p. 171.

14. Interstate Commerce Commission, Federal Trade Commission, Federal Communications Commission, Federal Power Commission, Securities and Exchange Commission, National Labor Relations Board.

15. Felix A. Nigro and Lloyd G. Nigro, *Modern Public Administration,* 5th ed. (New York: Harper and Row, 1980), pp. 93–95.

16. James O. Freedman, "Legislative Delegation to Regulator Agencies," *Proceedings of the Academy of Political Science* 34 (1981): 76–89; *U.S. News and World Report* (18 January 1982), pp. 62–63.

17. George J. Gordon, *Public Administration in America* (New York: St. Martin's, 1978), p. 13; Seidman, pp. 255–74.

18. Harold Orlans, ed., *Nonprofit Organizations: A Government Management Tool* (New York: Praeger, 1980).

19. Seidman, pp. 47–51.

20. Seidman, p. 47.

21. Seidman, p. 66.

22. Martha Derthick, "The Government's Use of Nonprofit Organizations for Social Demonstrations," in Orlans, p. 3.

23. Nigro and Nigro, pp. 286–322.

24. Mackenzie, pp. 123–40.

25. "Symposium: The Professions in Government," *Public Administration Review* 38 (March–April 1978): 105–50.

26. Seidman, pp. 154–56.

27. Richard P. Nathan, *The Plot That Failed: Nixon and the Administrative Presidency* (New York: Wiley, 1975).

28. Timothy B. Clark, "Here's One 'Midnight Regulation' That's Slipped Through Reagan's Net," *National Journal* (7 February 1981), pp. 221–24; *New York Times,* 21 September 1981, p. 17.

29. Morris P. Fiorina, "Congressional Control of the Bureaucracy: A Mismatch of Incentives and Capabilities," in Lawrence C. Dodd and Bruce I. Oppenheimer, *Congress Reconsidered,* 2nd ed. (Washington, D.C.: Congressional Quarterly Press, 1981), pp. 332–48.

30. Seidman, p. 144.

31. Robert F. DiClerico, *The American President* (Englewood Cliffs, N.J.: Prentice-Hall, 1979), p 109.

32. Samuel H. Beer, "Federalism, Nationalism, and Democracy in America," *American Political Science Review* 72 (March 1978): 17.

33. Alfred Marcus, "Environmental Protection Agency," in James Q. Wilson, ed., *The Politics of Regulation* (New York: Basic Books, 1980).

34. J. Dicken Kirschten, "Environmentalists Come in from the Cold in Carter Administration," *National Journal* (12 March 1977), pp. 382–84.

35. Dick Kirschten, "Ruckelshaus May Find EPA's Problems Are Budgetary as Much as Political," *National Journal* (26 March 1983), pp. 659–60.

SUGGESTED READINGS

CRAIG, BARBARA. *The Legislative Veto: Congressional Control of Regulation.* Boulder, Colorado: Westview Press, 1983.

HECLO, HUGH. *A Government of Strangers.* Washington, D.C.: Brookings Institution, 1977.

KAUFMAN, HERBERT. *Are Government Organizations Immortal?* Washington, D.C.: Brookings Institution, 1976.

NATHAN, RICHARD P. *The Plot That Failed: Nixon and the Administrative Presidency.* New York: Wiley, 1975.

REDFORD, EMMETTE S. *Democracy in the Administrative State.* New York: Oxford University Press, 1969.

RIPLEY, RANDALL, AND FRANKLIN, GRACE. *Congress, the Bureaucracy, and Public Policy.* Rev. ed. Homewood, Ill.: Dorsey, 1980.

ROURKE, FRANCIS E. *Bureaucracy, Politics, and Public Policy.* 2nd ed. Boston: Little, Brown, 1976.

SEIDMAN, HAROLD. *Politics, Position, and Power.* 3rd ed. New York: Oxford University Press, 1980.

WILSON, JAMES Q. *The Politics of Regulation.* New York: Basic Books, 1980.

Chapter Ten

THE COURTS

In June 1982 Allan P. Bakke graduated from medical school in the glare of national publicity. Ordinarily, graduation exercises don't make national news, but this was different. Bakke's name is inscribed on one of the most celebrated pieces of judicial policymaking in recent memory.

Back in 1973 Bakke applied to medical school at the University of California at Davis. At thirty-two, he was a little older than the typical applicant, but he had spent four years in the marine corps after graduating from the University of Minnesota in 1962 with an engineering degree. For the last several years he had been working for NASA at the Ames Research Center just south of San Francisco. Nevertheless, like thousands of others, it was Bakke's ambition to become a medical doctor. And, like thousands of others, Bakke's application was rejected. This was not, however, the end of Bakke's efforts to get into medical school. He sued the university, charging that its admissions policies violated the constitutions of the United States and of the State of California.

Each year the medical school admitted one hundred applicants, but sixteen of these positions were set aside for members of a "minority group"—blacks, Hispanics, Asians, or American Indians. The applications were physically separated into two groups, minority and majority applicants, and the top sixteen minority candidates were admitted. Then the remaining minority applications were mixed with the others and the other eighty-four positions were filled.

Since Bakke is a white male, he was not allowed to compete for the sixteen medical-school slots reserved for minorities. Also, he was not selected for any of the other places in the class. He charged in his lawsuit, however, that his objective qualifications were superior to those of some of the minority applicants the university did accept. Were he a minority-group member, Bakke argued, he would have been admitted. Consequently, the university was guilty of discrimination—"reverse" discrimination—and he asked a state court to order him admitted.

The medical school defended its procedures. There is a serious shortage of doctors in the minority communities, it argued, so training minority physicians is a legitimate, justifiable goal for a state university. The school further argued that decisions on admissions standards should be left to universities and not be set for them by judges.

For the next several years, the controversy worked its way through the courts. In 1974 a California trial court ruled the university's admissions program invalid, but it refused to order Bakke's admission. He was only entitled to be considered without regard to race, the court said. Neither Bakke nor the university was satisfied with that decision, however, and both appealed to the Supreme Court of the State of California. In 1976, that court ruled in behalf of Bakke. It ordered the medical school not to consider race in making admissions decisions and ordered Bakke admitted. The university appealed to the United States Supreme Court. The case was

Allan Bakke, subject of one of the most famous court cases of recent times, shown here chatting with a fellow student after his first day of classes at medical school.

titled *Regents of the University of California* v. *Bakke,* and the agenda was set for the Supreme Court to make a major policy decision.[1]

The Role of the Courts

The courts are like the other branches of government in that they are political participants in the policymaking process, but they work in a different setting and under a different set of ground rules. Let's examine the work of the courts and see how it fits into the policy process.

SETTLING DISPUTES

The everyday task of courts around the nation is settling disputes. In **criminal cases** a law allegedly has been violated and an individual, the defendant, stands accused of the crime. Meanwhile, the **prosecutor** represents the government through the office of a local district attorney, a state's attorney general, or even the United States Justice Department. The court guides and referees the dispute. Ultimately, a judge and/or jury rule on the defendant's guilt or innocence and, if the verdict is guilty, assess punishment.

Criminal cases are divided into two classifications, according to their severity. **Misdemeanors** are relatively less serious criminal offenses, such as a minor traffic violation. They are punishable by a relatively small fine and/or a relatively brief time in jail, generally less than a year. In contrast, **felonies** are more serious crimes, such as murder, rape, or burglary. Convicted felons may be assessed heavy fines and/or be sentenced to long prison terms. In some thirty-four states, persons convicted of murder may be sentenced to death. This is known as **capital punishment.**

Courts are also involved in settling civil disputes. In **civil cases,** the issue isn't the violation of a law, but rather a private conflict between two parties—individuals, corporations, or even government agencies. One party, the **plaintiff,** believes that he or she has been wronged by the other, the **defendant,** and files suit to ask a court to award monetary damages or to order the defendant to remedy the wrong. Allan Bakke, you recall, asked a court to order his admission to medical school.

There are two types of civil cases, **contracts** and **torts.** Contract cases involve disputes over written or implied contracts. For example, a homeowner might sue a roofing company over a faulty repair job, or one spouse might sue the other to dissolve the marriage contract. In the meantime, torts involve personal injury or damage to property. One automobile driver, for instance, might sue another over a traffic accident.

Every year the nation's courts are called upon to settle thousands of criminal and civil cases. Most of these are heard in the state courts rather than in the federal-court system. Federal criminal cases are rather narrowly confined to those matters that have some direct or indirect connection with federal activity or federal authority under the Constitution, such as postal theft, bank robbery, counterfeiting, or threatening to harm the president. Thanks to the interstate commerce clause of the Constitution, criminal activity that transcends state borders can also become a federal offense. Nevertheless, the great bulk of criminal cases, including most murders, rapes, robberies, thefts, and misdemeanor offenses, involve state laws only and are handled by state courts. Similarly, the overwhelming majority of civil actions are also decided in state courts. Federal civil actions are limited to such matters as bankruptcy petitions, customs, some tax disputes, patents, and certain civil cases involving citizens from different states.

The typical image of a court at work is that of a trial with a judge, jury, witnesses, and evidence. The two parties in the case, the **litigants,** are represented by counsel engaging in an **adversary proceeding.** This means that each attorney musters evidence and arguments to bolster his or her client's position, while ignoring information that might support the other side. Theoretically, it's a process that helps the judge and/or jury determine the real facts of the dispute.

In practice, most legal disputes are settled not by trials but through a process of negotiation and compromise between the parties involved. In civil cases, litigants generally decide that it's quicker and less costly to "settle out of court" than to go through the trial process. Meanwhile, most criminal cases are resolved through a **plea-bargaining** agreement between the prosecutor and the defendant. This usually involves the defendant agreeing to plead guilty to a lesser offense than the one with which he or she was originally charged.

Second, some of the most important judicial decisions aren't made at the original trial, but rather on appeal. The *Bakke* case, for example, was appealed from a California trial court to the state supreme court. From there, it was appealed to the United States Supreme Court. The purpose of a trial is to determine the facts of a case. What were the terms of the contract? Where was the defendant on the night in question? In contrast, an appeal focuses on points of law. Did the trial judge err in allowing the jury to see certain evidence? Did the judge improperly interpret the law or the Constitution in making a ruling? The most important judicial policymaking decisions involve an appellate court interpreting the law and the Constitution.

POLICYMAKING

Every time a court acts it is making policy, although most judicial decisions are quite mundane. After all, the course of history doesn't hinge on the adjudication of the typical traffic ticket, divorce proceeding, or personal-injury lawsuit. At times, however, seemingly ordinary cases can become instruments for policy decisions whose importance far transcends the particulars of the case involved. Remember the illustration of Clarence Earl Gideon from chapter 2? He was the Florida man who was sentenced to prison for breaking and entering. The United States Supreme Court overturned Gideon's conviction, ruling that the constitutional right to counsel meant that the state had to provide Gideon with an attorney since he could not afford to retain one himself.[2] The circumstances of the *Gideon* case were quite unremarkable, but it became a vehicle for the Court to make a major constitutional decision. The same can be said of the *Bakke* case.

One job of the courts is to apply the law to the particular circumstances of contemporary legal disputes, but the law is often broadly phrased. Sometimes the language of the law reflects the inevitable compromises of the legislative process when precise language loses out to political expediency. At other times, lawmakers are unsure or unable to agree on just what they want, so the law is drafted in general terms, and it is left to the bureaucracy and the courts to iron out the details. Then, there are occasions when circumstances arise that lawmakers were simply unable to foresee. In each of these instances, the courts can interpret the law and therefore make policy.

Take the example of the *Bakke* case. The judges of the U.S. Supreme Court asked the lawyers for Bakke and the university to submit **briefs** (that is, written legal arguments) arguing the merits of the case in light of Title VI of the federal Civil Rights Act of 1964. That law reads as follows:

> *No person in the United States shall, on the ground of race, color or national origin be excluded from participation in, be denied the benefits of or be subjected to discrimination under any program or activity receiving Federal financial assistance.*[3]

No one denied that the University of California at Davis was receiving federal funds and was therefore covered by the law, but the two sides disagreed about its applicability in this case. Bakke's lawyer argued that his client was indeed subjected to discrimination on account of race. The university countered by asserting that Congress' motives in passing the law were to protect racial minorities. To use the law as a basis for invalidating a program designed to compensate for past discrimination would be an ironic and unsupportable twist of the law's original intent.

Another job of the courts is to interpret the Constitution and, when the occasion arises, to review the actions of the various branches and bodies of government in light thereof. This, as we mentioned in chapter 2, is called the power of judicial review. It's a power that is not explicitly spelled out in the Constitution. The Supreme Court (through interpretation) simply assumed the power in the case of *Marbury* v. *Madison* in 1803.[4] Since then, when cases have arisen, the Court has reviewed the actions of Congress, the president, the bureaucracy, the other federal courts, and the various units of state government and occasionally found those actions to be unconstitutional and therefore null and void. Altogether, the Court has overturned at least one provision in more than two hundred federal laws (counting the one hundred or so laws affected by the legislative-veto decision) and more than one thousand state laws. In *Marbury,* for example, the Court reviewed and invalidated an act of Congress, a section of the Judiciary Act of 1789. In the case of *United States* v. *Nixon* in 1974, the Supreme Court rejected President Nixon's claim that "executive privilege" entitled him to refuse to turn over Watergate tapes to special prosecutor Leon Jaworski.[5] In the *Gideon* case, the Court ruled on trial procedures in the state of Florida. Then, in *Bakke,* the Court considered the policies of a state-supported university in California.

Bakke argued that the medical school's admissions procedures violated the equal-protection clause of the Fourteenth Amendment to the United States Constitution, which reads, "No State shall . . . deny to any person within its jurisdiction the equal protection of the laws." The Fourteenth Amendment was ratified in 1868 as an effort to protect the civil rights of newly freed blacks in the South. It meant that states were required to deal equally with all persons and not have one set of laws and regulations for whites and another set for blacks. Bakke argued that he was denied equal protection since minorities could compete for all one hundred places in the class while he was eligible for only eighty-four. In response, the university defended its policy, saying that the equal-protection clause was written to protect blacks from discrimination. Since the school was clearly not engaged in discrimination against blacks, the amendment did not apply. The policy, the university argued, was constitutional.

Such were the complicated legal and constitutional issues facing the courts in the *Bakke* case. Granted, most cases don't raise the kinds of complex questions presented by *Bakke,* but some do and they provide the opportunity for the courts, particularly the U.S. Supreme Court, to make important public-policy decisions.

THE SUPREME COURT AND POLICYMAKING

Throughout most of its history the Supreme Court has been an active participant in some of the nation's most important public-policy controversies. In its first decade, however, the Court was relatively unimportant in the policy process. There were even occasions when some of it members resigned in order to take other, better jobs.

Then came John Marshall, and the Supreme Court's role in the policy process began to take shape. Under Chief Justice Marshall (1801–35) the Court claimed the power of judicial review (*Marbury* v. *Madison*) and decided a number of landmark cases on commercial law and the nature of the federal system. In these the Court came out strongly in favor of property rights and a powerful central government.

The Supreme Court continued the pattern of the Marshall years during Chief Justice Roger Taney's tenure (1836–64). Eventually, the Court, like the rest of the nation, became engulfed in the slavery controversy. The Court's involvement culminated in the infamous *Dred Scott* decision in

Roger Taney, chief justice at the time of the famous Dred Scott *decision.*

which it declared the Missouri Compromise unconstitutional, saying the federal government lacked the power to prohibit slavery in the territories. The Court held that blacks had no rights under the Constitution. The role of the national government, it said, was to protect slavery everywhere in the United States.[6]

After the Civil War and Reconstruction, the nation got about the business of economic expansion, and the Supreme Court concentrated on reviewing the constitutionality of government efforts to regulate business activity. At first, the Court's positions were mixed, but by the 1930s the Court had grown increasingly hostile to government regulation. It scrutinized state and federal taxing and regulatory policies and found many of them unconstitutional, including child-labor laws and the Agricultural Adjustment Act (AAA) and the National Recovery Administration (NRA) of the New Deal period. Consequently, the Court became the object of liberal attack.

Who benefited from the Supreme Court's policy posture in this period? Business corporations—the advantaged interests of society. Meanwhile, disadvantaged groups, such as blacks, were ignored. The years around the turn of the century were a time when blacks were being segregated and disenfranchised, but the Supreme Court did nothing to help. Many states passed **Jim Crow laws** requiring the social segregation of blacks in separate and usually very unequal facilities. At the same time, many states were adopting fiendishly clever devices to prevent blacks from voting. The Supreme Court responded by legitimizing segregation (*Plessy* v. *Ferguson*[7]) and generally overlooking disenfranchisement. Ironically, the Fourteenth Amendment, which was enacted to protect the civil rights of freed blacks, was now used by the Court to protect business corporations.

Beginning in 1937, however, the Supreme Court changed its tune and its agenda. It began upholding the constitutionality of New Deal legislation. Since then, with only a few exceptions, the Court has left economic policymaking to the other branches of government. It has shifted its attention to civil-liberties and civil-rights issues. No longer is the Court the single-minded protector of big business. It has turned to other issues, including those involving the interests of the individual, the socially and economically disadvantaged, criminal defendants, and people with unpopular views.

The heyday of the new liberal Court came during the Warren years. Under Chief Justice Earl Warren (1953-69), the Court strengthened the First Amendment rights of freedom of expression and freedom of religion, broadened the procedural rights of the criminally accused, and ruled decisively for civil rights of blacks and other minorities. The Supreme Court had become an instrument of social reform. Consequently, it became the target of conservative critics.[8]

Since Warren's retirement the Supreme Court has been much more difficult to characterize. The Court's agenda has remained primarily civil liberties and civil rights, but its policy preferences are neither consistently liberal nor consistently conservative. Critics say it lacks direction. In some

JIM CROW LAW.

UPHELD BY THE UNITED STATES SUPREME COURT.

Statute Within the Competency of the Louisiana Legislature and Railroads—Must Furnish Separate Cars for Whites and Blacks.

Washington, May 18.—The Supreme Court today in an opinion read by Justice Brown, sustained the constitutionality of the law in Louisiana requiring the railroads of that State to provide separate cars for white and colored passengers. There was no interstate commerce feature in the case for the railroad upon which the incident occurred giving rise to case—Plessey vs. Ferguson—East Louisiana railroad, was and is operated wholly within the State, to the laws of Congress of many of the States. The opinion states that by the analogy of the laws of Congress, and of many of states requiring establishment of separate schools for children of two races and other similar laws, the statute in question was within competency of Louisiana Legislature, exercising the police power of the State. The judgment of the Supreme Court of State upholding law was therefore upheld.

Mr. Justice Harlan announced a very vigorous dissent saying that he saw nothing but mischief in all such laws. In his view of the case, no power in the land had right to regulate the enjoyment of civil rights upon the basis of race. It would be just as reasonable and proper, he said, for states to pass laws requiring separate cars to be furnished for Catholic and Protestants, or for descendants of those of Teutonic race and those of Latin race.

Homer Adolph Plessy, a black man, tested a Louisiana law forbidding blacks to sit with whites on trains. The Supreme Court's 1896 decision, Plessy v. Ferguson, *upheld Louisiana's right to require "separate but equal" facilities for the two races.*

policy areas, such as procedural rights for criminal defendants, the Court has limited or qualified Warren Court positions. In other fields, however, including abortion rights, capital punishment, education for the children of illegal aliens, school busing, and sex discrimination, the Court has broken new ground.[9]

The Organization of the Federal Courts

The Constitution says little about the organization of the federal courts. It mentions a chief justice and a Supreme Court, but leaves most of the details to the discretion of Congress. "The judicial Power of the United States," it says in Article III, Section 1, "shall be vested in one supreme Court, and in such inferior Courts as the Congress may from time to time ordain and establish." Consequently, for the most part, the present organization of the judicial branch is the work of Congress, which has frequently acted on the initiative of the president and the urging of the judiciary itself.

TRIAL COURTS

The district courts are the basic trial courts of the federal system. There are ninety-four of them, with at least one in each of the fifty states and one each in the District of Columbia, Guam, Puerto Rico, and the Virgin Islands. Only one judge presides in each courtroom, but most of the districts have enough business to warrant several courtrooms, each with its own judge. The number of judges per district ranges from one to twenty-seven. Altogether there are some 600 district-court judges plus more than 100 semiretired senior-district-court judges. In addition, for each district there is a clerk's office, a United States marshal's office, and one or more bankruptcy judges, United States magistrates, probation officers, and court reporters.

The jurisdiction of district courts includes both civil and criminal matters. In sheer volume, their biggest jobs are the naturalization of aliens and the granting of passport applications. District courts also have jurisdiction over bankruptcy cases filed under federal law, civil cases involving more than $10,000 in which the United States government is a party, and, if either party requests it, lawsuits in which there is a diversity of citizenship (i.e., the litigants are from different states) and there is more than $10,000 at stake.

As for criminal matters, district courts try all cases involving federal crimes and offenses occurring on federal territory, federal reservations, or the high seas. District judges must also handle a great many **habeas corpus** petitions filed by convicts in both state and federal prisons. These petitions allege that the prisoner is being held contrary to law and ask the court to inquire into the matter. For example, a convict's attorney may charge that a trial court erred in admitting certain evidence, therefore violating the Fifth and Fourteenth Amendments to the United States Constitution. If the judge thinks there is any merit in the petitioner's complaint, he or she can direct the jailer to reply, and the suit will be joined.[10] *Habeas corpus* petitions are sometimes used by prisoners on death row hoping to avoid or at least delay their execution.

In addition to the district courts, Congress has created a number of specialized trial courts to deal with some of the more complex areas of federal law. These include the claims court, the court of international trade, and the tax court. Also, on occasion a special three-judge district court will be assembled to hear one particular case. This is sometimes employed in cases where the constitutionality of a state law or an act of Congress is under challenge, although this type of court has fallen into disuse in recent years and Chief Justice Burger has proposed its elimination.

Federal judges are appointed by the president subject to Senate confirmation by majority vote. Supreme Court appointments are some of the most important and highly publicized nominations a president gets to make, but appointments to the lower federal bench receive considerably less attention. When there is a vacancy, the deputy attorney general begins gathering the names of potential nominees to submit to the president. District judges generally must live in their court's district, so state party leaders, senators, and members of Congress are consulted. The American Bar Association (ABA) Committee on the Federal Judiciary will likely be asked to evaluate the qualifications of potential nominees. Eventually, the deputy attorney general will suggest a name or perhaps a short list of names for the president's consideration.

What kinds of individuals do presidents appoint to the lower federal bench? The foremost answer seems to be that presidents favor judges from their own political party. The overwhelming majority of President Carter's judicial appointments were Democrats. President Reagan, however, much prefers Republicans. Second, presidents tend to appoint white, Anglo-Saxon, middle-aged men, from middle and upper-middle class families. Most have had legal training and political experience. The exception to this pattern of appointment was Jimmy Carter, who named more women, blacks, and Hispanics to the federal courts than any president in history. Of Carter's 265 appointments to the federal bench, 41 were women, 58 were black, and 16 were Hispanic. In contrast, nearly all of Ronald Reagan's appointees have been white males, despite the celebrated selection of Sandra Day O'Connor to the Supreme Court. Through early 1984, Reagan had made 88 appointments. These included only 13 women, 2 blacks, and 7 Hispanics.[11]

Once the president settles on a nominee, he submits it to the Senate where it is referred to the Judiciary Committee. The committee staff will conduct a background check and a hearing may be held to allow the nominee and any interested parties an opportunity to be heard. The confirmation process for district judges is usually a fairly quiet affair, but there can be real trouble if one of the nominee's home-state senators from the president's political party opposes the nomination. The long-standing custom of **senatorial courtesy** holds that the Senate will reject any district-court nominee opposed by a senator representing the state involved, provided the senator is from the president's party. Presidents know all about senatorial courtesy and make it a point to consult the appropriate senator or senators before a nomination is submitted. In practice, this means that senators from the president's party have at least a veto on district-judge appointments from their states and often suggest the candidates the president eventually nominates. Most federally appointed judges enjoy lifetime tenure (see **PERSPECTIVE** on page 282).

COURTS OF APPEAL

The United States Courts of Appeal (also known as circuit courts of appeal) are the primary intermediate appellate courts in the federal system. There are thirteen of them, one for each of the eleven judicial "circuits," or regions, one for the District of Columbia, and a thirteenth circuit called the United States Court of Appeals for the Federal Circuit. The latter specializes in customs and patent appeals from the district courts. The map on page 280 shows how the United States is divided among the circuits. The number of judges for each of the circuits ranges from three to twenty-four. Altogether, there are 144 appellate-court judges plus an additional forty or so senior judges. In addition to the courts of appeal, the court of military appeals is the appeals court for the military-justice system.

"Appeals! Appeals! Why isn't anyone satisfied?"

Judges on the courts of appeal are chosen in a manner similar to that used for naming district judges, with some modifications. The White House probably exercises more care in the selection of circuit judges since there are fewer of them and since their positions are considered more important than district judges. Also, senatorial courtesy isn't a factor since each of the circuits includes several states.

The courts of appeal are exclusively appellate courts, hearing cases in panels of three judges each. Cases are appealed to them by the tax court and the court of international trade, but their largest source of business is the United States district courts. About 8 percent of district-court cases are appealed. The courts of appeal also hear appeals on the decisions of the regulatory commissions. Of these, the decisions of the National Labor Relations Board (NLRB) produce the most appeals. The courts of appeal decide cases with three types of rulings. They may *affirm* the decision of the lower court, *reverse* it, or *remand* (send) it back to the lower court for reconsideration in light of the court's instructions.

FIGURE 10.1   *United States Courts of Appeals and United States District Courts*

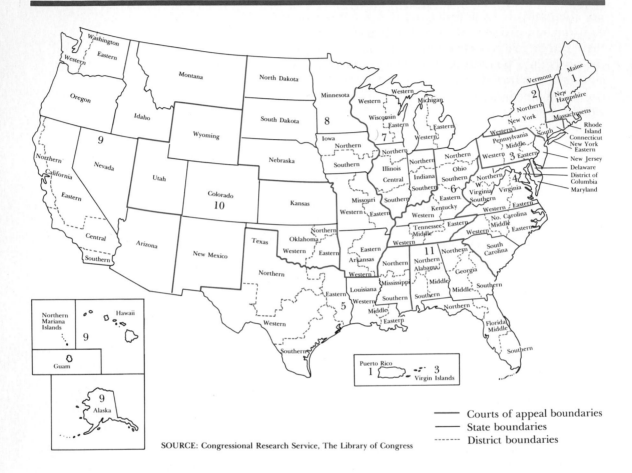

SOURCE: Congressional Research Service, The Library of Congress

——— Courts of appeal boundaries
——— State boundaries
------- District boundaries

SUPREME COURT

The United States Supreme Court is the highest court in the land. Through the years, Congress has varied its size from as few as five to as many as ten justices, but its present size of nine has been in effect for more than a century. Back in the 1930s, Franklin Rooosevelt's attempt to enlarge the Court so he could appoint justices friendly to the New Deal was popularly attacked as a "court-packing plan" and defeated by Congress. Since then, no serious attempts have been made to change the Court's size.

Today's Court includes the chief justice and eight associate justices. The justices are equal and independent, like nine separate law firms, but the chief justice is first among them. Among other powers and responsibilities, the chief presides over public sessions and private conferences. He can call special sessions of the Court and he has a role in the administration of the federal-court system. In practice, however, the relative influence of the chief justice depends more on his leadership abilities and the personalities of the other justices than it does on his formal powers. Earl Warren, for example, was clearly the Court's leader during his tenure as chief from 1953 to 1969. However, his successor, Warren Burger, has been unable to fill Earl Warren's shoes on a Court that often seems to lack direction.

Selection of judges.   Nominating individuals for the Supreme Court is one of the president's most important responsibilities. For one thing it's an opportunity that may not come along very often. Richard Nixon was able to appoint four judges in less than six years in office, but Jimmy Carter was unable to make any appointments during his four-year term. Second, each appointment has the potential to affect public policy for years to come, particularly if the Court is closely divided or if the president has the chance to name a new chief justice.

The formal procedures of appointment and confirmation of Supreme Court justices are similar to those for lower-court judges, except they are generally performed more carefully and receive considerably more publicity. The attorney general is usually assigned the task of compiling a list of possible nominees. This time the American Bar Association and other interest groups are much more active in trying to influence the selection. Sometimes, a potential nominee may actually shill a bit for his own cause, subtly and behind-the-scenes, of course. Former President William Howard Taft, for example, was not above campaigning for nomination as chief justice and in 1921 got his wish, thanks to President Harding. Once the president narrows the list of possible nominees to only a few names, the FBI is asked to run a background check on each.

In selecting Supreme Court justices, presidents may employ several criteria. First, they look for competence and ethics. Most Supreme Court justices have been scholarly and honorable. Some, such as Justices Benjamin Cardozo and Oliver Wendell Holmes, have been brilliant. On the other hand, some justices, including Chief Justice Burger, have been criticized for a lack of scholarly acumen. On occasion, ethical questions have arisen. In 1969, for example, Associate Justice Abe Fortas was forced to resign in the face of accusations of conflict of interest.

Second, presidents generally prefer nominees who share their policy preferences: conservative presidents seek conservative judges; liberals look for liberals. When Franklin Roosevelt finally had the chance to make appointments to the Supreme Court, he was careful to find men sympathetic to the New Deal. President Nixon took pains to be sure his Court selections were conservative.[12]

Sometimes, however, presidents are surprised and disappointed at the performance of their nominees on the Court. Liberal Woodrow Wilson, for example, was responsible for appointing James MacReynolds, one of the crustiest conservatives ever to sit on the Court. On the other hand, the relatively conservative Dwight Eisenhower chose Chief Justice Warren and

Associate Justice William Brennan, two of the more liberal justices of recent times. What was Ike's reaction? Asked if he had made any mistakes as president, Eisenhower replied, "Yes, two, and they are both sitting on the Supreme Court."[13]

Third, presidents occasionally hand out Supreme Court appointments as rewards for political support or personal friendship. In 1952, Earl Warren, who was then governor of California, was instrumental in helping Dwight Eisenhower win the Republican presidential nomination. Consequently, Eisenhower owed him a favor and paid it back when he chose Warren to be chief justice. In the 1960s both John Kennedy and Lyndon Johnson appointed old friends and political allies to the Court. Kennedy named Byron White and LBJ picked Abe Fortas. There's a saying that a judge is a lawyer who knows the president.

Finally, presidents sometimes make appointments in hopes of scoring political points. For example, Eisenhower's appointment of the Catholic William Brennan before the 1956 election may have been timed to influence the Catholic vote. Certainly Lyndon Johnson was not unaware of the political significance of nominating Thurgood Marshall as the nation's first black Supreme Court justice, and Ronald Reagan's appointment of Sandra O'Connor, the first woman to serve on the Court, was done partly to fulfill a campaign promise.

Perspective
JUDICIAL TENURE

The framers of America's Constitution intended for federal judges to be insulated from political pressure. Consequently, they included the following language in Article III, Section 1: "The Judges . . . shall hold their Offices during good Behaviour, and shall . . . receive for their Services, a Compensation, which shall not be diminished during their Continuance in Office." This means that federal judges enjoy life appointments. They may not be retired involuntarily or removed for political reasons. The phrase "during good Behaviour" implies that they are subject to impeachment by the House and removal by the Senate, but this is rare. Historically, only six district-court judges have ever been impeached and only three have been convicted and removed. Also, the Constitution protects federal judges from having their salaries reduced during their time in office. Table 10.1 lists the salaries of the various federal judges.

These constitutional provisions apply only to those judgeships created under the authority of

TABLE 10.1 *The Salaries of Federal Judges, 1983*

Judge	Salary
Chief Justice of the United States	$100,000
Supreme Court Associate Justice	96,700
Court of Appeals Judge	77,300
District Court Judge	73,100

SOURCE: Congressional Research Service, "Update of *The United States Courts: Their Jurisdictions and Work*," (Washington, D.C.: U.S. Government Printing Office, 1983).

The Senate looks far more closely at Supreme Court nominations than it does at the president's lower-court appointments. The Judiciary Committee staff and the staffs of individual senators carefully explore the nominee's background and past statements on policy issues. A hearing is held at which the nominees, interest-group spokespersons, and other interested parties have their say. Then the Senate as a whole debates the nomination on the floor before voting to confirm or reject.

The entire process is highly political. The administration and interest groups of various stripes roll out their heaviest lobbying artillery to try to sway the vote. In 1969 and 1970, Richard Nixon's ill-fated nominations of Clement Haynesworth and G. Harrold Carswell turned into a political tug-of-war between civil-rights and civil-liberties groups and the White House. Nixon lost those two, but in 1971 he won another confirmation fight when the Senate approved his selection of William Rehnquist despite considerable opposition.

In the end, most presidential nominations to the Supreme Court are confirmed by the Senate, although there have been notable exceptions. Overall, the scorecard reads 113 confirmations out of 139 nominations; in the twentieth century it's 45 out of 53.[14] The most recent rejected nominees have been Haynesworth, Carswell, and Abe Fortas. In 1968, after Earl Warren announced his retirement, President Johnson sought to elevate

---

Article III. This includes all Supreme Court and appellate-court judges and most district-court judges. These provisions do not apply, however, to judges on the tax court, the court of military appeals, or the district courts for Guam, Puerto Rico, and the Virgin Islands. Congress has created these courts under the authority of Article I of the Constitution. These judges are appointed by the president to fixed terms set by Congress, and they are not protected against diminution of their salaries during their term of office. The district judges in the territories, for example, serve eight-year terms. Judges on the tax court and the court of military appeals serve for fifteen years.

In the early 1980s, an intriguing constitutional/political controversy arose over the status of the bankruptcy judges attached to the federal district courts. When Congress reformed the federal bankruptcy laws in 1978, it broadened the authority of the bankruptcy judges, putting them on a par with federal district judges but without the latter's tenure or salary protection. In June 1982 the Supreme Court held this reform invalid and gave Congress a fall deadline either to restrict the authority of the bankruptcy judges or to give them life tenure. Congress missed that deadline and another one as well. Congress finally resolved the problem in June 1984 by restricting the power of bankruptcy judges, subordinating them to the federal district judges.[1]

[1]Morrow Cater, "Manville Bankruptcy Case May Prompt Congress to Close 'Loopholes' in Law," *National Journal* (27 November 1982), pp. 2029–30; Ronald Brownstein, "Going Bankrupt—Is It Just a Way to Get Out of Labor Contracts?" *National Journal* (12 November 1983), pp. 2353–56.

The swearing in of Sandra Day O'Connor, the first woman justice to sit on the United States Supreme Court.

Associate Justice Fortas to the post of chief justice. The nomination became embroiled in election-year politics and charges of political cronyism, though, and fell victim to a filibuster on the Senate floor.

Historically, Supreme Court justices have been a fairly homogeneous group. All of them have been lawyers, many graduating from the nation's most prestigious universities and law schools. Most of them have been middle and upper-middle class white, male, Anglo-Saxon Protestants. In recent years, however, the make up of the Court has shown more diversity. A number of Catholics and several Jews have served on the Court. Then, in 1967 Thurgood Marshall became the Court's first black member and in 1981 Sandra O'Connor became its first woman.

Supreme Court justices come to the bench from a variety of career backgrounds, but most are no strangers to politics. O'Connor, for example, was a state judge immediately before she was named to the Supreme Court, but earlier in her career she was a Republican leader in the Arizona legislature. Burger was a federal appeals-court judge, but had once been a Republican organizer in Minnesota and an assistant attorney general in the Eisenhower Administration. Not all politics is party politics, of course. Louis Powell was a past national president of the ABA, and Marshall was head of the NAACP's Legal Defense Fund. There are also justices whose backgrounds are less political. Harry Blackmun and John Paul Stevens were relatively apolitical federal judges before their appointments to the Court.

As with other federal judges, members of the Supreme Court enjoy the ultimate in job security. With "good Behaviour" they can serve for life and many have continued on the bench well past normal retirement age. Associate Justice Hugo Black, for example, served until age eighty-five;

William O. Douglas lasted until he was seventy-seven. Justices can be impeached and removed from office, but this is very unlikely unless there is clear evidence of misconduct. Politics or even old age and senility probably aren't reason enough. During the Warren years, some of the Court's most conservative critics launched a billboard campaign to "Impeach Earl Warren" and Congressman Gerald Ford called for the impeachment of Douglas, but neither effort got very far. In 1969, however, Justice Fortas resigned under fire over conflict-of-interest allegations.

Jurisdiction.   Technically, the Supreme Court can be both a trial court and an appellate court, but in practice it is almost exclusively appellate. The Constitution says the Court's **original jurisdiction** (that is, those cases it may hear as a trial court) extends to "Cases affecting Ambassadors, other public Ministers and Consuls, and those in which a State shall be Part," provided the state has initiated the case. The Supreme Court never conducts trials, however. The Court shares jurisdiction with the federal district courts on these matters and leaves most of the cases for the district courts to handle. Even for those few cases in original jurisdiction that the justices consider worth their while, the Supreme Court doesn't hold a trial. Instead, the Court appoints a special master to conduct a hearing to determine the facts before it decides the legal issues raised.

The Court's appellate jurisdiction is set by law, and through the years Congress has seen fit to make the United States Supreme Court the nation's highest appellate court for both the federal and the state judicial systems (see Figure 10.2). In the federal system, the most important source of appeals by far is the courts of appeal, but cases may also come on appeal from the court of military appeals and the special three-judge district courts. From the state systems, appeals can be made to the U.S. Supreme

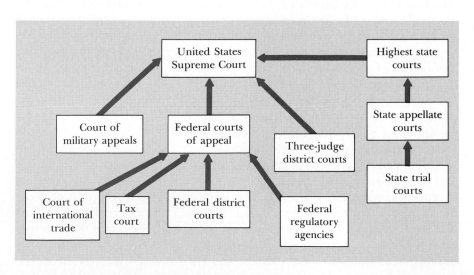

FIGURE 10.2
The Federal Court System (connecting lines indicate path of appeals).

Court from the highest court in each of the states, usually the state supreme court. The *Bakke* case, for example, was appealed from the California Supreme Court.

What Congress gives, Congress can take away. After the Civil War,
Congress removed the authority of the Supreme Court to review the
constitutionality of Reconstruction legislation. Since then, however, Congress has been fairly reluctant to tamper with the jurisdiction of the federal
courts on the grounds that it would interfere with the independence of the
judicial branch. In recent years, for example, attempts to limit the federal
courts' jurisdiction in cases involving such controversial issues as abortion,
school prayer, busing, and the rights of criminal defendants have all failed.

Deciding to decide. Each year the Supreme Court meets in regular
session from the first Monday in October until the end of June or early
July. The summer months are a time for vacation and individual study by
the Court's members, although the chief justice has the power to call a
special session to consider particularly pressing matters. The Nixon Watergate tapes case, for example, was dealt with in a special session.

Once in session, one of the most important activities of the Court is
determining what cases to decide. Each year some four or five thousand
cases are appealed to the Supreme Court, far more than the one to two
hundred cases the Court can reasonably handle. Consequently, the justices
must screen the cases brought to them to decide which ones merit their
attention.

The process begins with lawyers filing petitions to the Court and submitting briefs explaining why their client's case deserves to be reviewed by the
Supreme Court. There's a $200 filing fee and a requirement of forty copies
of the paperwork, but the Court will waive these requirements when a
litigant is too poor to hire an attorney and cover the expenses of the appeal.
Many of these petitions, filed *in forma pauperis,* as the procedure is called,
arrive at the Court written in longhand on Big Chief notebook paper.
Frequently, they are from prison inmates who spend their time studying
lawbooks and preparing appeals as a sort of occupational therapy. Most of
these appeals are rejected summarily by the Court, but a few, including the
Gideon case, make the Court's docket for full examination. In these instances, the Court appoints an attorney to prepare and argue the case for
the indigent petitioner. During the Court's 1982–83 term, for example,
about half of the roughly 4000 petitions were filed *in forma pauperis.* The
rest were "paid." The Court agreed to hear ten of the pauper petitions and
169 of the paid cases.[15]

When petitions arrive at the Court, the justices' law clerks go over them,
searching for cases of interest to their bosses. The chief and the five most
senior associate justices have four clerks apiece—the others three—all
hired from a pool of applicants that includes many of the best and brightest
young law-school graduates in the nation. As you might imagine, it's quite a

prestigious job and a big boost to a young lawyer's career. There are anecdotes about the clerks shaping policy on the Court, and to some degree they do influence decisionmaking there, but most of their work is routine, such as reading through stacks of petitions.

With the help of his clerks, the chief justice prepares and circulates among his colleagues a "discuss list" of cases he thinks are worth discussing. Any of the other justices can add a case to the discuss list, but only about 30 percent of the cases make it this far. Based on the list, the justices then select the cases to be granted **certiorari,** or **appeals,** the technical terms for the Court's decision to hear arguments and make a ruling in a case. The other appeals are rejected without a hearing, and the lower court's decision is upheld.

The selection process takes place in **conference,** a closed meeting attended only by the justices. Decisions are based on the **Rule of Four**—if four of the nine justices agree to hear a case, it will be heard. Fewer than 5 percent of all cases appealed to the Supreme Court are actually granted *certiorari* or appeals.

What kinds of cases does the Court accept? Important ones, of course. These include cases with legal issues of national importance that the Court has not already decided; cases involving conflicts among appeals courts or between a lower court and the Supreme Court; and cases in which the constitutionality of a state or federal law is under attack. Congress requires the Court to hear cases in which a state supreme court has found a federal law unconstitutional and cases in which a federal appeals court has found a state law unconstitutional. The Court rejects cases it considers trivial or local in scope, or that raise issues already decided by earlier Court rulings. The Court won't accept appeals from state courts, for example, unless the litigant can demonstrate that a substantial national constitutional principle is involved.

All of this is vague enough to leave a great deal of discretion to the justices. They set their own rules for deciding what to decide, and follow or violate them as they see fit. For years the Supreme Court refused to get involved in the question of how members of Congress and state legislatures are chosen. It was a "political question," the Court said. However, in 1962 in *Baker* v. *Carr,* the "one person, one vote" decision, the Court conveniently overlooked its "political questions doctrine" and got involved anyway.[16]

Another example of judicial discretion is the *De Funis* case. It offered the Court the chance to decide issues similar to those raised by the *Bakke* case back in 1974. Marco de Funis had applied to law school and had been rejected under circumstances similar to those of Allan Bakke. The Supreme Court refused to grant *certiorari,* however, because a lower court had ordered De Funis admitted to law school pending appeal. By the time the case reached the Supreme Court, De Funis was about to graduate. The case was moot, said the Court.[17] Or, perhaps, too hot to handle. Only the year

What kinds of cases does the Court accept? Even seemingly insignificant issues are heard by the Court and can come to have large implications and consequences. The tiny snail darter was an endangered species and so qualified for protection under federal law. When the Tennessee Valley Authority sought to build a $116 million dam threatening the fish's critical habitat, the Supreme Court ordered a halt to construction.

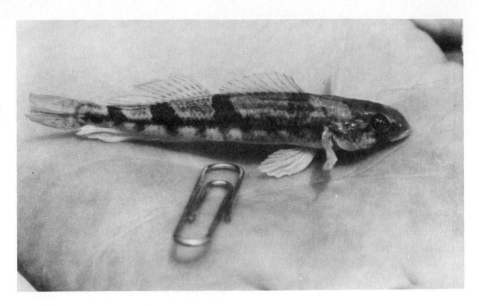

before, however, in *Roe* v. *Wade,* the Court accepted and decided a case challenging the constitutionality of state laws outlawing abortion even though one suspects that the fetus in question had long since been born or aborted by the time the case reached the Court.[18] Deciding what to decide is a political decision.

Deciding the case.   The cases the Court agrees to decide are generally dealt with in one of two ways. About half of them are decided without oral arguments. The Court issues its ruling, accompanied by an unsigned, unanimous written opinion briefly explaining the Court's decision. These **per curiam opinions,** as they are called, may be used, for example, to reverse a lower-court ruling that is contrary to an earlier decision of the Supreme Court.

The other half of the cases receive the Court's full treatment. Briefs are submitted arguing the merits of the case and oral arguments are scheduled. The briefs come from the litigants, but also, with the Court's permission, from a variety of other parties who have an interest in the outcome of the case. These **amicus curiae** or "friend of the court" **briefs** offer the justices more input than they would otherwise receive and provide interest groups an opportunity to lobby the Court. In the *Bakke* case, for example, *amicus* briefs supporting Bakke were submitted by a number of groups, including the American Federation of Teachers, the American Jewish Committee, the U.S. Chamber of Commerce, and the National Medical and Dental Association. Meanwhile, the university's friends included the American Bar Association, the NAACP, the United Mine Workers, Harvard University, the ACLU, NOW, the Mexican-American Legal Defense and Education Fund, the YWCA, and the federal government.[19]

The oral arguments are presented publicly to the nine justices in the courtroom of the Supreme Court building. The two attorneys in the case are usually allotted half an hour each to make their case and answer any questions the justices may ask. In *Bakke,* however, each side was given an hour, and the counsel for the university shared his time with the solicitor general, the Justice Department attorney who argues cases before the Supreme Court on behalf of the government.

A few days after the oral arguments, the justices meet in closed conference to discuss the case and take a tentative vote. If the chief justice is part of the initial majority, he assigns himself or some other justice to begin drafting a **majority opinion.** If the chief is with the minority, however, the responsibility for opinion assignment falls to the most senior justice with the majority. The majority opinion is the official voice of the Court. It justifies the Court's ruling in the case, explains the legal reasoning behind it, and offers guidance to lower courts in dealing with similar cases later.

At this point, everything is tentative. A great deal of negotiating and haggling usually takes place before the Court is ready to hand down its ruling. Over the next several months some justices may switch sides on the vote, and others will threaten to switch if the majority opinion isn't written to their liking. The justice drafting the majority opinion searches for language to satisfy a majority of the Court's members. Inevitably, it will be a negotiated document, reflecting compromises among the justices.[20] Meanwhile, other justices may be preparing and circulating **concurring** or **dissenting** opinions. Concurring opinions reach the same outcome as the majority opinion, but follow a different logic to get there. Dissenting opinions disagree with both the decision and the logic of the majority. Only the majority opinion has legal force, however.

The decision.   Eventually, the justices' positions harden or coalesce and the Court is ready to announce its decision. This is done in open court and the final versions of the justices' opinions—majority, concurring, and dissenting—are published in the *United States Reports.* Majority rules on the Court. Cases can be decided nine-to-zero, five-to-four, or anything in between (assuming, of course, that the Court is fully staffed and every justice participates). Most observers believe, however, that the strength of the Court's decision depends on its unanimity.

Take the example of *Brown* v. *Board of Education of Topeka,* the great school desegregation case decided in 1954.[21] The Court's decision was unanimous; the death or resignation of one or two justices wasn't going to reverse the majority on the issue. Also, there was only one opinion, the majority opinion written by Chief Justice Warren. Consequently, there was no aid and comfort to anyone looking for a weakness of will on the Court.[22]

In contrast, the Court was badly divided on the *Bakke* case and its decision muddled. Four of the justices—Burger, Stevens, Rehnquist, and Potter Stewart—agreed that Bakke should be admitted and that the university's quota system was a violation of the 1964 Civil Rights Act. "Race cannot be the basis of excluding anyone from participating in a federally-funded program," they argued.[23] Four other justices—Brennan, White, Marshall, and Blackmun—wanted to uphold the admissions program and support the school's decision to reject Bakke. "We . . . conclude that Davis' goal of admitting minority students disadvantaged by the effects of past discrimination is sufficiently important to justify use of race-conscious admissions criteria."[24]

That left Justice Lewis Powell as the swing man and the author of the majority opinion. First, Powell joined Burger, Stevens, Rehnquist, and Stewart to rule five-to-four in support of Bakke's admission and in opposition to racial quotas in medical-school admissions. "Preferring members of one group for no reason other than race or ethnic origin," Powell wrote, "is discrimination for its own sake. This the Constitution forbids." Powell based his decision on the equal-protection clause of the Fourteenth Amendment.[25]

Second, Powell joined Brennan, White, Marshall, and Blackmun to form another majority of five in support of admissions decisions that consider race as long as there is no hard-and-fast quota system. A diverse student body is a worthy goal, Powell said. Harvard, for example, aims for a student body that includes a variety of economic, racial, and ethnic groups. Race may tip the balance in favor of a particular applicant, but so may geographic origin or life spent on a farm. The Harvard admissions program is acceptable because it is flexible; it treats applicants as individuals.[26]

As you can see, the Court was badly split over the issues raised by *Bakke.* Only Powell supported all the main points of the majority opinion. The other eight justices agreed in part, dissented in part. Also, Burger, Stevens, Rehnquist, and Stewart wrote a concurring opinion, saying they would have preferred to decide the case on the basis of the Civil Rights Act rather than on the Fourteenth Amendment, as Powell did. In sum, *Bakke* is a confused decision and that makes for weak law and uncertain public policy.

POLITICS, THE LAW, AND THE COURTS

The courts have a unique role in America's policy process because of their status as both legal and political institutions. Consequently, in some respects they are different from the other institutions of American government, while in others they are very similar.

THE LAW AND THE COURTS

The courts are different because they are legal bodies. This means they work under different ground rules than the Congress, the president, or the federal bureaucracy. Certainly, the atmosphere is different. There's a reserve, almost a reverence for judicial proceedings not found among members of the other political institutions. As Justice Harold Burton replied when he was asked about his appointment to the Supreme Court after serving in Congress, "Have you ever gone direct from a circus to a monastery?"[27]

As legal institutions, courts must make decisions within the framework of the law and the Constitution. Sometimes the courts are limited by the plain meaning of the law or the Constitution. For example, the Constitution clearly states that no one less than thirty-five years old may become president. The courts could hardly rule otherwise. At other times, the courts find themselves restricted by clear legislative intent. Take the example of the Second Amendment. Did the founders adopt this to insure the individual's right to own and carry firearms? Or were they concerned that state governments be permitted to maintain militias? Historians tell us that it is the latter, and the courts have consistently so ruled. Also, the courts, especially the lower courts, are bound by earlier judicial decisions. This is known as the principle of **stare decisis.** Court decisions set precedents for future cases involving the same issues. There are times when the Supreme Court consciously decides to overturn a precedent (the *Brown* decision reversed a precedent set in 1896),[28] but it doesn't do so frivolously. Moreover, the lower courts are expected to work within the precedents set by the Supreme Court.

The law and the Constitution serve as frameworks for judicial action, but they aren't straitjackets. As we have seen, the Constitution's meaning isn't always plain; it's frequently vague. Room is left for interpretation. In a sense the Supreme Court is an ongoing constitutional convention, interpreting and reinterpreting the Constitution (see the **PERSPECTIVE** on page 292). The intent of lawmakers and constitution writers isn't always clear either. Historians cannot agree, for example, on the precise intent behind the Fourteenth Amendment. Also, in many cases courts may choose among several different precedents, each producing a different outcome. Consequently, there is room for courts to maneuver in decisionmaking.

If the other branches of government think the courts have gone too far afield, however, the law and the Constitution can be used to rein them in. In 1978, for example, the Supreme Court ruled that the completion of a federal dam on the Little Tennessee River would violate the Endangered Species Act because it threatened a tiny fish called the snail darter.[29] The very next year Congress legislated to reverse the Court. Amending the Constitution to overrule the courts is a more difficult procedure, of course, but it has been done. For example, the Twenty-sixth Amendment giving eighteen-year-olds the right to vote was passed and ratified after the Supreme Court ruled that Congress could not legislatively lower the voting age because of constitutional restrictions.[30]

Another judicial ground rule is that courts must wait for a case before they can rule on an issue. We have seen that the members of the Supreme Court essentially decide which cases they will hear, but their choices are limited to those that come to them on appeal. During the Civil War, for example, Chief Justice Taney and perhaps a majority of the Supreme Court believed the draft law unconstitutional. They never had the opportunity to rule, however, since no case challenging the law ever reached the Court. Today, questions have been raised about the constitutionality of the War Powers Act's limitations on the president's prerogatives as commander in chief. The issue remains undecided, though, since a case has yet to arise under the law.

Still another important feature of the judicial process is that court decisions aren't self-enforcing. Instead, the courts must rely upon the other branches of government either to enforce or to comply with their rulings. Nonetheless, direct disobedience is rare; court actions enjoy considerable symbolic legitimacy. When the Supreme Court ordered President Nixon to deliver the key Watergate tapes to special prosecutor Leon Jaworski, for example, Nixon complied. We suspect that if the president had made a bonfire of them, as some suggested, he would have been impeached on those grounds. On the other hand, unpopular Supreme Court decisions are often met with delay and subtle evasion. One study reports that ten years after the *Brown* school-desegregation decision there wasn't one state in the deep South where as many as 10 percent of black students attended school with any white students.[31] Another study found widespread evasion of the Supreme Court's rulings against government-prescribed school prayers.[32]

Perspective
JUDICIAL RESTRAINT VS. JUDICIAL ACTIVISM

One of the Supreme Court's oldest and most significant debates involves the question of **judicial restraint** versus **judicial activism.** Those who advocate judicial restraint believe that judges should avoid substituting their own policy judgments for the judgments of legislators and executives. In contrast, judicial activists argue that judges' responsibility to interpret and apply the Constitution force them to invalidate any actions that violate the Constitution as they understand it.

Consider first the position of Associate Justice Felix Frankfurter, who was a leading proponent of judicial restraint.

As a member of this Court I am not justified in writing my private notions of policy into the Constitution, no matter how deeply I may cherish them or how mischievous I may deem their disregard. . . . It can never be emphasized too much that one's own opinion about the wisdom or evil of a law should be excluded altogether when one is doing one's duty on the bench.[1]

Now consider the views of another associate justice, Benjamin Cardozo, who was an advocate of judicial activism.

If you ask how [the judge] is to know when one interest outweighs another, I can only answer that he must get his knowledge just as the legislator gets it; from experience and study and reflection; in brief, from life itself. Here, indeed is the point of contact between the legislator's work and his. . . . Each indeed is legislating within the limits of his competence.[2]

[1]*West Virginia State Board of Education* v. *Barnette*, 319 U.S. 624 (1943), dissenting opinion.
[2]Benjamin N. Cardozo, *The Nature of the Judicial Process* (New Haven: Yale University Press, 1921), quoted in Robert H. Salisbury, *Governing America* (New York: Appleton-Century-Crofts, 1973), p. 163.

Judges also work within the framework of the norms of their institution. These include the concepts of justice, fairness, reverence for the Constitution, respect for the law, and deference to precedent. Most judges take seriously the notion that it is their job to interpret rather than to rewrite the law and the Constitution.

POLITICS AND THE COURTS

There's a fiction that courts and judges are somehow above politics, but nothing could be further from the truth. The courts function in a different environment, but they are probably as political as the other institutions of American government. Politics plays a role in the selection of judges and affects the kinds of cases that come before the courts. It influences which cases the Supreme Court chooses to hear and affects the way judges decide cases. It helps to shape popular reaction and response to judicial decisions and determines how vigorously courts' rulings will be enforced.

As with the other political institutions of government, the courts are subject to political pressures from a number of sources. Consider the relationship between interest groups and the courts. Direct lobbying, such as occurs in Congress and the executive branch, is thought highly inappropriate. However, interest groups use other methods to influence the judicial process, including lobbying for or against the selection of individual judges and submitting *amicus* briefs. Sometimes interest groups promote and finance cases through the court system in hopes of seeing the Supreme Court rule favorably to their cause. The *Brown* case, for example, was just such a **test case.** Linda Brown and her parents were real people, and she was indeed denied the opportunity to attend a "whites only" school nearest their home, but the resources for carrying the case through the long and expensive process of trial and appeals were supplied by an interest group, the NAACP.

The courts sometimes face a great deal of pressure from public opinion. During the 1930s, for example, the members of the Supreme Court were frequently attacked as "nine unelected old men" by liberals unhappy with their rulings against New Deal measures. In the 1950s and '60s, though, it was the conservatives' turn to complain. One critic, James J. Kilpatrick, found in the Warren Court "a trail of abuses, usurpations, and invasions of power. One pursues . . . the Chief Justice along a littered road of fallen landmarks and abandoned precedents. Here every principle of jurisprudence lies discarded. It is as if gypsies had passed through, leaving a bad picnic behind."[33]

Pressures can come from Congress and the executive branch as well. Life tenure gives federal judges a certain amount of insulation from political pressure, but Congress can threaten to limit the jurisdiction of the federal courts or to change the size of the Supreme Court. Congress and the president can also propose changes in the law or even constitutional

Linda Brown, whose attempt to attend a "whites-only" school was part of a larger effort to "test" the validity of the old separate-but-equal doctrine.

The social-activist stance of the Warren Court brought a flood of criticism and abuse from conservative persons and groups. The bottom of this sign once read, "Nine men against America."

amendments to override court decisions. Perhaps the most effective long-range instrument Congress and the president have for influencing the judicial branch is the appointment of judges.

How important are political pressures in shaping court rulings and policy decisions? Probably very important, but it's impossible to say just how significant they are or to state with any precision the relative importance of legal/constitutional factors and political factors in judicial decision-making. We suspect, however, that legal/constitutional factors have their greatest impact in everyday civil and criminal disputes handled by trial courts. The importance of political influences probably increases in major policy cases heard by the courts of appeal and the Supreme Court.

We can cite some examples, however, when courts and judges *appear* to have marched to the beat of a political drum and others when legal/constitutional tempos seemed more important. In the 1930s, Roosevelt's court-packing plan failed, but the Supreme Court nonetheless began upholding New Deal legislation. Observers spoke wryly of the Court's reading the election returns. In the 1970s and '80s, the Court has no longer been as predictably liberal as the Warren Court, thanks perhaps to the addition of four appointees by Richard Nixon. On the other hand, since *Brown* v. *Board of Education* many federal district judges, such as Frank Johnson of Alabama, have courageously ordered the desegregation of local schools despite enormous political and social pressures against them and their families. Alabama Governor George Wallace, for one, was fond of saying that Johnson ought to be given a "barbed wire enema."

Finally, at times it is difficult to determine whether the courts are acting on the basis of political motives, legal/constitutional principles, or both. Take the example of the "flag-salute" cases, decided in the 1940s. In the early days of World War II, a number of states passed laws requiring school children to salute the flag. The Jehovah's Witnesses, however, refused to permit their children to obey, saying flag salutes violated their religious beliefs. Some children were expelled for refusing to salute, and the dispute reached the Supreme Court in 1940. The Court ruled eight-to-one against the Witnesses. The right of the states to promote national unity took precedence, the Court said. Subsequently, Jehovah's Witnesses stuck to their principles, and their children frequently suffered expulsion. There was even some mob violence directed against the Witnesses. But there was also a great deal of criticism aimed at the Court in newspaper editorials and law-journal articles. The justices began to reconsider. In 1943 the Court accepted another flag case and simply reversed itself. This time the Court held that the compulsory flag-salute laws violated the First Amendment's freedom-of-religion clause.[34]

In these cases, was the Supreme Court acting as a political institution or was it a dispassionate arbiter of the Constitution? Was the first ruling based on constitutional principles, or was it a political response to the national mood during time of international crisis? In the second decision, did the Court rectify a constitutional error or was it simply responding to criticism. Perhaps both politics and the law were involved in each of the decisions.

But that's the point. The courts are both legal/constitutional institutions and political institutions. That is the fact that must be remembered if we are to understand the role of the courts in America's public-policy process today.

CONCLUSION: PUBLIC POLICY AND THE POLICYMAKING STRUCTURES

We have come to the end of Part Three. In the last four chapters we have studied the structures of American government—the Congress, the presidency, the federal bureaucracy, and the courts. We have examined how each of these institutions is part of the policymaking process and what factors are involved in that process. Now, before we turn to Part Four, let's briefly consider how the institutions of national government participate in the five stages of the policy process.

The agenda of American government is remarkably diverse, ranging from the MX Missile to religious freedom for Jehovah's Witnesses, but the various components of government tend to specialize on particular issue areas. Since the 1930s, the Supreme Court has concentrated on civil-liberties and civil-rights matters while the bureaucracy has specialized in regulatory policy. The president has to be somewhat of a generalist, but economic and foreign policy probably occupy the greatest share of his time. Taken as a whole, Congress is a generalist, but with its committees and subcommittees, it too is specialized.

Who proposes items for the public agenda? An array of groups, organizations, and individuals as diverse as the agenda itself. It includes interest groups, such as those we discussed in chapter 6. It includes states, cities, and federal agencies. It even includes individuals, ranging from the president of the United States to Clarence Earl Gideon, a convict in a Florida jail.

Influence isn't spread evenly, of course. Groups with greater financial and membership resources have a big advantage, but the specialization of government (read *fragmentation*) means that groups have innumerable opportunities to influence the policy issues that matter to them. Also, the modern Supreme Court has provided an arena for some "orphan groups" that are too weak and unpopular to get much of a hearing from the other branches of government. These include civil-rights groups, communists, Jehovah's Witnesses, atheists, criminal defendants, illegal aliens, and the poor.

Policy formulation on any broadscale basis in American government is the work of the president. He proposes the budget; he's the primary architect of foreign policy; and he usually takes the lead in major domestic policy areas. Others participate in the policy formulation process, but their contributions tend to be fragmented and piecemeal. The committees of Congress and the agencies of the bureaucracy stick to their areas of specialization, each committee and agency developing its own options and alternatives with little direction or coordination. Meanwhile, the courts are forced to deal with issues on a case-by-case basis.

Policy adoption is the most visible and dramatic stage of the policy process. Congress passes a bill. The president announces a foreign-policy initiative. A federal agency adopts new regulatory standards. The Supreme Court hands down a major decision. Formal adoption gets the publicity, but it is usually the results of a complicated behind-the-scenes bargaining process. A great deal of public policy isn't made publicly. Negotiations take place within branches of government—among Supreme Court justices or senators, for example. They occur between branches, such as between the White House and Congress or between an agency and the Congress. They take place between levels of government—the states or the cities and the federal government. Also, bargaining occurs between interest groups and governmental bodies, such as the auto industry and the Environmental Protection Agency.

Implementation is a particularly important part of the policy process, but it receives relatively little attention. Stories of Congress passing a bill or the president proposing the budget or the Supreme Court announcing a decision make front-page news. Stories of bureaucrats putting programs into operation or city governments spending revenue-sharing dollars or lower federal courts applying Supreme Court precedents are relegated to the back pages of the Sunday supplements.

Implementation may not be dramatic, but it is important. Those who adopt policies frequently give a great deal of leeway to those who carry them out. One reason for this involves practicality. The Congress, the president, and the Supreme Court recognize that they may be too far removed from the day-to-day operation of government to foresee every eventuality. Consequently, they adopt policies that leave room for discretion in implementation.

A second reason is that policies often reflect compromise among those who adopt them. When members of Congress or the Supreme Court or the administration can't agree, the details of policy are often left intentionally vague. That way everyone can claim a policy victory.

A third reason policy implementers frequently enjoy considerable discretion is that policymakers like to avoid controversial decisions. They allow the bureaucracy or the lower federal courts or state and local government officials to make the tough decisions and then take the criticism.

There's an important point to be made here about the nature of politics. Elected officials frequently complain about unelected officials making policy decisions. The truth is that controversial issues, such as abortion, busing, and nuclear energy, often wind up in the laps of judges and bureaucrats because those issues are too hot politically for elected officials to handle. The elected officials may criticize the courts and the bureaucracy, but these same elected officials are often secretly delighted to see the courts and bureaucrats step in.

Finally, we come to the last stage of the policy process, evaluation. On the one hand, government evaluates itself, or, perhaps more accurately, one arm of government evaluates another. The General Accounting Office, the Office of Management and Budget, and congressional committees all play a formal role in the process. Informally, virtually the whole of government makes some sort of evaluation of policy. On the other hand, policy evaluation also comes from outside the government, from the press, interest groups, the academic community, and other interested observers. It's a game any number can play. We'll try our hand at it in Part Four.

KEY TERMS

ADVERSARY PROCEEDING (273)

AMICUS CURIAE BRIEF (288)

APPEAL (287)

BRIEFS (274)

CAPITAL PUNISHMENT (272)

CERTIORARI (287)

CIVIL CASE (272)

CONCURRING OPINION (289)

CONFERENCE (287)

CONTRACT CASE (272)

CRIMINAL CASE (272)

DEFENDANT (272)

DISSENTING OPINION (289)

FELONY (272)

NOTES

1. *New York Times,* 29 June 1978, p. 22.
2. *Gideon* v. *Wainwright,* 372 U.S. 335 (1963).
3. Quoted in *New York Times,* 29 June 1976, p. 20.
4. *Marbury* v. *Madison,* 1 Cranch 137 (1803).
5. *United States* v. *Nixon,* 418 U.S. 683 (1974).
6. *Dred Scott* v. *Sandford,* 19 Howard 393 (1857).
7. *Plessy* v. *Ferguson,* 163 U.S. 537 (1896).
8. Lawrence Baum, *The Supreme Court* (Washington, D.C.: Congressional Quarterly Press, 1981), pp. 17–23; Alfred H. Kelly and Winfred A. Harbison, *The American Constitution: Its Origins and Development,* 5th ed. (New York: W. W. Norton, 1976).
9. A. E. Dick Howard, "The Burger Court: A Judicial Nonet Plays the Enigma Variations," *Law and Contemporary Problems* 43 (Summer 1980): 7–28.
10. Glendon Schubert, *Judicial Policy-Making: The Political Role of the Courts* (Glenview, Ill.: Scott, Foresman, 1974), p. 119.
11. *New York Times,* 22 April 1984, p. E4.
12. Baum, pp. 35–36.
13. Henry J. Abraham, *Justice and Presidents: A Political History of Appointments to the Supreme Court* (New York: Oxford University Press, 1974), p. 246.
14. Baum, p. 25.
15. *Houston Chronicle,* 3 January 1984, Sec. 1, p. 8.
16. *Baker* v. *Carr,* 369 U.S. 186 (1962).
17. *De Funis* v. *Odegaard,* 416 U.S. 312 (1974).
18. *Roe* v. *Wade,* 410 U.S. 208 (1973).
19. Baum, p. 75.

20. Bob Woodward and Scott Armstrong, *The Brethren* (New York: Simon and Schuster, 1979).

21. *Brown* v. *Board of Education of Topeka,* 347 U.S. 483 (1954).

22. S. Sidney Ulmer, "Earl Warren and the *Brown* Decision," *Journal of Politics* 33(1971): 689–702.

23. *Regents of the University of California* v. *Bakke,* 438 U.S. 265 (1978).

24. Ibid.

25. Ibid.

26. Ibid.

27. Mary Francis Berry, *Stability, Security, and Continuity: Mr. Justice Burton and Decision-Making in the Supreme Court 1945–1958* (Westport, Conn.: Greenwood, 1978), p. 27.

28. *Plessy* v. *Ferguson,* 163 U.S. 537 (1896).

29. *Tennessee Valley Authority* v. *Hill,* 437 U.S. 153 (1978).

30. *Oregon* v. *Mitchell,* 400 U.S. 112 (1970).

31. Harrell R. Rodgers, Jr. and Charles S. Bullock, III, *Law and Social Change* (New York: McGraw-Hill, 1977), p. 75.

32. H. Frank Way, Jr., "Survey Research on Judicial Decisions: The Prayer and Bible Reading Cases," *Western Political Quarterly* 21(June 1968): 189–205.

33. James J. Kilpatrick, "A Very Different Constitution," *National Review* (12 August 1969), p. 795. Quoted in Howard.

34. *Minersville School District* v. *Gobitis,* 310 U.S. 586 (1940); and *West Virginia State Board of Education* v. *Barnette,* 319 U.S. 624 (1943).

SUGGESTED READINGS

ABRAHAM, HENRY J. *The Judicial Process,* 4th ed. New York: Oxford University Press, 1980.

BAUM, LAWRENCE. *The Supreme Court.* Washington, D.C.: Congressional Quarterly Press, 1981.

CORWIN, EDWARD S. *The Constitution and What It Means Today.* 14th ed. Rev. by Harold W. Chase and Craig R. Ducat. Princeton: Princeton University Press, 1978.

HODDER-WILLIAMS, RICHARD. *The Politics of the U.S. Supreme Court.* Winchester, Mass.: Allen & Unwin, 1980.

LEWIS, ANTHONY. *Gideon's Trumpet.* New York: Random House, 1964.

MURPHY, WALTER F. *Elements of Judicial Strategy.* Chicago: University of Chicago Press, 1964.

SCHUBERT, GLENDON. *Judicial Policy-Making: The Political Role of the Courts.* Glenview: Scott, Foresman, 1974.

WOODWARD, BOB, AND ARMSTRONG, SCOTT. *The Brethren.* New York: Simon and Schuster, 1979.

Part Four

PUBLIC POLICIES

Beginning journalism students are taught that straight news stories should include the "who, what, when, where, why, and how" of events. In the next few chapters, we will discuss the who, what, when, where, why, and how of public policy in five substantive policy areas. Chapter 11 focuses on public economics while chapter 12 examines regulatory policy. Chapter 13 looks at civil-liberties policy. In chapter 14, the subject is government policy toward women and minorities. Finally, chapter 15 considers foreign and defense policy.

Each chapter begins with an example of policymaking in the area under study. These illustrate the relevance of policy to contempo-

rary American government and point out some of the characteristics of policymaking in the area. Then we discuss how policy in that area is made. How is the agenda set? Who formulates policy? How is it adopted and then implemented? What mechanisms are there for policy evaluation? Finally, we conclude each chapter with a discussion of the politics of policymaking as applied to the area under consideration.

In studying the next five chapters, you should consider what you are learning in light of the first three parts of this book. In Part One, you recall, we discussed the background of policymaking in America. As you study Part Four, consider how policymaking

in each of the five areas of study has been shaped by historical, philosophical, constitutional, and socioeconomic factors.

Part Two dealt with participation. As you read the last part of this book, ask yourself who participates in each area of policymaking. What means of participation are used by which groups? With what effect? Finally, ask what all of this means for democracy. Is policy made by the many for the good of all, or is it made by an elite for the benefit of a few?

In Part Three, we examined the role played by Congress, the president, the federal bureaucracy, and the federal courts in the policymaking process. As you read the next five chapters, consider the role played by each in making policy in the different policy areas. Which institutions are more important in each policy area? In which areas are each of the institutions of government most important?

So you see Part Four serves two purposes in our study of public policymaking in America. First, it describes and analyzes the substance of policy and the dynamics of policymaking in several important political spheres. Second, it illustrates what we learned about policymaking in the first three parts of our text.

Chapter Eleven

PUBLIC ECONOMICS

It was December 23, 1982—almost Christmas—and the United States Congress was finally able to adjourn. For two weeks the Senate had been tied down by a series of bitter, last-ditch filibusters against a proposed five-cent-a-gallon increase in the federal gasoline tax. Now the filibuster had been broken. The bill was passed and sent to President Reagan, who signed it into law.

Congress' session had ended much as it had begun: arguing economic policy. For the last year Congress had debated the budget, taxes, and spending; despite the passage of the gasoline tax, much was left undone. The government's 1983 **fiscal year,** or budget year, had begun on October 1, but Congress had passed only seven of the thirteen appropriations bills that provide money for various programs. Without appropriations the government would be forced to shut down. Consequently, two weeks before Christmas, Congress hastily lumped together more than $400 billion worth of spending into a single "**continuing resolution.**" In the rush to adjourn, one amendment after another was tacked onto the bill, amendments providing special projects for the home folks or some special favors to certain interest groups. Most members probably didn't even know the details of the final bill presented to them by the conference committee. Although it was some three hundred pages long, there were only thirty-five copies to go around. Nevertheless, it passed. It wasn't Congress' finest hour.[1]

Year in and year out, the federal budget is the single most important economic and political document the president and Congress must enact. Yet, there is basic disagreement over what economic policies the government should be following and deep dissatisfaction with the current economic policymaking process. Congress' budget problems in late 1982 were manifestations of both. Let's begin our study of public economics by examining the substance of contemporary economic policy.

A PROFILE OF THE BUDGET

The most striking feature of the federal budget is its size: more than $900 billion. But how big is that? The number itself is large beyond comprehension. Table 11.1 lists budget figures for various years since the turn of the century. Certainly the budgets of the 1980s are dramatically higher than the budgets of earlier years, but we need to place them in context. For one thing, the numbers aren't comparable because of inflation. A billion dollars today simply isn't worth as much as a billion dollars in 1970, 1960, or 1940—not by a long shot. Second, the economy has grown. There are more Americans now, producing more goods and services, earning larger incomes, paying more taxes, and demanding more services from government. A larger economy means a larger budget.

Perhaps the best way to evaluate the size of the federal budget is to consider it as a proportion of the nation's gross national product (GNP), which is a standard measure of the size of a nation's economy. Table 11.1 shows that, using this measure, the most dramatic increase in federal spending came with the New Deal and the Second World War. Before the 1930s, the federal budget accounted for less than 10 percent of the GNP; by 1942 it was up to 22 percent. After World War II, federal spending declined to about 17 percent of GNP and leveled off until the late 1960s. By 1970, it had risen to 20 percent of the GNP, and by 1980 it was up to 22.5 percent.

The size of the budget is a matter of great political debate. Liberals argue that the budget is large because society's needs are great; a major federal financial commitment is required to provide services for the people. Also, liberals point out that government spending in the United States is proportionally less than it is in many other industrialized countries, including Great Britain, West Germany, and France.[2]

In contrast, conservatives attack the budget as symbolic of a government that has gotten far too big. During the 1980 election campaign Ronald Reagan took every opportunity to attack what he called the "bloated federal budget" and promised to halt the growth of government. As you can see from Table 11.1, however, the relative size of the budget has continued to grow during the early years of the Reagan presidency. For 1985, Reagan proposed a budget that was equivalent to 24.2 percent of the GNP. In

TABLE 11.1

Federal Government Expenditures, 1902–1985

Year	Expenditures (billions of $)	As Pct. of GNP
1902	.57	2 %
1922	3.8	5
1932	4.3	7
1942	35.5	22
1950	43.1	17
1955	68.5	17
1960	92.2	18
1965	118.4	17
1970	196.6	20
1975	326.1	22
1980	579.6	22.5
1982	727.7	23.5
1984	853.8	24.4
1985*	925.5	24.2

*proposed
SOURCES: Historical Statistics of the U.S., U.S. Department of Commerce, Bureau of the Census, Treasury Department, Office of Management and Budget, reported in Adam Gifford, Jr., and Gary J. Santoni, *Public Economics* (Hinsdale, Ill.: Dryden, 1979), p. 61; *National Journal* (13 February 1982), and *National Journal* (4 February 1984), pp. 217–18.

The federal budget is always of interest to public and media alike, and inevitably arouses intense debate. Here officials rush to distribute copies of President Reagan's proposed 1985 budget.

SOURCE: *The White House*

practice, the Reagan economic program has been less a reduction of government spending than a shift of priorities. We can best examine this by turning our attention to the details of the budget.

BUDGET EXPENDITURES

The actual budget document runs over a thousand telephone book pages in small type, so it's necessary for us to group items together into broad categories if we are to describe it briefly. Table 11.2 breaks the federal budget down into eighteen functional categories and compares spending for these items through the last budget of the Carter years (1980) and into the Reagan presidency. As you can see from the table, national defense, Social Security and Medicare, interest on the debt, and income security are the budget's big-ticket items.

National defense.   The defense budget is one of the largest and fastest-growing components of the federal budget. In the 1960s, defense spending made up more than 40 percent of the budget, but it declined proportionally during the 1970s as the Vietnam war wound down and as social programs claimed an ever larger piece of the federal pie. By the late 1970s, the defense budget had declined proportionally to less than 25 percent of the total budget. The feeling was growing, however, that the nation's military machine needed an overhaul. President Carter proposed and Congress passed sizable increases in the defense budget. President Reagan asked for even more substantial increases than his predecessor. Although Congress trimmed Reagan's defense requests a bit, by the middle 1980s the Pentagon's share of the budget was approaching 30 percent.[3]

TABLE 11.2

Federal Expenditures, Fiscal 1981–1985 (Billions of Dollars)

Category	1981	1982	1983	1984	1985*
National defense	$160	$187	$211	$238	$270
International affairs	11	10	9	14	18
General science, space, technology	6	7	8	8	9
Energy	10	5	4	4	3
Natural resources, environment	14	13	13	12	11
Agriculture	6	15	22	11	14
Commerce, housing credit	4	4	4	4	1
Transportation	23	21	21	26	27
Community, regional development	9	7	7	8	8
Education, jobs, social services	31	26	27	29	28
Health	27	27	29	31	33
Social Security and Medicare	179	203	223	240	260
Income security	86	92	106	96	114
Veterans' benefits, services	23	24	25	26	27
Administration of justice	5	5	5	6	6
General government	4	5	5	6	6
General purpose fiscal assistance	7	6	7	7	7
Interest on debt	69	85	90	108	116

*proposed
SOURCE: *National Journal* (4 February 1984), p. 217.

The defense budget is the focus of one of Washington's livelier policy debates. Conservatives contend that a defense buildup is necessary to counter a growing Soviet threat. Many liberals in Congress have agreed that some additional defense spending is necessary, but they argue that the large increases proposed by Reagan are wasteful and unnecessary. They believe that the nation's security can be ensured for less money and that the nation would be stronger if some of the defense dollars were spent elsewhere or not spent at all. We will consider defense policy in more detail in chapter 15.

Social Security and Medicare. Another large and rapidly growing budget item is Social Security and Medicare. We will discuss Social Security first and then mention Medicare.

Social Security was begun in the 1930s to provide limited coverage to workers in industry and commerce at their retirement at age sixty-five. Through the years, however, Congress has extended the program's coverage and increased its benefits. Even before the first benefit checks were mailed, Congress had expanded coverage to include the aged spouses and the children of retired workers as well as the young children and spouses of covered workers upon the worker's death. In 1956, disability insurance was added to the package.

Congress has also increased the amounts of benefits, especially in the last fifteen years. Benefits were raised 15 percent in 1970, 10 percent in 1971, and 20 percent in 1972. Then, beginning in 1975, benefits were indexed to the **consumer price index (CPI),** a measure of inflation. Thus, if the CPI shows a 7-percent annual inflation rate, Social Security payments automatically go up 7 percent. All of this has made Social Security a large and rapidly growing program. As of April 1982, some 36-million Social Security recipients collected more than $160 billion a year. The average monthly benefit for a retired worker and aged spouse was $692.[4]

Social Security is financed by a payroll tax shared equally by the wage earner and the employer. Although many Americans have the impression that Social Security works like a pension plan, in fact it's a pay-as-you-go program. The taxes withheld from your paycheck today will be paid out next month in benefits.

For years, Social Security tax rates were relatively low. In the beginning, an employee's share was one percent of the first $3000 in wages earned. The most a worker could pay in a year was only $30. For decades, the demographic gods smiled and the system prospered. Birth rates were high; women were entering the work force; the economy was strong; and wages were rising. Consequently, the Social Security trust funds were blessed with healthy surpluses.

Now all that has changed. Birth rates are down. People are living longer. A stagnant economy has held down wage increases, and inflation has pushed up benefits. To keep the system solvent, Congress increased taxes in the 1970s and built in more increases for the 1980s. By 1990, the worker's share was set at 7.65 percent on wages up to $57,000.[5] By the early 1980s, however, the trust fund once again flirted with bankruptcy. President Reagan appointed a commission to study the problem and, based on its recommendations, in early 1983 Congress passed, and the president signed, legislation to rescue the system. The bailout plan included a number of provisions to increase tax revenues and to slow increases in benefits. Some already-scheduled tax increases were sped up while cost-of-living benefit increases were delayed for six months, from June 1983 to January 1984. Federal workers were added to the system, and provisions were made to raise the retirement age by small annual increments after the year 2000 until the age reaches sixty-seven. Also, the legislation provided for the taxation of half the benefits of upper-income recipients.

Despite these reforms, the Social Security system remains in deep trouble. In 1945, fifty workers paid taxes for every beneficiary drawing benefits. By 1982 the ratio was three to one. By 2035, when the baby-boom generation has retired, it will be less than two to one. Consequently, it is estimated that the Social Security system has an "unfunded liability" of $7 trillion.[6] This means that under present benefit schedules and tax rates, the system is obligated to pay out $7 trillion more in benefits to workers already in the system than it can expect to collect in taxes. Inevitably,

Social Security is a budgetmaker's nightmare partly because politicians shy away from an association with the benefit cutbacks or tax hikes that might alienate voters.

policymakers sooner or later will have to make some extraordinarily difficult political choices involving tax increases, benefit reductions, and possibly a complete overhaul of the system.[7]

There are innumerable proposals for resolving the Social Security dilemma, but three will probably receive the most attention in the years ahead. First, politically active groups of senior citizens argue that benefits need to be increased not decreased; if that means higher taxes, so be it. Although many economists believe that the nation cannot afford to devote such a large proportion of its resources to the elderly, the growing political clout of older Americans guarantees that this view will get a hearing.

Second, some conservatives would like to see government play less of a role in this area. Instead, they believe government should encourage private-pension funds and individual retirement accounts (IRAs). This approach leaves unresolved the problem of what to do with the millions of Americans who now rely on Social Security. Also, it would penalize lower-income people who may be unable to save for retirement.

Finally, a third approach would change Social Security explicitly into a welfare program, paying benefits only on the basis of need. This plan would save billions of dollars while providing income security to those most in need, but it would arouse the political wrath of middle- and upper-income taxpayers who believe they are entitled to receive benefits when they retire.

Medicare is a federal health-insurance program for the elderly, the disabled, and those with end-stage kidney disease whose treatment is extraordinarily expensive. Like Social Security, Medicare is financed by payroll taxes and, like Social Security, it is nearing financial insolvency. Thanks to runaway inflation in the health-care industry, the cost of Medicare has risen dramatically. Although recent administrations have tried various approaches to holding down the cost of the program, they have had little success.

Social Security and Medicare are politically popular programs that have benefited millions of Americans, but they are facing financial collapse, if not in the short run, certainly in the long run. Unfortunately, this is a policy problem that has no easy answers and so far, at least, Congress and the president have been unable or unwilling to agree on a long-term solution.

Interest on the debt.   A third large and growing item in the budget is interest paid on the national debt. The federal government's budget is seldom balanced. Sometimes revenues exceed expenditures and we say there is a **budget surplus.** More frequently, however, the government spends more than it takes in, a **budget deficit.** Historically, deficits haven't been unusual. There were twenty-nine in the nineteenth century and nineteen in the first forty years of this century. Recently, though, they have become the norm. The last surplus was in fiscal 1969, a tidy $3.2 billion.

Since then government officials have seen nothing but red ink, especially in the last few years. President Reagan's tax cut, coupled with a big increase in defense spending and a deep recession that held down economic growth, produced record-setting deficits in the early 1980s. The 1982 deficit was $110 billion; in 1983 it was $195 billion. What's more, administration projections forecast deficits exceeding $100 billion for every budget year for the remainder of the decade. The **national debt** is the cumulative deficit minus the cumulative surplus. Today, the debt exceeds $1.5 trillion and is growing rapidly.

Few subjects are more misunderstood than the national debt. A debt so large doesn't mean the nation is bankrupt any more than a family's $40,000 mortgage means that it is bankrupt. The actual number is enormous, of course, but, *as a proportion of GNP,* the debt is actually smaller today than it was after World War II. Then, the debt nearly equaled the nation's GNP; now it is just less than half. Also, much of the debt is held by the Federal Reserve and other government accounts. For example, surpluses in federal-employee pension funds are used to purchase government securities. So a substantial part (more than 30 percent) of the government's debt is owed to itself. The rest is held by banks, insurance companies, brokers, state and local governments, nonprofit institutions, and individuals.

Nevertheless, most Americans and many economists are troubled by deficits, particularly the record-high deficits of the early 1980s. Some economists believe that deficits lead to inflation. Others say they drive up interest rates and thus retard economic growth. High interest rates in turn contribute to the strength of the U.S. dollar against foreign currencies. This makes American goods less competitive with foreign goods, once again hurting American business. Also, as you saw in Table 11.2, the

These Californians are signing petitions calling for, in essence, an end to the federal deficit. The high deficit levels of the early 1980s were of deep concern to many citizens.

accumulated deficits are expensive to finance. In 1984, the government paid more than $100 billion in interest on the debt.[8]

Income security. The last of the four big-ticket items in the federal budget is income security. This category includes such so-called welfare programs as Food Stamps, Aid to Families with Dependent Children (AFDC), Medicaid, housing assistance, and Supplemental Security Income (SSI). Many of these programs have been primary targets of President Reagan's budget-cutting knife. As you can see from Table 11.2, federal spending for income-security programs has grown during the Reagan presidency. However, it has not increased as rapidly as it otherwise would have. A study by the Congressional Budget Office (CBO) estimates that these programs would have been 10 percent larger were it not for budget reductions.[9]

As with the other major items in the budget, spending levels for income security programs are the focus of political conflict. Conservatives contend that these programs are a major source of waste. They support the idea of a "social safety net" to protect the truly needy, but they call for tightening eligibility requirements on these programs to eliminate the less-than-needy. In contrast, liberals charge that the Reagan cuts are unfair. The Pentagon budget has grown fat, they say, at the expense of the poor.

Other expenditures. The other budget categories in Table 11.2 are relatively smaller than our "big four," but they all add up. To paraphrase the late Senator Everett Dirksen, a billion dollars here, a billion dollars there, and pretty soon we're talking about real money. Many of these other items were also the targets of Reagan budget cuts in the early 1980s, including various programs in the areas of energy, natural resources and the environment, housing, community and regional development, and education, jobs, and social services. As you can see from the table, spending in these areas leveled off, or even declined, between the 1981 and 1985 budgets.

Other federal financial activities merit our attention, but they aren't part of the formal budget. These **off-budget operations** are loans and loan guarantees made available by the federal government to a broad array of individuals and institutions, great and small. Chrysler Corporation, Lockheed Aircraft, and New York City are recipients of federal loan guarantees. The Student Loan Marketing Association lends money to college students. The Small Business Administration makes business loans, and the Farm Credit Administration lends to farmers. The VA and the FHA insure home loans.

The total amount of money loaned is substantial—more than $80 billion in 1980—and it's a money-losing operation, at least for the government. Since the budget is in deficit, all money for off-budget lending has to be borrowed at rates that have recently been well in excess of 10 percent. That money is then loaned out at much lower rates, sometimes only 1 to 3 percent. Consequently, the government loses money. In 1980, the total amount of money lost on off-budget operations was $14.2 billion.[10]

REVENUES

Now that we have studied the expenditure side of the budget, let's consider revenues. Where does the government's money come from? Figure 11.1 shows the major sources of revenue. We have already discussed two of these, Social Security payroll taxes (29 percent) and borrowing (20 percent). The largest single source of federal revenue, however, is the individual income tax.

The income tax is a **progressive tax** on an individual's taxable income. The higher an individual's taxable income, the higher the tax rate. As you

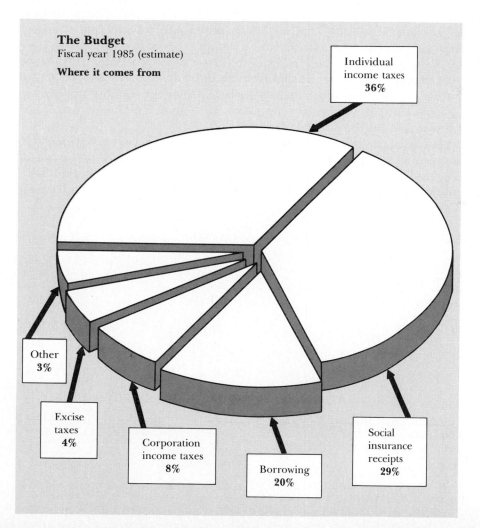

The Budget
Fiscal year 1985 (estimate)

Where it comes from

Individual income taxes
36%

Other
3%

Excise taxes
4%

Corporation income taxes
8%

Borrowing
20%

Social insurance receipts
29%

FIGURE 11.1
The 1985 Federal Revenue Dollar

can see from Table 11.3, the effective tax rate varies rather dramatically from low- to upper-income taxpayers.

The progressive income tax has been with us for more than half a century, but it still sparks controversy. Its advocates say that upper-income persons are better able to pay taxes than lower-income individuals. Also, the tax helps to reduce income differentials between the poor and the well-to-do. On the other hand, critics argue that the only truly fair tax is one in which everyone pays the same percentage, a **proportional** or **flat-rate tax** of say 15 percent across the board. What's more, they say, the current tax system discourages middle- and upper-income persons from working harder to make more money because most of it would only go to the government.

Another controversial aspect of the income tax is **tax preferences.** Because of a variety of exclusions and deductions, two persons earning the same income may pay significantly different tax bills. Some types of income are excluded from taxation, including most Social Security and veterans' benefits, pension contributions and earnings, and interest earned on state and local government bonds. Other items are **tax deductible.** This means their amount may be subtracted from an individual's gross income before computing the tax owed. These deductions include home-mortgage interest payments, charitable contributions, state and local taxes paid, and interest paid on consumer loans.

Critics say tax preferences have seriously eroded taxpayer confidence in the income tax. The tax code is so intricate that professional tax preparation has become a major industry. In 1982, some 40 percent of all individuals hired professionals to fill out their returns, an expense, incidentally,

TABLE 11.3 *Individual Income Tax Liability, 1980 and 1984*	Adjusted Gross Income Class	Effective Tax Rate	
		1980	*1984*
	0–$5000	1.3%	1.0%
	5–10,000	6.9	5.3
	10–15,000	10.5	7.9
	15–20,000	12.8	9.6
	20–25,000	14.3	10.6
	25–50,000	16.4	12.0
	50–100,000	23.4	17.3
	100–200,000	33.7	24.3
	200–500,000	40.8	30.9
	500–1,000,000	44.9	32.4
	1,000,000 and over	47.2	33.5

SOURCE: John Karl Scholz, "Individual Income Tax Provisions of the 1981 Tax Act," in Joseph A. Pechman, ed., *Setting National Priorities: The 1983 Budget* (Washington, D.C.: Brookings Institution, 1982).

that is itself tax deductible. Tax preferences also reduce tax receipts. In 1982 alone, revenue losses amounted to $266 billion. Finally, critics charge that "tax loopholes" frequently allow the wealthy to pay little or no taxes. In practice, they say, the income tax is not very progressive at all.

Every tax preference has its defenders, however. One person's loophole is another person's sacred right. Homeowners, wage earners, the elderly, churches, schools, businesses, and many others benefit from one tax preference or another. Consequently, any wholesale revision of tax preferences is likely to invite an earthshaking political battle.

Perhaps the most controversial feature of the income tax is its size. No one likes to pay taxes, of course, but until 1981 the pain of paying income taxes was growing sharper every year. In 1965, the average taxpayer's **marginal rate,** the rate of tax imposed on the last dollar earned, was 21 percent. In 1981, without a major tax increase, it had jumped to 32 percent. The culprit was the inflation that pushed taxpayers into higher and higher brackets while their real earnings did not increase. Ronald Reagan made rising taxes a major issue in the 1980 presidential election, proposing a 30-percent income-tax cut spread over three years. In 1981, Reagan made the tax cut a key part of his economic program, and Congress responded by slicing the income tax 5 percent in July 1981, 10 percent in 1982, and 10 percent more in 1983. What's more, the highest marginal rate was reduced from 70 percent to 50 percent. Congress also decided to index tax rates to inflation to prevent "bracket creep" from increasing taxes all over again. While they were at it, Congress significantly reduced taxes as well.

That's the good news for taxpayers. The bad news is that much of the individual income tax cut was wiped out by inflation, higher state and local taxes, increases in Social Security taxes, and higher excise taxes. (**Excise taxes** are levied on the manufacture, sale, or consumption of some particular commodity.) In 1982, Congress passed, and President Reagan signed, a major tax bill increasing many federal excise taxes, including levies on cigarettes, telephone bills, airline tickets, air freight shipments, aviation fuel, truck tires, diesel fuel, and gasoline.

THE GOALS OF ECONOMIC POLICY

An underlying cause of the great debate about economic policy in America is a fundamental disagreement over the goals of that policy. The most obvious goal of economic policy is the financing of government services, but, as we have seen, people disagree about the appropriate level of federal government activity in general, and disputes arise over spending priorities among the many governmental activities. Let's discuss some of the other goals of economic policy and consider the political debates that surround them.

INCENTIVES AND DISINCENTIVES
FOR PRIVATE ACTION

One aim of economic policy is to provide incentives or disincentives for private action. Government promotes certain activities by means of a variety of direct and indirect financial subsidies. Farmers, you recall, are the beneficiaries of an elaborate network of price supports and subsidy programs. The programs' advocates speak wistfully of the virtues of an agrarian lifestyle and argue forcefully that agriculture is an essential industry that needs to be kept strong; national security demands it. More cynical observers suggest that the farm lobby's influence depends more on political clout than nostalgia.

Government subsidies also support America's merchant marine. America's ship-building and shipping industries are not competitive in the world market, primarily because of the high cost of labor. The federal government has kept the industry afloat, however, by funneling government contracts through American shipyards and subsidizing the salaries of American crews. In 1983, for example, Uncle Sam shelled out $454 million for salary subsidies. The rationale for all of this is, once again, national security.   Ship-builders and ship crews, the argument goes, are vital to the nation's defense. Politics plays a role, too, of course. The merchant-marine lobby is one of the most powerful in Washington.[12]

The list of subsidy recipients goes on and on (See **PERSPECTIVE** on page 315). Publishers and bulk-rate advertisers are subsidized by the Postal Service, which charges them rates below cost and then makes up the losses by charging more for first-class mail. Beekeepers benefit too. During the decade of the '70s, the federal government gave them more than $30 million as compensation for bees killed by federally registered pesticides.[13]

Many private activities are promoted through tax incentives. The 1981 tax-cut bill, for example, provided for a variety of tax exemptions and credits for business aimed at encouraging investment and thereby enhancing economic growth. Tax exemptions for home-mortgage interest and state and local property taxes promote home ownership. Similarly, exemptions for charitable contributions help a broad range of educational, religious, and charitable institutions.

Taxes can also be used to discourage certain activities. The 1982 nickle-a-gallon increase in the federal gasoline tax was designed to raise money for highway construction and maintenance, but it also promoted energy conservation by making fuel more expensive. Similarly, at least part of the rationale behind taxes on alcohol and tobacco is to discourage their use.

In the 1980s, subsidies and tax incentives have become part of a lively debate about the course of economic policy in America. Budget deficits and recession have forced policymakers to reconsider the cost and effect of a number of these programs. Although proponents of a flat-rate tax would like to see most, if not all, of the tax-deduction incentives eliminated, a major overhaul is unlikely. The opposition political forces are too strong.

INCOME REDISTRIBUTION

Another goal of federal economic policy is the redistribution of income. Since the New Deal, the federal government has become a mammoth instrument for redistributing wealth, that is, taking from some groups of Americans and giving to others. A number of federal programs are geared to helping those at the lower end of the income spectrum. Supplemental Security Income (SSI) and Aid to Families with Dependent Children (AFDC) are **cash-transfer programs** directed to helping the poor. Food Stamps, the School Lunch Program, subsidized housing, and Medicaid are federal programs that provide **in-kind benefits** to individuals on the basis of need.

These programs are very important to poor Americans. People in the poorest fifth of the income spectrum now receive more than half their

Perspective
THE POLITICS OF ANTHRACITE COAL

Through the years, Congress has passed dozens of measures giving indirect subsidies to American industries. Consider the politics of anthracite coal. Since 1982, Congress has required that only American coal can be used to heat United States military bases in Europe. Consequently, the Pentagon is forced to purchase coal in the United States and pay to have it shipped across the Atlantic. This costs the government about $15 million a year more than it would simply to purchase the coal in Europe.

The major beneficiary of the coal policy is the anthracite-coal industry of eastern Pennsylvania. Anthracite coal was once the primary fuel used in the eastern United States, but the industry has been in decline for years. Most modern industries and power plants are designed to use less expensive bituminous coal or

fuel oil. Anthracite coal, however, is perfect for the Pentagon's power plants in Western Europe, which have not been converted to use cheaper fuels because of congressional restrictions. Now, thanks to Congress' intervention, the government has become the single largest purchaser of anthracite coal, purchasing more than $25 million of coal a year.

The politics behind the anthracite-coal program are similar to those behind other subsidy programs. It's not surprising that the program has the backing of senators and representatives from Pennsylvania, but support comes from other areas as well. Because some bituminous coal is also purchased by the government, the program is supported by members of Congress from a dozen states where coal is mined. Lobbying support comes from the United Mine Workers

Union, whose members mine the coal, the railroads, which carry the coal to port, and the maritime industry, which transports the coal to Europe. United States cargo-preference laws require the Pentagon to ship on American vessels even though they are twice as expensive as foreign shippers, another indirect subsidy to an American industry.

As with other subsidy programs, the anthracite-coal program is the subject of an ongoing policy debate. Critics of the program call it a special-interest boondoggle that increases the deficit while making government inefficient. The program's defenders say that it is necessary to keep the anthracite-coal industry alive, a goal that is, they argue, in the national interest. Regardless of the policy arguments, for now, at least, the program's defenders have the upper hand politically.[1]

[1]Michael Isikoff, "The Coal Coup: A Dying Industry's Lobbying Clout," *Washington Post*, National Weekly Edition, 26 March 1984, pp. 6–7.

incomes from Washington. It is estimated that without federal-assistance programs, the proportion of Americans living below the poverty level in 1981 would have been 23 percent rather than 14 percent.[14]

The poor, however, are not the only beneficiaries of federal largess. The largest and most expensive federal benefit programs—Social Security, Medicare, civil-service pensions, military pensions, and unemployment compensation—go to persons without regard for need. These programs help many poor persons, of course, but they also put dollars in the pockets of middle- and upper-income individuals. In fact, former Secretary of Commerce Pete Peterson says that federal programs end up "subsidizing the middle class far more than the poor."[15]

Taxes are another tool for redistributing income. Historically, the progressive income tax has played a major role in narrowing the gap between rich and poor. Those in the lowest income brackets pay almost no income tax while the upper income groups pay a sizable proportion of their earnings in taxes. Other federal taxes tend to be **regressive,** however, falling more heavily on lower-income persons. Excise taxes are the same for all purchasers of an item, but the poor generally devote a *greater proportion* of their incomes to these items than upper-income individuals. Social Security payroll taxes are proportional to a certain wage level, and then they too become regressive.

Income redistribution has always been controversial and it remains so today. On the one side are those who speak of the moral duty of society to aid the poor. The job is too great for private charity and state and local governments, they say; the federal government must step in. Others express distrust for those of great wealth and argue that significant differences of income are unhealthy for society.

On the other hand, there are those who hold that differences in ability and initiative are natural; some persons will inevitably do better and grow wealthier than others. The poor will always be with us. Is it fair for government to tax away the wealth of the successful achievers to give to nonachievers? To be sure, there should be a safety net of aid programs for the truly needy, but, they say, it doesn't help the poor to make them dependent on the federal government. Also, the high taxes necessary to support federal programs dampen the economy and, in the long run, hurt everyone.

Philosophically, the Reagan Administration has been more in tune with the latter view than the former. In general, its policies have worked to widen the gap between the rich and the poor. The Reagan income-tax cuts provided significantly more relief for upper-income taxpayers than persons on the lower end of the income spectrum. In addition, the 1982 excise-tax increases redistributed some of the tax burden to lower-income persons since excise taxes tend to be regressive.

The poor also felt the pinch of the federal spending cuts more seriously. In general, the cash-transfer and in-kind assistance programs that Reagan's budget cuts hit hardest were those that awarded benefits on the basis of need: Food Stamps, school lunches, subsidized housing, Medicaid, AFDC, and SSI. The larger programs that provide benefits regardless of need, the programs Pete Peterson says subsidize the middle class, escaped almost untouched by the Reagan cuts.[16]

The Congressional Budget Office estimated that the net effect of the Reagan policies was less for the poor, more for the wealthy. Altogether, those families earning $10,000 and less a year wound up $240 worse off after Reagan's programs were enacted than before. In contrast, families in the $80,000-plus bracket found themselves $15,000 better off than before.[17]

ECONOMIC STABILIZATION

A further goal of economic policy is to stabilize the economy with steady growth, a stable dollar, and low unemployment. The 1980s, however, have been a time of economic malaise. The decade began with double-digit inflation and 6-percent unemployment. The next couple of years saw inflation cool, but at the expense of a deep recession and double-digit unemployment that reached 10.8 percent in late 1982, a new postwar high. The economy recovered from recession in 1983 and 1984, but high interest rates and huge federal deficits had many economists worried about the future. What policies should the government adopt to ensure prosperity?

THEORIES OF ECONOMIC POLICY

Historically, American economic policy has been guided by a number of different economic theories. Let's examine some of those approaches and consider their implications for government action.

LAISSEZ-FAIRE ECONOMICS

Before the Great Depression, the working theory behind American economic policy was **laissez-faire**—leave the economy alone. According to this theory, the economic ups and downs of the **business cycle** are corrected naturally, without government intervention. Suppose, for instance, that there is an economic downturn, a **recession** or, more severely, a **depression.** As sales of goods and services drop, workers in manufacturing plants are laid off. Without a paycheck coming in, these unemployed workers and their families reduce their purchases. Consequently, more workers are laid off. It becomes a vicious circle.

At some point, however, market forces intervene to reverse the process. Since demand for goods and services has fallen, their price falls as well. Consequently, consumers eventually begin making purchases again. Similarly, the falling demand for labor drives down wage rates. Eventually,

Economic Policymaking in America: Who Wins and Who Loses?

A CONVERSATION WITH PROFESSOR JOHN PATRICK PLUMLEE, UNIVERSITY OF NORTH FLORIDA.

Q. What does it mean to win or lose in terms of economic policy?

A. Winners in economic policy decisions are those who benefit the most from the policy; losers are those who get fewer or no benefits. That seems reasonably simple, but it is sometimes difficult to determine who benefits the most from an economic policy. One problem is that we don't always know what the effects of a policy decision will be, hence there may be unanticipated winners and losers. Another problem is balancing relative versus absolute benefits. For example, if a tax policy adds $5000 a year to the income of a millionaire, does that increment mean as much as an additional $500 per year to the person who only makes $10,000? In absolute terms, the millionaire is better off. In percentage or relative terms, the person with the $10,000 per year income gains more. So it is difficult to say who has won or lost in a situation like that. Many economic policy proposals create similar difficulties.

Q. In the case you just mentioned, wouldn't the fair solution be to develop policies that would benefit everyone approximately equally?

A. You could design a policy that would benefit practically

Patrick Plumlee, Associate Professor and Coordinator of the Master of Public Administration degree program at the University of North Florida, has published in a variety of professional journals and has served as a consultant for many public and private institutions. His research interests include professionalization in administration and executive decision-making. Professor Plumlee currently teaches a course on the American presidency.

everyone equally in percentage terms, but there would still be big absolute differences because people's incomes differ so greatly. In actual practice, though, the government has been reluctant to try to achieve equality even in percentage terms. The progressive income tax, for example, takes a larger percentage of the income of the more affluent. In contrast, state and local sales taxes are regressive; they take a higher percentage of the income of the less affluent.

Q. What then is the basis for government decisions to treat people unequally in economic policymaking?

A. Politics. Public policies are designed to accomplish certain things, such as reducing inflation or lowering unemployment. The things we want to accomplish, and the way in which we want to accomplish them, are strongly influenced by our values. But all of us don't share the same values. There are conflicts in society about what is desirable social or economic policy. Politics serves as a mechanism for sorting out and resolving these value conflicts.

Q. Can you give an example of what you mean?

A. One good economic policy example is a trade-off between two goals, each of which is highly valued by most Americans. These two goals are economic equality and economic efficiency.

Since the 1930s, the federal government has intervened substantially in the national economy for the purpose of promoting greater economic equality. The government has provided both direct benefits, such as unemployment, welfare, or old-age payments, and indirect benefits, such as affirmative-action programs, to help many Americans improve their economic status, or at least to avoid impoverishment. This intervention has taken place because Americans were unwilling to let the market totally determine the living conditions for millions of the less fortunate. Of course, this meant higher taxes and bigger government, which led to concerns about economic efficiency.

One of the fundamental tenets of our economic philosophy in the United States is that it is unwise and even dangerous for government to interfere too greatly with what we like to call the "free-enterprise system." Government intervention is viewed as a threat to the efficient allocation of resources and that affects almost everyone adversely.

So a paradox emerges. In order to achieve greater equality, we have increased governmental intervention in the economy. In doing so, we have heightened threats to economic efficiency. Consequently, if economic efficiency is of greater importance to us than some higher level of equality, a certain amount of equality may have to be sacrificed, or vice versa. That is why our values are so important— they influence the extent to which we are willing to trade off one goal for another.[1] The policy process is where these values are exchanged and translated into governmental action.

Q. What is the current state of this trade-off?

A. On the whole, we have tended to defer a great deal to the idea of economic efficiency in developing economic policy. The achievement of such efficiency is strongly supported by the business community. Charles Lindblom says that business, in turn, enjoys a "privileged position" in having its values widely accepted in economic policy debates.[2]

Q. Is the Reagan Administration committed more to economic efficiency or to economic equality?

A. President Reagan undoubtedly believes that economic equality will be enhanced more through the actions of the market than through the actions of government. The supply-side approach relies heavily on the market.

Q. Are you saying that this approach will not work?

A. No, not at all. The strategy may work very well, or it may not work at all. The more important point is that we really don't know which approach works best, or what the best mix of policies is. In short, we often have to make unpleasant choices about the distribution of benefits in an environment of considerable uncertainty. Some people may suffer quite a lot from the choices that are made. As a consequence, we tend to make changes piecemeal and rather slowly.

Unfortunately, chipping away at big problems doesn't always bring us closer to solving them. But it is understandable that we are more comfortable with continued irresolution than with risking major changes that might turn out to be disastrous.

[1]A readable and thought-provoking discussion of these and other points about equality and efficiency can be found in Arthur M. Okun, *Equality and Efficiency: The Big Tradeoff* (Washington, D.C.: Brookings Institution, 1975).

[2]Charles Lindblom, *Politics and Markets: The World's Political-Economic Systems* (New York: Basic Books, 1977).

wages fall to the point where employers begin rehiring. The economy begins to recover.

At the apex of the business cycle, the economy works at full capacity, and there is full employment. Since unemployment does not exist, employers offer higher and higher wages as they compete for the limited number of available employees. With higher incomes, workers and their families increase their purchases of goods and services. This increased demand drives up prices. With the economy already moving at full throttle, supply cannot be increased. The general increase in wages and prices is called **inflation.**

Once again, the invisible hand of the market comes to the rescue. Sooner or later prices become so high that purchases slack off. Some producers can no longer afford so many employees at the current high wage level; they lay off a few. Both wages and prices stabilize as the economy cools.

Such is the world of *laissez-faire* economics. There are good times and bad, but the market is self-correcting. There is no need for government intervention. In fact, intervention is thought to do more harm than good.

In the early part of this century, many economists believed that the *laissez-faire* model was an accurate reflection of how the system worked. In practice, American government in the late nineteenth and early twentieth centuries intervened in the economy rather regularly, generally with the aim of promoting business growth. There were subsidies—for the railroads, for example—and tariffs to protect American manufactured goods. Also, state and local governments consistently intervened on the side of management in labor disputes.

The Great Depression forced American policymakers to rethink the theory and practice of *laissez-faire* economics. The economy collapsed, terribly, and it did not rebound. Where was the benevolent invisible hand of the marketplace?

KEYNESIAN ECONOMICS

Onto the scene stepped John Maynard Keynes, a British economist, with a new theory that offered a solution to the Depression. He suggested that recessions and depressions are caused by a lack of demand in the economy, or too little spending. The remedy is for government to stimulate demand by putting money into the economy. It does this by running a deficit.

When government taxes, it takes money out of the economy. It returns the money through expenditures, either by giving cash to individuals, such as Social Security recipients, or by purchasing goods and services, such as tanks for the military or medical care for the elderly. When the budget is balanced, this process of taking and returning money evens out. When the government runs a deficit, however, it puts more money into the economy than it withdraws.

The latter, said Keynes, is precisely what government should do to combat depression/recession. By cutting taxes and/or increasing expendi-

John Maynard Keynes

tures, government should pump cash into the economy. People will then have more money to spend; demand for goods and services will rise. Manufacturers will then begin rehiring workers to make goods to meet the increased demand. The economy will recover.[18]

During the 1930s, policymakers around the world turned to **Keynesian economics** for a way out of the Depression. In the United States, the New Deal put Keynes' theories into practice and Franklin Roosevelt spoke of "pump priming" as the government put money into circulation to get the economy moving again.

By the late 1940s, the economic theories of Keynes and his disciples had become the new economic orthodoxy. Classic *laissez-faire* economics said leave the economy alone and it will correct itself. The Keynesians, on the other hand, said government can successfully intervene to correct the imbalances of recession and inflation by careful manipulation of **fiscal policy,** taxes and spending, and **monetary policy,** the control of the money supply.

Monetary policy involves the amount of money in circulation in the economy. Fluctuations in the money supply affect interest rates. **Interest,** you recall, is money paid for the use of money. The laws of supply and demand stipulate that interest rates will rise and fall with the money supply. If money is tight, interest rates rise. If money is easy, they fall.

Interest rates have an important effect on the economy. Low interest rates encourage investment and discourage savings. High interest rates do the opposite. Suppose you are a business person with $500,000 in cash. You can either invest the money by using it as a down payment on a new manufacturing plant or you can save it by purchasing a certificate of deposit at the bank. The higher the interest rates, the more likely you are to put the money in the bank. Why borrow at high interest rates when you can collect those rates yourself without the risks involved in expanding your business? In contrast, lower interest rates make saving less attractive, investment more attractive. Consequently, monetary policy can be used to stimulate an economy in recession or cool down an inflationary boom.

Thus, two weapons in the Keynesian arsenal may be used by policymakers against unemployment and inflation: fiscal and monetary policy. During times of recession, government can intervene by running a budget deficit and/or loosening the money supply to lower interest rates. If inflation is the problem, however, government may take the opposite approach—a budget surplus and/or a **tight-money policy** to raise interest rates.

In 1958, Alban W. H. Phillips, a New Zealander at the London School of Economics, introduced his famous **Phillips curve** as a corollary to the Keynesians' thinking. He presented the concept that full employment and stable prices aren't compatible in a mixed economy, such as that of the United States or Great Britain. At full employment, he said, competition for labor drives up wages and, eventually, prices as well. Consequently,

FIGURE 11.2

Sample Phillips Curve

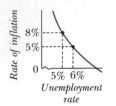

inflation is the price we pay for full employment. It can be reduced, but only at the cost of more unemployment. (A sample Phillips curve is shown in Figure 11.2.) We have to accept a trade-off. For policymakers, the trick is to "fine tune" the economy to balance an acceptable level of inflation with moderate unemployment.[19]

Until the late 1960s, the Keynesian explanation of economic reality seemed accurate. It appeared that both inflation and unemployment could be managed; the fluctuations of the business cycle seemed under control. Then something went wrong. The nation began experiencing **"stagflation,"** high rates of unemployment and inflation simultaneously. In the early 1960s, rates of inflation and unemployment were generally less than 4 percent. The 1970s, though, saw inflation soar to more than 10 percent in some years and unemployment top the 8-percent mark. The trade-off didn't seem to be working. What had happened to the government's ability comfortably to manage the economy?

THE MONETARIST SCHOOL

Keynesian economics has always had its critics, but now the critics received a wider, more receptive audience. The attack was led by Milton Friedman, an economist at the University of Chicago, who directly challenged some of the major tenets of the Keynesian orthodoxy. Keynes, writing in the midst of the Depression, considered unemployment to be the result of an inadequate demand for labor. The remedy was for government to stimulate demand. Friedman argued that much unemployment doesn't fit the Keynesian mold. Many of the unemployed are young people, looking for their first jobs. Others are between jobs and are out of work only temporarily. Still others lack skills or have skills that are out of date. Consequently, there's a "natural" level of unemployment in the economy that isn't going to be reduced by government efforts to stimulate demand.

The only result of those efforts, according to Friedman, will be inflation, which in the long run won't even subside during a recession. Conventional economic thinking holds that wages and prices level off during a recession because of decreased demand. In Friedman's view, chronic inflation upsets this process. After years of inflation, workers and business people get wise; they expect more inflation. Consequently, workers ask for big wage increases to compensate them for future inflation, even during a recession. Employers anticipate more inflation as well, so they grant the increases and raise their prices. The net result is that wages and prices continue to rise as inflationary expectations become a self-fulfilling prophecy.

The basic disagreement between Friedman and his associates and the Keynesians is over the efficacy of government action to solve economic problems. The Keynesians argue that monetary and fiscal policy can be used to reduce unemployment and control inflation. Friedman argues that government intervention in the economy *causes* problems rather than solves them. For example, minimum-wage laws, unemployment compensation, and welfare programs increase the natural level of unemployment because they reduce incentives for people to accept low-paying jobs. Other government policies, such as Social Security, progressive tax rates, and interest-rate ceilings discourage savings that are essential for investment and economic growth.

The major focus of Friedman and the Chicago School, however, is monetary policy. Consequently, their approach is frequently called **monetarism.** They argue that the only cure for inflation is for the Federal Reserve to pursue a policy of moderate, steady, predictable growth of the money supply. If the money supply is allowed to expand too rapidly, inflation results; too slowly means recession. According to the monetarists, the Great Depression could have been prevented or ameliorated significantly had the Federal Reserve expanded the money supply in a timely fashion. On the other hand, a major cause of the great inflation of the 1970s, they say, was a too-rapid growth in the money supply. The message of the monetarists, then, is less government intervention and more reliance on free-market forces. This means fewer regulations, lower taxes, less spending, a balanced budget, and moderate, steady growth of the money supply.[20]

Milton Friedman

By the end of the 1970s the monetarist school had won quite a following in academic circles, and Milton Friedman became the nation's best-known economist, winning the Nobel Prize in 1976. Among the converts was Ronald Reagan, who found in monetarism an economic philosophy complementary to his political conservatism. Consequently, it was natural for Reagan as president to support a tight-money policy by the Federal Reserve Board. The policy did indeed shrink the inflation rate, but it also produced record-setting interest rates approaching 20 percent. This brought on a severe recession with unemployment rates exceeding 10 percent, a new postwar high. Not until 1983 did the economy begin a recovery, but only after the Federal Reserve had begun to allow the money supply to grow more rapidly.

Critics of monetarism pointed to the recession as proof that the approach is wrongheaded. The monetarists' defenders argued back that recession is the price for years of inflation. Friedman himself contended that the Federal Reserve failed to follow monetarist principles consistently. Others might point out that President Reagan looked elsewhere for inspiration for his fiscal policy—to **supply-side economics.**

SUPPLY-SIDE ECONOMICS

Supply-side economic theory is similar in many ways to monetarism, but with a unique twist or, shall we say, curve. That is the **Laffer curve,** named after Arthur B. Laffer, a business professor at the University of Southern California. The Laffer curve, pictured in Figure 11.3, shows the relationship between tax revenues and tax rates. When the tax rate is zero, there are no tax revenues, of course. As the tax rate increases, revenues rise, but

FIGURE 11.3
The Laffer Curve

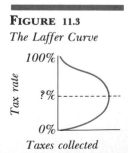

Taxes collected

only to a certain point. Eventually, taxes become so high they discourage investment and worker productivity. Why work harder to earn more money if the government is going to tax away most of it? Consequently, tax receipts decline even though the tax rate is rising. Finally, the tax rate reaches 100 percent and revenues are once again zero. Why work if *all* earnings go for taxes? The underlying concept of supply-side economics is that government policy, taxes in this case, not only affects demand, as the Keynesians point out, but it also affects the *supply* of goods and services in the economy. Hence, the name: supply-side.[21]

In the late 1970s, Laffer and his followers argued that taxes in the U.S. had gotten so high as to discourage productivity. A tax cut, they said, would provide an economic stimulus so great that tax revenues would actually rise. Among those who accepted the supply-siders' argument was Ronald Reagan, who endorsed a tax-cut bill introduced in Congress by Representative Jack Kemp and Senator Philip Roth. The so-called Kemp-Roth tax cut provided for a 30-percent reduction in tax rates spread over three years. Congress responded in 1981 by passing a three-year, 25-percent cut. The result was somewhat less than the economic boom and balanced budget that the supply-siders predicted. In 1982, the country was in the throes of a deep recession. Meanwhile, the budget was more than $100 billion in the red with predictions of much higher deficits in the years to come.

Supply-side economics had always been the object of a great deal of skepticism. Many professional economists suggested that the relationship between tax rates and tax revenues is less a curve than a tangle. In his 1980

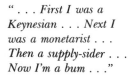

" . . . First I was a Keynesian . . . Next I was a monetarist . . . Then a supply-sider . . . Now I'm a bum . . ."

campaign for the Republican presidential nomination, George Bush described supply-side economics as "voodoo economics."[22]

After the recession of 1982, however, the wolves came out in force. Lawrence Klein, a Keynesian economist who won the Nobel Prize for economics in 1980, said this about the supply-siders: "They pulled a vast swindle on the American public—so much so that I've often thought that if there were Nuremberg trials for economists, supply-siders would be in the dock."[23] Other critics used phrases like "snake-oil economics" and "economic laetrile." Some economists sought for new ways to approach our economic problems (see the **PERSPECTIVE** on page 326). Nevertheless, supply-side still had at least one advocate after 1982, and a very important one at that—Ronald Reagan.[24]

ECONOMIC POLICYMAKING

Economic policymaking is exceedingly complex. It involves scores of decisionmakers, guided by contradictory theories, using imprecise data, and pressured by a host of interest groups. To top it all off, the decisionmaking process is so complicated and fragmented that it makes the adoption of any coherent, consistent economic policy well-nigh impossible.

AGENDA BUILDING

Nearly everyone has a stake in economic policy and many make their voices heard. The general public favors "good times," of course, low unemployment and stable prices, and are wont to vote their pocketbooks. Presidents and parties that preside over hard times usually pay an electoral price, as did Herbert Hoover and the Republican party during the Great Depression. More recently, Jimmy Carter's reelection campaign was badly damaged by public unhappiness over inflation, unemployment, and high taxes.

There are many attentive publics with specific demands. They, too, vote their economic interests. The elderly, for example, fret about receiving their Social Security checks. Woe be to any politician who dares suggest reducing benefits. Farmers worry about farm prices. College students and their parents are interested in student-loan programs. Veterans' groups are concerned with veterans' programs. Many poor persons depend on government-assistance programs.

Meanwhile, there are thousands of interest groups, each promoting its own special programs. Defense contractors favor defense spending. Highway contractors support more money for road construction. Truckers oppose increased road-use taxes.

Some of the most active lobbying on economic issues comes from the public sector, from the government itself. First, state and local officials lobby Washington over federal programs. When these are cut back, as they were in the early 1980s, state and local governments must either raise taxes or cut services. Neither is a pleasant prospect politically. Second, pressure comes from the federal bureaucracy. Program managers and bureau chiefs see their current expenditure levels (including an increment for inflation) as their *base*. They lobby for more money and resist vigorously any effort to give them less.

POLICY FORMULATION

Since the 1930s, the president has taken the initiative in economic policymaking. The primary instrument of presidential influence in economic policy is the budget. It outlines presidential priorities for spending and taxation. Also, it is a tool for presidential control of the executive branch. The president can reward cooperation and punish recalcitrance by propos-

Perspective
POST-KEYNESIAN ECONOMICS

Within the last few years, liberal economists such as Lester Thurow, Robert Lekachman, Robert Heilbroner, Felix Rohatyn, and others have begun to articulate a major redefinition of economic theory that has acquired the title of "post-Keynesian economics." These economists argue that the source of America's economic malaise is to be found in the corporate strategies of major corporations, particularly multinational corporations, and in the weakness of labor unions and government to counterbalance corporate power. Instead of reinvesting profits in new plants and machinery, corporate managers, say the post-Keynesians, have funneled their resources into foreign investment, speculation, and mergers. In 1984, for example, Standard Oil of California (SOCAL) spent $13.4 billion purchasing Gulf

Oil. More than $13 billion were spent, but no new wells were drilled, no plants were built, and no jobs were created. According to the post-Keynesians, these kinds of corporate management policies have undermined major sectors of the American economy as well as the economic base of many regions of the country. For all intents and purposes, they say, the United States has become "deindustrialized." The post-Keynesian economists recommend that government loan and subsidy programs that encourage these damaging corporate policies should be changed in favor of a national industrial policy that will promote reinvestment. Meanwhile, they argue, labor unions should be strengthened in order to help balance the political power of the giant corporations.

So far, the post-Keynesians'

views have had very little impact on American public policy. However, that situation may soon change. The Democratic party has been searching for an alternative economic policy to Reaganomics, a policy that won't bear the stigma of past failures. The post-Keynesian approach not only does that, it also offers the Democrats a policy that promises some modicum of economic security to those groups that support the party electorally. In fact, Walter Mondale, Gary Hart, and other Democratic leaders began discussing the ideas of the post-Keynesians during the 1984 election campaign. Should a Democrat move into the White House in the near future, it is likely that the theories of the post-Keynesian economists will help shape American economic policy.[1]

[1]Barry Bluestone and Bennett Harrison, *The Deindustrialization of America: Plant Closings, Community Abandonment and the Dismantling of Basic Industry* (New York: Basic Books, 1982); and Felix Rohatyn, "American Roulette," *New York Review* (29 March 1984), pp. 11–15.

ing an increase or decrease in an agency's budget. Finally, the president can use the budget to influence the economy.

Economic advisers.   Economic policy is complex, so the president frequently turns to others for assistance and advice. The Council of Economic Advisers (CEA) provides the president with information on the state of the economy and suggests policies to promote economic growth and stability. Meanwhile, the Office of Management and Budget (OMB), another agency in the Executive Office of the President, works out the details of the budget. It negotiates with agencies over final budget figures and prepares the final document to be sent to Congress.

The president also gets input on economic policy from his cabinet. The secretary of the treasury is usually a major adviser on tax policy. Other cabinet members participate in budget decisions affecting their departments, generally advocating increased expenditures for programs under their authority. In 1982, for example, Secretary of Transportation Drew Lewis was the author of an idea to increase the gasoline excise tax in order to raise funds for highway construction and maintenance.

The president's most influential economic advisers, however, may be members of the White House staff. They may know nothing about economic theory and have little background in budgeting, but they will have an eye for politics. After all, economic decisions are also political decisions. Economists worry about the long run, but the president wants to lower unemployment and control inflation by the next election. Timing is all-important. That means you cut taxes *before* an election and wait until later to reduce services. Increase services before; raise taxes to pay the bills afterward.

Constraints on budgetmaking.   The president is the chief architect of the budget, but he must operate under a number of constraints. First, the economic data he must use is often faulty. Estimates of current economic conditions are frequently proven wrong. Also, there are lags in compiling statistics. The country may be in or out of a recession for months before the data reveal it. In addition, no one can be sure about the reliability of economic indicators. Many experts argue that the consumer price index (CPI) is a poor indicator of inflation. Another measure, the **GNP deflator,** is probably superior, but it only comes out every three months. The unemployment index is criticized because it doesn't count discouraged workers who have given up trying to find a job. That could be corrected, of course, but no administration wants to admit to higher figures.

Second, economic forecasts are often worse than weather forecasts. Perhaps the complexity of the economy makes accurate prediction impossible. For example, international events can intervene to wreak havoc with the most careful prognostication. Economists could hardly have predicted the effects of the Arab oil embargo and subsequent price increases on America's inflation rate in the 1970s. Another problem is that administrations are notorious for making rosy predictions. The traditional political defense for a weak economy, of course, is to announce that prosperity is just around the corner.

Third, fiscal policy at best is a clumsy tool for stabilizing the economy. Preparation of any particular budget begins eighteen to twenty months before the start of the fiscal year. Who can foresee accurately what the economy will then be like? Also, Congress is slow. If the president asks for a tax cut to fight today's recession, it may not be passed and in place until recovery is well under way, just in time, perhaps, to fuel inflation.

Finally, more than three fourths of the expenditures in the budget are *uncontrollable;* that is, they are funds that must be spent because of contracts already signed or laws already on the books. This includes interest on the national debt and expenditures for weapons systems ordered in previous years. It also includes money for programs such as Social Security, Food Stamps, Medicare, AFDC, and veterans' benefits. These are known as **entitlement programs** because eligible recipients are entitled to receive benefits by law. Consequently, spending in these areas can't be significantly reduced without changing the law.

All of this leaves little room to maneuver. The part of the budget that is controllable can't easily be changed for political reasons. Every dollar in the budget has its supporters. Balance the budget, they say, but leave my pet programs alone. Also, there is a bias toward rising expenditures. Entitlements grow because the number of people eligible is increasing and benefits are often indexed to inflation. Then there's the "camel's nose" phenomenon. Many programs, especially weapons programs, start small but increase in subsequent years. To cut back means to risk wasting money already spent. In other words, once the camel has poked his nose inside the tent, it's hard to get him out again. Before long, the little program is a big one and the entire camel is in the tent. Consequently, the budget is less an economic plan than an estimate of what is likely to happen. The budget may not be completely out of control, but it certainly isn't *in* control.

The budget process.   The actual process of formulating a budget begins in the spring, a year and a half before the start of the fiscal year. The president consults with his advisers, setting economic goals and establishing overall revenue and expenditure levels. He may also map out plans for spending initiatives in some areas, retrenchment in others.

Around March, the Office of Management and Budget (OMB) sends out guidelines on spending levels to the various agencies of the executive branch. In the early summer, the agencies submit budget proposals to the OMB, proposals that invariably are over the ceiling. The OMB then cuts the requests. The agencies react with real or feigned horror. A period of negotiations follows, after which agencies may appeal to the deputy director of the OMB, the director, and, eventually, the president. The whole process isn't complete until Christmas or early January. The president then submits the budget to Congress.[25]

The Congressional Budget and Impoundment Control Act of 1974 was one of the most important events in the so-called "reassertion of Congress" in the 1970s. Before this law's enactment, Congress had largely reacted to the president's budget. Committees were responsible for authorizing spending and taxes and for appropriating the actual sums government could spend, but everything was done piecemeal. Congress made no general review of the entire budget. The 1974 legislation was designed to provide Congress with the means to become an active participant in the overall process.[26]

In practice, the reform has been a mixed blessing. Congress is better informed now about economic matters, thanks to the creation of the Congressional Budget Office (CBO), which compiles economic data and makes economic forecasts independently of the executive branch. The budget process itself, however, is more fragmented now than ever. The 1974 law created a Joint Economic Committee and new budget committees in each house to make recommendations on overall spending and taxing levels, but it only succeeded in superimposing new structures and procedures over the old. Consequently, there are now more steps in the

"Now that both sides have reached agreement on the basic money issues, let's see if we can decide who's going to accept the public opprobrium for it."

Drawing by Ed Fisher © 1981 The New Yorker Magazine Inc.

process, more power centers to be appeased, and more opportunity for jurisdictional disputes and petty jealousies to get in the way. The end result is that Congress exhausts itself on the details of the budget without ever really getting a handle on the overall product.

The budget process in Congress begins in November, eleven months before the start of the next fiscal year, when the president submits a **current services budget** to the Joint Economic Committee. This is simply an estimate of the cost of continuing present services at the current levels. Using this as a starting point, the Joint Economic Committee, which is composed of the members of the tax-writing and appropriations committees in each house, prepares its own recommendations to submit to the budget committees by year's end.

In late January, the president sends his budget to Congress and it is immediately chopped up, never to be wholly reassembled. Tax measures go to the Ways and Means Committee in the House and the Finance Committee in the Senate. Because the Constitution stipulates that revenue-raising bills must originate in the House, the Ways and Means Committee gets the first shot. Through the years, Ways and Means has developed a reputation for hard work, competence, and fairness. When it finishes its work on a tax bill, the general view in the House is that the experts have spoken. Since the Rules Committee normally sends tax bills to the floor under a closed rule—no amendments—the judgment of the Ways and Means Committee usually stands for the whole House. In the Senate, however, the Finance Committee has a reputation as a hospitality center for special-interest groups, tacking on amendments to benefit groups that were left out in the House bill. More amendments are added on the Senate floor.[27]

Before money can be spent, a program must be authorized and money appropriated. This means two sets of bills and two sets of committees. Authorization bills are considered by the standing legislative committees in each chamber, such as Agriculture and Armed Services. Entitlement programs are already in place, so funds for them go through the appropriations process only. Changes in entitlements and approval for new programs, however, must travel through the authorization process.

Appropriations bills are the responsibility of the appropriation committees in each chamber. By custom, the House committee considers the budget first. There it is broken down into thirteen parts, one for each of the thirteen standing subcommittees. Generally, subcommittee decisions are accepted by the full committee and the House as a whole. Subcommittee membership is fairly stable, so members become quite familiar with the agencies and programs under their jurisdiction. Consequently, they tend to view budgeting incrementally, focusing on the changes in budget requests from year to year. Another feature of the House Appropriations Committee is that its members tend to regard themselves as "guardians of the Treasury."

The Senate Appropriations Committee plays a role similar to that of the Finance Committee. It gets the budget after the House has done its work and functions as an appeals court for House decisions. Agencies and interest groups lobby to improve their budget fate every step of the way, but they are often more successful on the Senate side than in the House.[28]

While the authorization/appropriations process is in progress, the budget committees are at work. They were created by the 1974 budget-reform law to establish revenue and spending targets for the coming fiscal year. They work with information from the CBO, spending estimates from the various legislative committees, and recommendations from the Joint Economic Committee to prepare what is known as the **first concurrent resolution.** This sets nonbinding spending targets for the appropriations and authorization committees. Congress is to approve it by May 15.

By September 15, Congress is required to pass a **second concurrent resolution.** This reaffirms or revises the provisions of the first resolution on the basis of changing economic conditions and political developments. This time the ceilings are binding. For the next ten days the appropriations and legislative committees are to alter their previous actions to bring them in line with the resolution. This is called the **reconciliation process.** The final congressional budget, including all spending and tax measures, is to be passed by October 1, the start of the new fiscal year.[29]

The budget reforms of the 1970s were designed to impose some order on the intricate process of congressional budgetmaking, but it hasn't worked that way. The budget committees were designed to force Congress to focus on the results of its separate actions on spending and taxation. Congress soon learned, however, that it can't make decisions about budget totals without considering the various categories that make up the whole. Yet once the budget committees got involved in details, they became embroiled in debates over specifics. They became another arena for interest groups to appeal their causes and another stage for Congress to exhaust itself trying to formulate economic policy. Instead of unifying the congressional budget process, the reform of the 1970s succeeded in fragmenting it more than ever.[30]

POLICY ADOPTION

The adoption of fiscal policy is primarily the responsibility of Congress and the president. Measures to revise the tax laws, authorize spending, and appropriate money must all pass through the legislative process. The Congressional Budget and Impoundment Act of 1974 established a timetable to ensure the timely adoption of the budget, but Congress has met the deadline only once, in 1976, the first year it was fully operative. In 1982, you recall, Congress passed only three of the thirteen appropriations bills before the start of the fiscal year on October 1. Only seven were enacted by the end of the calendar year. Ironically, this was a better performance than that of the previous two years. When Congress fails to adopt the budget on time, it must pass a continuing resolution to continue agency funding, usually at current levels, until the budget is passed.

Monetary policy, however, is the domain of the **Federal Reserve Board,** the "Fed." This is an independent regulatory commission, headed by a seven-member board of governors appointed by the president and confirmed by the Senate to serve fixed, staggered terms of fourteen years. The president also names a chairperson of the board, with Senate approval, to serve a four-year term.

The idea behind this arrangement is to make the Fed independent of presidential and congressional control. In theory, the board sets monetary policy on the basis of economic considerations, not political ones. The problem with this independence, however, is that fiscal and monetary policy may not always mesh. They may even cancel one another. In 1981, for example, President Reagan and the Congress launched their great experiment in supply-side economics. By enacting a substantial tax cut they hoped to stimulate an economic boom. Meanwhile, the Federal Reserve, under Chairman Paul Volcker, was tightening the money supply to get a handle on inflation. This helped push up interest rates and slow down the economy. Consequently, business did not expand and the supply-side tax-cut stimulus never materialized.

In practice, however, the Fed is far from an apolitical body. It lobbies Congress and the executive and, in turn, receives pressure from Congress, the White House, and the banking community, among other interests. There is also evidence that the Fed bends with the political winds. One observer notes that the Fed appears to respond to the desires of the incumbent president.[31] Another finds that since 1960 the Federal Reserve has increased the money supply more rapidly in the two years preceding a presidential election than in the two years following, thereby stimulating the economy and presumably enhancing the president's reelection prospects.[32]

Paul Volcker, chairman of the Federal Reserve Board.

POLICY IMPLEMENTATION

The implementation of economic policy involves nearly the whole of government in America. For the most part, tax collection and borrowing is the responsibility of the Treasury Department. Monetary policy is implemented by the Federal Reserve and its member banks. Money is spent by the agencies of the executive branch and, through the federal system, by an array of state and local governments.

Before 1974, impoundment was a major issue in policy implementation. This was the power, claimed by the president, to impound, or refuse to spend, money appropriated by Congress. President Nixon pushed this further than any of his predecessors and Congress responded with the Budget and Impoundment Control Act of 1974 limiting the president's power to impound funds. Now, Congress must approve presidential requests to defer spending to some future year or to rescind an appropriation. In practice, Congress has generally allowed deferrals but rejected recisions.[33]

Sometimes problems arise in implementation unforeseen in the formulation/adoption process. The complexity of the tax laws, for example, have contributed to tax evasion, which the IRS estimates to be in the range of $92 billion a year.[34] Federal policy is also a major cause of runaway inflation in the health-care industry. Because of Medicare, Medicaid, and tax exemptions and deductions for medical care and health insurance, incentives to economize are greatly reduced. A final example of unforeseen problems in implementation involves the decision in the mid-1970s to index Social Security benefits to the CPI. The problem is that prices have gone up considerably faster than wages, so benefit costs have increased more rapidly than tax receipts.

POLICY EVALUATION

There are mechanisms within government itself for evaluating economic policy. The OMB assesses the operation of programs within the executive branch for the president. The General Accounting Office (GAO) fulfills that role for Congress, investigating agency activities and auditing expenditures. Outside of the GAO, however, Congress' efforts at oversight are haphazard and unsystematic. When they occur, they tend to focus on nickle-and-dime matters, such as expense accounts and limousine use, or on well-publicized abuses, such as cost overruns on the weapons systems purchased by the Pentagon.

CONCLUSION: ECONOMIC POLICY AND POLITICS

This is a chapter about economic policy, but the most important points we've made haven't been economic; they've been political. Consider the nature of America's economic crisis in the 1980s. For years, the economy has been beset by chronic inflation, high unemployment, and slow growth. A primary reason has been lack of sufficient business investment. American manufacturing plants are often years behind their Western European and Japanese competitors, and American companies spend comparatively little on research and development. Industrial productivity in the United States has virtually stopped growing. In 1980, for example, the United States purchased $10 billion more in Japanese goods than the Japanese bought from the U.S. In itself, that trade deficit is cause for concern, but the nature of the products traded is even more alarming. The major exports by Japan to America were motor vehicles, iron and steel plates, truck and tractor chassis, radios, motor bikes, and audio and video tape recorders. In contrast, the United States' major exports to Japan were

In recent years, Japan has become an increasingly important supplier of sophisticated technical and consumer goods to the United States. Controlling exports and imports is a critical economic issue for American policymakers.

soybeans, corn, fir logs, hemlock logs, coal, wheat, and cotton. In respect to our major economic competitor, the United States has been reduced to an agricultural supplier trying desperately (and unsuccessfully) to keep pace with the world's major supplier of sophisticated capital and consumer goods.[35] The nation's economy is in a decline that will reduce our standard of living and may threaten our way of life. The great irony, however, is that American economic policy isn't geared to solving the problem. Instead, it's making it worse.

Before there can be investment, there must be savings. Otherwise, cash will not be available for business to borrow in order to modernize and expand. Federal tax policy, though, discourages savings and encourages consumer borrowing. Income earned from dividends and interest is taxed at a high rate, but when consumers borrow money—for houses, cars, or stereos—the interest they pay is tax deductible. Consequently, it's hardly surprising that Americans have one of the lowest rates of saving in the industrialized world. During the 1970s, our gross savings rate was 19 percent, as opposed to an average of 26 percent for all industrialized nations. The savings rate in Japan was 35 percent.[36]

Other government policies divert the scarce investment resources available away from business investment. In the early 1980s, a substantial portion of the funds available for investment have gone to finance federal budget deficits exceeding $100 billion a year. What's more, when the government borrows that kind of money, it helps drive up interest rates, thus further discouraging business borrowing.

Other investment capital is being diverted into building homes, again thanks to the federal economic policy. Property taxes paid on homes and mortgage interest paid are both tax deductible. Capital gains from the sale of homes generally escape taxation. Also, a series of government agencies are in the business of insuring home loans so that Americans can purchase a home at 5-percent down. In contrast, a Japanese family usually pays 50-percent down. All of this costs the federal government more than $30 billion a year in lost revenue, but, more importantly, the housing industry is soaking up billions of precious investment dollars needed to rebuild American industry. We have chosen to build homes instead of factories.[37]

None of this may make economic sense, but politics has reasons that economics doesn't understand. Public opinion and powerful interest groups strongly support government policies that favor home purchases. After all, owning a home is part of the American dream.

How about the deficits? Conservatives like to blame welfare programs, such as Food Stamps and AFDC, but some of the largest and fastest-growing budget items are entitlement programs that are available to recipients without regard to financial need—Social Security, military and civil-service pensions, and Medicare, among others. Since most of these programs are indexed to inflation, their benefits have grown rapidly. Many retired government workers and military personnel actually draw more money in pensions than their replacements earn on the job today. These groups are so well organized politically, however, that their benefits seem impregnable to cost-cutting assault. Short-term politics takes precedence over long-term economics.

The best explanation for economic policy lies not in economic theory but in political reality. Democratic administrations generally favor policies designed to benefit their traditional support groups: organized labor, inner-city voters, the lower and lower-middle classes. Meanwhile, Republicans steer economic policy to favor their support groups: business people and professionals, suburban voters, the upper and upper-middle income groups. The Reagan tax cuts, you recall, benefited middle- and upper-income taxpayers the most while the spending cuts hit the poor and near-poor the hardest.

A strong case can be made that political leaders embrace particular economic theories not for their economic merit but for their political appeal. The Reagan economic program of big tax cuts, defense-spending increases, and reductions in social-welfare spending isn't based so much on economic theory as it is on conservative political doctrine. Meanwhile, Democratic talk of a national industrial policy is motivated by a desire to shift government policy in favor of Democratic support groups.

As we have seen, these aren't the brightest days for economic theory. Long-standing economic assumptions are under attack, and there is no general agreement on the best course for American economic policy. As in 1982, when Congress stayed in session nearly to Christmas debating economic policy, deep divisions remain over economic policy. The major division isn't so much over economic theory, however, as it is over politics. American policymakers are unable to agree on a consistent economic policy because they do not agree on the basic political questions of who should benefit and who should pay the bills.

KEY TERMS

BUDGET DEFICIT *(308)*

BUDGET SURPLUS *(308)*

BUSINESS CYCLE *(317)*

CASH-TRANSFER PROGRAMS *(315)*

CONSUMER PRICE INDEX *(307)*

CONTINUING RESOLUTION *(303)*

CURRENT SERVICES BUDGET *(330)*

DEPRESSION *(317)*

ENTITLEMENT PROGRAMS *(328)*

EXCISE TAXES *(316)*

FEDERAL RESERVE BOARD *(332)*

FIRST CONCURRENT RESOLUTION *(331)*

FISCAL POLICY *(321)*

FISCAL YEAR *(303)*

GNP DEFLATOR *(327)*

INFLATION *(320)*

IN-KIND BENEFIT PROGRAMS *(315)*

INTEREST *(321)*

KEYNESIAN ECONOMICS *(321)*

LAFFER CURVE *(323)*

LAISSEZ-FAIRE ECONOMICS *(317)*

MARGINAL RATE *(313)*

MONETARISM *(323)*

MONETARY POLICY *(321)*

NATIONAL DEBT *(309)*

OFF-BUDGET OPERATIONS *(310)*

PHILLIPS CURVE *(321)*

PROGRESSIVE TAX *(311)*

PROPORTIONAL (FLAT-RATE) TAX *(312)*

RECESSION *(317)*

RECONCILIATION PROCESS *(331)*

REGRESSIVE TAX *(316)*

SECOND CONCURRENT RESOLUTION *(331)*

STAGFLATION *(322)*

SUPPLY-SIDE ECONOMICS *(323)*

TAX DEDUCTIONS *(312)*

TAX PREFERENCE *(312)*

TIGHT-MONEY POLICY *(321)*

NOTES

1. *Washington Post*, 12 December 1982, p. 8; 24 December 1982, p. 1.
2. *Time* (28 March 1983), p. 32.
3. William W. Kaufmann, "The Defense Budget," in Joseph A. Pechman, ed., *Setting National Priorities: The 1982 Budget* (Washington, D.C.: Brookings Institution, 1981).
4. *National Journal* (9 October 1982), p. 1706.
5. Eli Ginzburg, "The Social Security System," *Scientific American* 246 (January 1982), pp. 51–57.
6. "The Future of Social Security: An Exchange," *New York Review* (17 March 1983), p. 57.

7. Hobart Rowan, "Ducking Social Security," *Washington Post,* National Weekly Edition, 27 February 1984, p. 5.

8. Robert W. Hartman, "The Budget Outlook," in Pechman, ed., *Setting National Priorities*; Robert J. Samuelson, "Deceptive Deficits," *National Journal* (7 August 1982), p. 1387.

9. *Houston Chronicle,* 26 August 1983, Sec. 1, p. 2.

10. William Barry Furlong, "America's Other Budget," *New York Times Magazine* (21 February 1982), pp. 32, 39, 60–74; and Andrew S. Carron, "Fiscal Activities Outside the Budget," in Pechman, ed., *Setting National Priorities*.

11. Timothy B. Clark, "Flat-Rate Income Tax Debate May Spur Attacks on Some Tax Breaks," *National Journal* (13 November 1982), pp. 1928–33.

12. *National Journal* (18 December 1982), pp. 2143, 2176.

13. Carl P. Chelf, *Public Policymaking in America* (Glenview, Il.: Scott, Foresman and Company, 1981), pp. 159–62.

14. Joel Havemann, "Sharing the Wealth: The Gap Between Rich and Poor Grows Wider," *National Journal* (23 October 1982), pp. 1788–95.

15. Peter G. Peterson, "No More Free Lunch for the Middle Class," *New York Times Magazine* (17 January 1982), pp. 40–41, 56–63.

16. Timothy B. Clark, "Betting on Prosperity," *National Journal* (4 February 1984), pp. 219–22.

17. *Newsweek* (5 April 1982), pp. 17–18.

18. John Maynard Keynes, *General Theory of Employment, Interest and Money* (New York: Harcourt, Brace & World, 1936).

19. A. W. H. Phillips, "The Relationship Between Unemployment and the Rate of Change in Money Wage Rates in the United Kingdom, 1862–1957," *Economica* (November 1958): 283–99.

20. Milton Friedman, "The Role of Monetary Policy," *American Economic Review* (March 1968): 1–17; and Milton Friedman and Anna J. Schwartz, *A Monetary History of the United States, 1867–1960* (Princeton, N.J.: Princeton University Press, 1963).

21. Jude Wanniki, *The Way the World Works: How Economies Fail—and Succeed* (New York: Basic Books, 1978); Jack Kemp, *An American Renaissance: A Strategy for the 1980s* (New York: Harper and Row, 1979); George Gilder, *Wealth and Poverty* (New York: Basic Books, 1981).

22. Martin Gardner, "Mathematical Games: The Laffer Curve and Other Laurels in Current Economics," *Scientific American* 245 (December 1981), pp. 18–34.

23. Quoted in *Time* (17 January 1983), p. 36.

24. John M. Berry, "Ronald Reagan: Almost the Last Administration Supply-Sider," *Washington Post,* National Weekly Edition, 27 February 1984, pp. 20–21.

25. Richard M. Pious, *The American Presidency* (New York: Basic Books, 1979), ch. 8; Chelf, ch. 3; George P. Shultz and Kenneth W. Dam, *Economic Policy Beyond the Headlines* (New York: W. W. Norton, 1977).

26. Douglas H. Shumavon, "Policy Impact of the 1974 Congressional Budget Act," *Public Administration Review* 41 (May/June 1981): 339–48.
27. Thomas J. Reese, *The Politics of Taxation* (Westport, Ct.: Quorum Books, 1980).
28. Lance T. LeLoup, *Budgetary Politics* (Brunswick, Ohio: King's Court Communications, 1977), ch. 8.
29. Ibid., ch. 7; Chelf, ch. 3.
30. Richard E. Cohen, "The Congressional Budget Process—Is It Worth All the Headaches?" *National Journal* (29 September 1979), pp. 1605–7.
31. Nathaniel Beck, "Presidential Influence on the Federal Reserve in the 1970s," *American Journal of Political Science* 26 (August 1982): 415–45.
32. Robert J. Shapiro, "Politics and the Federal Reserve," *Public Interest* 66 (Winter 1982): 119–39.
33. Pious, ch. 8.
34. *Houston Chronicle*, 8 April 1983, Sec. 1, p. 7.
35. Godfrey Hodgson, "State of the Nation," *Boston Globe Magazine* (18 January 1981), p. 16.
36. *New York Review* (17 March 1983), p. 57.
37. Peterson, "No More Free Lunch."

SUGGESTED READINGS

BOWLES, SAMUEL, GORDON, DAVID M., AND WEISSKOPF, THOMAS E. *Beyond the Wasteland: A Democratic Alternative to Economic Decline.* New York: Doubleday, 1983.

DOLBEARE, KENNETH M. *American Public Policy: A Citizen's Guide.* New York: McGraw-Hill, 1982.

FRIEDMAN, MILTON, AND SCHWARTZ, ANNA J. *A Monetary History of the United States, 1867–1960.* Princeton: Princeton University Press, 1963.

GILDER, GEORGE. *Wealth and Poverty.* New York: Basic Books, 1981.

HAVEMANN, JOEL. *Congress and the Budget.* Bloomington, Ind.: Indiana University Press, 1978.

HEILBRONER, ROBERT L., AND THUROW, LESTER C. *The Economic Problem.* Englewood Cliffs: Prentice-Hall, 1981.

KEYNES, JOHN MAYNARD. *General Theory of Employment, Interest and Money.* New York: Harcourt, Brace & World, 1936.

PECHMAN, JOSEPH A. *Federal Tax Policy.* 3rd ed. Washington, D.C.: Brookings Institution, 1977.

SHULTZ, GEORGE P., AND DAM, KENNETH W. *Economic Policy Beyond the Headlines.* New York: W. W. Norton, 1977.

SHICK, ALLEN. *Congress and Money: Budgeting, Spending and Taxing.* Washington, D.C.: Urban Institute, 1980.

WEINTRAUB, SIDNEY, AND GOODSTEIN, MARVIN. *Reaganomics in the Stagflation Economy.* Philadelphia: University of Pennsylvania Press, 1983.

Chapter Twelve

GOVERNMENT REGULATION

How much government regulation of business is enough? How much is too much? Consider the case of children's television advertising and the Federal Trade Commission, the FTC. In the middle 1970s, a coalition of health and children's advocacy groups, including Action for Children's Television, the American Dental Association, and the Center for Science in the Public Interest, began calling attention to television advertising aimed at children. Statistics show that the average child is exposed to about 21,000 commercials a year, some 57.5 a day. A third to a half of these are for food and soft-drink products. Many of the advertisements are aimed specifically at children. Saturday morning in particular is the domain of cartoon characters such as the Trix rabbit, Tony the Tiger, and Cookie Jarvis, who peddle candy and presweetened breakfast cereals to an audience of children. The advertisers hope the children will then talk their parents into purchasing the products.

Children, however, are an impressionable, unsophisticated audience, unable to evaluate maturely the true worth of sugar-coated cereals and candy. Consequently, the advertising for these products encourages children to develop poor nutritional habits and contributes to health problems, such as tooth decay, obesity, and diabetes. For remedy, the coalition turned to the FTC, which is charged by law with protecting the public from false or deceptive advertising. In 1977, coalition members filed petitions with the FTC asking it to curtail advertising for "sugary snack foods" aimed specifically at children.[1]

For years, the FTC had been known as the "little old lady of Pennsylvania Avenue." Critics claimed it spent too much time arguing trivial issues, such as whether Geritol should be allowed to claim it cured "tired blood," while avoiding major cases against big business. In the 1960s and 1970s, though, the FTC began to change as the consumer movement developed muscle. President Carter appointed Michael Pertschuk, a consumer activist, to head the agency in the late 1970s, and Pertschuk staffed it with aggressive young lawyers eager to do battle with big business.[2] Consequently, the coalition's petitions were received at the FTC with considerable sympathy.

On the other side of the issue was the breakfast-cereal industry with its $600 million worth of advertising. It charged that the FTC was trying to become a "national nanny." What's more, it argued, a ban on advertising would violate the advertisers' First Amendment right of freedom of expression and make it impossible to advertise new, improved products.

Both sides rolled out their heaviest artillery to try to influence the outcome of the controversy. The cereal industry won a round in the courts when a federal district judge barred FTC chairman Pertschuk from participating in the case because he had already expressed an opinion favoring a ban. The industry also went to work on Congress, and in 1978 an effort was made to attach an amendment to the FTC's appropriation prohibiting the agency from using any of its budget on an investigation of advertising directed at children. The coalition of interest groups supporting the ban

Should children be protected from breakfast-cereal advertisers? In 1980, Congress declared that the government could only prohibit "deceptive" advertising.

succeeded in defeating the amendment. Meanwhile, the coalition sought to enlist public support for their cause, asking adults to watch one hour of children's television and then write the commission with their opinion of the ads.[3]

The coalition's victory in Congress was short-lived, however. The FTC's activism on this and other issues in the late 1970s slowly turned a majority in Congress against it. Congressman Elliot Levitas of Georgia led the attack against the agency: "The FTC is really a minilegislature, but the people who compose it have never suffered the inconvenience of running for public office."[4]

In May 1980, Congress acted to put the FTC on a shorter leash. The agency was told that it must focus on ads that are "deceptive." Consequently, truthful ads were no longer part of the agency's jurisdiction, even if directed at children too young to understand them. The battle over children's TV advertising was over. The breakfast cereal industry had won.[5]

Our story illustrates a number of important points about the politics of regulation. First, the regulatory agencies of the executive branch aren't the only institutions involved in making regulatory policy. In this case, the courts and the Congress were also involved. In general, the courts, Congress, and the White House have become increasingly active participants in the regulatory process.

Second, a broad range of interest groups are frontline combatants in regulatory-policy battles. We expect the involvement of "special" interest groups representing business, labor, and the professions, but in the last few decades "public-interest" groups promoting consumer and environmentalist causes have also made their presence felt. Also, it is not foreordained that the big-business or big-labor groups always win. They did in this example, but in many cases the outcome has been reversed.

Finally, conflicts over regulatory policy involve fundamental questions about the role of government. How much government is enough? How much is too much? We will consider these issues as we study regulatory policymaking in America.

THE HISTORY OF REGULATION IN AMERICA

The federal government's involvement in regulating private enterprise dates to 1887 and the enactment of the Interstate Commerce Act. Before the late nineteenth century, Washington's relationship with business was relatively modest and generally aimed at promoting business growth. Tariffs were levied on imports to protect American products, and land grants were made to the railroads to further their expansion.

By the 1870s, however, many Americans had become increasingly concerned about the growing power of big business. Small-business people worried about being gobbled up by big business and complained about unfair competition. Farmers were angered by the railroads' rate policies for hauling grain and livestock to market. Meanwhile, reformers such as the Populists and Progressives feared the concentration of economic power in only a few hands.

At first, state governments tried to regulate big-business enterprise, but the results were unsatisfactory. A major problem was that the largest enterprises, particularly the railroads, were interstate operations. State-by-state regulation proved too piecemeal to work well. Then in 1886 the Supreme Court ruled in the *Wabash* case that states could not regulate the rates of interstate railroads.[6] The reformers had nowhere to turn but the federal government. Congress responded with the Interstate Commerce Act.

THE ICC AND OTHER INDEPENDENT REGULATORY COMMISSIONS

The Interstate Commerce Act created the Interstate Commerce Commission (ICC), an expert, nonpartisan agency designed to regulate the railroads "outside of politics." This was the first of the independent regulatory commissions. Its objective was to protect consumers by keeping prices low and preventing unfair acts or rates. It was given the power to set rates, grant routes, regulate service, and control entry into the industry.

Congress followed the creation of the ICC with other ventures in regulatory policymaking. In 1890 it passed the Sherman Antitrust Act, outlawing monopolies or attempts to monopolize a market and giving the Justice

Department enforcement powers. The Clayton Act of 1914 was passed to plug loopholes in the Sherman Act. Also, it gave the Justice Department the power to block business mergers that might prove monopolistic. In the same year, Congress enacted the Federal Trade Commission Act, creating the FTC and empowering it to safeguard against "unfair competition" and "deceptive trade practices."[7]

In subsequent years, Congress extended the scope of federal regulation, particularly during the 1930s. The ICC's jurisdiction was expanded to include interstate trucking as well as rail transportation, and the Civil Aeronautics Board (CAB) was created to regulate the airline industry. The Federal Communications Commission (FCC) was granted authority over interstate communications services, including television and radio broadcasting and interstate telephone and telegraph service. The Federal Maritime Commission (FMC) was set up to regulate electricity generation and transmission. The Securities and Exchange Commission (SEC) was empowered to regulate the exchange of stocks and bonds.

For the most part, Congress' efforts at regulation before the 1960s involved the creation of independent regulatory commissions with power to control competition and prices in a particular industry. As you recall from our discussion in chapter 9, independent regulatory commissions are headed by multimember boards whose members are appointed by the president (with Senate confirmation) to serve fixed, overlapping terms. Generally, then, in the years prior to the 1960s, Congress assigned regulatory authority to these boards in rather broad terms. Boards were to set rates that were "just and reasonable" or to regulate "in the public interest." The goals of regulation included breaking up excessive concentrations of economic power and restoring ideal market conditions.

" . . . and, as members of the FCC, we will thereby take whatever steps are necessary to prevent you from continuing to communicate in this manner without obtaining a proper license . . ."

NEWER REGULATORY AGENCIES

The emergence of politically powerful public interest groups in the early 1960s led to the creation of a new wave of federal regulatory agencies. Groups such as the Sierra Club, Friends of the Earth, and the various organizations begun by Ralph Nader mobilized strong public support behind federal action to protect consumers, the environment, workers, and the disabled. These groups lobbied Congress for the creation of new federal regulatory agencies, but they wanted the new agencies to be organized differently from the old agencies. For some time, Nader and other leaders of the public-interest lobby had been making the case that many of the older agencies, such as the ICC and CAB, had been "captured" by the industries they were charged with regulating. The agencies, Nader argued, frequently regulated on behalf of the industry, not in the public interest. Consequently, the public-interest groups pushed Congress to devise structures and procedures to keep these new agencies independent of industry control.

Congress responded in the 1960s and '70s by creating a series of new regulatory agencies that differed in several important respects from most of the older regulatory commissions. First, most of these new agencies were structurally different from their older counterparts. Although the Consumer Product Safety Commission was created as an independent regulatory commission, most of the new agencies, including the Environmental Protection Agency (EPA), the National Highway Traffic Safety Administration (NHTSA), and the Occupational Safety and Health Administration (OSHA), were made part of the executive branch. Their heads were to be appointed by the president with Senate approval to serve at the president's pleasure (that is, the president could remove them as he saw fit). This gave the president considerably more control over these agencies' operation than was the case with the independent regulatory commissions. The hope was that a president sympathetic to the goals of consumer safety, environmental protection, and the like, would use his authority to ensure against industry capture of new agencies.

Second, the newer agencies' goals were broader than the older commissions. The traditional regulatory effort aimed at ensuring reasonable rates and fair competition, while the regulatory efforts launched in the 1960s and '70s embraced social goals such as clean air, a safe workplace, pure water, and safe and effective products.

Third, the new agencies differed from most of their older counterparts in that they were given authority to regulate certain aspects of production across industry lines. Most of the older agencies had been established to regulate a single industry or a small number of related industries. The SEC, for example, was created to regulate the stock market. In contrast, the regulatory activities of the more recently established agencies affected a broad range of industries. OSHA, for example, was to regulate working conditions across industry lines. Consequently, the regulatory impact of the new agencies was felt more broadly than that of the older agencies.

Fourth, the newer agencies were generally given more specific and more rigid instructions than the older commissions. In general, the legislation authorizing the regulatory activities of the older agencies had been cast in broad, flexible language. Much was left to the discretion and expertise of the administrators. By the 1960s, however, the captured-agencies phenomenon had convinced many members of Congress that too much bureaucratic flexibility can lead to too much industry influence. Consequently, Congress passed legislation in the 1960s and 1970s that often mandated specific requirements and set deadlines for their fulfillment. Although Congress got the "tough" legislation it wanted, the legislation often left little room for flexibility in administration, and that too sometimes created problems. The Office of Endangered Species, for example, held up the completion of a major water project that threatened the tiny snail darter fish because the law gave it no option to make exceptions.[8]

Finally, the newer regulatory agencies were empowered to regulate the conditions under which goods and services were generated as well as the physical characteristics of the products produced. The older commissions had been generally limited to setting rates and controlling entry into an industry. The CAB, for instance, established air fares and granted routes to air carriers. The newer agencies, though, were given the power to set performance standards for products and production. The EPA, for example, was authorized to set pollution-emission standards for industry. The NHTSA was empowered to establish performance standards for automobiles.

DEREGULATION

By the latter 1970s, momentum had built for deregulation, at least in some areas. Liberals pushed for reforms in the older agencies, many of whose regulatory efforts, the liberals argued, only resulted in keeping prices high and protecting industry from competition. The liberals were joined in their efforts by some conservatives who were philosophically opposed to regulation in general. Consequently, during the Ford and Carter administrations, Congress approved the phased deregulation of the trucking, airline, and banking industries.

Meanwhile, conservative business groups had grown quite restive over what they saw as the "excessive regulation" of the newer regulatory agencies. In 1980, these groups gained a powerful ally when Ronald Reagan was elected to the White House. One of Reagan's first acts as president was to order that all new agency rules and regulations had first to be reviewed and cleared by the Office of Management and Budget (OMB) before taking effect. The basis of the review was to be **cost-benefit analysis.** This meant that the OMB would evaluate the expected benefits of a proposed regulation in light of its anticipated costs. In 1981, the OMB received 119 regulations already adopted but not yet in effect when Reagan took office. It killed 76 of them.[9]

Reagan set out to weaken some of the agencies that he considered most obnoxious by asking Congress to cut their budgets and by appointing vocal critics of regulation to their boards. Among Reagan's targets were the EPA, the FTC, OSHA, the NHTSA, and the Consumer Product Safety Commission. Between 1981 and 1983, for example, the Reagan Administration cut the EPA's budget for the enforcement of toxic-waste regulations from $11.4 million to $2.3 million; enforcement personnel were reduced from 311 to 75. In the meantime, Reagan appointed a man to head OSHA whose family's construction company had been cited forty-eight times by OSHA for safety violations. James Watt, whom Reagan named secretary of the interior, had led a private group in a fight against interior department restrictions on oil drilling on federal lands.[10] As might be expected, Reagan's actions were extremely controversial and were energetically opposed by the affected agencies and their friends.[11]

THE SCOPE OF REGULATION TODAY

Despite the recent moves toward deregulation, the regulatory hand of the federal government is still pervasive. In several industries, new firms must obtain government permission before they can begin doing business. Radio and television stations, for example, are licensed by the FCC, nuclear-power plants by the Nuclear Regulatory Commission. In other industries, new products must meet government standards. The Consumer Product Safety Commission sets safety standards for a long list of products ranging from lawn mowers to children's sleepwear. New drugs must be approved by the Food and Drug Administration (FDA).

Government regulations also affect a wide range of business operating procedures. Conditions in the workplace are regulated by OSHA. The EPA establishes and enforces regulations regarding air pollution, water pollution, and solid-waste disposal. Most employers are required to adhere to wage and hour laws and to provide their employees with a number of fringe benefits, including Social Security, workers' compensation, and unemployment insurance. Meanwhile, the Equal Employment Opportunity Commission (EEOC) enforces laws prohibiting discrimination on the basis of race, color, religion, sex, or national origin.

Finally, the government enforces an extensive series of regulations through its status as a major purchaser of goods and services. Some firms—defense contractors, for example—do nearly all of their business with the government; others do a significant share. Any company signing a contract of any significance with the government, however, must conform to a host of requirements. The Davis-Bacon Act, for example, requires that contractors pay prevailing wages (read *union* wages) on any project that is financed or subsidized by the federal government. Other regulations require government contractors to prefer American-made products in their purchases, to hire the disabled, to refrain from polluting, and to implement affirmative-action programs for hiring minorities.[12]

Government regulation reaches into many sectors of American life. OSHA is charged with regulating conditions in the workplace.

THE PROS AND CONS OF REGULATION

Regulation is controversial. For society, it offers the promise of safe products, a safe working place, a healthy environment, and fair prices. For the regulated, however, it may involve great expense and inconvenience. Let's examine some of the arguments for and against regulation.

THE CASE FOR REGULATION

One argument supporting regulation is that it is needed to control **monopoly** and **oligopoly**. A monopoly exists when a single firm is the sole producer of a good or a service. In oligopoly, only a few firms dominate an industry, and these few do not vigorously compete with one another.

Instead, they may formally or informally agree to a prearranged division of the market and/or a minimum price level.

Consumers are hurt by both monopoly and oligopoly. They have little or no choice in the price and quality of goods and services because there is no competition. Also, quality is likely to be lower and prices higher than would be the case in a competitive market.

The proponents of regulation say that government should intervene to break up monopolies and oligopolies and to prevent them from forming in the first place. This was the rationale behind the passage of the Sherman Act and the Clayton Act outlawing monopolies. Later, the Clayton Act was amended to give the FTC authority to police mergers of major corporations in order to prevent excessive concentrations of industry in large corporate entities.

One of the most recent examples of antitrust laws in action involved AT&T (American Telephone & Telegraph, *alias* Ma Bell). In 1974 the Justice Department filed suit against the phone company for violating antitrust laws and accused it of unfair competitive practices. The case was eventually settled in 1982, with the company agreeing to divest itself of local telephone-service operating companies. In the past, AT&T, the long-distance phone company, and the local phone companies (Southwestern Bell, Pacific Bell, etc.) were all part of the same company. Today, they are all separate.

Economists, however, tell us that there are times when a monopoly is inevitable, even desirable. For example, the local telephone company (as opposed to a nationwide conglomerate such as AT&T) is a **natural monopoly.** It would not be economically efficient for three or four different phone companies to string wires all over town. Customers would find it inconvenient and expensive to have to subscribe to each of the companies in order to call everyone they wished. Electricity and natural gas are two other industries that are often called natural monopolies or utilities.

In this case, the advocates of regulation say that government needs to step in to set rates and service standards in order to keep these companies from acting like monopolies. Also, government regulation can ensure a firm's profitability, making it easier for these types of companies to raise the enormous amounts of investment capital needed to provide service. On the federal level, the FCC sets interstate telephone rates while the Federal Power Commission regulates interstate gas and electric utilities. Intrastate regulation, however, is done by state and local agencies, often state public-utility commissions.

A second reason for regulation is to compensate for market imperfections or, to use an economist's phrase, to **"internalize the externalities."** Theoretically, the price of a good should include all of its costs—labor, raw materials, energy, and the like—plus a fair profit. Sometimes, however, the unregulated price of a product does not represent its true cost to society; there are external costs not included in the price.

Suppose a chemical plant is dumping effluent into a river, thereby polluting it. In this case, pollution is an external cost of production. The cost isn't included in the selling price of the chemicals. Instead, it is borne by people living downstream who can no longer use the river for drinking, irrigation, commercial fishing, or recreation. The river is damaged esthetically and may even be a health hazard.

The advocates of regulation argue that this is an instance where government should intervene to shift the external cost of pollution to the price of the product. Let those who purchase the chemicals pay all of the costs of production. Government can do this either by fining the plant's owners an amount equal to the cost of cleaning up the river or by requiring the plant to reduce dumping harmful waste into the river below a hazardous level.[13]

A third general reason for government regulation is to protect those who are economically weak. Child-labor laws, for example, are written to shelter children from exploitation, and minimum-wage laws are aimed at protecting unskilled workers. Truth-in-packaging requirements are designed to provide customers with information necessary for protecting themselves. The FTC tries to shield credulous consumers from false and deceptive advertising.

THE CASE AGAINST REGULATION

There is, of course, another side. The opponents of regulation make a number of arguments against particular regulations and against regulation in general. We will focus on some of their more important general points. First, regulation's opponents point out that regulation is expensive to implement and that the consumer pays the bill. For example, the Council on Environmental Quality estimates that EPA regulations alone cost the economy $40 billion a year.[14] A study prepared for the Joint Economic Committee concludes that federal regulations add more than $650 to the price tag of the average car and $1500 to $2000 to the cost of a home.[15] Another study claims that regulation pushes up the price of lawn mowers 30 percent or more.[16]

A second argument is that federal regulations are inevitably tangled in confusion and red tape. There are some famous illustrations. Take, for example, OSHA's well-known regulation for wooden ladders (since repealed): "the general slope of grain shall not be steeper than one in fifteen rungs and cleats. For all ladders cross-grain not steeper than one in twelve are permitted."[17] Other OSHA regulations (since repealed) have specified the diameter of toilet seats and how high above the floor fire extinguishers must be placed.[18] Bureaucratic red tape can also mean delay. The FDA spent ten years trying to set standards governing the percentage of peanuts in peanut butter. It took the NHTSA seven years to establish automobile brake standards.

A third argument against regulation is that it interferes with market forces. Consider the effects of price controls. In a free market, price is a marvelous mechanism for balancing supply and demand. Suppose that the demand for a certain commodity should increase. The law of supply and demand dictates that the commodity's price will then rise. A higher price has two effects—it dampens demand and encourages producers to increase supply. But what happens if government imposes a price ceiling? Demand rises faster than it would if the price were allowed to rise naturally. Meanwhile, there is no incentive for producers to work harder to increase supply. The net result is likely to be a shortage of the commodity. This is precisely what occurred in the oil and gas industry. Government price controls in the 1960s led to shortages and rationing in the 1970s.[19]

Another effect of regulation on the market is to divert investment funds away from capital expansion and research. This is particularly true for health, safety, and environmental regulations. The general regulatory approach in these areas has been for government to mandate the purchase of specific equipment. Consequently, the industries hardest hit by these requirements, particularly the chemical, petroleum, wood, paper, electric-utility, and auto industries, have been forced to spend significant amounts of money complying with government regulations, money they might otherwise have spent modernizing their plants or expanding research and development.

A final general argument against regulation is that there is little evidence it is achieving its goals. The ICC and CAB, for example, have apparently made the transportation industry less efficient and more expensive to consumers than they would be without regulation. One critic says this of the ICC: "It has held rates above their normal levels, inflated the cost of doing business, continued to shut out newcomers, encouraged inefficiency, and made a thorough mess of surface transportation."[20]

Similarly, analysts have been unable to find any significant reductions in accident and illness rates because of OSHA, NHTSA, and EPA regulations. Auto accident rates have declined, but most observers credit the 55 mph speed limit for this rather than auto-safety standards. As for environmental regulation, EPA controls have helped some rivers, and the air quality is better in some locations. Overall, however, the effect has been negligible.[21] In fact, sulfate pollution has worsened, increasing the incidence of acid rain.

Despite the efforts of the EPA, environmental problems continue to plague many parts of the United States. The nose and chin of this statue outside of the Field Museum in Chicago show the effects of acid rain. Acid rain results when sulfur dioxide (which can be produced when coal is burned) or nitrogen oxide combines with moisture in the atmosphere and falls back to earth in an acidic mixture.

REGULATORY POLICYMAKING

Regulatory policymaking in America is a complex process, involving a broad array of interest groups and political actors. Let's examine the process step-by-step.

SETTING THE AGENDA

Who sets the agenda for regulatory policymaking in America? Public opinion plays a role. The creation of the ICC in the 1880s and the Sherman

Antitrust Act in 1890 took place in an atmosphere of general public distrust toward big business and outright animosity toward the railroads. In the 1930s, public opinion once again supported an expansion of the federal regulatory role, this time to alleviate the Great Depression. Similarly, the great expansion of federal regulatory activity in the 1960s and 1970s was spurred by strong public support for the environmental and consumer movements. Public concern about the environment, for example, was aroused by "Earth Day" in 1970, an occasion proclaimed by environmental groups to call attention to the need to safeguard the environment.

In each of these cases, opinion leaders played an important role in shaping and organizing public opinion in support of government regulation. In the late nineteenth and early twentieth centuries, the Populist and Progressive movements led the way, preaching the gospel of reform. In the '30s, Franklin Roosevelt articulated remedies for the Depression that involved large doses of government regulation. Then, in the 1960s, Rachel Carson's *Silent Spring* and Ralph Nader's *Unsafe at Any Speed* helped stimulate public concern about the environment and consumer issues.[22]

Today, in the midst of growing public sentiment that government in general is too big and that federal regulation is often excessive, there is still support for many specific regulatory policies. Although polls show that most Americans favor deregulation of industry, especially if the deregulation promotes competition, they also show that there is still strong public support for many regulatory activities. A recent survey found that 88 percent of Americans prefer even tougher clean-air standards while 91 percent favor either maintaining or strengthening regulation on safety in the workplace.[23] Other polls have found that pocketbook-conscious consumers strongly favor price controls for natural gas and public-utility regulations.[24]

On the other hand, some areas of regulatory policy evoke in the general public only apathy or even hostility. If, for example, large numbers of Americans are enthusiastic about federal automobile seat-belt requirements, they haven't shown it by wearing them. Moreover, many people in the western part of the nation have mounted what's called the "Sagebrush Rebellion" in opposition to federal land-management policies.

Interest groups are also involved in setting the agenda for policymaking. Some of the most active of these are business groups. The general image is that business opposes government regulation, and this is often the case. Business lobbyists vigorously opposed the creation of OSHA and the EPA, for example, and regularly bemoan the burdens of bureaucratic paperwork.

Business isn't always opposed to regulation, however. Sometimes the business community is divided over particular regulatory policies. For instance, the Shipping Act, which created the Federal Maritime Commission, was opposed by shipowners but supported by shippers. At other times, Congress regulates in response to demands from the business community. The trucking industry lobbied for federal regulation by the ICC, and the airline industry asked Congress to create the CAB. When Congress was debating the deregulation of these two industries, the most vocal opponents were industry spokespersons.[25]

Business groups aren't the only voices heard in regulatory policymaking. Farmers supported the creation of the ICC, and organized labor backed the establishment of OSHA. In recent decades, public-interest groups have become vocal and visible advocates of government regulation to protect the environment and the public health and safety.

Another force involved in regulatory policy is the bureaucracy itself. The people who head the regulatory agencies and staff their offices have policy perspectives of their own and are frequently successful in implementing them. One of the major criticisms of the older regulatory agencies—the CAB, SEC, ICC, FDA, and, before the 1970s, the FTC—was that they were "captured" by the industries they regulate. For years, these regulatory agencies were generally staffed by lackluster commissioners whose major qualifications were friendships with powerful members of Congress. The agency heads were frequently former employees of the industries they were to regulate, and they often wound up in executive positions in those industries after they left government service.

In contrast, most of the newer regulatory agencies developed close ties to the public-interest groups that had lobbied for their creation. The EPA, for example, attracted career employees who often saw themselves as environmental advocates. The Architectural and Transportation Board, which sets standards governing access for disabled persons to federal facilities, came to be dominated by strong advocates of regulation. When Jimmy Carter became president, he appointed to head these agencies administrators who were often former spokespersons for public-interest groups.[26]

With the election of Ronald Reagan, many of the newer agencies have become political battlegrounds. In most cases, Reagan's appointed administrators have tried to reverse the approach to regulation these agencies have traditionally taken, but they have been resisted overtly and covertly by career employees. Consider the case of the Food and Drug Administration (FDA). The FDA's critics have long charged that the agency is too cautious about approving new drugs for use in the United States. One of the goals of the Reagan Administration has been to make the agency move faster. For the most part, however, the administration's efforts have been thwarted by career employees who continue to adhere to the agency's long-established procedures for testing and enforcement.[27]

POLICY FORMULATION AND ADOPTION

Federal regulatory policy formulation and adoption are fragmented, involving Congress, the president, the courts, and dozens of boards, agencies, and commissions. Consequently, these stages involve politics. As we discussed earlier in this chapter, some of the more recent regulatory legislation is quite specific because a majority in Congress wanted to write "tough" laws that bureaucrats could not subvert. The 1970 Clean Air Act Amendment, for example, mandated the elimination of pollution, regardless of cost.[28] At other times, though, Congress can't agree on the details of regulatory policy, so it adopts vague, general language, leaving the details of policy to the bureaucracy and, frequently, to the courts. In 1972, for example, Congress voted to outlaw discrimination based on sex in college and university programs receiving federal funds. The difficult job of interpretation and enforcement was left to the bureaucracy.[29]

The details of regulatory policy are often formulated and adopted by the administrative bureaucracy through the rulemaking process that we outlined in chapter 9. Rulemaking is not, however, merely a straightforward technical process of translating statutory language into detailed requirements for specific circumstances. Instead, it is frequently the occasion for intense political disputes. The conflicts that first appeared in Congress reappear in the rulemaking process and, frequently, become more intense as the bureaucracy struggles to make policy more specific.[30]

Consider the case of the NHTSA and inflatable airbags for automobile safety. In 1966, Congress authorized the NHTSA to issue "reasonable, practicable, and appropriate" safety regulations. In 1977, the NHTSA adopted a regulation requiring the installation of airbags beginning in 1982. The decision provoked a long debate. Then, in 1981, the Reagan Administration ordered the rule revoked. In 1983, however, the United States Supreme Court ruled that the NHTSA could not repeal the rule without new studies. The debate goes on.[31]

As this example suggests, the courts are quite active participants in the federal regulatory process. The Administrative Procedures Act makes agency actions subject to court review, and recent years have seen a flurry of lawsuits over such regulatory policies as strip-mining rules, efficiency standards for household appliances, content labeling for alcoholic beverages, and the relaxation of crash-worthiness standards for car bumpers.[32]

In general, the policy impact of the federal courts has been to expand the scope and effect of regulation. As one observer phrases it, "the judicial branch has given the 'green light' to many types of rules and regulations, and sometimes has prodded agencies and Congress into more forceful action, adding considerably to the sum total of regulation on its own."[33] Even today, when the political climate in Washington leans more toward deregulation than regulation, the federal judiciary continues to rule in favor of the expansion of regulatory activity and to throw up legal roadblocks to efforts to repeal regulations.[34]

This has been one important effect of the Supreme Court's legislative-veto decision. Because of the conflictual political nature of regulatory policymaking, Congress had tried to maintain a measure of control over the rulemaking process through the device of the legislative veto. In many cases, agency rules were subject to rescission by the vote of both houses of Congress, one house, or by designated committees. In 1982, for example,

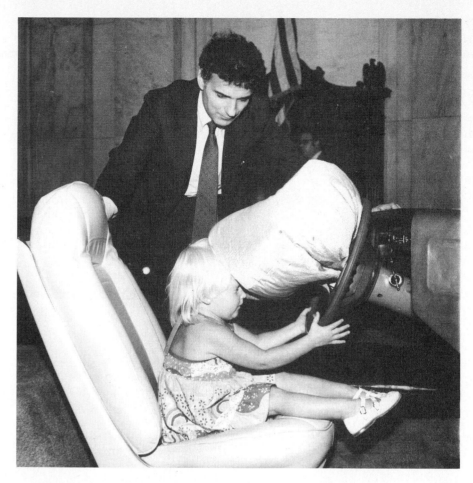

The issue of whether to require the use of airbags in automobiles has called forth varying responses from such diverse segments of government as the National Highway Traffic Safety Administration, the Reagan Administration, and the Supreme Court. Here, consumer advocate Ralph Nader demonstrates the effectiveness of the airbag.

Congress blocked an FTC rule that would have required used-car dealers to present customers with a written list of known defects in the cars they were considering. The Court's decision now invalidates this sort of action. In response, Congress has begun the process of reestablishing a direct check on the rulemaking process by other means.

Presidents are also actively involved in regulatory policy formulation and adoption. They appoint regulatory agency heads and have a direct hand in making regulatory policy in executive-branch agencies, such as the EPA or the Department of Education. Under the Reagan Administration, the president has added an important tool for controlling regulatory policy through the establishment of OMB clearance for agency rules.

POLICY IMPLEMENTATION

The implementation of regulatory policy is generally the responsibility of the bureaucratic agencies that formulated and adopted the policies ini-

The Legislative Veto and the Regulatory Process

A CONVERSATION WITH WILLIAM F. WEST, TEXAS A & M UNIVERSITY

Q. During the 1970s and early 1980s, before the Supreme Court's ruling in the *Chadha* case, the United States Congress turned frequently to the legislative veto as an instrument of administrative oversight. Would you explain how Congress used the veto to control regulatory policymaking in the federal bureaucracy?

A. The power of the bureaucracy to make regulatory policy is delegated to it by Congress. Frequently, Congress has seen fit to permit the bureaucracy considerable discretion in regulatory policy areas. Congress used the veto to reserve for itself the right to disapprove particular administrative decisions. The veto took a variety of forms, but in general it enabled one house, or both houses, or a particular committee or committees to approve or disapprove an administrative decision within a certain, fixed period of time. As a practical matter, the veto not only served

William F. West received his Ph.D. from Rice University and currently teaches political science at Texas A & M. His research interests include bureaucratic politics and administrative processes. Professor West has authored a book, Administrative Rulemaking: Politics and Processes, *and has contributed numerous articles to professional journals.*

as a "negative" means of control, but it was also a bargaining lever which legislators could use to

persuade bureaucrats to respond to Congress' wishes as they implemented regulatory policy.

Q. Would you give an example of Congress' use of the veto?

A. Yes. A good illustration would be Congress' veto of the incremental price rule for natural gas set by the Federal Energy Regulatory Commission, the FERC. The rule would have required large industry to pay more for natural gas than would residential users. As Congress was considering the FERC's regulation, it became convinced that a probable effect of the policy would have been to discourage exploration for new natural gas and thus exacerbate the national energy shortage. Another effect may ultimately have been to raise prices for residential users and small businesses by passing on to them a higher proportion of pipeline costs. In this instance, then, the legislature was able to block a regulation which, after

tially. Separation of powers does not prevail in the bureaucracy. Agencies enjoy considerable powers of enforcement. They frequently have the power to order the recall of defective products and even to ban hazardous ones. Advertisers can be forced to warn consumers about potential dangers or to retract misleading statements about their products. Agencies may file civil suits against violators, and the Justice Department may initiate criminal proceedings that could result in fines and even prison sentences for offenders.

In practice, however, implementation is the weak link of regulatory policymaking. In the environmental field, for example, extensive laws and regulations are on the books involving everything from drinking water to

some careful analysis, was felt to be ill-conceived.

Q. Do you think the veto was an effective tool? Did it lead to better or worse policy?

A. To be sure, Congress was not able to give thorough consideration to every regulation subject to veto review. The legislature simply lacks the resources—the time and the manpower—necessary to do that. The veto did, however, serve as a very powerful oversight tool which Congress could use on a selective basis. Some have criticized the veto as a device which Congress used to interject "political" influences into the administrative process (which should supposedly be neutral and rely only on factual and legal considerations). In reality, however, many agency decisions are inherently political in nature. I think that the veto led to good policy in this regard, since Congress should ultimately have control over political decisions. The Constitution gives Congress this responsibility and, in a more pragmatic vein, the legislature is simply better at achieving accommodation among competing interests than any administrative agency.

Q. Now that the Court has struck down many veto measures, where does this leave Congress' power to control regulatory policymaking?

A. Congress can still rely on traditional means of oversight, such as its control over the budget and its ability to amend legislation that delegates authority to the bureaucracy. In addition, it appears that Congress may experiment with some new devices designed to compensate for its loss of the veto. One rather extreme alternative, which would certainly be constitutional, would require both houses of Congress to approve and the president to sign into law proposed regulations. Congress could also pass two-house vetoes subject to the president's signature.

Q. Do you believe that these other approaches will be as effective as the legislative veto?

A. That's hard to say, but certainly the veto has decided advantages over the alternatives, at least from Congress' perspective. It is obviously much more flexible and much less burdensome than the alternative approaches. If two-house approval or rejection of regulatory rules subject to the president's signature were used on any widespread basis, it would impede the government's ability to react to problems. Also, this alternative approach to the legislative veto raises important questions about the relative balance of power between the legislature and the executive branches in the implementation of policy. This is a controversial area which has not been resolved by the courts.

---

hazardous-waste disposal to public-lands management, but enforcement is often weak and untimely. A similar story can be told in field after field.

A major part of the problem is the sheer size of the task. In America, there are 12,000 potentially hazardous waste sites to be monitored, 15,000 sewage treatment plants to be upgraded, nearly 300 species of plants and animals to be protected, and more than 3.5 million workplaces to be inspected.[35]

Another problem is that regulatory statutes often have been written without sufficient concern for implementation and enforcement. Congress passed the Clean Air Act Amendments of 1970 without regard to whether national air-quality standards could be met even under the best of circumstances.[36] Many wastewater treatment plants built to meet Congress' national standards haven't worked as expected because of technical problems.

Implementation is also hindered by scarce resources. Few agencies have the funds or the personnel to carry out their regulatory tasks effectively. This problem has been compounded by recent reductions in agency budgets and staffs.

Finally, implementation often faces political limitations. Agencies often have the power to withhold federal funds from state and local government programs or to shut down industrial plants that fail to comply. Politically, however, these types of sanctions are very difficult to impose. Members of Congress don't take kindly to reports that their communities are about to lose federal grant funds or that a major industrial plant employing many people in their district is about to be closed.[37]

EVALUATION

Who evaluates regulatory policy? The president, for one. Recent presidents have been particularly concerned about the effects of regulation on the economy. One of President Reagan's first acts in office was to appoint Vice-President George Bush to head a presidential task force on regulatory reform. The job of the task force was to evaluate federal regulatory policy and to recommend appropriate policy changes.

Congress is involved in evaluation. Besides the legislative veto, Congress has on occasion changed the law to reverse regulatory policies adopted by the bureaucracy. Take the case of the automobile interlock seat-belt system. The NHTSA required this device on all new cars sold in the United States, beginning with 1974 models. In 1975, however, Congress responded to adverse public reaction by legislating its end. Then there's the example of saccharin. After laboratory tests found a link between saccharin and the incidence of cancer in white rats, the FDA moved to ban its nonprescription use. In this case, the FDA was only following the law. Congress changed the law, however, allowing the continued use of saccharin but with a health warning.

The courts are also involved. In the early 1980s, federal district and appellate courts took much of the steam out of the Reagan Administration's efforts at reducing the federal regulatory burden. They held that agencies cannot repeal rules without "thorough, in-depth" documentation on the grounds for the change.[38] Consequently, the courts are not only an arena for appealing agency rules when they are first enacted; they can also have a say when an agency attempts to repeal rules already in effect. For example, the U.S. Court of Appeals for the District of Columbia rejected EPA efforts to relax regulations governing the Clean Air Act.[39]

Finally, many groups and individuals outside of the federal government are involved in the evaluation of regulatory policy. Evaluation comes from state and local governments directly affected by federal policies. The press is involved, albeit in a sporadic and haphazard fashion. Also, a growing number of scholarly evaluations have been done on the effects of regulatory policy on the nation's economy and society.

CONCLUSION: REGULATORY POLICY AND POLITICS

As with many other areas of public policy, regulatory policymaking combines questions of policy effectiveness, philosophy, and politics. First, there is the issue of effectiveness. Do regulatory policies accomplish their intended goals? Sometimes they do; sometimes they don't, but there is disagreement about which policies fit under which heading.

Many observers argue that regulatory policies should be evaluated in terms of a cost-benefit analysis. Are the benefits received sufficient to justify the costs of regulation? We suspect that product-safety standards to prevent infant crib deaths are worthwhile, and we have our doubts about OSHA pamphlets warning farmers about slipping on wet manure; other matters are less clear. How many millions of dollars of air-pollution abatement equipment are needed to balance how many cases of lung disease? At what point do clean air or safe products become too expensive? These are questions over which reasonable people may disagree.

A second aspect is philosophy. What role should government play? At one end of the spectrum are those who want to eliminate the heavy hand of government and rely on the free market. Let the market determine the price of natural gas, they say, not the government. Let the individual decide whether to use a seat belt, not the government. Let the consumer judge the merits of a product, not the government.

At the other end of the spectrum are those who believe that we don't so much suffer from too much regulation but from *bad* regulation. Ralph Nader, for example, believes that in some cases we have too little regulation.[40] The advocates of regulation argue that deregulating the price of natural gas will cost consumers billions of dollars while the industry reaps windfall profits. Deregulating the airlines, they say, has meant that some smaller cities are now left without service.[41] Reducing environmental, consumer, and worker-safety regulations will mean a threat to the health, safety, and welfare of a majority of Americans.

Between the philosophical extremes is another group that approaches regulation from a more pragmatic standpoint. Some regulations, they believe, should be eliminated or reduced because they only serve to protect industry from competition. Louis Engman, a former FTC chairman, described regulated industries as "federal protectorates, living in a cozy world of cost-plus, safely protected from the ugly spectres of competition, efficiency, and innovation."[42]

"Sorry I'm late, dear. . . . I was detained by the Consumer Product Safety Commission."

They also believe, however, that the free-market approach can be taken too far. An extreme example involves a decision taken by the FTC under its most recent chairman, James C. Miller III, a Reagan appointee and a strong advocate of the free-market approach. Under Miller, the FTC decided not to pursue a case involving the sale of hundreds of leaky survival suits marketed to protect persons in ocean accidents. The suits could have been repaired by the manufacturer quite inexpensively, but the FTC decided not to order a recall. The commission reasoned that the free market would remedy the situation. The relatives of people who drowned because of the leaky suits would sue the company, forcing it to clean up its act. Fortunately, the company decided to recall and repair the suits voluntarily after all of the publicity over the FTC's inaction.[43]

A final aspect of regulatory policy is politics: who gets what, when, and how. Groups tend to favor regulation that benefits them while opposing regulation that doesn't. The airlines welcomed regulation by the CAB; organized labor cheered the creation of OSHA. Business groups in general opposed the establishment of the Consumer Product Safety Commission and were unhappy with the FTC under the chairmanship of Michael Pertschuk.

Efficiency, philosophy, and politics mesh in the regulatory policymaking process in complex and fascinating ways. Let's return to our illustration of children's television advertising and the FTC. The dispute raised a number of technical questions. Are children impressed by commercials? Do they try to influence their parents to purchase particular brand-name products? Do parents respond to their children's requests? Are these products harmful to children's nutrition? Do these commercials have a beneficial effect in that they encourage children to eat breakfast?

Other questions involve the effect of a ban on children's television. After all, advertising foots the bill for television programs. If advertisers aren't allowed to direct their commercials specifically to children, will anyone want to buy advertising on children's programs? An unexpected result of a ban might have been fewer programs specifically for children.

The dispute also raises philosophical questions. What role should government play in such matters? Does government have a duty to protect children from the wiles of Madison Avenue? Or is that really the job of parents? How much government regulation is enough? How much is too much?

Finally, there's politics. The controversy pitted children's advocates and health groups against the breakfast-cereal and advertising industries. In the end, the latter won. How much did the dispute's outcome have to do with the facts of the case and reasoned debate about the legitimate role of government? How much depended on the relative political strength of the forces involved? All three aspects were intertwined, but that's the nature of regulatory policymaking in America. It is complicated and complex, combining politics with issues of philosophy and efficiency.

Key Terms

COST-BENEFIT ANALYSIS (345) *NATURAL MONOPOLY (347)*

INTERNALIZE THE EXTERNALITIES (347) *OLIGOPOLY (346)*

MONOPOLY (346)

NOTES

1. Linda E. Demkovitch, "Pulling the Sweet Tooth of Children's TV Advertising," *National Journal* (7 January 1978), pp. 24–26.
2. William F. West, "The Politics of Administrative Rulemaking," *Public Administration Review* 42 (September/October 1982): 420–26.
3. Linda E. Demkovitch, "Can Regulations Be Fair?" *National Journal* (18 November 1978), p. 1866.
4. *New York Times,* 6 September 1978, p. 36.
5. *New York Times,* 1 May 1980, Sec. IV, p. 1.
6. *Wabash, St. Louis & Pacific Railroad Co.* v. *Illinois,* 118 U.S. 557 (1886).
7. Carl P. Chelf, *Public Policymaking in America* (Glenview, Il.: Scott, Foresman, 1981), ch. 10.
8. David R. Beam, "From Law to Rule: Exploring the Maze of Intergovernmental Regulation," *Intergovernmental Perspective* 9 (Spring 1983): 7–22.
9. *Time* (29 August 1983), p. 13.
10. Ibid.
11. Michael Wines, "Administration, Critics Play Legal Cat and Mouse Game on Agency Rules," *National Journal* (18 December 1982), pp. 2157–60.
12. Murray L. Weidenbaum, *Business, Government, and the Public* (Englewood Cliffs: Prentice-Hall, 1977).
13. Stephen Breyer, *Regulation and its Reform* (Cambridge, Mass.: Harvard University Press, 1982), ch. 1.
14. Council on Environmental Quality, *Environmental Quality: Seventh Annual Report* (Washington, D.C.: U.S. Government Printing Office, 1976), p. 145.
15. Quoted in Chelf, p. 246.
16. *Reprints of Selected News Items* (Menlo Park, Cal.: Stanford Research Institute, 1975), p. 8; quoted in Weidenbaum, p. 26.
17. *U.S. Code of Regulation,* Title 29, Section 1910.25 (b) (3) (ii).
18. Timothy B. Clark, "What's All the Uproar Over OSHA's 'Nit-Picking' Rules," *National Journal* (7 October 1978), pp. 1594–96.
19. Paul H. MacAvoy, *The Regulated Industries and the Economy* (New York: W. W. Norton, 1979), pp. 47–58.
20. Stephen Chapman, "Too Much: The ICC and the Truckers," *Washington Monthly* (December 1977), p. 33.

21. MacAvoy, pp. 92–98.

22. Rachel Carson, *Silent Spring* (Boston: Houghton Mifflin, 1962); Ralph Nader, *Unsafe at Any Speed* (New York: Grossman, 1965).

23. *Time* (29 August 1983), p. 13.

24. *Gallup Report,* November 1982, p. 14.

25. Walter Adams, "The Rocky Road Toward Deregulation," in Thomas G. Gies and Werner Sichel, eds., *Deregulation: Appraisal Before the Fact* (Ann Arbor: University of Michigan, 1982), pp. 119–26.

26. "Building Access: Cost No Barrier?" *Regulation* (September/October 1982): 5–8.

27. *Time* (29 August 1983), p. 14.

28. Advisory Commission on Intergovernmental Relations, *Protecting the Environment: Politics, Pollution, and Federal Policy,* Report A–83 (Washington, D. C.: U.S. Government Printing Office, 1981), pp. 23–25, 52.

29. Andrew Fishel and Janice Pottker, *National Politics and Sex Discrimination in Education* (Lexington, Mass.: D.C. Heath and Co., 1977).

30. Beam.

31. Michael Wines, "It's Congress' Move," *National Journal* (9 July 1983), p. 1462.

32. Wines, "Administration, Critics Play Cat and Mouse."

33. Beam, p. 15.

34. Thomas J. Madden and David H. Remes, "The Courts and the Administration: Marching to Different Drummers," *Intergovernmental Perspective* 9 (Spring 1983): 23–29.

35. Beam, p. 17.

36. Charles O. Jones, *Clean Air: The Policies and Politics of Pollution Control* (Pittsburgh: University of Pittsburgh Press, 1975).

37. Beam.

38. *State Farm Mutual Automobile Insurance Co. et al.* v. *NHTSA,* 680 F. 2d 206 (1982).

39. *Natural Resources Defense Council* v. *Gorsuch,* 685 F 2d 718 (1982).

40. George Daly and David W. Brady, "Federal Regulation of Economic Activity: Failures and Reforms," in James E. Anderson, ed., *Economic Regulatory Policies* (Lexington, Mass.: Lexington Books, 1976), pp. 171–86.

41. Robert M. Kaus, "The Dark Side of Deregulation," *Washington Monthly* (May 1979), pp. 33–40.

42. Quoted in Adams, p. 120.

43. Michael Wines, "From Doctors to Dairy Farmers, Critics Gunning for the FTC Again," *National Journal* (29 January 1983), pp. 221–23.

SUGGESTED READINGS

ANDERSON, JAMES E. *Economic Regulatory Policies.* Lexington, Mass.: Lexington Books, 1976.

Breyer, Stephen. *Regulation and its Reform.* Cambridge, Mass.: Harvard University Press, 1982.

Davies, J. Clarence, iii, and Davies, Barbara S. *The Politics of Pollution.* 2nd ed. Indianapolis: Bobbs-Merrill, 1975.

Gies, Thomas G., and Sichel, Werner, eds. *Deregulation: Appraisal Before the Fact.* Ann Arbor: University of Michigan Press, 1982.

Jones, Charles O. *Clean Air: The Policies and Politics of Pollution Control.* Pittsburgh: University of Pittsburgh Press, 1975.

MacAvoy, Paul H. *The Regulated Industries and the Economy.* New York: W. W. Norton, 1979.

Stigler, George J. *The Citizen and the State: Essays on Regulation.* Chicago: University of Chicago Press, 1975.

Weidenbaum, Murray L. *Business, Government, and the Public.* Englewood Cliffs, N.J.: Prentice-Hall, 1977.

Wilson, James Q. *The Politics of Regulation.* New York: Basic Books, 1980.

Chapter Thirteen

CIVIL LIBERTIES

In 1977, Skokie, Illinois, became the setting for one of the most emotional **civil-liberties** controversies in recent memory. Skokie is a middle-class suburban community of some 70,000 people just north of Chicago. It is predominantly white and heavily Jewish. Skokie's brush with notoriety came when Frank Collin, the head of Chicago's branch of the American Nazi party, declared his group's intention to hold a march there on July 4, 1977, complete with Nazi uniforms, signs, and swastikas. Why Skokie? Because, the Nazis said, where you find the most Jews you find the most Jew-haters.

The Nazis' announcement raised cries of anguish and outrage in Skokie, whose Jewish community includes a sizable number of refugees from the Holocaust. Many Skokie residents had seen their mothers, fathers, brothers, and sisters murdered by the Nazis during World War II. Now the memory of those awful times was being revived by the prospect of brownshirted Nazis goose-stepping through their neighborhoods.

The Skokie Village Board responded by passing a series of ordinances designed to prevent the demonstration. One required that any group of fifty or more wishing to demonstrate on the city's streets must first obtain a permit. Another forbad "political organizations" from demonstrating in "military-style" uniforms. A third banned "symbols offensive to the community" and the distribution of literature that ascribes a "lack of virtue" to racially and ethnically identifiable groups.[1]

The Nazis went to court, represented by lawyers from the American Civil Liberties Union (ACLU), a public-interest group dedicated to the support of constitutional rights and liberties. The ACLU and others who defended the Nazis' right to demonstrate argued that free speech means free speech for everyone, even Nazis. However odious their views may be to most Americans, the Nazis' right to express them is guaranteed by the Constitution. There is no greater affirmation of freedom, one observer wrote, than to respect the rights of those who would destroy that freedom.[2]

Many others saw the issue differently. In fact, a substantial part of the ACLU's membership resigned over the organization's decision to defend the Nazis.[3] The Nazis aren't so much interested in the open exchange of views, they argued, as they are at spreading hatred and lacerating the feelings of Jews. Don't the people of Skokie have rights too? A free society should not be obliged to grant an absolute right of free speech and assembly to those who desire to destroy those freedoms.[4]

The battle in the courts was long and protracted. Initially, the state courts in Illinois were sympathetic to the Skokie Village Board. The Nazis appealed, however, and the United States Supreme Court ordered the Illinois courts to consider the First Amendment issues raised by the case. Ultimately, the Illinois supreme court and the lower federal courts ruled in favor of the Nazis.[5] The Skokie ordinances were struck down and the Nazis were free to march, swastikas and all. "The display of the swastika," said the Illinois supreme court, "as offensive to the principles of a free society as the memories it recalls may be, is symbolic speech intended to convey to the public the beliefs of those who display it."[6] Having made their point, the Nazis chose not to march in Skokie after all. Instead, they held a demonstration in front of the federal building in downtown Chicago.

The Skokie incident illustrates a number of important points about civil liberties and public policy in America. First, civil-liberties questions are often highly controversial. Theoretically, we hold high the banner of individual rights and liberties, but many of the groups and individuals demanding those freedoms are unpopular: Nazis, communists, prison inmates, persons accused of crimes, atheists, homosexuals, Jehovah's Witnesses, the Amish, and the owners of sexually oriented businesses. Particular civil-liberties issues are often divisive: abortion, capital punishment, school prayer, obscenity and pornography, privacy, and state aid to parochial schools.

Second, civil-liberties controversies inevitably focus on the Constitution as each side seeks constitutional justification for its point of view. What was the original intent of the relevant constitutional passages? What do they mean today? Frequently, the issue is laid to rest, at least temporarily, by invoking constitutional principles.

Third, the courts are major participants in civil-liberties policymaking.

Should an avowedly racist and anti-democratic organization receive First Amendment protection? The threat of a Nazi party march in heavily Jewish Skokie, Illinois, prompted a flurry of protests and counterdemonstrations. A barrage of eggs and stinkbombs hit the Nazi band when they marched at the Federal Center Plaza.

In our political system, controversial issues often wind up in the courts; constitutional ones almost always do. Consequently, most major civil-liberties questions eventually make their way to the U.S. Supreme Court.

Fourth, civil-liberties policymaking involves more participants than just the courts. It may include governmental bodies at all levels and the active participation of a broad range of interest groups. The Skokie controversy involved the Skokie Village Board and courts at the state and national level, as well as several interest groups including the ACLU and a number of Jewish organizations.

Finally, civil-liberties policymaking involves politics. Things of value were in dispute in the Skokie incident. The Nazis were looking for the opportunity to get the maximum possible publicity for their views while the citizens of Skokie wanted to be left in peace. The ACLU became involved in order to defend a constitutional principle they believed to be threatened. The dispute was fought in the political arena—the Skokie Village Board, the state courts of Illinois, the federal courts, and the media.

PHILOSOPHICAL ISSUES

Civil liberties concern the protection of the individual from the unrestricted power of government. The philosophical issues raised involve fundamental concepts about society, freedom, and order.

THE CASE FOR CIVIL LIBERTIES

Many eloquent statements have been made in support of individual liberty. Consider the words of Supreme Court Justice Robert H. Jackson:

> The very purpose of a Bill of Rights was to withdraw certain subjects from the vicissitudes of political controversy, to place them beyond the reach of majorities and officials and to establish them as legal principles to be applied by the courts. One's right to life, liberty, and property, to free speech, a free press, freedom of worship and assembly, and other fundamental rights may not be submitted to vote; they depend on the outcome of no election.[7]

One of the strongest arguments for individual liberty comes from the nineteenth-century English philosopher John Stuart Mill. Writing in *On Liberty*, Mill speaks forcefully for an absolute freedom of expression.[8] When society chooses to silence the views of a dissenter, argues Mill, then that society is assuming its own infallibility. Even if the dissenting opinion is entirely and utterly wrong, society will benefit from its expression. The truth is made clearer and its impression more lively because of its collision with error.

Mill asserts belief in complete freedom of expression, but he would place limits on action. Individuals should be free to act upon their opinions, he says, so long as it is at their own risk and not another's.

> *The liberty of the individual must be thus far limited; he must not make himself a nuisance to other people. But if he refrains from molesting others in what concerns them, and merely acts according to his own inclinations and judgment in things which concern himself . . . he should be allowed . . . to carry his opinions into practice at his own cost.*[9]

To use a modern example, we suspect that Mill would agree that individual adults have a right privately to indulge in alcohol or drugs as they choose. They do not have the right, however, then to drive an automobile, endangering others.

THE CASE FOR LIMITS ON CIVIL LIBERTIES

In America, there is not a substantial body of opinion philosophically opposed to individual freedom. Many, however, hold that certain limits must be placed upon individual liberty. The rights of the minority must be recognized, but not at the expense of society as a whole. Supreme Court Justice Felix Frankfurter makes the point this way:

> *The choice is not between order and liberty. It is between liberty with order and anarchy without either. There is danger that, if the court does not temper its doctrinaire logic with a little practical wisdom, it will convert the constitutional Bill of Rights into a suicide pact.*[10]

Even in a free society, the argument goes, conflicts arise between the rights of the individual and the rights of society as a whole. A distinction must be made between liberty and license; the line cannot be drawn so neatly as J. S. Mill suggests. Sometimes conflicts arise over the rights of the individual and the security of the state. Does freedom of speech entitle an individual to advocate the violent overthrow of the government? During wartime, should individuals be permitted to counsel avoidance of the draft? Many would say no, including Supreme Court Justice Oliver Wendell Holmes, Jr. "When a nation is at war," said Holmes, "many things that might be said in time of peace are such a hindrance to its effort that their utterance will not be endured."[11]

At other times, a tension exists between individual rights and the right of the majority to have the kind of society it wants. Consider the problem of pornography. Many believe that sexually explicit materials can undermine the moral fabric of society. They argue that society's interest in regulating pornography transcends the right of the individual to produce it, promote it, sell it, and purchase it.

Finally, the rights of different groups of individuals may sometimes come in conflict. Various religious groups claim the right to proselytize their faith by passing out pamphlets door-to-door and in public places such as airports. Many people on the other side argue that they have a right not to be disturbed at home or to be confronted with someone else's religion unless they desire it. Many women contend that they have the right to determine whether or not to terminate a pregnancy, but others ask about rights for the unborn. The Nazis in Chicago claimed a right to demonstrate; the residents of Skokie asked for the right to be left alone.

CIVIL LIBERTIES AND THE CONSTITUTION

The original Constitution includes a number of civil-liberties guarantees. Article I, Section 9 prohibits bills of attainder and ex post facto laws. It also guarantees the privilege of the writ of *habeas corpus* except in the extraordinary circumstances of rebellion or invasion. A bill of attainder, you recall, is a law that declares someone guilty and inflicts punishment without benefit of a trial. An ex post facto law is a retroactive law. Meanwhile, *habeas corpus* is a judge's order to determine whether a prisoner is being held lawfully. In Article IV, Section 3, the Constitution defines treason, sets standards for evidence, and establishes penalties. Article V, Section 2 provides for the extradition of criminal fugitives from one state to another. Finally, Article VII forbids the use of religious tests as a qualification for national office.

THE BILL OF RIGHTS

The original Constitution, however, did not include a list of individual rights and privileges—a bill of rights. There was some discussion of adding a bill of rights at the Constitutional Convention of 1787, but the general sentiment was that it would be unnecessary. The various state constitutions already had bills of rights, and at any rate the powers of the new federal government were to be quite limited.

The absence of a bill of rights became a point of controversy in the ratification debate in the states. The new Constitution's opponents, the Antifederalists, pointed out that the federal government would not be bound by the states' bills of rights; the absence of a bill of rights in the national constitution would therefore open the door to encroachments upon the liberties of the people. The Constitution's supporters, the Federalists, defended the document, but offered a compromise in order to win over some wavering opponents. They pledged the adoption of a bill of rights by amendment once the new government was established.

The Federalists proved true to their word. In Congress, James Madison took the lead in proposing changes to the original document. After some debate, a two-thirds majority of each house agreed to twelve proposed amendments and submitted them to the states in September 1789.

By November 1791 enough states had acted to determine the fate of the proposed amendments. Ten were ratified; two were rejected. The two that failed were less important than those that were adopted. One would have provided for a representative in the U.S. House for every fifty thousand persons. Obviously, that amendment would not have stood the test of time. The other amendment would have postponed any increase in salary for members of Congress until after the next election.[12]

The ten amendments that were ratified were added to the Constitution and are known as the Bill of Rights. Turn to the Appendix in the back of this text and read each of the amendments. The First Amendment guarantees freedom of religion, speech, press, and assembly. The second establishes a state's right to maintain a militia. The third forbids the quartering of soldiers in private homes during peacetime. The Fifth and Sixth Amendments list the rights of persons accused of crimes. The seventh provides for jury trials in civil suits exceeding twenty dollars. The Eighth Amendment prohibits excessive bail and excessive fines and forbids cruel and unusual punishments. The ninth states that the act of enumerating rights in the Constitution does not deny or disparage other rights the people may enjoy. Finally, the Tenth Amendment declares that the powers not delegated to the national government by the Constitution are reserved to the states, or to the people.

Federalist James Madison was instrumental in gaining the adoption of the Bill of Rights in the early days of the U.S. Congress.

The historical significance of the adoption of the Bill of Rights cannot be underestimated, but its early impact on public policy in America was not particularly significant. For one thing, it did not apply to the states; Congress intended the national Bill of Rights to apply only to the national government, and the Supreme Court so ruled in the case of *Barron* v. *Baltimore* in 1833.[13]

Second, the Bill of Rights failed to overturn one of the more serious abuses of individual rights in American history—the Sedition Act, passed by a Federalist-controlled Congress in 1798 and signed into law by President John Adams. The act made it illegal for any person to write, print, or publish any criticism of the government, the Congress, or the president, even if the criticism were true. The Adams Administration enforced the Sedition Act vigorously, prosecuting a number of opposition newspaper editors who dared criticize the Federalists. Nonetheless, the federal courts, staffed by Federalist judges, refused to find the act unconstitutional. It remained in effect until Adams and the Federalists were voted out of office in the election of 1800 and the new Congress repealed the Sedition Act.

THE FOURTEENTH AMENDMENT

The ratification of the Fourteenth Amendment in 1868 and its subsequent interpretation by the Supreme Court changed the constitutional basis for civil liberties in the federal system. Section 1 of the amendment first defines citizenship and then states the following:

No State shall make or enforce any law which shall abridge the privileges or immunities of citizens of the United States; nor shall any State deprive any person of life, liberty, or property, without due process of law; nor deny to any person within its jurisdiction the equal protection of the laws.

The historical intent of this section is one of the most hotly debated topics in constitutional history. We know that the amendment's framers wanted to protect the civil rights of blacks and that the phrase "life, liberty, or property, without due process of law" is quoted verbatim from the Fifth Amendment. Did the Congress intend to apply only the guarantees of the Fifth Amendment to the states? Did it intend to apply the entire Bill of Rights to the states? Or did it intend to apply a larger body of rights and privileges including but not limited to those found in the first ten amendments? That is the great debate for which there seems to be no certain answer.[14] For all practical purposes, however, the dispute has been settled by the interpretations of the Supreme Court.

The Supreme Court's first crack at interpreting the Fourteenth Amendment came in the Slaughterhouse cases of 1873. Ironically, the dispute had little to do with civil liberties. In 1869 the Louisiana state legislature, under corrupt influences, had granted the slaughterhouse business in New Orleans to a single firm. Consequently, more than 1000 other persons and firms were driven out of business. Some of these business owners filed suit, charging that the statute violated their "privileges or immunities" as citizens under the Fourteenth Amendment.

By a five-to-four vote, the Supreme Court upheld the constitutionality of the Louisiana law. The Court's majority drew a distinction between national citizenship and state citizenship, each of which enjoys certain distinct rights and privileges. Ordinary civil liberties, such as freedom of speech, press, and religion, are to be protected by the states, not the federal government. So, in the view of a majority on the Supreme Court, the Fourteenth Amendment hadn't really changed anything. The civil liberties protections of the Bill of Rights still did not apply to the states; the *Barron* precedent stood.[15]

THE SELECTIVE INCORPORATION OF THE BILL OF RIGHTS

In 1925, however, in the case of *Gitlow* v. *New York,* the U.S. Supreme Court began the process known as the "selective incorporation of the Bill of Rights" into the Fourteenth Amendment. On a case-by-case basis, the Court interpreted the **due-process clause** of the Fourteenth Amendment to mean that most of the guarantees of the Bill of Rights apply to the states as well as to the national government. The *Gitlow* case, for example, involved the validity of a New York law that made it a crime to advocate the

Benjamin Gitlow. In the case of Gitlow v. New York *(1925) the Supreme Court began the practice of selectively incorporating the Bill of Rights into the Fourteenth Amendment.*

violent overthrow of the government. Although the Court upheld the law, the majority opinion stated specifically that the First Amendment guarantees of free speech and press "are among the fundamental personal rights and 'liberties' protected by the Due Process Clause of the Fourteenth Amendment from impairment by the states."[16]

The incorporation process has been slow and sporadic, and at no point has the Supreme Court ruled that the entire Bill of Rights applies to the states. Through the years, however, the Court has nearly accomplished just that on a piecemeal basis. In 1931, the Supreme Court applied freedom of the press to the states.[17] In 1932, it was counsel in capital cases.[18] Freedom of religion was incorporated in 1934;[19] freedom of assembly and the right to petition the government in 1937.[20] The court added separation of church and state in 1947[21] and the right to a public trial in 1948.[22] Protection against unreasonable searches and seizures was incorporated in 1961.[23] The prohibition against cruel and unusual punishments was applied to the states in 1962.[24] In the *Gideon* case in 1963, the Court added right to counsel in noncapital cases.[25] In 1964 the Court applied the constitutional protection against self-incrimination to the states[26] and in 1965 added the right to confront witnesses.[27] The right to trial by an *impartial* jury came in 1966,[28] the right to a speedy trial in 1967.[29] Then, in 1968, the Court extended the right to trial by jury to the states.[30] Finally, the constitutional protection against double jeopardy was applied to the states in 1968.[31]

At times, the Supreme Court has interpreted the Fourteenth Amendment to include rights even beyond those in the Bill of Rights. In *Griswold* v. *Connecticut* (1965) the Court struck down state legislation that prohibited the use of contraceptives and the dispensing of birth control information. Justice William O. Douglas, writing for the Court, declared the law a violation of the constitutional "right to privacy." That phrase cannot be found in the Constitution, but Douglas said that the "specific guarantees in the Bill of Rights have penumbras, formed by emanations from those guarantees that help give them life and substance." According to the Court's majority, these "penumbras" guarantee zones of privacy upon which the states may not infringe. The decision was not unanimous, however. In dissent, Justice Hugo Black concluded that the Court was engaging in judicial "legislation." Justice Potter Stewart dissented as well. "To say that the Ninth Amendment has anything to do with this case," he said, "is to turn somersaults with history."[32] Nonetheless, the Court would return to its newly discovered constitutional right of privacy, notably in the abortion cases of 1973.[33]

THE DOUBLE STANDARD

A major consequence of the incorporation process has been to establish a national standard, set by the Court, for civil-liberties policy. Because of the

Gitlow precedent, for example, the Skokie Village ordinance enacted to prevent the Nazi demonstration could be challenged and overturned in the federal courts as a violation of the First and Fourteenth Amendments to the United States Constitution. Before the *Gitlow* ruling, these sorts of policy matters were left to the discretion of state and local governments. Today, thanks to the Supreme Court's incorporation policy, virtually the entire range of civil-liberties issues is subject to federal-court review.

The protection of individual rights and liberties has become the foremost item on the policy agenda of the modern Supreme Court. In the process, the Court has assumed a **double standard** for judging the constitutionality of legislation in the economic/regulatory sector as opposed to legislation dealing with civil rights and liberties. Since 1937, the Supreme Court has taken the position that all economic legislation is constitutional unless proven otherwise. In contrast, legislative and executive restrictions on the basic freedoms guaranteed by the Bill of Rights are presumed unconstitutional. The burden of proof is on the government to justify such restrictions constitutionally.[34]

What is the rationale for the double standard? Why should civil liberties enjoy a **preferred position,** as the doctrine is called? Because, the Court has said, certain rights, such as freedom of speech and assembly, are so basic that they make the exercise of other rights possible. Justice Jackson explained the Court's position in this way:

> *Ordinarily, legislation whose basis in economic wisdom is uncertain can be redressed by the processes of the ballot box or the pressure of public opinion. But when the channels of opinion or of peaceful persuasion are corrupted or clogged, these political correctives can no longer be relied on, and the democratic system is threatened at its most vital point. In that event the Court, by intervening, restores the processes of democratic government; it does not disrupt them.*[35]

The point is this: if government policy harms your business or threatens your income, you can act to change the policy through the political process. But, if government policy restricts your freedom of expression or your access to the political process, you are stymied. You have no way to complain, no means to redress the grievance. Thus the Court's double standard. The result is that economic policymaking in America primarily involves the legislative and executive branches of government. Civil-liberties policymaking, however, is very much the story of the judicial branch.

CIVIL LIBERTIES TODAY

Civil-liberties policy today reflects compromise among competing political interests and divergent philosophical viewpoints. As we have seen, many particular issues are highly controversial, often involving competing claims of the rights of the individual versus the rights of groups. A wide variety of political interest groups are also involved, each asserting its own position. Consequently, current civil-liberties policy usually involves a balancing of interests and a compromise of views.

RELIGIOUS LIBERTY

Americans are a religious people and a people of many religions. It is not surprising, then, that the relationship between the state and the church has been an ongoing source of civil-liberties controversies. The First Amendment addresses the issue with this well-known phrase: "Congress shall make no law respecting an establishment of religion, or prohibiting the free exercise thereof." This somewhat vague phrase has been the object of volumes of judicial interpretation as the Supreme Court has struggled to draw lines of distinction between competing interests and to balance divergent philosophies about the relationship between the government and religion.[36]

The free-exercise clause.   The Supreme Court has consistently held that freedom of religious *belief* is absolute, but it has drawn a distinction between belief and action. Freedom of religion does not mean an absolute freedom to put beliefs into practice. The Court has ruled, for example, that Mormons' religious beliefs do not justify polygamy.[37] Also, the Court has upheld state laws prohibiting the handling of poisonous snakes in religious ceremonies.[38]

For the most part, however, the Supreme Court has followed a liberal line in permitting the free exercise of religious beliefs. In the Flag Salute cases, you recall, the Court ruled that Jehovah's Witnesses may not be compelled to recite the pledge of allegiance in violation of their religious faith.[39] In other cases involving Jehovah's Witnesses, the Supreme Court has upheld their right to distribute religious pamphlets door-to-door and in public places without the permission of local authorities and without paying license taxes.[40]

The Amish are members of another religious sect that has participated in litigation involving the free exercise of religion. They fear that too much exposure to education will undermine their children's faith in their traditional religion. On religious grounds, they withdraw their children from school after completion of the eighth grade. This has brought them into conflict with state school-attendance laws and into court to argue the First Amendment. There they have won, as the Supreme Court has held that the free-exercise clause of the First Amendment outweighs the state's interest in education.[41]

The establishment-of-religion clause.   Perhaps the most controversial questions involving civil liberties have arisen under the establishment-of-religion clause. One of the more difficult issues has been that of state aid to parochial schools. Parents who send their children to private, church-related schools frequently complain that they are paying twice for their children's education. They pay taxes to support the public schools and then pay tuition for parochial school. Why can't the government help out a bit, they ask. The parochial school systems save taxpayers millions of dollars. Besides, many parochial school systems desperately need financial aid. On the other side of the issue are those who contend that taxpayers' money should not be used to support religious education. A wall of separation, they argue, should stand between the church and the state.

In terms of practical politics, the battle over public assistance to parochial schools generally begins in the state legislatures and school boards but winds up in the federal courts. In 1941, the New Jersey legislature authorized school districts to subsidize the transportation of students to and from school and, if they chose, to extend the benefit to parochial-school students as well. The Ewing Township district did just that, and a taxpayer named Everson sued, challenging the constitutionality of the act.

The Supreme Court's decision in *Everson* v. *Board of Education of Ewing Township* set an important precedent on the meaning of the establishment-of-religion clause. The vote was five-to-four to uphold the New Jersey statute, with the majority opinion written by Justice Hugo Black. "The 'establishment of religion' clause means at least this:" Black wrote, "Neither a state nor the Federal Government can set up a church. Neither can pass laws which aid one religion, aid all religions, or prefer one religion over another. . . ." Yet the New Jersey law did not violate the Constitution. Black drew a distinction between aid for the child and aid for the school. Transportation, said the Court's majority, is aid for the child and therefore constitutionally valid.

The Court's minority argued that the Court's ruling did not match Black's opinion. While the rhetoric of the opinion seemed to erect a wall of separation between church and state, the decision allowed New Jersey to breach the wall. In a well-known dissent, Justice Jackson likened the actions of the Court's majority to those of Julia, a heroine in one of Lord Byron's poems, who "whispering 'I will ne'er consent'—consented."[42]

Nevertheless, the Supreme Court has stuck with its child-benefit theory in upholding state laws providing textbooks[43] and therapeutic, remedial, and counseling services to students attending parochial schools.[44] These, the Court has reasoned, assist the student. In contrast, the Court has rejected other types of aid on the grounds that they benefit the school. These include loans of laboratory equipment and films,[45] and the provision of instructional resource materials, such as wall charts and slide projectors.[46]

In 1983, the Supreme Court developed another rationale for dealing with school-aid cases. The Court ruled five-to-four to uphold a Minnesota law that allowed parents a $700 tax deduction to send their children to private schools, including religious schools. The Court's majority reasoned that the statute was constitutional because it had the nonreligious purpose of ensuring good education for all citizens.[47]

The Supreme Court's position on state aid to parochial schools has generated some criticism for the Court, but it is a good example of the type of balancing act the Court frequently performs on tough civil-liberties issues. Critics might charge that the child-benefit approach makes a distinction without a difference. It isn't immediately obvious, for instance, that textbooks aid the child while lab equipment helps the school. Also, the Court has not followed the standard in regard to government aid to church-supported colleges and universities. That the judges have allowed.[48] As for the Court's recent ruling on tuition tax deductions, critics charge that the majority's promotion-of-good-education standard could be used to justify almost any type of aid. Perhaps the best way to interpret the Court's overall approach is to see it as a pragmatic attempt to mediate a thorny political/constitutional conflict. Does that mean that constitutional law reflects political compromise? Yes, sometimes it does.

The Supreme Court's efforts to balance divergent points of view and competing interests can be seen in other controversies involving the establishment-of-religion clause. For example, the Court has struck down a program for providing voluntary religious instruction for public-school children on public-school grounds,[49] but has upheld a similar program in which the religious instruction was held off school grounds.[50] The Court has upheld tax exemptions for church property[51] and ruled that imprinting "In God We Trust" on coins[52] and pledging allegiance to "one nation, under God"[53] do not violate the establishment clause. On the other hand, the Court has ruled that the voluntary recitation of official prayers in public-school classrooms violates the First Amendment. There is no end to the controversy generated by the school-prayer rulings.

The Supreme Court directly confronted the school prayer issue for the first time in 1962 in the case of *Engel* v. *Vitale*. This case involved the voluntary recitation of a prayer composed by New York's state board of regents. The brief prayer read as follows: "Almighty God, we acknowledge our dependence upon Thee, and we beg thy blessings upon us, our parents, our teachers and our country." By a six-to-one vote, the court ruled that the prayer's use was "wholly inconsistent with the Establishment Clause." Justice Black explained the majority's view:

> *The constitutional prohibition against laws respecting an establishment of religion must at least mean that . . . it is no part of the business of government to compose official prayers for any group of the American people to recite as part of a religious program carried on by the government.*[54]

Moreover, the voluntary nature of the prayer did not make it acceptable. "When the power, prestige and financial support of government is placed behind a particular religious belief," wrote Black, "the indirect coercive pressure upon religious minorities to conform to the prevailing officially approved religion is plain."

In 1963, the Supreme Court affirmed its position in two additional cases: *School District of Abington Township* v. *Schempp* and *Murray* v. *Curlett*. The *Schempp* case concerned a Pennsylvania law that required the classroom reading of at least ten verses from the King James Bible each day, followed by a recitation of the Lord's Prayer. The other case involved a suit by Madalyn Murray, the well-known atheist, and her son, William. They attacked a similar Bible-reading and prayer requirement in the city schools of Baltimore. In each case, the Court ruled eight-to-one that the Bible readings and prayers were unconstitutional. Government's role in the relationship between people and religion, said the Court, should be one of neutrality[55] (see the **PERSPECTIVE** on page 376).

FREEDOM OF EXPRESSION

The First Amendment guarantees freedom of expression. "Congress shall make no law . . . abridging the freedom of speech, or of the press; or the right of the people peaceably to assemble to petition the Government for a redress of grievances." Thanks to the Fourteenth Amendment and its case-by-case judicial interpretations, these guarantees apply against the states as well. Nevertheless, freedom of expression is not absolute in America. Some, including Justice Black, have argued that the First Amendment should be treated literally: " 'no law' . . . means . . . no law."[56] The prevailing view, however, has been that of Justice Oliver Wendell Holmes: "The . . . protection of free speech would not protect a man in falsely shouting fire in a theatre, and causing a panic."[57] The problem, of course, comes in applying this philosophy to the concrete circumstances of everyday events.

National security and free speech.   Consider the problem of national security. How far can the government go to protect itself from internal disorder and subversion? Through the years, the Supreme Court has adopted a number of approaches for judging at what point a form of expression becomes sufficiently threatening to society to justify its suppression or restraint. The most important of these approaches is the **clear-and-present-danger rule**, which was first stated in the *Schenck* case in 1919. This case involved the conviction, under the Federal Espionage Act of 1917, of the secretary of the American Socialist party for circulating anti-draft leaflets among newly inducted soldiers. The Court upheld Schenck's conviction unanimously with Justice Holmes writing for the Court.

> *The question in every case is whether the words are used in such circumstances and are of such a nature as to create a clear and present danger that they will bring about the substantive evils that Congress has a right to prevent. It is a question of proximity and degree. When a nation is at war many things that might be said in time of peace are such a hindrance to its effort that their utterance will not be endured.*[58]

Perspective
THE POLITICS OF PRAYER

The Supreme Court's rulings on school prayer have been extraordinarily controversial. When the rulings were first announced, they won support from some quarters, including a number of Jewish and community leaders. Others, however, attacked the Court for taking God out of the classroom. "The Supreme Court has made God unconstitutional," said Senator Sam Ervin of North Carolina.[1]

Today, more than twenty years after *Engel* v. *Vitale*, the school-prayer issue has become the focus of an important political movement led by fundamentalist Christian groups such as the Moral Majority and supported by Ronald Reagan. "Hasn't something gone haywire," asked Reagan, "when this great Constitution of ours is invoked to allow Nazis and Ku Klux Klansmen to march . . . but it supposedly prevents our children from . . . the saying of a simple prayer in their schools?"[2]

The issue came to a head in early 1984 when an amendment proposal was brought to a vote in the U.S. Senate. Prayer supporters conducted rallies and prayer meetings in the capital urging the amendment's passage. (Polls showed that upward of 60 percent of the public supported school prayer.)

The amendment's opponents argued forcefully against organized prayer in the schools. With so many religious traditions in America, they said, no one prayer could satisfy everyone and would surely offend many. Who would write the prayer, they asked. Students, teachers, the government? Also, the amendment's opponents pointed out that the Court hasn't outlawed prayer in the classroom, only spoken, organized prayer. And, as one member of Congress quipped, "As long as there are math tests, children will pray in school."[3]

When the prayer amendment came to a vote in the Senate, the count was fifty-six to forty-four in favor, but that was eleven votes shy of the two-thirds majority needed for passage. Although the amendment's supporters vowed to continue the fight, the battle in Congress was lost, at least for the 1984 session.

Down the street at the Supreme Court building, however, there were signs that the conservative religious groups' political activism was beginning to pay off. During the height of the prayer debate, the Court ruled five-to-four that the inclusion of a nativity scene in a city's decorative Christmas display did not violate the First Amendment. The Court's majority held that the crèche did not present "a real danger of establishment of a state church."[4] A number of observers suggested that the Court was acting to relieve the political pressures on itself over the prayer issue, and many predicted that the Court would eventually approve a daily moment of silent meditation.

[1]Quoted in Leo Pfeffer, *Church, State and Freedom*, rev. ed. (Boston: Beacon Press, 1967), p. 466.
[2]Quoted in *The Washington Post*, National Weekly Edition, 19 March 1984, p. 24.
[3]*Time* (19 March 1984), p. 15.
[4]Ibid., p. 14.

Judges decide cases, of course, not doctrines, and the Supreme Court has frequently strayed from or modified the rule established in *Schenck*. In the years after *Schenck*, the Court upheld a number of espionage and sedition convictions under circumstances involving less than a clear and present danger. In the *Abrams* case, for example, the Court upheld the conviction of a Russian-born immigrant for distributing two pamphlets in New York City critical of America's intervention in the Russian Civil War. The pamphlets were poorly produced and not widely circulated; one was even in Yiddish. In each of these cases, Justice Holmes joined by Justice Louis Brandeis dissented vigorously.[59]

The Court adopted a modification of the clear-and-present-danger doctrine in 1951 in *Dennis* v. *United States*. In 1948, the eleven top leaders of the American Communist party were convicted under the Smith Act for conspiring to teach and advocate the violent overthrow of the government and for organizing the Communist party with that purpose in mind. The Supreme Court upheld the convictions, stating that a danger need not be imminent. It is enough that there be a group willing to attempt the overthrow of the government if and when possible.[60]

In 1957, however, the Court significantly softened the impact of the *Dennis* ruling in the *Yates* case. This involved large-scale prosecutions against second-string Communist leaders and some party members. The Court reversed the convictions, holding that the government can outlaw only such advocacy of the overthrow of government as amounts to actual incitement to action.[61]

The best explanation for the Supreme Court's variations on national-security policy doesn't involve constitutional interpretation as much as it does contemporary politics. The *Schenck* and *Abrams* cases were decided during World War I; the *Dennis* case was decided in 1951, a time when many Americans felt threatened by communist subversion. In each of these cases the Supreme Court's decision to uphold the convictions of alleged "subversives" was in keeping with the national political mood. In contrast, the *Yates* case, which overturned several convictions, was decided in 1957, after fears of communist subversion had begun to recede.

In addition to the clear-and-present-danger doctrine, the Court has adopted a number of rules of thumb for interpreting the First Amendment's freedom-of-expression guarantee. First, freedom of expression is a broader concept than freedom of speech. For example, the Court has ruled in favor of high-school students who wanted to wear black armbands to protest the war in Vietnam.[62]

Second, the Court has generally ruled against prior restraints on publishing materials that might be considered harmful to the national interest. In the Pentagon Papers case, for example, the Supreme Court ruled that the government could not prevent the newspaper publication of excerpts from classified documents relating to the history of America's involvement in the Vietnam war. The Court hinted, though, that prior restraint might be permissible under extreme circumstances. Also, the government could

Pentagon Papers defendants Daniel Ellsberg and Anthony Russo talk with news reporters after the opening session of their trial in 1973. The Ellsberg case raised the question of the government's right to "prior restraint" of materials that might be considered harmful to the nation's security. The Court ruled in favor of the defendants.

have prosecuted the newspapers *after* publication, but it chose not to do so.[63]

Third, the Court has generally been more willing to accept limitations on speech that may lead to public disorder than limitations involving national security, but its record in this area is far from consistent. In 1949, for example, the Court overturned the conviction for disturbing the peace of a rabble-rousing defrocked priest whose speech incited a riot.[64] Two years later, however, the Court affirmed a similar conviction of a student whose harangue had angered only one passer-by.[65] In another example, in 1942 the Court upheld the conviction of a New Hampshire man who called a police officer "a G— d— racketeer" and "a d— Fascist." "Fighting words" that are so insulting as to provoke violence are not protected by the First Amendment, said the Court.[66] But, in 1972 the Court upheld the reversal of a conviction of a Georgia man who called a police officer an s.o.b.[67]

Finally, the Supreme Court has required that efforts to limit expression must conform to rigorous procedural guidelines. Statutes must not be so vague as to make it difficult for the average person to know whether he or she is in violation of them. Also, the laws must not be so broad as to restrain expression that is constitutionally protected.[68]

"If it turns me on, it's smut."

Drawing by Goldberg,
© 1972. The New Yorker
Magazine, Inc.

Obscenity.   The regulation of pornography is without a doubt one of the most controversial and difficult civil-liberties questions. On the one hand, there are those who agree with President Johnson's Commission on Obscenity and Pornography, whose 1970 report recommended lifting all restrictions on adults wishing to see books, pictures, or films. On the other hand, many share the view of the Reverend Billy Graham, who called the commission's work "one of the worst, most diabolical reports ever made by a presidential commission."[69]

The United States Supreme Court has long held that obscenity is not protected by the Constitution, but it has had a problem defining obscenity. As Justice John Marshall Harlan phrased it, "One man's vulgarity is another man's lyric."[70] And so it is. In the 1950s, Maryland's official movie censors found "The Moon Is Blue" to be "lewd" and "lascivious" because it contained the terms "pregnant" and "virginity."[71]

The Court's first effort to establish a yardstick came in 1957 in a pair of cases, *Roth* v. *United States* and *Alberts* v. *California*. In these cases the Court outlined its "prurient-interest" test for obscenity: "Whether to the average person, applying contemporary community standards, the dominant theme of the material taken as a whole, appeals to prurient interests."[72]

In subsequent years, the Court modified, refined, and in some ways revised its rule. The Court added "patently offensive" to its definition of obscenity in 1962[73] and in 1964 ruled that the material must be found "utterly without redeeming social importance."[74] In 1966 the Court held that a work's advertising could be considered in judging whether or not it appeals to "prurient interests,"[75] and in 1968 the Court said that it would not invalidate carefully drawn statutes aimed at protecting minors.[76] The Court has extended this precedent, upholding a New York law in 1982 that banned the distribution of material depicting sexual conduct by children.[77]

For a time, all of this qualification and equivocation left the Court in the position of having to act as a national censorship board. The judges spent a great deal of time in the film room, watching movies one lower court or another had ruled obscene. "I don't know how to define hardcore pornography," wrote Justice Potter Stewart, but "I know it when I see it."[78]

To get away from having to rule on every contested "girlie magazine" or "xxx movie," the Court took another stab at setting guidelines for obscenity in the *Miller* case in 1973. Chief Justice Burger outlined the Court's new rule. First, the material must depict or describe sexual conduct. Second, it must be such that the "average person, applying contemporary community standards, would find that the work taken as a whole appeals to prurient interest." Finally, the work taken as a whole must lack serious literary, artistic, political, or scientific value.[79]

The Court's majority in the *Miller* case resorted to local community standards rather than to a national standard. By this approach, the justices hoped to resolve obscenity questions at a level below the Supreme Court. Did it work? In 1973 the Court found itself involved in case-by-case adjudication once again as it reversed a jury decision in Georgia that declared the movie *Carnal Knowledge* obscene.[80]

In America's political system, a difficult question that cannot be resolved in other branches and levels of government frequently ends up in the Supreme Court. Although the Court may "resolve" the question with a ruling, the Court is usually unable to put the issue to rest. When there is no consensus in the nation on a policy issue, the Supreme Court is seldom able to manufacture one. Such is the case with the issue of obscenity. The Court has been unable to arrive at an approach to the question that is satisfactory to most groups concerned because the nation itself is badly divided on the issue.

DUE PROCESS OF LAW AND THE RIGHTS OF THE ACCUSED

Several provisions of the Bill of Rights are devoted to protecting the rights of persons under investigation for or accused of crimes, including the better part of the Fourth, Fifth, Sixth, and Eighth Amendments. The key constitutional phrase, however, is found in the Fifth Amendment: "No person shall . . . be deprived of life, liberty, or property, without due process of law. . . ." This phrase is used again—in the same words—in the Fourteenth Amendment, so it applies to the states as well as to the national government. But just what does it mean?

"Due process of law" is a broad and flexible concept, and cannot be defined precisely. Essentially, it means that government must be fair, that it must not act in an "arbitrary," "capricious," or "unreasonable" manner, and that its actions must take place within the confines of "fundamental principles of liberty and justice."[81]

In practice, there are two types of due process, substantive and procedural. **Substantive due process** refers to the actual content or subject matter of law. In the late nineteenth and early twentieth centuries, the Supreme Court relied on the doctrine of substantive due process to invalidate many government efforts to regulate business. Since 1937, though, the Court has used the concept quite sparingly and then primarily in civil-liberties matters. In 1942, for example, the Court relied on substantive due process to strike down an Oklahoma law that required the sterilization of felons who had been three times convicted of crimes involving "moral turpitude."[82] The federal courts have also used the notion of substantive due process to knock down many vagrancy, loitering, and public-nuisance laws for being unconstitutionally vague and arbitrary.[83]

Procedural due process involves the execution, administration, and interpretation of laws in accordance with accepted standards of justice. The Supreme Court has held on a case-by-case basis that due process incorporates most of the guarantees found in the Bill of Rights. Consequently, neither the federal government nor the states may resort to stacked juries, coerced confessions, self-incrimination, denial of counsel, cruel and unusual punishments, or unreasonable searches and seizures.

These constitutional guarantees were written to protect everyone in America from the arbitrary power of government, but in practice they most frequently arise in connection with criminal prosecutions. Some of those who benefit from their application are among the most unsavory individuals in society—murderers, rapists, and child molesters. As Justice Felix Frankfurter put it, "It is a fair summary of history to say that the safeguards of liberty have been forged in controversies involving not very nice people."[84] Consequently, the interpretation and application of the principles of due process of law have been quite controversial.

One of the more difficult due-process issues is the **exclusionary rule.** This is the doctrine that when the police err, violating an individual's constitutional right to protection from unreasonable searches and seizures or from self-incrimination, the evidence obtained as a result of the police misconduct or mistake cannot be used against a defendant. The exclusionary rule was established for federal prosecutions in the *Weeks* case in 1914. Weeks was arrested at his place of business and then the police searched his home. Both of these actions were taken without a warrant. Papers and articles seized in the search were used in federal court against Weeks and he was convicted. He appealed, arguing that the judge should not have admitted illegally seized materials into evidence. The Supreme Court agreed.

The tendency of those who execute the criminal laws of the country to obtain conviction by means of unlawful seizures and enforced confessions . . . should find no sanction in the judgment of the courts. . . . If letters and private documents can thus be seized and held and used in evidence against a citizen accused of an offense, the protection of the Fourth Amendment . . . might as well be stricken from the Constitution.[85]

In 1961, the Supreme Court applied the exclusionary rule to the states in the case of *Mapp* v. *Ohio*.[86]

As the crime rate in America has soared, criticism of the exclusionary rule has increased. Why should the criminal go free, critics ask, just because the police officer has erred? Justice is due the accused, but it is also due the victim. Among the strongest critics of the rule is Chief Justice Burger, and during his tenure the Court has somewhat modified the rule's application. In 1974, for example, the Court refused to apply the rule in grand-jury proceedings,[87] and in 1976 the Court held that the rule did not forbid the use, in federal civil proceedings, of evidence improperly seized by state officials acting in good faith.[88] Then, in July 1984 the Court went one step further by allowing the use of improperly seized evidence in criminal cases as long as the police had acted in good faith.

Another controversial due-process issue involves the right to counsel and the Fifth Amendment privilege against self-incrimination. In the *Gideon* case, you recall, the Supreme Court ruled that the right to counsel extends to indigent defendants in noncapital state prosecutions.[89] One year later, in 1964, the Court ruled five-to-four in *Escobedo* v. *Illinois* that a person has the right to consult an attorney as soon as he or she becomes the object of a police investigation.[90] The most controversial case in this area, however, is *Miranda* v. *Arizona*.[91]

Ernesto Miranda was arrested in connection with the kidnapping and rape of an eighteen-year-old girl. Under police questioning, Miranda confessed to the crime, but he was not informed of his constitutional rights to remain silent and to consult an attorney. On appeal, Miranda challenged the use of his confession as a violation of the Fifth Amendment's guarantee against self-incrimination.

In another five-to-four vote, the Supreme Court reversed Miranda's conviction. The Court's majority held that the prosecution may not use a statement against the accused in a court of law unless the authorities observe adequate procedural safeguards to ensure that the statement is obtained "voluntarily, knowingly, and intelligently." Before questioning, the accused must be warned that he has a right to remain silent, that any statement he makes may be used against him, and that he has the right to the presence of an attorney, either retained or appointed.

The immediate reaction to the *Miranda* decision was sharp criticism. Law-enforcement officials complained about having their hands tied. Once again, the critics charged, the Warren Court was releasing criminals on the basis of technicalities, and Richard Nixon attacked the ruling during his law-and-order campaign for the presidency in 1968.

As president, Nixon added to the Court several relatively conservative judges who joined with some of the dissenters from the original decision to chip away at the *Miranda* precedent. This is another example of the relationship between civil-liberties policy and contemporary politics. In a 1971 case, the Court held that the prosecution could use statements that don't meet the *Miranda* standards in cross-examining the accused.[92] The Court has also refused to extend *Miranda* to grand-jury proceedings.[93]

CIVIL-LIBERTIES POLICYMAKING

As we study the case law and the philosophical controversies of civil liberties, it is important to remember that we are also studying the public-policy process. Let's discuss the civil-liberties policy process in terms of the public-policy approach.

AGENDA SETTING

A number of political actors are involved in setting the agenda for civil-liberties policymaking. Interest groups are particularly important. Conservative groups such as the Moral Majority call on government to get tough on pornography and crime. Groups with unpopular views, such as the Nazis and the Ku Klux Klan, initiate public debate on the First Amendment by attempting to march and demonstrate. Meanwhile, many of the civil-liberties disputes reaching the Supreme Court are test cases initiated by interest groups, such as the ACLU and the Jehovah's Witnesses. The latter, for example, have been responsible for more than fifty cases involving religious liberty. They have won 90 percent of them.[94] Also, interest groups ranging from the Chamber of Commerce to B'nai Brith join other civil-liberties cases by means of the *amicus* brief.

Individuals can also raise civil-liberties issues to the public agenda. Many due-process/criminal-justice disputes arise from appeals filed by convicted felons, such as Ernesto Miranda or Clarence Earl Gideon, who aren't so much interested in the great principles of civil liberties as they are in saving their own hides. One individual who does act on the basis of principle, however, is Madalyn Murray O'Hair (formerly Madalyn Murray). She has become famous (or infamous, depending on your point of view) for initiating test cases to challenge what she sees as unconstitutional government support for religion.

For the most part, the views of the general public are too unfocused to set the public agenda on civil liberties in any specific fashion. Public opinion can, however, set some guidelines. It may not have been a coincidence that the liberal era of the Warren Court took place at a time when polls showed increasing public support for civil liberties, even when exercised by unpopular groups.[95] Also, the Burger Court's more conservative approach toward the rights of the criminally accused coincided with a rapidly rising crime rate and increased public concern about crime.

Madalyn Murray and her sons, William J. Murray III, and Garth Murray (center), on the steps of the U.S. Supreme Court, 1963. Mrs. Murray sought a court order discontinuing the use of the Lord's Prayer and the reading of the Bible in the Baltimore schools. On June 17, the Court ruled the prayer requirement unconstitutional, thereby setting off a national debate that continues to this day.

A number of attentive publics can play a direct role in setting the civil-liberties agenda. The Jewish community was important in the Skokie dispute. Many conservative Christians are quite interested in the school-prayer issue. One of the most important attentive publics is the legal profession. As a group, lawyers are well-informed about civil liberties and enjoy a greater access to judicial decisionmakers than most other groups. After all, judges are lawyers too. They read the legal journals and often feel a kinship with other members of the profession.

Government officials also play a role in setting the civil-liberties agenda. For example, the Flag Salute cases came about because a school board in West Virginia decided to require students to recite the pledge of allegiance and refused to make exceptions for Jehovah's Witnesses. Police-officer associations have lobbied Congress and state legislatures to eliminate legal "technicalities," such as the exclusionary rule.

The government officials who have the most influence in civil-liberties agenda setting, however, are judges, particularly the justices on the Supreme Court. As we have seen, the members of the Court essentially set their own agenda, picking and choosing from among the thousands of cases appealed to them. Civil liberties have become the primary agenda items of the modern Supreme Court in large part because the Court's justices have wanted it that way.

POLICY FORMULATION AND ADOPTION

Many civil-liberties policies are formulated and adopted in the courts, ultimately the Supreme Court, but the courts aren't the only political institutions involved. After all, the Supreme Court is a reactive institution. It rules on the validity of the actions of other governmental bodies, and then only when there is a lawsuit before it. The *Miranda* case, for example, involved the procedures of law-enforcement officials and state courts in Arizona. Similar procedures had been fairly standard practice around the country for decades. Public policy dealing with police interrogations and confessions and the use of those confessions in state courts had been set at the state and local levels until the *Miranda* case reached the Supreme Court and a majority of the justices decided to establish a national policy. When we study civil liberties, we spend much of our time examining Supreme Court decisions, but these are only important insofar as they serve as guidelines for the other institutions of government. If we are to understand civil-liberties policy formulation and adoption, we must also study the president, state governors, mayors, Congress, state legislatures, city councils, school boards, school superintendents, chiefs of police, the lower federal courts, and state courts.[96]

POLICY IMPLEMENTATION AND EVALUATION

These "other" units of government are also the ones primarily responsible for the implementation of civil-liberties policies. The Supreme Court can't enforce its own rulings. Consider, for example, the difficulty in enforcing the Court's school-prayer rulings. For years, a public high school in a suburb of Houston, Texas, used a school song that was essentially a prayer set to music. It asked God's blessing and guidance and ended with the phrase, "In Jesus' name we pray. Amen." Despite *Engel* v. *Vitale* and the other Supreme Court decisions, the school was still using its song in the early 1980s. Who was to enforce the Court's rulings? Federal marshals are not assigned to review school songs. Eventually, a federal judge ordered the song's use discontinued but only after several offended parents brought a lawsuit to the federal courts. Had no one objected to the song and, just as importantly, had no one been willing to go to the expense and to endure the public pressure to file a lawsuit, the students in that school would be singing that prayer/song at official school functions today. We suspect that, even as you attend class at your college or university, prayers are being said and sung in many public schools across the nation.[97]

The evaluation of civil-liberties policies is a subject that has received relatively little study. Part of the reason may be the difficulty of conducting such studies and the degree of subjectivity inherent in them. After all, how does one evaluate religious liberty or the constitutional protection from unreasonable searches and seizures? Still, a number of interesting evaluation studies have been made on certain aspects of civil-liberties policy. One study argues that the *Zorach* decision, which involved the issue of religious instruction during school time but off school grounds, had a major effect on attitudes concerning church-state relations.[98] A number of studies suggest that the primary impact of the *Miranda* decision may have been psychological. One study has found that the ruling had little appreciable effect on confessions and convictions.[99] Another observer says that *Miranda* has had no measurable impact on reducing police misconduct.[100]

CONCLUSION: CIVIL LIBERTIES AND POLITICS

Civil-liberties policymaking is political. Many of us entertain the notion that civil-liberties questions are somehow above politics because they involve constitutional law and the courts. That, however, is not the case. First, civil-liberties policymaking involves "political actors" who operate much as they do in economic and regulatory policymaking. Interest groups lobby for their cause. Congress and state legislatures consider civil-liberties legislation as part of their regular legislative processes. Executives at the various levels of the federal system participate as well.

Second, many civil-liberties issues are the focus of political controversy. Issues such as abortion, school prayer, pornography, and the rights of the criminally accused have been major campaign issues in recent elections.

Third, the courts are not apolitical. In chapter 10, you recall, we made the point that the federal courts are both political and legal institutions. Their membership is chosen through the political process of presidential selection and Senate confirmation. Their internal decisionmaking processes at the appellate level reflect bargaining and compromise. The implementation of judicial decisions involves political processes.

Finally, the substance of civil-liberties policies reflects politics: who gets what, when, and how. In the early nineteenth century, for example, the Federalist-controlled Congress passed the Sedition Act to use against political enemies and the Federalist-dominated judiciary vigorously enforced it, despite the Bill of Rights. In the 1930s, the Supreme Court shifted its agenda to focus on civil liberties only after the electoral triumph of New Deal liberalism. Even so, the Supreme Court took time out from its defense of civil liberties to legitimize the government's internment of 120,000 American citizens of Japanese descent in the early part of World War II.[101] The Court said the Japanese-Americans presented a "clear and present danger," but history indicates that the motivations for internment included greed, racism, mass hysteria, and politics—and not primarily a desire to protect national security.

Civil liberties aren't above politics. They depend very much on political factors, specifically the support of government officials and the politically active segment of the population, and, at the least, the acquiescence of the general public. When these factors are absent, as they were in the days of the Sedition Act or the Japanese-American internment, the civil liberties enumerated in the Bill of Rights don't mean much. Civil-liberties policy in America today is shaped by the Constitution and the tradition of freedom in America. But it is also the product of contemporary politics.

KEY TERMS

CIVIL LIBERTIES (363)

CLEAR-AND-PRESENT-DANGER RULE (375)

DOUBLE STANDARD (371)

DUE-PROCESS CLAUSE (369)

EXCLUSIONARY RULE (380)

PREFERRED POSITION (371)

PROCEDURAL DUE PROCESS (380)

SUBSTANTIVE DUE PROCESS (380)

NOTES

1. Carl Cohen, "Right to Be Offensive: Skokie—The Extreme Test," *Nation* (15 April 1978), pp. 422–28.
2. William Safire, *New York Times*, 27 March 1978, p. 19.
3. J. Anthony Lucas, "The ACLU Against Itself," *New York Times Magazine* (9 July 1978), p. 9.
4. George F. Will, "Nazis: Outside the Constitution," *Washington Post*, 2 February 1978, p. A–19.
5. *Village of Skokie* v. *National Socialist Party*, 97 S. Ct. 2205 (1977); 366 N.E. 2d 349 (1977); and 373 N.E. 2d 21 (1978).
6. Quoted in Cohen, p. 423.
7. *West Virginia State Board of Education* v. *Barnette*, 319 U.S. 624 (1943).
8. John Stuart Mill, *On Liberty* (New York: Appleton-Century-Crofts, 1947), originally published 1859.
9. Ibid.
10. *Terminiello* v. *Chicago*, 337 U.S. 1 (1949).
11. *Schenck* v. *United States*, 249 U.S. 47 (1919).
12. Alfred H. Kelly and Winfred A. Harbison, *The American Constitution: Its Origins and Development*, 5th ed. (New York: W. W. Norton, 1976), chs. 6–7; Irving Brandt, *The Bill of Rights* (Indianapolis: Bobbs-Merrill Co., 1965).
13. *Barron* v. *Baltimore*, 7 Peters 243 (1833).
14. Henry J. Abraham, *Freedom and the Courts*, 4th ed. (New York: Oxford University Press, 1982), ch. 3.

15. Slaughterhouse cases, 16 Wallace 36 (1873).
16. *Gitlow* v. *New York,* 268 U.S. 652 (1925).
17. *Near* v. *Minnesota,* 283 U.S. 697 (1931).
18. *Powell* v. *Alabama,* 287 U.S. 45 (1932).
19. *Hamilton* v. *Regents of the University of California,* 293 U.S. 245 (1934).
20. *De Jonge* v. *Oregon,* 299 U.S. 353 (1937).
21. *Everson* v. *Board of Education of Ewing Township,* 330 U.S. 1 (1947).
22. *In re Oliver,* 333 U.S. 257 (1948).
23. *Mapp* v. *Ohio,* 367 U.S. 643 (1961).
24. *Robinson* v. *California,* 370 U.S. 660 (1962).
25. *Gideon* v. *Wainwright,* 372 U.S. 335 (1963).
26. *Malloy* v. *Hogan,* 378 U.S. 1 (1964).
27. *Pointer* v. *Texas,* 380 U.S. 400 (1965).
28. *Parker* v. *Gladden,* 385 U.S. 363 (1966).
29. *Klopfer* v. *North Carolina,* 368 U.S. 213 (1967).
30. *Duncan* v. *Louisiana,* 391 U.S. 145 (1968).
31. *Benton* v. *Maryland,* 392 U.S. 925 (1968).
32. *Griswold* v. *Connecticut,* 381 U.S. 479 (1965).
33. *Roe* v. *Wade,* 410 U.S. 113; and *Doe* v. *Bolton,* 410 U.S. 179, both 1973.
34. *United States* v. *Carolene Products Co.,* 304 U.S. 144 (1938).
35. Robert H. Jackson, *The Struggle for Judicial Supremacy* (New York: Random House, 1941), pp. 284–85, quoted in *The Supreme Court and Individual Rights* (Washington, D.C.: Congressional Quarterly Press, 1980), p. 6.
36. Leo Pfeffer, *God, Caesar and the Constitution: The Court as Referee of Church-State Confrontation* (Boston: Beacon Press, 1974).
37. *Reynolds* v. *United States,* 98 U.S. 145 (1879).
38. *State* v. *Bunn,* 336 U.S. 942 (1949).
39. *Minersville School District* v. *Gobitis,* 310 U.S. 586 (1940), and *West Virginia State Board of Education* v. *Barnette,* 319 U.S. 624 (1943).
40. *Martin* v. *Struthers,* 319 U.S. 141 (1943) and *Jones* v. *Opelika,* 316 U.S. 584 (1942).
41. *Wisconsin* v. *Yoder,* 406 U.S. 205 (1972).
42. *Everson* v. *Board of Education of Ewing Township,* 330 U.S. 1 (1947).
43. *Board of Education* v. *Allen,* 392 U.S. 236 (1968).
44. *Wolman* v. *Walter,* 97 S. Ct. 2593 (1977).
45. *Meek* v. *Pittenger,* 421 U.S. 349 (1975).
46. *Wolman* v. *Walter.*
47. *New York Times,* 30 June 1983, p. 1.
48. *Tilton* v. *Richardson,* 403 U.S. 672 (1971), and *Roemer* v. *Maryland Public Works Board,* 426 U.S. 736 (1976).
49. *Illinois ex rel. McCollum* v. *Board of Education,* 333 U.S. 203 (1948).
50. *Zorach* v. *Clausen,* 343 U.S. 306 (1952).
51. *Walz* v. *Tax Commission of City of New York,* 397 U.S. 664 (1970).
52. *O'Hair* v. *Blumenthal* (1979).

53. *Lewis* v. *Allen*, 379 U.S. 923 (1964).
54. *Engel* v. *Vitale*, 370 U.S. 421 (1962).
55. *Abington School District* v. *Shempp*, and *Murray* v. *Curlett*, 374 U.S. 203 (1963).
56. *Smith* v. *California*, 361 U.S. 147 (1959).
57. *Schenck* v. *United States*, 249 U.S. 47 (1919).
58. Ibid.
59. *Abrams* v. *United States*, 250 U.S. 616 (1919).
60. *Dennis* v. *United States*, 341 U.S. 494 (1951).
61. *Yates* v. *United States*, 354 U.S. 298 (1957).
62. *Tinker* v. *Des Moines Independent Community School District*, 393 U.S. 503 (1969).
63. *New York Times* v. *United States*, 403 U.S. 713 (1971).
64. *Terminiello* v. *Chicago*.
65. *Feiner* v. *New York*, 340 U.S. 315 (1951).
66. *Chaplinsky* v. *New Hampshire*, 315 U.S. 568 (1942).
67. *Gooding* v. *Wilson*, 405 U.S. 518 (1972).
68. *Stromberg* v. *California*, 283 U.S. 359 (1931); *Shelton* v. *Tucker*, 364 U.S. 479 (1960); and *Coates* v. *California*, 402 U.S. 611 (1971).
69. *New York Times*, 14 October 1970, p. 30.
70. *Cohen* v. *California*, 403 U.S. 15 (1971).
71. Abraham, p. 188.
72. *Roth* v. *United States*, and *Alberts* v. *California*, 354 U.S. 476 (1957).
73. *Manual Enterprise* v. *Day*, 370 U.S. 478 (1962).
74. *Jacobellis* v. *Ohio*, 378 U.S. 184 (1964).
75. *Ginzburg* v. *U.S.*, 383 U.S. 463 (1966).
76. *Ginsburg* v. *United States*, 390 U.S. 629 (1968).
77. *New York* v. *Ferber*, 102 S. Ct. 3348 (1982).
78. *Jacobellis* v. *Ohio*.
79. *Miller* v. *California*, 413 U.S. 15 (1973).
80. *Jenkins* v. *Georgia*, 418 U.S. 153 (1974).
81. Abraham, ch. 4; *Palko* v. *Connecticut*, 302 U.S. 319 (1937).
82. *Skinner* v. *Oklahoma*, 316 U.S. 535 (1942).
83. Abraham, ch. 4.
84. *United States* v. *Rabinowitz*, 339 U.S. 56 (1950).
85. *Weeks* v. *United States*, 232 U.S. 383 (1914).
86. *Mapp* v. *Ohio*, 367 U.S. 643 (1961).
87. *United States* v. *Calandra*, 414 U.S. 338 (1974).
88. *United States* v. *Janis*, 428 U.S. 433 (1976).
89. *Gideon* v. *Wainwright*.
90. *Escobedo* v. *Illinois*, 378 U.S. 478 (1964).
91. *Miranda* v. *Arizona*, 384 U.S. 436 (1966).
92. *Harris* v. *New York*, 401 U.S. 222 (1971).
93. *United States* v. *Mandujano*, 425 U.S. 564 (1976).
94. Abraham, p. 236.

95. David G. Lawrence, "Procedural Norms and Tolerance: A Reassessment," *American Political Science Review* 70(March 1976): 80–100.

96. Lucius J. Barker and Turley W. Barker, Jr., *Civil Liberties and the Constitution* (Englewood Cliffs: Prentice-Hall, 1978).

97. H. Frank Way, Jr., "Survey Research on Judicial Decisions: The Prayer and Bible Reading Cases," *Western Political Quarterly* 21(June 1968): 189–205.

98. Frank J. Sorauf, "*Zorach* v. *Clausen*: The Impact of a Supreme Court Decision," *American Political Science Review* 53(September 1959): 777–91.

99. Otis H. Stephens, Jr. *The Supreme Court and Confessions of Guilt* (Knoxville: The University of Tennessee Press, 1973).

100. Donald L. Horowitz, *The Courts and Social Policy* (Washington, D.C.: Brookings Institution, 1977), p. 223.

101. *Korematsu* v. *United States*, 323 U.S. 214 (1944).

SUGGESTED READINGS

ABRAHAM, HENRY J. *Freedom and the Courts.* 4th ed. New York: Oxford University Press, 1982.

BARKER, LUCIUS J., AND BARKER, TURLEY W., JR. *Civil Liberties and the Constitution.* Englewood Cliffs, N.J.: Prentice-Hall, 1978.

BERNS, WALTER. *The First Amendment and the Future of American Democracy.* New York: Basic Books, 1976.

CASPER, JONATHAN. *The Politics of Civil Liberties.* New York: Basic Books, 1976.

HOROWITZ, DONALD L. *The Courts and Social Policy.* Washington, D.C.: Brookings Institution, 1977.

O'BRIEN, DAVID M. *Privacy, Law, and Public Policy.* New York: Praeger, 1979.

SHAPIRO, MARTIN. *Freedom of Speech: The Supreme Court and Judicial Review.* Englewood Cliffs, N.J.: Prentice-Hall, 1966.

SIGLER, JAY A. *American Rights Policies.* Homewood, Ill.: Dorsey, 1975.

Chapter Fourteen

MINORITIES AND WOMEN

Chicago is a town known for its politics. For years, Mayor Richard J. Daley ran Chicago as the boss of the last of the big-city Democratic political machines. The machine always delivered, even if the graveyard voted and ballot boxes sometimes mysteriously disappeared the day after the election.

But the 1983 mayoralty election was extraordinary, even by Chicago standards. First, the turnout was huge, almost 80 percent of the registered voters. Coming in an age when participation in *presidential* elections barely exceeds 50 percent, this is remarkable. Second, the Republican candidate, Bernard Epton, was a serious contender. Chicago last elected a Republican in 1927, and a Republican had not even run a close race in decades. Finally, the machine lost. Since the death of Boss Daley in 1976, the machine had grown rusty, and this year the mayor's son and heir apparent, Richie Daley, lost in the Democratic primary.

The man directly or indirectly responsible for each of these developments was Harold Washington, a two-term congressman who won the Democratic primary, defeating both Daley and incumbent Mayor Jane Byrne. Harold Washington is black. He won the primary because Daley and Byrne split the white vote while he received the support of Chicago's blacks, who make up about 40 percent of the Chicago population. That left him to face Republican Epton, a former state representative whom no one had given any chance of winning the mayor's job—at least not until Washington became the Democratic nominee.

The single, overwhelming issue in the election was race. There could have been other issues. As with most big cities, Chicago has problems, not the least of which is a severe financial crisis. And neither Washington nor Epton is a model of civic virtue and statesmanship. Washington once spent a few weeks in jail for failing to file income-tax returns and has a history of neglecting to pay his bills. Epton isn't much better. One newspaper columnist described him as "volatile and capricious, prone to inexplicable outbursts and fits of righteous indignation."[1] In any other year, these matters would have dominated the campaign, but not this year. The only issue that seemed to matter was that Washington was black and Epton white.

Both candidates said that race should not be an issue, but both tried to use race to their own advantage. When Washington announced his candidacy in November 1982, he made a racial appeal: "We've been giving white candidates our votes for years. . . . Now . . . it's our turn."[2] Then, after Washington won the Democratic primary, his supporters said, "We want it all."[3] Meanwhile, Epton's campaign sought to capitalize on white fears. "Epton now," his ads proclaimed, "before it's too late."

The campaign itself was a study in black and white. Some of the white Democratic ward bosses endorsed Epton while others remained neutral or gave Washington only lukewarm support. Some white Chicagoans wore campaign buttons showing a watermelon with a black slash across it. Others wore t-shirts proclaiming "Vote Right, Vote White." Then there was an ugly incident when Washington and former Vice-President Walter Mon-

Chicago mayoral candidates Harold Washington (left) and Bernard Epton (right) square off in a tele-vised debate in 1983. The Chicago election dramatized the impor-tance of minority politics in today's po-litical environment.

dale were driven from a white neighborhood by an angry crowd shouting racial epithets.[4]

The voting, too, was very much along racial lines. Washington carried the city's black wards with more than 95 percent of the vote, winning the Twenty-fourth Ward, for example, by 24,259 votes to 129 for Epton. In many white neighborhoods, Epton won victories almost as lopsided. The election was decided in the affluent white wards along the lakefront. There Washington got about 40 percent of the vote. Along with a majority of the Hispanic vote, that proved enough to provide Washington with a 51.8 percent majority.[5]

The Chicago mayoralty election illustrates some important points about minority politics in the 1980s. First, political issues involving the status of minorities and women are often quite controversial. The Chicago story illustrates that race is still a gut-wrenching issue, even in the mid-1980s.

Second, the Chicago election shows the potential power of minority voters, particularly in urban areas where they are a sizable voting bloc. Washington's political success was based on near-unanimous support among black voters and a good showing among Hispanics.

Third, Washington's election demonstrates that minorities usually need some support from white voters and white officeholders if they are to achieve their policy goals. Washington would not have won without the 18 percent of the white vote he received. Certainly, he would need white cooperation to be an effective mayor.

Finally, the Chicago election illustrates that minority politics is frequently imbedded in other political conflicts. Harold Washington was an outsider challenging Chicago's political establishment. Many of the forces that opposed him would have done so had he been white. Race was important, but it wasn't the only political factor involved in the election contest.

We will begin our study of the politics of minorities and women with an overview of the various equal-rights movements in America.

EQUAL-RIGHTS MOVEMENTS IN AMERICA

America's history is laced with accounts of ethnic, racial, and social groups struggling for equality. The black civil-rights movement has been the most prominent. Women aren't a numerical minority, of course, but they have had to fight long and hard for equal status with men. Two other groups, American Indians and Hispanics, have a long history in America, but their search for equality has only recently been "discovered" by the media. In recent years, several other groups have begun equal-rights campaigns, including Asian Americans, the elderly, the disabled, and gay people.

Each equal-rights movement is unique, but we can identify four broad, general stages of development that seem to apply to the various move-ments. The first stage is one of acceptance and adaptation to unequal treatment. Instead of working to secure equality, group members seem resigned to their fate and concentrate on adapting to the status quo. In the second stage, members of the group become increasingly sensitive to their second-class status and begin organizing to promote group goals. The third stage is marked by an active, aggressive equal-rights movement, emphasizing group unity and pride. Tactics may range from litigation to traditional election-oriented politics to militant protest, perhaps including violence. In the fourth stage, the group has won general recognition as a legitimate participant in social, economic, and political life. This doesn't mean that all of the group's goals have been achieved, but that it can go about pursuing them through conventional interest-group politics. Let's see how some of the more prominent equal-rights movements in America have fit this general pattern.

BLACKS

Until the middle of the nineteenth century, the fate of blacks in America was determined by others—slave traders, slave owners, state governments, and the federal government. During Reconstruction, however, Congress acted to abolish slavery and elevate blacks to full American citizenship. The Thirteenth Amendment ended slavery; the Fourteenth granted citizenship to blacks and guaranteed equal protection under state laws. The Fifteenth Amendment granted the freedmen the right to vote. What's more, Congress passed four civil-rights laws to enforce the provisions of the amendments.

This Currier and Ives print from the Reconstruction era shows some of the first black legislators to serve in the U.S. Congress. From left to right: Senator H. R. Revels, Mississippi; Representatives B. S. Turner, Alabama; Robert C. DeLarge, South Carolina; J. T. Wells, Florida; J. H. Long, Georgia; J. H. Rainey and R. B. Elliott, South Carolina.

Blacks responded by participating in Reconstruction-era politics in the South. The records are sketchy, but as many as 700,000 blacks may have registered to vote during Reconstruction. Also, blacks were elected to office. During Reconstruction, blacks held fourteen seats in the U.S. House, several Senate seats, and many seats in state legislatures.[6]

In 1877, however, federal troops were withdrawn from the South, and Reconstruction ended. White supremacy once again became the rule in southern political, economic, and social affairs. By the end of the century, southern blacks had been effectively deprived of the right to vote and to participate meaningfully in the political process, despite the Fifteenth Amendment. They were also segregated by law—in schools, rail cars, courts, libraries, parks, restrooms, water fountains, theaters, hotels, hospitals, ballparks, insane asylums, and cemeteries. New Orleans segregated prostitutes. Birmingham made it illegal for blacks and whites to play dominoes together. Interracial marriage was outlawed everywhere in the South.[7]

Booker T. Washington offered one kind of black response to the situation of the late nineteenth and early twentieth centuries. He counseled blacks to accept segregation and disenfranchisement. After all, there was really no other choice in the short run. Instead, he urged his black brethren to concentrate on vocational training to learn the skills necessary for the jobs open to them.

Not all blacks accepted Washington's conciliatory and gradualist philosophy. W. E. B. DuBois spoke out against disenfranchisement and segregation. In particular, he supported the idea of a liberal arts education for bright young blacks, the "talented tenth," as he put it, who could then uplift their brethren. In 1910, DuBois and a group of other black leaders and liberal whites founded the National Association for the Advancement of Colored People (NAACP) to further black interests.

Two important sociological developments in the first half of the twentieth century were to have a profound impact on the black civil-rights movement. The first was the great migration of blacks from the rural South to the big cities of the North. In the North blacks found better job and educational opportunities and the right to vote. With voting rights would come political influence. The second important development was the experience of millions of blacks in the armed forces during World Wars I and II. In the military, blacks gained skills, confidence, and pride. They came home far less willing to accept discrimination than when they left.[8]

The 1950s and '60s were the heyday of the black civil-rights movement. Hundreds of thousands of blacks and sympathetic whites joined together to attack discrimination on a number of fronts. The NAACP continued its assault on legal discrimination in the courts, while other organizations, including the Urban League, the Southern Christian Leadership Conference (SCLC), the Congress of Racial Equality (CORE), and the Student Nonviolent Coordinating Committee (SNCC), organized mass demonstrations, sit-ins, and boycotts to protest discrimination. Black leaders, es-

Rev. Jesse Jackson, speaking to the 1984 national Democratic convention. The first black candidate to run a serious national campaign for the presidency, Jackson brought a charismatic oratorical style to the hustings. The consequent heavy media coverage sparked a successful drive to register thousands of new black voters.

pecially Dr. Martin Luther King, Jr., spoke eloquently of shared dreams of brotherhood and justice, and stirred the conscience of the nation.

By the mid-1960s, blacks had achieved many of their political goals, but full equality was still far off for the millions of black Americans living in poverty. At times, black frustrations erupted into violence as riots broke out in several cities during the middle and late 1960s. Some black leaders, such as H. Rap Brown, went beyond talk of black pride to embrace the militant rhetoric of black power, while groups such as the Black Panthers promoted the idea of black separatism.

Today, the black civil-rights movement seems to be in a period of transition. Legal and political battles have been won against the most blatant forms of discrimination, but the war for equality is far from finished. As the 1983 mayoralty election in Chicago demonstrates, many Americans are not yet colorblind. On the other hand, black electoral turnout in Chicago and in the 1982 congressional elections was up significantly. In 1984, the presidential candidacy of Jesse Jackson spurred thousands of blacks to participate in politics for the first time. Perhaps we are on the threshold of a new season of black political activism.

WOMEN

Women in early America were to be seen but not heard. Under the common-law tradition of Britain and then America, women were accorded few legal rights, and were classified with children and imbeciles. A married woman surrendered what few rights she did possess to her husband. In the eyes of the law, she was little more than his personal property.

The women's movement began as a by-product of the abolitionist movement. It was acceptable for women in early America to become involved in religious and moral issues, so it was natural for many women to enlist in the struggle to abolish slavery. While working against slavery, women such as Lucretia Mott, Susan B. Anthony, and the Grimké sisters—Sarah and Angelina—began to recognize the inferiority of their own status. The catalyst was the World Anti-Slavery Convention, convened in London in 1840, which voted to exclude women as delegates. The American women were forced to sit in the balcony behind a partition.

In 1848, the women's-rights movement officially began with the convocation of the Women's Rights Convention in Seneca Falls, New York. The delegates there adopted a "Declaration of Rights and Sentiments" that proclaimed women's right to own property, to obtain a divorce, to enjoy access to educational and professional opportunities, and to vote. As it turned out, the early movement focused almost exclusively on the last of these goals. When women's suffrage was finally achieved in 1920 with the ratification of the Nineteenth Amendment, many women believed that the struggle had been won.[9]

But not everyone agreed. Some women's-rights advocates pointed out that discriminatory legislation remained in force in many states, covering such areas as labor, divorce, juror qualifications, property, and inheritance. In 1923 they proposed an equal-rights amendment to the Constitution that would wipe out discriminatory legislation, making men and women equal in the eyes of the law.[10]

Nonetheless, the women's movement did not become a serious political force again until the 1960s, after some important sociological changes had been wrought by the Second World War. With their husbands and brothers in the military, millions of women entered the work force to help build America's war machine. At work, "Rosie the Riveter" not only helped win the war, she also gained confidence, skill, and self-fulfillment. When the men came back from the war, women returned to the home, but many did not stay there. After the baby-boom generation was born and started in school, women returned to the work force. In 1947, some 32 percent of American adult women worked outside the home. The figure was 38 percent in 1962, 44 percent in 1972, and 50 percent in 1978.[11]

The beginning of the modern women's movement came in 1963 with the publication of *The Feminine Mystique* by Betty Friedan.[12] Millions of American women identified with Friedan's description of the lack of fulfillment experienced by contemporary women and found in the book's pages the incentive to change their own lives and work to change the society in which they lived. In 1966, Friedan founded the National Organization for Women (NOW), and soon other organizations, including the National Women's Political Caucus,[13] began to appear.

The modern women's movement embraced a broad set of goals aimed at securing political, economic, and social equality for women. It was the **Equal Rights Amendment** (ERA), however, that became the central focus of the movement. It was a short and simple statement, and read as follows:

The war effort of the 1940s brought forth numbers of "Rosie the Riveter," who were called upon to take over many of the jobs the men had left behind. Since World War II, the number of women in the work-place has steadily increased.

"Equality of rights under the law shall not be denied or abridged by the United States or any state on account of sex." Congress proposed the ERA in 1972 and sent it to the states where it won quick ratification in many areas. Momentum slowed, however, as conservative opposition mounted, led, ironically, by many women, most notably by Phyllis Schlafly of Illinois. Women's groups were forced to go back to Congress to ask for an extension of the deadline. Congress did extend the deadline for three additional years, but it was all to no avail. The time limit passed and the ERA failed, three states short of the three-fourths majority needed for ratification. In 1983, the amendment was reintroduced in Congress to begin the long process once again.

Today, the ERA is far from adoption, working women still earn only about two thirds of what their male counterparts make; and the movement lacks the freshness and enthusiasm it had during the 1960s and '70s. Nevertheless, the women's movement has not failed and is not dead. Many of the social and legal barriers to women's employment opportunities have been toppled, and women are more involved in politics now than ever before.[14] In 1984 women took a major step forward with the selection of Representative Geraldine Ferraro to run for vice-president on the Democratic ticket. The so-called "gender gap" provides evidence that women are beginning to vote as a bloc for the first time.

MEXICAN AMERICANS

Mexican Americans have long had a problem gaining recognition as a disadvantaged minority group. In 1969, a bill was introduced in the U.S. House of Representatives with the heading, "Establish an Inter-Agency

Committee on Mexican American Affairs." Some months later the bill's sponsors thought it had vanished. They finally located it, in the Foreign Affairs Committee, to which it had been mistakenly referred by Speaker John McCormack of Massachusetts.[15]

Many people living outside the southwestern United States may not be particularly aware of them, but large numbers of Mexican Americans have lived in this country since the annexation of Texas and the Treaty of Guadalupe Hidalgo. As a group, they have never been as poor as blacks, but their position has always been clearly inferior to that of the white majority. In most areas of the Southwest, Mexican Americans have been informally segregated and accorded inferior educational and job opportunities. They have been denied the opportunity effectively to participate in politics everywhere except in New Mexico.

The initial response of Mexican Americans to their second-rate status was to adapt and try to prove themselves good Americans. Their attitude was symbolized in the name of one of the earliest Mexican American organizations, the League of United Latin American Citizens (LULAC), founded in 1929. The founders used the term *Latin American* instead of *Mexican American* because of the perceived negative connotations of the latter name. Also, note the inclusion of the word *citizen*.

As with other minority groups, World War II played an important role in politicizing the Mexican American community. The war meant better jobs and better opportunities. After the war, Mexican Americans who had fought for their country were unwilling again to be relegated to an inferior status. They formed a number of organizations to defend their cause, including the American GI Forum, the Political Association of Spanish-Speaking Organizations (PASO), and the Mexican American Political Association (MAPO). These organizations used tactics such as electoral politics and litigation.

In the 1960s, the Mexican American equal-rights movement turned more militant with the emergence of the *Chicano* movement. Chicanos emphasized ethnic unity and pride, reaching out to make common cause with other Hispanic Americans such as Cubans in South Florida and Puerto Ricans in the cities of the Northeast. The Chicano movement's leaders included Cesar Chavez, who organized farm workers in California, and José Angel Gutiérrez in Texas, who founded a third-party political movement, La Raza Unida ("the race united").

Today, the more militant aspects of the Chicano movement seem to have passed. Cesar Chavez is out of the headlines and La Raza Unida is moribund. As with other equal-rights causes, the Mexican American movement seems to be in transition between the militancy of the 1960s and early '70s and whatever is to come.[16]

There are some signs, however, that Mexican Americans are beginning to establish themselves in some areas as legitimate, influential participants in the political process. Traditionally, Mexican Americans have been closely allied with the Democratic party. The identification has been so close, in fact, that some Chicano leaders charge Democrats with taking Mexican American votes for granted. In 1980, however, the Republican presidential ticket concentrated harder on winning Mexican American votes than Republicans have ever done in the past, and with some success. Mexican Americans may now find themselves in the enviable position of being wooed by both major parties.

A second major development has taken place at the local level, in San Antonio, Texas. San Antonio is a big city with a Mexican American majority that had long been governed by Anglos. In 1981, however, the city elected its first Mexican American mayor, Henry Cisneros. So far, at least, the results seem very positive. Mexican Americans are more involved in city politics than ever before, but not at the expense of alienating the city's other ethnic groups or the business community.

Finally, Mexican American voting power is on the rise. In Texas, for example, 590,000 Mexican Americans were registered to vote in 1978. By 1982, that number had grown to 830,000—a 41-percent increase in four years. Moreover, the potential for increasing Mexican American voting power remains considerable as hundreds of thousands of Mexican American adults are still unregistered.[17]

AMERICAN INDIANS

Since their conquest by the United States cavalry, American Indians have been at the mercy of the federal government. At times, federal policy has been well-meaning, albeit paternalistic; at other times it has been indifferent or avaricious. Treaties granted Indians reservation land, but it was invariably dusty, barren land no white settler would want. When minerals were discovered on reservation land, ways were devised to separate the Indians from their land. For example, the General Allotment Act of 1887 provided for the division of reservation land into individual parcels. Many Indians sold their shares or were swindled out of them, and vast amounts of Indian land were lost forever, including most reservation property in oil-rich Oklahoma. Between 1887 and 1934, when the program ended, Indian lands shrank from 139 million acres to 48 million acres.[18]

Indians living on the reservation have been the recipients of federal largess, but they have also had to pay a considerable price. The federal government provides social services, welfare, education, and health care to reservation Indians, and grants direct subsidies to tribal governments. Historically, however, Indians have had little to say about how these services are administered. Indian children have often been sent hundreds of miles from their homes and forbidden to speak their native tongue to encourage assimilation into white society. Tribal governments haven't even been allowed to manage their own lands. For years, the Bureau of Indian Affairs (BIA) negotiated mineral contracts with companies wanting to

Henry Cisneros, Hispanic mayor of San Antonio, Texas.

The militancy of certain American Indian groups was demonstrated in 1969, when a party of 250 Indians seized control of the abandoned prison on Alcatraz in San Francisco Bay. The Indians ultimately made a peaceful exit from the island, escorted by federal marshals.

develop Indian lands. (The government was afraid that the simple Indian would be an easy mark for fast-talking developers.) Unfortunately for the Indians, the BIA neglected to put escalation or termination clauses in the contracts. Consequently, today Indian coal often sells for as little as 15¢ a ton while the going price is about ten times higher.[19]

What's more, the life of many American Indians today is poor, nasty, brutish, and short. Suicide, alcoholism, and unemployment rates are higher for Indians than for any other ethnic group in America. Unemployment on the reservation ranges between 40 and 80 percent, and the average per capita income is only about $1000 a year. Indians who have left the reservation are little better off, crowded into red ghettos in Minneapolis, Chicago, Los Angeles, and other cities.

During the 1960s and '70s, Indians began to organize to assert their rights. Militant groups such as AIM, the American Indian Movement, received considerable publicity for occupying Alcatraz Island and BIA offices in Washington, D.C., and for provoking a violent confrontation with federal marshals at Wounded Knee, South Dakota. These events gained attention, but on the whole Indians have been more successful in the courtroom. In 1974, a federal judge ruled that an old treaty entitled Indians to half the West Coast salmon catch. Then, in 1975, federal courts upheld tribal claims to the northern two thirds of Maine.[20]

In general, however, Indian efforts have been severely hampered by political weakness and internal divisions. Indians are too few and too disorganized to be politically influential. Also, Indians are divided by ancient tribal rivalries and by disagreements about the basic goals of any Indian-rights movement. Some Indians believe that the future lies in the development of the vast coal, uranium, and oil deposits located on reservation land. Groups such as CERT, the Council of Energy Resources Tribes, want to turn these resources into economic power. Other Indians, however, are more concerned with preserving their traditional way of life. They regard plans for developing reservation mineral resources as a blueprint for "spiritual and physical genocide."

ISSUES AND POLICY

Women and minority groups share many concerns about public policy, but four broad areas of interest loom largest; equality before the law, the right to participate and be represented in the political process, freedom from discrimination, and economic equality. Let's examine each of these four areas, focusing on the development of public policy in each.

EQUALITY BEFORE THE LAW

Minorities and women demand equality before the law. They want the law and the judicial system to deal with them as it deals with others, without brutality and without bias. They want to be taxed fairly and, in turn, to receive their fair share of public services.

The Constitution guarantees equal protection under the law in the Fourteenth Amendment, ratified in 1868. "No State," it says, "shall . . . deny to any person within its jurisdiction the equal protection of the laws." But, as Chief Justice Charles Evans Hughes once said, the Constitution only means what the Supreme Court says it does. In the latter part of the nineteenth century, a number of states, particularly in the South, enacted statutes called **Jim Crow laws** requiring rigid legal racial separation in most aspects of life. Everything was segregated, went an old saying, except the highways. Nevertheless, the justices on the United States Supreme Court did not find this in conflict with the equal-protection clause.

The key case was *Plessy* v. *Ferguson*, decided in 1896. Homer Plessy challenged a Louisiana law that required "equal but separate" accommodations for black and white railway passengers. The Court ruled that the law was constitutional as long as the black passengers were furnished accommodations equal to those of whites. **"Separate but equal,"** said the Court, was sufficient to satisfy the Constitution. In lone dissent, Justice John Marshall Harlan eloquently called the decision "a compound of bad logic, bad history, bad sociology, and bad constitutional law. . . . Our Constitution is color-blind," he said, "and neither knows nor tolerates classes among citizens."[21]

Subsequently, the Court demonstrated that its definition of "equal" was a broad one indeed. In 1899 it held that the separate-but-equal doctrine did not require a county to provide a high school for "colored children" even though there was one for whites.[22] In another case, the Court allowed a Mississippi school district to require a girl of Chinese descent to attend a black school in a neighboring district rather than a nearby "whites only" school.[23]

American society was changing, however, and eventually the Supreme Court responded. In 1938 it began chipping away at the *Plessy* precedent in the *Gaines* case, one of a long line of test cases argued by the NAACP. Gaines, a black citizen of Missouri, had been denied admission to the University of Missouri law school. The state offered, however, to pay his tuition at a law school in a neighboring state, a school that would admit blacks. Gaines sued, charging that this arrangement violated the equal-protection clause, and the Court agreed. Separate-but-equal had to be in the same state.[24]

The Supreme Court further undermined the *Plessy* decision in two important cases decided in 1950. In *Sweatt* v. *Painter*, the Court ruled that Texas' hasty creation of a black law school did not satisfy the constitutional criterion of equal protection.[25] Then, in *McLaurin* v. *Oklahoma State Regents* the Court ruled against segregation within an institution. McLaurin, a black, was admitted to graduate school at the University of Oklahoma, but he was forced to sit in a particular row, study in a particular carrel, and eat at a particular table in the cafeteria. All of these facilities were labeled

"Reserved for Colored." The Court ordered that McLaurin be treated as other students.[26]

In 1954, the Court took the final step, unanimously overturning *Plessy* in the great case of *Brown* v. *Board of Education of Topeka*. The Court ruled that segregation denies to blacks equal educational opportunity. "Segregation of white and colored children in public schools has a detrimental effect upon the colored children," wrote Chief Justice Warren. "A sense of inferiority affects the motivation of a child to learn." In essence, the Court was now saying that separate-but-equal is a contradiction in terms. Once the law requires racial separation, it stamps the badge of inferiority on the minority race; separate therefore is inherently unequal.[27]

It is difficult to think of a more important judicial ruling in this century than the *Brown* decision, but the Court's opinion left two important questions unresolved. One involved the distinction between **de jure** and **de facto segregation.** *De jure* means segregation *by law*. In *Brown*, the Court ruled *de jure* segregation unconstitutional. But how about *de facto* segregation, which is caused not by force of law but because of housing or other unofficial patterns? The *Brown* decision failed to address that question.

Before the Brown v. Board of Education *decision,* de jure *segregation, supported by a host of overtly segregationist customs and traditions, was the norm throughout the South.*

IMPERIAL LAUNDRY CO.

WE WASH FOR WHITE PEOPLE ONLY

PRIVATE
M W WHITE

The other problem was implementation. How was desegregation to be achieved and at what pace? The Court delayed its implementation order until 1955. Then it ordered the lower federal courts to oversee the transition to a nondiscriminatory system "with all deliberate speed."[28]

Implementation proved far more deliberate than speedy. There was some progress in the border states, but in the South the Court's ruling was met by delay, evasion, defiance, and massive resistance. Alabama Governor George Wallace spoke for many white southerners: "I say segregation now, segregation tomorrow, segregation forever."[29]

The Supreme Court had gone too far beyond public opinion and the other branches of the federal government for its decision to be enforced. Congress did nothing. President Eisenhower stood silent. Only in 1957 did the president display a willingness to enforce the *Brown* ruling when he ordered federal troops into Little Rock, Arkansas, to enforce school desegregation against a stubborn Governor Orval Faubus and an angry mob. For years the *Brown* ruling was only a hollow victory for civil-rights forces. In 1964 only 68,850 black pupils out of 2,988,264 (2.1 percent) were enrolled in public schools with any whites in the eleven states of the old Confederacy.[30]

Then the nation began to catch up with the Court on the issue of black civil rights. Black protest demonstrations, vividly displayed on the television evening news, moved public opinion to support the cause. Presidents Kennedy and Johnson called for action, and Congress responded with the Civil Rights Act of 1964. Title VI of the act authorized the Department of Health, Education, and Welfare (HEW) to cut off federal assistance to school districts practicing segregation. HEW set guidelines, and some tentative progress was made.

In 1969, the Supreme Court stepped in to speed up the process. It ruled an end to "all deliberate speed" and ordered immediate desegregation.[31] This also meant, however, that the Court had to deal with other questions left unresolved by the original *Brown* case. How could integration be achieved? In *Swann* v. *Charlotte-Mecklenburg Board of Education,* decided in 1971, the court unanimously ruled that busing, racial quotas, pairing or grouping schools, and gerrymandering of attendance zones could all be used to eliminate the vestiges of state-supported segregation.[32] Then, in 1973 the Court expanded the definition of *de jure* segregation in the Keyes case. It ordered the integration of Denver schools not because they had been segregated by law, but because they had been segregated by policies. The local board, it seems, had manipulated attendance zones to produce segregation.[33]

Both of these decisions were quite controversial. One carried integration to the white suburbs; the other brought it north. Members of Congress from the North who had supported efforts to integrate southern schools now introduced resolutions to ban busing.

What's the status of school integration today? In the South, many black children attend school with whites, and official opposition to integration seems ended. In 1973, for example, Governor Wallace crowned a black homecoming queen at the University of Alabama. Not all attitudes have changed, however, and segregation often remains in practice. In fact, in many parts of the South a creeping "resegregation" has occurred. Many white students have enrolled in private academies, leaving the public schools nearly all black. Meanwhile, whites have maintained control of school boards and have worked to keep school taxes low. Consequently, the old southern system in which many black students attended separate, poorly financed schools has been recreated in many areas.[34]

In the North, controversy still rages. Because of housing patterns, integration often cannot be achieved without busing, and busing is highly controversial. It often leads to "white flight" to more distant suburbs and to private schools. In many instances, black children are the only ones bused, and little integration is achieved. The Detroit school system is now 82 percent black, for example. The Washington, D.C., system is 96 percent black.[35]

Nationally, the proponents of school integration find themselves on the defensive. In the Congress, civil-rights advocates have had to filibuster to try to defeat antibusing legislation. Moreover, in 1982 the U.S. Commission on Civil Rights issued a report denouncing the Reagan Administration's education policies, charging that they could mean a return to "separate and unequal" education for whites and blacks (see the **PERSPECTIVE** on page 405).

The desegregation of other public facilities has come about more smoothly and has been achieved more completely than school integration. In the late 1950s and early 1960s, segregated facilities were the targets of innumerable civil-rights protests and demonstrations in the South. For example, blacks would sit at a segregated dimestore lunch counter and refuse to leave until served. The police would then arrest the protesters, charging them with disturbing the peace or breaking the local Jim Crow ordinance. With NAACP assistance, the blacks would appeal the convictions, which would then be overturned by a federal court. This case-by-case approach succeeded in desegregating many public facilities, but it was slow and expensive.

The big breakthrough in desegregation came with the 1964 Civil Rights Act. Title II of the act outlawed discrimination based on race, religion, color, or national origin in hotels, restaurants, gas stations, and all other public accommodations that affect interstate commerce. In practice, the act has proved quite successful. For one thing, the courts have interpreted it broadly.[36] More importantly, however, business people have found it profitable to comply. People spend money regardless of race.

Blacks are not the only group demanding equal protection of the laws. After all, this is the demand that stands behind the proposed Equal Rights Amendment. The ERA was defeated, but the Supreme Court has recently demonstrated a willingness to apply the Fourteenth Amendment's equal-protection clause to women's issues. In 1973, for example, the Court declared unconstitutional a federal law requiring a different standard for spousal benefits for male and female service personnel.[37] Similarly, the Court has held that a state may not exclude women from jury duty.[38] The Court has applied equal protection to other groups as well. In 1982, for

Perspective

THE U.S. COMMISSION ON CIVIL RIGHTS AND THE REAGAN ADMINISTRATION

The United States Commission on Civil Rights was created in 1957 to monitor government enforcement of civil rights. Although the commission lacked the power either to make or enforce policy, it could conduct research on civil-rights issues and release reports. On many occasions, these reports called the nation's attention to particular civil-rights issues. Consequently, the commission played an important role in agenda setting.

From the beginning, the Civil Rights Commission was controlled by forces sympathetic to minority rights. Presidents from Eisenhower through Carter named liberals to the commission. In the eyes of many, the commission was the "national conscience" for civil rights.

In the early 1980s, however, the commission clashed with the Reagan Administration over civil-rights policy. Ronald Reagan came to the White House opposed to busing for purposes of school integration, opposed to hiring quotas for women and minorities, opposed to affirma-

tive action, and opposed to the ERA. The reaction of the Civil Rights Commission was to publish reports critical of administration policy. In response, Reagan fired several of the commission's more outspoken members. The firing touched off an uproar among certain members of Congress and among civil-rights advocates, who accused the president of trying to "politicize" the commission. Eventually, Congress and the White House reached a compromise. Congress and the president would appoint four commission members apiece, and the president would name the staff director.

By early 1984, however, it had become apparent that the compromise was really a victory for the White House. The new commission embarked on a new course, one much more akin to the Reagan philosophy. Under the leadership of Linda Chavez, the staff director appointed by Reagan, the commission decided not to release a study completed by the old commission showing that blacks in Alabama earned less than whites, were less well-

educated, and lived in poorer housing. This was no proof of discrimination, said Chavez. The commission canceled another study designed to measure the effect on minorities of the Reagan cuts in student aid. Meanwhile, the commission began a study to determine how affirmative action in higher education may have contributed to the "general decline in academic standards."

Today, the Commission on Civil Rights is the focus of debate over the course of civil-rights policy. Civil-rights advocates argue that the new commission is trying to turn back the clock on civil rights. Ms. Chavez replies that the commission is trying a new approach because old approaches have failed. "The problems facing minorities today," she says, "cannot be solved by civil-rights laws. Social problems like high unemployment, low educational attainment, a high rate of out-of-wedlock births are problems that are not amenable to solution by civil-rights laws or the Civil Rights Commission."[1]

[1] *Washington Post*, National Weekly Edition, 23 January 1984, p. 29.

example, the Supreme Court ruled that the equal-protection clause entitled the children of illegal aliens to a free public education.[39]

RIGHTS OF PARTICIPATION

Women and minorities want the opportunity to participate freely in politics and to be represented in elective and appointive office. Blacks won the constitutional right to vote with the passage of the Fifteenth Amendment, but after Reconstruction southern white authorities adopted a fiendishly clever array of devices for preventing them from exercising their right. These included literacy and understanding tests, and vouchers of good character. Poor persons of all races were discouraged from registering by **poll taxes** (taxes levied on the right to vote), and some southern states adopted **"white primary"** laws. These latter meant that only whites could vote in the Democratic primary, which, in the one-party South, was the only election that really mattered. If all else failed, local authorities could resort to out-and-out violence and intimidation to keep blacks from the polls. And they succeeded. As late as 1948, only 12 percent of voting-age blacks in the South were registered.[40]

The first assaults against disenfranchisement came in the courts. In 1915, the U.S. Supreme Court overturned Oklahoma's **"grandfather clause"** that allowed whites to escape literacy tests but not blacks. The clause required all prospective voters in Oklahoma to pass literacy tests, except those whose grandfathers had been eligible to vote in 1860. Consequently, whites could escape the test but not blacks.[41] Also, the Court eventually invalidated the white primary.[42] None of this led to significant increases in black political participation, however. That would require action from Congress and the executive.

Congress began responding to black demands for access to the ballot box in the late 1950s. The Civil Rights Act of 1957 empowered the attorney general to seek court injunctions against actions obstructing or depriving blacks of their right to vote. The act proved ineffective, however, because the Justice Department lacked sufficient manpower. Only three cases were filed. In 1960 another civil-rights bill authorized federal judges to appoint referees to oversee black voter registration. This, too, was too slow to have much effect. The 1964 Civil Rights Act specifically forbad the rejection of registrants for minor, immaterial errors on registration forms and required that a sixth-grade education be accepted as proof of literacy. The cumulative effect of these laws was that many blacks, especially in the border states, registered to vote.

The most important federal action in knocking down voting barriers, however, was the 1965 Voting Rights Act. In states and counties where voter participation was low (primarily in the South), the act prohibited all qualifications for voting except age, residence, and criminal record. It provided for the appointment of federal voting registrars and poll watchers. Also, all future changes in election laws and procedures would have to be cleared in advance by the Justice Department. The effect of the Voting Rights Act was the registration of hundreds of thousands of black voters. Subsequently, the act was amended to eliminate literacy tests nationwide and to extend its protections to language minorities, such as Mexican Americans, American Indians, Puerto Ricans, Cubans, and Eskimos. It also mandated bilingual ballots and bilingual election materials in covered areas.[43] Various landmark civil-rights laws are listed in Table 14.1.

Today, opportunities for minority participation are greater than at any other time in this century. Consequently, many blacks have won election to office. In 1983, 5606 blacks held elective office in America, as opposed to only 72 in 1965.[44] More than 2500 black officials were in the South. In recent decades, blacks have been elected mayor of some of the nation's largest cities, including Los Angeles, Detroit, Philadelphia, Newark, New Orleans, Birmingham, Richmond, Hartford, Atlanta, Gary, Oakland, Washington, D.C., Cleveland, and, of course, Chicago. Twenty-one blacks were elected to Congress in 1982 along with eleven Hispanics. What's more, blacks and Hispanics often find themselves holding the balance of electoral power between competing white candidates. As a result, white politicians now often find themselves campaigning to win black and brown votes.

For women, the ratification of the Nineteenth Amendment in 1920 brought down the legal obstacles to political participation, but many social and psychological barriers remained. Many men and women alike thought that women's place was in the home and not in the rough-and-tumble world of politics. Women voted, of course, but not in the same proportions as men, and they frequently took their voting cues from their husbands. Some women held elective and appointive offices, but many observers considered their role to be a marginal one.[45]

The modern women's movement has revolutionized public attitudes about the roles women can successfully perform in American society. Women hold seats in both houses of Congress as well as in many state and local governing bodies. Within the last fifteen years, women have been elected governor in the states of Washington, Connecticut, and Kentucky, and have captured the mayor's office in a number of major cities, including Chicago, Houston, San Antonio, San Francisco, and Austin, Texas. In 1984, a woman was the Democratic nominee for vice-president.

For American Indians, the question of participation hasn't focused so much on voting and winning office as it has on the issue of participation in the decisionmaking affecting Indians and reservations. Before 1934 and between 1953 and the early 1970s, federal policy toward Indians was one of assimilation. The government ran the reservations with the aim of getting out of the Indian business by pushing Indians to assimilate white culture. Many Indians deeply resented this approach, preferring instead a program of self-government bolstered by federal aid.

TABLE 14.1
Significant Civil-Rights Legislation

1957 Civil Rights Act.	Gives the Justice Department the power to seek court injunctions against voting-rights infractions. Creates a Civil Rights Division in the Justice Department and the U.S. Commission on Civil Rights.
1960 Civil Rights Act.	Authorizes federal judges to appoint referees to register qualified blacks to vote.
1964 Civil Rights Act.	Forbids discrimination based on race, color, sex, religion, or national origin either by employers or labor unions in business concerns of one hundred employees or more, dropping to twenty-five employees in 1968. Creates Equal Employment Opportunity Commission. Requires voting registrars to apply same standard to prospective black and white voters. Authorizes executive branch to halt federal funds to public or private programs or activities practicing discrimination based on race, color, or national origin. Outlaws discrimination because of race, religion, color, or national origin in hotels, restaurants, theaters, gas stations, and all other public accommodations that affect interstate commerce.
1965 Voting Rights Act.	Bars literacy tests and authorizes federal registrars and voting examiners in areas where voting rates are low. Provides criminal penalties for keeping qualified persons from voting. 1970 amendment extends ban on literacy tests to all fifty states and sets thirty-day residency requirement for presidential elections. 1975 amendment extends act's protections to language minorities and mandates bilingual ballots and election materials in covered areas.
1968 Civil Rights Act.	Provides federal protection to persons exercising their civil rights. Prohibits discrimination in the sale and rental of housing.
1972 Equal Employment Opportunities Enforcement Act.	EEOC given enforcement powers.

The current federal policy toward Indians was adopted in 1975, when Congress passed and President Ford signed the Indian Self-Determination and Education Assistance Act. This act commits the federal government to becoming a partner with Indians in the management of the reservation, rather than a big brother. It gives the authority for running reservations to tribal councils and allows them to contract with government agencies for the administration of their community programs.

FREEDOM FROM DISCRIMINATION

Women and minorities want freedom from discrimination in public accommodations and employment. During Reconstruction, Congress acted to outlaw discrimination in all public accommodations with the passage of the Civil Rights Act of 1875. The law had little practical effect, however, because it was held unconstitutional by the Supreme Court in the Civil Rights Cases of 1883. The Court said that the Fourteenth Amendment protected the individual from discrimination by the state, but not by private individuals.[46] Consequently, the door was open for private individuals and firms to discriminate against blacks, Hispanics, women, and other minorities in housing, employment, and a broad range of public accommodations.

It took more than eighty years for the civil-rights movement to overcome the precedent set in the Civil Rights Cases. In the 1964 Civil Rights Act, you recall, the Congress outlawed discrimination in most public accommodations, using its powers under the interstate-commerce clause. This law has been fairly effective, but certain types of discrimination have been difficult to eradicate.

One of the most invidious of these is housing discrimination. For decades, blacks and other minorities were severely limited in their choice of housing and neighborhoods. In 1917, the Supreme Court ruled that cities could not establish exclusive residential zones for whites and blacks.[47] In many instances, however, the same effect was accomplished through private deed restrictions or restrictive covenants that obliged a purchaser not to sell or lease the property to blacks or other minorities. These types of deeds were finally undercut in 1948 in the case of *Shelly* v. *Kraemer*. The Court held that private contracts calling for discrimination could be written, but the state courts could not enforce them. That would make the state a party to the discrimination.[48]

The *Shelly* case did not end housing discrimination. Blacks still had great difficulty purchasing or leasing homes in areas outside black neighborhoods. Further improvements awaited action by the executive and legislative branches. In 1962, President Kennedy issued an executive order banning discrimination in property owned, sold, or leased by the federal government. Then, Title IV of the 1964 Civil Rights Act extended nondiscrimination provisions to all public-housing and urban-renewal developments receiving federal assistance. The most important steps came in 1968, however, when Congress passed the Open Housing Act. It prohibited discrimination in all transactions involving realtors. Also, in the same year the Supreme Court interpreted the Civil Rights Act of 1866 to prohibit discrimination in all real estate.[49]

Today, the law of the land is on the side of nondiscrimination in housing, but many American communities remain starkly segregated, white from black. To be sure, deep-seated discrimination still exists, but there are other causes for this as well. Some involve peoples' attitudes. Many people—white, black, and brown alike—simply prefer living near others of their own racial and socioeconomic background. Another reason, however, is that many minority families simply cannot afford to move to the middle- and upper-income suburbs.

ECONOMIC EQUALITY

Women and minority groups want economic equality. Blacks, Hispanics, and Indians long for the day when the employment rate and average incomes for black, brown, and red Americans will be the same as for whites. Women demand equal pay with men for equal work.

Unfortunately, that is not the reality of the America of the 1980s. In 1981, the median family income for whites was $23,517; for Hispanics it was $16,402 and for blacks only $13,267. Median income for men was $13,470, but only $5460 for women.[50]

There are sociological and psychological reasons for these disparities. As a group, minority Americans are generally less well-educated than whites. School dropout rates are higher, and proportionally fewer minority youngsters go to college, graduate school, or professional school. Women have traditionally pursued careers in fields that pay relatively less than male-dominated professions. Also, many women take time out from their careers to raise families. Consequently, their opportunities for professional advancement are reduced.

The major reason for these disparities, however, is discrimination and its legacy. Segregated school systems relegated blacks and to a lesser extent Mexican Americans to separate and unequal schools. In many cases, the so-called women's professions, such as teaching and nursing, pay poorly *because* they have been dominated by women. Also, there has been a great deal of out-and-out discrimination in employment.

In recent decades, policy has come down strongly in favor of equal opportunity employment. Efforts to eliminate discrimination in federal hiring were begun in the Truman Administration. Later, John Kennedy ordered that the federal government take affirmative action to seek qualified women and minorities. The most important development for hiring by private employers was the 1964 Civil Rights Act. It outlawed job discrimination based on race, color, religion, sex, or national origin, and created the Equal Employment Opportunity Commission (EEOC). Then, in 1965, President Johnson issued an executive order prohibiting discrimination by any employer who received federal funds.[51] What's more, the courts have been toppling the barriers that have kept women from nontraditional jobs, such as casino dealers, iron workers, and prison guards. In general, employers must prove why women cannot perform "men's work."[52]

Even if all educational and employment barriers were eliminated today, great disparities in the socioeconomic status of women, minorities, and white males would still exist. Moreover, these disparities would almost certainly persist for decades to come. That is the legacy of discrimination. What is government's role in properly compensating for these disparities? Many Americans argue that government should have little or no role in promoting economic equality. They note that the American creed calls for equality of *opportunity*, not equality of *results*. Also, the constitutional foundation for governmental action in this area is not nearly as strong as it is regarding voting rights or equality under the law. In contrast, other Americans believe that government has an obligation to enact policies to compensate disadvantaged groups for the errors of the past.

This brings us to the controversial issues of affirmative action, quotas, and reverse discrimination. **Affirmative action** is the legal requirement that an organization take positive steps to increase the number of women and/or minority-group members in its membership or employment. **Quotas** refer to the legal requirement that an organization include within its membership or employment a specific proportion of women and/or minority-group members. **Reverse discrimination** charges that the practice of favoring women and/or minority-group members effectively discriminates against white males. Presidents Kennedy and Johnson ordered affirmative action in federal employment and hiring by government contractors, but their orders had little practical effect until the late 1960s. At that time, Nixon appointees in the Labor Department began requiring government contractors to employ certain percentages of women and minorities.

For the next ten years affirmative action took on a momentum all its own. For some, affirmative action meant nondiscrimination. For others, it meant seeking out qualified women and minorities. For still others, it meant hiring a certain percentage of women and minorities regardless of their qualifications—a quota system. All the while, employers carefully kept records of how many women, blacks, Cubans, Mexican Americans, Puerto Ricans, American Indians, Alaskan natives, Asians, Pacific Islanders, Vietnam veterans, and disabled persons were part of their operation.

Supporters of affirmative action say that it is the most effective tool available for fighting discrimination. They point to recent increases in the percentage of women and minorities in graduate school and in many occupations as proof of their point. On the other hand, critics argue that government should be blind to such distinctions as race and sex. Otherwise, public policy sanctions reverse discrimination.

The Supreme Court has tried to deal with this thorny controversy on

Preferential Treatment and Affirmative Action

A CONVERSATION WITH CHARLES V. HAMILTON, COLUMBIA UNIVERSITY

Q. Is it fair to favor one racial group over another?

A. Generally, no.

Q. Then how can affirmative action be justified?

A. If affirmative action is viewed as a means of correcting past practices of discrimination, it can be seen as a justifiable remedy.

Q. But doesn't that put the matter on a group basis and not on an individual basis? Doesn't that overlook the fact that some people, say, blacks or women, or Hispanics, who are favored in 1984, might not really be victims—*in 1984*—of discrimination, and some white males who are not favored might never have been perpetrators of discriminatory acts? Aren't the latter being "punished" or at least penalized for the sins of their forefathers?

Charles V. Hamilton, Wallace S. Sayre Professor of Government at Columbia University, has served widely as a consultant in government and industry, and has written extensively on such issues as voting rights and the black experience in America. Professor Hamilton is an active member and a past vice-president of the American Political Science Association.

A. Yes.

Q. Is that fair?

A. Yes, if you agree with President Lyndon Johnson's speech in 1965, in which he stated that it was not fair to cripple a people for centuries, set them free, and then tell them to run the competitive race with others who have had preferential favors throughout their history. In addition, it could be argued that while individual white males have not engaged in discrimination, they have certainly belonged to a group that has benefited from discrimination. It is correct to say that this focuses on groups, not on individuals, but it is also correct to note that "groups" were discriminated against, not individuals. Segregation signs read "whites only" and "no colored." They did not spec-

several recent occasions. In the *Bakke* case in 1978, you recall, a badly divided Court ruled that race could be considered in medical-school admissions as long as there were no hard and fast quotas.[53] The following year the Court decided a case involving an on-the-job training program agreed upon by Kaiser Aluminum and the Kaiser employees' labor union. Half of the places in the program were to be awarded on the basis of seniority; the other half were reserved for blacks. A white worker, Brian Weber, filed suit, charging that the quota system violated the 1964 Civil Rights Act. By a five-to-four vote, however, the Supreme Court ruled against him. The main concern of the statute, wrote Justice Brennan in the majority opinion, is "the plight of the Negro in our economy." It would be an ironic twist if it were now used to prohibit "all voluntary private, race-conscious efforts to abolish traditional patterns" of discrimination.[54] Then, in 1980, the Court upheld a congressional statute that set aside 10 percent of a $4-billion public-works program for "minority business enterprises."[55] In 1984, how-

ify which whites or which coloreds.

Q. But there are now laws on the books that guard against that behavior. Why isn't it sufficient to simply enforce the laws equally now?

A. Again, that sounds like equality. But is it? Going back to Johnson, is it equity? Is it really dealing with reality, past and present? If we simply start now to behave as if there had not been 350 years of history, wouldn't that be engaging in political fiction? And isn't it the case that this country has, in fact, recognized the need at times to make restitution? Isn't veterans' preference a form of preferential treatment?

Q. Yes, but for specific *individuals* who served their country

and were denied other opportunities in the process.

A. True. But aren't they given a preference over all others, even though those others might have wanted to serve, but could not for various reasons—age, for example? In addition, we have seen covert forms of affirmative action on a group basis in our age-old tradition of ticket-balancing. Put an Irish Catholic on the ticket, or an Italian, or a Jew in order to appeal to the voters of those groups.

Q. But these are not codified into law. Perhaps it is best not to put such things in hard and fast statutory terms. Wouldn't you agree?

A. Perhaps, but then we must recognize that we are engaging in what I prefer to call the political wink. We are willing to

accept some forms of preferential treatment—even quotas—in public life as long as we either do not call it that or do not overtly call attention to it. That smacks of hypocrisy to me. And isn't that the sort of dishonesty we ought to be trying to get away from? Isn't it really better to face up to our history and our current practices, and be blatantly honest about what it might take to really make this a truly egalitarian society?

Q. You have neatly reversed the question-and-answer. Let's get back to the original format.

A. Fair enough. But what's sauce for the goose—and so forth.

Q. What about the argument that goes affirmative action, yes; quotas, no?
(to next page)

---

ever, the Court ruled that the city of Memphis must follow the principle of "last hired, first fired" in laying off workers even if women and minorities were dismissed in disproportionate numbers.

CIVIL-RIGHTS POLICYMAKING

The civil-rights policymaking process involves a wide variety of groups and the whole range of political institutions in America. Let's consider the various stages of the process.

SETTING THE AGENDA

Public opinon has played an important role in setting the public agenda for civil-rights policy in America. Unlike many other areas of public policy, the

A. Some people say they have no objection to affirmative action as long as it means reaching out, casting the net wider, making sure that previously excluded groups are brought into consideration. Fine. But this is obviously what ought to be done anyway. The question is how to measure the results of this policy. Where prior discrimination has been established, why not have firm measures—numbers, quotas, if you will—by which to determine if progress has been made and, indeed, to determine, when it is possible to *stop* according special treatment? In other words, quotas are useful policy tools. They permit policymakers a chance to monitor their policies. They permit the evaluation of policy with clear, nonarbitrary standards and guidelines. They put substance to the statements

of good intentions and good will. In a society that prides itself on quantification, quotas provide a means to satisfy that inclination. Who was it who said, "If it cannot be counted, it probably doesn't count?"

Q. OK, but, assuming that, isn't it also the case that—knowing what we know about political realities—once established, such quotas will likely never be rescinded? That while they might be seen as temporary, they could become permanent?

A. Possibly, but hopefully not. And given the tense political debates around this subject, it is hardly likely that such will happen.

Q. That is probably too idealistic and too much wishful thinking.

But let's move to another point. What about the issue of stigma? Wouldn't some blacks or women who received preferential treatment always be concerned that they were appointed because of their race or sex, not because of their merit or qualifications? Look at the initial criticisms around selecting Congresswoman Geraldine Ferraro as the Democratic vice-presidential candidate in 1984. Some say she was chosen solely because she is a woman. Wouldn't this tend to make her defensive about her substantive qualifications? Won't she always have to wonder whether she was selected for her talents or her gender?

A. Yes. But this is unavoidable. The only way she or one in her position can *possibly* overcome such notions in the minds of

issues of minority rights and the status of women are ones that command large attentive publics. Public policy here affects the lives of millions of Americans in ways the average person recognizes. Many of the issues are emotionally charged.

The recent public-policy gains by minorities and women have been paralleled by a dramatic shift in public opinion. Survey research shows that since the early 1960s there has been a significant increase in public approval of racial integration and equality between the sexes.[56] The national conscience has become an ally of equal rights.

Many groups and individuals are actively involved in setting the agenda for civil-rights policy in America. Some of these groups are more effective than others at claiming a place on the policy agenda. In large part, a group's success depends on its ability to mobilize political and economic power. This, in turn, depends on numbers, organization, and group unity. Women, of course, would be the most powerful of all groups, if they were united and organized. Blacks as a group are more united and better

others is by performing well. Plus, let's face it, the perception basically starts with whites or with males. They simply are not prepared, psychologically or otherwise, to admit that—fiction, again—many of them have received their positions because of ascriptive characteristics, not solely because they were "qualified." Now, to say that merit will be the sole criterion is a little bit disingenuous, don't you think?

Q. Hasn't this entire matter created more friction (fiction aside) than harmony, more splintering than coalescing? Is it reasonable to expect people to accept what is, in fact, a zero-sum policy?

A. Yes to the first. No to the second. Yes, there is strong rejection of quotas, especially.

Some people basically see them as excluding a group, not as including a group, arguments of history and other practices notwithstanding. Likewise, it may not be reasonable, but we have seen staunch behavior turned around in this field. Once, southern governors stood in the school-house door and said "Segregation yesterday, segregation today, segregation forever." Just twenty-plus years ago, incidentally. Once, people could not imagine Congress passing a law requiring a ten-percent set-aside in contracts for minority businesses. And the U.S. Supreme Court has upheld this law. Affirmative action in its most overt form—quotas—will likely never be overwhelmingly popular, and likely not be accepted as permanent policy. But in this field, we know that change does not al-

ways come about in the least painful way, without rather considerable initial furor, dissent, disagreement, and, indeed, turmoil. No society can expect to have the blatant history of human denials this one has, all the while articulating grand ideas of freedom and justice, and still expect the path to progress to be painlessly peaceful. That would be an expectation embedded in immaturity, unrealism, and self-delusion. At some point, for the sake of our own legitimacy, we should stop winking.

organized than women, but they lack the numbers and economic resources to enjoy very much influence nationally, at least in terms of congressional representation. Nevertheless, they are effective in areas of concentration, including most large urban centers and the southern states. And, thanks to the electoral college, blacks can be quite influential in presidential elections. In 1976, for example, black voters provided Jimmy Carter with his margin of victory in many close states in the South and Northeast. Mexican Americans are handicapped by a lack of unity and organization, but they have the numbers to enjoy some influence in the states of the Southwest. The politics of the electoral college means that they cannot be ignored by the national parties, particularly in big states such as Texas and California. Finally, American Indians lack most of the resources necessary to be politically effective. Still, mineral wealth on the reservation offers the potential for influence.

Some groups, however, are able to win influence despite the absence of conventional sources of political power. The NAACP, the Mexican American Legal Defense Fund (MALDEF), and many Indian tribes have found in the federal courts a forum to seek redress of grievances. Other groups have been able to arouse public support for their positions. We suspect, for example, that few politicians would be able to withstand a televised protest demonstration by a half-dozen Americans in wheelchairs.

POLICY FORMULATION AND ADOPTION

Civil-rights policy formulation and adoption often involves action by the president, Congress, the federal bureaucracy, and the courts. Consider the case of bilingual education. **Bilingual education** involves the teaching of academic subjects, such as history and mathematics, in two languages. In a school district with a large Hispanic population, for example, bilingual education would require instruction in both English and Spanish in the same classroom. The advocates of bilingual education say that it allows students whose native tongue is not English to learn academic subjects unhindered by language barriers. Opponents point out that English is the country's basic language, and they argue that bilingual education can be a crutch for students who don't speak English well, preventing them from developing the English skills they need.

The statutory background for bilingual education is found in two laws. Title VI of the Civil Rights Act of 1964 prohibited discrimination on the basis of national origin. It said nothing about bilingual education, but in 1970 the Department of Health, Education, and Welfare (HEW) used it as authority for a memorandum suggesting that school districts take "affirmative action" to aid students with language difficulties. The second law was the Bilingual Education Act of 1968 that provided grant funds for programs designed to assist students with limited English. The act said nothing, however, about teaching basic subjects in any language but English.[57]

In 1974, the United States Supreme Court made its contribution to the bilingual education process in the case of *Lau* v. *Nichols*. The Court ruled unanimously that the 1970 HEW memorandum interpreting the 1964 Civil Rights Act did entitle children with English-language deficiencies to special instructional assistance. The Court did not require bilingual education.[58]

Congress responded, however, by amending the Bilingual Education Act to provide financial aid to bilingual programs. Then, in 1975, HEW issued guidelines establishing bilingual education as the favored strategy for dealing with students with limited English ability. The Department of Education expanded the guidelines in 1980.

The Reagan Administration has been hostile to bilingual education. In 1981, the administration withdrew the 1980 guidelines. Subsequently, Reagan proposed amendments to the Bilingual Education Act that would provide federal funds for alternative approaches to the language problems of minority students. The debate and the policy process go on.[59]

POLICY IMPLEMENTATION AND EVALUATION

The history of minority politics in America illustrates well the importance of implementation in the policymaking process. For decades, the noble words of the Fourteenth and Fifteenth Amendments were empty promises to black Americans. For years, the school desegregation ruling of the *Brown* case stood unenforced. As we have seen, the effectiveness of laws and court rulings depends upon how vigorously they are enforced by the executive branch, the lower federal courts, and the state and local governments.

It would be impossible to evaluate all the economic, social, and psychological effects of the changes that have been made in public policy toward women and minorities in the last several decades, but we can make a few observations. There are some obvious pluses. Jim Crow legislation is dead; public accommodations are open to all. Blacks now register and vote in proportions nearly equal to those of whites. Blacks, Hispanics, and women are better represented in higher education and the professions than ever before. Women and minorities hold more elective and appointive offices than ever before. In sum, the nation no longer wastes such a large proportion of the human talent available to it.

On the other hand, the proportion of women and minorities in professional school, elective office, and top management in business is still far below their proportion in the population. Women are still paid less than men for doing similar work, and blacks and Hispanics are much more likely to live in poverty than white Americans.

Also, controversy persists over the effectiveness of one of the most basic civil-rights goals—school integration.[60] In 1966, sociologist James S. Cole-

School desegregation, although it has been accomplished in some areas, remains for many communities a dream rather than a reality.

man issued a well-publicized report in which he presented evidence on the effect of integrating a minority of disadvantaged children into a classroom dominated by middle-class white children. The disadvantaged children improved their performance, he found, without hurting that of the middle-class youngsters.[61] In 1975, however, Coleman amended his views to conclude that the problems have further separated blacks from whites. Desegregation methods such as busing have accelerated white flight, he said, and have led to greater segregation.[62]

The evaluation of government policy toward women and minorities illustrates an important point about public policy—it has its limitations. Policy debates frequently revolve around questions concerning the proper role of government. It is just as important, however, to ask what government can do effectively. Consider the effectiveness of various public policies aimed at the problems of racial minorities and women. Some problems have proved amenable to public-policy solutions. Thanks to government action, most legal barriers to political participation by minorities and women have been knocked down. Most public accommodations, such as hotels, restaurants, gasoline stations, and shops have been opened to blacks and other minorities.

Other problems have been amenable only to partial solutions. For example, the days of legally segregated schools are now gone, but many schools remain virtually all white or all black. Although school integration has been accompanied by a dramatic rise in SAT scores by black students,[63] white flight to private schools in many areas has led to reduced public support for public schools. That has frequently translated into reduced tax support.

Finally, some of the problems of women and minorities are apparently immune to public-policy solutions. Despite a century of public-policy "solutions," the economic and social status of American Indians remains quite depressed. Serious inequalities in economic position and social lifestyle remain for other groups as well. It is problematical whether such deep-seated problems are really amenable to government-imposed solutions.

CONCLUSION: POLITICS AND CIVIL RIGHTS

In general, policymaking in America combines both idealistic and selfish qualities. On the one hand, there is the search for good public policy, fairness, and justice. On the other, there is the struggle for personal or group advantage of one sort or another. Civil-rights policymaking is no exception to this rule.

Civil-rights policymaking has always involved a heavy component of group politics. Minorities and women have demanded a larger share of the political pie; white males often haven't wanted to share. Many times political leaders on all sides have found a personal interest in fanning controversy rather than resolving it. In the Chicago mayoralty contest, you recall, both candidates found an advantage in promoting racial-bloc voting insofar as it aided their own cause.

In the 1960s it was easier to make judgment calls about the merits of civil-rights issues than it is today. It was not difficult to see the injustice in laws that kept blacks in the back of the bus and away from the ballot box. How fair was a system that kept women and minorities out of better-paying occupations? Who could support policies that effectively cheated American Indians of their traditional homelands?

Today, however, the issues are more complex and more difficult to evaluate. In the 1960s, school integration was the controversy; today it's busing. Then it was educational opportunities for Hispanics; now it's bilingual education. In the '60s, the issue was equal employment opportunity, but now the question is affirmative action and quotas.

Today's complex issues not only divide the nation, they divide minority communities as well. Some blacks and many Hispanics oppose busing. Indians are split over the issue of developing reservation resources or preserving traditional ways. Mexican Americans are divided over immigration and bilingual education. Women's groups disagree about the merits of the ERA.

Consequently, civil-rights politics today more than ever resemble the politics of group interests. In the eyes of many Americans, women and minorities aren't so much "masses yearning to be free" as they are competitors for scarce resources. To be sure, there are still injustices to be corrected, and there are worthy gains to be preserved, but in many cases the politics of women and minorities have become politics as usual. There's right and wrong on both sides and a good deal of scrambling to protect self-interest. That doesn't make these kinds of issues any less controversial, though, nor does it make them any easier to resolve.

KEY TERMS

AFFIRMATIVE ACTION (411)

BILINGUAL EDUCATION (416)

DE FACTO SEGREGATION (402)

DE JURE SEGREGATION (402)

EQUAL RIGHTS AMENDMENT (ERA) (396)

GRANDFATHER CLAUSE (406)

JIM CROW LAWS (401)

POLL TAX (406)

QUOTAS (411)

REVERSE DISCRIMINATION (411)

"SEPARATE BUT EQUAL" (401)

WHITE PRIMARY (406)

NOTES

1. David Axelrod, "GOP's Epton Must Temper his Tantrums," *Chicago Tribune*, 3 April 1983, Sec. 2, p. 10.

2. *Time* (25 April 1983), p. 12.
3. Joseph Kraft, "Politics Turns Ugly in Chicago," syndicated column in *Houston Post,* 12 April 1983, p. D-2.
4. *Time* (11 April 1983), p. 15.
5. *Time* (25 April 1983), p. 12.
6. Kenneth M. Stampp, *The Era of Reconstruction, 1865–1877* (New York: Knopf, 1965).
7. J. Harvie Wilkinson, III, *From Brown to Bakke: The Supreme Court and School Integration: 1954–1978* (New York: Oxford University Press, 1979), pp. 17–18.
8. August Meier and Elliot Rudwick, *From Plantation to Ghetto,* rev. ed. (New York: Hill and Wang, 1970).
9. Gerda Lerner, *The Woman in American History* (Menlo Park, Cal.: Addison-Wesley, 1971).
10. Sarah D. Becker, *The Origin of the Equal Rights Amendment* (Westport, Ct.: Greenwood Press, 1981).
11. Cynthia B. Lloyd and Beth T. Niemi, *The Economics of Sex Differentials* (New York: Columbia University Press, 1979).
12. Betty Friedan, *The Feminine Mystique* (New York: W. W. Norton, 1963).
13. David Broder, *Changing the Guard: Power and Leadership in America* (New York: Simon and Schuster, 1980).
14. Barbara Haber, ed. *The Women's Annual/1980: The Year in Review* (Boston: G. K. Hall, 1981).
15. Jerry Rankin, "Mexican Americans and National Policy-Making: An Aborted Relationship," in Rudolph O. de la Garza, Z. Anthony Kruszewski, and Tomás A. Arciniega, eds., *Chicanos and Native Americans* (Englewood Cliffs: Prentice-Hall, 1973).
16. F. Chris Garcia and Rudolph O. de la Garza, *The Chicano Political Experience* (North Scituate, Mass.: Duxbury, 1977) and Maurilio Virgil, *Chicano Politics* (Washington, D.C.: University Press, 1978).
17. Haynes Johnson and Thomas B. Edsall, "¡Arriba! The Rapid Rise of Hispanic Voting Power," *Washington Post,* National Weekly Edition, 9 April 1984, pp. 6–7.
18. Joyotpaul Chaudhuri and Jean Chaudhuri, "Emerging American Indian Politics: The Problem of Powerlessness," in *Chicanos and Native Americans,* de la Garza, et al., eds.
19. Jeanne Guillemin, "Federal Policies and Indian Politics," *Society* 17 (May/June 1980): 29–34.
20. Howell Raines, "American Indians: Struggling for Power and Identity," *New York Times Magazine* (February 11, 1979), Sec. IV, p. 21.
21. *Plessy* v. *Ferguson,* 163 U.S. 537 (1896).
22. *Cumming* v. *County Board of Education,* 175 U.S. 528 (1899).
23. *Gong Lum* v. *Rice,* 275 U.S. 78 (1927).
24. *Missouri ex rel. Gaines* v. *Canada,* 305 U.S. 337 (1938).
25. *Sweatt* v. *Painter,* 399 U.S. 629 (1950).

26. *McLaurin* v. *Oklahoma State Regents*, 339 U.S. 637 (1950).

27. *Brown* v. *Board of Education of Topeka*, 347 U.S. 483 (1954).

28. *Brown* v. *Board of Education of Topeka*, 349 U.S. 294 (1955).

29. Harrell R. Rodgers, Jr., and Charles S. Bullock, III, *Law and Social Change* (New York: McGraw-Hill, 1972), p. 71.

30. Carl P. Chelf, *Public Policymaking in America* (Glenview, Il.: Scott, Foresman, 1981).

31. *Alexander* v. *Holmes County Board of Education*, 396 U.S. 19 (1969).

32. *Swann* v. *Charlotte-Mecklenburg Board of Education*, 402 U.S. 1 (1971).

33. *Keyes* v. *School District #1, Denver, Colorado*, 413 U.S. 189 (1973).

34. Rick Atkinson, "New Segregation in the Old South," *Washington Post*, National Weekly Edition, 16 April 1984, pp. 8–9.

35. Chelf, p. 343.

36. *Heart of Atlanta Motel* v. *United States*, 379 U.S. 241 (1964), and *Katzenbach* v. *McClung*, 379 U.S. 294 (1964).

37. *Frontiero* v. *Richardson*, 411 U.S. 677 (1973).

38. *Taylor* v. *Louisiana*, 419 U.S. 522 (1975).

39. *New York Times*, 16 June 1982, Sec. IV, p. 1.

40. Henry J. Abraham, *Freedom and the Court*, 4th ed. (New York: Oxford University Press, 1982), p. 360.

41. *Guinn* v. *United States*, 238 U.S. 268 (1915).

42. *Smith* v. *Allwright*, 321 U.S. 649 (1944).

43. Rodgers and Bullock, pp. 32–38.

44. Milton D. Morris, "National Profile of Black Elected Officials," *Focus* (February 1984), pp. 3–6; Abraham, p. 300.

45. Marianne Githens and Jewel L. Prestage, eds. *A Portrait of Marginality* (New York: David M. McKay Co., 1977).

46. Civil Rights Cases, 109 U.S. 3 (1883).

47. *Buchanan* v. *Warley*, 245 U.S. 60 (1917).

48. *Shelly* v. *Kraemer*, 334 U.S. 1 (1948).

49. *Jones* v. *Mayer*, 392 U.S. 409 (1968).

50. *Houston Post*, 20 July 1982, p. 6A.

51. Rodgers and Bullock, ch. 5.

52. Peggy Simpson, "Politics and Law," in Haber, ed., p. 161.

53. *Regents of the University of California* v. *Bakke*, 438 U.S. 265 (1978).

54. *United Steelworkers of America* v. *Weber*, 443 U.S. 193 (1979).

55. *Fullilove* v. *Klutznick*, 48 LW 4979 (1980).

56. D. Garth Taylor, Paul B. Sheatsley, and Andrew M. Greeley, "Attitudes Toward Racial Integration," *Scientific American* 238 (June 1978), pp. 42–49.

57. Abigail M. Thernstrom, "E Pluribus Plura—Congress and Bilingual Education," *The Public Interest* 60 (Summer 1980): 4–5, 11–12.

58. *Lau* v. *Nichols*, 414 U.S. 563 (1974).

59. "Bilingual Education: Making (and Unmaking?) a Controversial Mandate," *Intergovernmental Perspective* 9 (Spring 1983): 13.

60. Lorenzo Middleton, "The Effects of School Desegregation: The Debate Goes On," *Chronicle of Higher Education,* 6 November 1978, pp. 1, 4–5.
61. James S. Coleman, *Equality of Educational Opportunity* (Washington, D.C.: U.S. Government Printing Office, 1966).
62. *New York Times,* 15 June 1975, Sec. 4, p. 16e.
63. *Houston Post,* 16 March 1983, p. 8A.

SUGGESTED READINGS

BRODER, DAVID. *Changing the Guard: Power and Leadership in America.* New York: Simon and Schuster, 1980.

FLEXNER, ELEANOR. *Century of Struggle: The Women's Rights Movement in the United States.* Rev. ed. Cambridge, Mass.: Harvard University Press, 1975.

GARCIA, F. CHRIS, and de la GARZA, RUDOLPH O. *The Chicano Political Experience.* North Scituate, Mass.: Duxbury, 1977.

de la GARZA, RUDOLPH O., KRUSZEWSKI, Z. ANTHONY, and ARCINIEGA, TOMÁS A., eds. *Chicanos and Native Americans.* Englewood Cliffs: Prentice-Hall, 1973.

LLOYD, CYNTHIA B., and NIEMI, BETH T. *The Economics of Sex Differentials.* New York: Columbia University Press, 1979.

ORFIELD, GARY. *Congressional Power: Congress and Social Change.* New York: Harcourt Brace Jovanovich, 1975.

RODGERS, HARRELL R., JR., and BULLOCK, CHARLES S., III. *Law and Social Change.* New York: McGraw-Hill, 1972.

WILKINSON, J. HARVIE, III. *From Brown to Bakke: The Supreme Court and School Integration: 1954–1978.* New York: Oxford University Press, 1979.

Chapter Fifteen

FOREIGN AND DEFENSE POLICY

On June 6, 1982, Israel invaded Lebanon. In a nuclear age, wars anywhere in the world are a concern to American policymakers, but this war was particularly troublesome. The Middle East has been a world trouble spot since 1948, when Israel was founded as a Jewish state in Palestine, a region that had been under British authority since 1923. Israel's Arab neighbors immediately declared war, attempting to crush the fledgling nation. Israel beat them back, however, and in the war's aftermath thousands of Palestinian Arabs emigrated from Israel, settling in refugee camps in the Arab countries bordering Israel.

The problems of 1948 are basically the problems of the Middle East today, despite several wars, innumerable negotiations, and the passage of more than thirty-five years. On the one hand, many Arab nations still refuse to recognize Israel, and Israeli borders are not secure, particularly from attacks by guerrillas of the Palestinian Liberation Organization (PLO). On the other hand, hundreds of thousands of Palestinian Arabs remain homeless, many still living in the crowded refugee camps.

The invasion of Lebanon was part of an effort by Israel to impose, on its own terms, a solution to the region's problems. The stated purpose of the invasion was to clear a twenty-five-mile zone of southern Lebanon of PLO guerrillas who threatened northern Israel with rocket attacks. Before long, however, it became apparent that Israel's goals were more ambitious. Its forces pushed sixty miles into Lebanon, defeating PLO forces and smashing units of the Syrian army that had been occupying eastern Lebanon. Eventually, the PLO guerrillas retreated to Beirut, the Lebanese capital, where they were encircled and besieged by the Israeli army.

As the siege of Beirut unfolded, American diplomats scrambled to end the fighting. United States Special Envoy Philip C. Habib was dispatched to the region to try to arrange a cease-fire. Also, evidence suggests that the Reagan Administration applied pressure on Israel not to invade West Beirut, where the PLO fighters were holding out. Why so much American involvement in a war fought so far away?

The Middle East is a key region for American foreign-policy interests. First, Israel is a long-standing friend and ally of the United States. It is the only democracy in the region, and many Americans, especially Jewish Americans, have always felt a particular affinity for the country. Through the years Israel has been the recipient of billions of dollars of American economic and military aid. Consequently, Israeli soldiers entered Lebanon driving American tanks, flying American aircraft, and firing American ammunition. The image of Israel acting aggressively, coupled with television footage of bombed-out homes and civilian casualties, left many Americans feeling uneasy.

Second, the United States has developed close ties to a number of nations in the Arab world, particularly Egypt and Saudi Arabia. The Lebanese invasion caught the U.S. in the middle—between Israel and its historic ties to America and the Arabs with their oil. America imports about half the oil it consumes each year, and much of that comes from the Middle East. Any interruption of that oil flow because of an enlarged war in the region or because of a political embargo would have grave consequences for the American economy.

Finally, the United States is concerned about a growing Soviet presence in the Middle East, particularly in Syria. Wars and rumors of wars provide opportunities for the Russians to expand their influence in the area—they like to fish in troubled waters. More seriously, however, the Israeli-Syrian clash raised the specter of a confrontation between the United States and the Soviet Union. While Israel is an ally of America, Syria has become an ally of the Soviet Union. Consequently, a conflict between Israel and Syria raises the danger of intervention by one, and then both, of the world's superpowers.

The American efforts failed to resolve the crisis in Lebanon. Ambassador Habib did manage to arrange a cease-fire, followed by the evacuation of the PLO fighters from the city. This was monitored by French and Italian troops operating under the auspices of the United Nations and a contingent of American marines. Unfortunately, the end of the siege of Beirut did not bring peace to the city. Shortly after the cease-fire, Lebanese president-elect Bashire Gemayal was assassinated, apparently by leftist gunmen. A bloody massacre of Palestinian civilians followed, apparently carried out by right-wing militiamen. Before long, the American marines became the targets of attacks by the rival military forces in the city; in late 1983 more than two hundred marines were killed in a terrorist bombing. When President Reagan finally ordered the withdrawal of the marines in early 1984, they left behind a badly divided city torn by violence and threatened by the danger of an all-out civil war.[1]

War-torn Lebanon, scene of much bloody conflict in recent years, is the setting for one of the most difficult challenges for American foreign-policy strategists.

The Israeli invasion of Lebanon illustrates a number of important points about American foreign policy. First, international affairs can be exceedingly complex. We must guard against the temptation to oversimplify complicated world events.

Second, international events are seldom direct confrontations between right and wrong. After studying the Middle East, we suspect that a neutral observer would have an understanding of and some sympathy for the points of view of the Israelis, the Palestinians, the Lebanese, and the Syrians as well. We must be careful not to regard every crisis as another battle in the war between good and evil.

Third, the United States is a principal actor on the world's stage, heavily involved in international affairs around the globe. In our illustration, the U.S. supplied arms to Israel, mediation to end the fighting, and marines to keep the peace. Also, American interests were directly involved in the dispute because of oil, because of the nation's historic ties to Israel, and because of concern over Soviet expansionism.

Fourth, American foreign policy and domestic policy are often closely linked. Public support for Israel, particularly among America's Jewish community, ensures that American policy toward Israel is inevitably a domestic political issue. America's dependence on imported oil makes the nation's relationship with the Arab oil producers important for domestic politics as well.

Finally, ultimate solutions to world problems are often difficult to obtain. The crisis in the Middle East dates from the 1940s. No end is in sight. International crises are often highly complex; problems are deep-seated. Quick and simple solutions seldom succeed.

AMERICA AND THE WORLD POLITICAL SYSTEM

In the world today there are more than 160 nations, and the United States maintains diplomatic relations with most of them. This means that we exchange ambassadors and other diplomatic personnel, and in most cases operate embassies in the various countries. There are a few nations, however, with whom America does not now have formal diplomatic relations, including Cuba, Vietnam, North Korea, Libya, and Iran.

In addition to the governments of the world, more than one hundred intergovernmental organizations are active on the international scene. The best known of these is the **United Nations (UN),** founded in 1945 as a diplomatic forum in which the world's nations could resolve their problems peacefully. The UN hasn't always been able to prevent war, but at times it has played a positive role in mediating disputes. UN peacekeeping forces helped oversee the withdrawal of the PLO from Beirut and then police the cease-fire. Some of the UN's most important accomplishments have come

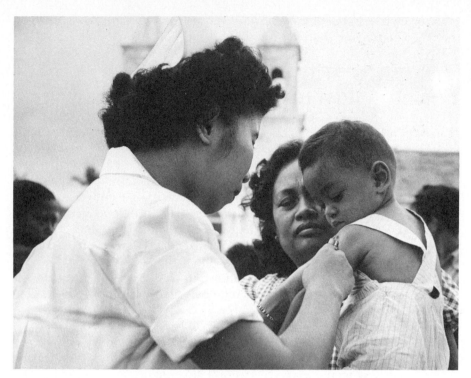

International organizations may sometimes accomplish important humanitarian goals. Here a nurse, using medical supplies and equipment provided by the United Nations, administers an anti-tuberculosis vaccine to a child in the Philippines.

in other areas, however, including assistance to refugees, agricultural programs, loan assistance to developing nations, and health programs. In particular, an agency of the UN, the World Health Organization (WHO), can be credited with the eradication of smallpox from the earth.

Other intergovernmental organizations are important to American foreign and defense policies as well. The **North Atlantic Treaty Organization (NATO)** is a regional defense alliance consisting of the United States, Canada, and their Western European allies. Similarly, the **Warsaw Pact** is a military alliance joining the Soviet Union and most of the countries of Eastern Europe. The **Organization of Petroleum Exporting Countries (OPEC)** is a thirteen-nation oil cartel that tries to set world oil prices.

Finally, there are a number of nongovernmental actors on the world stage. Thousands of multinational corporations, some of which have considerable resources and influence, play an important international role. Citibank, for example, operates in ninety-five countries and has made substantial loans to a number of governments. ITT has holdings in more than eighty countries, while the United Fruit Company is a major enterprise in a number of Latin American nations. Both Exxon and General Motors have sales exceeding the GNPs of all but twenty countries.[2] Other organizations capable of exerting influence internationally are the International Red Cross, the Roman Catholic Church, Amnesty International, a number of international unions, and even terrorist organizations, such as the Red Guards and, at times, the PLO.

THE ENDS AND MEANS OF FOREIGN POLICY

It is difficult to state the goals of American foreign policy, at least with specificity. For one thing, goals change over time. For years, America tried to isolate communist China, treating it as an outlaw state. All this changed, however, after President Nixon's visit to Peking. Also, the publicly stated goals of American policy may not be real goals. For example, the U.S. intervention in Colombia in support of Panamanian independence in the early twentieth century was justified as assistance to "freedom fighters" rather than a power play to acquire land for a canal. What's more, disagreements often occur among policymakers about the goals of foreign policy. Finally, foreign-policy goals are sometimes in conflict. Peace and national security are both frequently enunciated goals of American foreign policy, but they aren't always compatible in the real world.

Nevertheless, we will suggest three broad, general goals of American foreign policy that have been pursued rather consistently throughout the nation's history. The first is national security. A basic goal of American foreign policy is to preserve the nation's sovereignty and to protect the country's territorial integrity. During World War II, this meant defeating the Axis powers. In the postwar years, it meant containing Soviet aggression. A second broad goal is economic well-being. This involves trade and the promotion of American economic growth. One economic goal of the 1980s, for example, is to ensure a steady supply of imported oil at stable prices. A final general American foreign-policy goal is to promote American ideas and ideals abroad. A goal of World War I, you recall, was to make the world "safe for democracy." One of the goals behind the United States' intervention in Korea and Vietnam was to "preserve freedom" and promote democracy.

America's foreign-policy goals are pursued by a variety of means. First, foreign-policy goals can be achieved through military means. This may involve participation in defense alliances. Since World War II the United States has participated in a number of defense arrangements, including NATO and SEATO (the Southeast Asia Treaty Organization). They may also include the threat of force or actual military intervention. Since the 1940s the United States has conducted large-scale troop interventions in Korea, Lebanon, the Dominican Republic, Grenada, and Indochina. Through the Central Intelligence Agency (CIA), we have used force covertly in more than a dozen countries.

A second way to achieve foreign policy goals is by economic means. This may involve the promotion or the discouragement of trade. One of the means the United States employed in building relations with mainland China was to open the door to trade. On the other hand, the surcease of trade can be used as a foreign-policy weapon. When American hostages were taken in Iran in 1979, part of the U.S. response was to organize trade sanctions against Iran. The United States responded to the Soviet invasion of Afghanistan with a grain embargo. Another way of promoting foreign-policy objectives through the exercise of economic power is by use of foreign aid. In the years after World War II, the United States provided economic aid to Europe through the Marshall Plan, in order to strengthen European resistance to communist subversion.

Third, foreign-policy goals can be pursued by cultural means. This may include tourism, student exchanges, good-will tours, international athletic events, and even propaganda broadcasts. The process of improving relations between the United States and China, for example, has been facilitated by cultural exchanges. In fact, one of the first contacts between the two countries was the visit of an American table-tennis team to China—"ping-pong diplomacy," the pundits called it.

Finally, foreign-policy goals can be achieved through political action, such as diplomatic bargaining, negotiation, and compromise. This can be done through normal ambassadorial contacts or at the UN. Diplomacy can also be pursued through special negotiations or summit meetings among national leaders. In the Middle East, you recall, American envoy Philip Habib was dispatched to try to negotiate a cease-fire.

AMERICAN FOREIGN AND DEFENSE POLICIES

In his farewell address, retiring President George Washington warned the nation to avoid "entangling alliances." For nearly a century this served as the watchword of America's isolationist foreign policy toward Europe. President Monroe phrased the idea in his **Monroe Doctrine:** we would stay out of European affairs; the Europeans must stay out of ours. There was a practical aspect to this **isolationism.** In the early nineteenth century the United States was hardly a world power. Our energies were devoted to subduing and developing our own continent and, of course, we preferred doing it without European interference. But there was also an aspect of arrogance to America's policy of isolationism. We wanted to avoid spoiling ourselves by making alliances with our "corrupt" former colonizers. Instead, we would serve as a moral example to them. Finally, there was an aspect of hypocrisy to American isolationism. It did not apply to the Western Hemisphere. In fact, we reserved for ourselves the right to interfere in the affairs of the nations in the Americas.

And interfere we did. The war with Mexico was fought so that the United States could annex Mexico's northern provinces. Around the turn

of the century, Theodore Roosevelt intervened in Colombia to create the
nation of Panama so that the United States could build the canal. In the
twentieth century, the United States has directly intervened militarily in
several Latin American nations, including Cuba, El Salvador, Nicaragua,
Grenada, and the Dominican Republic. The U.S. has been involved indirectly in the political affairs of many other countries, including Chile,
Honduras, Venezuela, Guatemala, Ecuador, Brazil, and British Guiana.[3]
Meanwhile, American economic influence is felt everywhere in Latin
America.

America began to break out of its isolationism in the 1890s. First, the
treaty ending the Spanish-American War gave the United States a colonial
empire extending beyond this hemisphere to Guam and the Philippines.
Second, the U.S. had developed trading interests around the world, and it
now wanted to protect them. The so-called "Open Door" policy and intervention in China demonstrated this.

There were lapses in America's new internationalist policy, however,
notably in the years between the two world wars. Part of the reason for
America's return to isolationism was that Woodrow Wilson had oversold
World War I. It was "the war to end all wars" and "the war to make the
world safe for democracy." But idealism fades in the midst of bloody war,
and the results of the war were disillusioning. Another major reason for
the return of isolationism was the Great Depression. The country turned
inward as it tried to cope with economic collapse.

By 1945 America's romance with isolationism had ended, probably forever. Because of improved technology, isolationism was more difficult to
achieve. Modern communications and transportation meant that the world
had shrunk. More importantly, the United States emerged from World
War II as a great power, militarily and economically. It could no longer
afford retreat.

Since World War II, American foreign and defense policymaking has
been dominated principally by our relationship with the Soviet Union. By
the end of the 1940s, the two nations were locked in a bitter struggle for
dominant positions in the international arena. In the eyes of the Americans, the Soviets were hell-bent on expanding their control in Eastern
Europe and in Asia. Meanwhile, the Soviets regarded American actions,
particularly CIA activities in Eastern Europe, as a threat to their national
security.

The **Cold War** had begun. In part, the struggle was ideological: communism versus capitalism, dictatorship versus democracy. But the Cold War
can also be seen as a bipolar struggle between the world's two superpowers,
the U.S. and the U.S.S.R. There were no others; World War II had seen to
that. Germany and Japan were destroyed by the war; the nations of Western Europe were in ruins. That left a political vacuum which the war's
survivors, the United States and the Soviet Union, both sought to enter.
They were like two scorpions trapped in a jar. Some tension and conflict
were probably inevitable.[4]

America's foreign and defense policy after the war was based on the doctrine of **containment;** that is, keeping the Russians from expanding their sphere of control. One aspect of the policy involved providing economic assistance to nations threatened by communist subversion. The Marshall Plan, for example, provided billions of American dollars to the nations of Western Europe to rebuild their economies after the war. A second aspect of the policy was to maintain defense preparedness. This meant maintaining a substantial peacetime army equipped with the latest in weaponry, including nuclear weapons. Finally, the United States was willing to provide military assistance to halt the spread of communism. Sometimes, this entailed sending weapons shipments and financial aid to foreign countries, as we did to Greece and Turkey. At other times, it meant the commitment of American fighting forces, as in Korea and later Vietnam.

In the early 1950s, the Cold War entered a new phase. Before that time the struggle between the U.S. and the U.S.S.R. had been waged on the perimeters of Soviet influence—Eastern Europe, Berlin, China, Indochina, and Korea. Now, Nikita Khrushchev, a new and imaginative Soviet leader, adopted a different tactic. The Russians leapfrogged the old lines to push their cause well behind the American wall of containment—in Cuba, in Egypt, in the Congo, in Indonesia, and elsewhere in the developing world. Also, the Soviets now had nuclear weapons, and the launch of the Sputnik satellite in 1957 proved to the world that the U.S.S.R. was ahead of America in space technology.

The Cuban missile crisis of 1962 was another turning point. Despite Sputnik, the Soviet Union was still clearly inferior to the United States in

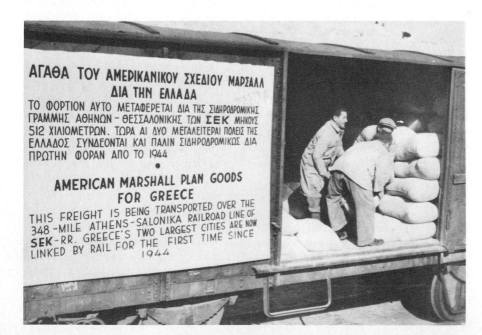

The Marshall Plan, designed to help rebuild the economies of Western Europe, was conceived as part of a larger effort to prevent the spread of communism.

The Cuban missile crisis provoked a tense Cold War confrontation between the United States and the U.S.S.R. The Soviet leader at the time was the fiery and contentious Nikita Khrushchev.

nuclear weaponry. To close the gap, Khrushchev elected to install missiles in Cuba, just ninety miles from American soil. When the U.S. discovered the Russian gambit, President Kennedy chose to respond with a naval blockade. The stage was set for a nuclear confrontation, but the Soviets backed down, withdrawing their missiles. The two nations were eyeball to eyeball, said Secretary of State Dean Rusk, and the Russians blinked.

AMERICAN DEFENSE POLICY AND THE ARMS RACE

The Cuban missile crisis provided the impetus for the Soviet Union to begin a massive buildup in both **strategic** (nuclear) and **conventional** (nonnuclear) **weapons** that has continued into the 1980s. The Russians were determined to catch up with the United States militarily, and catch up they have. Table 15.1 shows that the Soviet Union now has more missile launchers than the U.S., the same number of missile warheads, and nearly as many total warheads and bombs.

This is a case, however, when numbers don't tell the whole story. Other considerations are important as well. The Soviet warheads are bigger than the American, averaging three times the explosive power, but American missiles are considered more accurate, and a larger proportion are on alert at any given time.

The most important question about nuclear strength is whether a nation's nuclear arsenal is capable of deterring the other side from launching a nuclear attack. We must speak in terms of first-strike and second-strike capability. A **first strike** is the initial offensive move of a general nuclear war and is aimed at knocking out the other side's ability to retaliate. A **second strike** is a nuclear attack in response to an adversary's first strike. A second-strike capability refers to a nation's ability to absorb the full force of a first strike and still have enough nuclear firepower left to inflict unacceptable damage in response.[5]

America's nuclear strategy is based on the idea of **deterrence:** the Soviets will be deterred from venturing a first strike because the United States has a strong assured second-strike capability. Consequently, the U.S. must maintain a nuclear strike force that is both capable of penetrating Soviet defenses and relatively secure from being wiped out by a Russian first strike. The United States tries to achieve this through a **triad** of nuclear delivery systems. These include intercontinental ballistic missiles (ICBMs) stored in missile silos and ready for launch, missiles on nuclear submarines roaming the world's oceans, and B-52 manned bombers capable of delivering a nuclear payload to the Soviet Union.

So who's ahead in the nuclear arms race? No one knows for sure, not even the participants. There are too many variables and too many uncertainties. The best guess, though, is that there is a rough equivalence between the two sides. They have reached a macabre balance of terror in which each side is capable of destroying the other and, perhaps, civilization as well. As long as this balance persists, neither side will be tempted or frightened into launching a nuclear attack. At least that's the theory of deterrence. And the hope.

The Soviet military buildup that began after the Cuban missile crisis has encompassed conventional as well as strategic nuclear forces. As Table 15.2 shows, the Soviet war machine in the early 1980s has grown considerably larger than its American rival. Again, however, numbers don't mean everything. The Russians have an enormous advantage in tanks, for example— some 48,000 to our 11,560—but that doesn't necessarily translate into a battlefield victory. The United States and its NATO allies have stockpiled more than 200,000 antitank missiles.[6]Also, a substantial portion of the Soviet buildup has taken place in Asia, along the Chinese border, rather than in Europe.

On the other hand, there is cause for Americans to be concerned about their defense preparedness. Since World War II, American defense strategy has been predicated on the goal of containing Soviet power by means of U.S. and allied land, sea, and air forces. To accomplish this, American defense policymakers have adopted the concept of a **baseline force** with the capability of conducting one major campaign and one minor campaign simultaneously, anywhere in the world. The plan also calls for enough reserve stocks to last for forty-five days of intense combat.

By the end of the 1970s, however, many observers began questioning seriously whether the baseline force was still capable of fulfilling its mission. As Table 15.3 shows, defense expenditures had been on decline for more than twenty years, both as a proportion of GNP and as a percentage of the federal budget. Consequently, the American armed forces were beginning to show signs of disrepair. There were horror stories of ships in

| | 1962 | | 1972 | | 1982 | |
	US	USSR	US	USSR	US	USSR
Launchers						
ICBM	155	50	1050	1525	1050	1400
SLBM	145	100	650	500	550	950
Bombers	1300	155	450	150	400	350
Total	1600	305	2150	2175	2000	2700
Missile						
Warheads	300	150	3800	1900	7500	7500
Total Warheads						
and Bombers	5500	460	5600	2200	9000	8500

TABLE 15.1
Strategic Nuclear Forces

Abbreviations: ICBM: Intercontinental Ballistic Missile; SLBM: Submarine-Launched Ballistic Missile.
SOURCE: "Nuclear Arms and U.S. Security," in *Great Decisions '83* (New York: Foreign Policy Association, 1983).

TABLE 15.2
U.S.—U.S.S.R.
Conventional Force
Comparisons, 1981

Item	U.S.	U.S.S.R.
Large Warships	223	268
Tanks	11,560	48,000
Artillery	5140	19,300
Combat Aircraft	3988	4885
Manpower (millions)	2.09	4.84

SOURCE: John M. Collins, Congressional Research Service. Data cited in *Time* (27 July 1981).

drydock because the navy lacked the experienced personnel to staff them. Sometimes expensive military equipment had to be cannibalized because of shortages of spare parts.

One of the most serious concerns involved the question of mobility. With the turmoil in Iran and the Russian invasion of Afghanistan in 1979, American attention was directed toward the Middle East. If the Soviet Union were to launch an attack through Iran aimed at seizing the rich Persian Gulf oil fields, could the United States successfully defend the area without resorting to nuclear weapons? Many observers said no. The American response would be too little, too late.

In light of this and the continued Soviet military buildup, President Carter proposed increases in defense spending in order to upgrade both nuclear and conventional forces. He asked for money to modernize all three legs of America's triad of nuclear delivery systems and proposed the modernization of nonnuclear ground, naval, and air capabilities. In particular, Carter called for the creation of a Rapid Deployment Force to help solve the mobility problem. In general, Congress adopted Carter's defense proposals.[7]

Ronald Reagan came to the White House convinced that, in a dangerous world, America needed to do even more for defense. Carter had proposed defense spending increases between 1980 and 1985 averaging 5 percent in real terms (above the rate of inflation). Reagan asked for 8.4 percent. In general, President Reagan made no dramatic proposals for changing America's defense structure. Instead, he called for accelerating programs already in place or for adopting programs that had long been on the drawing board. These included the MX Missile and the B-1 Bomber. In 1981, Congress was quite receptive to Reagan's defense proposals, though in subsequent years it cut some of his spending requests.[8]

After all, the American military buildup is not without its critics. Some charge that billions of defense dollars are wasted because of the military brass' fascination with high-technology weapons. The high-tech weapons are often incredibly more expensive than the older model weapons they are designed to replace. Consequently, the Pentagon is spending more and more money buying fewer and fewer weapons. Allowing for inflation, the army spent the same amount of money purchasing tanks in 1983 that it did in 1953, some $2 billion in 1983 dollars. In 1953 that money bought 6735 tanks; in 1983 it purchased only 701. Similarly, in 1983 the military spent considerably more dollars (once again allowing for inflation) in buying 322 fighter planes than it did in 1951 purchasing 6300 planes.

The new high-tech weapons are so complex, service personnel often have difficulty operating them and the weapons tend to break down. The army's new M-1 tank, for example, breaks down five times more frequently than the older M-60. The air force's new F-15 fighter requires twenty-seven hours of maintenance for every hour of flight time, and system failures occur every 1.2 hours on the average.

Worst of all, the expensive and complicated weapons are sometimes less effective than cheap and simple ones. Consider the case of the Bradley Infantry Fighting Vehicle, the army's new armored personnel carrier. It's bigger and more expensive than the older model M-113 personnel carriers—$1,947,000 each versus $80,000 for the M-113—but it's not better. It is so big it has to be partially disassembled to fit into the standard army transport plane. Moreover, its armor can be easily penetrated by an enemy soldier firing a $150 antitank rocket. Then the Bradley's aluminum body vaporizes and burns, incinerating the soldiers it carries. The greatest irony is that the Bradley is so cramped only six infantrymen can fit inside. The older, cheaper, less complicated M-113 carries eleven.[9]

If it's any consolation, the Russians haven't had any better luck with their high-tech weapons. The standard Soviet battle tank is prone to engine overheating, and the inside space is so cramped crewmen can't be more than five feet, five inches tall and must load the gun with their left hand.

The defenders of high-tech weapons point out that the United States

Fiscal Year	As Pct. of GNP	As Pct. of Federal Outlays
1944	35.6%	78.7%
1950	4.4	27.4
1953	12.1	57.0
1962	9.1	46.3
1964	8.2	41.8
1968	9.3	43.3
1970	8.0	39.2
1974	5.6	28.8
1978	5.0	22.8
1980	5.1	22.7
1981	5.2	23.2
1982	5.6	24.3

TABLE 15.3
Defense Outlays, 1944–1982

SOURCE: William W. Kaufmann, "The Defense Budget," in Joseph A. Pechman, ed. *Setting National Priorities: The 1982 Budget* (Washington: Brookings Institution, 1981), p. 135.

must resort to sophisticated weapons to compensate for the greater strength in numbers of the Russians. If we don't win with technology, they argue, we may not win at all. Also, not every high-tech weapon is a white elephant. The cruise missile, for example, is a genuine success story. Even though the cruise is no bigger than a garbage can, it can carry a payload as big as the bomb that destroyed Hiroshima. It is self-programmed so the Russians can't jam its radio, and it can fly at treetop level so radar can't detect it. It is so easily launched that a B-52 flying near the Soviet border could release 120 of them. Best of all, the cruise is relatively inexpensive—only about a million dollars each.

A second general criticism of America's defense buildup involves the perennial question of priorities. While defense spending has increased, domestic spending programs have been cut and the federal budget has skyrocketed. A number of critics question whether the threat to America's security warrants the huge sums being spent on defense, especially when social programs are getting the ax and deficits are high.

Finally, a number of critics argue that America's military buildup is inconsistent with the search for peace. Instead of building more weapons, they say, the U.S. and U.S.S.R. should work for arms control. And this brings us back to our discussion of Soviet-American relations.

DÉTENTE AND THE CHANGING WORLD

The Cuban missile crisis brought the world to the verge of doomsday. Perhaps it had a sobering effect on the leaders of America and the Soviet Union, because not long thereafter a period of improved relations, called **détente,** began. To be sure, periods of conflict and tension still occurred between the superpowers (the war in Vietnam, for example), but in general the latter 1960s and early 1970s were a time of better communication and of visible efforts to relieve tensions.

One important aspect of détente involved arms control. Both the U.S. and the U.S.S.R. found advantage in slowing the arms race. Arms control saves money and, we hope, reduces the probability of nuclear war. Arms control is also good domestic politics, certainly in the United States and probably in Russia as well.

During the 1960s and '70s, the U.S. and U.S.S.R. agreed on a number of important arms-control measures. In 1963, the two superpowers and Great Britain signed a treaty banning above-ground testing of nuclear weapons. Subsequently, the U.S. and Russia agreed to ban nuclear weapons from outer space and from the ocean floor. In 1968 they agreed on a Non-proliferation Treaty to limit the spread of nuclear weapons to other countries.

Probably the most important arms-control agreement was the Strategic Arms Limitation Treaty (SALT), signed by President Nixon and Soviet Premier Leonid Brezhnev in 1972 and then ratified by the Senate. It limited the deployment of antiballistic missile systems and established a five-year agreement freezing the number of land- and sea-based missiles.

The SALT talks produced a second arms agreement in 1979: SALT II. This one was signed by Brezhnev and President Carter. It set limits on weapons, missiles, and long-range bombers. SALT II never came to a vote in the Senate, however. Many treaty opponents, including presidential candidate Ronald Reagan, argued that the U.S. had given up too much. Then, after the Soviet invasion of Afghanistan, relations with the U.S.S.R. soured to the point where the treaty stood no chance.

Détente also represented a recognition on the part of the superpowers that the conditions existing at the beginning of the Cold War no longer prevailed; that we no longer live in a bipolar world. For one thing, the Americans and Russians do not enjoy a nuclear monopoly. Six nations have now openly tested nuclear weapons—the U.S. (1945), the Soviet Union (1949), Britain (1952), France (1960), mainland China (1964), and India (1974). Several other countries may have the bomb secretly or be on the verge of developing it, including Israel, South Africa, Pakistan, Brazil, and Argentina.[10]

Second, economic power has shifted considerably since the late 1940s. America still has the world's largest economy, but it is hardly unchallenged. The economies of Japan and many Western European nations have grown more rapidly than the American economy in recent years, and in many fields American goods are no longer competitive on the world market. What's more, the emergence of OPEC and the dramatic increase in world oil prices have shifted great amounts of cash to a small number of oil-producing nations.

Third, the communist world is far from united behind Soviet leadership. In Eastern Europe, the communist governments of Yugoslavia and Albania have long traveled an independent road; the recent events in Poland demonstrate that there is unrest elsewhere. In Asia, communist nations have even gone to war with each other. In the 1970s a border war broke out between China and Vietnam, and Vietnam invaded and occupied Cambodia, another communist nation.

The most celebrated rift in the communist world, however, is that between Russia and China. The two communist giants have been at loggerheads for years; there even have been armed clashes along their common border. Meanwhile, the United States has tried to take advantage of the communist disunity. In particular, President Nixon made a dramatic visit to communist China, opening the door for eventual diplomatic relations between the two nations, a step that was completed during the Carter Administration.

Finally, the noncommunist world isn't united either. After World War II, the United States was clearly the leader of the Western democracies, but that is no longer the case. Japan and the nations of Western Europe no longer want to be led, especially along paths they consider naive or incompatible with their own interests. For example, President Carter's call for a boycott of the 1980 Moscow Olympics was ignored by a number of Western nations. President Reagan's effort to scuttle the construction of an oil pipeline between the Soviet Union and Western Europe was a complete failure. For its part, Moscow has taken advantage of Western disunity by increasing trade relations and other ties to Western Europe.

A Soviet pipeline in western Siberia, designed to supply gas to Western European countries such as Italy, France, and West Germany. Despite occasional protests from the U.S. government, many Western countries are seeking their own methods of accommodation with the communist nations, including the Soviet Union.

FOREIGN POLICY TODAY

The challenge of foreign policy in the 1980s is to deal with the changing realities of a complex and uncertain world. Our illustration of the Lebanese crisis illustrates how difficult that challenge can be.

Jimmy Carter promised to return morality to American foreign policy by making human rights the cornerstone of our relationship with other nations. American trade, aid, and alliances would be based on the way other governments treated their citizens. The United States would have a "foreign policy as good as the American people," Carter promised.

Unfortunately, human rights proved to be too simplistic a doctrine on which to base a global foreign-policy strategy. What if U.S. security interests and human rights conflicted? Would we sacrifice American defense interests in South Korea and the Philippines, for example, in the name of human rights? In practice, the answer turned out to be no. Consequently, the Carter Administration found itself accused of hypocrisy. Many observers saw overtones of arrogance in the policy as well. It seemed that Carter had adopted the role of a missionary, helping the poor abroad and bringing American values to those who suffer in the dark.

To be fair, the Carter Administration had its foreign policy successes— the Camp David peace treaty between Israel and Egypt, the Panama Canal Treaty, and improved relations with China. For the most part, however, the Carter foreign policy was incoherent. There were policy zigzags and erratic tactics. New policies would be solemnly adopted only to be abandoned when the first difficulties arose. There were even public debates among Carter's principal foreign-policy advisers.[11]

Ronald Reagan has based his foreign policy on a firm opposition to Soviet power. He sees world politics as a bipolar rivalry between the U.S. and the U.S.S.R., and there is no doubt who the bad guys are. The Soviet leaders, Reagan has said, reserve for themselves the right "to lie, to cheat, to commit any crime." To meet the challenge, President Reagan has called for a firm national will and a military buildup. Other than that, Reagan's policy is vague and unspecific.

In practice, the Reagan foreign policy has achieved few foreign-policy successes. Relations with China and the Soviet Union have worsened. Little progress has been made toward peace in the Middle East. The Lebanese adventure was a debacle. America's allies are critical of what they see as "amateurism" in America's approach to foreign policy. Among Reagan's foreign-policy advisers there are open, sometimes rancorous debates. And the nation may be slowly sinking into an unwanted involvement in a guerrilla war in Central America.[12]

It may be some consolation that Soviet foreign policy seems just as clumsy and unsophisticated. The Soviet Union has gotten itself involved in what is apparently a no-win guerrilla war in Afghanistan. Not only are Russian soldiers dying, but the invasion has been a propaganda disaster for the U.S.S.R. in the developing world, especially in Arab countries.

FOREIGN AND DEFENSE POLICYMAKING

American foreign and defense policy is made by means of a process involving the various branches of the national government as well as a number of interest groups. Let's examine the process in terms of the policymaking framework.

AGENDA SETTING

Agenda setting for foreign and defense policymaking is dominated by events and the executive branch. Some issues become important items on the policy agenda because of dramatic international events—the bombing of Pearl Harbor, the launch of Sputnik, the Arab oil embargo, or the takeover of the American embassy in Tehran, Iran.

At other times, however, international developments and defense issues become part of the policy agenda only after the president and others in the executive branch do a selling job. In 1947, for example, the Truman Administration, particularly Undersecretary of State Dean Acheson, had to convince congressional leaders that United States aid for Greece and Turkey was essential to American security. During the 1960s and '70s, a series of presidents and a procession of State Department and Pentagon spokespersons worked to convince the Congress and the nation of the importance of American intervention in Vietnam. Similarly, in the 1980s President Reagan has tried to make a case for American aid to oppose communist guerrillas in Central America.

Constitutionally, the president and Congress share the authority to formulate and adopt foreign and defense policy. The president negotiates treaties, but the treaties must be ratified by the Senate. The president has the power of diplomatic recognition, but the Senate must confirm ambassadorial appointments. The president may budget money for foreign aid and defense, but Congress must appropriate the funds. The president is commander in chief of the armed forces, but only the Congress can declare war.

In practice, however, the president is the prime mover in foreign and defense policymaking, while the Congress' role is usually to modify or, occasionally, to reject policies formulated in the executive branch. There are a number of reasons for the development of this rather uneven division of labor. First, the executive branch is better equipped to deal with international crises than the Congress. Unlike Congress, the president is always "in session," he can respond quickly to international events, and he can speak with one voice.

Second, the president has an advantage in that secret national security information from the CIA, the military, and the diplomatic corps flows directly to the president. A clever president can use this to keep Congress in the dark, or he can release information selectively to justify his policies.[13] During the 1980 presidential campaign, for example, President Carter leaked classified information on the development of the Stealth Bomber in order to counter criticism of his decision to shelve the B-1 Bomber project.

Third, the general public looks to the president for leadership in foreign and defense policymaking. As a rule, the public is neither well-informed nor particularly attentive to foreign affairs. There is a tendency, though, for Americans to rally round their president in times of international crises, at least in the short run. After the hostages were taken in Iran, you recall, Jimmy Carter's popularity experienced the greatest short-term rise in the history of the Gallup Poll.

Finally, the president has dominated foreign and defense policymaking because Congress has allowed it. Most members of Congress aren't interested in overall foreign policy and defense strategy. As an institution, Congress is decentralized. It focuses on the parts of policy but seldom on the whole. Meanwhile, individual members involve themselves only on the big issues that arouse public opinion, such as Vietnam, or on issues that are of particular concern to their constituents, such as trade policy or aid to Israel.

During the 1970s, Congress acted on a number of fronts to reassert its authority in foreign and defense policymaking. It passed the War Powers Act to limit the president's power to commit American forces abroad without congressional authorization and enacted the Military Sales Act to give itself a veto on arms sales overseas. It restrained the activities of the CIA, acted to control the spread of nuclear materials, and restricted development of trade relations with the U.S.S.R. It cut American aid to Chile and South Korea and voted to ban all aid to countries engaged in a pattern of human-rights violations unless the president determined and reported that aid would directly benefit the needy people of the country.

Each of these congressional actions was an important policymaking step, but their impact was generally to check the actions of the president. They were a reaction to the presidential excesses of the Vietnam era rather than a blueprint for a comprehensive foreign policy by Congress. What's more, by the end of the 1970s, Congress had begun to retreat a bit from its assertive line. It voted to resume aid to Chile and other nations accused of human-rights violations and relaxed its restrictions on military sales.[14]

Today, the president is still the primary architect of American foreign and defense policy, but Congress is hardly a rubber stamp. The congressional quiescence of the late 1960s and early 1970s is gone, perhaps forever. To be sure, Congress has not assumed the primary role in policy formulation, but it has adopted a more important role in checking and modifying presidential initiatives.

POLICY FORMULATION AND ADOPTION

Most foreign policies are formulated in the executive branch. The president plays the leading role in this process, but it is unusual for the American people to elect a president with very much foreign-policy experience or expertise. While Richard Nixon had long been a student of foreign affairs, Jimmy Carter and Ronald Reagan came to the White House with almost no foreign-policy experience at all.

Consequently, most presidents must rely heavily on others for information and advice. The president can look to the CIA, the diplomatic corps, and the military for information on developments abroad and defense matters. For advice, he can turn to the National Security Council (NSC), which includes the vice-president and the secretaries of state and defense. In addition, the director of the CIA, the chairman of the Joint Chiefs of

Ceremonial and official visits, such as this one at a historic archaelogical site in China, constitute a significant proportion of a president's schedule.

Staff, the director of the Arms Control and Disarmament Agency, and the national security adviser usually participate in its meetings.

In practice, however, most presidents don't use the NSC as a policymaking body, at least not as a group. Instead, they consult its members individually and other officials who are not part of the NSC, including members of the White House staff and various members of the cabinet. Usually, a president comes to rely upon one adviser or a small circle of advisers for counsel in formulating foreign and defense policy. In the Nixon and Ford Administrations, for example, it was National Security Adviser and then Secretary of State Henry Kissinger. For Jimmy Carter, it was Security Adviser Zbigniew Brzezinski and Secretary of State Cyrus Vance. President Reagan has apparently relied most heavily on his secretaries of state, Alexander Haig and then George Shultz; his secretary of defense, Caspar Weinberger; his secretary of the treasury, Donald Regan; his national security advisers, Richard Allen, William Clark, and then Robert McFarlane; and members of his White House staff, especially James Baker.

Some foreign and defense policies can be adopted in the executive branch alone, but most require congressional action as well. Foreign assistance and defense budgets must journey through the regular appropriations process. Treaties must be ratified and appropriations confirmed.

In practice, Congress more frequently modifies than blocks presidential initiatives. To be sure, there are times when a president has been rebuffed—Wilson and the League of Nations Treaty, for example—but even in that case the Senate would likely have ratified the treaty had Wilson been willing to compromise. There are many examples, however, of Congress supporting presidential initiatives in foreign policy with modifications. The Senate ratified the Panama Canal Treaty, but only after tacking on some twenty-four amendments, conditions, reservations, and understandings. In the 1980s, Congress acted on several occasions to restrain the Reagan Administration from too great an extension of American military involvement in Central America.

POLICY IMPLEMENTATION AND EVALUATION

The implementation of foreign policy is primarily the responsibility of the executive branch. The State Department, the Department of Defense, and the CIA are quite prominently involved, but many other agencies and departments play a role as well. The Agriculture Department, for example, promotes the sale of American agricultural products abroad. Student-exchange programs are administered through the Department of Education.

Foreign and defense policies may not always be implemented in the way the president and Congress originally intended or expected. As we have noted, bureaucrats sometimes have priorities of their own. Also, large bureaucracies tend to develop standard operating procedures (SOPs) that they follow in performing their tasks.

President Kennedy learned this lesson during the Cuban missile crisis. The U.S. navy procedures manual specifies that naval blockades be established no closer than ninety miles from the blockaded coast. This reduces the danger of attack from land-based enemy aircraft. Kennedy, however, specifically ordered the blockade set up closer to shore than that. With so much at stake, he wanted to delay the moment when an American warship would first stop a Soviet vessel. This would allow more time to reach a compromise and avert war. Subsequently, the president was perturbed to learn that the blockade had been established ninety miles out after all, just as naval SOPs specify.[15]

There is no systematic, ongoing governmental mechanism for evaluating foreign and defense policies. Congress monitors expenditures, but limits its policy oversight to the more salient policy areas, such as arms control and the Middle East. Other efforts at evaluation take place in the executive branch, in academia, and by the news media.

In general, however, foreign and defense policies are probably more difficult to evaluate than policies in other areas. It's not always possible to determine whether policy goals have been met. In the absence of war, for example, any evaluation of the effectiveness of particular defense strategies has to be at least somewhat speculative. Another problem is that many of the details of policy implementation are secret. Only now, years after the events took place, is information being made available so that historians can begin intelligently to evaluate American foreign policy in the years immediately following World War II.

CONCLUSION: POLITICS AND FOREIGN POLICY

There's a saying that "politics stops at the water's edge." This suggests that foreign and defense policy ought to be above partisan politics. Most American policymakers pay lip service to this idea and, we believe, most sincerely try to practice what they preach. Most presidents, members of Congress, military leaders, and civilian bureaucrats try to formulate, adopt, and implement foreign and defense policies that they believe are in the national interest. Inevitably, however, politics plays a major role in foreign and defense policymaking.

First, the actors involved in the foreign and defense policymaking process are political animals. Presidents often proclaim their commitment to keeping politics out of foreign policy and may privately instruct their advisers not to consider domestic political factors in their advice. Nevertheless, politics often enters beneath the surface. In the Cuban missile crisis, for example, President Kennedy had to weigh the risks of blowing up the planet against the risk of political attack at home.[16] For some months the Kennedy Administration had been fending off election-year attacks from the Republicans that Kennedy was soft on communism. There had even been allegations that the Russians were sneaking missiles into Cuba, but the administration strongly denied the allegations. Now that there was proof of the missiles, Kennedy had to respond vigorously or give the Republicans a major campaign issue.[17]

Kennedy faced another political dilemma in Vietnam. No president wants to be accused of letting a country "go communist," but none want to send American soldiers into combat either. Kennedy found himself trying to walk this thin line in Vietnam. In fact, Kenneth O'Donnell, one of Kennedy's advisers, reports that the president had planned the complete withdrawal of American troops from Vietnam, but decided to wait until 1965, after he was reelected.[18]

Congress, too, is a political institution. Some members of Congress have a broad, continuing interest in foreign affairs and national-security policy, but most are primarily concerned with domestic-policy matters. Foreign policy becomes important to them when it directly affects their constituents. Consequently, most senators and representatives focus their attention on the big issues of war and peace and on the small issues that directly touch their state or district. These may include tariffs to protect local manufacturers or defense contracts awarded to local firms.

Second, foreign and defense policy is the object of pressure-group politics, similar to other areas of public policy. Multinational corporations, such as energy companies and big banks, are acutely aware of and concerned about American foreign policy because it affects their business abroad. Other interests are concerned with trade policy. American auto and steel companies and their workers' unions lobby for tariffs to keep out what they see as "unfair" foreign competition. On the other hand, farmers and other American industries favor free trade because they benefit as exporters. Moreover, many companies, including General Dynamics, Lockheed, and McDonnell-Douglas, focus their lobbying on defense policy because of their role as major defense contractors.

A number of attentive publics are also involved in foreign policymaking. The American Jewish community, for example, pays close attention to United States policy toward Israel. Also, in recent years, hundreds of thousands of people in the United States and Western Europe have joined what's called the nuclear-freeze movement. They propose that the U.S. and the U.S.S.R. agree to a freeze on the testing, production, and development of nuclear weapons.

Third, foreign and defense policymaking, like domestic policymaking, requires political bargaining and compromise. For example, the Panama Canal Treaty ultimately passed the Senate because its backers were willing to compromise and accept reservations. The defense budget inevitably reflects the political compromises characteristic of the appropriations process.

Finally, there's the politics of bureaucracy. As we have said, military officers and civilian bureaucrats try to act in the national interest. As with everyone else, though, their view of the world is colored by their own experiences. Consequently, they tend to equate national security with the interest of their own organizations.[19]

For example, a perennial conflict simmers between the State Department and the White House over the conduct of foreign policy. Careerists in State believe that diplomacy is best conducted by career diplomats working through normal channels. They resent the interference of White House amateurs who come and go, and they think presidential diplomacy at summit meetings is nothing more than electioneering. Meanwhile, presidents frequently distrust the career officials in the State Department and rarely permit the secretary of state to manage foreign policy. The White House staff typically complains about State Department red tape and inefficiency.[20]

Defense policy is affected by the bureaucratic perspectives of military men. Consider the problem of mobility. The Achilles' heel of America's armed forces today is their inability to respond quickly and effectively to security threats in important, but relatively inaccessible, corners of the globe, such as the Persian Gulf region. The military needs to improve its transport and supply capability, but this has always been well down the Pentagon's list of priorities. Why? The top brass of the military just don't see transport and supply as their primary function.

The dominant view of air-force officers is that the primary mission of the air force is to fly combat airplanes designed for deploying nuclear weapons against the Soviet Union. Other tasks, such as flying ground support for combat troops or developing ICBMs, are secondary. After all, sitting in a silo can't compare with flying a bomber. Military airlift is the least glamorous of all. Consequently, in setting their own priorities, career air-force officers put manned bombers first, air transport last.

Meanwhile, naval officers see the essence of the navy as maintaining combat ships whose primary mission is to control the sea against potential enemies. There are disagreements within the navy over how this can best be accomplished. Some believe that big aircraft carriers are the key. Others advocate a large surface navy with less reliance on the carrier. Still others emphasize the submarine. Right now the carrier supporters have the upper hand. But no senior naval officers emphasize transport. Consequently, transport is at the bottom of the navy's list, too.[21]

As you can see, politics doesn't stop at the water's edge. Foreign and defense policy is made through the interplay of executive and legislative bodies, public and private interests, and personalities. And the process is highly political. In fact, foreign and defense policymaking is becoming more political. This is because the link between foreign and domestic politics has become closer.[22] For example, the nuclear-freeze movement has intensified the importance of arms control as a domestic political issue. Trade policy has heavy domestic political overtones because of its impact on jobs and local economies.

The intermix of foreign policy with domestic politics makes foreign and defense policymaking even more complicated. Let's consider again our illustration of the Israeli invasion of Lebanon. The Middle East presents American policymakers with a complex situation that is made even more complicated because domestic politics is involved. On the one hand, there is a strong pro-Israeli lobby in America, and any administration that dares come down too hard against Israel risks losing the Jewish vote. On the other hand, there's the energy problem. A cut-off of Arab oil supplies would wreak havoc with the American economy and probably doom a president's reelection chances.

In sum, the foreign-policy challenge to America in the 1980s is great. The world is an extraordinarily complex place whose problems resist simplistic diagnoses and simple-minded solutions. Meanwhile, the close link between foreign and defense policy and domestic politics complicates the policymaking process still further. Are public-policy makers in America up to the task? In a nuclear age, we can only hope that the answer is yes.

KEY TERMS

BASELINE FORCE (433)

COLD WAR (430)

CONTAINMENT (431)

CONVENTIONAL WEAPONS (432)

DÉTENTE (437)

DETERRENCE (432)

FIRST STRIKE (432)

ISOLATIONISM (429)

MONROE DOCTRINE (429)

NORTH ATLANTIC TREATY ORGANIZATION (NATO) (427)

ORGANIZATION OF PETROLEUM EXPORTING COUNTRIES (OPEC) (427)

SECOND STRIKE (432)

STRATEGIC WEAPONS (432)

TRIAD (432)

UNITED NATIONS (UN) (426)

WARSAW PACT (427)

NOTES

1. "Crusade in Lebanon," *Foreign Policy* 48 (Fall 1982): 94–121; Christopher Madison, "U.S. Balancing Act in the Middle East—Seeking Peace and Guarding the Oil," *National Journal* (28 November 1981), pp. 2104–2108; Thomas L. Friedman, "America's Failure in Lebanon," *New York Times Magazine* (8 April 1984), pp. 32–33, 36–37, 40–44, 62–68.

2. Thomas L. Brewer, *American Foreign Policy: A Contemporary Introduction* (Englewood Cliffs, N.J.: Prentice-Hall, 1980), p. 90.

3. Roger Morris, "The Aftermath of CIA Intervention," *Society* 3 (March/April 1975): 76–80; Morton H. Halperin, et al., *The Lawless State* (New

York: Penguin, 1976); Robert L. Borosage and John Marks, eds. *The CIA File* (New York: Grossman, 1976).

4. J. Samuel Walker, "Historians and Cold War Origins: The New Consensus," in Gerald K. Haines and J. Samuel Walker, eds., *American Foreign Relations: A Historiographical Review* (Westport, Ct.: Greenwood Press, 1981).

5. "Nuclear Arms and U.S. Security," *Great Decisions '83* (New York: Foreign Policy Association, 1983).

6. Brewer, p. 179.

7. William W. Kaufman, "The Defense Budget," in Joseph A. Pechman, ed., *Setting National Priorities: The 1982 Budget* (Washington, D.C.: Brookings Institution, 1981).

8. Barry R. Posen and Stephen Van Evera, "Defense Policy and the Reagan Administration," *International Security* 8 (Summer 1983): 3–45.

9. *Time* (7 March 1983), pp. 12–30.

10. Lewis A. Dunn, *Controlling the Bomb: Nuclear Proliferation in the 1980s* (New Haven: Yale University Press, 1982).

11. Stanley Hoffman, "Requiem," *Foreign Policy* 42 (Spring 1981): 3–26; Linda B. Miller, "Morality in Foreign Policy: A Failed Consensus," in Pechman, ed., *Setting National Priorities: The 1983 Budget.*

12. Leslie H. Gelb, "Is Reagan's Foreign Policy Overheated or Warming Up?" *New York Times*, 1 May 1983, Sec. 4, p. 1; Michael M. Harrison, "Reagan's World," *Foreign Policy* 42 (Summer 1981): 3–16; Jeffrey Record, "Jousting with Unreality: Reagan's Military Strategy," *International Security* 8 (Winter 1983/84): 3–18.

13. Richard M. Pious, *The American Presidency* (New York: Basic Books, 1979), p. 340.

14. David Leyton-Brown, "The Role of Congress in the Making of Foreign Policy," *International Journal* 38 (Winter 1982–83): 59–76; and Thomas M. Franck and Edward Weisband, *Foreign Policy by Congress* (New York: Oxford University Press, 1979).

15. Graham T. Allison, *Essence of Decision: Explaining the Cuban Missile Crisis* (Boston: Little, Brown, 1971).

16. Morton H. Halperin, *Bureaucratic Politics and Foreign Policy* (Washington, D.C.: Brookings Institution, 1974), ch. 4.

17. Allison.

18. Kenneth F. O'Donnell, "LBJ and the Kennedys," *Life* (7 August 1970), pp. 44–56.

19. Halperin, ch. 1.

20. Stanley J. Heginbotham, "Dateline Washington: The Rules of the Game," *Foreign Policy* 53 (Winter 1983–84): 157–72.

21. Halperin, pp. 26–32.

22. Charles W. Kegley, Jr. and Eugene R. Wittkopf, "Beyond Consensus: The Domestic Context of American Foreign Policy," *International Journal* 38 (Winter 1982–83): 77–106.

SUGGESTED READINGS

ALLISON, GRAHAM T. *Essence of Decision: Explaining the Cuban Missile Crisis.* Boston: Little, Brown, 1971.

BREWER, THOMAS L. *American Foreign Policy: A Contemporary Introduction.* Englewood Cliffs: Prentice-Hall, 1980.

CRABB, CECIL V., JR. *Policy-Makers and Critics: Conflicting Theories of American Foreign Policy.* New York: Praeger, 1976.

DESTLER, I. M. *Presidents, Bureaucrats, and Foreign Policy.* Princeton: Princeton University Press, 1972.

DUNN, LEWIS A. *Controlling the Bomb: Nuclear Proliferation in the 1980s.* New Haven: Yale University Press, 1982.

HALPERIN, MORTON H. *Bureaucratic Politics and Foreign Policy.* Washington, D.C.: Brookings Institution, 1974.

KEGLEY, CHARLES W., JR., and WITTKOPF, EUGENE R. *American Foreign Policy: Pattern and Process.* New York: St. Martins, 1979.

NATHAN, JAMES, and OLIVER, JAMES. *Foreign Policy-Making and the American Political System.* Boston: Little, Brown, 1982.

SPANIER, JOHN, and USLANER, ERIC M. *How American Foreign Policy Is Made.* New York: Praeger, 1974.

POLITICS
AND POLICY
IN AMERICA

John Gardner, a former cabinet member, once said that America's greatest problem is that she has too many uncritical lovers and too many unloving critics.[1] After fifteen chapters of this book, we hope you will be neither.

On the one hand, we hope that you now understand that the civics-book model of participatory democracy sometimes presented in Americanism courses in junior high really isn't the way America's government works. By now you know that many Americans are uninformed about the great public-policy debates of the day. In fact, barely half can even identify their representative in the House. Many Americans don't bother to vote and even fewer participate in politics through other means. Consequently, we know that the notion that public policy directly reflects the expressed will of the majority is naive.

On the other hand, we hope you haven't become a confirmed cynic who believes that democracy is a sham and that policy is made by a narrow elite. Not all Americans swing the same political weight, of course, but this does not mean that a small clique runs the country. After all, one of the major points of this book is that public policymaking in America is fragmented. Elites are important, but there are many different groups of elites whose influence varies according to time and place and from issue to issue.

How, then, should we go about understanding America's government? Political scientists like to use the term *pluralism* to describe policymaking in America. This is the idea that public policy results from political bargaining and compromise among different groups of power holders. Let's examine each of the elements of this definition.

First, public policy is the result of political bargaining and compromise. We have seen that political bargaining is a constant element of policymaking in America. It occurs in the Congress, in the executive branch, and among the justices of the Supreme Court. It takes place between the Congress and the president, between the courts and the Congress, and between the courts and the executive branch. It occurs among the levels of government within the federal system. What's more, we have learned that political bargaining is involved in every policy area. Nothing is "above politics." Politics affects economic policy, regulatory policy, civil-liberties policy, civil-rights policy, and foreign and defense policy.

Second, the process involves different groups of power holders. Another of the major points of this book is that a wide range of groups is involved in the policy process. There are business groups, professional associations, labor organizations, ethnic groups, public interest organizations, and single-issue groups, all competing to influence the making of public policy. We have also seen that some of the most active and successful participants in the policy process are government bureaucrats.

Not all groups are equally powerful, of course, but the fragmentation of the policy process in America means that groups that fail in one arena can win elsewhere. Some groups are most influential at the state and local level. Others are heard sympathetically in congressional committees. Still others are able to influence policymaking in the bureaucracy. Even small, unpopular groups with few sources of political influence can get a hearing in the federal courts and, as we have seen, sometimes win.

But where does pluralism leave democracy? Pluralism certainly isn't the kind of democracy described in Americanism texts, but it isn't the power elite either, as sociologist C. Wright Mills would put it.[2] One of the virtues of political fragmentation in America is that it permits participation by a diverse array of groups. To be sure, not all Americans are represented in the process and not all are represented equally, but power is spread more widely and more equitably than if there were a single ruling elite.

And how about elections? There isn't a one-to-one relationship between election outcomes and policy outputs, but elections are not a meaningless exercise. Some of the most vigorous group competition in America is over elections. The electorate may not directly determine policy through elections, but it frequently chooses among elites who do.

Now, It's Up to You

After all these pages, it's now time for you to take your place as an informed participant in America's pluralist democracy. We have tried to interest you in the process, and to pass some of its excitement along to you. We have tried to give you a tool for understanding and analyzing politics in America.

In the final analysis, though, it is up to you. The best way to learn about public policy in America is to test out by personal experience the insights you have gained. Get involved in the concerns and the politics of your community. Learn about government at all levels and discover how it affects you. Then learn how you can affect it. After all, that's the challenge of this book—for you to become an informed participant in America's public-policy process.

NOTES

1. John Gardner, *Self-Renewal* (New York: Harper and Row, 1964).
2. C. Wright Mills, *The Power Elite* (New York: Oxford University Press, 1956).

Appendix
THE 1984 ELECTION IN BRIEF

The 1984 presidential election ended, unofficially at least, at 7:00 P.M. (CST) on Election Day, November 7. Although the polls were still open in much of the country, the CBS television network, in the person of Dan Rather, declared that Ronald Reagan had won enough states to be assured of reelection to the presidency.

There was little suspense that night; Reagan had led from the earliest returns. He quickly piled up a popular vote landslide—53 million votes to 37 million—with a whopping margin of 59 percent to Mondale's 41 percent. The only question seemed to be whether Reagan would carry all fifty states! He didn't; Mondale carried his home state of Minnesota and the District of Columbia, for a total of 13 electoral votes. But Reagan won the largest electoral total in history: 49 states with 525 electoral votes.

The President's coattails proved to be short, however. Republicans had hoped to pick up 25 to 30 seats in the House of Representatives, but were only able to take 14 from the Democrats. In the Senate, the Democrats actually made a net gain of two seats. Meanwhile, despite the Reagan landslide, the GOP gained only one additional governorship. (See inside back and front cover for more election results.)

Early predictions of dramatic increases in voter turnout proved overly optimistic. Both parties had conducted vigorous voter registration drives, and some observers thought that the presence of Geraldine Ferraro on the Democratic ticket would swell the ranks of women voters. When all the ballots were counted, however, percentage turnout was up only slightly from 1980.

Why did Reagan win and Mondale lose? Let's begin with the battle for the Democratic nomination.

THE DEMOCRATS PICK A PRESIDENTIAL TICKET

Since President Reagan faced no serious challenge for the Republican nomination, the first skirmishes of the long political season were fought among Democrats. Eight hopefuls mounted serious campaigns for their party's presidential nomination: Former vice-president Walter Mondale; Senators John Glenn, Gary Hart, Alan Cranston, and Ernest Hollings; former Senator George McGovern; former Governor Reubin Askew of Florida; and black civil rights leader, Rev. Jesse Jackson.

Mondale and Glenn were early favorites, primarily because of name recognition, but when Glenn's campaign failed to get off the launching pad, Mondale became the front-runner. Mondale was preferred by Democratic party leaders and elected officials. He raised more money than his opponents and collected important endorsements from the AFL-CIO, National Organization of Women (NOW), and National Education Association (NEA). When Mondale swept to a big victory in the Iowa caucus in late February, many political observers pronounced him the party's nominee.

But Mondale had serious liabilities. His tenure as Jimmy Carter's vice-president gave his opponents the opportunity to link him with the failures of the Carter

Administration. Mondale's rivals attacked his endorsements, too, contending he promised too much to too many. What's more, Mondale often proved a lackluster campaigner.

The candidate best able to exploit Mondale's vulnerability was Senator Gary Hart. He attacked Mondale as the embodiment of the "old politics" and presented himself as the candidate of "new ideas." At first, Hart was just another face in a crowded field, but coming in second in the Iowa caucus gave him the media attention he needed to emerge from the pack. A week after Iowa, Hart pulled off a major upset, winning 37 percent of the New Hampshire primary vote to Mondale's 28 percent. For a while, it looked as if he might knock Mondale out of the race. But Mondale fought back. He used a hamburger chain's advertising slogan, "Where's the beef?" to attack the substance of Hart's new-ideas campaign. Mondale and Hart traded caucus and primary victories through March. The race for the Democratic nomination, once seen as a short sprint for Mondale, had turned into a marathon.

By now, all the other candidates except Jesse Jackson had dropped out. As the nation's first serious black candidate for president, Jackson was able to attract intense media attention. Although Jackson's campaign was poorly organized and underfunded, his personal magnetism attracted a sizable core of intensely loyal supporters in states with substantial black populations. By the end of March, Jackson was a strong third in the race for the nomination and prepared to go the distance. Nevertheless, Jackson's prospects of achieving a winning "rainbow coalition" of blacks, Hispanics, American Indians, and "progressive whites," and becoming the eventual nominee, were slim.

Mondale, Hart, and Jackson each appealed to different segments of the Democratic electorate. Polls showed that Mondale's support came from older, poorer, less well-educated voters who identified strongly with the Democratic party, and from organized labor. In contrast, Hart did best among young, urban professionals, called Yuppies by the pundits. Many of his supporters were independents who told pollsters they would vote for Reagan if Mondale were the Democratic nominee. Meanwhile, the predominant color in Jackson's rainbow coalition was black. He ran particularly well among younger black voters who had never before participated politically.

In the end, Mondale won the nomination, but it wasn't easy, and it wasn't without a price. Jackson won primaries in Louisiana and South Carolina, Hart gained victories in Ohio and California, but Mondale took Illinois, New York, Pennsylvania, Texas, and New Jersey. By mid-June Mondale had enough delegates on paper to win the nomination, unite the party, and build momentum for the fall campaign. In a historic move, he named Geraldine Ferraro, a congresswoman from New York, as his vice-presidential running mate. The Ferraro nomination succeeded in outflanking Hart, and wrapped up a first-ballot nomination for Mondale. It also helped to produce at least superficial unity at the Democratic convention, as both Hart and Jackson made conciliatory calls for party unity. The polls showed that a Mondale-Ferraro ticket had surged to within a few percentage points of the Reagan-Bush team. The stage was set for the presidential election campaign.

THE FALL CAMPAIGN

Unfortunately for the Democrats, they lost momentum even before the summer was over. First came some confusion and backtracking over naming a new Democratic national party chairman; the episode left Mondale appearing indecisive and reminded voters of some of the unhappier days of the Carter Administration. Another summer problem for the Democrats centered around vice-presidential candidate Ferraro's family finances. Federal law requires members of Congress to disclose all financial holdings. Not long after the Democratic convention, questions arose concerning the adequacy of Ferraro's financial disclosure statement, particularly in regard to her husband John Zaccaro's business investments. Each day brought more allegations and innuendos. Ferraro eventually quieted the controversy by releasing detailed financial statements for herself and her husband, and by answering questions in a marathon press conference. But for Mondale, who had hoped to go on the offensive against the Reagan Administration, the affair was both damaging and distracting.

Meanwhile, the Reagan campaign generated high enthusiasm. The Republican national convention was a made-for-television pep rally for the president. Speaker after speaker praised the accomplishments of the Reagan-Bush Administration, and newspaper headlines reinforced Republican optimism. Inflation rates remained low, unemployment fell, the economy grew, and the United States garnered a record number of medals at the 1984 Olympic games.

In the last weeks of the presidential election campaign of 1984, Reagan and Mondale faced off in two question-and-answer sessions, known as "the debates."

The Reagan strategy was to ride the crest of favorable news into the White House. The president claimed credit for economic recovery at home and peace through strength abroad, while labeling Mondale a prophet of doom and gloom who wanted to return the nation to the "failed policies of the Carter years."

Conversely, the Democrats tried to paint Reagan as a detached president, uninvolved, and uninformed on the issues of the day. Mondale hammered away at three issues on which he perceived Reagan to be vulnerable. First, Mondale attacked the Reagan economic program as both unfair and ineffective. He charged that Reaganomics gave lucrative tax breaks to the wealthy while crippling programs that helped the poor, aided education, and protected the environment. Worse, he said, the economic recovery was an illusion, nothing but "blue smoke and mirrors." Soon, Mondale warned, the huge federal budget deficits would drag the economy into a new, more severe recession. To reduce the deficit, Mondale announced he would raise taxes. Reagan responded by claiming that economic growth alone would be sufficient to reduce the deficit. As for Mondale's pledge to raise taxes, said Reagan, that was one promise Mondale could be counted on to keep.

Second, Mondale and the Democrats condemned the Reagan Administration for foreign policy failures. In the Middle East, Mondale charged, the president's inattention to detail left U.S. forces in Beirut unnecessarily vulnerable to terrorist bombings, which killed more than 250 marines. Mondale also suggested that Reagan's policies in Central America were slowly dragging the United States into guerrilla wars. Mondale's most persistent foreign policy criticisms focused on the issue of arms control. Instead of negotiating an arms control agreement, said Mondale, the Reagan Administration has stepped up the arms race, and the world has become a more dangerous place. Reagan responded to Mondale's attacks by asserting that the world is safer now because America is stronger. In contrast to the Carter-Mondale years, the United States now has the means and the will to defend her vital interests. What's more, Reagan argued, the Russians would soon be back at the negotiating table to discuss arms control because they respect strength.

A third issue on which the Democratic ticket hoped to gain ground was the thorny question of religion and politics. During the Republican convention, conservative Christian fundamentalist groups were quite conspicuous. President Reagan told one gathering of fundamentalists that religion and government are closely

The losers. . . .
Walter Mondale and
Geraldine Ferraro,
Democrats

related, and accused those opposed to organized school prayer of being intolerant of religion. Walter Mondale suggested that Reagan's ties to religious conservatives threatened the separation of church and state. "Do you want Jerry Falwell choosing Supreme Court justices?" Mondale asked. Attempting to defuse religion as an issue, Reagan vehemently denied any intention to breach the church/state wall.

Although the Democrats hoped to put Reagan on the defensive, it was Mondale and Ferraro who had trouble getting their campaigns in gear. Mondale's early crowds were small, and his speaking style was often flat. Ferraro generated some excitement in her campaign appearances, but she was dogged by antiabortion demonstrators wherever she went. Hecklers frequently disrupted appearances by both Democratic candidates.

No such problems beset the Republicans. Reagan's basic strategy was to run for reelection by being presidential. He met with foreign leaders and issued official statements; held no press conferences and limited his public appearances to speeches before carefully selected audiences of enthusiastic supporters, frequently at college campuses. The president left most of the political dirty work to Vice-President Bush, who characterized Mondale as "dull" and a "whiner."

Throughout September and early October, the polls showed Reagan ahead by twenty points or more nationwide, and leading in almost every state. Although Mondale scored higher on the issues of fairness to the poor, arms control, and religion, the polls showed that the voters credited Reagan's policies for holding down inflation and promoting economic growth. Meanwhile, Mondale's tax increase proposal received low marks. On the key question of leadership, the voters regarded Reagan as "stronger and more decisive" by a sizable margin.

Interest in the presidential and vice-presidential candidates' debates in October offered the Democrats their best and, perhaps, last chance to narrow Reagan's lead. The first Reagan-Mondale debate, on domestic policy, gave the Democratic campaign a boost. Mondale showed himself to be articulate and informed; Reagan appeared tired and, at times, confused. For the first time in the campaign, the press and, perhaps, voters began to take the Mondale candidacy seriously. His campaign appearances were met by larger and more enthusiastic crowds. For the Republicans the debate cast a small shadow over their campaign, the shadow of old age. At 73, was Reagan too old? The polls showed that Mondale had won the debate and considerably improved his image as a leader, but he still trailed far behind Reagan.

*The winners. . . .
Ronald Reagan and
George Bush,
Republicans*

In contrast to the Reagan-Mondale confrontation, the debate between the two vice-presidential candidates was almost anticlimactic. George Bush energetically defended Reagan's policies, while Geraldine Ferraro presented herself as cool and capable. Most observers judged, however, that the vice-presidential debate would change few votes in the long run.

For Mondale, the second debate—on foreign policy—was crucial. Behind in the polls, he needed a clearcut debate victory to have even an outside chance to win the election. He performed well; in fact, a panel of debate experts unanimously judged Mondale the victor on the issues. But on another dimension, Reagan did better. Although he made several misstatements of fact, the old Reagan style was back, allaying voters' fears on the issue of age.

THE VOTERS DECIDE

On Election Day, Reagan won, Mondale lost. Personalities, organization, and issues all played a role in the president's victory. First, Ronald Reagan had become the most popular figure in contemporary American politics. During the campaign, Democrats coined the phrase "Teflon president" to describe him. No matter what the problem—the bombings in Beirut, the severe recession of 1982, or scandals involving presidential appointees—Reagan's personal popularity among the voters seemed not to suffer. In contrast, Walter Mondale had difficulty establishing a positive image for himself. Before the first debate, news commentators sometimes described Mondale's image problem as the "wimp factor." Geraldine Ferraro added some spark to the Democratic ticket, but most voters based their voting choice on the presidential rather than the vice-presidential candidates.

Second, the Republicans ran the reelection campaign like a well-oiled machine, while Mondale and Ferraro always seemed to be struggling to overcome mistakes and misfortunes. Reagan did a masterful job of using his incumbency as a campaign tool. The White House took advantage of every opportunity to present Reagan as a strong and statesmanlike leader, whether it was the fortieth anniversary of D-Day or the opening of the Olympic Games at Los Angeles.

Finally, Reagan won on the issues, at least on the one issue that counted most in 1984—the economy. Compared to 1980, inflation and interest rates were down significantly. The unemployment rate was only slightly lower than in 1980, but it was much lower than it had been in 1982 in the midst of the recession, and it was still dropping. Although the federal deficit and the balance of payments deficit were at record high levels, neither of those economic statistics pinched the voters' pocketbooks in any immediately painful fashion. American presidential elections more often than not are decided on pocketbook issues and this one was no exception. A majority of voting Americans felt they were indeed better off in 1984 than in 1980 and, consequently, they voted for Reagan.

Moreover, Reagan promised further prosperity at no additional cost. For the president, economic growth is the ultimate solution. It would eliminate the deficit, uplift the poor, and ensure a strong defense. There would be no need for tax increases, reduction in Social Security, cutbacks in defense spending, or bothersome programs to conserve energy. Reagan preached the gospel of boundless optimism, and in 1984 that was the message Americans wanted to hear.

Mondale's message, on the other hand, was one of caution, restraint, and some sacrifice. He pointed out that many Americans—the poor, minorities, workers in depressed industries—had been bypassed by the recovery. He warned of huge budget and trade deficits, and he proposed a tax increase. Historians may one day tell us that Mondale's reading of America's future was more realistic, but it was not good politics, at least not in 1984. Ronald Reagan's message won the day.

THE 1984 ELECTION AND THE FUTURE OF AMERICAN POLITICS

Now that the 1984 election is history, we can begin to assess its impact on American politics. Is the balance changing between the parties? As you can see from the chart inside the front cover of this book, Reagan ran solidly among traditional Republican support groups: white Protestants, professionals, midwesterners, westerners, and upper-income earners. But he also did exceptionally well among groups that historically have been Democrats: Catholics, labor union members and their families, blue-collar workers, and Southern whites. Among those groups who compose the traditional Democratic coalition, only blacks, Hispanics, Jews, the very poor, and the unemployed stayed with Mondale in significant numbers.

For many Americans of the baby-boom generation, the factors that molded the original Democratic coalition are not relevant in the 1980s. Franklin D. Roosevelt is merely a historical figure, and the economic and social disaffection of the 1930s are no longer meaningful.

This, however, does not mean that America has embarked on an era of Republican dominance. Ronald Reagan's victory in 1984 was a personal triumph, rather than a party triumph. The election left the Democrats firmly entrenched in the U.S. House of Representatives, and in good position to wrest control of the U.S. Senate in 1986. Democrats also hold a majority of governorships.

Instead of indicating *realignment*, the 1984 election showed that America is in a period of party *dealignment*, as millions of voters opted for President Reagan and then cast their ballots for Democrats in congressional, state, and local races. This is an age of ticket-splitting independents; they vote less and less on the basis of party, and more and more on the basis of issues and personalities. In an era when political parties are becoming increasingly irrelevant to voters, the greatest challenge for the two parties in the last decade-and-a-half of the twentieth century may not be to attain majority-party status, but rather to survive.

Glossary

ADVERSARY PROCEEDING Legal procedure in which each side in a lawsuit presents evidence and arguments to bolster its position only, ignoring information that might support the other side.

AFFIRMATIVE ACTION The legal requirement that companies and other organizations take positive steps to increase the number of women and/or minority group members in their membership or employment.

AGENDA BUILDING The process whereby problems become matters of governmental concern.

AGENT Theory of representation in which members of Congress vote as the majority of their constituents would vote.

AGENTS OF SOCIALIZATION Factors that contribute to political socialization by shaping formal and informal learning about politics.

AMICUS CURIAE BRIEF In appellate cases, a brief submitted by parties not directly involved in the lawsuit.

ATTENTIVE PUBLIC Those people who have an active and continuing interest in an issue.

BASELINE FORCE The defense doctrine that the U.S. should maintain a military force capable of conducting one major military campaign and one minor campaign simultaneously.

BICAMERALISM The division of legislative power between two chambers.

BILINGUAL EDUCATION Teaching academic subjects in two languages—English and the native language of the students.

BILL OF ATTAINDER A law declaring a person guilty of a crime and providing for punishment without indictment or trial.

BILL OF RIGHTS The first ten amendments to the Constitution listing individual rights and privileges.

BLOCK GRANT A federal grants-in-aid program in which money is available for broad, general policy areas.

BRIEFS Written legal arguments.

BUDGET DEFICIT When budget expenditures exceed receipts.

BUDGET SURPLUS When budget receipts exceed expenditures.

BUSINESS CYCLE Cyclical phases of the economy, ranging from economic slump to economic boom.

CAPITAL PUNISHMENT The death penalty.

CAPITALISM An economy that conforms closely to the free market model.

CAPTURED AGENCIES Agencies that are allegedly controlled by the very economic interests they are supposed to be regulating.

CASH-TRANSFER PROGRAMS Government programs that give money directly to individuals.

CATEGORY GRANT A federal grants-in-aid program in which money is available for specific, narrow purposes.

CAUCUS[ES] Local and district political party meetings to select delegates for state and national nominating conventions.

CENTRALLY DIRECTED ECONOMY An economic system in which the basic decisions of what, how, and for whom to produce are made by the government.

CERTIORARI The technical term for the Supreme Court's decision to hear arguments and make a ruling in a case.

CHECKS AND BALANCES The system of the separation, overlapping, and limitation of powers among the branches of government.

CIVIL CASE A legal dispute between private parties.

CIVIL LIBERTIES The protection of the individual from the unrestricted power of government.

CIVILIAN SUPREMACY OF THE ARMED FORCES The concept that the armed forces should be under the direct control of civilian authorities.

CLEAR AND PRESENT DANGER RULE The point at which a form of expression becomes sufficiently threatening to the society to justify its restraint or suppression.

CLOTURE Procedure for shutting off a filibuster (requires 60 votes).

COATTAIL EFFECT Political phenomenon in which a strong presidential candidate gives a boost to fellow party members on the ballot.

COLD WAR Period of global tensions between the United States and the Soviet Union.

COMMUNISM   An economy that conforms fairly closely to the centrally directed economic model, usually combined with an authoritarian form of government.

CONCURRING OPINION   A judicial opinion that agrees with the majority opinion's decision but disagrees with its reasoning.

CONFEDERATION   A league of quasi-independent states.

CONFERENCE   Closed meeting of Supreme Court judges.

CONFERENCE COMMITTEE   Committee formed with members of both chambers of Congress, whose job is to reach a compromise when the House and Senate versions of a bill are not identical.

CONSERVATISM   A set of political beliefs calling for decreased government activity in the areas of social welfare and regulation of business, and increased government involvement in the area of social policy.

CONSTITUENCY   Those people represented in government by an elected official.

CONSUMER PRICE INDEX (CPI)   A measure of inflation used by the government for increasing Social Security and other payments indexed to inflation.

CONTAINMENT   The postwar policy of keeping the Soviets from expanding their sphere of control.

CONTINUING RESOLUTION   A provision to fund government programs pending the approval of the budget for the new fiscal year.

CONTRACT CASES   Litigation about a written or implied contract.

CONVENTIONAL WEAPONS   Nonnuclear weapons.

COOPERATIVE FEDERALISM   A period in which the relationship between the federal government and state and local governments is one of cooperation.

COST-BENEFIT ANALYSIS   An evaluation of a proposed policy based on comparing its expected benefits with its anticipated costs.

CRIMINAL CASE   A legal dispute between the prosecutor, representing the government, and the defendant, who is charged with breaking a law.

CURRENT SERVICES BUDGET   A budgetary estimate of the cost of continuing present government services at the current levels.

DE FACTO SEGREGATION   Racial segregation resulting from housing and other unofficial social patterns.

DE JURE SEGREGATION   Racial segregation required by law.

DEFENDANT   The person who stands accused in a criminal trial, or the person against whom suit is filed in a civil trial.

DELEGATED POWERS   The powers of the national government found in Article I, Section 8 of the Constitution.

DEMOCRACY   A government in which a majority of the people rule either directly (pure democracy) or through their representatives (representative democracy).

DEMOCRATIC ELITISM   Political phenomenon in which those people most politically active are the most supportive of democratic principles.

DEMOCRATIZATION   The process of opening the political process to participation by a broader spectrum of individuals and groups.

DEPRESSION   A very severe and prolonged economic decline.

DÉTENTE   A period of relative relaxation of tension in the relationship between the U.S. and the Soviet Union.

DETERRENCE   The U.S. doctrine that the Soviets will be deterred from launching a first strike because the U.S. has an assured second-strike capability.

DEVIATING ELECTION   An election in which short-term factors upset the normal party balance.

DISSENTING OPINION   A judicial opinion that expresses disagreement with the majority's decision and its reasoning.

DOUBLE STANDARD   The judicial doctrine that *economic legislation* is presumed constitutional unless proven otherwise, while *restrictions on the basic freedoms* guaranteed by the Bill of Rights are presumed unconstitutional, with the burden of proof on the government to justify their constitutionality.

DUAL FEDERALISM   The doctrine that the states are equal participants with the national government in the federal system.

DUE PROCESS CLAUSE   A broad and flexible concept stated in the Fifth Amendment and reiterated in the Fourteenth, protecting the individual against the deprivation of life, liberty, or property by arbitrary or unreasonable acts of federal or state governments.

ELECTORAL COLLEGE   A body of electors, popularly chosen in the separate states in presidential elections, who actually cast the state's electoral votes (one for each member of Congress) for the winning presidential candidate in their respective states.

ELITE THEORY   The concept that a relatively small cohesive group holds power in America.

ENLIGHTENMENT An eighteenth-century movement that put great trust in the ability of human beings to solve their problems through the use of reason.

ENTITLEMENT PROGRAMS Government programs such as Food Stamps and Social Security, so called because eligible recipients are entitled to receive benefits by law.

EQUAL RIGHTS AMENDMENT (ERA) Constitutional amendment proposed by women's rights groups.

EX POST FACTO LAW A retroactive law.

EXCISE TAXES Taxes levied on the manufacture, sale, or consumption of some particular commodity, such as gasoline or cigarettes.

EXCLUSIONARY RULE Judicial doctrine stating that when the police violate an individual's constitutional rights, the evidence obtained as a result of the police misconduct or error cannot be used against the defendant.

EXECUTIVE BRANCH The branch of government that is given the power to execute and enforce laws.

EXECUTIVE AGREEMENTS International agreements between the president and foreign nations that have the effect of treaties but do not require Senate ratification.

FEDERAL RESERVE BOARD Independent regulatory commission composed of seven members and appointed by the president for fourteen-year terms.

FEDERALISM A political system that divides power between a national government and the state governments.

FELONY A serious criminal offense, usually punishable by a large fine and/or more than a year in jail.

FILIBUSTER An effort to defeat a bill through unlimited debate on the floor of the Senate.

FIRST CONCURRENT RESOLUTION Congressional resolution setting nonbinding spending targets for the appropriations and authorizations committees.

FIRST STRIKE The initial offensive of a general nuclear war, aimed at knocking out the other side's ability to retaliate.

FISCAL POLICY The control of government spending and taxation for the purpose of achieving economic goals.

FISCAL YEAR The government's budgetary year, running from October 1 through September 30.

FORMULA GRANT A federal grants-in-aid program in which funds are awarded on the basis of a formula established by Congress.

FROSTBELT The northeastern and midwestern regions of the U.S.

GENDER GAP Difference in political opinion between men and women.

GENERAL REVENUE SHARING A federal grants-in-aid program in which money is provided to states and localities with few strings attached.

GERRYMANDERING Redrawing the boundaries of election districts to benefit a particular political party or group.

GNP DEFLATOR A measure of inflation.

GRANDFATHER CLAUSE Requirement that all prospective voters pass literacy tests, except those whose grandfathers had been eligible to vote in 1860. This clause allowed whites to vote without taking the test, but not blacks.

GRANTS-IN-AID Federal program providing funds to state and local governments for purposes determined in Washington, D.C.

GROSS NATIONAL PRODUCT (GNP) The sum total of the goods and services produced in the economy in a year—a standard measure of the economy's size.

HABEAS CORPUS, WRIT OF A court order requiring government authorities to show cause why a person is being held in custody.

HEAD OF STATE President's role as official head of the government.

HEROIC PRESIDENT The positive image of a strong president who leads the nation toward peace, prosperity, and justice for all.

IMPEACHMENT A constitutional process in which the House accuses the president of offenses for which he should be removed from office. The power to try and remove the president (by two thirds vote) is vested in the Senate.

IMPERIAL PRESIDENCY The negative image of a president who has grown too powerful and may misuse his power.

IMPLIED POWERS Powers not explicitly mentioned in Article I, Section 8 of the Constitution, but derived by interpretation of expressly mentioned powers.

IMPOUNDMENT The refusal of a president to spend funds already appropriated by Congress.

IN-KIND BENEFIT PROGRAMS Government programs that assign goods and services directly to individuals.

INFLATION A general increase in wages and prices representing a decline in the value of the nation's currency.

INITIATIVE   A process of initiating legislation by petitioning to place a proposal on the ballot, and then enacting or defeating the proposal by popular vote.

INNER CABINET   The Secretaries of State, Defense, and Treasury, and the Attorney General. These four cabinet members are most frequently asked for policymaking advice by the president.

INTEREST   Payment for the use of money.

INTEREST GROUP   An organization of people who join together voluntarily on the basis of some interest they share, for the purpose of influencing public policy.

INTERGOVERNMENTAL RELATIONS   The relationships among governments within the federal system.

INTERNALIZE THE EXTERNALITIES   Government action to ensure that all the economic and social costs of a good or service are reflected in its cost.

ISOLATIONISM   American foreign policy characterized by a pulling back from the affairs of other nations.

JIM CROW LAWS   Laws requiring rigid racial segregation in most aspects of life.

JOINT COMMITTEES   Congressional committees that include members from both houses.

JUDICIAL ACTIVISM   The view that the responsibility of judges to interpret and apply the Constitution force them to invalidate any actions that violate the Constitution as they understand it.

JUDICIAL BRANCH   The branch of government that is given the power to interpret laws.

JUDICIAL RESTRAINT   The view that judges should avoid substituting their own policy judgments for the judgment of legislators and executives.

JUDICIAL REVIEW   The power of courts to determine whether the acts of other governmental bodies conform to the Constitution.

JUDICIAL REVIEW   The power of the courts to review the actions of other branches and units of government to determine whether they are consistent with the Constitution and, if they are not, to declare them null and void.

JURISDICTION   The right or power of a court to decide a case or controversy.

KEYNESIAN ECONOMICS   An economic theory suggesting that government should use fiscal and monetary policy to solve economic problems.

LABOR PRODUCTIVITY   The amount of output generated per worker.

LAFFER CURVE   An economic model that purports to show the relationship between tax rates and total tax revenue as a bell-shaped curve.

LAISSEZ-FAIRE ECONOMICS   An economic theory suggesting that government intervention impedes the free-market forces that drive a healthy economy.

LEGISLATIVE BRANCH   The branch of government that is given the power to make laws.

LEGISLATIVE VETO   Provision in a bill that gives one or both houses of Congress, or a congressional committee, the power to invalidate an action by the executive branch.

LIBERALISM   A set of political beliefs calling for increased government activity in the areas of social welfare and regulation of business, and decreased government involvement in the area of social policy.

LITIGANTS   The parties involved in a legal dispute.

LOBBYIST   An interest group representative whose job is to present a group's point of view to government decision-makers.

MAINTAINING ELECTION   An election in which the normal party balance remains unchanged.

MAJESTIC VAGUENESS   Describes the nonspecific nature of America's Constitution, which leaves room for growth and adaptation to changing times.

MAJORITY LEADER   The leader of the majority party in the Senate; the second-in-command in the House.

MAJORITY OPINION   The judicial opinion expressing the official voice of the Supreme Court. It explains the Court's decision and gives guidance to lower federal courts in dealing with similar cases in the future.

MAJORITY WHIP   First assistant to the majority leader.

MANDAMUS, WRIT OF   A court order directing that a specific act or duty be performed.

MARGINAL RATE   The rate of tax imposed on the last dollar earned.

MARKET ECONOMY   An economic system in which the basic economic decisions of what, how, and for whom to produce are made by the market.

MASS PUBLIC   Those people who have little interest in a particular public issue.

MINORITY LEADER   The leader of the minority party in each chamber of Congress.

MINORITY RIGHTS   Individual freedom and rights not dependent on consensus. These rights are protected by the Bill of Rights in the Constitution.

Minority Whip   First assistant to the minority leader.

Misdemeanor   A criminal offense, less serious than a felony, usually punishable by a small fine and/or less than a year in jail.

Mixed Economy   An economic system that combines aspects of a centrally directed economy with a market economy.

Monetarism   An economic theory suggesting that government should rely almost exclusively on monetary policy to solve economic problems.

Monetary Policy   The control of the money supply for the purpose of achieving economic goals.

Monopoly   A single firm is the sole producer of a good or service.

Monroe Doctrine   The foreign policy doctrine enunciated by President James Monroe: the U.S. would stay out of European affairs and Europe must stay out of the Americas.

Multinational Corporation   A corporation that operates in several nations.

Multiple Advocacy System   Decisionmaking process in which the president solicits advice from a broad range of sources.

National Debt   The cumulative budget deficit minus the cumulative budget surplus.

National Supremacy Clause   The provision found in Article IV of the Constitution, declaring that the laws made under it, and the treaties of the United States are the supreme law of the land.

Natural Monopoly   An industry in which it would be impractical or economically inefficient for there to be more than one firm doing business in an area, such as the local (not long-distance) telephone company and the electricity and natural gas utilities.

Natural Rights   The theory that people possess certain rights, derived from a natural law, which cannot be taken away.

Necessary and Proper Clause   The last clause in Article I, Section 8 of the Constitution granting Congress the power to make all laws "necessary and proper" for carrying out the delegated powers.

Normal Vote   Election outcome reflecting the underlying party balance in the electorate.

North Atlantic Treaty Organization (NATO)   A regional defense alliance among the U.S., Canada, and their Western European allies.

Off-budget Operations   Federal financial operations involving loans and loan guarantees that are not included in the formal budget.

Official Agenda   The set of problems government chooses to tackle.

Oligopoly   Only a few producers affect the market for a particular good or service and these few do not compete vigorously with one another.

Opinion Leaders   Influential people who lead public opinion, make political decisions, and muster support for policies among both the attentive and the mass public.

Organization of Petroleum Exporting Countries (OPEC)   A thirteen-nation combination of oil producers that tries to keep world oil prices at a certain level.

Original Jurisdiction   Supreme Court's non-appellate jurisdiction, usually limited to cases initiated by the states.

Parity   Government-established price for farm products designed to maintain farmers' purchasing power.

Per Curiam Opinion   An unsigned judicial opinion.

Phillips Curve   An economic hypothesis suggesting that as the rate of inflation goes down, unemployment goes up.

Plaintiff   One who commences a civil lawsuit.

Platform   Statement of party principles and positions on issues.

Plea Bargaining   A process whereby a criminal defendant pleads guilty to a lesser offense than the one with which he or she was initially charged.

Pluralism, or Pluralist Democracy   The theory that political power is divided among competing groups of elites.

Pocket Veto   A method by which a president can kill a bill indirectly by not acting on it after Congress has adjourned.

Policy   *See* **Public Policy**

Policy Adoption   The formal decision by a governmental body to adopt a particular policy.

Policy Evaluation   The assessment and appraisal of public policies.

Policy Formulation   The development of governmental policies to deal with the problems on the official agenda.

Policy Implementation   The stage of the policy process in which policies are executed.

POLICY OUTCOMES The impact of public policies in operation.

POLICY OUTPUTS What government actually does.

POLICY TRIANGLES Three-sided political alliances among interest groups, agency officials, and key members of Congress.

POLITICAL ACTION COMMITTEE (PAC) An organization formed by an interest group to contribute money to political campaigns.

POLITICAL EFFICACY The extent to which individuals believe that they can influence the policymaking process.

POLITICAL PARTY A group of individuals who organize for the purpose of electing candidates to office and thereby influencing public policy.

POLITICAL SOCIALIZATION The process of acquiring political knowledge, attitudes, and beliefs.

POLITICS The allocation of power and authority; the process that determines who gets what, when, and how.

POLL TAX Tax levied on the right to vote.

POVERTY LINE An amount of money that measures the subsistence level for an individual or family.

PREFERRED POSITION Judicial doctrine that civil liberties are the basic rights that make all other rights possible. Hence, the Court presumes that governmental restrictions on these freedoms are unconstitutional unless proven otherwise.

PRESIDENT PRO TEMPORE A senator from the majority party selected to preside over the Senate in the absence of the vice-president.

PRIMARY ELECTION An election in which voters choose party candidates for the general election.

PRIVATE SECTOR Nongovernmental entities, such as corporations.

PROCEDURAL DUE PROCESS Refers to the execution, administration, and interpretation of laws in accordance with accepted standards of justice.

PROGRESSIVE TAX A tax that taxes higher-income groups at a higher rate than lower-income groups.

PROJECT GRANT A federal grants-in-aid program not based on a formula, in which state and local governments apply and compete for federal funds.

PROPORTIONAL OR FLAT-RATE TAX A tax that taxes all income groups at the same percentage rate.

PROSECUTOR The attorney representing the government in a criminal case.

PROSPECTIVE VOTING Voting decision based on the prospect that the candidate will adopt certain clear policy stances.

PUBLIC AGENDA The set of problems that are raised to the level of public concern.

PUBLIC POLICY How government decisionmakers respond or fail to respond to public issues.

PUBLIC POLICY PROCESS The making, enacting, and evaluation of public policy.

PUBLIC SECTOR Governmental entities.

QUOTAS The legal requirement that businesses and other organizations include within their membership or employment a certain percentage of women and/or minority group members.

RANDOM SAMPLE Sample in which every member of a universe has an equal chance to be included.

REALIGNING ELECTION An election in which voters change basic party loyalties.

REAPPORTIONMENT Redistribution of legislative seats to reflect population shifts.

RECESSION An economic downturn.

RECONCILIATION PROCESS Step in the budgetary process in which congressional committees alter appropriations and authorization measures to bring them in line with the Second Concurrent Resolution.

REDISTRICT To redraw the boundaries of election districts as population changes.

REFERENDUM Submission of a legislative proposal or popular initiative to a vote of the general electorate.

REGRESSIVE TAX A tax that exacts a lower rate from higher-income groups than from lower-income groups.

REINSTATING ELECTION An election that restores normal voting habits after a brief deviation.

RESPONSIBLE PARTIES Political parties that faithfully implement the policies proposed in their platforms.

RETROSPECTIVE VOTING Voting decision based on the voter's perception of a candidate's or party's performance in office.

REVERSE DISCRIMINATION The allegation that affirmative action efforts on behalf of women and minority group members effectively discriminate against white males.

RULE MAKING A regulatory process used by government agencies to enact legally binding regulations.

Rule of Four   Procedure in which the Supreme Court determines which cases to hear; four of the nine judges must agree.

Sample   Small group actually studied or questioned.

Second Concurrent Resolution   Congressional resolution setting binding ceilings for appropriations and authorizations; must be approved by September 15.

Second Strike   The ability of a nation to absorb the full force of a nuclear strike and still have enough nuclear firepower left to inflict unacceptable damage in response.

Select or Special Committees   Congressional committees established for a limited period.

Selective Incorporation of the Bill of Rights   The judicial interpretation that, on a piecemeal basis, selected parts of the Bill of Rights apply to state actions.

Senatorial Courtesy   The custom that senators from the president's party have a veto on judicial appointments from their states.

Separate but Equal   Judicial doctrine established by the Supreme Court in *Plessy* v. *Ferguson* (1896) holding that separate facilities for whites and blacks satisfy the Equal Protection Clause's requirements. Overturned in *Brown* v. *Topeka* (1954).

Separation of Powers   The division of power among the executive, legislative, and judicial branches of the U.S. government.

Single-issue Group   An interest group that focuses its political efforts on a single issue or a group of strongly related issues.

Social Democracy   A mixed economy that includes public ownership of basic industries and free market direction, combined with a democratic government.

Spoils System   A system of hiring government employees from among the friends and supporters of the elected officeholders.

Stagflation   Economic condition in which high unemployment and high rates of inflation exist at the same time.

Standing Committees   Permanent congressional committees.

Stare Decisis   The judicial principle stating that court decisions stand as precedents for future cases involving the same issues.

Statutory Law   Laws enacted by the legislative process.

Strategic Weapons   Nuclear weapons.

Substantive Due Process   Refers to actual content or subject matter of law.

Sunbelt   The southern and southwestern regions of the U.S.

Supergrades   The highest federal job classifications, GS 16–18.

Supply-side Economics   An approach to economic problems that focuses on factors, such as tax rates, that affect the supply of goods and services in the economy.

Tax Deduction   Expenditures, such as charitable contributions, that may be deducted from gross income before computing the tax owed.

Tax Preference   A tax deduction or exclusion that allows individuals to owe less tax than they would otherwise.

Test Case   A case put forward by an interest group in hopes of receiving a favorable judicial ruling.

Ticket Splitting   Voting for candidates from different parties in different races in the same election.

Tight-money Policy   Monetary policy of high interest rates.

Tort Case   Legal dispute over an injury to a person or to property.

Triad   The three-sided configuration of American defense systems: intercontinental ballistic missiles; submarine-launched missiles; and B-52 bombers.

Trustee   Theory of representation in which members of Congress use their own judgment to determine what is in their constituents' best interest.

"Two Presidencies"   Concept that there are two presidencies, a weaker one for domestic affairs and a more powerful one for foreign affairs.

Unitary System   A political system in which governmental authority is concentrated in a single national government.

United Nations (UN)   An international organization founded in 1945 as a diplomatic forum for conflict resolution among the world's nations.

Universe   In a survey research project, the population to be studied.

Veterans' Preference   Procedure by which veterans are given additional points on civil service exams.

Warsaw Pact   A regional military alliance between the Soviet Union and most of the nations of Eastern Europe.

"White Primary"   Electoral system in the South that prevented the participation of blacks in the Democratic primary.

The Declaration of Independence

IN CONGRESS, JULY 4, 1776

*The unanimous Declaration
of the thirteen united States of America.*

When in the Course of human events, it becomes necessary for one people to dissolve the political bands which have connected them with another, and to assume among the Powers of the earth, the separate and equal station to which the Laws of Nature and of Nature's God entitle them, a decent respect to the opinions of mankind requires that they should declare the causes which impel them to the separation.

We hold these truths to be self-evident, that all men are created equal, that they are endowed by their Creator with certain unalienable Rights, that among these are Life, Liberty and the pursuit of Happiness. That to secure these rights, Governments are instituted among Men, deriving their just powers from the consent of the governed. That whenever any Form of Government becomes destructive of these ends, it is the Right of the People to alter or to abolish it, and to institute new Government, laying its foundation on such principles and organizing its powers in such form, as to them shall seem most likely to effect their Safety and Happiness. Prudence, indeed, will dictate that Governments long established should not be changed for light and transient causes; and accordingly all experience hath shown, that mankind are more disposed to suffer, while evils are sufferable, than to right themselves by abolishing the forms to which they are accustomed. But when a long train of abuses and usurpations, pursuing invariably the same Object evinces a design to reduce them under absolute Despotism, it is their right, it is their duty, to throw off such Government, and to provide new Guards for their future security.—Such has been the patient sufferance of these Colonies; and such is now the necessity which constrains them to alter their former Systems of Government. The history of the present King of Great Britain is a history of repeated injuries and usurpations, all having in direct object the establishment of an absolute Tyranny over these States. To prove this, let Facts be submitted to a candid world.

He has refused his Assent to Laws, the most wholesome and necessary for the public good.

He has forbidden his Governors to pass Laws of immediate and pressing importance, unless suspended in their operation till his Assent should be obtained; and when so suspended, he has utterly neglected to attend to them.

He has refused to pass other Laws for the accommodation of large districts of people, unless those people would relinquish the right of Representation in the Legislature, a right inestimable to them and formidable to tyrants only.

He has called together legislative bodies at places unusual, uncomfortable, and distant from the depository of their Public Records, for the sole purpose of fatiguing them into compliance with his measures.

He has dissolved Representative Houses repeatedly, for opposing with manly firmness his invasions on the rights of the people.

He has refused for a long time, after such dissolutions, to cause others to be elected; whereby the Legislative Powers, incapable of Annihilation, have returned to the People at large for their exercise; the State remaining in the mean time exposed to all the dangers of invasion from without, and convulsions within.

He has endeavoured to prevent the population of these States; for that purpose obstructing the Laws for Naturalization of Foreigners; refusing to pass others to encourage their migrations hither, and raising the conditions of new Appropriations of Lands.

He has obstructed the Administration of Justice, by refusing his Assent to Laws for establishing Judiciary Powers.

He has made Judges dependent on his Will alone, for the tenure of their offices, and the amount and payment of their salaries.

He has erected a multitude of New Offices, and sent hither swarms of Officers to harass our people, and eat out their substance.

He has kept among us, in times of peace, Standing Armies without the Consent of our legislatures.

He has affected to render the Military independent of and superior to the Civil Power.

He has combined with others to subject us to a jurisdiction foreign to our constitution, and unacknowledged by our laws; giving his Assent to their acts of pretended Legislation:

For quartering large bodies of armed troops among us:

For protecting them, by a mock Trial, from Punishment for any Murders which they should commit on the inhabitants of these States:

For cutting off our Trade with all parts of the world:

For imposing taxes on us without our Consent:

For depriving us in many cases, of the benefits of Trial by Jury:

For transporting us beyond Seas to be tried for pretended offences:

For abolishing the free System of English Laws in a neighbouring Province, establishing therein an Arbitrary government, and enlarging its Boundaries so as to render it at once an example and fit instrument for introducing the same absolute rule into these Colonies:

For taking away our Charters, abolishing our most valuable Laws, and altering fundamentally the Forms of our Governments:

For suspending our own Legislatures, and declaring themselves invested with Power to legislate for us in all cases whatsoever.

He has abdicated Government here, by declaring us out of his Protection and waging War against us.

He has plundered our seas, ravaged our Coasts, burnt our towns, and destroyed the lives of our people.

He is at this time transporting large armies of foreign mercenaries to compleat the works of death, desolation and tyranny, already begun with circumstances of Cruelty & perfidy scarcely paralleled in the most barbarous ages, and totally unworthy the Head of a civilized nation.

He has constrained our fellow Citizens taken Captive on the high Seas to bear Arms against their Country, to become the executioners of their friends and Brethren, or to fall themselves by their Hands.

He has excited domestic insurrections amongst us, and has endeavoured to bring on the inhabitants of our frontiers, the merciless Indian Savages, whose known rule of warfare, is an undistinguished destruction of all ages, sexes and conditions.

In every stage of these Oppressions We have Petitioned for Redress in the most humble terms: Our repeated Petitions have been answered only by repeated injury. A Prince, whose character is thus marked by every act which may define a Tyrant, is unfit to be the ruler of a free people.

Nor have We been wanting in attentions to our British brethren. We have warned them from time to time of attempts by their legislature to extend an unwarrantable jurisdiction over us. We have reminded them of the circumstances of our emigration and settlement here. We have appealed to their native justice and magnanimity, and we have conjured them by the ties of our common kindred to disavow these usurpations which, would inevitably interrupt our connections and correspondence. They too have been deaf to the voice of justice and of consanguinity. We must, therefore, acquiesce in the necessity, which denounces our Separation, and hold them, as we hold the rest of mankind, Enemies in War, in Peace Friends.

We, therefore, the Representatives of the united States of America, in General Congress, Assembled, appealing to the Supreme Judge of the world for the rectitude of our intentions, do, in the Name, and by authority of the good People of these Colonies, solemnly publish and declare, That these United Colonies are, and of Right ought to be Free and Indepenent States; that they are Absolved from all Allegiance to the British Crown, and that all political connection between them and the State of Great Britain, is and ought to be totally dissolved; and that as Free and Independent States, they have full power to levy War, conclude Peace, contract Alliances, establish Commerce, and to do all other Acts and Things which Independent States may of right do. And for the support of this Declaration, with a firm reliance on the Protection of Divine Providence, we mutually pledge to each other our Lives, our Fortunes and our sacred Honor.

The Constitution
of the United States of America

We the People of the United States, in Order to form a more perfect Union, establish justice, insure domestic Tranquility, provide for the common defence, promote the general Welfare, and secure the Blessings of Liberty to ourselves and our Posterity, do ordain and establish this Constitution for the United States of America.

ARTICLE I

Section 1.

All legislative Powers herein granted shall be vested in a Congress of the United States, which shall consist of a Senate and House of Representatives.

Section 2.

The House of Representatives shall be composed of Members chosen every second Year by the People of the several States, and the Electors in each State shall have the Qualifications requisite for Electors of the most numerous Branch of the State Legislature.

No Person shall be a Representative who shall not have attained to the Age of twenty five Years, and been seven Years a Citizen of the United States, and who shall not, when elected, be an Inhabitant of that State in which he shall be chosen.

Representatives and direct Taxes shall be apportioned among the several States which may be included within this Union, according to their respective Numbers, which shall be determined by adding to the whole Number of free Persons, including those bound to Service for a Term of Years, and excluding Indians not taxed, three fifths of all other Persons.[1] The actual Enumeration shall be made within three years after the first Meeting of the Congress of the United States, and within every subsequent Term of ten Years, in such Manner as they shall by Law direct. The Number of Representatives shall not exceed one for every thirty Thousand, but each State shall have at Least one Representative; and until such enumeration shall be made, the State of New Hampshire shall be entitled to chuse three, Massachusetts eight, Rhode-Island and Providence Plantations one, Connecticut five, New-York six, New Jersey four, Pennsylvania eight, Delaware one, Maryland six, Virginia ten, North Carolina five, South Carolina five, and Georgia three.

When vacancies happen in the Representation from any State, the Executive Authority thereof shall issue Writs of Election to fill such Vacancies.

The House of Representatives shall chuse their Speaker and other Officers; and shall have the sole Power of Impeachment.

Section 3.

The Senate of the United States shall be composed of two Senators from each State, chosen by the Legislature thereof, for six Years; and each Senator shall have one Vote.

Immediately after they shall be assembled in Consequence of the first Election, they shall be divided as equally as may be into three Classes. The Seats of the Senators of the first Class shall be vacated at the Expiration of the second Year, of the second Class at the Expiration of the fourth Year, and of the third Class at the Expiration of the Sixth Year, so that one third may be chosen every second Year; and if Vacancies happen by Resignation, or otherwise, during the Recess of the Legislature of any State, the Executive thereof may make temporary Appointments until the next Meeting of the Legislature, which shall then fill such Vacancies.[2]

No Person shall be a Senator who shall not have attained to the Age of thirty Years, and been nine Years a Citizen of the United States, and who shall not, when elected, be an Inhabitant of that State for which he shall be chosen.

The Vice President of the United States shall be President of the Senate, but shall have no Vote, unless they be equally divided.

The Senate shall chuse their other Officers, and also a President pro tempore, in the Absence of the Vice President, or when he shall exercise the Office of President of the United States.

The Senate shall have the sole Power to try all impeachments. When sitting for that Purpose, they shall be on Oath or Affirmation. When the President of the United States is tried the Chief Justice shall preside: And no Person shall be convicted without the Concurrence of two thirds of the Members present.

Judgment in Cases of Impeachment shall not extend further than to removal from Office, and disqualification to hold and enjoy any Office of honor, Trust or Profit under the United States; but the Party convicted shall nevertheless be liable and subject to Indictment, Trial, Judgment and Punishment, according to Law.

Section 4.

The Times, Places and Manner of holding Elections for Senators and Representatives, shall be prescribed in each State by the Legislature thereof; but the Congress may at any time by Law make or alter such Regulations, except as to the Places of chusing Senators.

The Congress shall assemble at least once in every Year, and such Meeting shall be on the first Monday in December, unless they shall by Law appoint a different Day.[3]

Section 5

Each House shall be the Judge of the Elections, Returns and Qualifications of its own Members, and a Majority of each shall constitute a

---

[1]"Other Persons" being black slaves. Modified by Amendment XIV, Section 2.

[2]Provisions changed by Amendment XVII.

[3]Provision changed by Amendment XX, Section 2.

Quorum to do Business; but a smaller Number may adjourn from day to day, and may be authorized to compel the Attendance of absent Members, in such Manner, and under such Penalties as each House may provide.

Each House may determine the Rules of its Proceedings, punish its Members for disorderly Behaviour, and, with the Concurrence of two thirds, expel a Member.

Each House shall keep a Journal of its Proceedings, and from time to time publish the same, excepting such Parts as may in their Judgment require Secrecy; and the Yeas and Nays of the Members of either House on any question shall, at the Desire of one fifth of those Present, be entered on the Journal.

Neither House, during the Session of Congress, shall, without the Consent of the other, adjourn for more than three days, nor to any other Place than that in which the two Houses shall be sitting.

Section 6.

The Senators and Representatives shall receive a Compensation for their Services, to be ascertained by Law, and paid out of the Treasury of the United States. They shall in all Cases, except Treason, Felony and Breach of the Peace, be privileged from Arrest during their Attendance at the Session of their respective Houses, and in going to and returning from the same; and for any Speech or Debate in either House, they shall not be questioned in any other Place.

No Senator or Representative shall, during the Time for which he was elected, be appointed to any civil Office under the Authority of the United State, which shall have been created, or the Emoluments whereof shall have been encreased during such time; and no Person holding any Office under the United States, shall be a Member of either House during his Continuance in Office.

Section 7.

All Bills for raising Revenue shall originate in the House of Representatives; but the Senate may propose or concur with Amendments as on other Bills.

Every Bill which shall have passed the House of Representatives and the Senate, shall, before it become a Law, be presented to the President of the United States; If he approve he shall sign it, but if not he shall return it, with his Objections to that House in which it shall have originated, who shall enter the Objections at large on their Journal, and proceed to reconsider it. If after such Reconsideration two thirds of that House shall agree to pass the Bill, it shall be sent, together with the Objections, to the other House, by which it shall likewise to be reconsidered, and if approved by two thirds of that House, it shall become a Law. But in all such Cases the Votes of both Houses shall be determined by yeas and Nays, and the Names of the Persons voting for and against the Bill shall be entered on the Journal of each House respectively. If any Bill shall not be returned by the President within ten Days (Sundays excepted) after it shall have been presented to him, the Same shall be a Law, in like Manner as if he had signed it, unless the Congress by their Adjournment prevent its Return, in which Case it shall not be a Law.

Every Order, Resolution, or Vote to which the Concurrence of the Senate and House of Representatives may be necessary (except on a question of Adjournment) shall be presented to the President of the United States; and before the Same shall take Effect, shall be approved by him, or being disapproved by him, shall be repassed by two thirds of the Senate and House of Representatives, according to the Rules and Limitations prescribed in the Case of a Bill.

Section 8.

The Congress shall have Power To lay and collect Taxes, Duties, Imposts and Excises, to pay the Debts and provide for the common Defence and general Welfare of the United States; but all Duties, Imposts and Excises shall be uniform throughout the United States;

To borrow Money on the credit of the United States;

To regulate Commerce with foreign Nations, and among the several States, and with the Indian Tribes;

To establish an uniform Rule of Naturalization, and uniform Laws on the subject of Bankruptcies throughout the United States;

To coin Money, regulate the Value thereof, and of foreign Coin, and fix the Standard of Weights and Measures;

To provide for the Punishment of counterfeiting the Securities and current Coin of the United States;

To establish Post Offices and post Roads;

To promote the Progress of Science and useful Arts, by securing for limited Times to Authors and Inventors the exclusive Right to their respective Writings and Discoveries;

To constitute Tribunals inferior to the supreme Court;

To define and punish Piracies and Felonies committed on the high Seas, and Offences against the Law of Nations;

To declare War, grant Letters of Marque and Reprisal, and make Rules concerning Captures on Land and Water;

To raise and support Armies, but no Appropriation of Money to that Use shall be for a longer Term than two Years;

To provide and maintain a Navy;

To make Rules for the Government and Regulation of the land and naval Forces;

To provide for calling forth the Militia to execute the Laws of the Union, suppress Insurrections and repel Invasions;

To provide for organizing, arming, and disciplining, the Militia, and for governing such Part of them as may be employed in the Service of the United States, reserving to the States respectively, the Appointment of the Officers, and the Authority of training the Militia according to the discipline prescribed by Congress;

To exercise exclusive Legislation in all Cases whatsoever, over such District (not exceeding ten Miles square) as may, by Cession of particular States, and the Acceptance of Congress, become the Seat of the Government of the United States, and to exercise like Authority over all Places purchased by the Consent of the Legislature of the State in which the Same shall be, for the Erection of Forts, Magazines, Arsenals, dock-Yards, and other needful Buildings;—And

To make all Laws which shall be necessary and proper for carrying into Execution the foregoing Powers, and all other Powers vested by this Constitution in the Government of the United States, or in any Department or Officer thereof.

Section 9.

The Migration or Importation of such Persons as any of the States now existing shall think proper to admit, shall not be prohibited by the Congress prior to the Year one thousand eight hundred and eight, but a Tax, or duty may be imposed on such Importation, not exceeding ten dollars for each Person.

The Privilege of the Writ of Habeas Corpus shall not be suspended, unless when in Cases of Rebellion or Invasion the public Safety may require it.

No Bill of Attainder or ex post facto Law shall be passed.

No Capitation, or other direct, Tax shall be laid, unless in Proportion to the Census or Enumeration herein before directed to be taken.

No Tax or Duty shall be laid on Articles exported from any State.

No Preference shall be given by any Regulation of Commerce or Revenue to the Ports of one State over those of another; nor shall Vessels bound to, or from, one State, be obliged to enter, clear, or pay Duties in another.

No Money shall be drawn from the Treasury, but in Consequence of Appropriations made by Law; and a regular Statement and Account of the Receipts and Expenditures of all public Money shall be published from time to time.

No Title of Nobility shall be granted by the United States: And no Person holding any Office of Profit or Trust under them, shall, without the Consent of the Congress, accept of any present, Emolument, Office, or Title, of any kind whatever, from any King, Prince, or foreign State.

Section 10.

No State shall enter into any Treaty, Alliance, or Confederation; grant Letters of Marque and Reprisal; coin Money; emit Bills of Credit;

make any Thing but gold and silver Coin a Tender in Payment of Debts; pass any Bill of Attainder, ex post facto Law, or Law impairing the Obligation of Contracts, or grant any Title of Nobility.

No State shall, without the Consent of the Congress, lay any Imposts or Duties on Imports or Exports, except what may be absolutely necessary for executing its inspection Laws; and the net Produce of all Duties and Imposts, laid by any State on Imports or Exports, shall be for the Use of the Treasury of the United States; and all such Laws shall be subject to the Revision and Control of the Congress.

No State shall, without the Consent of Congress, lay any Duty of Tonnage, keep Troops, or Ships of War in time of Peace, enter into any Agreement or Compact with another State, or with a foreign Power, or engage in War, unless actually invaded, or in such imminent Danger as will not admit of delay.

ARTICLE II

Section 1.

The executive Power shall be vested in a President of the United States of America. He shall hold his Office during the Term of four Years, and, together with the Vice President, chosen for the same Term, be elected, as follows:

Each State shall appoint, in such Manner as the Legislature thereof may direct, a Number of Electors, equal to the whole Number of Senators and Representatives to which the State may be entitled in Congress; but no Senator or Representative, or Person holding an Office of Trust or Profit under the United States, shall be appointed an Elector.

The Electors shall meet in their respective States, and vote by Ballot for two Persons, of whom one at least shall not be an Inhabitant of the same State with themselves. And they shall make a List of all the Persons voted for, and of the Number of Votes for each; which List they shall sign and certify, and transmit sealed to the Seat of the Government of the United States, directed to the President of the Senate. The President of the Senate shall, in the Presence of the Senate and House of Representatives, open all the Certificates, and the Votes shall then be counted. The Person having the greatest Number of Votes shall be the President, if such Number be a Majority of the whole Number of Electors appointed; and if there be more than one who have such Majority, and have an equal Number of Votes, then the House of Representatives shall immediately chuse by Ballot one of them for President; and if no Person have a Majority, then from the five highest on the List the said House shall in like Manner chuse the President. But in chusing the President, the Votes shall be taken by States, the Representation from each State having one Vote; A quorum for this Purpose shall consist of a Member or Members from two thirds of the States, and a Majority of all the States shall be necessary to a Choice. In every Case, after the Choice of the President, the Person having the greatest Number of Votes of the Electors shall be the Vice President. But if there should remain two or more who have equal Votes, the Senate shall chuse from them by Ballot the Vice President.[4]

The Congress may determine the Time of chusing the Electors, and the Day on which they shall give their Votes; which Day shall be the same throughout the United States.

No Person except a natural born Citizen, or a Citizen of the United States, at the time of the Adoption of this Constitution, shall be eligible to the Office of President; neither shall any Person be eligible to that Office who shall not have attained to the Age of thirty five Years, and been fourteen Years a Resident within the United States.

In Case of the Removal of the President from Office, or of his Death, Resignation, or Inability to discharge the Powers and Duties of the said Office, the Same shall devolve on the Vice President, and the Congress may by Law provide for the Case of Removal, Death, Resignation or Inability, both of the President and Vice President, declaring what

Officer shall then act as President, and such Officer shall act accordingly, until the Disability be removed, or a President shall be elected.

The President shall, at stated Times, receive for his Services, a Compensation, which shall neither be encreased nor diminished during the Period for which he shall have been elected, and he shall not receive within that Period any other Emolument from the United States, or any of them.

Before he enter on the Execution of his Office, he shall take the following Oath or Affirmation:—"I do solemnly swear (or affirm) that I will faithfully execute the Office of President of the United States, and will to the best of my Ability, preserve, protect and defend the Constitution of the United States."

Section 2.

The President shall be Commander in Chief of the Army and Navy of the United States, and of the Militia of the several States, when called into the actual Service of the United States; he may require the Opinion, in writing, of the principal Officer in each of the executive Departments, upon any Subject relating to the Duties of their respective Offices, and he shall have Power to grant Reprieves and Pardons for Offences against the United States, except in Cases of Impeachment.

He shall have Power, by and with the Advice and Consent of the Senate, to make Treaties, provided two thirds of the Senators present concur; and he shall nominate, and by and with the Advice and Consent of the Senate, shall appoint Ambassadors, other public Ministers and Consuls, Judges of the supreme Court, and all other Officers of the United States, whose Appointments are not herein otherwise provided for, and which shall be established by Law: but the Congress may by Law vest the Appointment of such inferior Officers, as they think proper in the President alone, in the Courts of Law, or in the Heads of Departments.

The President shall have Power to fill up all Vacancies that may happen during the Recess of the Senate, by granting Commissions which shall expire at the end of their next Session.

Section 3.

He shall from time to time give to the Congress Information of the State of the Union, and recommend to their Consideration such Measures as he shall judge necessary and expedient; he may, on extraordinary Occasions, convene both Houses, or either of them, and in Case of Disagreement between them, with Respect to the Time of Adjournment, he may adjourn them to such Time as he shall think proper; he shall receive Ambassadors and other public Ministers; he shall take Care that Laws be faithfully executed, and shall Commission all the Officers of the United States.

Section 4.

The President, Vice President and all civil Officers of the United States, shall be removed from Office on Impeachment for, and Conviction of, Treason, Bribery, or other high Crimes and Misdemeanors.

ARTICLE III

Section 1.

The judicial Power of the United States, shall be vested in one supreme Court, and in such inferior Courts as the Congress may from time to time ordain and establish. The Judges, both of the supreme and inferior Courts, shall hold their Offices during good Behaviour, and shall, at stated Times, receive for their Services, a Compensation, which shall not be diminished during their Continuance in Office.

Section 2.

The judicial Power shall extend to all Cases in Law and Equity, arising under this Constitution, the Laws of the United States, and Treaties made, or which shall be made, under their Authority;—to all Cases affecting Ambassadors, other public Ministers and Consuls;—to all Cases of admiralty and maritime Jurisdiction;—to Controversies to

---

[4]Provisions superseded by Amendment XII.

which the United States shall be a Party;—to Controversies between two or more states;—between a State and Citizens of another State;—between Citizens of different States;—between Citizens of the same State claiming Lands under Grants of different States, and between a State, or the Citizens thereof, and foreign States, Citizens or Subjects.[5]

In all Cases affecting Ambassadors, other public Ministers and Consuls, and those in which a State shall be Party, the supreme Court shall have original Jurisdiction. In all the other Cases before mentioned, the supreme Court shall have appellate Jurisdiction, both as to Law and Fact, with such Exceptions, and under such Regulations as the Congress shall make.

The Trial of all Crimes, except in Cases of Impeachment, shall be by Jury; and such Trial shall be held in the State where the said Crimes shall have been committed, but when not committed within any State, the Trial shall be at such Place or Places as the Congress may by Law have directed.

Section 3.

Treason against the United States, shall consist only in levying War against them, or in adhering to their Enemies, giving them Aid and Comfort. No person shall be convicted of Treason unless on the Testimony of two Witnesses to the same overt Act, or on Confession in open Court.

The Congress shall have Power to declare the Punishment of Treason, but no Attainder of Treason shall work Corruption of Blood, or Forfeiture except during the Life of the Person attainted.

ARTICLE IV

Section 1.

Full Faith and Credit shall be given in each State to the public Acts, Records, and judicial Proceedings of every other State. And the Congress may by general Laws prescribe the Manner in which such Acts, Records and Proceedings shall be proved, and the Effect thereof.

Section 2.

The Citizens of each State shall be entitled to all Privileges and Immunities of Citizens in the several States.

A Person charged in any State with Treason, Felony, or other Crime, who shall flee from Justice, and be found in another State, shall on Demand of the executive Authority of the State from which he fled, be delivered up, to be removed to the State having Jurisdiction of the Crime.

No Person held to Service or Labour in one State, under the Laws thereof, escaping into another, shall, in Consequence of any Law or Regulation therein, be discharged from such Service or Labour, but shall be delivered up on Claim of the Party to whom such Service or Labour may be due.

Section 3.

New States may be admitted by the Congress into this Union; but no new State shall be formed or erected within the jurisdiction of any other State; nor any State be formed by the Junction of two or more States, or Parts of States, without the Consent of the Legislatures of the States concerned as well as of the Congress.

The Congress shall have Power to dispose of and make all needful Rules and Regulations respecting the Territory or other Property belonging to the United States; and nothing in this Constitution shall be so construed as to Prejudice any Claims of the United States, or of any particular State.

Section 4.

The United States shall guarantee to every State in this Union a Republican Form of Government, and shall protect each of them against Invasion; and on Application of the Legislature, or of the Executive (when the Legislature cannot be convened) against domestic Violence.

ARTICLE V

The Congress, whenever two thirds of both Houses shall deem it necessary, shall propose Amendments to this Constitution, or, on the Application of the Legislatures of two thirds of the several States, shall call a Convention for proposing Amendments, which, in either Case, shall be valid to all Intents and Purposes, as Part of this Constitution, when ratified by the Legislatures of three fourths of the several states, or by Conventions in three fourths thereof, as the one or the other Mode of Ratification may be proposed by the Congress; Provided that no Amendment which may be made prior to the Year One thousand eight hundred and eight shall in any Manner affect the first and fourth Clauses in the Ninth Section of the first Article; and that no State, without its Consent, shall be deprived of its equal Suffrage in the Senate.

ARTICLE VI

All Debts contracted and Engagements entered into, before the Adoption of this Constitution, shall be as valid against the United States under this Constitution, as under the Confederation.

This Constitution, and the Laws of the United States which shall be made in Pursuance thereof; and all Treaties made, or which shall be made, under the Authority of the United States, shall be the supreme Law of the Land; and the Judges in every State shall be bound thereby, any Thing in the Constitution or Laws of any State to the Contrary notwithstanding.

The Senators and Representatives before mentioned, and the Members of the several State Legislatures, and all executive and judicial Officers, both of the United States and of the several States, shall be bound by Oath or Affirmation, to support this Constitution; but no religious Test shall ever be required as a Qualification to any Office or public Trust under the United States.

ARTICLE VII

The Ratification of the Conventions of nine States shall be sufficient for the Establishment of this Constitution between the States so ratifying the Same.

done in Convention by the Unanimous Consent of the States present the Seventeenth Day of September in the Year of our Lord one thousand seven hundred and Eighty seven and of the Independence of the United States of America and the Twelfth[6] IN WITNESS whereof We have here unto subscribed our Names.

[names omitted]

---

[5]Clause changed by Amendment XI.

[6]The Constitution was submitted on September 17, 1787, by the Constitutional Convention, was ratified by the conventions of several states at various dates up to May 29, 1790, and became effective on March 4, 1789.

Amendments to the Constitution

(THE FIRST TEN AMENDMENTS FORM THE BILL OF RIGHTS)

[AMENDMENT I]

Congress shall make no law respecting an establishment of religion, or prohibiting the free exercise thereof; or abridging the freedom of speech, or of the press, or the right of the people peaceably to assemble, and to petition the Government for a redress of grievances.

[AMENDMENT II]

A well regulated Militia being necessary to the security of a free State, the right of the people to keep and bear Arms, shall not be infringed.

[AMENDMENT III]

No Soldier shall, in time of peace be quartered in any house, without the consent of the Owner, nor in time of war, but in a manner to be prescribed by law.

[AMENDMENT IV]

The right of the people to be secure in their persons, houses, papers, and effects, against unreasonable searches and seizures, shall not be violated, and no Warrants shall issue, but upon probable cause, supported by Oath or affirmation, and particularly describing the place to be searched, and the persons or things to be seized.

[AMENDMENT V]

No person shall be held to answer for a capital, or otherwise infamous crime, unless on a presentment or indictment of a Grand Jury, except in cases arising in the land or naval forces, or in the Militia, when in actual service in time of War or public danger; nor shall any person be subject for the same offense to be twice put in jeopardy of life or limb; nor shall be compelled in any criminal case to be a witness against himself, nor be deprived of life, liberty, or property, without due process of law; nor shall private property be taken for public use, without just compensation.

[AMENDMENT VI]

In all criminal prosecutions, the accused shall enjoy the right to a speedy and public trial, by an impartial jury of the State and district wherein the crime shall have been committed, which district shall have been previously ascertained by law, and to be informed of the nature and cause of the accusation; to be confronted with the witnesses against him; to have compulsory process for obtaining witnesses in his favor, and to have the Assistance of Counsel for his defence.

[AMENDMENT VII]

In Suits at common law, where the value in controversy shall exceed twenty dollars, the right of trial by jury shall be preserved, and no fact tried by a jury, shall be otherwise re-examined in any court of the United States, than according to the rules of the common law.

[AMENDMENT VIII]

Excessive bail shall not be required, nor excessive fines imposed, nor cruel and unusual punishments inflicted.

[AMENDMENT IX]

The enumeration in the Constitution, of certain rights, shall not be construed to deny or disparage others retained by the people.

[AMENDMENT X]

The powers not delegated to the United States by the Constitution, nor prohibited by it to the States, are reserved to the States respectively, or to the people.[7]

[AMENDMENT XI]

The Judicial power of the United States shall not be construed to extend to any suit in law or equity, commenced or prosecuted against one of the United States by Citizens of another State, or by Citizens or Subjects of any Foreign State.[8]

[AMENDMENT XII]

The Electors shall meet in their respective states, and vote by ballot for President and Vice-President, one of whom, at least, shall not be an inhabitant of the same state with themselves; they shall name in their ballots the person voted for as President, and in distinct ballots the person voted for as Vice-President, and they shall make distinct lists of all persons voted for as President, and of all persons voted for as Vice-President, and of the number of votes for each, which lists they shall sign and certify, and transmit sealed to the seat of the government of the United States, directed to the President of the Senate;—The President of the Senate shall, in the presence of the Senate and House of Representatives, open all the certificates and the votes shall then be counted;—The person having the greatest number of votes for President, shall be the President, if such number be a majority of the whole number of Electors appointed; and if no person have such majority, then from the persons having the highest numbers not exceeding three on the list of those voted for as President, the House of Representatives shall choose immediately, by ballot, the President. But in choosing the President, the votes shall be taken by states, the representation from each state having one vote; a quorum for this purpose shall consist of a member or members from two-thirds of the states, and a majority of all the states shall be necessary to a choice. And if the House of Representatives shall not choose a President whenever the right of choice shall devolve upon them, before the fourth day of March next following, then the Vice-President shall act as President, as in the case of the death or

---

[7]The first ten amendments were all proposed by Congress on September 25, 1789, and were ratified and adoption certified on December 15, 1791.

[8]Proposed by Congress on March 4, 1794, and declared ratified on January 8, 1798.

other constitutional disability of the President.—The person having the greatest number of votes as Vice-President, shall be the Vice-President, if such number be a majority of the whole number of Electors appointed, and if no person have a majority, then from the two highest numbers on the list, the Senate shall choose the Vice-President; a quorum for the purpose shall consist of two-thirds of the whole number of Senators, and a majority of the whole number shall be necessary to a choice. But no person constitutionally ineligible to the office of President shall be eligible to that of Vice-President of the United States.[9]

[AMENDMENT XIII]

Section 1.

Neither slavery nor involuntary servitude, except as a punishment for crime whereof the party shall have been duly convicted, shall exist within the United States, or any place subject to their jurisdiction.

Section 2. .

Congress shall have power to enforce this article by appropriate legislation.[10]

[AMENDMENT XIV]

Section 1.

All persons born or naturalized in the United States and subject to the jurisdiction thereof, are citizens of the United States and the State wherein they reside. No State shall make or enforce any law which shall abridge the privileges or immunities of citizens of the United States; nor shall any State deprive any person of life, liberty, or property, without due process of law; nor deny to any person within its jurisdiction the equal protection of the laws.

Section 2.

Representatives shall be apportioned among the several States according to their respective numbers counting the whole number of persons in each State, excluding Indians not taxed. But when the right to vote at any election for the choice of electors for President and Vice-President of the United States, Representatives in Congress, the Executive and Judicial officers of a State, or the members of the Legislature thereof, is denied to any of the male inhabitants of such State being twenty-one years of age and citizens of the United States, or in any way abridged, except for participation in rebellion or other crime, the basis of representation therein shall be reduced in the proportion which the number of such male citizens shall bear to the whole number of male citizens twenty-one years of age in such State.

Section 3.

No person shall be a Senator or Representative in Congress, or elector of President and Vice President or hold any office, civil or military, under the United States or under any State, who, having previously taken an oath, as a member of Congress, or as an officer of the United States, or as a member of any State legislature, or as an executive or judicial officer of any State to support the Constitution of the United States, shall have engaged in insurrection or rebellion against the same, or given aid or comfort to the enemies thereof. But Congress may by a vote of two-thirds of each House, remove such disability.

Section 4.

The validity of the public debt of the United States authorized by law, including debts incurred for payment of pensions and bounties for services in suppressing insurrection or rebellion, shall not be questioned. But neither the United States nor any State shall assume or pay any debt or obligation incurred in aid of insurrection or rebellion against the United States, or any claim for the loss or emancipation of any slave; but all such debts, obligations and claims shall be held illegal and void.

Section 5.

The Congress shall have power to enforce, by appropriate legislation, the provisions of this article.[11]

[AMENDMENT XV]

Section 1.

The right of citizens of the United States to vote shall not be denied or abridged by the United States or by any State on account of race, color, or previous condition of servitude.

Section 2.

The Congress shall have power to enforce this article by appropriate legislation.[12]

[AMENDMENT XVI]

The Congress shall have power to lay and collect taxes on incomes, from whatever source derived, without apportionment among the several States, and without regard to any census or enumeration.[13]

[AMENDMENT XVII]

The Senate of the United States shall be composed of two Senators from each State, elected by the people thereof, for six years; and each Senator shall have one vote. The electors in each State shall have the qualifications requisite for electors of the most numerous branch of the State legislatures.

When vacancies happen in the representation of any State in the Senate, the executive authority of such State shall issue writs of election to fill such vacancies: *Provided*, That the legislature of any State may empower the executive thereof to make temporary appointments until the people fill the vacancies by election as the legislature may direct.

This amendment shall not be so construed as to affect the election or term of any Senator chosen before it becomes valid as part of the Constitution.[14]

[AMENDMENT XVIII]

Section 1.

After one year from the ratification of this article the manufacture, sale, or transportation of intoxicating liquors within, the importation thereof into, or the exportation thereof from the United States and all territory subject to the jurisdiction thereof for beverage purposes is hereby prohibited.

---

[9]Proposed by Congress on December 9, 1803; declared ratified on September 25, 1804; supplemented by Amendments XX and XXIII.

[10]Proposed by Congress on January 31, 1865; declared ratified on December 18, 1865.

[11]Proposed by Congress on June 13, 1866; declared ratified on July 28, 1868.

[12]Proposed by Congress on February 26, 1869; declared ratified on March 30, 1870.

[13]Proposed by Congress on July 12, 1909; declared ratified on February 25, 1913.

[14]Proposed by Congress on May 13, 1912; declared ratified on May 31, 1913.

Section 2.

The Congress and the several States shall have concurrent power to enforce this article by appropriate legislation.

Section 3.

This article shall be inoperative unless it shall have been ratified as an amendment to the Constitution by the legislatures of the several States, as provided in the Constitution, within seven years from the date of the submission hereof to the States by the Congress.[15]

[AMENDMENT XIX]

The right of citizens of the United States to vote shall not be denied or abridged by the United States or by any State on account of sex.

Congress shall have power to enforce this article by appropriate legislation.[16]

[AMENDMENT XX]

Section 1.

The terms of the President and Vice President shall end at noon on the 20th day of January, and the terms of Senators and Representatives at noon on the 3d day of January, of the years in which such terms would have ended if this article had not been ratified; and the terms of their successors shall then begin.

Section 2.

The Congress shall assemble at least once in every year, and such meeting shall begin at noon on the 3d day of January, unless they shall by law appont a different day.

Section 3.

If, at the time fixed for the beginning of the term of the President, the President elect shall have died, the Vice President elect shall become President. If a President shall not have been chosen before the time fixed for the beginning of his term, or if the President elect shall have failed to qualify, then the Vice President elect shall act as President until a President shall have qualified; and the Congress may by law provide for the case wherein neither a President elect nor a Vice President elect shall have qualified, declaring who shall then act as President, or the manner in which one who is to act shall be selected, and such person shall act accordingly until a President or Vice President shall have qualified.

Section 4.

The Congress may by law provide for the case of the death of any of the persons from whom the House of Representatives may choose a President whenever the right of choice shall have devolved upon them, and for the case of the death of any of the persons from whom the Senate may choose a Vice President whenever the right of choice shall have devolved upon them.

Section 5.

Sections 1 and 2 shall take effect on the 15th day of October following the ratification of this article.

Section 6.

This article shall be inoperative unless it shall have been ratified as an amendment to the Constitution by the legislatures of three-fourths of the several States within seven years from the date of its submission.[17]

[AMENDMENT XXI]

Section 1.

The eighteenth article of amendment to the Constitution of the United States is hereby repealed.

Section 2.

The transportation or importation into any States, Territory, or possession of the United States for delivery or use therein of intoxicating liquors, in violation of the laws thereof, is hereby prohibited.

Section 3.

This article shall be inoperative unless it shall have been ratified as an amendment to the Constitution by conventions in the several States, as provided in the Constitution, within seven years from the date of the submission hereof to the States by the Congress.[18]

[AMENDMENT XXII]

Section 1.

No person shall be elected to the office of the President more than twice, and no person who has held the office of President, or acted as President, for more than two years of a term to which some other person was elected President shall be elected to the office of the President more than once. But this Article shall not apply to any person holding the office of President when the Article was proposed by the Congress, and shall not prevent any person who may be holding the office of President, or acting as President, during the term within which this Article becomes operative from holding the office of President or acting as President during the remainder of such term.

Section 2.

This article shall be inoperative unless it shall have been ratified as an amendment to the Constitution by the legislatures of three-fourths of the several States within seven years from the date of its submission to the States by the Congress.[19]

[AMENDMENT XXIII]

Section 1.

The District constituting the seat of Government of the United States shall appoint in such manner as the Congress shall direct:

A number of electors of President and Vice President equal to the whole number of Senators and Representatives in Congress to which the District would be entitled if it were a State, but in no event more than the least populous State; they shall be in addition to those appointed by the States, but they shall be considered, for the purposes of the election of President and Vice President, to be electors appointed by a State; and they shall meet in the District and perform such duties as provided by the twelfth article of amendment.

Section 2.

The Congress shall have power to enforce this article by appropriate legislation.[20]

---

[15]Proposed by Congress on December 18, 1917; declared ratified on January 29, 1919; repealed by Amendment XXI.

[16]Proposed by Congress on June 4, 1919; declared ratified on August 26, 1920.

[17]Proposed by Congress on March 2, 1932; declared ratified on February 6, 1933.

[18] Proposed by Congress on February 20, 1933; declared ratified on December 5, 1933.

[19] Proposed by Congress on March 24, 1947; declared ratified on March 1, 1951.

[20] Proposed by Congress on June 16, 1960; declared ratified on April 3, 1961.

[AMENDMENT XXIV]

Section 1.

The right of citizens of the United States to vote in any primary or other election for President or Vice President, for electors for President or Vice President, or for Senator or Representative in Congress, shall not be denied or abridged by the United States or any state by reason of failure to pay any poll tax or other tax.

Section 2.

The Congress shall have the power to enforce this article by appropriate legislation.[21]

[AMENDMENT XXV]

Section 1.

In case of the removal of the President from office or his death or resignation, the Vice President shall become President.

Section 2.

Whenever there is a vacancy in the office of the Vice President, the President shall nominate a Vice President who shall take the office upon confirmation by a majority vote of both houses of Congress.

Section 3.

Whenever the President transmits to the President pro tempore of the Senate and the Speaker of the House of Representatives his written declaration that he is unable to discharge the powers and duties of his office, and until he transmits to them a written declaration to the countrary, such powers and duties shall be discharged by the Vice President as Acting President.

Section 4.

Whenever the Vice President and a majority of either the principal officers of the executive departments or of such other body as Congress may by law provide, transmit to the President pro tempore of the Senate and the Speaker of the House of Representatives their written declaration that the President is unable to discharge the powers and duties of his office, the Vice President shall immediately assume the powers and duties of the office as Acting President.

Thereafter, when the President transmits to the President pro tempore of the Senate and the Speaker of the House of Representatives his written declaration that no inability exists, he shall resume the powers and duties of his office unless the Vice President and a majority of either the principal officers of the executive department or of such other body as Congress may by law provide, transmit within four days to the President pro tempore of the Senate and the Speaker of the House of Representatives their written declaration that the President is unable to discharge the powers and duties of his office. Thereupon Congress shall decide the issue, assembling within 48 hours for that purpose if not in session. If the Congress, within 21 days after receipt of the latter written declaration, or, if Congress is not in session, within 21 days after Congress is required to assemble, determines by two-thirds vote of both houses that the President is unable to discharge the powers and duties of his office, the Vice President shall continue to discharge the same as Acting President; otherwise, the President shall resume the powers and duties of his office.[22]

[AMENDMENT XXVI]

Section 1.

The right of citizens of the United States, who are 18 years of age or older, to vote shall not be denied or abridged by the United States or any state on account of age.

Section 2.

The Congress shall have the power to enforce this article by appropriate legislation.[23]

---

[21] Proposed by Congress on August 27, 1962; declared ratified on January 23, 1963.

[22] Proposed by Congress on July 6, 1965; declared ratified on February 10, 1967.

[23] Proposed by Congress on March 23, 1971; declared ratified on June 30, 1971.

Credits

Index

1984 ELECTION RESULTS
GOVERNORSHIPS

	Before 1984 Election	After 1984 Election	Net Gain/Loss
Democrats	35	34	−1
Republicans	15	16	+1

State-by-State Results (winners in **bold type**)

	Democrat	Republican
Arkansas	**Bill Clinton***	Woody Freeman
Delaware	William T. Quillen	**Mike Castle**
Indiana	Wayne Townsend	**Robert Orr***
Missouri	Kenneth Rothman	**John Ashcroft**
Montana	**Ted Schwinden***	Pat Goodover
New Hampshire	Chris Spirou	**John Sununu***
North Carolina	Rufus Edmisten	**Jim Martin**
North Dakota	**George Sinner**	Allen Olson*
Rhode Island	Anthony Solomon	**Edward DiPrete**
Utah	Wayne Owens	**Norman Bangerter**
Vermont	**Madeleine Kunin**	John Easton, Jr.
Washington	**Booth Gardner**	John Spellman*
West Virginia	Clyde See	**Arch Moore, Jr.**

SENATE

	Before 1984 Election	After 1984 Election	Net Gain/Loss
Democrats	45	47	+2
Republicans	55	53	−2

State-by-State Results (winners in **bold type**)

	Democrat	Republican		Democrat	Republican
Alabama	**Howell Heflin***	Albert Lee Smith, Jr.	New Hampshire	Norman D'Armours	**Gordon Humphrey***
Alaska	John Havelock	**Ted Stevens***	New Jersey	**Bill Bradley***	Mary Mochary
Arkansas	**David Pryor***	Ed Bethune	New Mexico	Judy Pratt	**Pete Domenici***
Colorado	Nancy Dick	**William Armstrong***	North Carolina	Jim Hunt	**Jesse Helms***
Delaware	**Joseph Biden***	John Burris	Oklahoma	**David Boren***	Will Crozier
Georgia	**Sam Nunn***	Mike Hicks	Oregon	Margie Hendriksen	**Mark Hatfield***
Idaho	Peter Busch	**James McClure***	Rhode Island	**Claiborne Pell***	Barbara Leonard
Illinois	**Paul Simon**	Charles Percy*	South Carolina	Melvin Purvis	**Strom Thurmond***
Iowa	**Tom Harkin**	Roger Jepson*	South Dakota	George Cunningham	**Larry Pressler***
Kansas	James Maher	**Nancy Kassebaum***	Tennessee	**Albert Gore, Jr.**	Victor Ashe
Kentucky	Walter Huddleston*	**Mitch McConnell***	Texas	Lloyd Doggett	**Phil Gramm**
Louisiana	**J. Bennett Johnston***	Winner decided in open primary 9/29/84	Virginia	Edythe Harrison	**John Warner***
Maine	Elizabeth Mitchell	**William Cohen***	West Virginia	**Jay Rockefeller**	John Raese
Massachusetts	**John Kerry**	Ray Shamie	Wyoming	Victor Ryan	**Alan Simpson***
Michigan	**Carl Levin***	Jack Lousma		* = incumbents	
Minnesota	Joan Growe	**Rudy Boschwitz***			
Mississippi	William Winter	**Thad Cochran***			
Montana	**Max Baucus***	Chuck Cozzens			
Nebraska	**James Exon***	Nancy Hoch			